Sources of the Western Tradition

Sources of the Western Tradition

From the Scientific Revolution to the Present
Volume II

Marvin Perry
Baruch College, City University of New York

Joseph R. Peden
Baruch College, City University of New York

Theodore H. Von Laue
Clark University

George W. Bock, Editorial Associate

HOUGHTON MIFFLIN COMPANY   BOSTON
DALLAS GENEVA, ILLINOIS LAWRENCEVILLE, NEW JERSEY PALO ALTO

Credits

Cover: Color plate from Dickinson Brothers, *Dickinson's Comprehensive Pictures of the Great Exhibition of 1851*, London, 1854, by permission of the Houghton Library, Harvard University.

The Great Exhibition opened in the Crystal Palace in Hyde Park, London, on May 1, 1851. Designed by Sir Joseph Paxton, the Crystal Palace was constructed of prefabricated parts forming a network of iron rods that supported walls of clear glass. The exhibition drew more than six million visitors.

Chapter openers: Chapter 1: Galileo in his observatory; Alinari/The Mansell Collection. *Chapter 2:* Madame Geoffrin's salon; Malmaison/Giraudon/Art Resource. *Chapter 3:* Storming the Bastille, July 14, 1789; Musée Carnavalet, Paris/Photo Flammarion. *Chapter 4:* Barricades in Berlin, night of March 18–19, 1848; Bildarchiv Preussischer Kulturbesitz. *Chapter 5:* Linen manufacture, 1783; The Mansell Collection. *Chapter 6:* Collecting hut tax in Natal, South Africa; *Illustrated London News*, 1879/ Culver Pictures. *Chapter 7:* Finches from Galapagos Archipelago, with which Darwin illustrated natural selection; the Fotomas Index. *Chapter 8:* "Trenches in Winter, 1915–1916, Souchez" (detail), by François Flameng; Editions Tallandier Phototothèque. *Chapter 9:* Collective farming in the Ukraine, 1929; Novosti Press Agency. *Chapter 10:* Hitler and his retinue, November 9, 1938; The Bettmann Archive. *Chapter 11:* The Berlin Wall, with the Brandenburg Gate, West Berlin; UPI/Bettmann Newsphotos.

Credits continued on page 393.

Printed in the U.S.A.
Library of Congress Catalog Card Number: 86-81593
ISBN: 0-395-35032-8
BCDEFGHIJ-VB-8987

Contents

Preface

Teachers of the Western Civilization survey have long recognized the pedagogical value of primary sources, which are the raw materials of history. *Sources of the Western Tradition* contains a wide assortment of documents — over 300 and virtually all primary sources — that have been carefully selected and edited to fit the needs of the survey and to supplement standard texts.

We have based our choice of documents on several criteria. In order to introduce students to those ideas and values that characterize the Western tradition, *Sources of the Western Tradition* emphasizes primarily the works of the great thinkers. While focusing on the great ideas that have shaped the Western heritage, however, the reader also provides a balanced treatment of political, economic, and social history. We have tried to select documents that capture the characteristic outlook of an age and that provide a sense of the movement and development of Western history. The readings are of sufficient length to convey their essential meaning, and we have carefully extracted those passages that focus on the documents' main ideas.

An important feature of the reader is the grouping of several documents that illuminate a single theme; such a constellation of related readings reinforces understanding of important themes and invites comparison, analysis, and interpretation. In Volume I, Chapter 5, for example, Selection 6, "Third-Century Crisis," contains three readings: "Caracalla's Extortions" (from Dio Cassius), "Petition to Emperor Philip," and "Extortions of Maximinus" (from Herodian). In Volume II, Chapter 10, Selection 6, "The Anguish of the Intellectuals," contains readings by Johan Huizinga, José Ortega y Gasset, Thomas Mann, and Arthur Koestler.

An overriding concern of the editors in preparing this compilation was to make the documents accessible — to enable students to comprehend and to interpret historical documents on their own. We have provided several pedagogical features to facilitate this aim. Introductions of three types explain the historical setting, the authors' intent, and the meaning and significance of the readings. First, introductions to each of the twenty-two chapters provide comprehensive overviews to periods. Second, introductions to each numbered selection or grouping treat the historical background for the reading(s) that follow(s). Third, each reading has a brief headnote that provides specific details about that reading.

Within some readings, italicized Interlinear Notes, clearly set off from the text of the document, serve as transitions and suggest the main themes of the passages that follow. Used primarily in longer extracts of the great thinkers, these interlinear notes help to guide students through the readings.

To aid students' comprehension, brief, bracketed editorial definitions or notes that explain unfamiliar or foreign terms are inserted into the running text. When terms or concepts in the documents require fuller explanations, these appear at the bottom of pages as editors' footnotes. Where helpful, we have retained the notes of authors, translators, or editors from whose works the documents were acquired. (The latter have asterisks, daggers, etcetera, to distinguish them from our explanatory notes.) The Review Questions that appear at the end of selections enable students to check their understanding of the documents; sometimes the questions ask for comparisons with other readings, linking or contrasting key concepts.

For ancient sources, we have generally selected recent translations that are both faithful to the text and readable. For some seventeenth- and eighteenth-century English documents, the archaic spelling has been retained, when this does not preclude comprehension, in order to show students how the English language has evolved over time.

The pictures that open each chapter illustrate an important theme covered in the chapter; they are identified on the copyright page. In addition, in each volume there is a five-page section (between Chapters 3 and 4 in Volume I and between Chapters 8 and 9 in Volume II) devoted to art. In Volume I, "Elements of Classical, Medieval, and Renaissance Art" samples sculptural and architectural styles. Volume II's "Developments in Painting from Impressionism to the Abstract" samples the varied styles of painting in the late nineteenth and early twentieth centuries.

Volume I, *From Ancient Times to the Enlightenment*, contains thirteen chapters that cover the period from the rise of civilizations in the ancient Near East to the philosophes of the eighteenth century. Volume II, *From the Scientific Revolution to the Present*, incorporates the last two chapters of Volume I, "The Scientific Revolution" and "The Enlightenment," and has eleven chapters. Marvin Perry, senior editor of the project, researched both volumes. Joseph R. Peden contributed to Volume I and Theodore H. Von Laue to Volume II.

We wish to thank the following instructors for their critical reading of the manuscript and for their many valuable suggestions.

Ronald D. Cassell, *University of North Carolina*
James Cottom, *Massasoit Community College*
Manfred J. Enssle, *Colorado State University*
Paula S. Fichtner, *Brooklyn College, City University of New York*
Carole K. Fink, *University of North Carolina*
James Gump, *University of San Diego*
Donald G. Kyle, *University of Texas at Arlington*
Lyle Linville, *Prince George's Community College*
Curtis Porter, *Troy State University*
Harry Rosenberg, *Colorado State University*

Julius R. Ruff,   *Marquette University*
Francis W. Wcislo,   *Vanderbilt University*

We are also appreciative of the efforts of the Houghton Mifflin staff, who with their usual competent professionalism, guided the project from its inception. I wish to thank Angela Von Laue, who helped to research several chapters in Volume II and carefully read the galleys for that volume. I am especially grateful to George W. Bock, who worked closely with me in every phase of the reader's development, and to my wife, Phyllis Perry, for her encouragement.

M.P.

Early Modern Europe: New Views of Nature and Society

CHAPTER · 1

The Scientific Revolution

The Scientific Revolution of the sixteenth and seventeenth centuries replaced the medieval view of the universe with a new cosmology and produced a new way of investigating nature. It overthrew the medieval conception of nature as a hierarchical order ascending toward a realm of perfection. Rejecting reliance on authority, the thinkers of the Scientific Revolution affirmed the individual's ability to know the natural world through the method of mathematical reasoning and the direct observation of nature.

The medieval view of the universe had blended the theories of Aristotle and Ptolemy, two ancient Greek scientists, with Christian teachings. In that view, a stationary earth stood in the center of the universe just above hell. Revolving around the earth were seven planets: the moon, Mercury, Venus, the sun, Mars, Jupiter, and Saturn. Because people believed that earth did not move, it was not considered a planet. Each planet was attached to a transparent sphere that turned around the earth. Encompassing the universe was a sphere of fixed stars; beyond the stars lay three heavenly spheres, the outermost of which was the abode of God. An earth-centered universe accorded with the Christian idea that God had created the universe for men and women and that salvation was the aim of life.

Also agreeable to the medieval Christian view was Aristotle's division of the universe into a lower, earthly realm and a higher realm beyond the moon. Two sets of laws operated in the universe, one on earth and the other in the celestial realm. Earthly objects were composed of four elements: earth, water, fire, and air; celestial objects were composed of the divine ether — a substance too pure, too clear, too fine, too spiritual to be found on earth. Celestial objects naturally moved in perfectly circular orbits around the earth; earthly objects, composed mainly of the heavy elements of earth and water, naturally fell downward, whereas objects made of the lighter elements of air and fire, naturally flew upward toward the sky.

The destruction of the medieval world picture began with the publication in 1543 of *Revolutions of the Celestial Spheres,* by Nicolaus Copernicus, a Polish mathematician, astronomer, and clergyman. In Copernicus's system, the sun was in the center of the universe and the earth was another planet that moved around the sun. Most thinkers of the time, committed to the Aristotelian-Ptolemaic system and to the biblical statements that seemed to support it, rejected Copernicus's conclusions.

The work of Galileo Galilei, an Italian mathematician, astronomer, and physicist, was decisive in the shattering of the medieval cosmos and the shaping of the modern scientific outlook. Galileo advanced the modern view that knowledge of nature derives from direct observation and from mathematics. For Galileo, the universe was a "grand book which . . . is written in the language of mathematics, and its characters are triangles, circles, and other geometric figures without which it is humanly impossible to understand a single word of it." Galileo also pioneered experimental physics, advanced the modern idea that nature is uniform throughout the universe, and attacked reliance on scholastic authority rather than on experimentation in resolving scientific controversies.

Johannes Kepler (1571–1630), a contemporary of Galileo, discovered three laws of planetary motion that greatly advanced astronomical knowledge. Kepler showed that the path of a planet was an ellipse, not a circle as Ptolemy (and Copernicus) had believed, and that planets do not move at uniform speed but accelerate as they near the sun. He devised formulas to calculate accurately both a planet's speed at each point in its orbit around the sun and a planet's location at a particular time. Kepler's laws provided further evidence that Copernicus had been right, for they made sense only in a sun-centered universe, but Kepler could not explain why planets stayed in their orbits rather than flying off into space or crashing into the sun. The resolution of that question was left to Sir Isaac Newton.

Newton's great achievement was integrating the findings of Copernicus, Galileo, and Kepler into a single theoretical system. Newton uncovered the mechanical laws of motion and attraction that govern celestial and terrestrial objects.

The creation of a new model of the universe was one great achievement of the Scientific Revolution; another accomplishment was the formulation of the scientific method. The scientific method encompasses two approaches to knowledge, which usually complement each other: the empirical (inductive) and the rational (deductive). Although all sciences use both approaches, the inductive method is generally stressed more in such descriptive sciences as biology, anatomy, and geology, which rely on the accumulation of data. In the inductive approach, general principles are derived from analyzing external experiences — observations and the results of experiments. In the deductive approach, used in mathematics and theoretical physics, truths are derived in successive steps from indubitable axioms. Whereas the inductive method builds its concepts from an analysis of sense experience, the deductive approach constructs its ideas from self-evident principles that are conceived by the mind itself without external experience. The inductive and deductive approaches to knowledge, and their interplay, have been a constantly recurring feature in Western intellectual history since the rationalism of Plato and the empiricism of Aristotle. The success of the scientific method in modern times arose from the skillful synchronization of induction and deduction by such giants as Leonardo, Copernicus, Kepler, Galileo, and Newton.

The Scientific Revolution was instrumental in shaping the modern outlook. It destroyed the medieval conception of the universe and established the scientific method as the means for investigating nature and acquiring knowledge, even in areas having little to do with the study of the physical world. By demonstrating the powers of the human mind, the Scientific Revolution gave thinkers great confidence in reason and led eventually to a rejection of traditional beliefs in magic, astrology, and witches. In the eighteenth century, this growing skepticism led thinkers to question miracles and other Christian beliefs that seemed contrary to reason.

1 | The Copernican Revolution

In proclaiming that the earth was not stationary but revolved around the sun, Nicolaus Copernicus (1473–1543) revolutionized the science of astronomy. Fearing controversy and scorn, Copernicus long refused to publish his great work, *On the Revolutions of the Heavenly Spheres*. However, persuaded by friends, he finally relented and permitted publication; a copy of his book reached him on his deathbed. As Copernicus anticipated, his ideas aroused the ire of many thinkers.

Both Catholic and Protestant philosophers and theologians (including Martin Luther and John Calvin) attacked Copernicus for contradicting the Bible and Aristotle and Ptolemy, and they raised several specific objections. First, certain passages in the Bible imply a stationary earth and a sun that moves (for example, Psalm 93 says, "Yea, the world is established; it shall never be moved"; and in attacking Copernicus, Luther pointed out that "sacred Scripture tells us that Joshua commanded the sun to stand still, and not the earth"). Second, a body as heavy as the earth cannot move through space at such speed as Copernicus suggested. Third, if the earth spins on its axis, why does a stone dropped from a height land directly below instead of at a point behind where it was dropped? Fourth, if the earth moved, objects would fly off it. Finally, the moon cannot orbit both the earth and the sun at the same time.

NICOLAUS COPERNICUS

On the Revolutions of the Heavenly Spheres

On the Revolutions of the Heavenly Spheres was dedicated to Pope Paul III, whom Copernicus asked to protect him from vilification. In the dedication, Copernicus explains his reason for delaying publication of *Revolutions*.

To His Holiness, Pope Paul III,
Nicholas Copernicus' Preface
to His Books on the Revolutions

I can readily imagine, Holy Father, that as soon as some people hear that in this volume, which I have written about the revolutions of the spheres of the universe, I ascribe certain motions to the terrestrial globe, they will shout that I must be immediately repudiated together with this belief. For I am not so enamored of my own opinions that I disregard what others may think of them. I am aware that a philosopher's ideas are not subject to the judgement of ordinary persons, because it is his endeavor to seek the truth in all things, to the extent permitted to human reason by God. Yet I hold that completely erroneous views should be shunned. Those who know that the consensus of many centuries has sanctioned the conception that the earth remains at rest in the middle of the heaven as its center would, I reflected, regard it as an insane pronouncement if I made the opposite assertion that the earth moves. Therefore I debated with myself for a long time whether to publish the volume which I wrote to prove the earth's motion or rather to follow the example of the Pythagoreans[1] and certain others, who used to transmit philosophy's secrets only to kinsmen and friends, not in writing but by word of mouth. . . . And they did so,

---

[1] Pythagoreans were followers of Pythagoras, a Greek mathematician and philosopher of the sixth century B.C.; they were particularly interested in cosmology. (Throughout the text, the editors' notes carry numbers, whereas notes from the original sources are indicated by asterisks, daggers, etcetera.)

it seems to me, not, as some suppose, because they were in some way jealous about
their teachings, which would be spread
around; on the contrary, they wanted the
very beautiful thoughts attained by great
men of deep devotion not to be ridiculed
by those who are reluctant to exert themselves vigorously in any literary pursuit
unless it is lucrative; or if they are stimulated to the nonacquisitive study of philosophy by the exhortation and example
of others, yet because of their dullness of
mind they play the same part among philosophers as drones among bees. When I
weighed these considerations, the scorn
which I had reason to fear on account of
the novelty and unconventionality of my
opinion almost induced me to abandon
completely the work which I had undertaken.

But while I hesitated for a long time
and even resisted, my friends [encour-
aged me].[2] . . . Foremost among them
was the cardinal of Capua [a city in southern Italy], Nicholas Schönberg, renowned
in every field of learning. Next to him
was a man who loves me dearly, Tiede-
mann Giese, bishop of Chelmno [a city in
northern Poland], a close student of sacred letters as well as of all good literature. For he repeatedly encouraged me
and, sometimes adding reproaches, ur-
gently requested me to publish this volume and finally permit it to appear after
being buried among my papers and lying
concealed not merely until the ninth year
but by now the fourth period of nine years.
The same conduct was recommended to
me by not a few other very eminent scholars. They exhorted me no longer to refuse, on account of the fear which I felt,
to make my work available for the general
use of students of astronomy. The cra-
zier my doctrine of the earth's motion now
appeared to most people, the argument

ran, so much the more admiration and
thanks would it gain after they saw the
publication of my writings dispel the fog
of absurdity by most luminous proofs.
Influenced therefore by these persuasive
men and by this hope, in the end I allowed my friends to bring out an edition
of the volume, as they had long besought
me to do.

However, Your Holiness will perhaps
not be greatly surprised that I have dared
to publish my studies after devoting so
much effort to working them out that I
did not hesitate to put down my thoughts
about the earth's motion in written form
too. But you are rather waiting to hear
from me how it occurred to me to venture
to conceive any motion of the earth, against
the traditional opinion of astronomers and
almost against common sense. I have accordingly no desire to conceal from Your
Holiness that I was impelled to consider a
different system of deducing the motions
of the universe's spheres for no other reason than the realization that astronomers
do not agree among themselves in their
investigations of this subject. . . . [Co-
pernicus then describes some of the problems connected with the Ptolemaic system. These problems would not have
arisen had scientists] followed sound
principles. For if the hypotheses assumed by them were not false, everything
which follows from their hypotheses would
be confirmed beyond any doubt. Even
though what I am now saying may be obscure, it will nevertheless become clearer
in the proper place.

For a long time, then, I reflected on
this confusion in the astronomical traditions concerning the derivation of the
motions of the universe's spheres. I began to be annoyed that the movements of
the world machine, created for our sake
by the best and most systematic Artisan of
all [God], were not understood with
greater certainty by the philosophers, who
otherwise examined so precisely the most
insignificant trifles of this world. For this
reason I undertook the task of rereading
the works of all the philosophers which I

---

[2]Throughout the text, words in brackets have
been added as glosses by the editors. Brackets
around glosses from the original sources have
been changed to parentheses to distinguish
them.

could obtain to learn whether anyone had ever proposed other motions of the universe's spheres than those expounded by the teachers of astronomy in the schools. And in fact first I found in Cicero that Hicetas supposed the earth to move. Later I also discovered in Plutarch[2] that certain others were of this opinion. I have decided to set his words down here, so that they may be available to everybody:

> Some think that the earth remains at rest. But Philolaus[3] the Pythagorean believes that, like the sun and moon, it [the earth] revolves around the fire in an oblique circle. Heraclides of Pontus and Ecphantus the Pythagorean[4] make the earth move, not in a progressive motion, but like a wheel in a rotation from west to east about its own center.

Therefore, having obtained the opportunity from these sources, I too began to consider the mobility of the earth. And even though the idea seemed absurd, nevertheless I knew that others before me had been granted the freedom to imagine any circles whatever for the purpose of explaining the heavenly phenomena. Hence I thought that I too would be readily permitted to ascertain whether explanations sounder than those of my predecessors could be found for the revolution of the celestial spheres on the assumption of some motion of the earth.

Having thus assumed the motions which I ascribe to the earth later on in the volume, by long and intense study I finally found that if the motions of the other planets are correlated with the orbiting of the earth, and are computed for the revolution of each planet, not only do their phenomena follow therefrom but also the order and size of all the planets and spheres, and heaven itself is so linked together that in no portion of it can anything be shifted without disrupting the remaining parts and the universe as a whole. Accordingly in the arrangement of the volume too I have adopted the following order. In the first book I set forth the entire distribution of the spheres together with the motions which I attribute to the earth, so that this book contains, as it were, the general structure of the universe. Then in the remaining books I correlate the motions of the other planets and of all the spheres with the movement of the earth so that I may thereby determine to what extent the motions and appearances of the other planets and spheres can be saved if they are correlated with the earth's motions. I have no doubt that acute and learned astronomers will agree with me if, as this discipline especially requires, they are willing to examine and consider, not superficially but thoroughly, what I adduce in this volume in proof of these matters. However, in order that the educated and uneducated alike may see that I do not run away from the judgement of anybody at all, I have preferred dedicating my studies to Your Holiness rather than to anyone else. For even in this very remote corner of the earth where I live you are considered the highest authority by virtue of the loftiness of your office and your love for all literature and astronomy too. Hence by your prestige and judgement you can easily suppress calumnious attacks although, as the proverb has it, there is no remedy for a backbite.

Perhaps there will be babblers who claim to be judges of astronomy although completely ignorant of the subject and, badly distorting some passage of Scripture to their purpose, will dare to find fault with my undertaking and censure it. I

[2] Hicetas, a Pythagorean philosopher of the fourth century B.C., taught that the earth rotated on its axis while the other heavenly bodies were at rest. Cicero was a Roman statesman of the first century B.C. Plutarch (A.D. c. 50–c. 120) was a Greek moral philosopher and biographer.

[3] Philolaus (fifth century B.C.) taught that the universe was centered on a fire, around which the earth, sun, and other bodies revolved.

[4] Heraclides of Pontus (first century A.D.) was a Greek grammarian and poet, and Ecphantus (fifth century B.C.) was a Pythagorean philosopher who taught that the earth was spherical.

disregard them even to the extent of despising their criticism as unfounded. For it is not unknown that Lactantius,[5] otherwise an illustrious writer but hardly an as-

---

[5] Renaissance humanists admired Lactantius (c. 240–c. 320), a Latin rhetorician and Christian apologist, for his classical, Ciceronian literary style.

tronomer, speaks quite childishly about the earth's shape, when he mocks those who declared that the earth has the form of a globe. Hence scholars need not be surprised if any such persons will likewise ridicule me. Astronomy is written for astronomers. To them my work too will seem, unless I am mistaken, to make some contribution.

GIOVANNI MARIA TOLOSANI
Heaven and the Elements

Shortly after *Revolutions'* publication, Giovanni Maria Tolosani (c. 1471–1549), a Dominican friar, condemned Copernicus's work because it contradicted Aristotle and Holy Writ. Excerpts that follow come from an appendix, *Heaven and the Elements,* which Tolosani later added to his treatise *On the Truth of Holy Scripture* (1544). The *italic* notes were written by Edward Rosen, a leading authority on Copernicus.

The book by Nicholas Copernicus . . . was printed not long ago and published in recent days. In it he tries to revive the teaching of certain Pythagoreans concerning the earth's motion, a teaching which had died out in times long past. Nobody accepts it now except Copernicus. In my judgment, he does not regard that belief to be true. On the contrary, in this book of his he wanted to show others the keenness of his mind rather than expound the truth of the matter.

Since Tolosani, other anti-Copernicans have similarly made the baseless charge that Copernicus did not believe what he wrote.

As far as I could judge by reading his book, he is a man with a keen mind. He understands Latin and Greek, and expresses himself eloquently in those languages, not however without an obscurity in his phraseology since he uses unfamiliar words too often. He is also an expert in mathematics and astronomy, but he is very deficient in physics and dialectics. Moreover he seems to be unfamiliar with Holy Scripture since he contradicts some of its principles, not without the risk to himself and to the readers of his book of straying from the faith. . . .

Thoroughly familiar with the Bible, Copernicus farsightedly warned against allowing

distortions of Biblical passages to impede the development of science.

Hence, since Copernicus does not understand physics and dialectics, it is not surprising if he is mistaken in this opinion and accepts the false as true, through ignorance of those sciences. Summon men educated in all the sciences, and let them read Copernicus, Book I, on the moving earth and the motionless starry heaven. Surely they will find that his arguments have no solidity and can be very easily refuted. For it is stupid to contradict a belief accepted by everyone over a very long time for extremely strong reasons, unless the naysayer uses more powerful and incontrovertible proofs, and completely rebuts the opposed reasoning. Copernicus does not do this at all. For he does not undermine the proofs, establishing necessary conclusions, advanced by Aristotle the philosopher and Ptolemy the astronomer.

Then let experts read Aristotle, *On the Heavens,* Book II, and the commentaries of those who have written about it . . . and they will find that Aristotle absolutely destroyed the arguments of the Pythagoreans. . . .

Hence Copernicus, copying the Pythagoreans in part, leans on a cane of fragile reed which easily pierces his hand, or on an imaginary fabrication by which the truth cannot be proved. Therefore he is often mistaken. For in his imagination he changes the order of God's creatures in his system when . . . he (seeks) to raise the earth, heavier than the other elements, from its lower place to the sphere where everybody by common consent correctly locates the sun's sphere, and to cast that sphere of the sun down to the place of the earth, contravening the rational order and Holy Writ, which declares that heaven is up, while the earth is down. . . .

Almost all the hypotheses of this author Copernicus contain something false, and very many absurdities follow from them. . . . For by a foolish effort [he] tries to revive the contrived Pythagorean belief, long since deservedly buried, since it explicitly contradicts human reason and opposed Holy Writ. Pythagoreanism could easily give rise to quarrels between Catholic expounders of Holy Writ and those persons who might wish to adhere with stubborn mind to this false belief. I have written this little work for the purpose of avoiding this scandal.

After Chapter 2, with which Tolosani orig- *inally intended to conclude his Heaven and the* *Elements, he began Chapter 3 as follows:*

Although I have ended my remarks, nevertheless having been urged on by the advice of learned men, I think that some statements must still be added. For I have sent my reader to peruse the text of Aristotle, *On the Heavens,* Book II. It is not easy, however, for everybody to have that book in his own possession, together with the commentaries on it. Therefore, in order that readers may more readily learn that Nicholas Copernicus neither read nor understood the arguments of Aristotle the philosopher and Ptolemy the astronomer, for that reason I shall briefly adduce here their arguments and refutations of the opinion opposed by them. . . .

Toward the end of Chapter 4 Tolosani re- *marked:*

Read Book I of Nicholas Copernicus' *Revolutions* and from what I have written here you will clearly recognize into how many and how great errors he has tumbled, even contrary to Holy Writ. Where he wished to show off the keenness of his mind in the book he published, by his own words and writings he rather revealed his own ignorance.

Review Questions

1. Why did Copernicus fear to publish his theory about the earth's motion?
2. Why did Copernicus dedicate his work to Pope Paul III?
3. What facts encouraged Copernicus to investigate the motions of the universe's spheres?
4. What methods did Copernicus employ in investigating the earth's motion?
5. On what grounds did Giovanni Tolosani reject the Copernican theory?

2 | Expanding the New Astronomy

The brilliant Italian scientist Galileo Galilei (1564–1642), rejected the medieval division of the universe into higher and lower realms and proclaimed the modern idea of nature's uniformity. Learning that a telescope had been invented in Holland, Galileo built one for himself and used it to investigate the heavens. Through his telescope, Galileo saw craters and mountains on the moon; he concluded that celestial bodies were not pure, perfect, and immutable, as had been believed. There was no difference in quality between heavenly and earthly bodies; nature was the same throughout.

GALILEO GALILEI
The Starry Messenger

In the following reading, Galileo reported the findings observed through his telescope, which led him to proclaim the uniformity of nature.

About ten months ago a report reached my ears that a certain Fleming [a native of Flanders]* had constructed a spyglass by means of which visible objects, though very distant from the eye of the observer, were distinctly seen as if nearby. Of this truly remarkable effect several experiences were related, to which some persons gave credence while others denied them. A few days later the report was confirmed to me in a letter from a noble Frenchman at Paris, Jacques Badovere,† which caused me to apply myself wholeheartedly to inquire into the means by which I might arrive at the invention of a similar instrument. This I did shortly afterwards, my basis being the theory of refraction. First I prepared a tube of lead, at the ends of which I fitted two glass lenses, both plane on one side while on the other side one was spherically convex and the other concave. Then placing my eye near the concave lens I perceived objects satisfactorily large and near, for they appeared three times closer and nine times

larger than when seen with the naked eye alone. Next I constructed another one, more accurate, which represented objects as enlarged more than sixty times. Finally, sparing neither labor nor expense, I succeeded in constructing for myself so excellent an instrument that objects seen by means of it appeared nearly one thousand times larger and over thirty times closer than when regarded with our natural vision.

It would be superfluous to enumerate the number and importance of the advantages of such an instrument at sea as well as on land. But forsaking terrestrial observations, I turned to celestial ones, and first I saw the moon from as near at hand as if it were scarcely two terrestrial radii [a measure of distance, obscure today] away. After that I observed often with wondering delight both the planets and the fixed stars, and since I saw these latter to be very crowded, I began to seek (and eventually found) a method by which I might measure their distances apart. . . .

Now let us review the observations made during the past two months, once more inviting the attention of all who are eager for true philosophy to the first steps of such important contemplations. Let us speak first of that surface of the moon which faces us. For greater clarity I distinguish two parts of this surface, a lighter and a darker; the lighter part seems to surround and to pervade the whole hemisphere, while the darker part discolors the

---

*Credit for the original invention is generally assigned to Hans Lipperhey, a lens grinder in Holland who chanced upon this property of combined lenses and applied for a patent on it in 1608.

†Badovere studied in Italy toward the close of the sixteenth century and is said to have been a pupil of Galileo's about 1598. When he wrote concerning the new instrument in 1609 he was in the French diplomatic service at Paris, where he died in 1620.

moon's surface like a kind of cloud, and makes it appear covered with spots. Now those spots which are fairly dark and rather large are plain to everyone and have been seen throughout the ages; these I shall call the "large" or "ancient" spots, distinguishing them from others that are smaller in size but so numerous as to occur all over the lunar surface, and especially the lighter part. The latter spots had never been seen by anyone before me. From observations of these spots repeated many times I have been led to the opinion and conviction that the surface of the moon is not smooth, uniform, and precisely spherical as a great number of philosophers believe it (and the other heavenly bodies) to be, but is uneven, rough, and full of cavities and prominences, being not unlike the face of the earth, relieved by chains of mountains and deep valleys. . . .

———————→ •◆• ←———————

With his telescope, Galileo discovered four moons orbiting Jupiter, an observation that overcame a principal objection to the Copernican system. Galileo showed that a celestial body could indeed move around a center other than the earth; that earth was not the common center for all celestial bodies; that a celestial body (earth's moon or Jupiter's moons) could orbit a planet at the same time that the planet revolved around another body (namely, the sun).

———————→ •◆• ←———————

On the seventh day of January in this present year 1610, at the first hour of night, when I was viewing the heavenly bodies with a telescope, Jupiter presented itself to me; and because I had prepared a very excellent instrument for myself, I perceived (as I had not before, on account of the weakness of my previous instrument) that beside the planet there were three starlets, small indeed, but very bright. Though I believed them to be among the host of fixed stars, they aroused my curiosity somewhat by appearing to lie in an exact straight line parallel to the ecliptic, and by their being more splendid than others of their size. Their arrange-

ment with respect to Jupiter and each other was the following:

East   ✳   ✳   ○   ✳   *West*

that is, there were two stars on the eastern side and one to the west. The most easterly star and the western one appeared larger than the other. I paid no attention to the distances between them and Jupiter, for at the outset I thought them to be fixed stars, as I have said.‡ But returning to the same investigation on January eighth — led by what, I do not know — I found a very different arrangement. The three starlets were now all to the west of Jupiter, closer together, and at equal intervals from one another as shown in the following sketch:

East   ○   ✳   ✳   ✳   *West*

On the tenth of January, however, the stars appeared in this position with respect to Jupiter:

East   ✳   ✳   ○   *West*

that is, there were but two of them, both easterly, the third (as I supposed) being hidden behind Jupiter. . . . There was no way in which such alterations could be attributed to Jupiter's motion, yet being certain that these were still the same stars I had observed . . . my perplexity was now transformed into amazement. I was sure that the apparent changes belonged not to Jupiter but to the observed stars, and I resolved to pursue this investigation with greater care and attention. . . .

I had now decided beyond all question

———————

‡The reader should remember that the telescope was nightly revealing to Galileo hundreds of fixed stars never previously observed. His unusual gifts for astronomical observation are illustrated by his having noticed and remembered these three merely by reason of their alignment, and recalling them so well that when by chance he happened to see them the following night he was certain that they had changed their positions.

that there existed in the heavens three stars wandering about Jupiter as do Venus and Mercury about the sun, and this became plainer than daylight from observations on similar occasions which followed. Nor were there just three such stars; four wanderers complete their revolutions about Jupiter. . . .

Here we have a fine and elegant argument for quieting the doubts of those who, while accepting with tranquil mind the revolutions of the planets about the sun in the Copernican system, are might-

ily disturbed to have the moon alone revolve about the earth and accompany it in an annual rotation about the sun. Some have believed that this structure of the universe should be rejected as impossible. But now we have not just one planet rotating about another while both run through a great orbit around the sun; our own eyes show us four stars which wander around Jupiter as does the moon around the earth, while all together trace out a grand revolution about the sun in the space of twelve years.

Review Questions

1. What role did technological innovation play in advancing the possibility of new scientific knowledge?

2. What was the implication for modern astronomy of Galileo's observation of the surface of the moon? Of the moons of Jupiter?

3. What methods did Galileo use in his scientific investigations?

3 | Critique of Authority

Galileo appealed to the Roman Catholic authorities asking them to halt their actions against the theories of Copernicus, but was unsuccessful. His support of Copernicus aroused the ire of both clergy and scholastic philosophers. In 1616, the church placed Copernicus's book on the Index of forbidden books, and Galileo was ordered to cease his defense of the Copernican theory. In 1632, Galileo published *Dialogue Concerning the Two Chief World Systems* in which he upheld the Copernican view. Widely distributed and acclaimed, the book antagonized Galileo's enemies, who succeeded in halting further printing. Summoned to Rome, the aging and infirm scientist was put on trial by the Inquisition and ordered to abjure the Copernican theory. Galileo bowed to the Inquisition, which condemned the *Dialogue* and sentenced him to life imprisonment — largely house arrest at his own villa near Florence, where he was treated humanely.

GALILEO GALILEI

Letter to the Grand Duchess Christina and Dialogue Concerning the Two Chief World Systems — Ptolemaic and Copernican

The first reading illustrates Galileo's active involvement in a struggle for freedom of inquiry many years before the *Dialogue* was published. In 1615, in a letter ostensibly addressed to Grand Duchess Christina of Tuscany, Galileo argued that passages from the Bible had no authority in scientific disputes.

The second reading (from the *Dialogue*) reveals Galileo's views on Aristotle. Medieval scholastics regarded Aristotle as the supreme authority on questions concerning nature, an attitude that was perpetuated by early modern scholastics. Galileo insisted that such reliance on authority was a hindrance to scientific investigation, that it is through observation, experiment, and reason that one arrives at physical truth.

[Biblical Authority]

Some years ago, as Your Serene Highness well knows, I discovered in the heavens many things that had not been seen before our own age. The novelty of these things, as well as some consequences which followed from them in contradiction to the physical notions commonly held among academic philosophers, stirred up against me no small number of professors — as if I had placed these things in the sky with my own hands in order to upset nature and overturn the sciences. They seemed to forget that the increase of known truths stimulates the investigation, establishment, and growth of the arts; not their diminution or destruction.

Showing a greater fondness for their own opinions than for truth, they sought to deny and disprove the new things which, if they had cared to look for themselves, their own senses would have demonstrated to them. To this end they hurled various charges and published numerous writings filled with vain arguments, and they made the grave mistake of sprinkling these with passages taken from places in the Bible which they had failed to understand properly, and which were ill suited to their purposes. . . .

. . . Men who were well grounded in astronomical and physical science were persuaded as soon as they received my first message. There were others who denied them or remained in doubt only because of their novel and unexpected character, and because they had not yet had the opportunity to see for themselves. These men have by degrees come to be satisfied. But some, besides allegiance to their original error, possess I know not what fanciful interest in remaining hostile not so much toward the things in question as toward their discoverer. No longer being able to deny them, these men now take refuge in obstinate silence, but being more than ever exasperated by that which has pacified and quieted other men, they divert their thoughts to other fancies and seek new ways to damage me. . . .

. . . Possibly because they are disturbed by the known truth of other propositions of mine which differ from those commonly held, and therefore mistrusting their defense so long as they confine themselves to the field of philosophy, these men have resolved to fabricate a shield for their fallacies out of the mantle of pretended religion and the authority of the Bible. These they apply, with little judgment, to the refutation of arguments that they do not understand and have not even listened to.

First they have endeavored to spread the opinion that such propositions in general are contrary to the Bible and are consequently damnable and heretical. . . . Hence they have had no trouble in finding men who would preach the damnability and heresy of the new doctrine from their very pulpits with unwonted confidence, thus doing impious and inconsiderate injury not only to that doctrine and its followers but to all mathematics and mathematicians in general. . . .

. . . They go about invoking the Bible, which they would have minister to their deceitful purposes. Contrary to the sense of the Bible and the intention of the holy [Church] Fathers, if I am not mistaken, they would extend such authorities until even in purely physical matters — where faith is not involved — they would have us altogether abandon reason and the evidence of our senses in favor of some biblical passage, though under the surface meaning of its words this passage may contain a different sense.

I hope to show that I proceed with much greater piety than they do, when I argue not against condemning this book, but against condemning it in the way they suggest — that is, without understanding it, weighing it, or so much as reading it. For Copernicus never discusses matters of religion or faith, nor does he use arguments that depend in any way upon the authority of sacred writings which he might have interpreted erroneously. He stands always upon physical conclusions pertaining to the celestial motions, and deals with them by astronomical and geometrical demonstrations, founded primarily upon sense experiences and very exact observations. He did not ignore the Bible, but he knew very well that if his doctrine were proved, then it could not contradict the Scriptures when they were rightly understood. . . .

The reason produced for condemning the opinion that the earth moves and the sun stands still is that in many places in the Bible one may read that the sun moves and the earth stands still. Since the Bible cannot err, it follows as a necessary consequence that anyone takes an erroneous and heretical position who maintains that the sun is inherently motionless and the earth movable.

With regard to this argument, I think in the first place that it is very pious to say and prudent to affirm that the holy Bible can never speak untruth — whenever its true meaning is understood. But I believe nobody will deny that it is often very abstruse, and may say things which are quite different from what its bare words signify. Hence in expounding the Bible if one were always to confine oneself to the unadorned grammatical meaning, one might fall into error. . . .

. . . Now the Bible, merely to condescend to popular capacity, has not hesitated to obscure some very important

pronouncements, attributing to God himself some qualities extremely remote from (and even contrary to) His essence. Who, then, would positively declare that this principle has been set aside, and the Bible has confined itself rigorously to the bare and restricted sense of its words, when speaking but casually of the earth, of water, of the sun, or of any other created thing? Especially in view of the fact that these things in no way concern the primary purpose of the sacred writings, which is the service of God and the salvation of souls — matters infinitely beyond the comprehension of the common people.

This being granted, I think that in discussions of physical problems we ought to begin not from the authority of scriptural passages, but from sense-experiences and necessary demonstrations. . . . Nothing physical which sense-experience sets before our eyes, or which necessary demonstrations prove to us, ought to be called in question (much less condemned) upon the testimony of biblical passages which may have some different meaning beneath their words. . . .

. . . I do not feel obliged to believe that that same God who has endowed us with senses, reason, and intellect has intended to forgo their use and by some other means to give us knowledge which we can attain by them. He would not require us to deny sense and reason in physical matters which are set before our eyes and minds by direct experience or necessary demonstrations. . . .

It is obvious that such [anti-Copernican] authors, not having penetrated the true senses of Scripture, would impose upon others an obligation to subscribe to conclusions that are repugnant to manifest reason and sense, if they had any authority to do so. God forbid that this sort of abuse should gain countenance and authority, for then in a short time it would be necessary to proscribe all the contemplative sciences. People who are unable to understand perfectly both the Bible and the sciences far outnumber those who do understand. The former, glancing superficially through the Bible, would arrogate to themselves the authority to decree upon every question of physics on the strength of some word which they have misunderstood, and which was employed by the sacred authors for some different purpose. And the smaller number of understanding men could not dam up the furious torrent of such people, who would gain the majority of followers simply because it is much more pleasant to gain a reputation for wisdom without effort or study than to consume oneself tirelessly in the most laborious disciplines.

Galileo attacked the unquestioning acceptance of Aristotle's teachings in his Dialogue Concerning the Two Chief World Systems — Ptolemaic and Copernican. *In the dialogue, Simplicio is an Aristotelian and Salviati is a spokesman for Galileo; Sagredo, a third participant, introduces the problem of relying on the authority of Aristotle.*

[Aristotelian Authority]

SAGREDO One day I was at the home of a very famous doctor in Venice, where many persons came on account of their studies, and others occasionally came out of curiosity to see some anatomical dissection performed by a man who was truly no less learned than he was a careful and expert anatomist. It happened on this day that he was investigating the source and origin of the nerves, about which there exists a notorious controversy between the Galenist and Peripatetic doctors.[1] The anatomist showed that the great trunk of nerves, leaving the brain and passing through the nape, extended on down the spine and then branched out through the

whole body, and that only a single strand as fine as a thread arrived at the heart. Turning to a gentleman whom he knew to be a Peripatetic philosopher, and on whose account he had been exhibiting and demonstrating everything with unusual care, he asked this man whether he was at last satisfied and convinced that the nerves originated in the brain and not in the heart. The philosopher, after considering for awhile, answered: "You have made me see this matter so plainly and palpably that if Aristotle's text were not contrary to it, stating clearly that the nerves originate in the heart, I should be forced to admit it to be true." . . .

SIMPLICIO But if Aristotle is to be abandoned, whom shall we have for a guide in philosophy? Suppose you name some author.

SALVIATI We need guides in forests and in unknown lands, but on plains and in open places only the blind need guides. It is better for such people to stay at home, but anyone with eyes in his head and his wits about him could serve as a guide for them. In saying this, I do not mean that a person should not listen to Aristotle; indeed, I applaud the reading and careful study of his works, and I reproach only those who give themselves up as slaves to him in such a way as to subscribe blindly to everything he says and take it as an inviolable decree without looking for any other reasons. This abuse carries with it another profound disorder, that other people do not try harder to comprehend the strength of his demonstrations. And what is more revolting in a public dispute, when someone is dealing with demonstrable conclusions, than to hear him interrupted by a text (often written to some quite different purpose) thrown into his teeth by an opponent? If, indeed, you wish to continue in this method of studying, then put aside the name of philosophers and call yourselves historians, or memory experts; for it is not proper that those who never philosophize should usurp the honorable title of philosopher.

---

[1]Galenist doctors followed the medical theories of Galen (129–c. 199 A.D.), a Greek anatomist and physician whose writings had great authority among medieval and early modern physicians. Peripatetic doctors followed Aristotle's teachings.

Review Questions

1. Why was Galileo convinced that, if Copernicus's theories proved scientifically valid, they could not contradict the Bible?

2. What point was Galileo making in telling the story of the anatomical dissection?

3. What was Galileo's view on the use of Aristotle's works as a basis for scientific endeavors?

4 | Prophet of Modern Science

Sir Francis Bacon (1561–1626), an English statesman and philosopher, vigorously supported the advancement of science and the scientific method. He believed that increased comprehension and mastery of nature would improve living conditions for people and therefore wanted science to encompass systematic research; he urged the state to fund scientific institutions. Bacon denounced universities for merely repeating Aristotelian concepts and discussing problems — Is matter formless? Are all natural substances composed of matter? — that did not increase understanding of nature or contribute to human betterment. The webs spun by these scholastics, he said, were ingenious but valueless. Bacon wanted an educational program that stressed direct contact with nature and fostered new discoveries.

Bacon was among the first to appreciate the new science's value and to explain its method clearly. Like Leonardo da Vinci, Bacon gave supreme value to the direct observation of nature; for this reason he is one of the founders of the empirical tradition in modern philosophy. Bacon upheld the inductive approach — careful investigation of nature, accumulation of data, and experimentation — as the way to truth and useful knowledge. Because he wanted science to serve a practical function, Bacon praised artisans and technicians who improved technology.

FRANCIS BACON

The New Organon, or True Directions Concerning the Interpretation of Nature

Bacon was not himself a scientist; he made no discoveries and had no laboratory. Nevertheless, for his advocacy of the scientific method, Bacon is deservedly regarded as a prophet of modern science. In these excerpts from *The New Organon (Novum Organum)*, Bacon criticized contemporary methods used to inquire into nature. He expressed his ideas in the form of aphorisms — concise statements of principles or general truths.

I. Man, being the servant and interpreter of Nature, can do and understand so much and so much only as he has observed in fact or in thought of the course of nature: beyond this he neither knows anything nor can do anything.

VIII. . . . The sciences we now possess are merely systems for the nice ordering and setting forth of things already invented; not methods of invention or directions for new works.

XII. The logic now in use serves rather to fix and give stability to the errors which have their foundation in commonly received notions than to help the search after truth. So it does more harm than good.

XVIII. The discoveries which have hitherto been made in the sciences are such as lie close to vulgar notions, scarcely beneath the surface. In order to penetrate into the inner and further recesses of nature, it is necessary that both notions and axioms [self-evident, obvious truths] be derived from things by a more sure and guarded way; and that a method of intellectual operation be introduced altogether better and more certain.

XIX. There are and can be only two ways of searching into and discovering truth. The one flies from the senses and particulars to the most general axioms, and from these principles, the truth of which it takes for settled and immoveable, proceeds to judgment and to the discovery of middle axioms. And this way is now in fashion. The other derives axioms from the senses and particulars, rising by a gradual and unbroken ascent, so that it arrives at the most general axioms last of all. This is the true way, but as yet untried.

XXIII. There is a great difference between . . . certain empty dogmas, and the true signatures and marks set upon the works of creation as they are found in nature.

XXIV. It cannot be that axioms established by argumentation should avail for the discovery of new works; since the subtlety of nature is greater many times over than the subtlety of argument. But axioms duly and orderly formed from particulars easily discover the way to new particulars, and thus render sciences active.

C. But not only is a greater abundance of experiments to be sought for and procured, and that too of a different kind from those hitherto tried; an entirely different method, order, and process for carrying on and advancing experience must also be introduced. For experience, when it wanders in its own track is, as I have already remarked, mere groping in the dark, and confounds men rather than instructs them. But when it shall proceed in accordance with a fixed law, in regular order, and without interruption, then may better things be hoped of knowledge.

CIX. There is therefore much ground for hoping that there are still laid up in the womb of nature many secrets of excellent use, having no affinity or parallelism with any thing that is now known, but lying entirely out of the beat of the imagination, which have not yet been found out. They too no doubt will some time or other, in the course and revolution of many ages, come to light of themselves, just as the others did; only by the method of which we are now treating they can be speedily and suddenly and simultaneously presented and anticipated.

Review Questions

1. What intellectual attitude did Francis Bacon believe hampered new scientific discoveries in his time?

2. What method of scientific inquiry did Bacon advocate?

3. What did Bacon assume would follow from the adoption of his new method of scientific inquiry?

5 | The Autonomy of the Mind

René Descartes (1596–1650), a French mathematician and philosopher, united the new currents of thought initiated during the Renaissance and the Scientific Revolution. Descartes said that the universe was a mechanical system whose inner laws could be discovered through mathematical thinking and formulated in mathematical terms. With Descartes's assertions on the power of thought, human beings became fully aware of their capacity to comprehend the world through their mental powers. For this reason he is regarded as the founder of modern philosophy.

The deductive approach stressed by Descartes presumes that inherent in the mind are mathematical principles, logical relationships, the principle of cause and effect, concepts of size and motion, and so on — ideas that exist independently of human experience with the external world. Descartes, for example, would say that the properties of a right-angle triangle ($a^2 + b^2 = c^2$) are implicit in human consciousness prior to any experience one might have with a triangle. These innate ideas, said Descartes, permit the mind to give order and coherence to the physical world. Descartes held that the mind arrives at truth when it "intuits" or comprehends the logical necessity of its own ideas and expresses these ideas with clarity, certainty, and precision.

RENÉ DESCARTES
Discourse on Method

In the *Discourse on Method,* Descartes proclaimed the mind's inviolable autonomy and importance, and its ability and right to comprehend truth. In this work he offered a method whereby one could achieve certainty and thereby produce a comprehensive understanding of nature and human culture. In the following passage from the *Discourse on Method,* he explained the purpose of his inquiry. How he did so is almost as revolutionary as the ideas he wished to express. He spoke in the first person, autobiographically, as an individual employing his own reason, and he addressed himself to other individuals, inviting them to use their reason. He brought to his narrative an unprecedented confidence in the power of his own judgment and a deep disenchantment with the learning of his times.

Part One

From my childhood I lived in a world of books, and since I was taught that by their help I could gain a clear and assured knowledge of everything useful in life, I was eager to learn from them. But as soon as I had finished the course of studies which usually admits one to the ranks of the learned, I changed my opinion completely. For I found myself saddled with so many doubts and errors that I seemed to have gained nothing in trying to edu-

cate myself unless it was to discover more and more fully how ignorant I was.

Nevertheless I had been in one of the most celebrated schools in Europe, where I thought there should be wise men if wise men existed anywhere on earth. I had learned there everything that others learned, and, not satisfied with merely the knowledge that was taught, I had perused as many books as I could find which contained more unusual and recondite knowledge. . . . And finally, it did not seem to me that our own times were less flourishing and fertile than were any of the earlier periods. All this led me to conclude that I could judge others by myself, and to decide that there was no such wisdom in the world as I had previously hoped to find. . . .

I revered our theology, and hoped as much as anyone else to get to heaven, but having learned on great authority that the road was just as open to the most ignorant as to the most learned, and that the truths of revelation which lead thereto are beyond our understanding, I would not have dared to submit them to the weakness of my reasonings. I thought that to succeed in their examination it would be necessary to have some extraordinary assistance from heaven, and to be more than a man.

I will say nothing of philosophy except that it has been studied for many centuries by the most outstanding minds without having produced anything which is not in dispute and consequently doubtful. I did not have enough presumption to hope to succeed better than the others; and when I noticed how many different opinions learned men may hold on the same subject, despite the fact that no more than one of them can ever be right, I resolved to consider almost as false any opinion which was merely plausible. . . .

This is why I gave up my studies entirely as soon as I reached the age when I was no longer under the control of my teachers. I resolved to seek no other knowledge than that which I might find within myself, or perhaps in the great book of nature. I spent a few years of my adolescence traveling, seeing courts and armies, living with people of diverse types and stations of life, acquiring varied experience, testing myself in the episodes which fortune sent me, and, above all, thinking about the things around me so that I could derive some profit from them. For it seemed to me that I might find much more of the truth in the cogitations which each man made on things which were important to him, and where he would be the loser if he judged badly, than in the

cogitations of a man of letters in his study, concerned with speculations which produce no effect, and which have no consequences to him. . . .

. . . After spending several years in thus studying the book of nature and acquiring experience, I eventually reached the decision to study my own self, and to employ all my abilities to try to choose the right path. This produced much better results in my case, I think, than would have been produced if I had never left my books and my country. . . .

Part Two

. . . As far as the opinions which I had been receiving since my birth were concerned, I could not do better than to reject them completely for once in my lifetime, and to resume them afterwards, or perhaps accept better ones in their place, when I had determined how they fitted into a rational scheme. And I firmly believed that by this means I would succeed in conducting my life much better than if I built only upon the old foundations and gave credence to the principles which I had acquired in my childhood without ever having examined them to see whether they were true or not. . . .

. . . Never has my intention been more than to try to reform my own ideas, and rebuild them on foundations that would be wholly mine. . . . The decision to abandon all one's preconceived notions is not an example for all to follow. . . .

As for myself, I should no doubt have . . . [never attempted it] if I had had but a single teacher or if I had not known the differences which have always existed among the most learned. I had discovered in college that one cannot imagine anything so strange and unbelievable but that it has been upheld by some philosopher; and in my travels I had found that those who held opinions contrary to ours were neither barbarians nor savages, but that many of them were at least as reasonable as ourselves. I had considered how the same man, with the same capacity for reason, becomes different as a result of being brought up among Frenchmen or Germans than he would be if he had been brought up among Chinese or cannibals; and how, in our fashions, the thing which pleased us ten years ago and perhaps will please us again ten years in the future, now seems extravagant and ridiculous; and I felt that in all these ways we are much more greatly influenced by custom and example than by any certain knowledge. Faced with this divergence of opinion, I could not accept the testimony of the majority, for I thought it worthless as a proof of anything somewhat difficult to discover, since it is much more likely that a single man will have discovered it than a whole people. Nor, on the other hand, could I select anyone whose opinions seemed to me to be preferable to those of others, and I was thus constrained to embark on the investigation for myself.

Nevertheless, like a man who walks alone in the darkness, I resolved to go so slowly and circumspectly that if I did not get ahead very rapidly I was at least safe from falling. Also, I did not want to reject all the opinions which had slipped irrationally into my consciousness since birth, until I had first spent enough time planning how to accomplish the task which I was then undertaking, and seeking the true method of obtaining knowledge of everything which my mind was capable of understanding. . . .

Descartes's method consists of four principles that place the capacity to arrive at truth entirely within the province of the human mind. First one finds a self-evident principle, such as a geometric axiom. From this general principle, other truths are deduced through logical reasoning. This is accomplished by breaking a problem down into its elementary components and then step by step moving toward more complex knowledge.

. . . I thought that some other method [beside that of logic, algebra, and geome-

try] must be found to combine the advantages of these three and to escape their faults. Finally, just as the multitude of laws frequently furnishes an excuse for vice, and a state is much better governed with a few laws which are strictly adhered to, so I thought that instead of the great number of precepts of which logic is composed, I would have enough with the four following ones, provided that I made a firm and unalterable resolution not to violate them even in a single instance.

The first rule was never to accept anything as true unless I recognized it to be evidently such: that is, carefully to avoid precipitation and prejudgment, and to include nothing in my conclusions unless it presented itself so clearly and distinctly to my mind that there was no occasion to doubt it.

The second was to divide each of the difficulties which I encountered into as many parts as possible, and as might be required for an easier solution.

The third was to think in an orderly fashion, beginning with the things which were simplest and easiest to understand, and gradually and by degrees reaching toward more complex knowledge, even treating as though ordered materials which were not necessarily so.

The last was always to make enumerations so complete, and reviews so general, that I would be certain that nothing was omitted. . . .

What pleased me most about this method was that it enabled me to reason in all things, if not perfectly, at least as well as was in my power. In addition, I felt that in practicing it my mind was gradually becoming accustomed to conceive its objects more clearly and distinctly. . . .

Descartes was searching for an incontrovertible truth that could serve as the first principle of philosophy. His arrival at the famous dictum "I think therefore I am" marks the beginning of modern philosophy.

Part Four

. . . As I desired to devote myself wholly to the search for truth, I thought that I should . . . reject as absolutely false anything of which I could have the least doubt, in order to see whether anything would be left after this procedure which could be called wholly certain. Thus, as our senses deceive us at times, I was ready to suppose that nothing was at all the way our senses represented them to be. As there are men who make mistakes in reasoning even on the simplest topics in geometry, I judged that I was as liable to error as any other, and rejected as false all the reasoning which I had previously accepted as valid demonstration. Finally, as the same precepts which we have when awake may come to us when asleep without their being true, I decided to suppose that nothing that had ever entered my mind was more real than the illusions of my dreams. But I soon noticed that while I thus wished to think everything false, it was necessarily true that I who thought so was something. Since this truth, *I think, therefore I am*, was so firm and assured that all the most extravagant suppositions of the sceptics[1] were unable to shake it, I judged that I could safely accept it as the first principle of the philosophy I was seeking.

[1] The skeptics belonged to the ancient Greek philosophic school that held true knowledge to be beyond human grasp and treated all knowledge as uncertain.

Review Questions

1. Why did René Descartes conclude that the teachings of his contemporaries did not conform to true reality?
2. Why did Descartes exclude religious truths from his rational analysis?
3. Why was Descartes skeptical about truth being found among the philosophers?
4. What eventually became Descartes's sole object of investigation?
5. What did Descartes discover about the basis of commonly held opinions?
6. What method for rational inquiry did Descartes finally choose? Why did he choose it?
7. What convinced Descartes that the skeptic philosophers were wrong?
8. Compare the methods of Descartes with those advocated by Bacon and Galileo?

6 | The Mechanical Universe

By demonstrating that all bodies in the universe — earthly objects as well as moons, planets, and stars — obey the same laws of motion and gravitation, Sir Isaac Newton (1646–1723) completed the destruction of the medieval view of the universe. The idea that the same laws governed the movement of earthly and heavenly bodies was completely foreign to medieval thinkers, who drew a sharp division between a higher celestial world and a lower terrestrial one. In the *Principia Mathematica* (1687), Newton showed that the same forces that hold celestial bodies in their orbits around the sun make apples fall to the ground. For Newton, the universe was like a giant clock, all of whose parts obeyed strict mechanical principles and worked together in perfect precision. To Newton's contemporaries, it seemed as if mystery had been banished from the universe.

ISAAC NEWTON
Principia Mathematica

In the following passage from *Principia Mathematica*, Newton stated the principle of universal law and lauded the experimental method as the means of acquiring knowledge.

Rules of Reasoning in Philosophy. — Rule I. We are to admit no more causes of natural things than such as are both true and sufficient to explain their appearances.

To this purpose the philosophers say that Nature does nothing in vain, and more is in vain when less will serve; for Nature is pleased with simplicity, and affects not the pomp of superfluous causes.

Rule II. Therefore to the same natural effects we must, as far as possible, assign the same causes.

As to respiration in a man and in a beast; the descent of stones [meteorites] in *Europe* and in *America;* the light of our culinary fire and of the sun; the reflection of light in the earth, and in the planets.

Rule III. The qualities of bodies, which admit neither [intensification] *nor remission of degrees, and which are found to belong to all bodies within the reach of our experiments, are to be esteemed the universal qualities of all bodies whatsoever.*

For since the qualities of bodies are only known to us by experiments, we are to hold for universal all such as universally agree with experiments; and such as are not liable to diminution can never be quite taken away. We are certainly not to relinquish the evidence of experiments for the sake of dreams and vain fictions of our own devising; nor are we to recede from the analogy of Nature, which [is] . . . simple, and always consonant to itself. We no other way know the extension of bodies than by our senses, nor do these reach it in all bodies; but because we perceive extension in all that are sensible, therefore, we ascribe it universally to all others also. That

abundance of bodies are hard, we learn by experience; and because the hardness of the whole arises from the hardness of the parts, we, therefore, justly infer the hardness of the undivided particles not only of the bodies we feel but of all others. That all bodies are impenetrable, we gather not from reason, but from sensation. The bodies which we handle we find impenetrable, and thence, conclude impenetrability to be an universal property of all bodies whatsoever. That all bodies are moveable, and endowed with certain powers (which we call . . . *[inertia]*) of persevering in their motion, or in their rest, we only infer from the like properties observed in the bodies which we have seen. The extension, hardness, impenetrability, mobility, . . . of the whole, result from the extension, hardness, impenetrability, mobility, . . . of the parts; and thence we conclude the least particles of all bodies to be also all extended, and hard and impenetrable, and moveable, . . . And this is the foundation of all philosophy. . . .

Lastly, if it universally appears, by experiments and astronomical observations, that all bodies about the earth gravitate towards the earth, and that in proportion to the quantity of matter which they severally contain; that the moon likewise, according to the quantity of its matter, gravitates towards the earth; that, on the other hand, our sea gravitates towards the moon; and all the planets mutually one towards another; and the comets in like manner towards the sun; we must, in consequence of this rule, universally allow that all bodies whatsoever are endowed with a principle of mutual gravitation. . . .

Rule IV. In experimental philosophy we are to look upon propositions collected by general induction from phænomena as accurately or very nearly true, notwithstanding any contrary hy- *potheses that may be imagined, till such time as other phænomena occur, by which they may either be made more accurate, or liable to exceptions.*

This rule we must follow, that the argument of induction may not be evaded by hypotheses.

Review Questions

1. What method did Isaac Newton use to guide his scientific investigations?
2. What would cause Newton to reject a previously held scientific truth?
3. How did Newton's method fulfil the demands set forth both by Bacon and by Descartes?
4. What kind of universe did Newton's rules of reasoning assume?

7 | The Circulation of the Blood

William Harvey (1578–1657), a British physician, showed that blood circulates in the body because of the pumping action of the heart muscle. Previous belief derived from Galen's theories. Galen (c. 138–c. 201), a Greco-Roman physician, claimed that there were two centers of blood, with the liver being the source of blood in the veins, and the heart being the source of arterial blood. In contrast, Harvey demonstrated that all blood passes through a single central organ, the heart, flowing away from the heart through the arteries and back to it through the veins, and that this constant, rotating circulation is caused by the rhythmic contractions of the heart muscle acting as a pump.

This discovery of the circulation of blood marked a break with medieval medical ideas (inherited from the ancient world) and signified the emergence of modern physiology. Harvey employed the inductive method championed by Sir Francis Bacon; he drew conclusions after carefully observing and experimenting with living animals.

WILLIAM HARVEY

The Motion of the Heart and Blood in Animals

In *The Motion of the Heart and Blood in Animals* (1628), Harvey described the heart as a mechanical pump, a description that corresponded to Newton's view that the universe was a mechanical system. In this reading, Harvey discussed his reasons for writing the book and provided insights into his method.

When I first gave my mind to vivisections [cutting live animals open for experimen- tation], as a means of discovering the motions and uses of the heart, and sought to discover these from actual inspection, and not from the writings of others, I found the task so truly arduous, so full of difficulties, that I was almost tempted to think . . . that the motion of the heart was only to be comprehended by God. For I could neither rightly perceive at first when the systole and when the diastole took place, nor when and where dilatation and contraction occurred,[1] by reason of the rapidity of the motion, which in many animals is accomplished in the twinkling of an eye, coming and going like a flash of lightning; so that the systole presented itself to me now from this point, now from that; the diastole the same; and then everything was reversed, the motions occurring, as it seemed, variously and confusedly together. My mind was therefore greatly unsettled, nor did I know what I should myself conclude, nor what believe from others. . . .

At length, and by using greater and daily diligence, having frequent recourse to vivisections, employing a variety of animals for the purpose, and collating numerous observations, I thought that I had attained to the truth, that I should extricate myself and escape from this labyrinth [a maze, a confused state], and that I had discovered what I so much desired, both the motion and the use of the heart and arteries; since which time I have not hesitated to expose my views upon these subjects, not only in private to my friends, but also in public, in my anatomical lectures, after the manner of the Academy[2] of old.

These views, as usual, pleased some more, others less; some chid and calumniated me, and laid it to me as a crime that I had dared to depart from the pre-

cepts and opinion of all anatomists; others desired further explanations of the novelties, which they said were both worthy of consideration, and might perchance be found of signal use. At length, yielding to the requests of my friends, that all might be made participators in my labours, and partly moved by the envy of others, who, receiving my views with uncandid minds and understanding them indifferently, have essayed to traduce me publicly, I have been moved to commit these things to the press, in order that all may be enabled to form an opinion both of me and my labours. . . .

But lest any one should say that we give them words only, and make mere specious assertions without any foundation, and desire to innovate without sufficient cause, three points present themselves for confirmation, which being stated, I conceive that the truth I contend for will follow necessarily, and appear as a thing obvious to all. First, — the blood is incessantly transmitted by the action of the heart from the vena cava to the arteries in such quantity, that it cannot be supplied from the ingesta,[3] and in such wise that the whole mass must very quickly pass through the organ; Second, — the blood under the influence of the arterial pulse enters and is impelled in a continuous, equable, and incessant stream through every part and member of the body, in much larger quantity than were sufficient for nutrition, or than the whole mass of fluids could supply; Third, — the veins in like manner return this blood incessantly to the heart from all parts and members of the body. These points proved, I conceive it will be manifest that the blood circulates, revolves, propelled and then returning, from the heart to the extremities, from the extremities to the heart, and thus that it performs a kind of circular motion.

Let us assume either arbitrarily or from

---

[1] In dilatation, the heart muscle is relaxed, creating the diastole, or expansion of the heart's chambers, during which they fill with blood. The heart's contraction, or systole, forces blood out of the chambers in a pumping action.
[2] *The Academy* refers to the Athens school founded by Plato at which public lectures were given.

---

[3] The vena cava is the major vein that carries blood returning from the body into the heart. Ingesta refers to solid or liquid nutrients taken into the body.

experiment, the quantity of blood which the left ventricle[4] of the heart will contain when distended to be, say two ounces, three ounces, one ounce and a half — in the dead body I have found it to hold upwards of two ounces. Let us assume further, how much less the heart will hold in the contracted than in the dilated state; and how much blood it will project into the aorta[5] upon each contraction; — and all the world allows that with the systole something is always projected, a necessary consequence demonstrated in the third chapter, and obvious from the structure of the valves; and let us suppose as approaching the truth that the fourth, or fifth, or sixth, or even but the eighth part of its charge is thrown into the artery at each contraction; this would give either half an ounce, or three drachms, or one drachm [dram: ⅛ ounce] of blood as propelled by the heart at each pulse into the aorta; which quantity, by reason of the valves at the root of the vessel, can by no means return into the ventricle. Now in the course of half an hour, the heart will have made more than one thousand beats, in some as many as two, three, and even

four thousand. Multiplying the number of drachms propelled by the number of pulses, we shall have either one thousand half ounces, or one thousand times three drachms, or a like proportional quantity of blood, according to the amount which we assume as propelled with each stroke of the heart, sent from this organ into the artery; a larger quantity in every case than is contained in the whole body! In the same way, in the sheep or dog, say that but a single scruple [⅓ dram, ¹⁄₂₄ ounce] of blood passes with each stroke of the heart, in one half hour we should have one thousand scruples, or about three pounds and a half of blood injected into the aorta; but the body of neither animal contains above four pounds of blood, a fact which I have myself ascertained in the case of the sheep.

Upon this supposition, therefore, assumed merely as a ground for reasoning, we see the whole mass of blood passing through the heart, from the veins to the arteries, and in like manner through the lungs.

But let it be said that this does not take place in half an hour, but in an hour, or even in a day; any way it is still manifest that more blood passes through the heart in consequence of its action, than can either be supplied by the whole of the ingesta, or than can be contained in the veins at the same moment.

----

[4] The heart consists of four chambers: a left and right ventricle (the lower chambers) and a left and right atrium (the upper chambers).
[5] The aorta is the major artery that carries blood out of the heart to the body.

Review Questions

1. What evidence led William Harvey to conclude that blood constantly circulates through the heart?

2. What method did he use to reach his conclusions?

3. Why did some of Harvey's colleagues refuse to believe his conclusions?

4. Why did Harvey publish his book?

CHAPTER 2

The Enlightenment

The Enlightenment of the eighteenth century culminated the movement toward modernity that started in the Renaissance era. The thinkers of the Enlightenment, called *philosophes*, attacked medieval otherworldliness, dethroned theology from its once-proud position as queen of the sciences, and based their understanding of nature and society on reason alone, unaided by revelation or priestly authority.

From the broad spectrum of Western history, several traditions flowed into the Enlightenment: the rational spirit born in classical Greece, the Stoic emphasis on natural law that applies to all human beings, and the Christian belief that all individuals are equal in God's eyes. A more immediate influence on the Enlightenment was Renaissance humanism, which focused on the individual and worldly human accomplishments and which criticized medieval theology-philosophy for its preoccupation with questions that seemed unrelated to the human condition. In many ways, the Enlightenment grew directly out of the Scientific Revolution. The philosophes praised both Newton's discovery of the mechanical laws that govern the universe and the scientific method that made this discovery possible. They wanted to transfer the scientific method — the reliance on experience and the critical use of the intellect — to the realm of society. They maintained that independent of clerical authority, human beings through reason — just as Newton had uncovered the laws of nature that operate in the physical world — could grasp the natural laws that govern the social world. The philosophes said that those institutions and traditions that could not meet the test of reason, because they were based on authority, ignorance, or superstition, had to be reformed or dispensed with.

For medieval philosophers, reason had been subordinate to revelation; the Christian outlook determined the medieval concept of nature, morality, government, law, and life's purpose. During the Renaissance and Scientific Revolution, reason increasingly asserted its autonomy. For example, Machiavelli rejected the principle that politics should be based on Christian teachings; he recognized no higher world as the source of a higher truth. Galileo held that on questions regarding nature, one should trust to observation, experimentation, and mathematical reasoning, and should not rely on Scripture. Descartes had rejected reliance on past authority and maintained that through thought alone one could attain knowledge that has absolute certainty. Agreeing with Descartes that the mind is self-sufficient, the philosophes rejected the guidance of revelation and its priestly interpreters. They believed that through the use of reason, individuals could comprehend and reform society.

Eighteenth-century thinkers were particularly influenced by John Locke's advocacy of religious toleration, his reliance on experience as the source of knowledge, and his concern for individual liberty. In his first *Letter Concerning Toleration,* Locke declared that Christians who persecute others in the name of their religion violate Christ's teachings. In his *Essay Concerning Human Understanding,* a work of immense significance in the history of philosophy, Locke argued that human beings are not born with innate ideas (the idea of God and principles of good and evil, for example) divinely implanted in their minds. Rather, said Locke, the human mind at birth is a blank slate upon which are imprinted sensations derived from contact with the world. These sensations, combined with the mind's reflections on them, are the source of ideas. In effect, knowledge is derived from experience. In the tradition of Francis Bacon, Locke's epistemology (theory of knowledge) implied that people should not dwell on unknowable questions, particularly sterile theological issues, but should seek practical knowledge that promotes human happiness and enlightens human beings and gives them control over their environment. Locke's empiricism, which aspired to useful knowledge and stimulated an interest in political and ethical questions that focused on human concerns, helped to mold the utilitarian and reformist spirit of the Enlightenment. If there are no innate ideas, said the philosophes, then human beings are not born with original sin, contrary to what Christians believed. All that individuals are derive from their particular experiences. If people are provided with a proper environment and education, they will become intelligent and productive citizens. This was how the reform-minded philosophes interpreted Locke. They preferred to believe that evil stemmed from faulty institutions and poor education, both of which could be remedied, rather than from a defective human nature. Locke himself favored this outlook. In his treatise on education, he wrote, "of all the men we meet with, nine . . . of ten are what they are, good or evil, useful or not, by their education."

The Enlightenment philosophes articulated basic principles of the modern outlook: confidence in the self-sufficiency of the human mind, belief that individuals possess natural rights that governments should not violate, and the desire to reform society in accordance with rational principles.

1 | The Enlightenment Outlook

The critical use of the intellect was the central principle of the Enlightenment. The philosophes rejected beliefs and traditions that seemed to conflict with reason and attacked clerical and political authorities for interfering with the free use of the intellect.

IMMANUEL KANT

What Is Enlightenment?

The German philosopher Immanuel Kant (1724–1804) is a giant in the history of modern philosophy. Several twentieth-century philosophic movements have their origins in Kantian thought, and many issues raised by Kant still retain their importance. For example, in *Metaphysical Foundations of Morals* (1785), Kant set forth the categorical imperative that remains a crucial principle in moral philosophy. Kant asserted that when confronted with a moral choice, people should ask themselves: "Canst thou also will that thy maxim should be a universal law?" By this, Kant meant that people should ponder whether they would want the moral principle underlying their action to be elevated to a universal law that would govern others in similar circumstances. If their conclusion was no, it should not, then the maxim should be rejected and the action avoided.

Kant valued the essential ideals of the Enlightenment and viewed the French Revolution, which put these ideals into law, as the triumph of liberty over despotism. In an essay entitled "What Is Enlightenment?" (1784), he contended that the Enlightenment marked a new way of thinking and eloquently affirmed the Enlightenment's confidence in and commitment to reason.

Enlightenment is man's leaving his self-caused immaturity. Immaturity is the incapacity to use one's intelligence without the guidance of another. Such immaturity is self-caused if it is not caused by lack of intelligence, but by lack of determination and courage to use one's intelligence without being guided by another. *Sapere Aude!* [Dare to know!] Have the courage to use your own intelligence! is therefore the motto of the enlightenment.

Through laziness and cowardice a large part of mankind, even after nature has freed them from alien guidance, gladly remain immature. It is because of laziness and cowardice that it is so easy for others to usurp the role of guardians. It is so comfortable to be a minor! If I have a book which provides meaning for me, a pastor who has conscience for me, a doctor who will judge my diet for me and so on, then I do not need to exert myself. I do not have any need to think; if I can pay, others will take over the tedious job for me. The guardians who have kindly undertaken the supervision will see to it that by far the largest part of mankind, including the entire "beautiful sex," should consider the step into maturity, not only as difficult but as very dangerous.

After having made their domestic animals dumb and having carefully prevented these quiet creatures from daring to take any step beyond the lead-strings to which they have fastened them, these guardians then show them the danger which threatens them, should they attempt to walk alone. Now this danger is not really so very great; for they would presumably learn to walk after some stumbling. However, an example of this kind intimidates and frightens people out of all further attempts.

It is difficult for the isolated individual to work himself out of the immaturity which has become almost natural for him. He has even become fond of it and for the time being is incapable of employing his own intelligence, because he has never been allowed to make the attempt. Statutes and formulas, these mechanical tools of a serviceable use, or rather misuse, of his natural faculties, are the ankle-chains of a continuous immaturity. Whoever threw it off would make an uncertain jump over the smallest trench because he is not accustomed to such free movement. Therefore there are only a few who have pursued a firm path and have succeeded in escaping from immaturity by their own cultivation of the mind.

But it is more nearly possible for a public to enlighten itself: this is even inescapable if only the public is given its freedom. For there will always be some people who think for themselves, even among the self-appointed guardians of the great mass who, after having thrown off the yoke of immaturity themselves, will spread about them the spirit of a reasonable estimate of their own value and of the need for every man to think for himself. . . . a public can only arrive at enlightenment slowly. Through revolution, the abandonment of personal despotism may be engendered and the end of profit-seeking and domineering oppression may occur, but never a true reform of the state of mind. Instead, new prejudices, just like the old ones, will serve as the guiding reins of the great, unthinking mass. . . .

All that is required for this enlightenment is *freedom;* and particularly the least harmful of all that may be called freedom, namely, the freedom for man to make *public use* of his reason in all mat-

ters. But I hear people clamor on all sides: Don't argue! The officer says: Don't argue, drill! The tax collector: Don't argue, pay! The pastor: Don't argue, believe! . . . Here we have restrictions on freedom everywhere. Which restriction is hampering enlightenment, and which does not, or even promotes it? I answer: The *public use* of a man's reason must be free at all times, and this alone can bring enlightenment among men. . . .

I mean by the public use of one's reason, the use which a scholar makes of it before the entire reading public. . . .

The question may now be put: Do we live at present in an enlightened age? The answer is: No, but in an age of enlightenment. Much still prevents men from being placed in a position or even being placed into position to use their own minds securely and well in matters of religion. But we do have very definite indications that this field of endeavor is being opened up for men to work freely and reduce gradually the hindrances preventing a general enlightenment and an escape from self-caused immaturity. . . .

I have emphasized the main point of enlightenment, that is of man's release from his self-caused immaturity, primarily *in matters of religion.* I have done this because our rulers have no interest in playing the guardian of their subjects in matters of arts and sciences. Furthermore immaturity in matters of religion is not only most noxious but also most dishonorable. But the point of view of a head of state who favors freedom in the arts and sciences goes even farther; for he understands that there is no danger in legislation permitting his subjects to make *public* use of their own reason and to submit *publicly* their thoughts regarding a better framing of such laws together with a frank criticism of existing *legislation.*

Review Questions

1. Why did Immanuel Kant believe most persons never reached maturity?
2. What did Kant mean by the term "enlightenment"?

3. What was Kant's explanation for the existence of the "guardians" in Western society?

4. What did Kant think to be the function of statutes and customs?

5. How did Kant propose to increase the maturity of individuals?

6. For Kant, what role did public liberties play in the progress of enlightenment?

7. Why was freedom in matters of religion of crucial importance to Kant?

2 | Political Liberty

John Locke (1632–1704), a British physician, statesman, philosopher, and political theorist, was a principal founder of the Enlightenment. Locke's political philosophy as formulated in the *Two Treatises on Government* complements his theory of knowledge, described in the introduction to this chapter; both were rational and secular attempts to understand and improve the human condition. The Lockean spirit pervades the American Declaration of Independence, the Constitution, and the Bill of Rights and is a principal source of the liberal tradition that aims to protect individual liberty from despotic state authority.

Viewing human beings as brutish and selfish, Thomas Hobbes (see Chapter 11, Volume I) had prescribed a state with unlimited power; only in this way, he said, could people be protected from each other and civilized life preserved. Locke, regarding people as essentially good and humane, developed a conception of the state differing fundamentally from Hobbes's. Locke held that human beings are born with natural rights of life, liberty, and property; they establish the state to protect these rights. Consequently, neither executive nor legislature, neither king nor assembly has the authority to deprive individuals of their natural rights. Whereas Hobbes justified absolute monarchy, Locke explicitly endorsed constitutional government in which the power to govern derives from the consent of the governed and the state's authority is limited by agreement.

JOHN LOCKE
Second Treatise on Government

Locke said that originally, in establishing a government, human beings had never agreed to surrender their natural rights to any state authority. The state's founders intended the new polity to preserve these natural rights and to implement the people's will. Therefore, as the following passage from Locke's *Second Treatise on Government* illustrates, the power exercised by magistrates cannot be absolute or arbitrary:

. . . *Political power* is that power, which every man having in the state of nature, has given up into the hands of the society, and therein to the governors, whom the society hath set over itself, with this express or tacit trust, that it shall be employed for their good, and the preserva- tion of their property: now this *power*, which every man has *in the state of nature*, and which he parts with to the society in all such cases where the society can secure him, is to use such means, for the pre- serving of his own property, as he thinks good, and nature allows him; and to punish the breach of the law of nature in others, so as (according to the best of his reason) may most conduce to the preservation of himself, and the rest of mankind. So that the *end and measure of this power,* when in every man's hands in the state of nature, being the preservation of all of his society, that is, all mankind in general, it can have no other *end or measure,* when in the hands of the magistrate, but to preserve the members of that society in their lives, liberties, and possessions; and so cannot be an absolute, arbitrary power over their lives and fortunes, which are as much as possible to be preserved; but a *power to make laws,* and annex such *penalties* to them, as may tend to the preservation of the whole, by cutting off those parts, and those only, which are so corrupt, that they threaten the sound and healthy, without which no severity is lawful. And this *power has its original only from compact,* and agreement, and the mutual consent of those who make up the community. . . .

These are the *bounds,* which the trust, that is put in them by the society, and the law of God and nature, have *set to the legislative* power of every common-wealth, in all forms of government.

First, They are to govern by *promulgated established laws,* not to be varied in particular cases, but to have one rule for rich and poor, for the favourite at court, and the country man at plough.

Secondly, These *laws* also ought to be designed *for* no other end ultimately, but *the good of the people.*

Thirdly, They must *not raise taxes* on the *property of the people, without the consent of the people,* given by themselves, or their deputies. And this properly concerns only such governments, where the *legislative* is always in being, or at least where the people have not reserved any part of the legislative to deputies, to be from time to time chosen by themselves.

Fourthly, The *legislative* neither must *nor can transfer the power of making laws* to any body else, or place it any where, but where the people have. . . .

◆ ·◆· ◆

If government fails to fulfill the end for which it was established — the preservation of the individual's right to life, liberty, and property — the people have a right to dissolve that government.

◆ ·◆· ◆

. . . The *legislative acts against the trust* reposed in them, when they endeavour to invade the property of the subject, and to make themselves, or any part of the community, masters, or arbitrary disposers of the lives, liberties, or fortunes of the people.

The reason why men enter into society, is the preservation of their property; and the end why they chuse and authorize a legislative, is, that there may be laws made, and rules set, as guards and fences to the properties of all the members of the society, to limit the power, and moderate the dominion of every part and member of the society: for since it can never be supposed to be the will of the society, that the legislative should have a power to destroy that which every one designs to secure, by entering into society, and for which the people submitted themselves to legislators of their own making; whenever the *legislators endeavour to take away, and destroy the property of the people,* or to reduce them to slavery under arbitrary power, they put themselves into a state of war with the people, who are thereupon absolved from any farther obedience, and are left to the common refuge, which God hath provided for all men, against force and violence. Whensoever therefore the *legislative* shall transgress this fundamental rule of society; and either by ambition, fear, folly or corruption, *endeavour to grasp* themselves, *or put into the hands of any other, an absolute power* over the lives, liberties, and estates of the people; by this breach of trust they *forfeit the power* the people had put into their hands for quite contrary ends, and it devolves to the people, who have a right to resume their original liberty, and, by the establishment of a new legislative, (such as they shall think fit) provide for their own safety and security, which is the end for which they are in society. What I have said here, concerning the legislative in general, holds true also concerning the supreme executor, who having a double trust put in him, both to have a part in the legislative, and the supreme execution of the law, acts against both, when he goes about to set up his own arbitrary will as the law of the society. He *acts* also *contrary to his trust,* when he either employs the force, treasure, and offices of the society, to corrupt the *representatives,* and gain them to his purposes; or openly pre-engages the *electors,* and prescribes to their choice, such, whom he has, by sollicitations, threats, promises, or otherwise, won to his designs; and employs them to bring in such, who have promised beforehand what to vote, and what to enact. . . .

Locke responds to the charge that his theory will produce "frequent rebellion." Indeed, says Locke, the true rebels are the magistrates who, acting contrary to the trust granted them, violate the people's rights.

. . . Such *revolutions happen* not upon every little mismanagement in public affairs. *Great mistakes* in the ruling part, many wrong and inconvenient laws, and all the *slips* of human frailty, will be *borne by the people* without mutiny or murmur. But if a long train of abuses, prevarications and artifices, all tending the same way, make the design visible to the people, and they cannot but feel what they lie under, and see whither they are going; it is not to be wondered at, that they should then rouze themselves, and endeavour to put the rule into such hands which may secure to them the ends for which government was at first erected. . . .

. . . I answer, that *this doctrine* of a power in the people of providing for their safety a-new, by a new legislative, when their legislators have acted contrary to their trust, by invading their property, is *the best [de]fence against rebellion,* and the probablest means to hinder it: for *rebellion* being an opposition, not to persons, but authority, which is founded only in the constitutions and laws of the government; those, whoever they be, who by force break through, and by force justify their violation of them, are truly and properly *rebels:* for when men, by entering into society and civil government, have excluded force, and introduced laws for the preservation of property, peace, and unity amongst themselves, those who set up force again in opposition to the laws, do *rebellare,* that is, bring back again the state of war, and are properly rebels: which they who are in power, (by the pretence they have to authority, the temptation of force they have in their hands, and the flattery of those about them) being likeliest to do; the properest way to prevent the evil, is to shew them the danger and injustice of it, who are under the greatest temptation to run into it.

The end of government is the good of mankind; and which is *best for mankind,* that the people should be always exposed to the boundless will of tyranny, or that the rulers should be sometimes liable to be opposed, when they grow exorbitant in the use of their power, and employ it for the destruction, and not the preservation of the properties of their people?

Review Questions

1. According to John Locke, what were the purposes for which governments might legitimately be formed?

2. According to Locke's theory, where did sovereignty rest in the state of nature? Where did it reside after governments were formed?

3. According to Locke, what limits bound legislators in any government?

4. What did Locke believe were the rights of a people in face of a government that failed to protect their lives, liberties, and possessions?

5. Compare the views of Locke with those of Thomas Hobbes (Chapter 11, Volume I).

6. In what respect were Locke's views similar to those of the Levellers (Chapter 11, Volume I)?

7. Compare Locke's theory of natural rights with the principles stated in the American Declaration of Independence.

3 | Attack on the Old Regime

François Marie Arouet (1694–1778), known to the world as Voltaire, was the recognized leader of the French Enlightenment. Few of the philosophes had a better mind and none had a sharper wit. A relentless critic of the Old Regime (the social structure in prerevolutionary France), Voltaire attacked superstition, religious fanaticism and persecution, censorship, and other abuses of eighteenth-century French society. Spending more than two years in Great Britain, Voltaire acquired a great admiration for English liberty, toleration, commerce, and science. In *Letters Concerning the English Nation* (1733), he drew unfavorable comparisons between a progressive Britain and a reactionary France.

Voltaire's angriest words were directed against established Christianity, to which he attributed many of the ills of modern society. Voltaire regarded Christianity as "the Christ-worshiping superstition" that someday would be destroyed "by the weapons of reason." He rejected revelation and the church hierarchy and was repulsed by Christian intolerance, but he accepted Christian morality and believed in God as the prime mover who set the universe in motion.

VOLTAIRE
A Plea for Tolerance and Reason

The following passages compiled from Voltaire's works — grouped according to topic — provide insight into the outlook of the philosophes. The excerpts come from sources that include his *Candide* (1759), *Treatise on Tolerance* (1763), and *The Philosophical Dictionary* (1764).

Tolerance

It does not require any great art or studied elocution to prove that Christians ought to tolerate one another. I will go even further and say that we ought to look upon all men as our brothers. What! call a Turk, a Jew, and a Siamese, my brother? Yes, of course; for are we not all children of the same father, and the creatures of the same God?

What is tolerance? It is the portion of humanity. We are all full of weakness and errors; let us mutually pardon our follies. This is the first law of nature. . . .

It is clear that every private individual who persecutes a man, his brother, because he is not of the same opinion, is a monster. . . .

Of all religions, the Christian ought doubtless to inspire the most tolerance, although hitherto the Christians have been the most intolerant of all men.

•

. . . Tolerance has never brought civil war; intolerance has covered the earth with carnage. . . .

What! Is each citizen to be permitted to believe and to think that which his reason rightly or wrongly dictates? He should indeed, provided that he does not disturb the public order; for it is not contingent on man to believe or not to believe; but it is contingent on him to respect the usages of his country; and if you say that it is a crime not to believe in the dominant religion, you accuse then yourself the first Christians, your ancestors, and you justify those whom you accuse of having martyred them.

You reply that there is a great difference, that all religions are the work of men, and that the Apostolic Roman Catholic Church is alone the work of God. But in good faith, ought our religion because it is divine reign through hate, violence, exiles, usurpation of property, prisons, tortures, murders, and thanksgivings to God for these murders? The more the Christian religion is divine, the less it pertains to man to require it; if God made it, God will sustain it without you. You know that intolerance produces only hypocrites or rebels; what distressing alternatives! In short, do you want to sustain through executioners the religion of a God whom executioners have put to death and who taught only gentleness and patience?

•

I shall never cease, my dear sir, to preach tolerance from the housetops, despite the complaints of your priests and the outcries of ours, until persecution is no more. The progress of reason is slow, the roots of prejudice lie deep. Doubtless, I shall never see the fruits of my efforts, but they are seeds which may one day germinate.

Dogma

. . . Is Jesus the Word? If He be the Word, did He emanate from God in time or before time? If He emanated from God, is He co-eternal and consubstantial with Him, or is He of a similar substance? Is He distinct from Him, or is He not? Is He made or begotten? Can He beget in His turn? Has He paternity? or productive virtue without paternity? Is the Holy Ghost made? or begotten? or produced? or proceeding from the Father? or proceeding from the Son? or proceeding from both? Can He beget? can He produce? is His hypostasis consubstantial with the hypostasis of the Father and the Son? and how is it that, having the same nature — the same essence as the Father and the Son, He cannot do the same things done by these persons who are Himself?

Assuredly, I understand nothing of this; no one has ever understood any of it, and that is why we have slaughtered one another.

The Christians tricked, cavilled, hated, and excommunicated one another, for some of these dogmas inaccessible to human intellect.

Fanaticism

Fanaticism is to superstition what delirium is to fever, what rage is to anger. He who has ecstasies and visions, who takes dreams for realities, and his own imaginations for prophecies is an enthusiast; he who reinforces his madness by murder is a fanatic. . . .

The most detestable example of fanaticism is that exhibited on the night of St. Bartholomew,[1] when the people of Paris rushed from house to house to stab, slaughter, throw out of the window, and

---

[1] St. Bartholomew refers to the day when the populace of Paris, instigated by King Charles IX at his mother's urging, began a week-long slaughter of Protestants that began on August 24, 1572.

tear in pieces their fellow citizens who did not go to mass.

There are some cold-blooded fanatics; such as those judges who sentence men to death for no other crime than that of thinking differently from themselves. . . .

Once fanaticism has infected a brain, the disease is almost incurable. I have seen convulsionaries who, while speaking of the miracles of Saint Paris [a fourth-century Italian bishop], gradually grew heated in spite of themselves. Their eyes became inflamed, their limbs shook, fury disfigured their face, and they would have killed anyone who contradicted them.

There is no other remedy for this epidemic malady than that philosophical spirit which, extending itself from one to another, at length softens the manners of men and prevents the access of the disease. For when the disorder has made any progress, we should, without loss of time, flee from it, and wait till the air has become purified.

Persecution

What is a persecutor? He whose wounded pride and furious fanaticism arouse princes and magistrates against innocent men, whose only crime is that of being of a different opinion. "Impudent man! you have worshipped God; you have preached and practised virtue; you have served man; you have protected the orphan, have helped the poor; you have changed deserts, in which slaves dragged on a miserable existence, into fertile lands peopled by happy families; but I have discovered that you despise me, and have never read my controversial work. You know that I am a rogue; that I have forged G's signature, that I have stolen. You might tell these things; I must anticipate you. I will, therefore, go to the confessor [spiritual counselor] of the prime minister, or the magistrate; I will show them, with outstretched neck and twisted mouth, that you hold an erroneous opinion in relation to the cells in which the Septuagint was

studied; that you have even spoken disrespectfully ten years ago of Tobit's dog,[2] which you asserted to have been a spaniel, while I proved that it was a greyhound. I will denounce you as the enemy of God and man!" Such is the language of the persecutor; and if precisely these words do not issue from his lips, they are engraven on his heart with the pointed steel of fanaticism steeped in the bitterness of envy. . . .

O God of mercy! If any man can resemble that evil being who is described as ceaselessly employed in the destruction of your works, is it not the persecutor?

Superstition

In 1749 a woman was burned in the Bishopric of Würzburg [a city in central Germany], convicted of being a witch. This is an extraordinary phenomenon in the age in which we live. Is it possible that people who boast of their reformation and of trampling superstition under foot, who indeed supposed that they had reached the perfection of reason, could nevertheless believe in witchcraft, and this more than a hundred years after the so-called reformation of their reason?

In 1652 a peasant woman named Michelle Chaudron, living in the little territory of Geneva [a large city in Switzerland], met the devil going out of the city. The devil gave her a kiss, received her homage, and imprinted on her upper lip and right breast the mark that he customarily bestows on all whom he recognizes as his favorites. This seal of the devil is a little mark which makes the skin insensitive, as all the demonographical jurists of those times affirm.

The devil ordered Michelle Chaudron

---

[2] The Septuagint, the version of the Hebrew Scriptures used by Saint Paul and other early Christians, was a Greek translation done by Hellenized Jews in Alexandria sometime in the late third or the second century B.C. *Tobit's dog* appears in the Book of Tobit, a Hebrew book contained in the Catholic version of the Bible.

to bewitch two girls. She obeyed her master punctually. The girls' parents accused her of witchcraft before the law. The girls were questioned and confronted with the accused. They declared that they felt a continual pricking in certain parts of their bodies and that they were possessed. Doctors were called, or at least, those who passed for doctors at that time. They examined the girls. They looked for the devil's seal on Michelle's body — what the statement of the case called *satanic marks*. Into them they drove a long needle, already a painful torture. Blood flowed out, and Michelle made it known, by her cries, that satanic marks certainly do not make one insensitive. The judges, seeing no definite proof that Michelle Chaudron was a witch, proceeded to torture her, a method that infallibly produces the necessary proofs: this wretched woman, yielding to the violence of torture, at last confessed every thing they desired.

The doctors again looked for the satanic mark. They found a little black spot on one of her thighs. They drove in the needle. The torment of the torture had been so horrible that the poor creature hardly felt the needle; thus the crime was established. But as customs were becoming somewhat mild at that time, she was burned only after being hanged and strangled.

In those days every tribunal of Christian Europe resounded with similar arrests. The faggots were lit everywhere for witches, as for heretics. People reproached the Turks most for having neither witches nor demons among them. This absence of demons was considered an infallible proof of the falseness of a religion.

A zealous friend of public welfare, of humanity, of true religion, has stated in one of his writings on behalf of innocence, that Christian tribunals have condemned to death over a hundred thousand accused witches. If to these judicial murders are added the infinitely superior number of massacred heretics, that part

of the world will seem to be nothing but a vast scaffold covered with torturers and victims, surrounded by judges, guards and spectators.

------♦•♦------

The following passage is from Candide, *Voltaire's most famous work of fiction. The king of the Bulgarians goes to war with the king of the Abares, and Candide is caught in the middle of the conflict.*

------♦•♦------

War

Nothing could be smarter, more splendid, more brilliant, better drawn up than the two armies. Trumpets, fifes, hautboys [oboes], drums, cannons, formed a harmony such as has never been heard even in hell. The cannons first of all laid flat about six thousand men on each side; then the musketry removed from the best of worlds some nine or ten thousand blackguards who infested its surface. The bayonet also was the sufficient reason for the death of some thousands of men. The whole might amount to thirty thousand souls. Candide, who trembled like a philosopher, hid himself as well as he could during this heroic butchery. At last, while the two Kings each commanded a Te Deum[3] in his camp, Candide decided to go elsewhere to reason about effects and causes. He clambered over heaps of dead and dying men and reached a neighboring village, which was in ashes; it was an Abare village which the Bulgarians had burned in accordance with international law. Here, old men dazed with blows watched the dying agonies of their murdered wives who clutched their children to their bleeding breasts; there, disemboweled girls who had been made to satisfy the natural appetites of heroes gasped

------

[3] A Te Deum is a special liturgical hymn praising and thanking God for granting some special favor, like a military victory or the end of a war.

their last sighs; others, half-burned, begged to be put to death. Brains were scattered on the ground among dismembered arms and legs. Candide fled to another village as fast as he could; it belonged to the Bulgarians, and Abarian heroes had treated it in the same way. Candide, stumbling over quivering limbs or across ruins, at last escaped from the theater of war. . . .

Review Questions

1. What argument did Voltaire offer in favor of a policy of religious toleration?
2. Why was religious toleration of such central importance to enlightened philosophes like Voltaire?
3. Why did Voltaire ridicule Christian theological disputation?
4. What did Voltaire mean by the term *fanaticism*? How was it to be cured?
5. According to Voltaire, what moral evils arose from persecuting people for having differing opinions?
6. According to Voltaire, how did religion, science, and law contribute to the evil of persecuting ideological dissenters in society?
7. What did Voltaire imply about the rationality and morality of war?

4 | Attack on Religion

Christianity came under severe attack during the eighteenth century. The philosophes rejected Christian doctrines that seemed contrary to reason. Deism, the dominant religious outlook of the philosophes, taught that religion should accord with reason and natural law. To deists, it seemed reasonable to believe in God, for this superbly constructed universe required a creator in the same manner that a watch required a watchmaker. But, said the deists, after God had constructed the universe, he did not interfere in its operations; the universe was governed by mechanical laws. Deists denied that the Bible was God's work, rejected clerical authority, and dismissed miracles — like Jesus walking on water — as incompatible with natural law. To them, Jesus was not divine but an inspiring teacher of morality. Many deists still considered themselves Christians; the clergy, however, viewed the deists' religious views with horror.

THOMAS PAINE
The Age of Reason

Exemplifying the deist outlook was Thomas Paine (1737–1809), an Englishman who moved to America in 1774. Paine's *Common Sense* (1776) was an eloquent appeal for American independence. Paine is also famous for *The Rights of Man* (1791–1792), included in the next chapter, in which he defended the French Revolution. In *The Age of Reason* (1794–1795), he denounced Christian mysteries, miracles, and prophecies as superstition, and called for a natural religion that accorded with reason and science.

I believe in one God, and no more; and I hope for happiness beyond this life.

I believe in the equality of man; and I believe that religious duties consist in doing justice, loving mercy, and endeavoring to make our fellow-creatures happy.

But, lest it should be supposed that I believe many other things in addition to these, I shall, in the progress of this work, declare the things I do not believe, and my reasons for not believing them.

I do not believe in the creed professed by the Jewish church, by the Roman church, by the Greek church, by the Turkish church, by the Protestant church, nor by any church that I know of. My own mind is my own church. . . .

When Moses told the children of Israel that he received the two tables of the [Ten] commandments from the hands of God, they were not obliged to believe him, because they had no other authority for it than his telling them so; and I have no other authority for it than some historian telling me so. The commandments carry no internal evidence of divinity with them; they contain some good moral precepts, such as any man qualified to be a lawgiver, or a legislator, could produce himself, without having recourse to supernatural intervention. . . .

When also I am told that a woman called the Virgin Mary, said, or gave out, that she was with child without any co-habitation with a man, and that her betrothed husband, Joseph, said that an angel told him so, I have a right to believe them or not; such a circumstance required a much stronger evidence than their bare word for it; but we have not even this — for neither Joseph nor Mary wrote any such matter themselves; it is only reported by others that *they said so* — it is hearsay upon hearsay, and I do not choose to rest my belief upon such evidence.

It is, however, not difficult to account for the credit that was given to the story of Jesus Christ being the son of God. He was born when the heathen mythology had still some fashion and repute in the world, and that mythology had prepared the people for the belief of such a story. Almost all the extraordinary men that lived under the heathen mythology were reputed to be the sons of some of their gods. It was not a new thing, at that time, to believe a man to have been celestially begotten; the intercourse of gods with women was then a matter of familiar opinion. Their Jupiter [chief Roman god], according to their accounts, had cohabited with hundreds: the story, therefore, had nothing in it either new, wonderful, or obscene; it was conformable to the opinions that then prevailed among the people called Gentiles, or Mythologists, and it was those people only that believed it. The Jews who had kept strictly to the belief of one God, and no more, and who had always rejected the heathen mythology, never credited the story. . . .

Nothing that is here said can apply, even with the most distant disrespect, to the real character of Jesus Christ. He was a virtuous and an amiable man. The morality that he preached and practised was of the most benevolent kind; and though similar systems of morality had been preached by Confucius [Chinese philosopher], and by some of the Greek philosophers, many years before; by the Quakers [members of the Society of Friends] since; and by many good men in all ages, it has not been exceeded by any. . . .

. . . The resurrection and ascension [of Jesus Christ], supposing them to have taken place, admitted of public and ocular demonstration, like that of the ascension of a balloon, or the sun at noon-day, to all Jerusalem at least. A thing which everybody is required to believe, requires that the proof and evidence of it should be equal to all, and universal; and as the public visibility of this last related act was the only evidence that could give sanction to the former part, the whole of it falls to the ground, because that evidence never was given. Instead of this, a small number of persons, not more than eight or nine, are introduced as proxies for the whole world, to say they saw it, and all the rest of the world are called upon to believe it. But it appears that Thomas [one of Jesus' disciples] did not believe the resurrection, and, as they say, would not believe without having ocular and manual demonstration himself. *So neither will I,* and the reason is equally as good for me, and for every other person, as for Thomas.

It is in vain to attempt to palliate or disguise this matter. The story, so far as relates to the supernatural part, has every mark of fraud and imposition stamped upon the face of it. Who were the authors of it is as impossible for us now to know, as it is for us to be assured that the books in which the account is related were written by the persons whose names they bear; the best surviving evidence we now have respecting this affair is the Jews. They are regularly descended from the people who lived in the times this resurrection and ascension is said to have happened, and they say, *it is not true.*

BARON D' HOLBACH
Good Sense

More extreme than the deists were the atheists, who denied God's existence altogether. The foremost exponent of atheism was Paul-Henri Thiry, Baron d' Holbach (1723–1789), a prominent contributor to the *Encyclopedia* (see selection 5). Holbach hosted many leading intellectuals, including Diderot, Rousseau, and Condorcet (all represented later in this chapter), at his country estate outside of Paris. He regarded the idea of God as a product of ignorance, fear, and superstition and said that terrified by natural phenomena — storms, fire, floods — humanity's primitive ancestors attributed these occurrences to unseen spirits, whom they tried to appease through rituals. In denouncing religion, Holbach was also affirming core Enlightenment ideals, as the following passage from *Good Sense* reveals.

In a word, whoever will deign to consult common sense upon religious opinions, and will bestow on this inquiry the attention that is commonly given to any objects we presume interesting, will easily perceive that those opinions have no foundation; that Religion is a mere castle in the air. Theology is but the ignorance of natural causes reduced to a system; a long tissue of fallacies and contradictions. In every country, it presents us with romances void of probability. . . .

Savage and furious nations, perpetually at war, adore, under divers names, some God, conformable to their ideas, that is to say, cruel, carnivorous, selfish, bloodthirsty. We find, in all the religions of the earth, "a God of armies," a "jealous God," an "avenging God," a "destroying God," a "God," who is pleased with carnage, and whom his worshippers consider it as a duty to serve to his taste. Lambs, bulls, children, men, heretics, infidels, kings, whole nations, are sacrificed to him. Do not the zealous servants of this barbarous God think themselves obliged even to offer up themselves as a sacrifice to him? Madmen may every where be seen who, after meditating upon their terrible God, imagine that to please him they must do themselves all possible injury, and inflict on themselves, for his honour, the most exquisite torments. The gloomy ideas more usefully formed of the Deity, far from consoling them under the evils of life, have every where disquieted their minds, and produced follies destructive to their happiness.

How could the human mind make any considerable progress, while tormented with frightful phantoms, and guided by men, interested in perpetuating its ignorance and fears? Man has been forced to vegetate in his primitive stupidity: he has been taught nothing but stories about invisible powers upon whom his happiness was supposed to depend. Occupied solely by his fears, and by unintelligible reveries, he has always been at the mercy of his priests, who have reserved to themselves the right of thinking for him, and directing his actions.

Thus man has remained a child without experience, a slave without courage, fearing to reason, and unable to extricate himself from the labyrinth, in which he has so long been wandering. He believes himself forced to bend under the yoke of his gods, known to him only by the fabulous accounts given by his ministers, who, after binding each unhappy mortal in the chains of his prejudice, remain his masters, or else abandon him defenceless to the absolute power of tyrants, no less terrible than the gods, of whom they are the representatives upon earth.

Oppressed by the double yoke of spiritual and temporal power, it has been impossible for the people to know and pursue their happiness. As Religion, so Politics and Morality became sacred things, which the profane were not permitted to handle. Men have had no other Morality, than what their legislators and priests brought down from the unknown regions of heaven. The human mind, confused by its theological opinions ceased to know its own powers, mistrusted experience, feared truth and disdained reason, in order to follow authority. Man has been a mere machine in the hands of tyrants and priests, who alone have had the right of directing his actions. Always treated as a slave, he has contracted the vices of a slave.

Such are the true causes of the corruption of morals, to which Religion opposes only ideal and ineffectual barriers. Ignorance and servitude are calculated to make men wicked and unhappy. Knowledge, Reason, and Liberty, can alone reform them, and make them happier. But every thing conspires to blind them and to confirm them in their errors. Priests cheat them, tyrants corrupt, the better to enslave them. Tyranny ever was, and ever will be, the true cause of man's depravity, and also of his habitual calamities. Almost always fascinated by religious fic-

tion, poor mortals turn not their eyes to the natural and obvious causes of their misery; but attribute their vices to the imperfection of their natures, and their unhappiness to the anger of the gods. They offer up to heaven vows, sacrifices, and presents, to obtain the end of their sufferings, which in reality, are attributable only to the negligence, ignorance, and perversity of their guides, to the folly of their customs, to the unreasonableness of their laws, and above all, to the general want of knowledge. Let men's minds be filled with true ideas; let their reason be cultivated; let justice govern them; and there will be no need of opposing to the passions, such a feeble barrier, as the fear of the gods. Men will be good, when they are well instructed, well governed, and when they are punished or despised for the evil, and justly rewarded for the good, which they do to their fellow citizens.

To discover the true principles of Morality, men have no need of theology, of revelation, or of gods: They have need only of common sense. They have only to commune with themselves, to reflect upon their own nature, to consult their visible interests, to consider the objects of society, and of the individuals who compose it; and they will easily perceive, that virtue is advantageous, and vice disadvantageous to such beings as themselves. Let us persuade men to be just, beneficent, moderate, sociable; not because such conduct is demanded by the gods, but, because it is pleasure to men. Let us advise them to abstain from vice and crime; not because they will be punished in the other world, but because they will suffer for it in this. — *There are*, says a great man, [Montesquieu], *means to prevent crimes, and these means are punishments; there are means to reform manners, and these means are good examples.* . . .

. . . Men are unhappy, only because they are ignorant; they are ignorant, only because every thing conspires to prevent their being enlightened; they are wicked, only because their reason is not sufficiently developed.

Review Questions

1. What positive religious beliefs were held by a deist like Thomas Paine?
2. What Christian beliefs did Paine reject?
3. How did Paine use the new rules of scientific methodology to attack Christian beliefs?
4. What was Baron d' Holbach's view of religion?
5. Compare the views of Holbach with those of Kant (at the beginning of this chapter) on most human beings' intellectual and psychological development.
6. How did Holbach propose to change people's views on religion, politics, and morals?

5 | Compendium of Knowledge

A 38-volume *Encyclopedia*, whose 150 or more contributors included leading Enlightenment thinkers, was undertaken in Paris during the 1740s as a monumental effort to bring together all human knowledge and to propagate Enlightenment ideas. The *Encyclopedia*'s numerous articles on science and technology and its limited coverage of theological questions attest to the new interests of eighteenth-century intellectuals. Serving as principal editor, Denis Diderot (1713–1784) steered the project through difficult periods, including the suspension of publication by French authorities. After the first two volumes were published, the authorities denounced the work for containing "maxims that would tend to destroy royal authority, foment a spirit of independence and revolt, . . . and lay the foundations for the corruption of morals and religion." In 1759, Pope Clement XIII condemned the *Encyclopedia* for having "scandalous doctrines [and] inducing scorn for religion." It required careful diplomacy and clever ruses to finish the project and still incorporate ideas considered dangerous by religious and governmental authorities. With the project's completion in 1772, Diderot and Enlightenment opinion triumphed over clerical censors and powerful elements at the French court.

DENIS DIDEROT
The Encyclopedia

The *Encyclopedia* was a monument to the Enlightenment, as Diderot himself recognized. "This work will surely produce in time a revolution in the minds of man, and I hope that tyrants, oppressors, fanatics, and the intolerant will not gain thereby. We shall have served humanity." Some articles from the *Encyclopedia* follow.

Encyclopedia . . . In truth, the aim of an *encyclopedia* is to collect all the knowledge scattered over the face of the earth, to present its general outlines and structure to the men with whom we live, and to transmit this to those who will come after us, so that the work of past centuries may be useful to the following centuries, that our children, by becoming more educated, may at the same time become more virtuous and happier, and that we may not die without having deserved well of the human race. . . .

. . . We have seen that our *Encyclopedia* could only have been the endeavor of a philosophical century. . . .

I have said that it could only belong to a philosophical age to attempt an *encyclopedia;* and I have said this because such a work constantly demands more intellectual daring than is commonly found in [less courageous periods]. All things must be examined, debated, investigated without exception and without regard for anyone's feelings. . . . We must ride roughshod over all these ancient puerilities, overturn the barriers that reason never erected, give back to the arts and sciences the liberty that is so precious to them. . . . We have for quite some time needed a reasoning age when men would no longer seek the rules in classical authors but in nature. . . .

Fanaticism . . . is blind and passionate zeal born of superstitious opinions, causing people to commit ridiculous, unjust, and cruel actions, not only without any shame or remorse, but even with a kind of joy and comfort. *Fanaticism,* therefore, is only superstition put into practice. . . .

Fanaticism has done much more harm to the world than impiety. What do impious people claim? To free themselves of a yoke, while *fanatics* want to extend their chains over all the earth. Infernal zealomania! . . .

Government . . . The good of the people must be the great purpose of the *government.* The governors are appointed to fulfill it; and the civil constitution that invests them with this power is bound therein by the laws of nature and by the law of reason, which has determined that purpose in any form of *government* as the cause of its welfare. The greatest good of the people is its liberty. Liberty is to the body of the state what health is to each individual; without health man cannot enjoy pleasure; without liberty the state of welfare is excluded from nations. A patriotic governor will therefore see that the right to defend and to maintain liberty is the most sacred of his duties. . . .

If it happens that those who hold the reins of *government* find some resistance when they use their power for the destruction and not the conservation of things that rightfully belong to the people, they must blame themselves, because the public good and the advantage of society are the purposes of establishing a *government.* Hence it necessarily follows that power cannot be arbitrary and that it must be exercised according to the established laws so that the people may know its duty and be secure within the shelter of laws, and so that governors at the same time should be held within just limits and not be tempted to employ the power they have in hand to do harmful things to the body politic. . . .

History . . . *On the usefullness of history.* The advantage consists of the comparison that a statesman or a citizen can make of foreign laws, morals, and customs with those of his country. This is what stimulates modern nations to surpass one another in the arts, in commerce, and in agriculture. The great mistakes of the past are useful in all areas. We cannot describe too often the crimes and misfortunes caused by absurd quarrels. It is certain that by refreshing our memory of these quarrels, we prevent a repetition of them. . . .

Humanity . . . is a benevolent feeling for all men, which hardly inflames anyone without a great and sensitive soul. This sublime and noble enthusiasm is troubled by the pains of other people and by the necessity to alleviate them. With these sentiments an individual would wish to cover the entire universe in order to abolish slavery, superstition, vice, and misfortune. . . .

Intolerance . . . Any method that would tend to stir up men, to arm nations, and to soak the earth with blood is impious.

It is impious to want to impose laws upon man's conscience: this is a universal rule of conduct. People must be enlightened and not constrained. . . .

What did Christ recommend to his disciples when he sent them among the Gentiles? Was it to kill or to die? Was it to persecute or to suffer? . . .

Which is the true voice of humanity, the persecutor who strikes or the persecuted who moans?

Peace . . . War is the fruit of man's depravity; it is a convulsive and violent sickness of the body politic. . . .

If reason governed men and had the influence over the heads of nations that it deserves, we would never see them inconsiderately surrender themselves to the fury of war; they would not show that ferocity that characterizes wild beasts. . . .

Political Authority No man has received from nature the right to command others. Liberty is a gift from heaven, and each individual of the same species has the right to enjoy it as soon as he enjoys the use of reason. . . .

The prince owes to his very subjects the *authority* that he has over them; and this *authority* is limited by the laws of nature and the state. The laws of nature and the state are the conditions under which they have submitted or are supposed to have submitted to its government. . . .

Moreover the government, although hereditary in a family and placed in the hands of one person, is not private property, but public property that consequently can never be taken from the people, to whom it belongs exclusively, fundamentally, and as a freehold. Consequently it is always the people who make the lease or the agreement: they always intervene in the contract that adjudges its exercise. It is not the state that belongs to the prince, it is the prince who belongs to the state: but it does rest with the prince

to govern in the state, because the state has chosen him for that purpose: he has bound himself to the people and the administration of affairs, and they in their turn are bound to obey him according to the laws. . . .

The Press . . . People ask if freedom of the *press* is advantageous or prejudicial to a state. The answer is not difficult. It is of the greatest importance to conserve this practice in all states founded on liberty. I would even say that the disadvantages of this liberty are so inconsiderable compared to its advantages that this ought to be the common right of the universe, and it is certainly advisable to authorize its practice in all governments. . . .

The Slave Trade [This trade] is the buying of unfortunate Negroes by Europeans on the coast of Africa to use as slaves in their colonies. This buying of Negroes, to reduce them to slavery, is one business that violates religion, morality, natural laws, and all the rights of human nature.

Negroes, says a modern Englishman full of enlightenment and humanity, have not become slaves by the right of war; neither do they deliver themselves voluntarily into bondage, and consequently their children are not born slaves. Nobody is unaware that they are bought from their own princes, who claim to have the right to dispose of their liberty, and that traders have them transported in the same way as their other goods, either in their colonies or in America, where they are displayed for sale.

If commerce of this kind can be justified by a moral principle, there is no crime, however atrocious it may be, that cannot be made legitimate. Kings, princes, and magistrates are not the proprietors of their subjects: they do not, therefore, have the right to dispose of their liberty and to sell them as slaves.

On the other hand, no man has the right to buy them or to make himself their master. Men and their liberty are not objects of commerce; they can be neither sold nor bought nor paid for at any price. We must conclude from this that a man whose slave has run away should only blame himself, since he had acquired for money illicit goods whose acquisition is prohibited by all the laws of humanity and equity.

There is not, therefore, a single one of these unfortunate people regarded only as slaves who does not have the right to be declared free, since he has never lost his freedom, which he could not lose and which his prince, his father, and any person whatsoever in the world had not the power to dispose of. Consequently the sale that has been completed is invalid in itself. This Negro does not divest himself and can never divest himself of his natural right; he carries it everywhere with him, and he can demand everywhere that he be allowed to enjoy it. It is, therefore, patent inhumanity on the part of judges in free countries where he is transported, not to emancipate him immediately by declaring him free, since he is their fellow man, having a soul like them.

Review Questions

1. Why was the publication of the *Encyclopedia* a vital step in the philosophes' hopes for reform?

2. What was the *Encyclopedia*'s view on the nature of liberty?

3. To what extent were John Locke's political ideals reflected in the *Encyclopedia*?

4. Why did the *Encyclopedia* recommend the study of history for the "enlightened" mind?

5. What moral ideals did the authors of the *Encyclopedia* promote for "great and sensitive" souls?

6. Why was freedom of the press of such significance to the enlightened philosophes?

7. Why did the philosophes condemn slavery?

6 | Critique of Christian Sex Mores

Diderot reviewed Louis Antoine de Bouganville's *Voyage Around the World* (1771) and later wrote *Supplement to the Voyage of Bouganville.* In this work, Diderot explored some ideas, particularly the sex habits of Tahitians, treated by the French explorer. Diderot also denounced European imperialism and the exploitation of non-Europeans, and questioned traditional Christian sexual standards.

DENIS DIDEROT
Supplement to the Voyage of Bouganville

In *Supplement,* Diderot constructed a dialogue between a Tahitian (Orou), who possesses the wisdom of a French philosophe, and a chaplain, whose defense of Christian sexual mores reveals Diderot's critique of the Christian view of human nature. Diderot thus used a representative of an alien culture to attack those European customs and beliefs that the philosophes detested. In the opening passage, before Orou's dialogue, a Tahitian elder rebukes Bouganville and his companions for bringing the evils of European civilization to his island.

"We [Tahitians] are free — but see where you [Europeans] have driven into our earth the symbol of our future servitude. You are neither a god nor a devil — by what right, then, do you enslave people? Orou! You who understand the speech of these men, tell every one of us, as you have told me, what they have written on that strip of metal — 'This land belongs to us.' This land belongs to you! And why? Because you set foot in it? If some day a Tahitian should land on your shores, and if he should engrave on one of your stones or on the bark of one of your trees: 'This land belongs to the people of Tahiti,' what would you think? You are stronger than we are! And what does that signify? When one of our lads carried off some of the miserable trinkets with which your ship is loaded, what an uproar you made, and what revenge you took! And at that very moment you were plotting, in the depths of your hearts, to steal a whole country! You are not slaves; you would suffer death rather than be enslaved, yet you want to make slaves of us! Do you believe, then, that the Tahitian does not know how to die in defense of his liberty? This Tahitian, whom you want to treat as a chattel, as a dumb animal — this Tahitian is your brother. You are both children of Nature — what right do you have over him that he does not have over you?

"You came; did we attack you? Did we plunder your vessel? Did we seize you and expose you to the arrows of our enemies? Did we force you to work in the fields alongside our beasts of burden? We respected our own image in you. Leave us our own customs, which are wiser and more decent than yours. We have no wish to barter what you call our ignorance for your useless knowledge. We possess already all that is good or necessary for our existence. Do we merit your scorn because we have not been able to create su-perfluous wants for ourselves? When we are hungry, we have something to eat; when we are cold, we have clothing to put on. You have been in our huts — what is lacking there, in your opinion? You are welcome to drive yourselves as hard as you please in pursuit of what you call the comforts of life, but allow sensible people to stop when they see they have nothing to gain but imaginary benefits from the continuation of their painful labors. If you persuade us to go beyond the bounds of strict necessity, when shall we come to the end of our labor? When shall we have time for enjoyment? We have reduced our daily and yearly labors to the least possible amount, because to us nothing seemed more desirable than leisure. Go and bestir yourselves in your own country; there you may torment yourselves as much as you like; but leave us in peace, and do not fill our heads with a hankering after your false needs and imaginary virtues. Look at these men — see how healthy, straight and strong they are. See these women — how straight, healthy, fresh and lovely they are. Take this bow in your hands — it is my own — and call one, two, three, four of your comrades to help you try to bend it. I can bend it myself. I work the soil, I climb mountains, I make my way through the dense forest, and I can run four leagues [about 12 miles] on the plain in less than an hour. Your young comrades have been hard put to it to keep up with me, and yet I have passed my ninetieth year. . . .

"Woe to this island! Woe to all the Tahitians now living, and to all those yet to be born, woe from the day of your arrival! We used to know but one disease — the one to which all men, all animals and all plants are subject — old age. But you have brought us a new one [venereal disease]: you have infected our blood. We shall perhaps be compelled to exterminate with our own hands some of our young girls, some of our women, some of our children, those who have lain with your women, those who have lain with your men. Our fields will be spattered with the foul blood that has passed from your veins into ours. Or else our children, condemned to die, will nourish and perpetuate the evil disease that you have given their fathers and mothers, transmitting it forever to their descendants. . . .

———————— ◆ •●• ◆ ————————

Before the arrival of Christian Europeans, love-making was natural and enjoyable. Europeans introduced an alien element, guilt.

———————— ◆ •●• ◆ ————————

But a while ago, the young Tahitian girl blissfully abandoned herself to the embraces of a Tahitian youth and awaited impatiently the day when her mother, authorized to do so by her having reached the age of puberty, would remove her veil and uncover her breasts. She was proud of her ability to excite men's desires, to attract the amorous looks of strangers, of her own relatives, of her own brothers. In our presence, without shame, in the center of a throng of innocent Tahitians who danced and played the flute, she accepted the caresses of the young man whom her young heart and the secret promptings of her senses had marked out for her. The notion of crime and the fear of disease have come among us only with your coming. Now our enjoyments, formerly so sweet, are attended with guilt and terror. That man in black [a priest], who stands near to you and listens to me, has spoken to our young men, and I know not what he has said to our young girls, but our youths are hesitant and our girls blush. Creep away into the dark forest, if you wish, with the perverse companion of your pleasures, but allow the good, simple Tahitians to reproduce themselves without shame under the open sky and in broad daylight.

———————— ◆ •●• ◆ ————————

In the following conversation between Orou and the chaplain, Christian sexual mores and the

concept of God are questioned. Orou addresses the chaplain.

———————— ◆ •●• ◆ ————————

[OROU] "You are young and healthy and you have just had a good supper. He who sleeps alone, sleeps badly; at night a man needs a woman at his side. Here is my wife and here are my daughters. Choose whichever one pleases you most, but if you would like to do me a favor, you will give your preference to my youngest girl, who has not yet had any children."

The mother said: "Poor girl! I don't hold it against her. It's no fault of hers."

The chaplain replied that his religion, his holy orders, his moral standards and his sense of decency all prevented him from accepting Orou's invitation.

Orou answered: "I don't know what this thing is that you call 'religion,' but I can only have a low opinion of it because it forbids you to partake of an innocent pleasure to which Nature, the sovereign mistress of us all, invites everybody. It seems to prevent you from bringing one of your fellow creatures into the world, from doing a favor asked of you by a father, a mother and their children, from repaying the kindness of a host, and from enriching a nation by giving it an additional citizen. I don't know what it is that you call 'holy orders,' but your chief duty is to be a man and to show gratitude. . . . I hope that you will not persist in disappointing us. Look at the distress you have caused to appear on the faces of these four women — they are afraid you have noticed some defect in them that arouses your distaste. But even if that were so, would it not be possible for you to do a good deed and have the pleasure of honoring one of my daughters in the sight of her sisters and friends? Come, be generous!"

THE CHAPLAIN You don't understand — it's not that. They are all four of them equally beautiful. But there is my religion! My holy orders! . . .

. . . [God] spoke to our ancestors and gave them laws; he prescribed to them the way in which he wishes to be honored; he ordained that certain actions are good and others he forbade them to do as being evil.

OROU I see. And one of these evil actions which he has forbidden is that of a man who goes to bed with a woman or girl. But in that case, why did he make two sexes?

THE CHAPLAIN In order that they might come together — but only when certain conditions are satisfied and only after certain initial ceremonies have been performed. By virtue of these ceremonies one man belongs to one woman and only to her; one woman belongs to one man and only to him.

OROU For their whole lives?

THE CHAPLAIN For their whole lives.

OROU So that if it should happen that a woman should go to bed with some man who was not her husband, or some man should go to bed with a woman that was not his wife . . . but that could never happen because the workman [God] would know what was going on, and since he doesn't like that sort of thing, he wouldn't let it occur.

THE CHAPLAIN No. He lets them do as they will, and they sin against the law of God (for that is the name by which we call the great workman) and against the law of the country; they commit a crime.

OROU I should be sorry to give offense by anything I might say, but if you don't mind, I'll tell you what I think.

THE CHAPLAIN Go ahead.

OROU I find these strange precepts contrary to nature, and contrary to reason. . . . Furthermore, your laws seem to me to be contrary to the general order of things. For in truth is there anything

so senseless as a precept that forbids us to heed the changing impulses that are inherent in our being, or commands that require a degree of constancy which is not possible, that violate the liberty of both male and female by chaining them perpetually to one another? Is there anything more unreasonable than this perfect fidelity that would restrict us, for the enjoyment of pleasures so capricious, to a single partner — than an oath of immutability taken by two individuals made of flesh and blood under a sky that is not the same for a moment, in a cavern that threatens to collapse upon them, at the foot of a cliff that is crumbling into dust, under a tree that is withering, on a bench of stone that is being worn away? Take my word for it, you have reduced human beings to a worse condition than that of the animals. I don't know what your great workman is, but I am very happy that he never spoke to our forefathers, and I hope that he never speaks to our children, for if he does, he may tell them the same foolishness, and they may be foolish enough to believe it. . . .

OROU Are monks faithful to their vows of sterility?

THE CHAPLAIN No.

OROU I was sure of it. Do you also have female monks?

THE CHAPLAIN Yes.

OROU As well behaved as the male monks?

THE CHAPLAIN They are kept more strictly in seclusion, they dry up from unhappiness and die of boredom.

OROU So nature is avenged for the injury done to her! Ugh! What a country! If everything is managed the way you say, you are more barbarous than we are.

Review Questions

1. According to Denis Diderot, why did European imperialism violate natural law?

2. How did Europeans influence the health and sexual mores of the Tahitians?

3. How did Diderot attempt to use the Tahitians to criticize the sexual morals of Europeans?

4. How did Diderot use the concept of the law of nature to undermine Christian sexual morality?

7 | Educational Reform

To the philosophes, advances in the arts were hallmarks of progress. The French philosopher Jean Jacques Rousseau (1712–1778) argued that the accumulation of knowledge improved human understanding but corrupted the morals of human beings. In *A Discourse on the Arts and Sciences* (1750) and *A Discourse on the Origin of Inequality* (1755), Rousseau diagnosed the illnesses of modern civilization. He said that human nature, which was originally good, had been corrupted by society. As a result, he stated at the beginning of *The Social Contract* (1762), "Man is born free; and everywhere he is in chains." How can humanity be made moral and free again? In *The Social Contract*, Rousseau suggested one cure: reforming the political system. He argued that in the existing civil society, the rich and powerful who controlled the state oppressed the majority. Rousseau admired the small ancient Greek city-state (polis), where citizens participated actively and directly in public affairs. A small state modeled after the ancient Greek polis, said Rousseau, would be best able to resolve the tensions between individual freedom and the requirements of the collective community.

JEAN JACQUES ROUSSEAU
Émile

In *The Social Contract*, Rousseau, who had only contempt for absolute monarchy, sought to provide a theoretical foundation for political liberty. In *Émile* (1762), he suggested another cure for the ills of modern society: educational reforms that would instill in children self-confidence, self-reliance, and emotional security. Rousseau understood that children should not be treated like little adults. He railed against chaining young children to desks and filling their heads with rote learning. Instead, he urged that children experience direct contact with the world to develop their ingenuity, resourcefulness, and imagination so that they might become productive and responsible citizens. Excerpts from Rousseau's influential treatise on education follow.

When I thus get rid of children's lessons, I get rid of the chief cause of their sorrows, namely their books. Reading is the curse of childhood, yet it is almost the only occupation you can find for children. Emile, at twelve years old, will hardly know what a book is. "But," you say, "he must, at least, know how to read." When reading is of use to him, I admit he must learn to read, but till then he will only find it a nuisance.

If children are not to be required to do anything as a matter of obedience, it follows that they will only learn what they perceive to be of real and present value, either for use or enjoyment; what other motive could they have for learning? . . .

People make a great fuss about discovering the best way to teach children to read. They invent "bureaux"* and cards, they turn the nursery into a printer's shop. Locke would have them taught to read by means of dice. What a fine idea! And the pity of it! There is a better way than any of those, and one which is generally overlooked — it consists in the desire to learn. Arouse this desire in your scholar [a student who is taught by a "learned tutor"] and have done with your "bureaux" and your dice — any method will serve.

Present interest, that is the motive power, the only motive power that takes us far and safely. Sometimes Emile receives notes of invitation from his father or mother, his relations or friends; he is invited to a dinner, a walk, a boating expedition, to see some public entertainment. These notes are short, clear, plain, and well written. Some one must read them to him, and he cannot always find anybody when wanted; no more consideration is shown to him than he himself showed to you yesterday. Time passes, the chance is lost. The note is read to him at last, but it is too late. Oh! if only he had known how to read! He receives other notes, so short, so interesting, he would like to try to read them. Sometimes he gets help, sometimes none. He does his best, and at last he makes out half the note; it is something about going to-morrow to drink cream — Where? With whom? He cannot tell — how hard he tries to make out the rest! I do not think Emile will need a "bureau." Shall I proceed to the teaching of writing? No, I am ashamed to toy with these trifles in a treatise on education. . . .

If, in accordance with the plan I have

sketched, you follow rules which are just the opposite of the established practice, if instead of taking your scholar far afield, instead of wandering with him in distant places, in far-off lands, in remote centuries, in the ends of the earth, and in the very heavens themselves, you try to keep him to himself, to his own concerns, you will then find him able to perceive, to remember, and even to reason; this is nature's order. . . . Give his body constant exercise, make it strong and healthy, in order to make him good and wise; let him work, let him do things, let him run and shout, let him be always on the go; make a man of him in strength, and he will soon be a man in reason.

Of course by this method you will make him stupid if you are always giving him directions, always saying come here, go there, stop, do this, don't do that. If your head always guides his hands, his own mind will become useless. . . .

It is a lamentable mistake to imagine that bodily activity hinders the working of the mind, as if these two kinds of activity ought not to advance hand in hand, and as if the one were not intended to act as guide to the other. . . .

. . . Your scholar is subject to a power which is continually giving him instruction; he acts only at the word of command; he dare not eat when he is hungry, nor laugh when he is merry, nor weep when he is sad, nor offer one hand rather than the other, nor stir a foot unless he is told to do it; before long he will not venture to breathe without orders. What would you have him think about, when you do all the thinking for him? . . .

As for my pupil, or rather Nature's pupil, he has been trained from the outset to be as self-reliant as possible, he has not formed the habit of constantly seeking help from others, still less of displaying his stores of learning. On the other hand, he exercises discrimination and forethought, he reasons about everything that concerns himself. He does not chatter, he acts. Not a word does he know of

---

Translator's note — The "bureau" was a sort of case containing letters to be put together to form words. It was a favourite device for the teaching of reading and gave its name to a special method, called the bureau-method, of learning to read.

what is going on in the world at large, but he knows very thoroughly what affects himself. As he is always stirring he is compelled to notice many things, to recognise many effects; he soon acquires a good deal of experience. Nature, not man, is his schoolmaster, and he learns all the quicker because he is not aware that he has any lesson to learn. So mind and body work together. He is always carrying out his own ideas, not those of other people, and thus he unites thought and action; as he grows in health and strength he grows in wisdom and discernment.

Review Questions

1. What was Jean Jacques Rousseau's basic approach in educating a child?
2. What was Rousseau's view of human nature, and how did it influence his theories of education?

8 | Humanitarianism

A humanitarian spirit pervaded the philosophes' outlook. Showing a warm concern for humanity, they attacked militarism, slavery, religious persecution, torture, and other violations of human dignity, as seen in foregoing passages from the *Encyclopedia* and Voltaire's works in this chapter.

CAESARE BECCARIA
On Crimes and Punishments

In *On Crimes and Punishments* (1764), Caesare Beccaria (1738–1794), an Italian economist and criminologist, condemned torture, commonly used to obtain confessions in many European countries, as irrational and inhuman.

The true relations between sovereigns and their subjects, and between nations, have been discovered. Commerce has been reanimated by the common knowledge of philosophical truths diffused by the art of printing, and there has sprung up among nations a tacit rivalry of industriousness that is most humane and truly worthy of rational beings. Such good things we owe to the productive enlightenment of this age. But very few persons have studied and fought against the cruelty of punishments and the irregularities of criminal procedures, a part of legislation that is as fundamental as it is widely neglected in almost all of Europe. Very few persons have undertaken to demolish the accumulated errors of centuries by rising to general principles, curbing, at least, with the sole force that acknowledged truths possess, the unbounded course of ill-directed power which has continually produced a long and authorized example of the most cold-blooded barbarity. And yet the groans of the weak, sacrificed to cruel ignorance and to opulent indolence; the barbarous torments, multiplied with lavish and useless severity, for crimes either not proved or wholly imaginary; the filth and horrors of a prison, intensified by that cruellest tormentor of the miserable, uncertainty — all these ought to have roused that breed of magistrates who direct the opinions of men. . . .

But what are to be the proper punishments for such crimes?

Is the death-penalty really *useful* and *necessary* for the security and good order of society? Are torture and torments *just,* and do they attain the *end* for which laws are instituted? What is the best way to prevent crimes? Are the same punishments equally effective for all times? What influence have they on customary behavior? These problems deserve to be analyzed with that geometric precision which the mist of sophisms, seductive eloquence, and timorous doubt cannot withstand. If I could boast only of having been the first to present to Italy, with a little more clarity, what other nations have boldly written and are beginning to practice, I would account myself fortunate. But if, by defending the rights of man and of unconquerable truth, I should help to save from the spasm and agonies of death some wretched victim of tyranny or of no less fatal ignorance, the thanks and tears of one innocent mortal in his transports of joy would console me for the contempt of all mankind. . . .

A cruelty consecrated by the practice of most nations is torture of the accused during his trial, either to make him confess the crime or to clear up contradictory statements, or to discover accomplices, or to purge him of infamy in some metaphysical and incomprehensible way, or, finally, to discover other crimes of which he might be guilty but of which he is not accused.

No man can be called *guilty* before a judge has sentenced him, nor can society deprive him of public protection before it has been decided that he has in fact violated the conditions under which such protection was accorded him. What right is it, then, if not simply that of might, which empowers a judge to inflict punishment on a citizen while doubt still remains as to his guilt or innocence? Here is the dilemma, which is nothing new: the fact of the crime is either certain or uncertain; if

certain, all that is due is the punishment established by the laws, and tortures are useless because the criminal's confession is useless; if uncertain, then one must not torture the innocent, for such, according to the laws, is a man whose crimes are not yet proved. . . .

. . . The impression of pain may become so great that, filling the entire sensory capacity of the tortured person, it leaves him free only to choose what for the moment is the shortest way of escape from pain. The response of the accused is then as inevitable as the impressions of fire and water. The sensitive innocent man will then confess himself guilty when he believes that, by so doing, he can put an end to his torment. Every difference between guilt and innocence disappears by virtue of the very means one pretends to be using to discover it. (Torture) is an infallible means indeed — for absolving robust scoundrels and for condemning innocent persons who happen to be weak. Such are the fatal defects of this so-called criterion of truth, a criterion fit for a cannibal. . . .

Of two men, equally innocent or equally guilty, the strong and courageous will be acquitted, the weak and timid condemned, by virtue of this rigorous rational argument: "I, the judge, was supposed to find you guilty of such and such a crime; you, the strong, have been able to resist the pain, and I therefore absolve you; you, the weak, have yielded, and I therefore condemn you. I am aware that a confession wrenched forth by torments ought to be of no weight whatsoever, but I'll torment you again if you don't confirm what you have confessed." . . .

A strange consequence that necessarily follows from the use of torture is that the innocent person is placed in a condition worse than that of the guilty, for if both are tortured, the circumstances are all against the former. Either he confesses the crime and is condemned, or he is declared innocent and has suffered a punishment he did not deserve. The guilty man, on the contrary, finds himself in a favorable situation; that is, if, as a consequence of having firmly resisted the torture, he is absolved as innocent, he will have escaped a greater punishment by enduring a lesser one. Thus the innocent cannot but lose, whereas the guilty may gain. . . .

It would be superfluous to intensify the light, here, by citing the innumerable examples of innocent persons who have confessed themselves criminals because of the agonies of torture; there is no nation, there is no age that does not have its own to cite.

Review Questions

1. What were Caesare Beccaria's arguments against the use of torture in judicial proceedings?
2. What philosophic ideals of the Enlightenment philosophes are reflected in Beccaria's arguments?

9 | On the Progress of Humanity

Marie Jean-Antoine-Nicolas Caritat, Marquis de Condorcet (1743–1794) was a French mathematician and historian of science. He contributed to the *Encyclopedia* and campaigned actively for religious toleration and the abolition of slavery. During the French Revolution, Condorcet attracted the enmity of the dominant Jacobin party and in 1793 was forced to go into hiding. Secluded in Paris, he wrote *Sketch for a Historical Picture of the Progress of the Human Mind.* Arrested in 1794, Condorcet died during his first night in prison from either exhaustion or self-inflicted poison.

MARQUIS DE CONDORCET
Progress of the Human Mind

Sharing the philosophes' confidence in human goodness and in reason, Condorcet was optimistic about humanity's future progress. Superstition, prejudice, intolerance, and tyranny — all barriers to progress in the past — would gradually be eliminated, and humanity would enter a golden age. The following excerpts are from Condorcet's *Sketch.*

. . . The aim of the work that I have undertaken, and its result will be to show by appeal to reason and fact that nature has set no term to the perfection of human faculties; that the perfectibility of man is truly indefinite; and that the progress of this perfectibility, from now onwards independent of any power that might wish to halt it, has no other limit than the duration of the globe upon which nature

has cast us. This progress will doubtless vary in speed, but it will never be reversed as long as the earth occupies its present place in the system of the universe, and as long as the general laws of this system produce neither a general cataclysm nor such changes as will deprive the human race of its present faculties and its present resources. . . .

. . . It will be necessary to indicate by

what stages what must appear to us today a fantastic hope ought in time to become possible, and even likely; to show why, in spite of the transitory successes of prejudice and the support that it receives from the corruption of governments or peoples, truth alone will obtain a lasting victory; we shall demonstrate how nature has joined together indissolubly the progress of knowledge and that of liberty, virtue and respect for the natural rights of man. . . .

After long periods of error, after being led astray by vague or incomplete theories, publicists have at last discovered the true rights of man and how they can all be deduced from the single truth, that *man is a sentient being, capable of reasoning and of acquiring moral ideas.* . . .

At last man could proclaim aloud his right, which for so long had been ignored, to submit all opinions to his own reason and to use in the search for truth the only instrument for its recognition that he has been given. Every man learnt with a sort of pride that nature had not forever condemned him to base his beliefs on the opinions of others; the superstitions of antiquity and the abasement of reason before the transports of supernatural religion disappeared from society as from philosophy.

Thus an understanding of the natural rights of man, the belief that these rights are inalienable and indefeasible, a strongly expressed desire for liberty of thought and letters, of trade and industry, and for the alleviation of the people's suffering, for the proscription of all penal laws against religious dissenters and the abolition of torture and barbarous punishments, the desire for a milder system of criminal legislation and jurisprudence which should give complete security to the innocent, and for a simpler civil code, more in conformance with reason and nature, indifference in all matters of religion which now were relegated to the status of superstitions and political impostures, a hatred of hypocrisy and fanaticism, a contempt for prejudice, zeal for the propagation

of enlightenment: all these principles, gradually filtering down from philosophical works to every class of society whose education went beyond the catechism and the alphabet, became the common faith . . . [of enlightened thinkers]. In some countries these principles formed a public opinion sufficiently widespread for even the mass of the people to show a willingness to be guided by it and to obey it. . . .

Force or persuasion on the part of governments, priestly intolerance, and even national prejudices, had all lost their deadly power to smother the voice of truth, and nothing could now protect the enemies of reason or the oppressors of freedom from a sentence to which the whole of Europe would soon subscribe. . . .

Our hopes for the future condition of the human race can be subsumed under three important heads: the abolition of inequality between nations, the progress of equality within each nation, and the true perfection of mankind. Will all nations one day attain that state of civilization which the most enlightened, the freest and the least burdened by prejudices, such as the French and the Anglo-Americans [by virtue of their revolutions], have attained already? Will the vast gulf that separates these peoples from the slavery of nations under the rule of monarchs, from the barbarism of African tribes, from the ignorance of savages, little by little disappear? . . .

Is the human race to better itself, either by discoveries in the sciences and the arts, and so in the means to individual welfare and general prosperity; or by progress in the principles of conduct or practical morality; or by a true perfection of the intellectual, moral, or physical faculties of man, an improvement which may result from a perfection either of the instruments used to heighten the intensity of these faculties and to direct their use or of the natural constitution of man?

In answering these three questions we shall find in the experience of the past, in the observation of the progress that the sciences and civilization have already made, in the analysis of the progress of the human mind and of the development of its faculties, the strongest reasons for believing that nature has set no limit to the realization of our hopes. . . .

The time will therefore come when the sun will shine only on free men who know no other master but their reason; when tyrants and slaves, priests and their stupid or hypocritical instruments will exist only in works of history and on the stage; and when we shall think of them only to pity their victims and their dupes; to maintain ourselves in a state of vigilance by thinking on their excesses; and to learn how to recognize and so to destroy, by force of reason, the first seeds of tyranny and superstition, should they ever dare to reappear amongst us.

Review Questions

1. What image of human nature underlies the Marquis de Condorcet's theory of human progress?

2. According to Condorcet, what economic, political, and cultural policies were sought by enlightened philosophes?

3. According to Condorcet, what had to occur before other peoples were to achieve the goal of sharing in an enlightened civilization?

4. Was the Enlightenment philosophy an alternative moral order to that of Christianity? Or was it an internal reformation of the Christian moral order?

PART · II

Modern Europe

CHAPTER · 3

The French Revolution

In 1789, many participants and observers viewed the revolutionary developments in France as the fulfillment of the Enlightenment's promise — the triumph of reason over tradition and ignorance, of liberty over despotism. It seemed that the French reformers were eliminating the abuses of an unjust system and creating a new society founded on the ideals of the philosophes.

Eighteenth-century French society, the Old Regime, was divided into three orders, or estates. The First Estate (the clergy) and the Second Estate (the nobility) enjoyed special privileges sanctioned by law and custom. The church collected tithes (taxes on the land), censored books regarded as a threat to religion and morality, and paid no taxes to the state (although the church did make a "free gift" to the royal treasury). Nobles were exempt from most taxes, collected manorial dues from peasants (even from free peasants), and held the highest positions in the church, the army, and the government. Peasants, urban workers, and members of the bourgeoisie belonged to the Third Estate, which comprised about 96 percent of the population.

The bourgeoisie — which included merchants, bankers, professionals, and government officials below the top ranks — provided the leadership and ideology for the French Revolution. In 1789 the bourgeoisie possessed wealth and talent, but had no political power; they were denied equality with the aristocracy, for whom the highest positions in the land were reserved on the basis of birth. By 1789 the bourgeoisie wanted to abolish the special privileges of the nobility and to open prestigious positions to men of talent regardless of their birth. They wanted to give France a constitution that limited the monarch's power, established a parliament, and protected the rights of the individual.

The immediate cause of the French Revolution was a financial crisis. The wars of Louis XIV and subsequent foreign adventures, including French aid to the American colonists during their revolution, had emptied the royal treasury. The refusal of the clergy and the nobles to surrender their tax exemptions compelled Louis XVI to call a meeting of the Estates General — a medieval assembly that had last met in 1614 — to deal with impending bankruptcy. The nobility intended to use the Estates General to weaken the French throne and regain powers lost a century earlier under the absolute rule of Louis XIV. But the nobility's expectations were misguided; their revolt against the crown paved the way for the Third Estate's eventual destruction of the Old Regime.

Between June and November 1789 the bourgeoisie, aided by uprisings of the common people of Paris and the peasants in the countryside, gained control over the state and instituted reforms. During this opening, moderate phase of the Revolution (1789–1791), the bourgeoisie abolished the special privileges of the aristocracy and clergy, formulated a declaration of human rights, subordinated the church to the state, reformed the country's administrative and judicial systems, and drew up a constitution creating a parliament and limiting the king's power.

Between 1792 and 1794 came a radical stage. Three principal factors propelled the Revolution in a radical direction: pressure from the urban poor, the *sans-culottes*, who wanted the government to do something about their poverty; a counterrevolution led by clergy and aristocrats who wanted to undo the reforms of the Revolution; and war with the European powers which sought to check French expansion and to stifle the revolutionary ideals of liberty and equality.

The dethronement of Louis XVI, the establishment of a republic in September 1792, and the king's execution in January 1793 were all signs of growing radicalism. As the new Republic tottered under the twin blows of internal insurrection and foreign invasion, the revolutionary leadership grew more extreme. In June 1793 the Jacobins took power. Tightly organized, disciplined, and fiercely devoted to the Republic, the Jacobins mobilized the nation's material and human resources to defend it against the invading foreign armies. To deal with counterrevolutionaries, the Jacobins unleashed the Reign of Terror, which took the lives of some 20,000 to 40,000 people, many of them innocent of any crime against the state. Although the Jacobins succeeded in saving the Revolution, their extreme measures aroused opposition. In the last part of 1794, power again passed into the hands of the moderate bourgeoisie who wanted no part of Jacobin radicalism.

In 1799, Napoleon Bonaparte, a popular general with an inexhaustible yearning for power, overthrew the government and pushed the Revolution in still another direction, toward military dictatorship. Although Napoleon subverted the revolutionary ideal of liberty, he preserved the social gains of the Revolution — the abolition of the special privileges of the nobility and the clergy.

The era of French Revolution was a decisive period in the shaping of the modern West. By destroying aristocratic privileges and opening careers to talent, it advanced the cause of equality under the law. By weakening the power of the clergy, it promoted the secularization of society. By abolishing the divine right of monarchy, drafting a constitution, and establishing a parliament, it accelerated the growth of the liberal-democratic state. By eliminating serfdom and the sale of government office and by reforming the tax system, it fostered a rational approach to administration. In the nineteenth century, the ideals and reforms of the French Revolution spread in shock waves across Europe; in country after country, the old order was challenged by the ideals of liberty and equality.

1 | Abuses of the Old Regime

The roots of the French Revolution lay in the aristocratic structure of French society. The Third Estate resented the special privileges of the aristocracy, a legacy of the Middle Ages, and the inefficient and corrupt methods of government. To many French people influenced by the ideas of the philosophes, French society seemed an affront to reason. By 1789, reformers sought a new social order based on rationality and equality.

ARTHUR YOUNG
Plight of the French Peasants

French peasants in the late eighteenth century were better off than the peasants of eastern and central Europe, where serfdom predominated. The great majority of France's 21 million peasants were free; many owned their own land, and some were prosperous. Yet the countryside was burdened with severe problems, which sparked a spontaneous revolution in 1789.

A rising birthrate led to the continual subdivision of French farms among peasant sons; on the resulting small holdings, peasants struggled to squeeze out a living. Many landless peasants, who were forced to work as day laborers, were also hurt by the soaring population. An oversupply of rural day laborers reduced many of the landless to beggary. An unjust and corrupt tax system also contributed to the peasants' poverty. Peasants paid excessive taxes to the state, church, and lords; taxes and obligations due the lords were particularly onerous medieval vestiges, since most peasants were no longer serfs. Inflation and a poor harvest in 1788–1789 worsened conditions.

Arthur Young (1741–1820), an English agricultural expert with a keen eye for detail, traveled through France just prior to the Revolution. In *Travels During the Years 1787, 1788, and 1789,* he reported on conditions in the countryside.

. . . The abuses attending the levy of taxes were heavy and universal. The kingdom was parceled into generalities [administrative units], with an intendant at the head of each, into whose hands the whole power of the crown was delegated for everything except the military authority; but particularly for all affairs of finance. The generalities were subdivided into elections, at the head of which was a *sub-delegue* appointed by the intendant. The rolls of the *taille,* capitation, *vingtiemes,*[1] and other taxes, were distributed among districts, parishes, and individuals, at the pleasure of the intendant, who could exempt, change, add, or diminish at pleasure. Such an enormous power, constantly acting, and from which no man was free, must, in the nature of things, degenerate in many cases into absolute tyranny. It must be obvious that the friends, acquaintances, and dependents of the intendant, and of all his *sub-delegues,* and the friends of these friends, to a long chain of dependence, might be favoured in taxation at the ex-

---

[1] A *taille* was a tax levied on the value of a peasant's land or wealth. A capitation was a head or poll tax paid for each person. A *vingtieme* was a tax on income and was paid chiefly by peasants.

pense of their miserable neighbours; and that noblemen in favour at court, to whose protection the intendant himself would naturally look up, could find little difficulty in throwing much of the weight of their taxes on others, without a similar support. Instances, and even gross ones, have been reported to me in many parts of the kingdom, that made me shudder at the oppression to which numbers must have been condemned, by the undue favours granted to such crooked influence. But, without recurring to such cases, what must have been the state of the poor people paying heavy taxes, from which the nobility and clergy were exempted? A cruel aggravation of their misery, to see those who could best afford to pay, exempted because able! . . . The *corvees* [taxes paid in labor, often road building], or police of the roads, were annually the ruin of many hundreds of farmers; more than 300 were reduced to beggary in filling up one vale in Lorraine: all these oppressions fell on the *tiers etat* [Third Estate] only; the nobility and clergy having been equally exempted from *tailles*, militia and *corvees*. The penal code of finance makes one shudder at the horrors of punishment inadequate to the crime. . . .

1. Smugglers of salt, armed and assembled to the number of five, in Provence, a fine of 500 liv. [*livres*, French coins] and nine years galleys [sentenced to backbreaking labor — rowing sea vessels] in all the rest of the kingdom, death.

2. Smugglers, armed, assembled, but in number under five, a fine of 300 liv. and three years galleys. Second offense, death. . . .

10. Buying smuggled salt, to resell it, the same punishments as for smuggling. . . .

The *Capitaineries* [lords' exclusive hunting rights] were a dreadful scourge on all the occupiers of land. By this term is to be understood the paramountship of certain districts, granted by the king to princes of the blood, by which they were put in possession of the property of all game, even on lands not belonging to them. . . . In speaking of the preservation of the game in these *capitaineries*, it must be observed that by game must be understood whole droves of wild boars, and herds of deer not confined by any wall or pale, but wandering at pleasure over the whole country, to the destruction of crops; and to the peopling of the galleys by the wretched peasants, who presumed to kill them in order to save that food which was to support their helpless children. . . . Now an English reader will scarcely understand it without being told, that there were numerous edicts for preserving the game which prohibited weeding and hoeing, lest the young partridges should be disturbed; . . . manuring with night soil, lest the flavour of the partridges should be injured by feeding on the corn so produced; mowing hay, etc., before a certain time, so late as to spoil many crops; and taking away the stubble, which would deprive the birds of shelter. The tyranny exercised in these *capitaineries*, which extended over 400 leagues[2] of country, was so great that many *cahiers* [lists of the Third Estate's grievances] demanded the utter suppression of them. Such were the exertions of arbitrary power which the lower orders felt directly from the royal authority; but, heavy as they were, it is a question whether the [abuses], suffered [indirectly] through the nobility and the clergy, were not yet more oppressive. Nothing can exceed the complaints made in the *cahiers* under this head. They speak of the dispensation of justice in the manorial courts, as comprising every species of despotism; the districts indeterminate — appeals endless — irreconcilable

---

[2] Various units of distance were called leagues, and their length was from about 2.4 to 4.6 miles.

to liberty and prosperity — and irrevocably [condemned] in the opinion of the public — augmenting litigations — favouring every [form of trickery] — ruining the parties — not only by enormous expenses on the most petty objects, but by a dreadful loss of time. The judges, commonly ignorant pretenders, who hold their courts in *cabarets* [taverns], and are absolutely dependent on the seigneurs [lords]. Nothing can exceed the force of expression used in painting the oppressions of the seigneurs, in consequence of their feudal powers. . . . The countryman is tyrannically enslaved by it. . . . In passing through many of the French provinces, I was struck with the various and heavy complaints of the farmers and little proprietors of the feudal grievances, with the weight of which their industry was [burdened]; but I could not then conceive the multiplicity of the shackles which kept them poor and depressed. I understood it better afterwards.

Grievances of the Third Estate

At the same time that elections were held for the Estates General, the three estates drafted *cahiers de doléances,* the lists of grievances that deputies would take with them when the Estates General convened. The cahiers from all three estates expressed loyalty to the monarchy and the church and called for a written constitution and an elected assembly. The cahiers of the clergy and the nobility insisted on the preservation of traditional rights and privileges. The Cahier of the Third Estate of Dourdan, in the *généralité* of Orléans (one of the thirty-four administrative units into which prerevolutionary France was divided), expressed the reformist hopes of the Third Estate. Some of the grievances in the cahier follow.

29 March, 1789

The order of the third estate of the City, *Bailliage* [judicial district], and County of Dourdan, imbued with gratitude prompted by the paternal kindness of the King, who deigns to restore its former rights and its former constitution, forgets at this moment its misfortunes and impotence, to harken only to its foremost sentiment and its foremost duty, that of sacrificing everything to the glory of the *Patrie* [nation] and the service of His Majesty. It supplicates him to accept the grievances, complaints, and remonstrances which it is permitted to bring to the foot of the throne, and to see therein only the expression of its zeal and the homage of its obedience.

It wishes:

1. That his subjects of the third estate, equal by such status to all other citizens, present themselves before the common father without other distinction which might degrade them.

2. That all the orders [the three estates], already united by duty and a common desire to contribute equally to the needs of the State, also deliberate in common concerning its needs.

3. That no citizen lose his liberty except according to law; that, consequently, no one be arrested by virtue of special orders, or, if imperative circumstances necessitate such orders, that the prisoner be handed over to the regular courts of justice within forty-eight hours at the latest.

4. That no letters or writings intercepted in the post [mails] be the cause of the detention of any citizen, or be produced in court against him, except in case of conspiracy or undertaking against the State.

5. That the property of all citizens be

inviolable, and that no one be required to make sacrifice thereof for the public welfare, except upon assurance of indemnification based upon the statement of freely selected appraisers. . . .

15. That every personal tax be abolished; that thus the *capitation* and the *taille* and its accessories be merged with the *vingtièmes*[1] in a tax on land and real or nominal property.

16. That such tax be borne equally, without distinction, by all classes of citizens and by all kinds of property, even feudal and contingent rights.

17. That the tax substituted for the *corvée* [taxes paid in labor] be borne by all classes of citizens equally and without distinction. That said tax, at present beyond the capacity of those who pay it and the needs to which it is destined, be reduced by at least one-half. . . .

Justice

1. That the administration of justice be reformed, either by restoring strict execution of ordinances, or by reforming the sections thereof that are contrary to the dispatch and welfare of justice. . . .

7. That venality [sale] of offices be suppressed. . . .

8. That the excessive number of offices in the necessary courts be reduced in just measure, and that no one be given an office of magistracy if he is not at least twenty-five years of age, and until after a substantial public examination has verified his morality, integrity, and ability. . . .

10. That the study of law be reformed; that it be directed in a manner analogous to our legislation, and that candidates for degrees be subjected to rigorous tests which may not be evaded; that no dispensation of age or time be granted.

11. That a body of general customary law be drafted of all articles common to all the customs of the several provinces and *bailliages*. . . .

12. That deliberations of courts and companies of magistracy which tend to prevent entry of the third estate thereto be rescinded and annulled as injurious to the citizens of that order, in contempt of the authority of the King, whose choice they limit, and contrary to the welfare of justice, the administration of which would become the patrimony of those of noble birth instead of being entrusted to merit, enlightenment, and virtue.

13. That military ordinances which restrict entrance to the service to those possessing nobility be reformed.

That naval ordinances establishing a degrading distinction between officers born into the order of nobility and those born into that of the third estate be revoked, as thoroughly injurious to an order of citizens and destructive of the competition so necessary to the glory and prosperity of the State.

Finances

1. That if the Estates General considers it necessary to preserve the fees of *aides* [tax on commodities], such fees be made uniform throughout the entire kingdom and reduced to a single denomination. . . .

2. That the tax of the *gabelle* [tax on salt] be eliminated if possible, or that it be regulated among the several provinces of the kingdom. . . .

3. That the taxes on hides, which have totally destroyed that branch of commerce and caused it to go abroad, be suppressed forever.

4. That . . . all useless offices, either in police or in the administration of justice, be abolished and suppressed.

Agriculture

4. That the right to hunt may never affect the property of the citizen; that, accordingly, he may at all times travel over his lands, have injurious herbs uprooted,

---

[1] For an explanation of taxes, see footnote 1 on page 61.

and cut *luzernes* [alfalfa], *sainfoins* [fodder], and other produce whenever it suits him; and that stubble may be freely raked immediately after the harvest. . . .[2]

11. . . . That individuals as well as communities be permitted to free themselves from the rights of *banalité* [peasants were required to use the lord's mill, winepress, and oven] and *corvée*, by payments in money or in kind, at a rate likewise established by His Majesty on the basis of the deliberations of the Estates General. . . .

15. That the militia, which devastates the country, takes workers away from husbandry, produces premature and ill-matched marriages, and imposes secret and arbitrary taxes upon those who are subject thereto, be suppressed and replaced by voluntary enlistment at the expense of the provinces.

---

[2]See the discussion of nobles' hunting rights and the peasants' hatred of this practice in the preceding reading by Arthur Young.

EMMANUEL SIEYÈS

Bourgeois Disdain for Special Privileges of the Aristocracy

In a series of pamphlets, including *The Essay on Privileges* (1788) and *What Is the Third Estate?* (1789), Abbé Emmanuel Sieyès (1748–1836) expressed the bourgeoisie's disdain for the nobility. Although educated at Jesuit schools to become a priest, Sieyès had come under the influence of Enlightenment ideas. In *What Is the Third Estate?* he denounced the special privileges of the nobility, asserted that the people are the source of political authority, and maintained that national unity stands above estate or local interests. The ideals of the Revolution — liberty, equality, and fraternity — are found in Sieyès's pamphlet, excerpts of which follow.

The plan of this book is fairly simple. We must ask ourselves three questions.

1) What is the Third Estate? *Everything.*

2) What has it been until now in the political order? *Nothing.*

3) What does it want to be? *Something.* . . .

. . . Only the well-paid and honorific posts are filled by members of the privileged order [nobles]. Are we to give them credit for this? We could do so only if the Third Estate was unable or unwilling to fill these posts. We know the answer. Nevertheless, the privileged have dared to preclude the Third Estate. "No matter how useful you are," they said, "no matter how able you are, you can go so far and no further. Honors are not for the like of you.". . .

. . . Has nobody observed that as soon as the government becomes the property of a separate class, it starts to grow out of all proportion and that posts are created not to meet the needs of the governed but of those who govern them? . . .

It suffices to have made the point that the so-called usefulness of a privileged order to the public service is a fallacy; that, without help from this order, all the arduous tasks in the service are performed by the Third Estate; that without this order the higher posts could be infinitely better filled; that they ought to be the natural prize and reward of recognised ability and service; and that if the privileged have succeeded in usurping all well-paid and honorific posts, this is both a hateful iniquity towards the generality of citizens and an act of treason to the commonwealth.

Who is bold enough to maintain that the Third Estate does not contain within itself everything needful to constitute a complete nation? It is like a strong and robust man with one arm still in chains. If the privileged order were removed, the nation would not be something less but something more. What then is the Third Estate? All; but an "all" that is fettered and oppressed. What would it be without the privileged order? It would be all; but free and flourishing. Nothing will go well without the Third Estate; everything would go considerably better without the two others. . . .

. . . The privileged, far from being useful to the nation, can only weaken and injure it; . . . the nobility may be a *burden* for the nation. . . .

The nobility, however, is . . . a foreigner in our midst because of its *civil and political* prerogatives.

What is a nation? A body of associates living under *common* laws and represented by the same *legislative assembly*, etc.

Is it not obvious that the nobility possesses privileges and exemptions which it brazenly calls its rights and which stand distinct from the rights of the great body of citizens? Because of these special rights, the nobility does not belong to the common order, nor is it subjected to the common laws. Thus its private rights make it a people apart in the great nation.

Review Questions

1. What abuses did Arthur Young see in the French systems of taxation and justice?

2. Why did Young consider the *capitaineries* to be a particularly "dreadful scourge" on the peasants?

3. The principle of equality pervaded the cahiers of the Third Estate. Discuss this statement.

4. How did the Cahier of the Third Estate of Dourdan try to correct some of the abuses discussed by Arthur Young?

5. How important did Sieyès say the nobility (the privileged order) were to the life of the nation?

6. What importance did Sieyès attach to the contribution of the Third Estate (the bourgeoisie) to the life of the nation?

7. How did Sieyès define the nation? Why did he believe that the privileged order was a barrier to national unity?

2 | The Role of the Philosophes

The Enlightenment thinkers were not themselves revolutionaries. However, by subjecting the institutions and values of the Old Regime to critical scrutiny and by offering the hope that society could be reformed, the philosophes created the intellectual precondition for revolution.

ALEXIS DE TOCQUEVILLE
Critique of the Old Regime

The following passage from *The Old Regime and the French Revolution*, by Alexis de Tocqueville (1805–1859), treats the role of the philosophes in undermining the Old Regime. Born of a noble family, de Tocqueville was active in French politics. After traveling in the United States, he wrote *Democracy in America* (1835), a great work of historical literature. In 1856, he published *The Old Regime and the French Revolution*, which explored the causes of the French Revolution.

France had long been the most literary of all the nations of Europe; although her literary men had never exhibited such intellectual powers as they displayed about the middle of the 18th century, or occupied such a position as that which they then assumed. Nothing of the kind had ever been seen in France, or perhaps in any other country. They were not constantly mixed up with public affairs as in England: at no period, on the contrary, had they lived more apart from them. They were invested with no authority whatever, and filled no public offices in a society crowded with public officers; yet they did not, like the greater part of their brethren in Germany, keep entirely aloof from the arena of politics and retire into the regions of pure philosophy and polite literature. They busied themselves incessantly with matters appertaining to government, and this was, in truth, their special occupation. Thus they were continually holding forth on the origin and primitive forms of society, the primary rights of the citizen and of government, the natural and artificial relations of men, the wrong or right of customary laws, and the principles of legislation. While they thus penetrated to the fundamental basis of the constitution of their time, they examined its structure with minute care and criticised its general plan.

. . . [The thinkers of the Enlightenment] all agreed that it was expedient to substitute simple and elementary rules, deduced from reason and natural law, for the complicated traditional customs which governed the society of their time. Upon a strict scrutiny it may be seen that what might be called the political philosophy of the eighteenth century consisted, properly speaking, in this one notion.

These opinions were by no means novel; for three thousand years they had unceasingly traversed the imaginations of mankind, though without being able to stamp themselves there. How came they at last to take possession of the minds of all the writers of this period? Why, instead of progressing no farther than the heads of a few philosophers, as had frequently been the case, had they at last reached the masses, and assumed the strength and the fervour of a political passion to such a degree, that general and abstract theories upon the nature of society became daily topics of conversation, and even inflamed the imaginations of women and of the peasantry? How was it that literary men, possessing neither rank, nor honours, nor fortune, nor responsibility, nor power, became, in fact, the principal political men of the day. . . .

It was not by chance that the philosophers of the 18th century . . . coincided in entertaining notions so opposed to those which still served as bases to the society of their time: these ideas had been naturally suggested to them by the aspect of the society which they had all before their eyes. The sight of so many unjust or absurd privileges, the [burden] of which was more and more felt whilst their cause was less and less understood, urged, or rather precipitated the minds of one and all to the idea of the natural equality of man's condition. Whilst they looked upon so many strange and irregular institutions, born of other times, which no one had attempted either to bring into harmony with each other or to adapt to modern wants, and which appeared likely to perpetuate their existence though they had lost their worth, they learned to abhor what was ancient and traditional, and naturally became desirous of re-constructing the social edifice of their day upon an entirely new plan — a plan which each one traced solely by the light of his reason. . . .

Had [the French] been able, like the English, gradually to modify the spirit of their ancient institutions by practical experience without destroying them, they would perhaps have been less inclined to invent new ones. But there was not a man who did not daily feel himself injured in his fortune, in his person, in his comfort, or his pride by some old law, some ancient political custom, or some other remnant of former authority, without perceiving at hand any remedy that he could himself apply to his own particular hardship. It appeared that the whole constitution of the country must either be endured or destroyed.

The French, however, had still preserved one liberty amidst the ruin of every other: they were still free to philosophize almost without restraint upon the origin of society, the essential nature of governments, and the primordial rights of mankind.

All those who felt themselves aggrieved by the daily application of existing laws were soon enamoured of these literary politics. The same taste soon reached even those who by nature or by their condition of life seemed the farthest removed from abstract speculations. Every taxpayer wronged by the unequal distribution of the *taille*[1] was fired by the idea that all men ought to be equal; every little landowner devoured by the rabbits of his noble neighbour was delighted to be told that all privileges were without distinction contrary to reason. Every public passion thus assumed the disguise of philosophy; all political action was violently driven back into the domain of literature; and the writers of the day, undertaking the guidance of public opinion, found themselves at one time in that position which the heads of parties commonly hold in free countries. No one in fact was any longer in a condition to contend with them for the part they had assumed. . . .

If now it be taken into consideration that this same French nation, so ignorant of its own public affairs, so utterly devoid of experience, so hampered by its institutions, and so powerless to amend them, was also in those days the most lettered and witty nation of the earth, it may readily be understood how the writers of the time became a great political power, and ended by being the first power in the country.

Above the actual state of society — the constitution of which was still traditional, confused, and irregular, and in which the laws remained conflicting and contradictory, ranks sharply sundered, the conditions of the different classes fixed whilst their burdens were unequal — an imaginary state of society was thus springing up, in which everything appeared simple and co-ordinate, uniform, equitable, and agreeable to reason. The imagination of the people gradually deserted the former state of things in order to seek refuge in the latter. Interest was lost in what was, to foster dreams of what might be; and men thus dwelt in fancy in this ideal city, which was the work of literary invention. . . .

This circumstance, so novel in history, of the whole political education of a great people being formed by its literary men, contributed more than anything perhaps to bestow upon the French Revolution its peculiar stamp, and to cause those results which are still perceptible.

---

[1] See footnote 1 on page 61.

Review Questions

1. According to de Tocqueville, how did the philosophes undermine the Old Regime?
2. Why did de Tocqueville believe the French people were receptive to the philosophes' ideas?

3 | Liberty, Equality, Fraternity

In August 1789 the French National Assembly adopted the Declaration of the Rights of Man and of Citizens, which expressed the liberal and universal ideals of the Enlightenment. The Declaration proclaimed that sovereignty derives from the people, that is, that the people are the source of political power; that men are born free and equal in rights; and that it is the purpose of government to protect the natural rights of the individual. Because these ideals contrasted markedly with the outlook of an absolute monarchy, a privileged aristocracy, and an intolerant clergy, some historians view the Declaration of Rights as the death knell of the Old Regime. Its affirmation of liberty, reason, and natural rights inspired liberal reformers in other lands.

Declaration of the Rights of Man and of Citizens

Together with John Locke's *Second Treatise on Government*, the American Declaration of Independence, and the Constitution of the United States, the Declaration of the Rights of Man and of Citizens, which follows, is a pivotal document in the development of modern liberalism.

The Representatives of the people of FRANCE, formed into a NATIONAL ASSEMBLY, considering that ignorance, neglect, or contempt of human rights, are the sole causes of public misfortunes and corruptions of Government, have resolved to set forth in a solemn declaration, these natural, imprescriptible, and unalienable rights: that this declaration, being constantly present to the minds of the members of the body social, they may be ever kept attentive to their rights and their duties: that the acts of the legislative and executive powers of Government, being capable of being every moment compared with the end of political institutions, may be more respected: and also, that the future claims of the citizens, being directed by simple and incontestible principles, may always tend to the maintenance of the Constitution, and the general happiness.

For these reasons the NATIONAL ASSEMBLY doth recognize and declare, in the presence of the Supreme Being, and with the hope of his blessing and favor, the following *sacred* rights of men and of citizens:

I. *Men are born, and always continue, free,*

and equal in respect of their rights. Civil distinctions, therefore, can be founded only on public utility.

II. *The end of all political associations, is, the preservation of the natural and imprescriptible rights of man; and these rights are liberty, property, security, and resistance of oppression.*

III. *The nation is essentially the source of all sovereignty; nor can any* INDIVIDUAL, *or* ANY BODY OF MEN, *be entitled to any authority which is not expressly derived from it.*

IV. Political Liberty consists in the power of doing whatever does not injure another. The exercise of the natural rights of every man, has no other limits than those which are necessary to secure to every *other* man the free exercise of the same rights; and these limits are determinable only by the law.

V. The law ought to prohibit only actions hurtful to society. What is not prohibited by the law, should not be hindered; nor should any one be compelled to that which the law does not require.

VI. The law is an expression of the will of the community. All citizens have a right to concur, either personally, or by their representatives, in its formation. It should be the same to all, whether it protects or punishes; and *all being equal in its sight, are equally eligible to all honors, places, and employments, according to their different abilities, without any other distinction than that created by their virtues and talents.*

VII. No man should be accused, arrested, or held in confinement, except in cases determined by the law, and according to the forms which it has prescribed. All who promote, solicit, execute, or cause to be executed, arbitrary orders, ought to be punished; and every citizen called upon or apprehended by virtue of the law, ought immediately to obey, and renders himself culpable by resistance.

VIII. The law ought to impose no other penalties but such as are absolutely and evidently necessary: and no one ought to be punished, but in virtue of a law pro-

mulgated before the offence, and legally applied.

IX. Every man being presumed innocent till he has been convicted, whenever his detention becomes indispensible, all rigor [harshness] to him, more than is necessary to secure his person, ought to be provided against by the law.

X. No man ought to be molested on account of his opinions, not even on account of his *religious* opinions, provided his avowal of them does not disturb the public order established by the law.

XI. The unrestrained communication of thoughts and opinions being one of the most precious rights of man, every citizen may speak, write, and publish freely, provided he is responsible for the abuse of this liberty in cases determined by the law.

XII. A public force being necessary to give security to the rights of men and of citizens, that force is instituted for the benefit of the community, and not for the particular benefit of the persons with whom it is entrusted.

XIII. A common contribution being necessary for the support of the public force, and for defraying the other expenses of government, it ought to be divided equally among the members of the community, according to their abilities.

XIV. Every citizen has a right, either by himself or his representative, to a free voice in determining the necessity of public contributions, the appropriation of them, and their amount, mode of assessment and duration.

XV. Every community has a right to demand of all its agents, an account of their conduct.

XVI. Every community in which a separation of powers and a security of rights is not provided for, wants a constitution.

XVII. The rights to property being inviolable and sacred, no one ought to be deprived of it, except in cases of evident public necessity, legally ascertained, and on condition of a previous just indemnity.

Review Questions

1. What purpose did the writers of the Declaration of Rights intend the document to have? Was it supposed to describe reality as it was? Was it a law to be obeyed? Was it a standard against which to measure reality?

2. According to the Declaration, what do all men share by birth and what makes it possible for them to differ from one another in public life?

3. What does the Declaration say about the nature of political liberty? What are its limits, and how are they determined?

4. How does the Declaration show the influence of John Locke (see Chapter 2 in this volume)?

5. The ideals of the Declaration have become deeply embedded in the Western outlook. Discuss this statement.

4 | The Revolution Debated

There were mixed reactions to the French Revolution among thinkers and statesmen in Europe and the United States. In *Reflections on the Revolution in France* (1790), Edmund Burke (1729–1797), a leading British statesman and political thinker, attacked the violence and fundamental principles of the Revolution. Thomas Paine (1737–1809), a prominent figure in the American Revolution — his *Common Sense* (1776) was a stirring appeal for independence — responded to Burke's attack on the French Revolution in his *Rights of Man* (1791–1792).

EDMUND BURKE

Reflections on the Revolution in France

Burke regarded the revolutionaries as wild-eyed fanatics who had uprooted all established authority, tradition, and institutions, thereby plunging France into anarchy. Not sharing the faith of the philosophes in human goodness, Burke held that without the restraints of established authority, people revert to savagery. For Burke, monarchy, aristocracy, and Christianity represented civilizing elements that tamed the beast in human nature. By undermining venerable institutions, he said, the French revolutionaries had opened the door to anarchy and terror. Burke's *Reflections*, excerpts of which follow, was instrumental in the shaping of conservative thought.

. . . You [revolutionaries] chose to act as if you had never been moulded into civil society, and had every thing to begin anew. You began ill, because you began by despising every thing that belonged to you. . . . If the last generations of your country appeared without much lustre in your eyes, you might have passed them by, and derived your claims from a more early race of ancestors. Under a pious predilection for those ancestors, your imaginations would have realized in them a standard of virtue and wisdom, beyond the vulgar practice of the hour: and you would have risen with the example to whose imitation you aspired. Respecting your forefathers, you would have been taught to respect yourselves. You would not have chosen to consider the French as a people of yesterday, as a nation of low-born servile wretches, until the emancipating year of 1789. . . . By following wise examples you would have given new examples of wisdom to the world. You would have rendered the cause of liberty venerable in the eyes of every worthy mind in every nation. . . . You would have had a free constitution; a potent monarchy; a disciplined army; a reformed and venerated clergy; a mitigated but spirited nobility, to lead your virtue. . . .

Compute your gains: see what is got by those extravagant and presumptuous speculations which have taught your leaders to despise all their predecessors, and all their contemporaries, and even to despise themselves, until the moment in which they became truly despicable. By following those false lights, France has bought undisguised calamities at a higher price than any nation has purchased the most unequivocal blessings! . . . France, when she let loose the reins of regal authority, doubled the licence, of a ferocious dissoluteness in manners, and of an insolent irreligion in opinions and practices; and has extended through all ranks of life. . . . all the unhappy corruptions that usually were the disease of wealth and power. This is one of the new principles of equality in France. . . .

. . . The science of government being therefore so practical in itself, and intended for such practical purposes, a matter which requires experience, and even more experience than any person can gain in his whole life, however sagacious and observing he may be, it is with infinite caution that any man ought to venture upon pulling down an edifice which has answered in any tolerable degree for ages the common purposes of society, or on building it up again, without having models and patterns of approved utility before his eyes. . . .

. . . The nature of man is intricate; the objects of society are of the greatest possible complexity; and therefore no simple disposition or direction of power can be suitable either to man's nature, or to the quality of his affairs.

When ancient opinions of life are taken away, the loss cannot possibly be estimated. From that moment we have no compass to govern us; nor can we know distinctly to what port we steer. . . .

. . . Nothing is more certain than that our manners, our civilization, and all the good things which are connected with manners and with civilization have, in this European world of ours, depended for ages upon two principles and were, indeed, the result of both combined: I mean the spirit of a gentleman and the spirit of religion. . . .

———————————→ •◦• ←———————————

Burke next compares the English people with the French revolutionaries.

———————————→ •◦• ←———————————

. . . Thanks to our sullen resistance to innovation, thanks to the cold sluggishness of our national character, we still bear the stamp of our forefathers. . . . We are not the converts of Rousseau; we are not the disciples of Voltaire; Helvetius has made no progress amongst us.[1] Atheists are not our preachers; madmen are not our lawgivers. We know that *we* have made no discoveries, and we think that no discoveries are to be made, in morality nor many in the great principles of government. . . . We fear God; we look up with awe to kings, with affection to parliaments, with duty to magistrates, with reverence to priests, and with respect to nobility. . . .

. . . We are afraid to put men to live and trade each on his own private stock of reason, because we suspect that this

---

[1] Rousseau, Voltaire, and Helvetius were French philosophes of the eighteenth century noted, respectively, for advocating democracy, attacking the abuses of the Old Regime, and applying scientific reason to moral principles.

stock in each man is small, and that the individuals would do better to avail themselves of the general bank and capital of nations and of ages.

THOMAS PAINE

Rights of Man

In his *Rights of Man,* excerpted below, Thomas Paine argued that reason, not tradition, was the proper foundation of government. He defended the principle of natural rights and insisted that as a form of government, a republic was superior to hereditary monarchy or aristocracy.

Among the incivilities by which nations or individuals provoke and irritate each other, Mr. Burke's pamphlet on the French Revolution is an extraordinary instance. . . . There is scarcely an epithet of abuse to be found in the English language with which Mr. Burke has not loaded the French nation and the National Assembly. Everything which rancor, prejudice, ignorance, or knowledge could suggest are poured forth in the copious fury of near four hundred pages. . . .

The two modes of government which prevail in the world are, first, government by election and representation; secondly, government by hereditary succession. The former is generally known by the name of republic; the latter by that of monarchy and aristocracy.

Those two distinct and opposite forms erect themselves on the two distinct and opposite bases of reason and ignorance. As the exercise of government requires talents and abilities, and as talents and abilities cannot have hereditary descent, it is evident that hereditary succession requires a belief from man to which his reason cannot subscribe and which can only be established upon his ignorance; and the more ignorant any country is, the better it is fitted for this species of government.

On the contrary, government in a well-constituted republic requires no belief from man beyond what his reason can give. He sees the rationale of the whole system, its origin and its operation; and as it is best supported when best understood, the human faculties act with boldness and acquire, under this form of government, a gigantic manliness.

. . . Each of those forms acts on a different base — the one moving freely by the aid of reason, the other by ignorance. . . .

All hereditary government is in its nature tyranny. A heritable crown or a heritable throne, or by what other fanciful name such things may be called, have no other significant explanation than that mankind are heritable property. To inherit a government is to inherit the people, as if they were flocks and herds. . . .

We have heard the rights of man called a *leveling* system,[1] but the only system to which the word "leveling" is truly applicable is the hereditary monarchical system. It is a system of *mental leveling.* It indiscriminately admits every species of character to the same authority. Vice and virtue, ignorance and wisdom, in short, every quality, good or bad, is put on the same level. Kings succeed each other, not as [rational men], but as animals. It signifies not what their mental or moral characters are.

Passing over, for the present, all the evils and mischiefs which monarchy has occasioned in the world, nothing can more effectually prove its uselessness in a state of *civil government* than making it hereditary. Would we make any office heredi-

---

[1] To aristocratic critics, the principle of the rights of man reduced those who were naturally better to the level of their inferiors.

tary that required wisdom and abilities to fill it? . . .

It requires some talents to be a common mechanic, but to be a king requires only the animal figure of a man — a sort of breathing automaton. This sort of superstition may last a few years more, but it cannot long resist the awakened reason and interest of man. . . .

As this is the order of nature, the order of government must necessarily follow it, or government will, as we see it does, degenerate into ignorance. The hereditary system, therefore, is as repugnant to human wisdom as to human rights and is as absurd as it is unjust.

As the republic of letters brings forward the best literary productions by giving to genius a fair and universal chance, so the representative system of government is calculated to produce the wisest laws by collecting wisdom where it can be found. I smile to myself when I contemplate the ridiculous insignificance into which literature and all the sciences would sink were they made hereditary, and I carry the same idea into governments. A hereditary governor is as inconsistent as a hereditary author. I know not whether Homer or Euclid[2] had sons, but I will venture an opinion that if they had, and had left their works unfinished, those sons could not have completed them.

Do we need a stronger evidence of the absurdity of hereditary government than is seen in the descendants of those men, in any line of life, who once were famous? Is there scarcely an instance in which there is not a total reverse of character? It appears as if the tide of mental faculties flowed as far as it could in certain channels, and then forsook its course and arose in others. How irrational then is the hereditary system which establishes channels of power, in company with which wisdom refuses to flow! By continuing this absurdity, man is perpetually in contradiction with himself; he accepts for a king or a chief magistrate or a legislator a person whom he would not elect for a constable.

----

[2] Homer, ancient Greek epic poet, composed the *Odyssey* and the *Iliad*. Euclid was a Greek mathematician of the third century B.C. who systematized the principles of geometry.

Review Questions

1. Why was Edmund Burke opposed to the French Revolution?
2. Why did Burke regard "resistance to innovation" and the "cold sluggishness of our national character" as virtues?
3. On what grounds did Thomas Paine defend the French Revolution?
4. According to Paine, how did the two modes of government that prevailed in the world — monarchy and republic — differ from one another?
5. Compare and contrast the attitudes of Burke and Paine toward (1) the historical past, (2) liberty and natural rights, (3) reason, and (4) the philosophes.

5 | Robespierre and the Reign of Terror

In the summer of 1793 the French Republic was threatened with internal insurrection and foreign invasion. During this period of acute crisis, the Jacobins provided strong leadership. They organized a large national army of citizen soldiers who, imbued with love for the nation, routed the invaders on the northern frontier. To deal with internal enemies, the Jacobins instituted the Reign of Terror, in which Maximilien Robespierre (1758–1794) played a pivotal role.

Most Jacobins, including Robespierre, supported terror not because they were bloodthirsty or power mad. Rather, they were idealists who believed that terror was necessary to rescue the Republic and the Revolution from destruction. Deeply committed to republican democracy, Robespierre viewed himself as the bearer of a higher faith, molding a new society founded on reason, good citizenship, patriotism, and virtue. Robespierre viewed those who prevented the implementation of this new society as traitors and sinners who had to be killed for the good of humanity.

MAXIMILIEN ROBESPIERRE

Republic of Virtue

The new declaration of rights proposed by Robespierre in April 1793 sets forth his vision of the Republic of Virtue, the new society that would serve as a model for all humanity.

[A Declaration of Rights]

The representatives of the French people, assembled in National Convention, recognizing that human laws which do not derive from the eternal laws of justice and of reason are only the outrages of ignorance or despotism against humanity; convinced that forgetfulness and contempt of the natural rights of man are the sole causes of the crimes and misfortunes of the world, have resolved to set forth in a solemn declaration these sacred and inalienable rights, in order that all citizens, being able constantly to compare the acts of the government with the aim of every social institution, may never allow themselves to be oppressed and degraded by tyranny, in order that the people always may have before their eyes the bases of their liberty and welfare; the magistrate, the rule of his duties; the legislator, the object of his mission.

Accordingly, the National Convention proclaims in the presence of the Universe, and before the eyes of the Immortal Legislator, the following declaration of the rights of man and citizen.

1. The aim of every political association is the maintenance of the natural and inalienable rights of man, and the development of all their attributes.

2. The principal rights of man are those of providing for the preservation of his existence and his liberty.

3. These rights appertain equally to all men, whatever the difference in their physical and moral powers.

4. Equality of rights is established by nature; society, far from impairing it, guarantees it against the abuse of power which renders it illusory.

5. Liberty is the power which appertains to man to exercise all his faculties at will; it has justice for rule, the rights of others for limits, nature for principle, and the law for a safeguard.

6. The right to assemble peaceably, the right to manifest one's opinions, either by means of the press or in any other manner, are such necessary consequences of the principle of the liberty of man, that the necessity of enunciating them presumes either the presence or the recent memory of despotism.

7. The law may forbid only whatever is injurious to society; it may order only whatever is useful thereto.

8. Every law which violates the inalienable rights of man is essentially

unjust and tyrannical; it is not a law at all.

9. Property is the right of each and every citizen to enjoy and to dispose of the portion of property guaranteed to him by law.

10. The right of property is limited, as are all others, by the obligation to respect the property of others.

11. It may not be detrimental to the security, or the liberty, or the existence, or the property of our fellowmen.

12. All dealings which violate this principle are essentially illicit and immoral.

13. Society is obliged to provide for the subsistence of all its members, either by procuring work for them, or by assuring the means of existence to those who are unable to work. . . .

16. Society must favor with all its power the progress of public reason, and must place education within reach of all citizens.

17. The law is the free and solemn expression of the will of the people. . . .

20. The law must be equal for all. . . .

27. Resistance to oppression is the consequence of the other rights of man and citizen. . . .

29. When the government violates the rights of the people, insurrection is the most sacred of rights and the most indispensable of duties for the people, and for each and every portion thereof. . . .

34. The men of all countries are brothers, and the different peoples must help one another, according to their power, as citizens of the same State.

35. Whoever oppresses a single nation declares himself the enemy of all.

36. Whoever make war on a people in order to check the progress of liberty and annihilate the rights of man must be prosecuted by all, not as ordinary enemies, but as assassins and rebellious brigands.

In the following speech before the National Convention in December 1793, Robespierre proposed a theory of revolutionary government to deal with foreign and domestic enemies.

[On Revolutionary Government]

The theory of revolutionary government is as new as the Revolution that created it. It is as pointless to seek its origins in the books of the political theorists, who failed to foresee this revolution, as in the laws of the tyrants, who are happy enough to abuse their exercise of authority without seeking out its legal justification. And so this phrase is for the aristocracy a mere subject of terror or a term of slander, for tyrants an outrage and for many an enigma. It behooves us to explain it to all in order that we may rally good citizens, at least, in support of the principles governing the public interest.

It is the function of government to guide the moral and physical energies of the nation toward the purposes for which it was established.

The object of constitutional government is to preserve the Republic; the object of revolutionary government is to establish it.

Revolution is the war waged by liberty against its enemies; a constitution is that which crowns the edifice of freedom once victory has been won and the nation is at peace.

The revolutionary government has to summon extraordinary activity to its aid precisely because it is at war. It is subjected to less binding and less uniform regulations, because the circumstances in which it finds itself are tempestuous and shifting, above all because it is compelled to deploy, swiftly and incessantly, new resources to meet new and pressing dangers.

The principal concern of constitutional government is civil liberty; that of revolutionary government, public liberty. Under a constitutional government little more is required than to protect the individual against abuses by the state, whereas revolutionary government is obliged to defend the state itself against the factions that assail it from every quarter.

To good citizens revolutionary government owes the full protection of the state; to the enemies of the people it owes only death.

————————→ •◆• ←————————

In a series of notes written in the summer of 1793, Robespierre expressed his policy toward counterrevolutionaries.

————————→ •◆• ←————————

[Despotism in Defense of Liberty]

What is our goal? The enforcement of the constitution for the benefit of the people.

Who will our enemies be? The vicious and the rich.

What means will they employ? Slander and hypocrisy.

What things may be favorable for the employment of these? The ignorance of the *sans-culottes*.[1]

The people must therefore be enlightened. But what are the obstacles to

the enlightenment of the people? Mercenary writers who daily mislead them with impudent falsehoods.

What conclusions may be drawn from this? 1. These writers must be proscribed as the most dangerous enemies of the people. 2. Right-minded literature must be scattered about in profusion.

What are the other obstacles to the establishment of liberty? Foreign war and civil war.

How can foreign war be ended? By putting republican generals in command of our armies and punishing those who have betrayed us.

How can civil war be ended? By punishing traitors and conspirators, particularly if they are deputies or administrators; by sending loyal troops under patriotic leaders to subdue the aristocrats of Lyon, Marseille, Toulon, the Vendée, the Jura, and all other regions in which the standards of rebellion and royalism have been raised; and by making frightful examples of all scoundrels who have outraged liberty and spilled the blood of patriots.

1. Proscription of perfidious and counter-revolutionary writers and propagation of proper literature.
2. Punishment of traitors and conspirators, particularly deputies and administrators.
3. Appointment of patriotic generals; dismissal and punishment of others.
4. Sustenance and laws for the people.

---

[1] *Sans-culottes* literally means without the fancy breeches worn by the aristocracy. The term refers generally to a poor city dweller (who wore simple trousers). Champions of equality, the sans-culottes hated the aristocracy and the powerful bourgeoisie.

Review Questions

1. Compare and contrast Maximilien Robespierre's vision of the Republic of Virtue with the ideals of the Declaration of the Rights of Man and of Citizens in Selection 3.

2. What distinction did Robespierre draw between constitutional and revolutionary government?

3. On what grounds did Robespierre justify terror?

4. Like medieval inquisitors, Robespierre regarded people with different views not as opponents but as sinners. Discuss this statement.

6 | Napoleon's Genius for Psychological Warfare

Napoleon Bonaparte (1769–1821) — later Napoleon I, emperor of France — was a brilliant military commander who carefully planned each campaign and resorted to speed, deception, and surprise to confuse and demoralize his opponents. By rapid marches, Napoleon would concentrate a superior force against a segment of the enemy's strung-out forces. Recognizing the importance of good morale, he sought to inspire his troops by appealing to their honor, their vanity, and their love of France.

NAPOLEON BONAPARTE

Proclamations to French Troops in Italy

In 1796, Napoleon, then a young officer, was given command of the French army in Italy. In the Italian campaign, he demonstrated a genius for propaganda and psychological warfare, as the following proclamations to his troops indicate.

[March 27, 1796]

Soldiers, you are naked, ill fed! The Government owes you much; it can give you nothing. Your patience, the courage you display in the midst of these rocks, are admirable; but they procure you no glory, no fame is reflected upon you. I seek to lead you into the most fertile plains in the world. Rich provinces, great cities will be in your power. There you will find honor, glory, and riches. Soldiers of Italy, would you be lacking in courage or constancy?

[April 26, 1796]

Soldiers:

In a fortnight you have won six victories, taken twenty-one standards, fifty-five pieces of artillery, several strong positions, and conquered the richest part of Piedmont [a region in northern Italy]; you have captured 15,000 prisoners and killed or wounded more than 10,000 men. . . .

. . . You have won battles without cannon, crossed rivers without bridges, made forced marches without shoes, camped without brandy and often without bread. Soldiers of liberty, only republican phalanxes [infantry troops] could have endured what you have endured. Soldiers, you have our thanks! The grateful *Patrie* [nation] will owe its prosperity to you. . . .

The two armies which but recently attacked you with audacity are fleeing before you in terror; the wicked men who laughed at your misery and rejoiced at the thought of the triumphs of your enemies are confounded and trembling.

But, soldiers, as yet you have done nothing compared with what remains to be done. . . .

. . . Undoubtedly the greatest obstacles have been overcome; but you still have battles to fight, cities to capture, rivers to cross. Is there one among you whose courage is abating? . . . No. . . . All of you are consumed with a desire to extend the glory of the French people; all of you long to humiliate those arrogant kings who dare to contemplate placing us in fetters; all of you desire to dictate a glorious peace, one which will indemnify the *Patrie* for the immense sacrifices it has made; all of you wish to be able to say with pride as you return to your villages, "I was with the victorious army of Italy!"

Friends, I promise you this conquest; but there is one condition you must swear to fulfill — to respect the people whom you liberate, to repress the horrible pillaging committed by scoundrels incited by our enemies. Otherwise you would not be the liberators of the people; you would be their scourge. . . . Plunderers will be shot without mercy; already, several have been. . . .

Peoples of Italy, the French army comes to break your chains; the French people is the friend of all peoples; approach it with confidence; your property, your religion, and your customs will be respected.

We are waging war as generous enemies, and we wish only to crush the tyrants who enslave you.

Review Questions

1. In these proclamations how did Napoleon Bonaparte try to raise the morale of his troops?

2. How did Napoleon try to appeal to the Italians?

7 | Napoleonic Indoctrination

In several ways, Napoleon anticipated the strategies of twentieth-century dictators. He concentrated power in his own hands, suppressed opposition, and sought to mold public opinion by controlling the press and education.

NAPOLEON I
Imperial Catechism of 1806

The following Imperial Catechism of 1806, which school children were required to memorize and recite, is a pointed example of Napoleonic indoctrination.

Lesson VII. Continuation of the Fourth Commandment.

Q. What are the duties of Christians with respect to the princes who govern them, and what in particular are our duties towards Napoleon I, our Emperor?

A. Christians owe to the princes who govern them, and we owe in particular to Napoleon I, our Emperor, *love, respect, obedience, fidelity, military service* and the tributes laid for the preservation and defence of the Empire and of his throne; we also owe to him fervent prayers for his safety and the spiritual and temporal prosperity of the state.

Q. Why are we bound to all these duties towards our Emperor?

A. First of all, because God, who creates empires and distributes them according to His will, in loading our Emperor with gifts, both in peace and in war, has established him as our sovereign and has made him the minister of His power and His image upon the earth. *To honor and to serve our Emperor is then to honor and to serve God himself.* Secondly, because our Lord Jesus Christ by His doctrine as well as by His example, has Himself taught us what we owe to our sovereign: He was born the subject of Caesar Augustus;[1] He paid the prescribed impost; and just as He ordered to render to God that which belongs to God, so He ordered to render to Caesar that which belongs to Caesar.

Q. Are there not particular reasons which ought to attach us more strongly to Napoleon I, our Emperor?

A. Yes; for it is he whom God has raised up under difficult circumstances to re-establish the public worship of the holy religion of our fathers and to be the protector of it. He has restored and preserved public order by his profound and active wisdom; he defends the state by his powerful arm; he has become the anointed of the Lord through the consecration which he received from the sovereign pontiff, head of the universal church.

Q. What ought to be thought of those who may be lacking in their duty towards our Emperor?

A. According to the apostle Saint Paul, they would be resisting the order established by God himself and would render themselves *worthy of eternal damnation.*

Q. Will the duties which are required of us towards our Emperor be equally binding with respect to his lawful successors in the order established by the constitutions of the Empire?

A. Yes, without doubt; for we read in the holy scriptures, that God, Lord of heaven and earth, by an order of His supreme will and through His providence, gives empires not only to one person in particular, but also to his family.

---

[1] Caesar Augustus (27 B.C.–A.D. 14) was the Roman emperor at the time that Jesus was born.

Review Questions

1. What was the purpose of Napoleon's Imperial Catechism of 1806?

2. How did the appeal to religion serve to help fulfill the underlying purpose of the catechism?

3. Does the catechism suggest to you what Napoleon's true religious convictions may have been? What were they?

4. Do you see any similarities of method in Napoleon's proclamations to his troops and the Imperial Catechism? Any differences?

CHAPTER · 4

Romanticism, Reaction, Revolution

In 1815 the European scene had changed. Napoleon was exiled to the island of St. Helena, and a Bourbon king, in the person of Louis XVIII, again reigned in France. The Great Powers of Europe, meeting at Vienna, had drawn up a peace settlement that awarded territory to the states that had fought Napoleon and restored to power some rulers dethroned by the French emperor. The Congress of Vienna also organized the Concert of Europe to guard against a resurgence of the revolutionary spirit that had kept Europe in turmoil for some twenty-five years. The conservative leaders of Europe wanted no more Robespierres who resorted to terror and no more Napoleons who sought to dominate the continent.

However, reactionary rulers' efforts to turn the clock back to the Old Regime could not contain the forces unleashed by the French Revolution. Between 1820 and 1848 a series of revolts rocked Europe. The principal causes were liberalism (which demanded constitutional government and the protection of the freedom and rights of the individual citizen) and nationalism (which called for the reawakening and unification of the nation and its liberation from foreign domination).

In the 1820s, the Concert of Europe crushed a quasi-liberal revolution in Spain and liberal uprisings in Italy, and Tsar Nicholas I subdued liberal aristocrats who challenged tsarist autocracy. The Greeks, however, successfully fought for independence from the Ottoman Turks.

Between 1830 and 1832, another wave of revolutions swept over Europe. Italian liberals and nationalists failed to free Italy from foreign rule or to wrest reforms from autocratic princes, and the tsar's troops crushed a Polish bid for independence from Russian rule. But in France, rebels overthrew the reactionary Bourbon Charles X in 1830 and replaced him with a more moderate ruler, Louis Philippe; a little later Belgium gained its independence from Holland.

The year 1848 was decisive in the struggle for liberty and nationhood. In France, democrats overthrew Louis Philippe and established a republic that gave all men the right to vote. However, in Italy and Germany, revolutions attempting to unify each land failed, as did a bid in Hungary for independence from the Hapsburg empire. After enjoying initial successes, the revolutionaries were crushed by superior might, and their liberal and nationalist objectives remained largely unfulfilled. By 1870, however, many nationalist aspirations had been realized. The Hapsburg empire granted Hungary autonomy in 1867, and during 1870–1871, the period of the Franco-Prussian War, Germany and Italy became unified states. That authoritarian and militaristic Prussia unified Germany, rather than liberals like those who had fought in the revolutions of 1848, affected the future of Europe.

In the early nineteenth century a new cultural orientation, romanticism, emphasized the liberation of human emotions and the free expression of personality in artistic creations. The romantics' attack on the rationalism of the Enlightenment and their veneration of the past influenced conservative thought, and their concern for a people's history and traditions contributed to the development of nationalism. By encouraging innovation in art, music, and literature, the romantics greatly enriched European cultural life.

1 | Romanticism

Romantics attacked the outlook of the Enlightenment, protesting that the philosophes' excessive intellectualizing and their mechanistic view of the physical world and human nature distorted and fettered the human spirit and thwarted cultural creativity. The rationalism of the philosophes, said the romantics, had reduced human beings into soulless thinking machines, and vibrant nature into lifeless wheels, cogs, and pulleys. In contrast to the philosophes' scientific and analytic approach, the romantics asserted the intrinsic value of emotions and imagination and extolled the spontaneity, richness, and uniqueness of the human spirit. To the philosophes, the emotions obstructed clear thinking.

For romantics, feelings and imagination were the human essence, the source of cultural creativity, and the avenue to true understanding. Their beliefs led the romantics to rebel against strict standards of esthetics that governed artistic creations. They held that artists, musicians, and writers must trust their own sensibilities and inventiveness and must not be bound by textbook rules; the romantics focused on the creative capacities inherent in the emotions and urged individuality and freedom of expression in the arts. In the Age of Romanticism, the artist and poet succeeded the scientist as the arbiters of Western civilization.

WILLIAM WORDSWORTH
Preface to The Lyrical Ballads

The works of the great English poet William Wordsworth (1770–1850) exemplify many tendencies of the Romantic Movement. In the interval during which he tried to come to grips with his disenchantment with the French Revolution, Wordsworth's creativity reached its height. In the preface to *The Lyrical Ballads* (1798), excerpted below, Wordsworth produced what has become known as the manifesto of romanticism. He wanted poetry to express powerful feelings and also contended that because it is a vehicle for the imagination, poetry is the source of truth. Wordsworth thus represented a shift in perspective comparable to the shift begun by Descartes in philosophy, but for Wordsworth imagination and feeling, not mathematics and logic, yielded highest truth.

Taking up the subject, then, upon general grounds, I ask what is meant by the word Poet? What is a Poet? To whom does he address himself? And what language is to be expected from him? He is a man speaking to men: a man, it is true, [endowed] with more lively sensibility, more enthusiasm and tenderness, who has a greater knowledge of human nature, and a more comprehensive soul, than are supposed to be common among mankind; a man pleased with his own passions and volitions, and who rejoices more than other men in the spirit of life that is in him; delighting to contemplate similar volitions and passions as manifested in the goings-on of the Universe, and habitually impelled to create them where he does not find them. To these qualities he has added a disposition to be affected more than other men by absent things as if they were present; an ability of conjuring up in himself passions, which are indeed far from being the same as those produced by real events, yet (especially in those parts of the general sympathy which are pleasing and delightful) do more nearly resemble the passions produced by real events, than any thing which, from the motions of their own minds merely, other men are accustomed to feel in themselves. . . .

. . . Aristotle, I have been told, hath said, that Poetry is the most philosophic of all writing: it is so: its object is truth, not individual and local, but general, and operative; not standing upon external testimony, but carried alive into the heart by passion; truth which is its own testimony, which gives strength and divinity to the tribunal to which it appeals, and receives them from the same tribunal. Poetry is the image of man and nature. . . .

To this knowledge which all men carry about with them, and to these sympathies in which without any other discipline than that of our daily life we are fitted to take delight, the Poet principally directs his attention. He considers man and nature as essentially adapted to each other, and the mind of man as naturally the mirror of the fairest and most interesting qualities of nature. . . . The Man of Science seeks truth as a remote and unknown benefactor; he cherishes and loves it in his soli-

tude: the Poet, singing a song in which all human beings join with him, rejoices in the presence of truth as our visible friend and hourly companion. Poetry is the breath and finer spirit of all knowledge: it is the impassioned expression which is in the countenance of all Science. Emphatically may it be said of the Poet, as Shakespeare hath said of man, "that he looks before and after." He is the rock of defence of human nature; an upholder and preserver, carrying every where with him relationship and love. In spite of difference of soil and climate, of language and manners, of laws and customs, in spite of things silently gone out of mind and things violently destroyed, the Poet binds together by passion and knowledge the vast empire of human society, as it is spread over the whole earth, and over all time. The objects of the Poet's thoughts are every where; though the eyes and senses of men are, it is true, his favourite guides, yet he will follow wheresoever he can find an atmosphere of sensation in which to move his wings. Poetry is the first and last of all knowledge — it is as immortal as the heart of man.

WILLIAM WORDSWORTH
Lines Composed a Few Miles Above Tintern Abbey

The philosophes had regarded nature as a giant machine, all of whose parts worked in perfect precision and whose laws could be uncovered through the scientific method. The romantics rejected this mechanical model. To them, nature was a living organism filled with beautiful forms whose inner meaning was grasped through the human imagination; they sought from nature a higher truth than mechanical law. In "Tintern Abbey," Wordsworth expresses this interconnection between nature and human imagination.

            . . . For I have learned
To look on nature, not as in the hour
Of thoughtless youth; but hearing
   oftentimes
The still, sad music of humanity,
Nor harsh nor grating, though of ample
   power

To chasten and subdue. And I have felt
A presence that disturbs me with the joy
Of elevated thoughts; a sense sublime
Of something far more deeply
   interfused,
Whose dwelling is the light of setting
   suns,

And the round ocean and the living air,
And the blue sky, and in the mind of
    man:
A motion and a spirit, that impels
All thinking things, all objects of all
    thought,
And rolls through all things. Therefore
    am I still
A lover of the meadows and the woods,
And mountains; and of all that we
    behold
From this green earth; of all the mighty
    world
Of eye, and ear, — both what they half
    create,
And what perceive; well pleased to
    recognise
In nature and the language of the sense
The anchor of my purest thoughts, the
    nurse,
The guide, the guardian of my heart,
    and soul
Of all my moral being.
                    .   .   .

. . . and this prayer I
    make,
Knowing that Nature never did betray
The heart that loved her; 'tis her privilege,
Through all the years of this our life, to
    lead
From joy to joy: for she can so inform
The mind that is within us, so impress
With quietness and beauty, and so feed
With lofty thoughts, that neither evil
    tongues,
Rash judgments, nor the sneers of selfish
    men,
Nor greetings where no kindness is, nor
    all
The dreary intercourse of daily life,
Shall e'er prevail against us, or disturb
Our cheerful faith, that all which we
    behold
Is full of blessings. Therefore let the moon
Shine on thee in thy solitary walk;
And let the misty mountain-winds be free
To blow against thee. . . .

WILLIAM BLAKE

Milton

William Blake (1757–1827) was a British engraver, poet, and religious mystic. He
also affirmed the creative potential of the imagination and expressed distaste for the
rationalist-scientific outlook of the Enlightenment, as is clear from these lines in his
poem "Milton."

. . . the Reasoning Power in Man:
This is a false Body; an Incrustation over
    my Immortal
Spirit; a Selfhood, which must be put off
    & annihilated alway
To cleanse the Face of my Spirit by Self-
    examination.
To bathe in the Waters of Life, to wash
    off the Not Human,
I come in Self-annihilation & the
    grandeur of Inspiration,
To cast off Rational Demonstration by
    Faith in the Saviour,
To cast off the rotten rags of Memory by
    Inspiration,

To cast off Bacon, Locke & Newton
    from Albion's covering,[1]
To take off his filthy garments & clothe
    him with Imagination,
To cast aside from Poetry all that is not
    Inspiration,
That it no longer shall dare to mock with
    the aspersion of Madness
Cast on the Inspired by the tame high
    finisher of paltry Blots

---

[1] Bacon, Locke, and Newton were British
thinkers who valued reason and science, and
Albion is an ancient name for England.

Indefinite, or paltry Rhymes, or paltry
    Harmonies,
Who creeps into State Government like a
    catterpiller to destroy;
To cast off the idiot Questioner who is
    always questioning
But never capable of answering, who sits
    with a sly grin
Silent plotting when to question, like a
    thief in a cave,
Who publishes doubt & calls it
    knowledge, whose Science is Despair,
Whose pretence to knowledge is Envy,
    whose whole Science is
To destroy the wisdom of ages to gratify
    ravenous Envy
That rages round him like a Wolf day &
    night without rest:
He smiles with condescension, he talks of
    Benevolence & Virtue,

And those who act with Benevolence &
    Virtue they murder time on time.
These are the destroyers of Jerusalem,
    these are the murderers
Of Jesus, who deny the Faith & mock at
    Eternal Life,
Who pretend to Poetry that they may
    destroy Imagination
By imitation of Nature's Images drawn
    from Remembrance.
These are the Sexual Garments, the
    Abomination of Desolation,
Hiding the Human Lineaments as with
    an Ark & Curtains
Which Jesus rent & now shall wholly
    purge away with Fire
Till Generation is swallow'd up in
    Regeneration.

Review Questions

1. What was William Wordsworth's attitude toward reason, feeling, imagination, and freedom, as expressed in the preface to *The Lyrical Ballads*?

2. How did Wordsworth feel that the human mind could arrive at truth? In what way did science and poetry diverge in the way they attained truth?

3. According to Wordsworth, how could the human being achieve goodness?

4. What did Wordsworth believe the role of the poet was?

5. In "Tintern Abbey," what connection did Wordsworth see between nature and the human mind? How did his idea of nature differ from that of the scientist's? According to Wordsworth, what effect did nature have on the imagination?

6. Why did William Blake attack reason?

---

2 | Conservatism

In the period after 1815, conservatism was the principal ideology of those who repudiated the Enlightenment and the French Revolution. Conservatives valued tradition over reason, aristocratic and clerical authority over equality, and the community over the individual. Edmund Burke's *Reflections on the Revolution in France* (see page 71) was instrumental in shaping the conservative outlook. Another leading conservative was Joseph De Maistre (1753–1821) who fled his native Sardinia in 1792 (and again in 1793) after it was invaded by the armies of the new French Republic. De Maistre denounced the Enlightenment for spawning the French Revolution, defended the church as a civilizing agent that made individuals aware of their social obligations, and affirmed tradition as a model more valuable than instant reforms embodied in "paper constitutions."

The symbol of conservatism in the first half of the nineteenth century was Prince Klemens von Metternich (1773–1859) of Austria. A bitter opponent of Jacobinism and Napoleon, he became the pivotal figure at the Congress of Vienna (1814–1815) where European powers met to redraw the map of Europe after their victory over France. Metternich said that the Jacobins had subverted the pillars of civilization and that Napoleon, by harnessing the forces of the Revolution, had destroyed the traditional European state system. No peace was possible with Napoleon, who championed revolutionary doctrines and dethroned kings, and whose rule rested not on legitimacy but on conquest and charisma. No balance of power could endure such an adventurer who obliterated states and sought European domination.

KLEMENS VON METTERNICH
Confession of Political Faith

Two decades of revolutionary warfare had shaped Metternich's political thinking. After the fall of Napoleon, Metternich worked to restore the European balance and to suppress revolutionary movements. The following excerpt from his *Memoirs*, a memorandum to Tsar Alexander I, dated December 15, 1820, reveals Metternich's conservative outlook.

"L'Europe," a celebrated writer has recently said, *"fait aujourd'hui pitié à l'homme d'esprit et horreur à l'homme vertueux."*[1]

It would be difficult to comprise in a few words a more exact picture of the situation at the time we are writing these lines!

Kings have to calculate the chances of their very existence in the immediate future; passions are let loose, and league together to overthrow everything which society respects as the basis of its existence; religion, public morality, laws, customs, rights, and duties, all are attacked, confounded, overthrown, or called in question. . . .

What is the cause of all these evils? By what methods has this evil established itself, and how is it that it penetrates into every vein of the social body?

Do remedies still exist to arrest the progress of this evil, and what are they? . . .

Let us examine the matter!

Metternich denounces the French philosophes for their "false systems" and "fatal errors" that weakened the social fabric and gave rise to the French Revolution. In their presumption, the philosophes forsook the experience and wisdom of the past, trusting only their own thoughts and inclinations.

The progress of the human mind has been extremely rapid in the course of the last three centuries. This progress having been accelerated more rapidly than the growth of wisdom (the only counterpoise to passions and to error); a revolution prepared by the false systems, the fatal errors into which many of the most illustrious sovereigns of the last half of the eighteenth century fell, has at last broken out in a century advanced in knowledge, and enervated by pleasure, in a country inhabited by a people whom one can only

---

[1] Europe today arouses pity in an intelligent man and horror in a man of virtue.

regard as frivolous, from the facility with which they comprehend and the difficulty they experience in judging calmly. . . .

. . . There were . . . some men [the philosophes], unhappily endowed with great talents, who felt their own strength, and were not slow to appraise the progressive course of their influence, taking into account the weakness or the inertia of their adversaries; and who had the art to prepare and conduct men's minds to the triumph of their detestable enterprise — an enterprise all the more odious as it was pursued without regard to results, simply abandoning themselves to the one feeling of hatred of God and of His immutable moral laws.

France had the misfortune to produce the greatest number of these men. It is in her midst that religion and all that she holds sacred, that morality and authority, and all connected with them, have been attacked with a steady and systematic animosity, and it is there that the weapon of ridicule has been used with the most ease and success.

Drag through the mud the name of God and the powers instituted by His divine decrees, and the revolution will be prepared! Speak of a social contract,[2] and the revolution is accomplished! The revolution was already completed in the palaces of Kings, in the drawing-rooms and boudoirs of certain cities, while among the great mass of the people it was still only in a state of preparation. . . .

. . . The French Revolution broke out, and has gone through a complete revolutionary cycle in a very short period, which could only have appeared long to

its victims and to its contemporaries. . . .

. . . The revolutionary seed had penetrated into every country. . . . It was greatly developed under the *régime* of the military despotism of Bonaparte. His conquests displaced a number of laws, institutions, and customs; broke through bonds sacred among all nations, strong enough to resist time itself; which is more than can be said of certain benefits conferred by these innovators. From these perturbations it followed that the revolutionary spirit could in Germany, Italy, and later on in Spain, easily hide itself under the veil of patriotism. . . .

Metternich attacks the middle class for adopting and spreading these dangerous ideas.

It is principally the middle classes of society which this moral gangrene has affected, and it is only among them that the real heads of the party are found. . . .

In all four countries [France, Germany, Italy, and Spain] the agitated classes are principally composed of wealthy men — real cosmopolitans, securing their personal advantage at the expense of any order of things whatever — paid State officials, men of letters, lawyers, and the individuals charged with public education. . . .

We see this intermediary class abandon itself with a blind fury and animosity which proves much more its own fears than any confidence in the success of its enterprises, to all the means which seem proper to assuage its thirst for power, applying itself to the task of persuading Kings that their rights are confined to sitting upon a throne, while those of the people are to govern, and to attack all that centuries have bequeathed as holy and worthy of man's respect — denying, in fact, the value of the past, and declaring themselves the masters of the future. We see this class take all sorts of disguises, uniting and subdividing as occasion offers, helping each other in the hour of danger, and

---

[2] The social contract theory consisted essentially of the following principles: (1) people voluntarily enter into an agreement to establish a political community; (2) government rests on the consent of the governed; (3) people possess natural freedom and equality, which they do not surrender to the state. These principles were used to challenge the divine right of kings and absolute monarchy.

the next day depriving each other of all their conquests. It takes possession of the press, and employs it to promote impiety, disobedience to the laws of religion and the State, and goes so far as to preach murder as a duty for those who desire what is good. . . .

Metternich wants governments to band to-gether to suppress dangerous ideas, the free press, and secret societies and to preserve religious principles.

We are convinced that society can no longer be saved without strong and vigorous resolutions on the part of the Governments still free in their opinions and actions.

We are also convinced that this may be, if the Governments face the truth, if they free themselves from all illusion, if they join their ranks and take their stand on a line of correct, unambiguous, and frankly announced principles.

By this course the monarchs will fulfil the duties imposed upon them by Him who, by entrusting them with power, has charged them to watch over the maintenance of justice, and the rights of all, to avoid the paths of error, and tread firmly in the way of truth. . . .

There is a rule of conduct common to individuals and to States, established by the experience of centuries as by that of everyday life. This rule declares "that one must not dream of reformation while agitated by passion; wisdom directs that at such moments we should limit ourselves to maintaining."

Let the monarchs vigorously adopt this principle; let all their resolutions bear the impression of it. Let their actions, their measures, and even their words announce and prove to the world this determination — they will find allies everywhere. The Governments, in establishing the principle of *stability*, will in no wise exclude the development of what is good, for stability is not immobility. . . .

If the same elements of destruction which are now throwing society into convulsions have existed in all ages — for every age has seen immoral and ambitious men, hypocrites, men of heated imaginations, wrong motives, and wild projects — yet ours, by the single fact of the liberty of the press, possesses more than any preceding age the means of contact, seduction, and attraction whereby to act on these different classes of men.

We are certainly not alone in questioning if society can exist with the liberty of the press, a scourge unknown to the world before the latter half of the seventeenth century, and restrained until the end of the eighteenth, with scarcely any exceptions but England — a part of Europe separated from the continent by the sea, as well as by her language and by her peculiar manners.

The first principle to be followed by the monarchs, united as they are by the coincidence of their desires and opinions, should be that of maintaining the stability of political institutions against the disorganised excitement which has taken possession of men's minds; the immutability of principles against the madness of their interpretation; and respect for laws actually in force against a desire for their destruction. . . .

. . . The first and greatest concern for the immense majority of every nation is the stability of the laws, and their uninterrupted action — never their change. Therefore let the Governments govern, let them maintain the groundwork of their institutions, both ancient and modern; for if it is at all times dangerous to touch them, it certainly would not now, in the general confusion, be wise to do so. . . .

Let them maintain religious principles in all their purity, and not allow the faith to be attacked and morality interpreted according to the *social contract* or the visions of foolish sectarians.

Let them suppress Secret Societies, that gangrene of society. . . .

To every great State determined to survive the storm there still remain many chances of salvation, and a strong union between the States on the principles we have announced will overcome the storm itself.

Review Questions

1. What was Klemens von Metternich's opinion of "the progress of the human mind . . . in the . . . last three centuries" and its effect upon the society of his times?

2. What did Metternich mean by "Drag through the mud the name of God and the powers instituted by His decrees, and the revolution will be prepared!"?

3. How did Metternich regard the middle classes?

4. What strategy did Metternich propose to bring stability back to political life?

---

3 | Liberalism

Conservatism was the ideology of the old order that was hostile to the Enlightenment and the French Revolution; in contrast, liberalism aspired to carry out the promise of the philosophes and the Revolution. Liberals called for a constitution that protected individual liberty and denounced censorship, arbitrary arrest, and other forms of repression. They believed that through reason and education, social evils could be remedied. Liberals rejected an essential feature of the Old Regime — the special privileges of the aristocracy and the clergy — and held that the individual should be judged on the basis of achievement, not of birth. At the core of the liberal outlook lay the conviction that the individual would develop into a good and productive human being and citizen if not coerced by governments and churches.

BENJAMIN CONSTANT
On the Limits of Popular Sovereignty

Benjamin Constant (1767–1830), a leading French liberal theorist, feared the danger posed to liberty by democratic revolutionaries like Robespierre and his fellow Jacobins, who would exercise unlimited authority to establish liberty. Constant embraced the principle of popular sovereignty (that government derives its legitimacy and authority from the people), but warned against the danger of unlimited popular sovereignty. Neither the people as a whole nor their delegated representatives, said Constant, can possess total authority over the lives of individuals.

Unlimited popular sovereignty creates . . . a degree of power in human society too great by definition, which is an evil no matter in whose hands it is placed. Whether it is entrusted to a single man, to several, or to all, it will be found equally an evil. . . . There are weights too heavy for human hands. . . .

In a society founded on popular sovereignty it is certain that no individual, no class, may subject the rest to its particular will; but it is false to say that society as a whole exercises unlimited sovereignty over its members.

The totality of the citizenry is sovereign in the sense that no individual, party, or group may arrogate sovereignty to itself if it has not been delegated to it. But it does not follow that the totality of citizens, or those who are invested with sovereignty by it, may wilfully dispose of the lives of individuals. There is, on the contrary, a part of human life which of necessity remains individual and independent and which as of right remains outside the jurisdiction of society. Sovereignty exists only in a limited and relative way. The jurisdiction of this sovereignty stops at the point where the independence of individual life starts. If society crosses this border it becomes as culpable as the despot whose title rests only on the sword of destruction. . . . The consent of the majority by no means suffices in all cases to make its acts legitimate; there are some acts that nothing can make legitimate. When any authority commits acts of this sort it matters little from what source it claims to derive; it matters little whether it is called an individual or a nation; it might be the entire nation with the exception of the citizen whom it oppresses, and the act would still not be legitimate. . . .

When sovereignty is not limited there is no means of protecting individuals from governments. . . . No political organization can avert this danger. You can try a division of powers; but if the sum total of powers is unlimited the divided powers have only to form a coalition for despotism to be installed without remedy. What is important for us is not that our rights may not be violated by one power without the approval of another, but rather that such a violation be forbidden to all powers. . . . The important truth, the eternal principle to be established is that sovereignty is limited, and that there are desires that neither the people nor their delegates have the right to entertain.

No authority on earth is unlimited, neither the people's, nor that of the men who claim to be their representatives, nor that of kings whatever their title to rule, nor that of the law which, being nothing but the expression of the will of the people or the prince, according to the form of government, must be kept within the same bounds as the authority from which it emanates.

These boundaries are fixed by justice and by the rights of individuals. Not even the will of an entire people can make just that which is unjust. The representatives of a nation do not have the right to do what the nation itself has not the right to do. . . . The consent of a people cannot make legitimate what is illegitimate, since a people can delegate to nobody an authority it does not have. . . .

————————◆·●·◆————————

To limit sovereignty, Constant supports a system of separation of powers in which no branch of government can exceed the authority granted to it. Secondly, if the principle of limited sovereignty is regarded as a general rule that applies to all states, "then nobody will ever dare to claim such [unlimited] power."

————————◆·●·◆————————

One objection presents itself to the limitation of sovereignty. Is it possible to limit it? Is there a force that can prevent it from breaking through the barriers prescribed for it? It will be said that by ingenious devices power can be restrained by dividing it. Its various parts can be placed in opposition and in equilibrium. But by what means can the sum total be prevented from being limitless? How can power be reined in other than by power?

Undoubtedly limitation of power in the abstract is not sufficient. We must look for the foundations of political institutions which will so combine the interests of the various guardians of power that their most obvious, most lasting, and most assured advantage lies in each one of them remaining within the limits of his respective functions. Nevertheless, the first problem remains the competence and the limitation of sovereignty; for before we can organize anything we must determine its nature and extent.

In the second place, without wishing, as philosophers have done only too frequently, to exaggerate the influence of truth, we can state that when certain principles are completely and clearly demonstrated they serve in a sense as their own guarantees. A universal opinion is formed concerning the evidence which soon becomes victorious. If it is recognized that sovereignty is not without limits, that is to say, that there is no unlimited power on earth, then nobody will ever dare to claim such a power. This has already been proved by experience. For example, society as a whole is no longer given the right to put anyone to death without trial. No modern government, therefore, claims to exercise such a right. . . .

Limitation of sovereignty is therefore both genuine and possible. It will be safeguarded, first of all by the force that safeguards all truths recognized by public opinion, and second, more precisely, by the distribution and balance of powers. . . . Everything else is nothing but crude charlatanism, practised from century to century for the benefit of some and to the misery and shame of the rest.

JOHN STUART MILL
On Liberty

Freedom of thought and expression were principal concerns of nineteenth-century liberals. The classic defense of intellectual freedom is *On Liberty* (1859) written by John Stuart Mill (1806–1873), a prominent British philosopher. Mill argued that no individual or government has a monopoly on truth, for all humans are fallible. Therefore, the government and the majority have no legitimate authority to suppress views, however unpopular; they have no right to interfere with a person's liberty so long as that person's actions do no injury to others. Nothing is more absolute, contended Mill, than the inviolable right of all adults to think and live as they please so long as they respect the rights of others. For Mill, toleration of opposing and unpopular viewpoints is a necessary trait in order for a person to become rational, moral, and civilized.

The object of this essay is to assert one very simple principle, as entitled to govern absolutely the dealings of society with the individual. . . . That principle is that the sole end for which mankind are warranted, individually or collectively, in interfering with the liberty of action of any of their number is self-protection. That the only purpose for which power can be rightfully exercised over any member of a civilized community, against his will, is to prevent harm to others. His own good, either physical or moral, is not a sufficient warrant. He cannot rightfully be compelled to do or forbear because it will be better for him to do so, because it will make him happier, because, in the opinions of others, to do so would be wise or even right. These are good reasons for remonstrating with him, or reasoning with him, or persuading him, or entreating him, but not for compelling him or visiting him with any evil in case he do otherwise. To justify that, the conduct from which it is desired to deter him must be calculated to produce evil to someone else. The only part of the conduct of anyone for which he is amenable to society is that which concerns others. In the part which merely concerns himself, his independence is, of right, absolute. Over himself, over his own body and mind, the individual is sovereign. . . .

. . . This, then, is the appropriate region of human liberty. It comprises, first, the inward domain of consciousness, demanding liberty of conscience in the most comprehensive sense, liberty of thought and feeling, absolute freedom of opinion and sentiment on all subjects, practical or speculative, scientific, moral, or theological. The liberty of expressing and publishing opinions may seem to fall under a different principle, since it belongs to that part of the conduct of an individual which concerns other people, but, being almost of as much importance as the liberty of thought itself and resting in great part on the same reasons, is practically inseparable from it. Secondly, the principle requires liberty of tastes and pursuits, of framing the plan of our life to suit our own character, of doing as we like, subject to such consequences as may follow, without impediment from our fellow creatures, so long as what we do does not harm them, even though they should think our conduct foolish, perverse, or wrong. Thirdly, from this liberty of each individual follows the liberty, within the same limits, of combination among individuals; freedom to unite for any purpose not involving harm to others: the persons combining being supposed to be of full age and not forced or deceived.

No society in which these liberties are not, on the whole, respected is free, whatever may be its form of government; and none is completely free in which they do not exist absolute and unqualified. The only freedom which deserves the name is that of pursuing our own good in our own way, so long as we do not attempt to deprive others of theirs or impede their efforts to obtain it. Each is the proper guardian of his own health, whether bodily *or* mental and spiritual. Mankind are greater gainers by suffering each other to live as seems good to themselves than by compelling each to live as seems good to the rest. . . .

. . . Let us suppose, therefore, that the government is entirely at one with the people, and never thinks of exerting any power of coercion unless in agreement with what it conceives to be their voice. But I deny the right of the people to exercise such coercion, either by themselves or by their government. The power itself is illegitimate. The best government has no more title to it than the worst. It is as noxious, or more noxious, when exerted in accordance with public opinion than when in opposition to it. If all mankind minus one were of one opinion, mankind would be no more justified in silencing that one person than he, if he had the power, would be justified in silencing mankind. Were an opinion a personal possession of no value except to the owner, if to be obstructed in the enjoyment of it were simply a private injury, it would make some difference whether the injury was inflicted only on a few persons or on many. But the peculiar evil of silencing the expression of an opinion is that it is robbing the human race, posterity as well as the existing generation — those who dissent from the opinion, still more than those who hold it. If the opinion is right, they are deprived of the opportunity of exchanging error for truth; if wrong, they lose, what is almost as great a benefit, the clearer perception and livelier impression of truth produced by its collision with error.

Review Questions

1. Benjamin Constant held that the consent of a people cannot make legitimate what is illegitimate. What implications did his statement that "the jurisdiction of sovereignty stops at the point where the independence of individual life starts" have for liberalism and the prevailing ideas about majority rule?

2. How did Constant propose to limit popular sovereignty?

3. What was the purpose of John Stuart Mill's essay?

4. For Mill, what is the "peculiar evil of silencing the expression of an opinion," however unpopular?

5. On what grounds would Mill permit society to restrict individual liberty?

4 | Nationalism and Repression in Germany

Nationalism espoused the individual's allegiance to the national community and sought to unify divided nations and to liberate subject peoples. In the early nineteenth century, most nationalists were liberals who viewed the struggle for unification and freedom from foreign oppression as an extension of the struggle for individual rights. Few liberals recognized that nationalism was a potentially dangerous force that could threaten liberal ideals of freedom and equality.

By glorifying a nation's language and ancient traditions and folkways, romanticism contributed to the evolution of modern nationalism, particularly in Germany. German romantics longed to create a true folk community in which the individual's soul would be immersed in the nation's soul. Through the national community, individuals could find the meaning in life for which they yearned. The romantic veneration of the past produced a mythical way of thinking about politics and history, one that subordinated reason to powerful emotions. In particular, German romantics attacked the liberal-rational tradition of the Enlightenment and the French Revolution as hostile to the true German spirit.

ERNST MORITZ ARNDT
The War of Liberation

The Napoleonic wars kindled nationalist sentiments in the German states. Hatred of the French occupier evoked a feeling of outrage and a desire for national unity among some Germans, who before the occupation had thought not of a German fatherland but of their own states and princes. These Germans called for a war of liberation against Napoleon. Attracting mostly intellectuals, the idea of political unification had limited impact on the rest of the people, who remained loyal to local princes and local territories. Nevertheless, the embryo of nationalism was conceived in the German uprising against Napoleon in 1813. The writings of Ernst Moritz Arndt (1769–1860) vividly express the emerging nationalism. The following excerpts describe Arndt's view of the War of Liberation and present his appeal for German unity.

Fired with enthusiasm, the people rose, "with God for King and Fatherland." Among the Prussians there was only one voice, one feeling, one anger and one love, to save the Fatherland and to free Germany. The Prussians wanted war; war and death they wanted; peace they feared be- cause they could hope for no honorable peace from Napoleon. War, war, sounded the cry from the Carpathians [mountains] to the Baltic [Sea], from the Niemen to the Elbe [rivers]. War! cried the noble- man and landed proprietor who had be- come impoverished. War! the peasant who was driving his last horse to death. . . . War! the citizen who was growing exhausted from quartering soldiers and paying taxes. War; the widow who was sending her only son to the front. War! the young girl who, with tears of pride and pain, was leaving her betrothed. Youths who were hardly able to bear arms, men with gray hair, officers who on account of wounds and mutilations had long ago been honorably discharged, rich landed proprietors and officials, fathers of large families and managers of extensive businesses — all were unwilling to remain behind. Even young women, under all sorts of disguises, rushed to arms; all wanted to drill, arm themselves and fight and die for the Fatherland. . . .

The most beautiful thing about all this holy zeal and happy confusion was that all differences of position, class, and age were forgotten . . . that the one great feeling for the Fatherland, its freedom and honor, swallowed all other feelings, caused all other considerations and relationships to be forgotten.

In another passage, Arndt appealed for German unity.

German man, feel again God, hear and fear the eternal, and you hear and fear also your *Volk* [folk, people, nation]; you feel again in God the honor and dignity of your fathers, their glorious history rejuvenates itself again in you, their firm and gallant virtue reblossoms in you, the whole German Fatherland stands again before you in the august halo of past centuries! Then, when you feel and fear and honor all this, then you cry, then you lament, then you wrathfully reproach yourself that you have become so miserable and evil: then starts your new life and your new history. . . . From the North Sea to the Carpathians from the Baltic [Sea] to the Alps, from the Vistula to the Schelde [rivers], one faith, one love, one courage, and one enthusiasm must gather again the whole German folk in brotherly community; they must learn to feel how great, mighty, and happy their fathers were in obedience to one German emperor and one Reich, at a time when the many discords had not yet turned one against the other, when the many cowards and knaves had not yet betrayed them; . . . above the ruins and ashes of their destroyed Fatherland they must weepingly join hands and pray and swear all to stand like one man and to fight until the sacred land will be free. . . . Feel the infinite and sublime which slumbers hidden in the lap of the days, those light and mighty spirits which now glimmer in isolated meteors but which soon will shine in all suns and stars; feel the new birth of times, the higher, cleaner breath of spiritual life and do not longer be fooled and confused by the insignificant and small. No longer Catholics and Protestants, no longer Prussians and Austrians, Saxons and Bavarians, Silesians and Hanoverians, no longer of different faith, different mentality, and different will — be Germans, be one, will to be one by love and loyalty, and no devil will vanquish you.

HEINRICH VON GAGERN
The Call for German Unity

Heinrich von Gagern (1799–1880) was a liberal who helped to organize the *Burschenschaften*, German student fraternities dedicated to national unity. In the passage that follows, von Gagern explained the nationalist purpose of the German student movement.

It is very hard to explain the spirit of the student movement to you, but I shall try, even though I can only give you a few characteristics. . . .

. . . Those who share in this spirit have [a] . . . tendency in their student life, Love of Fatherland is their guiding principle. Their purpose is to make a better future for the Fatherland, each as best he can, to spread national consciousness, or to use the much ridiculed and maligned Germanic expression, more folkishness, and to work for better constitutions. . . .

. . . We want more sense of community among the several states of Germany, greater unity in their policies and in their principles of government; no separate policy for each state, but the nearest possible relations with one another; above all, we want Germany to be considered *one* land and the German people *one* people. In the forms of our student comradeship we show how we want to approach this as nearly as possible in the real world. Regional fraternities are forbidden, and we live in a German comradeship, one people in spirit, as we want it for all Germany in reality. We give our selves the freest of constitutions, just as we should like Germany to have the freest possible one, insofar as that is suitable for the German people. We want a constitution for the people that fits in with the spirit of the times and with the people's own level of enlightenment, rather than what each prince gives his people according to what he likes and what serves his private interest. Above all, we want the princes to understand and to follow the principle that they exist for the country and not the country for them. In fact, the prevailing view is that the constitution should not come from the individual states at all. The main principles of the German constitution should apply to all states in common, and should be expressed by the German federal assembly. This constitution should deal not only with the absolute necessities, like fiscal administration and justice, general administration and church and military affairs and so on; this constitution ought to be extended to the education of the young, at least at the upper age levels, and to many other such things.

Karlsbad Decrees

In 1819, Metternich and representatives from other German states meeting at Karlsbad drew up several decrees designed to stifle liberalism and nationalism. The Karlsbad Decrees called for the dissolution of the *Burschenschaft,* the censoring of books and newspapers, and the dismissal of professors who spread liberal doctrines.

Provisional Decree relative to the Measures to be taken concerning the Universities.
Sect. 1. The Sovereign shall make choice for each university of an extraordinary commissioner, furnished with suitable instructions and powers, residing in the place where the university is established. . . .

The duty of this commissioner shall be to . . . observe carefully the spirit with which the professors and tutors are guided in their public and private lectures; . . . and to devote a constant attention to every thing which may tend to the maintenance of morality, good order and decency among the youths.

Sect. 2. The governments of the states, members of the confederation, reciprocally engage to remove from their universities and other establishments of instruction, the professors and other public teachers, against whom it may be proved, that in departing from their duty, in overstepping the bounds of their duty, in abusing their legitimate influence over the minds of youth, by the propagation of pernicious dogmas, hostile to order and public tranquility, or in sapping the foundation of existing establishments, they have shown themselves incapable of executing the important functions entrusted to them. . . .

A professor or tutor thus excluded, cannot be admitted in any other state of the confederation to any other establishment of public instruction.

Sect. 3. The laws long since made against secret or unauthorized associations at the universities, shall be maintained in all their force and rigour, and shall be particularly extended with so much the more severity against the well-known society formed some years ago under the name of the General Burgenschaft, as it has for its basis an idea, absolutely inadmissible, of community and continued correspondence between the different universities.

The governments shall mutually engage to admit to no public employment any individuals who may continue or enter into any of those associations after the publication of the present decree.

Decree relative to the Measures for preventing the Abuses of the Press.

Sect. 1. . . . No writing appearing in the form of a daily paper or periodical pamphlet . . . shall be issued from the press without the previous consent of the public authority. . . .

Sect. 7. The editor of a journal, or other periodical publication, that may be suppressed by command of the Diet, shall not be allowed, during the space of five years, to conduct any similar publication in any states of the confederation. . . .

Decree relative to the formation of a Central Commission, for the purpose of Ulterior Inquiry respecting Revolutionary Plots, discovered in some of the States of the Confederation.

Art. 1. In 15 days from the date of this decree, an extraordinary commission of inquiry, appointed by the Diet and composed of 7 members, including the President, shall assemble in the city of Mentz, a fortress of the confederation.

2. The object of this commission is, to make careful and detailed inquiries respecting the facts, the origin and the multiplied ramifications of the secret revolutionary and demagogic associations, directed against the political constitution and internal repose, as well of the confederation in general, as of the individual members thereof.

Review Questions

1. According to Ernst Arndt, what was the effect upon German people of different classes and ages of the rising feeling of nationalism?

2. Arndt's writings show the interconnection between Romanticism and nationalism. Discuss this statement.

3. What was the guiding principle behind Heinrich von Gagern's characterization of the German student movement? What were its political implications?

4. By what methods did the Karlsbad Decrees propose to preserve political stability, and on what grounds was this proposal made?

5. The Karlsbad Decrees seem to have assumed that unregulated ideas were powerful factors in disrupting civilization. If this is so, do you feel that the methods proposed to restrain ideas indicated a genuine understanding of their force and were equal to the task of repressing them? Discuss.

5 | The Spread of Liberalism and Nationalism

In 1821 the Greeks revolted against their Ottoman Turk overlords. The struggle, which ended with the granting of independence to Greece in 1830, captured the imagination of many European intellectuals who admired ancient Greece as the birthplace of Western civilization. These intellectuals raised money for the revolutionaries and glorified the struggle in their writings and paintings.

The Greek Proclamation of Independence

The Greek proclamation of independence, issued in 1822, clearly exemplifies the liberal and nationalist ideals that grew out of the French Revolution.

Declaration of Independence

The National Assembly to the Greeks.

The Greek Nation, wearied by the dreadful weight of Ottoman oppression, and resolved to break its yoke, though at the price of the greatest sacrifices, proclaims to-day, before God and men, by the organ of its lawful representatives, met in a national assembly, its independence.

Descendants of a generous and enlightened nation, witnesses of the happiness which the sacred ægis of law secures to the civilized nations of Europe! Ye all know, that the measure of our sufferings was full. It was impossible for us any longer to bear, without being charged with cowardice and stupidity, the cruel scourge of Ottoman rule. Has not the Turk, during four centuries, trampling under foot reason and justice, disposed of us as his caprice prompted? We flew to arms then, in order to avenge the injuries which an insolent tyrant had heaped on our country; injuries utterly unexampled, and which left far behind it all the various shapes of oppression which have ever desolated and dyed the earth with carnage.

Our warfare against the Turks, far from being the effect of a seditious and jacobinical movement, or the pretext of an ambitious faction, is a national war, undertaken for the sole purpose of reconquering our rights, and securing our existence and honour. In vain did injustice, by depriving us of all securities, hope to stifle in our hearts the conviction of their necessity. As if, formed out of the vilest materials, we were condemned by nature to perpetual servitude; doomed to crouch beneath the wild sway of ferocious tyrants, who came from afar to subdue and to crush us! No, a thousand ages of proscription would not bar the sacred rights, whose creation was the work of nature herself. They were torn from us by violence; and violence, more righteously directed, may one day win them back, and hold them forth in all their reviving brilliancy to the admiration of the universe. In a word, they are rights which we have never ceased reclaiming in the very heart of our country, by every method which occasional opportunities placed in our power.

Strong in these principles, and wishing to advance as the equals of the Christians of Europe, in the paths of civilization, we combined into one great war all the partial and secret conflicts which we had long waged against the Ottoman empire. We swore to conquer, and to behold our country governed by just laws, or to disappear from the face of the earth. During ten months God has blest our steps in this glorious but rugged road. Our arms have been often victorious, but often they have experienced resistance. We are struggling to remove the obstacles which retard our triumph. Our political organization was then deferred, and the nation, solely occupied in repelling a lasting danger, foresaw that appearance of disorder which ever follows great convulsions, and which the injudicious alone can make a matter of reproach against us.

As soon as circumstances allowed us to think of a plan of government, we saw the Greek continent of the east and west, the Peloponnesus, and the islands, successively proceed in their organization, and prepare the way for that general constitutional system which was necessary to direct the progress of our revolution. For this purpose, the deputies of the provinces and of the islands, being duly authorised, and having met in a national assembly, and after deliberately considering the state of the country, have decreed the basis and the provisional form of the government which is to preside over the future destinies of your country. This gov-

ernment, founded on justice, instituted by universal consent, is now the only legitimate and national government. The nations of Greece will therefore hasten to recognise it.

Two august bodies, the executive power and the senate, will be at the head of the administration, supported by the judicial power, which will discharge its duties quite independently of the former.

The assembly declares to the nation, that, having completed its task, it this day dissolves itself. It is the duty of the nation to submit to the laws and the authorities which emanate from it. Grecians! but a little while since, ye said, "no more slavery!" and the power of the tyrant has vanished. But it is concord alone which can consolidate your liberty and independence. The assembly offers up its prayers, that the mighty arm of the Most High may raise the nation towards the sanctuary of his eternal wisdom. Thus discerning their true interests, the magistrates, by a vigilant foresight, the people by a sincere devotion, will succeed in founding the long-desired prosperity of our common country.

The Revolt Against Tsarist Autocracy

The French Revolution sharpened the already profound cultural differences between Russia and western Europe. French ideas of constitutional government and individual liberty threatened the survival of the Russian Empire, which lacked a sense of national unity and was held together by force. In 1814, two years after the disastrous retreat of Napoleon's army from Moscow, the Russian army reached Paris. Russian officers brought home with them not only the ideas of the French Revolution but also a taste of the good life in western Europe. They now looked at their own country — at the miserable serfs, corrupt officials, tyrannical landlords — with westernized eyes and found it wanting. These officers aspired to create a Russia that could hold its own in comparison with western Europe.

Tsar Alexander I (1801–1825) raised the officers' hopes by making vague promises of reform and by granting a constitution of sorts to those parts of Poland that had been annexed by the Russian Empire. At the opening of the Polish national assembly, the Diet, Alexander held out hope for a Russian constitution and an end to serfdom. But by 1820, following the lead of the reactionary monarchs of central Europe, he strengthened autocratic rule. Alexander's tightening of autocracy drove the westernized officers to form secret societies and to engage in conspiracy. In

December 1824, shortly after Alexander's death, the officers led their soldiers in open rebellion just as the new tsar, Nicholas I (1825–1855), ascended the throne. Although the Decembrist uprising failed miserably, it marked the beginning of a western-oriented revolutionary movement in Russia born from the ever-widening cultural gap between western Europe and tsarist autocracy.

Arrested Decembrist conspirators testified before an official Commission of Inquiry. What follows is a portion of the testimony of Pavel Ivanovich Pestel, the leader of the uprising, and a letter written by a member of the revolutionary circle.

Extracts from Pestel's Testimony

QUESTION 6: How did the revolutionary ideas gradually develop and become implanted in men's minds? Who first conceived these ideas and continued to preach and spread them throughout the State?

ANSWER 6: This question is very difficult to answer, for it must go beyond the realm of discussion about the secret Society. However, in order to fulfill the demand of the Committee I shall try so far as I can to explain it.

Political books are in the hands of everyone; political science is taught and political news spread everywhere. These teach all to discuss the activities and conduct of the Government, to praise one thing and assail another. A survey of the events of 1812, 1813, 1814, and 1815, likewise of the preceding and following periods, will show how many thrones were toppled over, how many others were established, how many kingdoms were destroyed, and how many new ones were created; how many Sovereigns were expelled, how many returned or were invited to return and were then again driven out; how many revolutions were accomplished; how many coup d'états carried out — all these events familiarized the minds of men with the idea of revolutions, with their possibilities, and with the favorable occasions on which to execute them. Besides that, every century has its peculiar characteristic: ours is marked by revolutionary ideas. From one end of Europe to the other the same thing is observed, from Portugal to Russia, without the exception of a single state, not even England or Turkey, those two opposites. The same spectacle is presented also in the whole of America. The spirit of reform causes mental fermentation. . . . Here are the causes, I think, which gave rise to revolutionary ideas and which have implanted them in the minds of people. As to the cause of the spread of the spirit of reform through the country, it could not be ascribed to the Society, for the organization was still too small to have any popular influence.

Extract from a Letter of Kakhovsky to General Levashev

Your Excellency,
Dear Sir!

The uprising of December 14 is a result of causes related above. I see, Your Excellency, that the Committee established by His Majesty is making a great effort to discover all the members of the secret Society. But the government will not derive any notable benefit from that. We were not trained within the Society but were already ready to work when we joined it. The origin and the root of the Society one must seek in the spirit of the time and in our state of mind. I know a few belonging to the secret Society but am inclined to think the membership is not very large. Among my many acquaintances who do not adhere to secret societies very few are opposed to my opinions. Frankly I state that among thousands of young men there are hardly a hundred who do not passionately long for freedom. These youths, striving with pure and strong love for the welfare of their Fatherland, toward true enlightenment, are growing mature.

The people have conceived a sacred truth — that they do not exist for govern-

ments, but that governments must be organized for them. This is the cause of
struggle in all countries; peoples, after
tasting the sweetness of enlightenment and
freedom, strive toward them; and governments, surrounded by millions of bay-
onets, make efforts to repel these peoples
back into the darkness of ignorance. But
all these efforts will prove in vain;
impressions once received can never be
erased. Liberty, that torch of intellect and
warmth of life, was always and everywhere the attribute of peoples emerged
from primitive ignorance. We are unable
to live like our ancestors, like barbarians
or slaves.

Review Questions

1. Show how the Greek Proclamation of Independence gave expression to the
   ideas of the Enlightenment and the French Revolution.
2. Show how the proclamation was also an expression of romantic nationalism?
3. To what did Pestel and Kakhovsky attribute the rise of revolutionary ideas?

6 | The Call for Italian Unity

In 1815, Italy was a fragmented nation. Hapsburg Austria ruled Lombardy and
Venetia in the north and a Bourbon king sat on the throne of the Kingdom of the
Two Sicilies in the south. The duchies of Tuscany, Parma, and Modena were ruled
by Hapsburg princes subservient to Austria. The papal states in central Italy were
ruled by the pope. The House of Savoy, an Italian dynasty, ruled the Kingdom of
Piedmont, which became the cornerstone of Italian unification. Inspired by past
Italian glories — the Roman Empire and the Renaissance — Italian nationalists de-
manded an end to foreign occupation and the unification of the Italian peninsula.
As in other lands, national revival and unification appealed principally to intellectuals
and the middle class.

GIUSEPPE MAZZINI
Young Italy

A leading figure in the *Risorgimento* — the struggle for Italian nationhood — was
Giuseppe Mazzini (1805–1872). Often called the "soul of the Risorgimento," Mazzini
devoted his life to the creation of a unified and republican Italy; he believed that a
free and democratic Italy would serve as a model to the other nations of Europe. In
1831, he founded Young Italy, a society dedicated to the cause of Italian unity. The
following reading includes the oath taken by members of Young Italy.

Young Italy is a brotherhood of Italians
who believe in a law of Progress and Duty,
and are convinced that Italy is destined to
become one nation, — convinced also that
she possesses sufficient strength within
herself to become one, and that the ill
success of her former efforts is to be attributed not to the weakness, but to the

misdirection of the revolutionary elements within her, — that the secret of force lies in constancy and unity of effort. They join this association in the firm intent of consecrating both thought and action to the great aim of reconstituting Italy as one independent sovereign nation of free men and equals. . . .

Young Italy is Republican. . . . Republican, — Because theoretically every nation is destined, by the law of God and humanity, to form a free and equal community of brothers; and the republican is the only form of government that insures this future. . . .

The means by which Young Italy proposes to reach its aim are — education and insurrection, to be adopted simultaneously, and made to harmonize with each other. Education must ever be directed to teach by example, word, and pen the necessity of insurrection. Insurrection, whenever it can be realized, must be so conducted as to render it a means of national education. . . .

Insurrection — by means of guerrilla bands — is the true method of warfare for all nations desirous of emancipating themselves from a foreign yoke. This method of warfare supplies the want — inevitable at the commencement of the insurrection — of a regular army; it calls the greatest number of elements into the field, and yet may be sustained by the smallest number. It forms the military education of the people, and consecrates every foot of the native soil by the memory of some warlike deed. . . .

Each member will, upon his initiation into the association of Young Italy, pronounce the following form of oath, in the presence of the initiator:

In the name of God and of Italy;

In the name of all the martyrs of the holy Italian cause who have fallen beneath foreign and domestic tyranny;

By the duties which bind me to the land wherein God has placed me, and to the brothers whom God has given me;

By the love — innate in all men — I bear to the country that gave my mother birth, and will be the home of my children;

By the hatred — innate in all men — I bear to evil, injustice, usurpation, and arbitrary rule;

By the blush that rises to my brow when I stand before the citizens of other lands, to know that I have no rights of citizenship, no country, and no national flag;

By the aspiration that thrills my soul towards that liberty for which it was created, and is impotent to exert; towards the good it was created to strive after, and is impotent to achieve in the silence and isolation of slavery;

By the memory of our former greatness, and the sense of our present degradation;

By the tears of Italian mothers for their sons dead on the scaffold, in prison, or in exile;

By the sufferings of the millions, —

I, . . . believing in the mission intrusted by God to Italy, and the duty of every Italian to strive to attempt its fulfillment; convinced that where God has ordained that a nation shall be, He has given the requisite power to create it; that the people are the depositaries of that power, and that in its right direction for the people, and by the people, lies the secret of victory; convinced that virtue consists in action and sacrifice, and strength in union and constancy of purpose: I give my name to Young Italy, an association of men holding the same faith, and swear:

To dedicate myself wholly and forever to the endeavor with them to constitute Italy one free, independent, republican nation; to promote by every means in my power — whether by written or spoken word, or by action — the education of my Italian brothers towards the aim of Young Italy; towards association, the sole means of its accomplishment, and to virtue, which alone can render the conquest lasting; to abstain from enrolling myself in any other association from this time forth; to obey all the instructions, in conformity with the spirit of Young Italy, given me by those who represent with me the union of my

Italian brothers; and to keep the secret of these instructions, even at the cost of my life; to assist my brothers of the association both by action and counsel —
NOW AND FOREVER.

This do I swear, invoking upon my head the wrath of God, the abhorrence of man, and the infamy of the perjurer, if I ever betray the whole or a part of this my oath.

Review Questions

1. What bonds united members of Giuseppe Mazzini's Young Italy?
2. Why do you suppose many students were attracted to Young Italy?
3. Mazzini was a democrat, a nationalist, and a romantic. Discuss this statement.

7 | 1848: The Year of Revolutions

In 1848, revolutions for political liberty and nationhood broke out in many parts of Europe. An uprising in Paris set this revolutionary tidal wave in motion. In February 1848, democrats seeking to create a French republic and to institute universal manhood suffrage precipitated a crisis; the following uprising in Paris forced King Louis Philippe to abdicate. The leaders of the new French Republic championed political democracy but, with some notable exceptions like Louis Blanc (1811–1882), had little concern for the plight of the laboring poor.

The publication of the *Organization of Labor* (1839) had established Blanc as a leading French social reformer. Blanc urged the government to finance national workshops — industrial corporations, in which the directors would be elected by the workers — to provide employment for the urban poor. The government responded to Blanc's insistence that all workers have the "right to work" by indeed establishing national workshops, but these provided jobs for only a fraction of the unemployed, and many workers were given wages for doing nothing. Property owners regarded the workshops as a waste of government funds and as nests of working-class radicalism. When the government closed the workshops in June 1848, Parisian workers revolted.

ALEXIS DE TOCQUEVILLE
The June Days

To the French workers the June 1848 revolt was against poverty and for a fairer distribution of property. Viewing this uprising as a threat to property and indeed to civilization, the rest of France rallied against the workers, who were crushed after several days of bitter street fighting. In his *Recollections*, Alexis de Tocqueville (1805–1859), a leading statesman and political theorist, included a speech he made on January 29, 1848, before the French Chamber of Deputies, in which he warned the officials about the mood of the laboring poor.

. . . I am told that there is no danger because there are no riots; I am told that, because there is no visible disorder on the surface of society, there is no revolution at hand.

Gentlemen, permit me to say that I believe you are deceived. True, there is no actual disorder; but it has entered deeply into men's minds. See what is passing in the breasts of the working classes, who, I grant, are at present quiet. No doubt they are not disturbed by political passion, properly so-called, to the same extent that they have been; but can you not see that their passions, instead of political, have become social? Do you not see that there are gradually forming in their breasts opinions and ideas which are destined not only to upset this or that law, ministry, or even form of government, but society itself, until it totters upon the foundations on which it rests today? Do you not listen to what they say to themselves each day? Do you not hear them repeating unceasingly that all that is above them is incapable and unworthy of governing them; that the present distribution of goods throughout the world is unjust; that property rests on a foundation which is not an equitable foundation? And do you not realize that when such opinions take root, when they spread in an almost universal manner, when they sink deeply into the masses, they are bound to bring with them sooner or later, I know not when nor how, a most formidable revolution?

This, gentlemen, is my profound conviction: I believe that we are at this moment sleeping on a volcano. I am profoundly convinced of it. . . .

———————→ ·•· ←———————

Later in his Recollections, *de Tocqueville describes the second uprising in 1848, called the* June Days.

———————→ ·•· ←———————

I come at last to the insurrection of June, the most extensive and the most singular that has occurred in our history, and perhaps in any other: the most ex-

tensive, because, during four days, more than a hundred thousand men were engaged in it; the most singular, because the insurgents fought without a war-cry, without leaders, without flags, and yet with a marvellous harmony and an amount of military experience that astonished the oldest officers.

What distinguished it also, among all the events of this kind which have succeeded one another in France for sixty years, is that it did not aim at changing the form of government, but at altering the order of society. It was not, strictly speaking, a political struggle, in the sense which until then we had given to the word, but a combat of class against class, a sort of Servile War [slave uprising in ancient Rome]. It represented the facts of the Revolution of February in the same manner as the theories of Socialism represented its ideas; or rather it issued naturally from these ideas, as a son does from his mother. We behold in it nothing more than a blind and rude, but powerful, effort on the part of the workmen to escape from the necessities of their condition, which had been depicted to them as one of unlawful oppression, and to open up by main force a road towards that imaginary comfort with which they had been deluded. It was this mixture of greed and false theory which first gave birth to the insurrection and then made it so formidable. These poor people had been told that the wealth of the rich was in some way the produce of a theft practised upon themselves. They had been assured that the inequality of fortunes was as opposed to morality and the welfare of society as it was to nature. Prompted by their needs and their passions, many had believed this obscure and erroneous notion of right, which, mingled with brute force, imparted to the latter an energy, a tenacity and a power which it would never have possessed unaided.

It must also be observed that this formidable insurrection was not the enterprise of a certain number of conspirators, but the revolt of one whole section of the population against another. Women took part in it as well as men. While the latter fought, the former prepared and carried ammunition; and when at last the time had come to surrender, the women were the last to yield. These women went to battle with, as it were, a housewifely ardour: they looked to victory for the comfort of their husbands and the education of their children. . . .

As we know, it was the closing of the national workshops that occasioned the rising. Dreading to disband this formidable soldiery at one stroke, the Government had tried to disperse it by sending part of the workmen into the country. They refused to leave. On the 22nd of June, they marched through Paris in troops, singing in cadence, in a monotonous chant, "We won't be sent away, we won't be sent away. . . ."

. . . The spirit of insurrection circulated from one end to the other of this immense class, and in each of its parts, as the blood does in the body; it filled the quarters where there was no fighting, as well as those which served as the scene of battle; it had penetrated into our houses, around, above, below us. The very places in which we thought ourselves the masters swarmed with domestic enemies; one might say that an atmosphere of civil war enveloped the whole of Paris, amid which, to whatever part we withdrew, we had to live. . . .

. . . It was easy to perceive through the multitude of contradictory reports that we had to do with the most universal, the best armed, and the most furious insurrection ever known in Paris. The national workshops and various revolutionary bands that had just been disbanded supplied it with trained and disciplined soldiers and with leaders. It was extending every moment, and it was difficult to believe that it would not end by being victorious, . . . all the great insurrections of the last sixty years

had triumphed. To all these enemies we were only able to oppose the battalions of the *bourgeoisie*, regiments which had been disarmed in February, and twenty thousand undisciplined lads of the Garde Mobile, who were all sons, brothers, or near relations of insurgents, and whose dispositions were doubtful.

But what alarmed us most was our leaders. The members of the Executive Commission filled us with profound distrust. On this subject I encountered, in the Assembly, the same feelings which I had observed among the National Guard. We doubted the good faith of some and the capacity of others. They were too numerous, besides, and too much divided to be able to act in complete harmony, and they were too much men of speech and the pen to be able to act to good purpose under such circumstances, even if they had agreed among themselves.

Nevertheless, we succeeded in triumphing over this so formidable insurrection; nay more, it was just that which rendered it so terrible which saved us. One might well apply in this case the famous phrase of the Prince de Condé [great French lord], during the wars of religion [in the seventeenth century]: "We should have been destroyed, had we not been so near destruction." Had the revolt borne a less radical character and a less ferocious aspect, it is probable that the greater part of the middle class would have stayed at home; France would not have come to our aid; the National Assembly itself would perhaps have yielded, or at least a minority of its members would have advised it; and the energy of the whole body would have been greatly unnerved. But the insurrection was of such a nature that any understanding with it became at once impossible, and from the first it left us no alternative but to defeat it or to be destroyed ourselves.

CARL SCHURZ
Revolution Spreads to the German States

The February Revolution in Paris was eagerly received by German liberals and nationalists who yearned for a Germany governed by a national parliament and a constitution that guaranteed basic liberties. In the following excerpt from his *Reminiscences,* Carl Schurz (1829–1906), then a student at the University of Bonn, recalled the expectations of German liberal-nationalists. After the revolution failed, Schurz fled to Switzerland and eventually went to the United States, where he had a distinguished career as a senator, cabinet member, and journalist.

One morning, toward the end of February, 1848, I sat quietly in my attic-chamber, working hard at my tragedy of "Ulrich von Hutten," when suddenly a friend rushed breathlessly into the room, exclaiming: "What, you sitting here! Do you not know what has happened?"

"No; what?"

"The French have driven away Louis Philippe and proclaimed the republic."

I threw down my pen — and that was the end of "Ulrich von Hutten." I never touched the manuscript again. We tore down the stairs, into the street, to the market-square, the accustomed meeting-place for all the student societies after their midday dinner. Although it was still forenoon, the market was already crowded with young men talking excitedly. There was no shouting, no noise, only agitated conversation. What did we want there? This probably no one knew. But since the French had driven away Louis Philippe and proclaimed the republic, something of course must happen here, too. Some of the students had brought their rapiers along, as if it were necessary at once to make an attack or to defend ourselves. We were dominated by a vague feeling as if a great outbreak of elemental forces had begun, as if an earthquake was impending of which we had felt the first shock, and we instinctively crowded together. Thus we wandered about in numerous bands . . . [and] fell into conversation with all manner of strangers, to find in them the same confused, astonished and expectant state of mind; then back to the market-square, to see what might be going on there; then again somewhere else, and so on, without aim and end, until finally late in the night fatigue compelled us to find the way home.

The next morning there were the usual lectures to be attended. But how profitless! The voice of the professor sounded like a monotonous drone coming from far away. What he had to say did not seem to concern us. The pen that should have taken notes remained idle. At last we closed with a sigh the notebook and went away, impelled by a feeling that now we had something more important to do — to devote ourselves to the affairs of the fatherland. And this we did by seeking as quickly as possible again the company of our friends, in order to discuss what had happened and what was to come. In these conversations, excited as they were, certain ideas and catchwords worked themselves to the surface, which expressed more or less the feelings of the people. Now had arrived in Germany the day for the establishment of "German Unity," and the founding of a great, powerful national German Empire. In the first line the convocation of a national parliament. Then the demands for civil rights and liberties, free speech, free press, the right of free assembly, equality before the law, a freely elected representation of the people with legislative power, responsibility of ministers, self-government of the communes, the right of the people to carry arms, the formation of a civic guard with elective officers, and so on — in short, that which was called a "constitutional form of government on a broad democratic basis." Republican ideas were at first only sparingly expressed. But the word democracy was soon on all tongues, and many, too, thought it a matter of course that if the princes should try to withhold from the people the rights and liberties demanded, force would take the place of mere petition. Of course the regeneration of the fatherland must, if possible, be accomplished by peaceable means. A few days after the outbreak of this commotion I reached my nineteenth birthday. I remember to have been so entirely absorbed by what was happening that I could hardly turn my thoughts to anything else. Like many of my friends, I was dominated by the feeling that at last the great opportunity had arrived for giving to the German people the liberty which was their birthright and to the German fatherland its unity and greatness, and that it was now the first duty of every German to do and to sacrifice everything for this sacred object. We were profoundly, solemnly in earnest. . . .

Exciting news came from all sides. In Cologne a threatening ferment prevailed. In the taverns and on the streets resounded the "Marseillaise" [French national anthem, symbol of the Revolution], which at that time still passed in all Europe as the "hymn of liberty." On the public places great meetings were held to consult about the demands to be made by the people. A large deputation, headed by the late lieutenant of artillery, August von Willich, forced its way into the hall of the city council, vehemently insisting that the municipality present as its own the demands of the people of Cologne to the king. The streets resounded with the military drumbeat; the soldiery marched upon the popular gatherings, and Willich, as well as another ex-artillery officer, Fritz Anneke, were arrested; whereupon increasing excitement. . . .

. . . In Coblenz, Düsseldorf, Aachen, Crefeld, Cleves and other cities on the Rhine similar demonstrations took place.

In South Germany — in Baden, Hessen-on-the Rhine, Nassau, Würtemberg, Bavaria — the same revolutionary spirit burst forth like a prairie-fire. In Baden the Grand Duke acceded almost at once to what was asked of him, and so did the rulers of Würtemberg, Nassau, and Hessen-Darmstadt. . . .

Great news came from Vienna. There the students of the university were the first to assail the Emperor of Austria with the cry for liberty and citizens' rights. Blood flowed in the streets, and the downfall of Prince Metternich was the result. The students organized themselves as the armed guard of liberty. In the great cities of Prussia there was a mighty commotion. Not only Cologne, Coblenz and Trier, but also Breslau, Königsberg and Frankfurt-on-the-Oder, sent deputations to Berlin to entreat the king. In the Prussian capital the masses surged upon the streets, and everybody looked for events of great import.

While such tidings rushed in upon us from all sides like a roaring hurricane, we in the little university town of Bonn were also busy preparing addresses to the sovereign, to circulate them for signature and to send them to Berlin. On the 18th of March we too had our mass demonstration. A great multitude gathered for a solemn procession through the streets of the town. The most respectable citizens, not a few professors and a great number of students and people of all grades marched in close ranks. At the head of the procession Professor Kinkel bore the tricolor, black, red and gold, which so long had been prohibited as the revolutionary flag. Arrived on the market-square he mounted the steps of the city hall and spoke to the assembled throng. He spoke with wonderful eloquence, his voice ringing out in its most powerful tones as he depicted a resurrection of German unity and greatness and of the liberties and rights of the German people, which now must be conceded by the princes or won by force by the people. And when at last he waved the black, red and gold banner, and predicted to a free German nation a magnificent future, enthusiasm without bounds broke forth. People clapped their hands, they shouted, they embraced one another, they shed tears. In a moment the city was covered with black, red and gold flags, and not only the Burschenschaft, but almost everybody wore a black-red-gold cockade on his hat. While on that 18th of March we were parading through the streets suddenly sinister rumors flew from mouth to mouth. It had been reported that the king of Prussia, after long hesitation, had finally concluded, like the other German princes, to concede the demands that were pouring upon him from all sides. But now a whispered report flew around that the soldiery had suddenly fired upon the people and that a bloody struggle was raging in the streets of Berlin.

Review Questions

1. According to Alexis de Tocqueville, why did Parisian workers revolt in 1848?

2. How did the goals of Parisian workers who revolted in 1848 differ from those of members of Mazzini's Young Italy?

3. In de Tocqueville's view, the most dangerous revolutions are invisible. Explain.

4. Why did the leaders of France resolve to crush the revolt and what enabled them to succeed?

5. De Tocqueville observed that what distinguished this revolt was that it aimed to change the order of society, not the form of government. What kind of revolt did this produce, and how did it differ from nationalist uprisings?

6. What effect did the news of Louis Philippe's overthrow and the founding of the French Republic have on Carl Schurz and the young students of his day? How did they behave?

7. What were the goals of Schurz and many of his colleagues? How did they seek to reconcile nationalism and liberalism?

8. Compare the goals of the German revolutionaries of 1848 with those of Young Italy's members.

CHAPTER 5

The Industrial Revolution

In the last part of the eighteenth century, as a revolution for liberty and equality swept across France and sent shock waves across Europe, a different kind of revolution, a revolution in industry, was transforming life in Great Britain. In the nineteenth century the Industrial Revolution spread to the United States and to the European continent. Today, it encompasses virtually the entire world; everywhere the drive to substitute machines for human labor continues at a rapid pace.

After 1760, dramatic changes occurred in Britain in the way goods were produced and labor organized. New forms of power, particularly steam, replaced animal strength and human muscle. Better ways of obtaining and using raw materials were discovered, and a new form of organizing production and workers — the factory — came into common use. In the nineteenth century, technology moved from triumph to triumph with a momentum unprecedented in human history. The resulting explosion in economic production and productivity transformed society with breathtaking speed.

Rapid industrialization caused hardships for the new class of industrial workers, many of them recent arrivals from the countryside. Arduous and monotonous, factory labor was geared to the strict discipline of the clock, the machine, and the production schedule. Employment was never secure. Sick workers received no pay and were often fired; aged workers suffered pay cuts or lost their jobs. During business slumps, employers lowered wages with impunity and laid-off workers had nowhere to turn for assistance. Because factory owners did not consider safety an important concern, accidents were frequent. Yet the Industrial Revolution was also a great force for human betterment. Ultimately it raised the standard of living, even for the lowest classes, lengthened life expectancy, and provided more leisure time and more possibilities for people to fulfill their potential.

The Industrial Revolution dramatically altered political and social life at all levels, but especially for the middle class, whose engagement in capitalist ventures brought greater political power and social recognition. During the course of the nineteenth century, the bourgeoisie came to hold many of the highest offices in western European states, completing a trend that had begun with the French Revolution.

Cities grew in size, number, and importance. Municipal authorities were unable to cope with the rapid pace of urbanization, and without adequate housing, sanitation, or recreational facilities, the exploding urban centers were another source of working-class misery. In preindustrial, Britain, most people had lived in small villages. They knew where their roots were; relatives, friends, and the village church gave them a sense of belonging. The industrial centers separated people from nature and from their places of origin, shattering traditional ways of life that had given men and women a sense of security.

The plight of the working class created a demand for reform, but the British government, committed to laissez-faire economic principles that militated against state involvement, was slow to act. In the last part of the nineteenth century, however, the development of labor unions, the rising political voice of the working class, and the growing recognition that the problems created by industrialization required government intervention speeded up the pace of reform. Rejecting the road of reform, Karl Marx called for a working-class revolution that would destroy the capitalist system.

1 | Early Industrialization

Several factors help to explain why the Industrial Revolution began in Great Britain. That country had an abundant labor supply, large deposits of coal and iron ore, and capital available for investing in new industries. A large domestic middle class and overseas colonies provided markets for manufactured goods. Colonies were also a source for raw materials, particularly cotton for the textile industry. The Scientific Revolution and an enthusiasm for engineering fostered a spirit of curiosity and inventiveness. Britain had enterprising and daring entrepreneurs who organized new businesses and discovered new methods of production.

EDWARD BAINES

Britain's Industrial Advantages and the Factory System

In 1835, Edward Baines (1800–1890), an early student of industrialization, wrote *The History of the Cotton Manufacture in Great Britain* — about one of the leading industries in the early days of the Industrial Revolution. In the passages that follow, Baines discusses the reasons for Britain's industrial transformation and the advantages of the factory system.

Three things may be regarded as of primary importance for the successful prosecution of manufactures, namely, waterpower, fuel, and iron. Wherever these exist in combination, and where they are abundant and cheap, machinery may be manufactured and put in motion at small cost; and most of the processes of making and finishing cloth, whether chemical or mechanical, depending, as they do, mainly on the two great agents of water and heat, may likewise be performed with advantage.

. . . A great number of streams . . . furnish water-power adequate to turn many hundred mills: they afford the element of water, indispensable for scouring, bleaching, printing, dyeing, and other processes of manufacture: and when collected in their larger channels, or employed to feed canals, they supply a superior inland navigation, so important for the transit of raw materials and merchandise.

Not less important for manufactures than the copious supply of good water, is the great abundance of coal. . . . This mineral fuel animates the thousand arms of the steam-engine, and furnishes the most powerful agent in all chemical and mechanical operations.

In mentioning the advantages which Lancashire [the major cotton manufacturing area] possesses as a seat of manufactures, we must not omit its ready communication with the sea by means of its well-situated port, Liverpool, through the medium of which it receives, from Ireland, a large proportion of the food that supports its population, and whose commerce brings from distant shores the raw materials of its manufactures, and again distributes them, converted into useful and elegant clothing, amongst all the nations of the earth. Through the same means a plentiful supply of timber is obtained, so needful for building purposes.

To the above natural advantages, we must add, the acquired advantage of a canal communication, which ramifies itself through all the populous parts of this county, and connects it with the inland counties, the seats of other flourishing manufactures, and the sources whence iron, lime, salt, stone, and other articles in which Lancashire is deficient, are obtained. By this means Lancashire, being already possessed of the primary requisites for manufactures, is enabled, at a very small expense, to command things of secondary importance, and to appropriate to its use the natural advantages of the whole kingdom. The canals, having been accomplished by individual enterprise, not by national funds, were constructed to supply a want already existing: they were not, therefore, original sources of the manufactures, but have extended together with them, and are to be considered as having essentially aided and accelerated that prosperity from whose beginnings they themselves arose. The recent introduction of railways will have a great effect in making the operations of trade more intensely active, and perfecting the division of labour, already carried to so high a point. By the railway and the locomotive engine, the extremities of the land will, for every beneficial purpose, be united.

In comparing the advantages of England for manufactures with those of other countries, we can by no means overlook the excellent commercial position of the country — intermediate between the north and south of Europe; and its insular situation, which, combined with the command of the seas, secures our territory from invasion or annoyance. The German ocean, the Baltic, and the Mediterranean are the regular highways for our ships; and our western ports command an unobstructed passage to the Atlantic, and to every quarter of the world.

A temperate climate, and a hardy race of men, have also greatly contributed to promote the manufacturing industry of England.

The political and moral advantages of this country, as a seat of manufactures, are not less remarkable than its physical advantages. The arts are the daughters of peace and liberty. In no country have these blessings been enjoyed in so high a degree, or for so long a continuance, as in England. Under the reign of just laws, personal liberty and property have been secure; mercantile enterprise has been allowed to reap its reward; capital has accumulated in safety; the workman has "gone forth to his work and to his labour until the evening;" and, thus protected and favoured, the manufacturing prosperity of the country has struck its roots deep, and spread forth its branches to the ends of the earth.

England has also gained by the calamities of other countries, and the intolerance of other governments. At different periods, the Flemish and French protestants, expelled from their native lands, have taken refuge in England, and have repaid the protection given them by practising and teaching branches of industry, in which the English were then less expert than their neighbours. The wars which have at different times desolated the rest of Europe, and especially those which followed the French revolution, (when mechanical invention was producing the most wonderful effects in England,) checked the progress of manufacturing improvement on the continent, and left England for many years without a competitor. At the same time, the English navy held the sovereignty of the ocean, and under its protection the commerce of this country extended beyond all former bounds, and established a firm connexion between the manufacturers of Lancashire and their customers in the most distant lands.

When the natural, political, and adventitious causes, thus enumerated, are viewed together, it cannot be [a] matter of surprise that England has obtained a preeminence over the rest of the world in manufactures.

A crucial feature of the Industrial Revolution was a new production system — the making of goods in factories. By bringing all the opera-

tions of manufacturing under one roof, industrialists made the process of production more efficient. Baines describes the factory system's advantages over former methods.

———————————◆·◈·◆—————————

. . . Hitherto the cotton manufacture had been carried on almost entirely in the houses of the workmen: the hand or stock cards,[1] the spinning wheel, and the loom, required no larger apartment than that of a cottage. A spinning jenny[2] of small size might also be used in a cottage, and in many instances was so used: when the number of spindles was considerably increased, adjacent work-shops were used. But the water-frame, the carding engine, and the other machines which [Richard] Arkwright brought out in a finished state, required both more space than could be found in a cottage, and more power than could be applied by the human arm. Their weight also rendered it necessary to place them in strongly-built mills, and they could not be advantageously turned by any power then known but that of water.

The use of machinery was accompanied by a greater division of labour than existed in the primitive state of the manufacture; the material went through many more processes; and of course the loss of time and the risk of waste would have been much increased, if its removal from house to house at every stage of the manufacture had been necessary. It became obvious that there were several important advantages in carrying on the numerous operations of an extensive manufacture in the same building. Where water power was required, it was economy to build one mill, and put up one water-wheel, rather than several. This arrangement also enabled the master spinner himself to superintend every stage of the manufacture: it gave him a greater security against the wasteful or fraudulent consumption of the material: it saved time in the transference of the work from hand to hand: and it prevented the extreme inconvenience which would have resulted from the failure of one class of workmen to perform their part, when several other classes of workmen were dependent upon them. Another circumstance which made it advantageous to have a large number of machines in one manufactory was, that mechanics must be employed on the spot, to construct and repair the machinery, and that their time could not be fully occupied with only a few machines.

All these considerations drove the cotton spinners to that important change in the economy of English manufactures, the introduction of the factory system; and when that system had once been adopted, such were its pecuniary advantages, that mercantile competition would have rendered it impossible, even had it been desirable, to abandon it.

———————————————————

[1] Prior to spinning, raw fibers had to be carded with a brushlike tool that cleaned and separated them.
[2] The spinning jenny, which was hand-powered, was the first machine that spun fiber onto multiple spindles at the same time; that is, it produced more thread or yarn in less time than the single-thread spinning wheel.

Review Questions

1. What natural assets for industrial development did England possess?
2. How did England's location in Europe and the world affect its industrial development?
3. What characteristics of English society and government contributed to the rise of the Industrial Revolution?
4. What was the role of British sea power in the Industrial Revolution?

5. What were the factory system's advantages over the domestic system of production?

2 | Industrialism and the Spirit of Capitalism

A vigorous spirit of enterprise and the opportunity for men of ability to rise from common origins to riches and fame help explain the growth of industrialism in England. These industrial capitalists adopted the attitude of medieval monks that "idleness is the enemy of the soul," to which they added "time is money."

EDWARD BAINES
The Career of Richard Arkwright

The spirit of enterprise is illustrated in the career of Richard Arkwright (1732–1792), one of the leading pioneers in the cotton industry. Arkwright began as an inventor of spinning machines and a promoter of factories and soon progressed to full-blown entrepreneurship. He was eventually knighted for his accomplishments. In the following excerpts from *The History of the Cotton Manufacture in Great Britain*, Edward Baines describes Arkwright's extraordinary rise to success and prominence.

Richard Arkwright rose by the force of his natural talents from a very humble condition in society. He was born at Preston on the 23d of December, 1732, of poor parents: being the youngest of thirteen children, his parents could only afford to give him an education of the humblest kind, and he was scarcely able to write. He was brought up to the trade of a barber at Kirkham and Preston, and established himself in that business at Bolton in the year 1760. Having become possessed of a chemical process for dyeing human hair, which in that day (when wigs were universal) was of considerable value, he travelled about collecting hair, and again disposing of it when dyed. In 1761, he married a wife from Leigh, and the connexions he thus formed in that town are supposed to have afterwards brought him acquainted with Highs's experiments in making spinning machines. He himself manifested a strong bent for experiments in mechanics, which he is stated to have followed with so much devotedness as to have neglected his business and injured his circumstances. His natural disposition was ardent, enterprising, and stubbornly persevering: his mind was as coarse as it was bold and active, and his manners were rough and unpleasing.

This uncouth mechanic produced a series of power-driven machines for all phases of textile manufacture from carding to spinning that revolutionized the industry and made him rich.

When this admirable series of machines was made known, and by their means yarns were produced far superior in quality to any before spun in England, as well as lower in price, a mighty impulse was communicated to the cotton manufacture. Weavers could now obtain an unlimited quantity of yarn, at a reasonable price; manufacturers could use warps [cross-threads in woven fabric] of cotton, which were much cheaper than the linen warps formerly used. Cotton fabrics could be sold lower than had ever before been known. The demand for them consequently increased. The shuttle [tool that carries thread in a loom] flew with fresh energy, and the weavers earned immoderately high wages. Spinning mills were erected to supply the requisite quantity of yarn. The fame of Arkwright resounded through the land; and capitalists flocked to him to buy his patent machines, or permission to use them. . . .

The most marked traits in the character of Arkwright were his wonderful ardour, energy, and perseverance. He commonly laboured in his multifarious concerns from five o'clock in the morning till nine at night; and when considerably more than fifty years of age, — feeling that the defects of his education placed him under great difficulty and inconvenience in conducting his correspondence, and in the general management of his business, — he encroached upon his sleep, in order to gain an hour each day to learn English grammar, and another hour to improve his writing and orthography [spelling]! He was impatient of whatever interfered with his favourite pursuits; and the fact is too strikingly characteristic not to be mentioned, that he separated from his wife not many years after their marriage, because she, convinced that he would starve his family . . . [because of the impracticality of some of his schemes], broke some of his experimental models of machinery. Arkwright was a severe economist of time; and, that he might not waste a moment, he generally travelled with four horses, and at a very rapid speed. His concerns in Derbyshire, Lancashire, and Scotland were so extensive and numerous, as to [show] at once his astonishing power of transacting business and his all-grasping spirit. In many of these he had partners, but he generally managed in such a way, that, whoever lost, he himself was a gainer. . . . His speculative schemes were vast and daring; he contemplated entering into the most extensive mercantile transactions, and buying up all the cotton in the world, in order to make an enormous profit by the monopoly: and from the extravagance of some of these designs, his judicious friends were of opinion, that if he had lived to put them in practice, he might have [impoverished himself].

Review Questions

1. What character traits enabled Richard Arkwright, a poor barber, to rise to knighthood, fortune, and fame?

2. What social, economic, and political conditions do you think made Arkwright's remarkable success possible?

3. What qualities made Arkwright a capitalist?

3 | Factory Discipline

For the new industries to succeed, workers needed to adopt the rigorous discipline exercised by the new industrial capitalists themselves. But adapting to labor with machines in factories proved traumatic for the poor, uneducated, and often unruly folk, who previously had toiled on farms and in village workshops and were used to a less demanding pace.

Factory Rules

The problem of adapting a preindustrial labor force to the discipline needed for coordinating large numbers of workers in the factory was common to all industrializing countries. The Foundry and Engineering Works of the Royal Overseas Trading Company, in the Moabit section of Berlin, issued the following rules in 1844. The rules aimed at instilling obedience and honesty as well as "good order and harmony" among the factory's workers. The rules not only stressed timekeeping (with appropriate fines for latecomers), but also proper conduct in all aspects of life and work in the factory.

In every large works, and in the co-ordination of any large number of workmen, good order and harmony must be looked upon as the fundamentals of success, and therefore the following rules shall be strictly observed.

Every man employed in the concern . . . shall receive a copy of these rules, so that no one can plead ignorance. Its acceptance shall be deemed to mean consent to submit to its regulations.

(1) The normal working day begins at all seasons at 6 A.M. precisely and ends, after the usual break of half an hour for breakfast, an hour for dinner and half an hour for tea, at 7 P.M., and it shall be strictly observed.

Five minutes before the beginning of the stated hours of work until their actual commencement, a bell shall ring and indicate that every worker employed in the concern has to proceed to his place of work, in order to start as soon as the bell stops.

The doorkeeper shall lock the door punctually at 6 A.M., 8.30 A.M., 1 P.M. and 4.30 P.M.

Workers arriving 2 minutes late shall lose half an hour's wages; whoever is more than 2 minutes late may not start work until after the next break, or at least shall lose his wages until then. Any disputes about the correct time shall be settled by the clock mounted above the gatekeeper's lodge.

These rules are valid both for time- and for piece-workers, and in cases of breaches of these rules, workmen shall be fined in proportion to their earnings. The deductions from the wage shall be entered in the wage-book of the gatekeeper whose duty they are; they shall be unconditionally accepted as it will not be possible to enter into any discussions about them.

(2) When the bell is rung to denote the end of the working day, every workman, both on piece- and on day-wage, shall leave his workshop and the yard, but is not allowed to make preparations for his departure before the bell rings. Every breach of this rule shall lead to a fine of five silver groschen [pennies] to the sick fund. Only those who have obtained special permission by the overseer may stay on in the workshop in order to work. — If a workman has worked beyond the closing bell, he must give his name to the gatekeeper on leaving, on pain of losing his payment for the overtime.

(3) No workman, whether employed by time or piece, may leave before the end of the working day, without having first received permission from the overseer and having given his name to the gatekeeper. Omission of these two actions shall lead to a fine of ten silver groschen payable to the sick fund.

(4) Repeated irregular arrival at work shall lead to dismissal. This shall also apply to those who are found idling by an official or overseer, and refuse to obey their order to resume work.

(5) Entry to the firm's property by any but the designated gateway, and exit by any prohibited route, e.g. by climbing fences or walls, or by crossing the Spree,

shall be punished by a fine of fifteen silver groschen to the sick fund for the first offences, and dismissal for the second.

(6) No worker may leave his place of work otherwise than for reasons connected with his work.

(7) All conversation with fellow-workers is prohibited; if any worker requires information about his work, he must turn to the overseer, or to the particular fellow-worker designated for the purpose.

(8) Smoking in the workshops or in the yard is prohibited during working hours; anyone caught smoking shall be fined five silver groschen for the sick fund for every such offence.

(9) Every worker is responsible for cleaning up his space in the workshop, and if in doubt, he is to turn to his overseer. — All tools must always be kept in good condition, and must be cleaned after use. This applies particularly to the turner, regarding his lathe.

(10) Natural functions must be performed at the appropriate places, and whoever is found soiling walls, fences, squares, etc., and similarly, whoever is found washing his face and hands in the workshop and not in the places assigned for the purpose, shall be fined five silver groschen for the sick fund.

(11) On completion of his piece of work, every workman must hand it over at once to his foreman or superior, in order to receive a fresh piece of work. Pattern makers must on no account hand over their patterns to the foundry without express order of their supervisors. No workman may take over work from his fellow-workman without instruction to that effect by the foreman.

(12) It goes without saying that all overseers and officials of the firm shall be obeyed without question, and shall be treated with due deference. Disobedience will be punished by dismissal.

(13) Immediate dismissal shall also be the fate of anyone found drunk in any of the workshops.

(14) Untrue allegations against supe-

riors or officials of the concern shall lead to stern reprimand, and may lead to dismissal. The same punishment shall be meted out to those who knowingly allow errors to slip through when supervising or stocktaking.

(15) Every workman is obliged to report to his superiors any acts of dishonesty or embezzlement on the part of his fellow workmen. If he omits to do so, and it is shown after subsequent discovery of a misdemeanour that he knew about it at the time, he shall be liable to be taken to court as an accessory after the fact and the wage due to him shall be retained as punishment. Conversely, anyone denouncing a theft in such a way as to allow conviction of the thief shall receive a reward of two Thaler [dollar equivalent], and, if necessary, his name shall be kept confidential. — Further, the gatekeeper and the watchman, as well as every official, are entitled to search the baskets, parcels, aprons etc. of the women and children who are taking the dinners into the works, on their departure, as well as search any worker suspected of stealing any article whatever. . . .

(18) Advances shall be granted only to the older workers, and even to them only in exceptional circumstances. As long as he is working by the piece, the workman is entitled merely to his fixed weekly wage as subsistence pay; the extra earnings shall be paid out only on completion of the whole piece contract. If a workman leaves before his piece contract is completed, either of his own free will, or on being dismissed as punishment, or because of illness, the partly completed work shall be valued by the general manager with the help of two overseers, and he will be paid accordingly. There is no appeal against the decision of these experts.

(19) A free copy of these rules is handed to every workman, but whoever loses it and requires a new one, or cannot produce it on leaving, shall be fined $2\frac{1}{2}$ silver groschen, payable to the sick fund.

Review Questions

1. How long was the working day in the Berlin factory? How much time off were the workers allowed?

2. Besides punctuality, what other aspects of factory work required official regulation?

3. Judging by the Berlin factory rules, what were the differences between preindustrial and industrial work routines?

4 | The Dark Side of Industrialization

Among the numerous problems caused by rapid industrialization, none aroused greater concern among humanitarians than child labor in factories and mines. In preindustrial times, children had always been part of the labor force, indoors and out, a practice that was continued during the early days of the Industrial Revolution. In the cotton industry, for instance, the proportion of children and adolescents under eighteen was around 40–45 percent of the labor force; in some large firms the proportion was even greater. Employers discovered early that youngsters adapted more easily to machines and factory discipline than did adults, who were used to traditional handicraft routines. Child labor took children away from their parents, undermined family life, and deprived children of schooling. Factory routines dulled their minds, and the long hours spent in often unsanitary environments endangered their health.

SADLER COMMISSION
Report on Child Labor

Due to concern about child labor, in 1832 a parliamentary committee chaired by Michael Thomas Sadler investigated the situation of children employed in British factories. The following testimonies are drawn from the records of the Sadler Commission.

Committee on Factories Bill: Minutes of Evidence.

[April 12,] 1832.
Michael Thomas Sadler, Esquire, in the Chair.
William Cooper, called in; and Examined.

What is your business? — I follow the cloth-dressing at present.[1]

What is your age? — I was eight-and-twenty last February.

When did you first begin to work in mills or factories? — When I was about 10 years of age.

With whom did you first work? — At Mr. Benyon's flax mills, in Meadowlane, Leeds.

What were your usual hours of working? — We began at five, and gave over at nine; at five o'clock in the morning.

And you gave over at nine o'clock? — At nine at night.

[1] In the original source, each paragraph was numbered; paragraphs 1–18 and 21–35 are in this section.

At what distance might you have lived from the mill? — About a mile and a half.

At what time had you to get up in the morning to attend to your labour? — I had to be up soon after four o'clock.

Every morning? — Every morning.

What intermissions had you for meals? — When we began at five in the morning, we went on until noon, and then we had 40 minutes for dinner.

Had you no time for breakfast? — No, we got it as we could, while we were working.

Had you any time for an afternoon refreshment, or what is called in Yorkshire your "drinking?" — No; when we began at noon, we went on till night; there was only one stoppage, the 40 minutes for dinner.

Then as you had to get your breakfast, and what is called "drinking" in that manner, you had to put in on one side? — Yes, we had to put it on one side; and when we got our frames doffed,[2] we ate two or three mouthfuls, and then put it by again.

Is there not considerable dust in a flax mill? — A flax mill is very dusty indeed.

Was not your food therefore frequently spoiled? — Yes, at times with the dust; sometimes we could not eat it, when it had got a lot of dust on.

What were you when you were ten years old? — What is called a bobbin-doffer;[3] when the frames are quite full, we have to doff them.

Then as you lived so far from home, you took your dinner to the mill? — We took all our meals with us, living so far off.

During the 40 minutes which you were allowed for dinner, had you ever to employ that time in your turn in cleaning the machinery? — At times we had to stop to clean the machinery, and then we got our dinner as well as we could; they paid us for that. . . .

Did you ever work even later than the time you have mentioned? — I cannot say that I worked later there. I had a sister who worked up stairs, and she worked till 11 at night, in what they call the card-room.[4]

At what time in the morning did she begin work? — At the same time as myself.

And they kept her there till 11 at night? — Till 11 at night.

You say that your sister was in the card-room? — Yes.

Is not that a very dusty department? — Yes, very dusty indeed.

She had to be at the mill at five, and was kept at work till eleven at night? — Yes.

During the whole time she was there? — During the whole time; there was only 40 minutes allowed at dinner out of that.

To keep you at your work for such a length of time, and especially towards the termination of such a day's labour as that, what means were taken to keep you awake and attentive? — They strapped [beat] us at times, when we were not quite ready to be doffing the frame when it was full.

Were you frequently strapped? — At times we were frequently strapped.

What sort of strap was it? — About this length (describing it).

What was it made of? — Of leather.

Were you occasionally very considerably hurt with the strap? — Sometimes it hurt us very much, and sometimes they did not lay on so hard as they did at others.

Were the girls strapped in that sort of way? — They did not strap what they called the grown-up women.

Were any of the female children strapped? — Yes; they were strapped in the same way as the lesser boys.

---

[2]*Frames* refers to the spinning machines, which were built on a bulky framework; *doff* means to lift off the spindles full of yarn.

[3]A bobbin-doffer was usually a child, whose job was to remove the spindles (bobbins) when filled with thread or yarn.

---

[4]In the card-room was a machine for separating fibers from one another, prior to being spun into yarn.

What were your wages at 10 years old at Mr. Benyon's? — I think it was 4 s. [shillings][5] a week.

[May 18,] 1832.
Michael Thomas Sadler, Esquire, in the chair.
Mr. Matthew Crabtree, called in; and Examined.

What age are you? — Twenty-two.[6]

What is your occupation? — A blanket manufacturer.

Have you ever been employed in a factory? — Yes.

At what age did you first go to work in one? — Eight.

How long did you continue in that occupation? — Four years.

Will you state the hours of labour at the period when you first went to the factory, in ordinary times? — From 6 in the morning to 8 at night.

Fourteen hours? — Yes.

With what intervals for refreshment and rest? — An hour at noon.

Then you had no resting time allowed in which to take your breakfast, or what is in Yorkshire called your "drinking"? — No.

When trade was brisk what were your hours? — From 5 in the morning to 9 in the evening.

Sixteen hours? — Yes.

With what intervals at dinner? — An hour.

How far did you live from the mill? — About two miles.

Was there any time allowed for you to get your breakfast in the mill? — No.

Did you take it before you left home? — Generally.

During those long hours of labour could you be punctual, how did you awake? — I seldom did awake sponta-neously. I was most generally awoke or lifted out of bed, sometimes asleep, by my parents.

Were you always in time? — No.

What was the consequence if you had been too late? — I was most commonly beaten.

Severely? — Very severely, I thought.

In whose factory was this? — Messrs. Hague & Cook's, of Dewsbury.

Will you state the effect that those long hours had upon the state of your health and feelings? — I was, when working those long hours, commonly very much fatigued at night, when I left my work, so much so that I sometimes should have slept as I walked if I had not stumbled and started awake again, and so sick often that I could not eat, and what I did eat I vomited.

Did this labour destroy your appetite? — It did.

In what situation were you in that mill? — I was a piecener.

Will you state to the Committee whether piecening is a very laborious employment for children, or not? — It is a very laborious employment. Pieceners are continually running to and fro, and on their feet the whole day.

The duty of the piecener is to take the cardings from one part of the machinery, and to place them on another? — Yes.

So that the labour is not only continual, but it is unabated to the last? — It is unabated to the last.

Do you not think, from your own experience, that the speed of the machinery is so calculated as to demand the utmost exertions of a child, supposing the hours were moderate? — It is as much as they could do at the best; they are always upon the stretch, and it is commonly very difficult to keep up with their work.

State the condition of the children towards the latter part of the day, who have thus to keep up with the machinery? — It is as much as they can do when they are not very much fatigued to keep up with their work, and towards the close of the day, when they come to be more fatigued,

---

[5] A shilling equals 12 pence or 1/20 of a British pound.
[6] Like the preceding section, each paragraph in this section is numbered in the original source: 2481–2519 and 2597–2604.

they cannot keep up with it very well, and the consequence is that they are beaten to spur them on.

Were you beaten under those circumstances? — Yes.

Frequently? — Very frequently.

And principally at the latter end of the day? — Yes.

And is it your belief that if you had not been so beaten, you should not have got through the work? — I should not if I had not been kept up to it by some means.

Does beating then principally occur at the latter end of the day, when the children are exceedingly fatigued? — It does at the latter end of the day, and in the morning sometimes, when they are very drowsy, and have not got rid of the fatigue of the day before.

What were you beaten with principally? — A strap.

Any thing else? — Yes, a stick sometimes; and there is a kind of roller which runs on the top of the machine called a billy, perhaps two or three yards in length, and perhaps an inch and a half, or more, in diameter; the circumference would be four or five inches, I cannot speak exactly.

Were you beaten with that instrument? — Yes.

Have you yourself been beaten, and have you seen other children struck severely with that roller? — I have been struck very severely with it myself, so much so as to knock me down, and I have seen other children have their heads broken with it.

You think that it is a general practice to beat the children with the roller? — It is.

You do not think then that you were worse treated than other children in the mill? — No, I was not, perhaps not so bad as some were. . . .

Can you speak as to the effect of this labour in the mills and factories on the morals of the children, as far as you have observed? — As far as I have observed with regard to morals in the mills, there is every thing about them that is disgusting to every one conscious of correct morality.

Do you find that the children, the females especially, are very early demoralized in them? — They are.

Is their language indecent? — Very indecent; and both sexes take great familiarities with each other in the mills, without at all being ashamed of their conduct.

Do you connect their immorality of language and conduct with their excessive labour? — It may be somewhat connected with it, for it is to be observed that most of that goes on towards night, when they begin to be drowsy; it is a kind of stimulus which they use to keep them awake; they say some pert thing or other to keep themselves from drowsiness, and it generally happens to be some obscene language.

Have not a considerable number of the females employed in mills illegitimate children very early in life? — I believe there are; I have known some of them have illegitimate children when they were between 16 and 17 years of age.

How many grown up females had you in the mill? — I cannot speak to the exact number that were grown up; perhaps there might be thirty-four or so that worked in the mill at that time.

How many of those had illegitimate children? — A great many of them, eighteen or nineteen of them, I think.

Did they generally marry the men by whom they had the children? — No, it sometimes happens that young women have children by married men, and I have known an instance, a few weeks since, where one of the young women had a child by a married man.

FRIEDRICH ENGELS

The Condition of the Working Class in England in 1844

Rapid industrialization produced a drastic change of environment for workers, who moved from the casual, slow-paced English villages and small towns to large, congested, and impersonal industrial cities. The familiar social patterns and cherished values by which preindustrial people had oriented themselves grew weak or disappeared, for these patterns and values clashed with the requirements of the new industrial age. Many people in England, from the highest to the lowest classes, still felt wedded to the old ways and hated the congested industrial centers. The miseries of the industrial towns distressed Friedrich Engels (1820–1895), a well-to-do German intellectual and son of a prosperous German manufacturer. In the early 1840s, Engels moved to Manchester, a great English industrial center, where he eventually established himself in business. In that decade, he also entered into a lifelong collaboration with Karl Marx, the founder of modern socialism (see page 138). Engels yearned for the fellowship and the pleasures of nature that he had experienced in preindustrial Germany. In the new urban centers, he found only alienation and human degradation — even in cosmopolitan London in 1844. The following passage is from his *Condition of the Working Class in England*.

. . . It is only when [a person] has visited the slums of this great city that it dawns upon him that the inhabitants of modern London have had to sacrifice so much that is best in human nature in order to create those wonders of civilisation with which their city teems. The vast majority of Londoners have had to let so many of their potential creative faculties lie dormant, stunted and unused in order that a small, closely-knit group of their fellow citizens could develop to the full the qualities with which nature has endowed them. The restless and noisy activity of the crowded streets is highly distasteful, and it is surely abhorrent to human nature itself. Hundreds of thousands of men and women drawn from all classes and ranks of society pack the streets of London. Are they not all human beings with the same innate characteristics and potentialities? Are they not all equally interested in the pursuit of happiness? And do they not all aim at happiness by following similar methods? Yet they rush past each other as if they had nothing in common. They are tacitly agreed on one thing only — that everyone should keep to the right of the pavement so as not to collide with the stream of people moving in the opposite direction. No one even thinks of sparing a glance for his neighbour in the streets. The more that Londoners are packed into a tiny space, the more repulsive and disgraceful becomes the brutal indifference with which they ignore their neighbours and selfishly concentrate upon their private affairs. We know well enough that this isolation of the individual — this narrow-minded egotism — is everywhere the fundamental principle of modern society. But nowhere is this selfish egotism so blatantly evident as in the frantic bustle of the great city. The disintegration of society into individuals, each guided by his private principles and each pursuing his own aims has been pushed to its furthest limits in London. Here indeed human society has been split into its component atoms.

From this it follows that the social conflict — the war of all against all — is fought in the open. . . . Here men regard their fellows not as human beings, but as pawns in the struggle for existence. Everyone exploits his neighbour with the result that the stronger tramples the weaker under foot. The strongest of all, a tiny group of capitalists, monopolise everything, while the weakest, who are in the vast majority, succumb to the most abject poverty.

What is true of London, is true also of all the great towns, such as Manchester, Birmingham and Leeds. Everywhere one finds on the one hand the most barbarous indifference and selfish egotism and on the other the most distressing scenes of misery and poverty. . . .

Every great town has one or more slum areas into which the working classes are packed. Sometimes, of course, poverty is to be found hidden away in alleys close to the stately homes of the wealthy. Generally, however, the workers are segregated in separate districts where they struggle through life as best they can out of sight of the more fortunate classes of society. The slums of the English towns have much in common — the worst houses in a town being found in the worst districts. They are generally unplanned wildernesses of one- or two-storied terrace houses built of brick. Wherever possible these have cellars which are also used as dwellings. These little houses of three or four rooms and a kitchen are called cottages, and throughout England, except for some parts of London, are where the working classes normally live. The streets themselves are usually unpaved and full of holes. They are filthy and strewn with animal and vegetable refuse. Since they have neither gutters nor drains the refuse accumulates in stagnant, stinking puddles. Ventilation in the slums is inadequate owing to the hopelessly unplanned nature of these areas. A great many people live huddled together in a very small area, and so it is easy to imagine the nature of the air in these workers' quarters.

Review Questions

1. According to the testimonies given the Sadler Commission, how young were the children employed in the factories? How many hours and at what times of day did they work?

2. What do you think were the reasons for the employment of children from the employers' point of view? From the parents' point of view?

3. What measures were employed in the factories to keep children alert at their tasks?

4. According to Friedrich Engels, how had the industrial city caused deterioration in the quality of human relationships? What did he mean by the statement that "human society has been split into its component atoms"?

5 | The Brighter Side of Industrialization

While rapid industrialization produced numerous instances of working-class distress, historians largely agree that the workers' standard of living generally increased over the short term and increased substantially over the long term. The new mechanical methods of production made it possible to feed and clothe an expanding population and ultimately reduced the burdens of heavy labor. Moreover, there were numerous examples of factory owners who treated their employees well.

ANDREW URE
Decent Working and Living Conditions

Andrew Ure (1778–1857), a scientist and an early observer of industrialization, challenged the pessimists of his day. In the following passages from his *Philosophy of Manufactures,* Ure disagreed with the testimony given to the Sadler Commission and stressed the benefits to workers accruing from the factory system.

Of all the common prejudices that exist with regard to factory labour, there is none more unfounded than that which ascribes to it excessive tedium and irksomeness above other occupations, owing to its being carried on in conjunction with the "unceasing motion of the steam-engine." In an establishment for spinning or weaving cotton, all the hard work is performed by the steam-engine which leaves for the attendant no hard labour at all, and literally nothing to do in general; but at intervals to perform some delicate operation, such as joining the threads that break, taking the cops off the spindles, &c. And it is so far from being true that the work in a factory is incessant, because the motion of the steam-engine is incessant, that the fact is, that the labour is not incessant on that very account, because it is performed in conjunction with the steam-engine. Of all manufacturing employments, those are by far the most irksome and incessant in which steam-engines are not employed, as in lace-running and stocking-weaving; and the way to prevent an employment from being incessant, is to introduce a steam-engine into it. These remarks certainly apply more especially to the labour of children in factories. Three-fourths of the children so employed are engaged in piecing at the mules.[1] "When the carriages of these have receded a foot and a half or two feet from the rollers," says Mr. Tufnell, "nothing is to be done, not even attention is required from either spinner or piecer." Both of them stand idle for a time, and in fine spinning particularly, for three-quarters of a minute, or more. Consequently, if a child remains at this business twelve hours daily, he has nine hours of inaction. And though he attends two mules, he has still six hours of non-exertion. Spinners sometimes dedicate these intervals to the perusal of books. The scavengers,[2] who in Mr. Sadler's report have been described as being "constantly in a state of grief, always in terror, and every moment they have to spare stretched all their length upon the floor in a state of perspiration," may be observed in cotton-factories idle for *four* minutes at a time, or moving about in a sportive mood, utterly unconscious of the tragical scenes in which they were dramatized.

Occupations which are assisted by steam-engines require for the most part a higher, or at least a steadier species of labour, than those which are not; the exercise of the mind being then partially substituted for that of the muscles, constituting skilled labour, which is always paid more highly than unskilled. On this principle we can readily account for the comparatively high wages which the inmates of a factory, whether children or adults, obtain. . . .

What I have myself witnessed at several times, both on Sundays and working-days, has convinced me that the population of Belper is, in reference to health, domestic comfort, and religious culture, in a truly enviable state, compared with

---

[1] Mules are machines that draw and twist fiber into thread and wind this into caps (pyramids of threads wound on tubes).

[2] Scavengers were children who collected the loose cotton lying on the floor and around the machinery.

the average of our agricultural villages. The factory rooms are well aired, and as clean as any gentleman's parlour. The children are well-complexioned, and work with cheerful dexterity at their respective occupations.

At Quarry Bank, near Wilmslow, in Cheshire, is situated the oldest of the five establishments belonging to the great firm of Messrs. Greg and Sons, of Manchester, who work up the one-hundredth part of all the cotton consumed in Great Britain. It is driven by an elegant water-wheel, 32 feet in diameter, and 24 feet broad, equivalent in power to 120 horses. The country round is beautiful, and presents a succession of picturesque wooded dells interspersed with richly cultivated fields. At a little distance from the factory, on a sunny slope, stands a handsome house, two stories high, built for the accommodation of the female apprentices. Here are well fed, clothed, educated, and lodged, under kind superintendence, sixty young girls, who by their deportment at the mill, as well as in Wilmslow Church on Sunday, where I saw them assembled, evince a degree of comfort most creditable to the humane and intelligent proprietors. . . .

Sufficient evidence has been adduced to convince the candid mind, that factories, more especially cotton-mills, are so organized as to afford as easy and comfortable occupation as anywhere can fall to the lot of the labouring classes.

What a pity it is that the party who lately declaimed so loudly about the inmates of factories being universally victims of oppression, misery, and vice, did not, from their rural or civic retreats, examine first of all into the relative condition of their own rustic operatives, and dispassionately see how the balance stood betwixt them! . . . It is, in fact, in the factory districts alone that the demoralizing agency of pauperism has been effectually resisted, and a noble spirit of industry, enterprise, and intelligence, called forth. What a contrast is there at this day, between the torpor and brutality which pervade very many of the farming parishes, as delineated in the official reports, and the beneficent activity which animates all the cotton factory towns, villages, and hamlets!

The regularity required in mills is such as to render persons who are in the habit of getting intoxicated unfit to be employed there, and all respectable manufacturers object to employ persons guilty of that vice; and thus mill-work tends to check drunkenness. Mr. Marshall, M.P. of Leeds, thinks that the health of persons employed in mills is better from the regularity of their habits, than of those employed at home in weaving.

Review Questions

1. How did Andrew Ure respond to the argument that factory work entailed incessant hard labor?

2. What was his opinion of the working and living conditions in the districts that he had visited? What comparison did he draw between factory districts and farming parishes?

6 | Demands for Reform

The abuses of industrialization led to demands for reform. Workers formed self-help societies to aid members who were unemployed and sick; unions, which became legal in England in 1825, evolved from these mutual-aid organizations. However, employer repression and prohibitions against strikes rendered British unions powerless in the first half of the nineteenth century. Still, parliamentary reports, which documented the suffering in factories and mines, led to the passage of a series of Factory Acts that regulated the hours of work of women and children. Starting in 1833, Parliament began to vote small sums of money for elementary education, and by 1869 about half of all British children of school age were in school.

THE CHARTISTS
An Appeal to the British Parliament

The failure of early British trade unions to generate social change and the passage of the Reform Bill of 1832, which granted the vote to the middle class but not to workers, led working-class leaders to pressure Parliament for reform. In 1838, they published a summary of demands in a document that came to be known as the "People's Charter," part of which follows. The charter petitioned for annual parliaments, universal manhood suffrage, the abolition of property qualifications for members of Parliament, pay for members of Parliament, equal electoral districts, and the secret ballot. Through such reforms the working class hoped to become a force in British politics. Although the Chartists' petition, which follows, contained more than a million signatures, it was rejected by the House of Commons in 1839, 1842, and 1848. The efforts of the working class to gain redress for their economic grievances through unified political action had failed, and the Chartist movement died out. Yet in ensuing decades, all the Chartists' demands, except the one for annual parliaments, were passed by parliament.

To the Honourable the Commons of Great Britain and Ireland, in Parliament assembled, the Petition of the undersigned, their suffering countrymen,
HUMBLY SHEWETH, —

That we, your petitioners, dwell in a land whose merchants are noted for their enterprise, whose manufacturers are very skilful, and whose workmen are proverbial for their industry. The land itself is goodly, the soil rich, and the temperature wholesome. It is abundantly furnished with the materials of commerce and trade. It has numerous and convenient harbours. In facility of internal communication it exceeds all others. For three and twenty years we have enjoyed a profound peace. Yet, with all the elements of national prosperity, and with every disposition and capacity to take advantage of them, we find ourselves overwhelmed with public and private suffering. . . . We have looked on every side; we have searched diligently in order to find out the causes of distress so sore and so long continued. We can discover none in nature or in Providence. Heaven has dealt graciously by the people, nor have the people abused its grace, but the foolishness of our rulers has made the goodness of God of none effect. The energies of a mighty kingdom have been wasted in building up the power of selfish and ignorant men, and its resources squandered for their aggrandisement. The good of a part has been advanced at the sacrifice of the good of the nation. The few have governed for the interest of the few, while the interests of the many have been sottishly neglected, or insolently and tyrannously trampled upon. It was the fond expectation of the friends of the people that a remedy for the greater part, if not for the whole of their grievances, would be found in the Reform Act of 1832. They regarded that Act as a wise means to a worthy end, as the machinery of an improved legislation, where the will of the masses would be at length potential. They have been bitterly and basely deceived. The fruit which looked so fair to the eye, has turned to dust and ashes when gathered. The Reform Act has effected a transfer of power from one domineering faction to another, and left the people as helpless as before. Our slavery has been exchanged for an apprenticeship to liberty, which has aggravated the painful feelings of our social degradation, by adding to them the sickening of still deferred hope. We come before your honourable house to tell you, with all humility, that this state of things must not be permitted to continue. That it cannot long continue, without very seriously endangering the stability of the throne, and the peace of the kingdom, and that if, by God's help, and all lawful and constitutional appliances, an end can be put to it, we are fully resolved that it shall speedily come to an end. We tell your honourable house, that the capital of the master must no longer be deprived of its due profit; that the labour of the workman must no longer be deprived of its due reward. That the laws which make food dear, and the laws which make money scarce, must be abolished. That taxation must be made to fall on property, not on industry. That the good of the many, as it is the only legitimate end, so must it be the sole study of the government. . . . Required, as we are universally, to support and obey the laws, nature and reason entitle us to demand that in the making of the laws the universal voice shall be implicitly listened to. We perform the duties of freemen; we must have the privileges of freemen. Therefore, we demand universal suffrage. The suffrage, to be exempt from the corruption of the wealthy and the violence of the powerful, must be secret. . . . The legislative and constituent powers, for correction and for instruction, ought to be brought into frequent contact. Errors which are comparatively light, when susceptible of a speedy popular remedy, may

produce the most disastrous effects when permitted to grow inveterate through years of compulsory endurance. To public safety, as well as public confidence, frequent elections are essential. Therefore, we demand annual parliaments. With power to choose, and freedom in choosing, the range of our choice must be unrestricted. We are compelled, by the existing laws, to take for our representatives men who are incapable of appreciating our difficulties, or have little sympathy with them; merchants who have retired from trade and no longer feel its harrassings; proprietors of land who are alike ignorant of its evils and its cure; lawyers by whom the notoriety of the senate is courted only as a means of obtaining notice in the courts. The labours of a representative who is sedulous in the discharge of his duty are numerous and burdensome. It is neither just, nor reasonable, nor safe, that they should continue to be gratuitously rendered. We demand that in the future election of members of your honourable house, the approbation of the constituency shall be the sole qualification, and that to every representative so chosen, shall be assigned out of the public taxes, a fair and adequate remuneration for the time which he is called upon to devote to the public service. The management of this mighty kingdom has hitherto been a subject for contending factions to try their selfish experiments upon. We have felt the consequences in our sorrowful experience. Short glimmerings of uncertain enjoyment, swallowed up by long and dark seasons of suffering. If the self-government of the people should not remove their distresses, it will, at least, remove their repinings. Universal suffrage will, and it alone can, bring true and lasting peace to the nation; we firmly believe that it will also bring prosperity. May it therefore please your honourable house, to take this our petition into your most serious consideration, and to use your utmost endeavours, by all constitutional means, to have a law passed, granting to every male of lawful age, sane mind, and unconvicted of crime, the right of voting for members of parliament, and directing all future elections of members of parliament to be in the way of secret ballot, and ordaining that the duration of parliament, so chosen, shall in no case exceed one year, and abolishing all property qualifications in the members, and providing for their due remuneration while in attendance on their parliamentary duties.

And your petitioners shall ever pray.

Petition to the Factory Owners of Cologne

As the Industrial Revolution spread to the European Continent, it produced the same social problems there that afflicted Britain. In April 1848, the workers of Cologne, Germany, presented the city's factory owners with a list of grievances and demands for reform.

The time for hypocrisy is over and done with. When you wanted to overcome the competition of foreign rivals you cut down our wages and you made no personal sacrifices. When you wanted to drive the goods of other German manufacturers from the home market it was the factory hands who had to work harder for longer hours. When you aimed at artificially raising the prices of manufactured goods you closed your works without turning a hair even although hundreds of workers were ruined.

Do you want proof? Your own enormous wealth and our extreme poverty — these facts speak louder than words. Our labour — the sweat of our brows and the ruin of our health — has made you rich. So it is to you that we look for redress. It is to you that we make the following demands:

(i) All factory workers dismissed since April 8 shall be reinstated at once unless it can be proved that they have violated the law.

(ii) The hours of work shall be from 6 A.M. to 6 P.M. Workers shall have half an hour for breakfast in the morning, half an hour for lunch at midday, and half an hour for coffee in the afternoon.

(iii) All overtime shall be paid for. The rate of pay shall be proportionate to normal day-rates.

(iv) If a worker clocks in late he shall either make up for lost time by working overtime or he shall forfeit a proportion of his day's pay — the money forfeited to be paid to the workers' association.

(v) The wives and children of workers absent from the factory owing to sickness shall receive half-pay for three months.

(vi) The minimum day wage of an adult worker shall be 20 silver groschens [pennies].

(vii) The authorities shall establish a board of arbitration composed of an equal number of masters and men. This board shall deal with all arbitrary actions for which either party is responsible.

We expect you to accept these demands in your own interests. Our distress is so serious that some desperate act of violence may occur. The responsibility is yours. The factory owners are asked to insert a notice in the *Cologne Gazette* within three days to fix the time and place of a meeting between the representatives of masters and men to discuss these demands.

Review Questions

1. To what did the Chartists attribute the sufferings of the working class?
2. What was the attitude of the Chartists toward the Reform Act of 1832?
3. Why did the Chartists want pay for members of Parliament?
4. What do the demands of the Cologne factory workers reveal about their conditions of employment?

7 | The New Science of Political Economy

Adam Smith (1723–1790) was a bright and thoughtful academic. After studying at Glasgow University in his native Scotland and then at Oxford University in England, he was appointed professor of logic at Glasgow at age twenty-eight and professor of moral philosophy at twenty-nine. In 1759 he published his first book, entitled *The Theory of Moral Sentiments*, which outlined the basic assumptions guiding his later work. In keeping with the industrial progress of the time, Smith thought of society as a moral system run like a "well-contrived machine," producing a natural harmony of individual and collective interests; pursuing their private affairs, people were guided by an "invisible hand" to promote the welfare of their community.

After some years of travel on the Continent, Smith wrote, over a span of ten years, his masterpiece. *An Inquiry into the Nature and Causes of the Wealth of Nations*, published in 1776, made him instantly famous.

In *The Wealth of Nations*, Smith's justification for leaving individuals to their own devices had profound consequences for economic policy. It led him to condemn government interference in economic life — so common in his days under the protectionist government policy of mercantilism, which sought to increase the nation's wealth by expanding exports while minimizing imports. From the condemnation of mercantilism, he went on to advocate free trade between nations based on an international division of labor.

ADAM SMITH
The Wealth of Nations

The Wealth of Nations is a difficult book to read; it contains some confused reasoning and many details. Nevertheless, it carries the important message of *laissez-faire*, which means that the government should intervene as little as possible in economic affairs and leave the market to its own devices. It advocates the liberation of economic production from all limiting regulation in order to benefit "the people and the sovereign," not only in Great Britain but in the community of countries. Admittedly, in his advocacy of free trade Smith made allowance for the national interest, defending, for instance, the Navigation Acts, which stipulated that goods brought from its overseas colonies into England be carried in British ships. Neither did he want to ruin established industries by introducing free trade too suddenly. His preference was clearly for economic cooperation among nations as a source of peace. Adam Smith was an eighteenth-century cosmopolitan who viewed political economy as an international system. He began *The Wealth of Nations* by analyzing the benefits of the division of labor — the system in which each worker performs a single set task or a single step in the manufacturing process.

The greatest improvement in the productive powers of Labour, and the greater skill, dexterity, and judgment with which it is anywhere directed, or applied, seem to have been the effects of the division of labour. . . .

This great increase of the quantity of work, which, in consequence of the division of labour, the same number of people are capable of performing, is owing to three different circumstances; first, to the increase of dexterity in every particular workman; secondly, to the saving of the time which is commonly lost in passing from one species of work to another; and lastly, to the invention of a great number of machines which facilitate and abridge labour, and enable one man to do the work of many. . . .

To take an example, therefore, from a very trifling manufacture; but one in which the division of labour has been very often taken notice of, the trade of the pin-maker; a workman not educated to this business (which the division of labour has rendered a distinct trade), nor acquainted with the use of the machinery employed in it (to the invention of which the same division of labour has probably given occasion), could scarce, perhaps, with his utmost industry, make one pin in a day, and certainly could not make twenty. But in the way in which this business is now carried on, not only the whole work is a peculiar trade, but it is divided into a number of branches, of which the greater part are likewise peculiar trades. One man draws out the wire, another straightens it, a third cuts it, a fourth points it, a fifth grinds it at the top for receiving the head; to make the head requires two or three distinct operations; to put it on is a peculiar business; to whiten the pins is an-

other; it is even a trade by itself to put them into the paper; and the important business of making a pin is, in this manner, divided into about eighteen distinct operations, which, in some manufactories, are all performed by distinct hands, though in others the same man will sometimes perform two or three of them. I have seen a small manufactory of this kind where ten men only were employed, and where some of them consequently performed two or three distinct operations. But though they were very poor, and therefore but indifferently accommodated with the necessary machinery, they could, when they exerted themselves, make among them about twelve pounds of pins in a day. There are in a pound upwards of four thousand pins of a middling size. Those ten persons, therefore, could make among them upwards of forty-eight thousand pins in a day. Each person, therefore, making a tenth part of forty-eight thousand pins, might be considered as making four thousand eight hundred pins in a day. But if they had all wrought separately and independently, and without any of them having been educated to this peculiar business, they certainly could not each of them have made twenty, perhaps not one pin in a day; that is, certainly, not the two hundred and fortieth, perhaps not the four thousand eight hundredth part of what they are at present capable of performing, in consequence of a proper division and combination of their different operations. . . .

The most important factor in the division of labor — not surprisingly in the age of Arkwright — was the invention and application of machinery. By raising productivity, the divi-

sion of labor was the source of all prosperity. That prosperity implies a tight interdependence of all people in society.

———————◆•◆◆———————

. . . Everybody must [recognize] how much labour is facilitated and abridged by the application of proper machinery. It is unnecessary to give any example. I shall only observe, therefore, that the invention of all those machines by which labour is so much facilitated and abridged, seems to have been originally owing to the division of labour. Men are much more likely to discover easier and readier methods of attaining any object, when the whole attention of their minds is directed towards that single object, than when it is dissipated among a great variety of things. But in consequence of the division of labour, the whole of every man's attention comes naturally to be directed towards some one very simple object. It is naturally to be expected, therefore, that some one or other of those who are employed in each particular branch of labour should soon find out easier and readier methods of performing their own particular work, wherever the nature of it admits of such improvement. A great part of the machines made use of in those manufactures in which labour is most subdivided, were originally the inventions of common workmen, who being each of them employed in some very simple operation, naturally turned their thoughts towards finding out easier and readier methods of performing it. . . .

All the improvements in machinery, however, have by no means been the inventions of those who had occasion to use the machines. Many improvements have been made by the ingenuity of the makers of the machines, when to make them became the business of a peculiar trade; and some by that of those who are called philosophers or men of speculation, whose trade it is, not to do anything, but to observe everything; and who, upon that account, are often capable of combining to-

gether the powers of the most distant and dissimilar objects. . . .

It is the great multiplication of the productions of all the different arts, in consequence of the division of labour, which occasions, in a well-governed society, that universal opulence which extends itself to the lowest ranks of the people. . . .

Observe the accommodation of the most common artificer or day-labourer in a civilized and thriving country, and you will perceive that the number of people of whose industry a part, though but a small part, has been employed in procuring him this accommodation, exceeds all computation. The woollen coat, for example, which covers the day-labourer, as coarse and rough as it may appear, is the produce of the joint labour of a great multitude of workmen. . . . Without the assistance and co-operation of many thousands, the very meanest person in a civilized country could not be provided, even according to what we very falsely imagine the easy and simple manner in which he is commonly accommodated. . . .

———————◆•◆◆———————

Smith holds that the pursuit of self-interest unwittingly also serves the common good. Thus, Smith justifies a policy of laissez-faire and free trade and attacks special interest groups that try to restrain international trade for their own advantage.

———————◆•◆◆———————

Every individual is continually exerting himself to find out the most advantageous employment for whatever capital he can command. It is his own advantage, indeed, and not that of the society, which he has in view. But the study of his own advantage, naturally, or rather necessarily, leads him to prefer that employment which is most advantageous to the society. . . .

. . . As every individual, therefore, endeavours as much as he can both to employ his capital in the support of do-

mestic industry, and so to direct that industry that its produce may be of the
greatest value, every individual necessarily labours to render the annual revenue
of the society as great as he can. He generally, indeed, neither intends to promote
the public interest, nor knows how much
he is promoting it. By preferring the
support of domestic to that of foreign industry, he intends only his own security;
and by directing that industry in such a
manner as its produce may be of the
greatest value, he intends only his own
gain, and he is in this, as in many other
cases, led by an invisible hand to promote
an end which was no part of his intention.
Nor is it always the worse for the society
that it was no part of it. By pursuing his
own interest he frequently promotes that
of the society more effectually than when
he really intends to promote it. I have
never known much good done by those
who affected to trade for the public
good. . . .

. . . The statesman who should attempt to direct private people in what
manner they ought to employ their capitals, would not only load himself with a
most unnecessary attention, but assume an
authority which could safely be trusted,
not only to no single person, but to no
council or senate whatever, and which
would nowhere be so dangerous as in the
hands of a man who had folly and presumption enough to fancy himself fit to
exercise it. . . .

. . . It is the maxim of every prudent
master of a family, never to attempt to
make at home what it will cost him more
to make than to buy. . . .

What is prudence in the conduct of
every private family, can scarce be folly in
that of a great kingdom. If a foreign
country can supply us with a commodity
cheaper than we ourselves can make it,
better buy it of them with some part of
the produce of our own industry, employed in a way in which we have some
advantage. The general industry of the
country . . . will not thereby be diminished, no more than that of the above-

mentioned artificers; but only left to find
out the way in which it can be employed
with the greatest advantage. . . .

. . . Each nation has been made to look
with an invidious eye upon the prosperity
of all the nations with which it trades, and
to consider their gain as its own loss.
Commerce, which ought naturally to be,
among nations as among individuals, a
bond of union and friendship, has become the most fertile source of discord and
animosity. The capricious ambition of
kings and ministers has not, during the
present and the preceding century, been
more fatal to the repose of Europe, than
the impertinent jealousy of merchants and
manufacturers. The violence and injustice of the rulers of mankind is an ancient
evil, for which, I am afraid, the nature of
human affairs can scarce admit of a remedy. But the mean rapacity, the monop-
olizing spirit of merchants and manufacturers, who neither are, nor ought to be,
the rulers of mankind, though it cannot
perhaps be corrected, may very easily be
prevented from disturbing the tranquill-
ity of anybody but themselves. . . .

The natural advantages which one
country has over another in producing
particular commodities are sometimes so
great, that it is acknowledged by all the
world to be in vain to struggle with them.
. . . Very good grapes can be raised in
Scotland, and very good wine too can be
made of them at about thirty times the
expense for which at least equally good
can be brought from foreign countries.
Would it be a reasonable law to prohibit
the importation of all foreign wines merely
to encourage the making of claret and
burgundy in Scotland? But if there would
be a manifest absurdity in turning towards
any employment thirty times more of the
capital and industry of the country than
would be necessary to purchase from foreign countries an equal quantity of the
commodities wanted, there must be an
absurdity, though not altogether so glaring, yet exactly of the same kind, in turning towards any such employment a thir-
tieth, or even a three hundredth part more

of either. Whether the advantages which   or acquired, is in this respect of no con-
one country has over another be natural   sequence. . . .

Review Questions

1. How, according to Adam Smith, did the division of labor lead to increased
   productivity?
2. What were Smith's objections to a policy of mercantilism?
3. What did Smith say were the results of a laissez-faire policy?
4. According to Smith, how did the division of labor promote peaceful cooperation among great numbers of people?
5. According to Smith, why was the production of wine in Scotland economically
   unjustified?

8 | Population Growth and Poverty

After Adam Smith, other thinkers advanced the science of political economy, among
them Thomas Robert Malthus (1766–1834). He too believed that "the study of it is
calculated to be of great practical use, and to prevent much positive evil." Yet he
felt that it "bears a nearer resemblance to the science of morals and politics than to
that of mathematics." A clergyman in the Church of England and a professor of
history and political economy at a small college run by the East India Company,
Malthus gave the study of political economy not only a moral but also a pessimistic
twist, which contrasted with the optimistic outlook of Adam Smith and other Enlightenment thinkers.

Malthus assumed that population tended forever to outgrow the resources needed
to sustain it. The balance between population and its life-sustaining resources was
elementally maintained, he gloomily argued, by famine, war, and other fatal calamities. As a clergyman, he believed in sexual abstinence as the means of limiting population growth. He also saw little need to better the condition of the poor, whom he
considered the most licentious part of the population, because he believed that they
would then breed faster and, by upsetting the population/resource balance, bring
misery to all. This view that poverty was an iron law of nature buttressed supporters
of strict laissez faire who opposed government action to aid the poor.

THOMAS R. MALTHUS
On the Principles of Population

Malthus contributed two books to the science of political economy. The first, *An
Essay on the Principle of Population, as It Affects the Future Improvement of Society,* was
published in 1798. It was followed in 1803 by *An Essay on the Principle of Population,
or, a View of Its Past and Present Effects on Human Happiness,* which discussed the checks
on population. The following passages state Malthus's principal conclusions, which
became collectively known as Malthusianism.

[Population's Effects on Society]

I have read some of the speculations on the perfectibility of man and of society with great pleasure. I have been warmed and delighted with the enchanting picture which they hold forth. I ardently wish for such happy improvements. But I see great and, to my understanding, unconquerable difficulties in the way to them. These difficulties it is my present purpose to state, declaring, at the same time, that so far from exulting in them, as a cause of triumphing over the friends of innovation, nothing would give me greater pleasure than to see them completely removed. . . .

[These difficulties are]

First, That food is necessary to the existence of man.

Secondly, That the passion between the sexes is necessary and will remain nearly in its present state.

These two laws, ever since we have had any knowledge of mankind, appear to have been fixed laws of our nature; and as we have not hitherto seen any alteration in them, we have no right to conclude that they will ever cease to be what they are now, without an immediate act of power in that Being who first arranged the system of the universe, and for the advantage of His creatures, still executes, according to fixed laws, all its various operations. . . .

Assuming, then, my postulata as granted, I say that the power of population is indefinitely greater than the power in the earth to produce subsistence for man.

Population, when unchecked, increases in a geometrical ratio. Subsistence only increases in an arithmetical ratio. A slight acquaintance with numbers will show the immensity of the first power in comparison of the second.

By that law of our nature which makes food necessary to the life of man, the effects of these two unequal powers must be kept equal.

This implies a strong and constantly operating check on population from the difficulty of subsistence. This difficulty must fall somewhere and must necessarily be severely felt by a large portion of mankind. . . .

This natural inequality of the two powers of population and of production in the earth, and that great law of our nature which must constantly keep their efforts equal, form the great difficulty that to me appears insurmountable in the way to perfectibility of society. . . .

Consequently, if the premises are just, the argument is conclusive against the perfectibility of the mass of mankind.

[Population's Effects on Human Happiness]

The ultimate check to population appears then to be a want of food, arising necessarily from the different ratios according to which population and food increase. But this ultimate check is never the immediate check, except in cases of actual famine.

The immediate check may be stated to consist in all those customs, and all those diseases, which seem to be generated by a scarcity of the means of subsistence; and all those causes, independent of this scarcity, which tend prematurely to weaken and destroy the human frame.

These checks to population, which are constantly operating with more or less force in every society, and keep down the number to the level of the means of subsistence, may be classed under two general heads — the preventive and the positive checks.

The preventive check, as far as it is voluntary, is peculiar to man, and arises from that distinctive superiority in his reasoning faculties which enables him to calculate distant consequences. Man cannot look around him and see the distress which frequently presses upon those who have large families; he cannot contemplate his present possessions or earnings which he now nearly consumes himself, and calculate the amount of each share, when with a little addition they must be divided, perhaps, among seven or eight, without feeling a doubt whether, if he follow the bent of his inclinations, he may be able to support the offspring which he will probably bring into the world. . . .

The conditions are calculated to prevent, and certainly do prevent, a great number of persons in all civilized nations from pursuing the dictate of nature in an early attachment to one woman. . . .

The positive checks to population are extremely various, and include every cause, whether arising from vice or misery, which in any degree contributes to shorten the natural duration of human life. Under this head, therefore, may be enumerated all unwholesome occupations, severe labor and exposure to the seasons, extreme poverty, bad nursing of children, great towns, excesses of all kinds, the whole train of common diseases and epidemics, wars, plague, and famine.

Review Questions

1. What are the "fixed laws" of human nature according to Thomas Malthus?
2. For Malthus, how did the power of population growth compare with that of the means to increase food?
3. What distinction did Malthus draw between preventive and positive checks to population growth?
4. Why is Malthus considered to have been a pessimist?

9 | The Socialist Revolution

After completing a doctorate at the University of Jena in 1841, Karl Marx (1818–1883) edited a newspaper that was suppressed by the Prussian authorities for its radicalism and atheism. He left his native Rhineland for Paris, where he became friendly with Friedrich Engels. Expelled from France at the request of Prussia, Marx went to Brussels. In 1848, Marx and Engels produced for the Communist League the *Communist Manifesto*, advocating the violent overthrow of capitalism and the creation of a socialist society. Marx returned to Prussia and participated in a minor way in the Revolutions of 1848 in Germany. Expelled from Prussia in 1849, he went to England. He spent the rest of his life there, writing and agitating for the cause of socialism.

The *Communist Manifesto* presented a philosophy of history and a theory of society that Marx expanded upon in his later works, particularly *Capital* (1867). In the tradition of the Enlightenment, he maintained that history, like the operations of nature, was governed by scientific law. To understand the past and the present and to predict the essential outlines of the future, said Marx, one must concentrate on economic forces, on how goods are produced and how wealth is distributed. Marx's call for a working-class revolution against capitalism and for the establishment of a classless society established the ideology of twentieth-century communist revolutionaries.

KARL MARX AND FRIEDRICH ENGELS
Communist Manifesto

In the opening section of the *Manifesto,* a basic premise of the Marxian philosophy of history is advanced: class conflict — the idea that the social order is divided into classes based on conflicting economic interests.

Bourgeois and Proletarians

The history of all hitherto existing society is the history of class struggles.

Freeman and slave, patrician and plebeian [aristocrat and commoner, in the ancient world], lord and serf, guild-master [master craftsman] and journeyman [who worked for a guild-master], in a word, oppressor and oppressed, stood in constant opposition to one another, carried on an uninterrupted, now hidden, now open fight, that each time ended, either in a revolutionary reconstitution of society at large, or in the common ruin of the contending classes.

In the earlier epochs of history we find almost everywhere a complicated arrangement of society into various orders, a manifold gradation of social rank. In ancient Rome we have patricians, knights, plebeians, slaves; in the Middle Ages, feudal lords, vassals [landowners pledged to lords], guild-masters, journeymen, apprentices, serfs; in almost all of these classes, again, subordinate gradations.

The modern bourgeois society that has sprouted from the ruins of feudal society, has not done away with class antagonisms. It has but established new forms of struggle in place of the old ones.

Our epoch, the epoch of the bourgeoisie [capitalist class], possesses, however, this distinctive feature; it has simplified the class antagonisms. Society as a whole is more and more splitting up into two great hostile camps, into two great classes directly facing each other: Bourgeoisie and Proletariat [industrial workers].

From the serfs of the middle ages sprang the chartered burghers of the earliest towns. From these burgesses the first elements of the bourgeoisie were developed.

The discovery of America, the rounding of the Cape, opened up fresh ground for the rising bourgeoisie. The East-Indian and Chinese markets, the colonization of America, trade with the colonies, the increase in the means of exchange and in commodities generally, gave to commerce, to navigation, to industry, an impulse never before known, and thereby, to the revolutionary element in the tottering feudal society, a rapid development.

The feudal system of industry, under which industrial production was monopolized by closed guilds, now no longer sufficed for the growing wants of the new market. The manufacturing system took its place. The guild-masters were pushed on one side by the manufacturing middle class; division of labor between the different corporate guilds vanished in the face of division of labor in each single workshop.

Meantime the markets kept ever growing, the demand ever rising. . . . Thereupon steam and machinery revolutionized industrial production. The place of manufacture was taken by the giant, Modern Industry, the place of the industrial middle class, by industrial millionaires, the leaders of whole industrial armies, the modern bourgeois.

Modern Industry has established the world's market, for which the discovery of America paved the way. This market has given an immense development to commerce, to navigation, to communication by land. This development has, in its turn, reacted on the extension of industry; and in proportion, as industry, commerce, navigation, railways extended, in the same proportion, the bourgeoisie developed, increased its capital, and pushed into the background every class handed down from the Middle Ages.

We see, therefore, how the modern bourgeoisie is itself the product of a long course of development, of a series of revolutions in the modes of production and of exchange.

Each step in the development of the bourgeoisie was accompanied by a corresponding political advance of that class. An oppressed class under the sway of the feudal nobility, an armed and self-governing association in the mediaeval commune [town], . . . the bourgeoisie has at last, since the establishment of Modern Industry and of the world's market, conquered for itself, in the modern representative State, exclusive political sway. The executive of the modern State is but a committee for managing the common affairs of the whole bourgeoisie.

The bourgeoisie, historically, has played a most revolutionary part.

The bourgeoisie, wherever it has got the upper hand, has put an end to all feudal, patriarchal, idyllic relations. It has pitilessly torn asunder the motley feudal ties that bound man to his "natural superiors," and has left remaining no other nexus between man and man than naked self-interest, than callous "cash payment." It has drowned the most heavenly ecstasies of religious fervor, of chivalrous enthusiasm, . . . in the icy water of egotistical calculation. It has resolved personal worth into exchange value, and in place of the numberless indefeasible chartered freedoms, has set up that single, unconscionable freedom — Free Trade. In one word, for exploitation, veiled by religious and political illusions, it has substituted naked, shameless, direct, brutal exploitation. . . .

---◆-◆-◆◄---

The bourgeoisie, states the Manifesto, *have subjected nature's forces to human control to an unprecedented degree and have replaced feudal organization of agriculture (serfdom) and manufacturing (guild system) with capitalist free competition. But the capitalists cannot control these "gigantic means of production and exchange." Periodically, capitalist society is burdened by severe economic crises; capitalism is afflicted with overproduction — more goods are produced than the market will absorb. In all earlier epochs, which were afflicted with scarcity, the* Manifesto *declares, such a condition "would have seemed an absurdity." To deal with the crisis, the capitalists curtail production, thereby intensifying the poverty of the proletariat. In capitalist society, the exploited worker suffers from physical poverty — a result of low wages — and spiritual poverty — a result of the monotony, regimentation, and impersonal character of the capitalist factory system. For the proletariat, work is not the satisfaction of a need but a repulsive means for survival. The products they help make bring them no satisfaction; they are alienated from their labor.*

---►-◆-◄---

In proportion as the bourgeoisie, *i.e.,* capital, is developed, in the same proportion is the proletariat, the modern working class, developed — a class of laborers, who live only so long as they find work, and who find work only so long as their labor increases capital. These laborers, who must sell themselves piecemeal, are a commodity, like every other article of commerce, and are consequently exposed to all the vicissitudes of competition, to all the fluctuations of the market.

Owing to the extensive use of machinery and to division of labor, the work of the proletarians has lost all individual character, and, consequently, all charm for the workman. He becomes an appendage of the machine, and it is only the most simple, most monotonous, and most easily acquired knack, that is required of him. Hence, the cost of production of a workman is restricted, almost entirely, to the means of subsistence that he requires for his maintenance, and for the propagation of his race. But the price of a commodity, and therefore also of labor, is equal to its cost of production. In proportion, therefore, as the repulsiveness of the work increases, the wage decreases. Nay more, in proportion as the use of machinery and division of labor increases, in the same proportion the burden of toil also increases, whether by prolongation of the working hours, by increase of the work exacted in a given time, or by increased speed of the machinery, etc.

Modern industry has converted the little workshop of the patriarchal master into the great factory of the industrial capitalist. Masses of laborers, crowded into the factory, are organized like soldiers. As privates of the industrial army they are placed under the command of a perfect hierarchy of officers and sergeants. Not only are they slaves of the bourgeois class, and of the bourgeois state; they are daily and hourly enslaved by the machine, by the overlooker, and, above all, by the individual bourgeois manufacturer himself. The more openly this despotism proclaims gain to be its end and aim, the more petty, the more hateful and the more embittering it is.

The less the skill and exertion of strength implied in manual labor, in other words, the more modern industry develops, the more is the labor of men superseded by that of women. Differences of age and sex have no longer any distinctive social validity for the working class. All are instruments of labor, more or less expensive to use, according to their age and sex.

No sooner has the laborer received his wages in cash, for the moment escaping exploitation by the manufacturer, than he is set upon by the other portions of the bourgeoisie, the landlord, the shopkeeper, the pawnbroker, etc. . . .

---◆•◆---

The exploited workers organize to defend their interests against the capitalist exploiters.

---◆•◆---

But with the development of industry the proletariat not only increases in number; it becomes concentrated in greater masses, its strength grows, and it feels that strength more. The various interests and conditions of life within the ranks of the proletariat are more and more equalized, in proportion as machinery obliterates all distinctions of labor and nearly everywhere reduces wages to the same low level. The growing competition among the bourgeois, and the resulting commercial crises, make the wages of the workers ever more fluctuating. The unceasing improvement of machinery, ever more rapidly developing, makes their livelihood more and more precarious: the collisions between individual workmen and individual bourgeois take more and more the character of collisions between two classes. Thereupon the workers begin to form combinations (trade unions) against the bourgeoisie; they club together in order to keep up the rate of wages; they found permanent associations in order to make provision beforehand for these occasional revolts. Here and there the contest breaks out into riots.

Now and then the workers are victorious, but only for a time. The real fruit of their battles lies, not in the immediate results, but in [their ever-expanding unity]. . . .

This organization of the proletarians into a class, and consequently into a political party, is continually being upset again by the competition between the workers themselves. But it ever rises up again, stronger, firmer, mightier. It compels legislative recognition of particular interests of the workers, by taking advantage of the divisions among the bourgeoisie itself. Thus the ten-hour bill[1] in England was carried. . . .

---◆•◆---

Increasingly, the proletariat, no longer feeling part of the old society, seeks to destroy it.

---◆•◆---

In the conditions of the proletariat, those of the old society at large are al-

---

[1] The Ten Hours Act (1847) provided a ten and a half hour day from 6 A.M. to 6 P.M., with an hour and a half for meals for women and children.

ready virtually swamped. The proletarian is without property; his relation to his wife and children has no longer anything in common with the bourgeois family relations; modern industrial labor, modern subjection to capital, the same in England as in France, in America as in Germany, has stripped him of every trace of national character. Law, morality, religion, are to him so many bourgeois prejudices, behind which lurk in ambush just as many bourgeois interests.

All the preceding classes that got the upper hand sought to fortify their already acquired status by subjecting society at large to their conditions of appropriation. The proletarians cannot become masters of the productive forces of society, except by abolishing their own previous mode of appropriation, and thereby also every other previous mode of appropriation. They have nothing of their own to secure and to fortify; their mission is to destroy all previous securities for, and insurances of, individual property.

All previous historical movements were movements of minorities, or in the interest of minorities. The proletarian movement is the self-conscious, independent movement of the immense majority, in the interest of the immense majority. The proletariat, the lowest stratum of our present society, cannot stir, cannot raise itself up, without the whole super-incumbent strata of official society being sprung into the air.

Though not in substance, yet in form, the struggle of the proletariat with the bourgeoisie is at first a national struggle. The proletariat of each country must, of course, first of all settle matters with its own bourgeoisie.

In depicting the most general phases of the development of the proletariat, we traced the more or less veiled civil war, raging within existing society, up to the point where that war breaks out into open revolution, and where the violent overthrow of the bourgeoisie lays the foundation for the sway of the proletariat. . . .

The modern laborer . . . instead of rising with the progress of industry, sinks deeper and deeper below the conditions of existence of his own class. He becomes a pauper, and pauperism develops more rapidly than population and wealth. And here it becomes evident that the bourgeoisie is unfit any longer to be the ruling class in society and to impose its conditions of existence upon society as an overriding law. It is unfit to rule because it is incompetent to assure an existence to its slave within his slavery, because it cannot help letting him sink into such a state that it has to feed him instead of being fed by him. Society can no longer live under this bourgeoisie, in other words its existence is no longer compatible with society.

The essential condition for the existence and for the sway of the bourgeois class, is the formation and augmentation of capital; the condition for capital is wage-labor. Wage-labor rests exclusively on competition between the laborers. The advance of industry, whose involuntary promoter is the bourgeoisie, replaces the isolation of the laborers, due to competition, by their revolutionary combination, due to association. The development of modern industry, therefore, cuts from under its feet the very foundation on which the bourgeoisie produces and appropriates products. What the bourgeoisie therefore produces above all, are its own gravediggers. Its fall and the victory of the proletariat are equally inevitable. . . .

Communists, says the Manifesto, *are the most advanced and determined members of working-class parties. Among the aims of the communists are organization of the working class into a revolutionary party; overthrow of bourgeois power and the assumption of political power by the proletariat; and an end to exploitation of one individual by another and the creation of a classless society. These aims will be achieved by the abolition of bourgeois private property (private ownership of the means of production) and the abolition of the bourgeoisie as a class.*

The Communists, therefore, are on the one hand, practically, the most advanced and resolute section of the working class parties of every country, that section which pushes forward all others; on the other hand, theoretically, they have over the great mass of the proletariat the advantage of clearly understanding the line of march, the conditions, and the ultimate general results of the proletarian movement.

The immediate aim of the Communists is the same as that of all the other proletarian parties: formation of the proletariat into a class, overthrow of the bourgeois supremacy, conquest of political power by the proletariat. . . .

The distinguishing feature of Communism is not the abolition of property generally, but the abolition of bourgeois property. But modern bourgeois private property is the final and most complete expression of the system of producing and appropriating products, that is based on class antagonisms, on the exploitation of the many by the few.

In this sense the theory of the Communists may be summed up in the single sentence: Abolition of private property. . . .

One argument leveled against communists by bourgeois critics, says the Manifesto, *is that the destruction of the bourgeoisie would lead to the disappearance of bourgeois culture, which is "identical with the disappearance of all culture," and the loss of all moral and religious truths. Marx insists that these ethical and religious ideals lauded by the bourgeoisie are not universal truths at all but are common expressions of the ruling class at a particular stage in history.*

That culture, the loss of which he [the bourgeois] laments, is for the enormous majority, a mere training to act as a machine.

But don't wangle with us so long as you [the bourgeoisie] apply to our [the communists] intended abolition of bourgeois property, the standard of your bourgeois notions of freedom, culture, law, etc. Your very ideas are but the outgrowth of the conditions of your bourgeois production and bourgeois property, just as your jurisprudence is but the will of your class made into a law for all, a will, whose essential character and direction are determined by the economical conditions of existence of your class.

The selfish misconception that induces you to transform into eternal laws of nature and of reason, the social forms springing from your present mode of production and form of property — historical relations that rise and disappear in the progress of production — this misconception you share with every ruling class that has preceded you. What you see clearly in the case of ancient property, what you admit in the case of feudal property, you are of course forbidden to admit in the case of your own bourgeois form of property. . . .

The charges against Communism made from a religious, a philosophical, and, generally, from an ideological standpoint, are not deserving of serious examination.

Does it require deep intuition to comprehend that man's ideas, views, and conceptions, in one word, man's consciousness changes with every change in the conditions of his material existence, in his social relations and in his social life?

What else does the history of ideas prove than that intellectual production changes its character in proportion as material production is changed? The ruling ideas of each age have ever been the ideas of its ruling class. . . .

. . . The ideas of religious liberty and freedom of conscience merely gave expression to the sway of free competition within the domain of knowledge.

"Undoubtedly," it will be said, "religious, moral, philosophical, and juridical ideas have been modified in the course of historic development. But religion, morality, philosophy, political science, and law, constantly survived this change.

"There are besides, eternal truths, such

as Freedom, Justice, etc., that are common to all states of society. But Communism abolishes eternal truths, it abolishes all religion and all morality, instead of constituting them on a new basis; it therefore acts as a contradiction to all past historical experience."

What does this accusation reduce itself to? The history of all past society has consisted in the development of class antagonisms, antagonisms that assumed different forms at different epochs.

But whatever form they may have taken, one fact is common to all past ages, *viz.,* the exploitation of one part of society by the other. No wonder, then, that the social consciousness of past ages, despite all the multiplicity and variety it displays, moves within certain common forms, or general ideas, which cannot completely vanish except with the total disappearance of class antagonisms.

The Communist revolution is the most radical rupture with traditional property relations; no wonder that its development involves the most radical rupture with traditional ideas.

—————————◆•◆•◆—————————

Aroused and united by communist intellectuals, says the Manifesto, *the proletariat will wrest power from the bourgeoisie and overthrow the capitalist system that has oppressed them. In the new society, people will be fully free.*

—————————◆•◆•◆—————————

But let us have done with the bourgeois objections to Communism.

We have seen above that the first step in the revolution by the working class is to raise the proletariat to the position of the ruling class, to win the battle of democracy.

The proletariat will use its political supremacy to wrest, by degrees, all capital from the bourgeoisie; to centralize all instruments of production in the hands of the State, *i.e.,* of the proletariat organized as the ruling class; and to increase the total of productive forces as rapidly as possible. . . .

When, in the course of development, class distinctions have disappeared and all production has been concentrated in the hands of a vast association of the whole nation, the public power will lose its political character. Political power, properly so called, is merely the organized power of one class for oppressing another. If the proletariat during its contest with the bourgeoisie is compelled, by the force of circumstances, to organize itself as a class, if, by means of a revolution, it makes itself the ruling class, and, as such, sweeps away by force the old conditions of production, then it will, along with these conditions, have swept away the conditions for the existence of class antagonism, and of classes generally, and will thereby have abolished its own supremacy as a class.

In place of the old bourgeois society with its classes and class antagonisms we shall have an association in which the free development of each is the condition for the free development of all. . . .

The Communist disdain to conceal their views and aims. They openly declare that their ends can be attained only by the forcible overthrow of all existing social conditions. Let the ruling classes tremble at a communistic revolution. The proletarians have nothing to lose but their chains. They have a world to win.

Working men of all countries, unite!

Review Questions

1. What do Karl Marx and Friedrich Engels mean by the term *class conflict*? What historical examples of class conflict are provided?

2. According to the *Manifesto,* what role has the state played in the class conflict?

3. How does the *Manifesto* describe the condition of the working class under capitalism?

4. According to the *Manifesto,* why is capitalism doomed? What conditions will bring about the end of capitalism?

5. "The ruling ideas of each age have ever been the ideas of its ruling class." What is meant by this statement? Do you agree or disagree? Explain.

6. What does the culture of an age owe to its mode of material production, according to the *Manifesto?*

CHAPTER 6

Politics and Society, 1850–1914

In the years just prior to World War I, Europe reached the climax of its power and influence in the world. These were peaceful and unprecedentedly prosperous years, and only vaguely disturbed by battles at the periphery — the Russo-Japanese War (1904–1905), wars in the Balkans stemming from the decline of the Ottoman Empire, and conflicts in European overseas empires. Europe had not experienced a major war since the Franco-Prussian War (1870–1871), and no general European war since the time of Napoleon. More numerous than ever and concentrated in ever-growing cities, the peoples of Europe interacted with each other in a busy exchange of goods, ideas, and services, which led to remarkable creativity in industry, science, and the arts. The physical sciences flourished; medical services advanced; the psychoanalytic method developed under Sigmund Freud. New technologies speeded communication and transportation, which intensified human contact and competition. Industrialization, promoted by capitalist enterprise, spread throughout Europe and the United States, raising the standard of living and advancing expectations among the poor for a better life. The new mobility and social interdependence provided greater opportunity for individual gain, but they also increased social tensions.

One source of tension was the agitation for women's rights to be equal with those of men in education and politics. Although women faced strenuous resistance with regard to suffrage, they fought toward that goal, gaining minor concessions. Conflict also arose over social justice for workers — for their material security and their right to vote and organize. In England, improvement for the working class resulted from joint efforts by the workers, members of the privileged classes, and the government. In Germany the state, afraid of revolution, took a more active role, organizing the first social security program for workers. Meanwhile, among workers able to improve their lot by voting and organizing, desire for revolution receded. Higher living standards created working-class parties loyal to the capitalist order; even workers aspired to bourgeois respectability. And rather than falling prey to all-consuming monopolies, as Marx had predicted, the middle classes thrived, at least in the countries of western and central Europe.

In Eastern Europe, social and political tensions were greater. In the Austro-Hungarian Empire, reaching east from the Alps into the Balkans, nationalist agitation was on the rise. The Slavic peoples, resenting their domination by Germans and Magyars, threatened the very survival of that multinational monarchy, one of the major states of Europe. A sociopolitical crisis also threatened the Russian Empire. Contact with western Europe convinced the tsarist government of the need to modernize the country's backward economy and catch up to "the West," as Russians called the richer lands of Europe. In the absence of capable capitalists, the government assumed direct responsibility for industrialization. At the same time, the workers, prompted by westernized intellectuals, compared their lot with that of their counterparts in western Europe and saw themselves as exploited. Like privileged Russians familiar with western Europe, they blamed their country's backwardness on the tsars; disaffected, they called for a constitutional government with universal suffrage. When Japan defeated Russia in 1905, revolution broke out, spearheaded by the workers of St. Petersburg. The revolution failed, but weakened the tsarist regime and strengthened the resolve of the revolutionaries. Russia's woeful conditions encouraged an especially militant brand of revolutionary Marxism.

Meanwhile the traditional rivalry of the major European states spread from Europe to the world at large. The Spanish and Portuguese empires had faded, but the British had long gloried in their overseas expansion. They used extravagant — even racist — language to justify their ambition, claiming to be the fittest in the struggle for survival. But in the newly united Germany, intellectuals and politicians enviously asked why their country should not be equal to Great Britain. They too wanted a world-spanning empire. Against the militant promoters of imperialism in Britain, Germany, and other aspiring powers, antiimperialists speaking on behalf of the conquered peoples and peaceful relations among nations made little headway. The power competition between the major states of Europe grew to global dimensions.

In 1884, virtually all of Africa not yet under colonial rule was divided among England, France, and Germany. Africans trying to resist lacked the resources of the Europeans, who quickly overpowered them. In the Far East, too, along the Chinese coast, ports and spheres of influence were carved out of the tottering Chinese Empire.

By the early 1900s, European civilization had produced impressive achievements in all spheres of human activity, and European states dominated the globe. Yet the great advances also increasingly divided Europe; competition for wealth and power heightened international rivalries. Nationalist ambitions, backed in most countries by popular support, and an arms race further worsened international relations. Although few people at the time recognized it, Europe's period of peace and security was ending. World War I, which broke out in 1914, was on the horizon.

1 | Progress of Science and Technology

The century before World War I witnessed unprecedented advances in all branches of science and technology. As new discoveries and inventions were quickly put to practical use, industrial productivity also soared, continuing the Industrial Revolution. Iron gave way to stronger and more resilient steel, which was indispensable in technical progress. Steam engines now pulled trains, and steam ships gave ocean travel independence from wind and weather. Transport became even faster after the discovery of petroleum and the invention of the internal combustion engine for automobiles.

New industries rose, like the chemical industry, which produced dyes for textiles, a great variety of medicines (thanks in part to discoveries in biology), and also dynamite, which was a major asset in blasting railway lines through mountains. Perhaps the most impressive industries were those that developed the uses of electricity, pioneering first the telegraph, then the telephone, and after the turn of the century, the radio. Electricity powered street lighting, street cars, and subway trains. All industries benefited from advances and refinements in the mechanical arts, exemplified in labor-saving devices like the sewing machine for factory and domestic use and the typewriter, which revolutionized office work.

The advances of science, technology, and industry were viewed as triumphs of human ingenuity; they inspired confidence, giving human beings new powers over nature and over their own destiny. They improved the material conditions of life, opened up opportunities for individuals, and enhanced political power in times of both peace and war, particularly the latter. The industrial arts produced breechloading rifles and guns, and by the end of the century, the machine gun. Industrialism also incited national ambition. By midcentury England was called "the workshop of the world"; by the end of the century Germany and the United States had forged ahead in key branches of industry.

The Crystal Palace Exhibit of 1851

No other event in this period so clearly showed the pride and hopes associated with the advance of industry as the great "Exhibit of Industry of All Nations," which opened in London's Hyde Park in 1851. Housed in a magnificent building of iron and glass called the Crystal Palace, the exhibit was hailed as "the Congress of the world's genius of industry." It proudly displayed crafts, arts, and industries from around the world, but also "augmented the fame of British manufacturers" and manifested British superiority "in every branch of Industrial Art." Its *Illustrated Catalogue* — the source of the following reading — reflected the significance attached to the worldwide development of industry as well as the pride of the exhibit's organizers. The Crystal Palace Exhibition grandly demonstrated nineteenth-century faith in science and technology as the source of human progress.

The experiment of an Exhibition of the Industry of all the civilised Nations of the World has been tried, and has succeeded beyond the most sanguine expectations of its projectors. It is, indeed, scarcely possible to instance any great enterprise of modern date which has so completely satisfied the anticipations which had been formed of its results. . . .

Other nations have devised means for the display and encouragement of their own arts and manufactures; but it has been reserved for England to provide an arena for the exhibition of the industrial triumphs of the whole world. She has offered an hospitable invitation to surrounding nations to bring the choicest products of their industry to her capital, and there to enter into amicable competition with each other and with herself; and she has endeavoured to secure to them the certainty of an impartial verdict on their efforts. Whatever be the extent of the benefit which this great demonstration may confer upon the Industrial Arts of the world, it cannot fail to soften, if not to eradicate altogether, the prejudices and animosities which have so long retarded the happiness of nations. . . .

Man — placed upon a strangely constituted globe, covered with all that is necessary for the sustenance of life — is compelled by the necessities of his condition, to exert his intellectual powers in devising means by which he may be sheltered from the summer heats and the winter colds. This impulsive power drives him to the study of nature — he cannot create, but everything which is created he can fashion to his desire; but to do this he must obey the great physical laws, by which the conditions of all matter is determined, and to obey them they must be known, and to be known, natural phenomena must be attentively observed. . . .

Man witnesses a fact, it recurs again and again, experience thus gives him information concerning the things around him, and eventually, — the progress is commonly slow, — he perceives that by the knowledge of that one fact, he may improve upon nature to his own advantage. Some baked clay taught the potter his useful art, and the *accidental* fusion of sea-sand instructed man in the manufacture

of glass. By a similar class of observations man has ever advanced his knowledge. Science has been the staff by which he has been helped forward, but for many ages he was ignorant of the nature of his aid. . . .

We have long boasted of our age as a most remarkable one; the number of useful applications which we have made within a comparatively limited period, are no doubt more numerous than were ever before made within the same time. What has been the cause of this? Why have we such vast improvements in steam machinery? Why the electrotype, the electric telegraph, and other aids of which we are so justly proud? Watt observed a small fact connected with the expansion of steam, . . . Oersted studied the movement of a magnet,[1] in the proximity of a wire, through which an electric current was traversing; and from the observations of simple facts great laws were deduced, and great ends have been attained. . . .

. . . In the Exhibition we perceive the germs of lasting good. Believing that the entire world, from China in the east to Chili [sic] and California in the west, will feel the exciting tremors of vitality which spring from the industrial heart of the world in 1851, beating within the Crystal Palace of Hyde Park, we content ourselves, in conclusion with that excellent maxim chosen by the Illustrious Prince [Albert, husband of Queen Victoria], . . . "Say not the discoveries we make are our own; the germs of every art are implanted within us, and God, our instructor, from hidden sources, develops the faculties of invention. . . ."

One of the most exciting novelties of the age, duly displayed at the exhibit, was electricity.

---

[1] James Watt (1736–1819), a Scottish engineer, developed the first practical steam engine, and H. C. Oersted (1777–1851) was a Danish physicist who discovered the link between magnetism and electricity.

Electricity — that power which, from its fearfully destructive force, was regarded as the manifestation of Almighty power . . . from which men still retreat in terror, has, by the force of human intelligence, directed in a philosophic spirit, been subdued to perform the most important tasks for man. Through space it passes, without note of time, to convey the expression of our thoughts and feelings. India by its means will soon be united [by telegraph] with England, and the merchant in London may instantaneously communicate with his agent in Calcutta, or the lover with his mistress. Thus, breaking through the barriers of distance, remote lands will be united together. The march of civilisation is in unison with the advance of science; and few things prove more convincingly the harmonious arrangements of Universal rule than the fact, that the physical agents which determine the condition of matter, which regulate the structural arrangements of the earth's crust, its rocks and its metalliferous deposits, and which myste-riously influence every organic change, are destined to work upon the spiritual part of creation, and to produce psychological phenomena, — which shall result in the production of order and the spread of peace. Bring people together, — let them know one another, — they develop the latent good which is in every human breast. Thus the gathering of nations in the Industrial Palace of Hyde Park cannot but be for good; and those small instruments which are exhibited in its north-western gallery are world-embracing in their influences, and must assimilate more closely the thoughts of those nations which they may bring into communion. . . .

The civilisation of the world has advanced to a certain point which is marked by the triumphs man has achieved over nature and the applications, to use and ornaments, of the crude material which he derives from their native source. The Great Exhibition stands a striking record of all that the world has done — it marks a point to which mankind has arrived — and indicates what he has yet to subdue.

Review Questions

1. What does the excerpt from the *Illustrated Catalogue* reveal about the British public's attitude toward industrialization? What does the *Catalogue* imply about English attitudes toward the rest of the world?

2. What evidence, if any, do you see of English nationalism in the *Catalogue*? Of English imperialism? Explain.

3. According to the *Catalogue,* what advantages were expected from the application of electricity to communications?

4. How does the *Catalogue* say the industrial arts will benefit civilization?

2 | The Evolution of Liberalism

The principal concern of early-nineteenth-century liberalism was protecting the rights of the individual against the demands of the state. For this reason, liberals advocated a constitution that limited the state's authority and a bill of rights that stipulated the citizen's basic freedoms. Believing that state interference in the economy endangered individual liberty and private property, liberals were strong advocates of laissez-faire — leaving the market to its own devices. And convinced that the un-propertied and uneducated masses were not deeply committed to individual free-dom, liberals approved property requirements for voting and office holding.

In the last part of the nineteenth century, however, liberalism changed substan-tially as many liberals came to support government reforms to deal with the problems created by unregulated industrialization. By the early twentieth century, liberalism — not without reservation and opposition on the part of some liberals — had evolved into social democracy, which maintains that government has an obligation to assist the needy.

HERBERT SPENCER
Man versus the State

Committed to a traditional laissez-faire policy, however, some liberals attacked state intervention as a threat to personal freedom and a betrayal of central liberal princi-ples. In *Man versus the State,* British philosopher Herbert Spencer (1820–1903) warned that increased government regulation would lead to socialism and slavery.

The extension of this policy . . . [of gov-ernment legislation] fosters everywhere the tacit assumption that Government should step in whenever anything is not going right. "Surely you would not have this misery continue!" exclaims some one, if you hint . . . [an objection] to much that is now being said and done. Observe what is implied by this exclamation. It takes for granted. . . . that every evil can be re-moved: the truth being that with the ex-isting defects of human nature, many evils can only be thrust out of one place or form into another place or form — often being increased by the change. The exclama-tion also implies the unhesitating belief, here especially concerning us, that evils of all kinds should be dealt with by the State. . . . Obviously, the more numerous gov-ernmental interventions become, the more confirmed does this habit of thought grow, and the more loud and perpetual the de-mands for intervention.

Every extension of the regulative pol-icy involves an addition to the regulative agents — a further growth of officialism and an increasing power of the organiza-tion formed of officials. . . .

. . . Moreover, every additional State-interference strengthens the tacit as-sumption that it is the duty of the State to

deal with all evils and secure all benefits. Increasing power of a growing adminis-trative organization is accompanied by decreasing power of the rest of the society to resist its further growth and con-trol. . . .

"But why is this change described as 'the coming slavery'?" is a question which many will still ask. The reply is simple. All socialism involves slavery. . . .

Evidently then, the changes made, the changes in progress, and the changes urged, will carry us not only towards State-ownership of land and dwellings and means of communication, all to be ad-ministered and worked by State-agents, but towards State-usurpation of all indus-tries: the private forms of which, disad-vantaged more and more in competition with the State, which can arrange every-thing for its own convenience, will more and more die away; just as many volun-tary schools have, in presence of Board-schools. And so will be brought about the desired ideal of the socialists. . . .

. . . It is a matter of common remark, often made when a marriage is impend-ing, that those possessed by strong hopes habitually dwell on the promised plea-sures and think nothing of the accom-panying pains. A further exemplification of this truth is supplied by these political enthusiasts and fanatical revolutionists. Impressed with the miseries existing under our present social arrangements, and not regarding these miseries as caused by the ill-working of a human nature but partially adapted to the social state, they imagine them to be forthwith curable by this or that rearrangement. Yet, even did their plans succeed it could only be by substituting one kind of evil for another. A little deliberate thought would show that under their proposed arrangements, their liberties must be surrendered in proportion as their material welfares were cared for.

For no form of co-operation, small or great, can be carried on without regulation, and an implied submission to the regulating agencies. . . .

. . . So that each [individual] would stand toward the governing agency in the relation of slave to master.

"But the governing agency would be a master which he and others made and kept constantly in check; and one which therefore would not control him or others more than was needful for the benefit of each and all."

To which reply the first rejoinder is that, even if so, each member of the community as an individual would be a slave to the community as a whole. Such a relation has habitually existed in militant communities, even under quasi-popular forms of government. In ancient Greece the accepted principle was that the citizen belonged neither to himself nor to his family, but belonged to his city — the city being with the Greek equivalent to the community. And this doctrine, proper to a state of constant warfare, is a doctrine which socialism unawares re-introduces into a state intended to be purely industrial. The services of each will belong to the aggregate of all; and for these services, such returns will be given as the authorities think proper. So that even if the administration is of the beneficent kind intended to be secured, slavery, however mild, must be the outcome of the arrangement. . . .

The function of Liberalism in the past was that of putting a limit to the powers of kings. The function of true Liberalism in the future will be that of putting a limit to the powers of Parliaments.

THOMAS HILL GREEN
Liberal Legislation and Freedom of Contract

Arguing that laissez-faire enabled the powerful to exploit the weak, Thomas Hill Green (1836–1882), a British political theorist, urged legislation to promote better conditions of labor, education, and health. In a truly liberal society, said Green, individuals have the opportunity to develop their moral and intellectual abilities. But poor education, inadequate housing, and unhealthy living and working environments deprive people of the opportunity for self-enhancement. For these people, freedom is an empty word. Green insisted that the liberal state must concern itself not just with individual rights but with the common good. The following reading is excerpted from his lecture, "Liberal Legislation and Freedom of Contract," delivered in 1881.

We shall probably all agree that freedom, rightly understood, is the greatest of blessings; that its attainment is the true end of all our effort as citizens. But when we thus speak of freedom, we should consider carefully what we mean by it. . . . When we speak of freedom as something to be so highly prized, we mean a positive power or capacity of doing or enjoying something worth doing or enjoying, and that, too, something that we do or enjoy in common with others. We mean by it a power which each man exercises through the help or security given him by his fellow-men, and which he in turn helps to secure for them. When we measure the progress of a society by its growth in freedom, we measure it by the increasing development and exercise on the whole of those powers of contributing to social good with which we believe the members of the society to be endowed; in short, by the greater power on the part of the citizens as a body to make the most and best of themselves. . . . If the ideal of true freedom is the maximum of power for all members of human society alike to make the best of themselves, we are right in refusing to ascribe the glory of freedom to a state in which the apparent elevation of the few is founded on the degradation of the many. . . .

If I have given a true account of that freedom which forms the goal of social effort, we shall see that freedom of contract, freedom in all the forms of doing what one will with one's own, is valuable only as a means to an end. That end is what I call freedom in the positive sense; in other words, the liberation of the powers of all men equally for contributions to a common good. No one has a right to do what he will with his own [property] in such a way as to contravene this end [the common good]. It is only through the guarantee which society gives him that he has property at all, or, strictly speaking, any right to his possessions. This guarantee is founded on a sense of common interest. Every one has an interest in securing to every one else the free use and enjoyment and disposal of his possessions, so long as that freedom on the part of one does not interfere with a like freedom on the part of others, because such freedom contributes to that equal development of the faculties of all which is the highest good for all. This is the true and the only justification of rights of property. Rights of property, however, have been and are claimed which cannot be thus

justified. We are all now agreed that men cannot rightly be the property of men. The institution of property being only justifiable as a means to the free exercise of the social capabilities of all, there can be no true right to property of a kind which debars one class of men from such free exercise altogether. We condemn slavery no less when it arises out of a voluntary agreement on the part of the enslaved person. A contract by which any one agreed for a certain consideration to become the slave of another we should reckon a void contract. Here, then, is a limitation upon freedom of contract which we all recognise as rightful. No contract is valid in which human persons, willingly or unwillingly, are dealt with as commodities, because such contracts of necessity defeat the end for which alone society enforces contracts at all.

Green argued that the state must correct abuses in society for people to develop their capacities and reap the harvest of freedom. For all members of society to make the best of themselves, it is necessary to place some limits on individual freedom. For instance, Green denied the freedom to contract for labor in a way that is detrimental to health. When people injure themselves, they also damage the community at large.

Are there no other contracts which, less obviously perhaps but really, are open to the same objection? In the first place, let us consider contracts affecting labour. Labour, the economist tells us, is a commodity exchangeable like other commodities. This is in a certain sense true, but it is a commodity which attaches in a peculiar manner to the person of man. Hence restrictions may need to be placed on the sale of this commodity which would be unnecessary in other cases, in order to prevent labour from being sold under conditions which make it impossible for the person selling it ever to become a free contributor to social good in any form. This is most plainly the case when a man bargains to work under conditions fatal to health, *e.g.* in an unventilated factory. Every injury to the health of the individual is, so far as it goes, a public injury. It is an impediment to the general freedom; so much deduction from our power, as members of society, to make the best of ourselves. Society is, therefore, plainly within its right when it limits freedom of contract for the sale of labour, so far as is done by our laws for the sanitary regulations of factories, workshops, and mines. It is equally within its right in prohibiting the labour of women and young persons beyond certain hours. If they work beyond those hours, the result is demonstrably physical deterioration; which, as demonstrably, carries with it a lowering of the moral forces of society. For the sake of that general freedom of its members to make the best of themselves, which it is the object of civil society to secure, a prohibition should be put by law, which is the deliberate voice of society, on all such contracts of service as in a general way yield such a result. The purchase or hire of unwholesome dwellings is properly forbidden on the same principle. Its application to compulsory education may not be quite so obvious, but it will appear on a little reflection. Without a command of certain elementary arts and knowledge, the individual in modern society is as effectually crippled as by the loss of a limb or a broken constitution. He is not free to develop his faculties. With a view to securing such freedom among its members it is as certainly within the province of the state to prevent children from growing up in that kind of ignorance which practically excludes them from a free career in life, as it is within its province to require the sort of building and drainage necessary for public health.

Our modern legislation then with reference to labour, and education, and health, involving as it does manifold interference with freedom of contract, is justified on the ground that it is the business of the state, not indeed directly to promote moral goodness, for that, from the very nature of moral goodness, it can-

not do, but to maintain the conditions without which a free exercise of the human faculties is impossible. . . . But there are some political speculators . . . [who] think that the individual ought to be left much more to himself than has of late been the case. Might not our people, they ask, have been trusted to learn in time for themselves to eschew unhealthy dwellings, to refuse dangerous and degrading employment, to get their children the schooling necessary for making their way in the world? Would they not for their own comfort, if not from more chivalrous feeling, keep their wives and daughters from overwork? Or, failing this, ought not women, like men, to learn to protect themselves? Might not all the rules, in short, which legislation of the kind we have been discussing is intended to attain, have been attained without it; not so quickly, perhaps, but without tampering so dangerously with the independence and self-reliance of the people?

Now, we shall probably all agree that a society in which the public health was duly protected, and necessary education duly provided for, by the spontaneous action of individuals, was in a higher condition than one in which the compulsion of law was needed to secure these ends. But we must take men as we find them. Until such a condition of society is reached, it is the business of the state to take the best security it can for the young citizens growing up in such health and with so much knowledge as is necessary for their real freedom. . . . It was the overworked women, the ill-housed and untaught families, for whose benefit they [laws] were intended. And the question is whether without these laws the suffering classes could have been delivered quickly or slowly from the condition they were in. Could the enlightened self-interest or benevolence of individuals, working under a system of unlimited freedom of contract, have ever brought them into a state compatible with the free development of the human faculties? No one considering the facts can have any doubt as to the answer to this

question. Left to itself, or to the operation of casual benevolence, a degraded
population perpetuates and increases itself. Read any of the authorised accounts, given before royal or parliamentary commissions, of the state of the
labourers, especially of the women and
children, as they were in our great industries before the law was first brought to
bear on them, and before freedom of
contract was first interfered with in them.
Ask yourself what chance there was of a
generation, born and bred under such
conditions, ever contracting itself out of

them. . . . If labour is to be had under
conditions incompatible with the health or
decent housing or education of the la-
bourer, there will always be plenty of people to buy it under those conditions. . . .
Either the standard of well-being on the
part of the sellers of labour must prevent
them from selling their labour under those
conditions, or the law must prevent it.
With a population such as ours was forty
years ago, and still largely is, the law must
prevent it and continue the prevention for
some generations, before the sellers will
be in a state to prevent it for themselves.

Review Questions

1. What was Herbert Spencer's answer to the argument that government legislation is necessary to relieve human misery?

2. What did Spencer mean by the dictum, "All socialism involves slavery"?

3. According to Spencer, what was true liberalism? Compare his conception of
   liberalism with that of Thomas Hill Green.

4. How did Green define freedom? Do you agree or disagree with his definition?
   Explain.

5. On what basis would Green restrict property rights?

6. On what basis does he justify state intervention in social and economic life?

3 | Equal Rights for Women

Inspired by the ideals of equality voiced in the Enlightenment and the French Revolution, women in nineteenth-century Europe and the United States began to demand equal rights. In the United States, the Women's Suffrage Movement held its
first convention in 1848 in Seneca Falls, New York. The women passed a Declaration of Principles that said in part: "We hold these truths to be self-evident: that all
men and women are created equal." The struggle for equal rights and voting privileges continued, and by the end of the century, women were voting in a few state
elections. Finally, in 1920, the Nineteenth Amendment gave women voting privileges throughout the United States.

In England, having failed to persuade Parliament in the mid-1860s to give them
the vote, women organized reform societies, drew up petitions, and protested unfair
treatment. The Women's Social and Political Union (WSPU), organized by Emmeline Pankhurst, employed militant tactics.

During World War I, women worked in offices, factories, and service industries
at jobs formerly held by men. Their wartime service made it clear that women played
an essential role in the economic life of nations, and many political leaders argued

for the extension of the vote to them. In 1918, British women over the age of thirty gained the vote, and in 1928, Parliament lowered the voting age for British women to twenty-one, the same as for men.

The first countries to permit women to vote were New Zealand in 1893 and Australia in 1902. In Europe, women were granted voting rights by stages, first for municipal elections, later for national ones. Finland extended voting rights to women in 1906; the other Scandinavian countries followed suit, but the majority of European countries did not allow women to vote until after World War I.

JOHN STUART MILL
The Subjection of Women

John Stuart Mill (1806–1873), a British philosopher and a liberal, championed women's rights. In 1867, Mill, as a member of Parliament, proposed that the suffrage be extended to women (the proposal was rejected by a vote of 194 to 74). In *The Subjection of Women* (1869), written in collaboration with his stepdaughter Helen Taylor, Mill argued that male dominance of women constituted a flagrant abuse of power. He maintained that female inequality, "a single relic of an old world of thought and practice exploded in everything else," violated the principle of individual rights and hindered the progress of humanity. Excerpts from Mill's classic in the history of feminism follow.

The object of this Essay is to explain, as clearly as I am able, the grounds of an opinion which I have held from the very earliest period when I had formed any opinions at all on social or political matters, and which, instead of being weakened or modified, has been constantly growing stronger by the progress of reflection and the experience of life: That the principle which regulates the existing social relations between the two sexes — the legal subordination of one sex to the other — is wrong in itself, and now one of the chief hindrances to human improvement; and that it ought to be replaced by a principle of perfect equality, admitting no power or privilege on the one side, nor disability on the other. . . .

. . . In the first place, the opinion in favour of the present system, which entirely subordinates the weaker sex to the stronger, rests upon theory only; for there never has been trial made of any other: so that experience, in the sense in which it is vulgarly opposed to theory, cannot be pretended to have pronounced any verdict. And in the second place, the adop-

tion of this system of inequality never was the result of deliberation, or forethought, or any social ideas, or any notion whatever of what conduced to the benefit of humanity or the good order of society. It arose simply from the fact that from the very earliest twilight of human society, every woman (owing to the value attached to her by men, combined with her inferiority in muscular strength) was found in a state of bondage to some man. . . .

But, it will be said, the rule of men over women differs from all these others in not being a rule of force: it is accepted voluntarily; women make no complaint, and are consenting parties to it. In the first place, a great number of women do not accept it. Ever since there have been women able to make their sentiments known by their writings (the only mode of publicity which society permits to them), an increasing number of them have recorded protests against their present social condition: and recently many thousands of them, headed by the most eminent women known to the public, have petitioned Parliament for their admission to the parliamentary suffrage. The claim of women to be educated as solidly, and in the same branches of knowledge, as men, is urged with growing intensity, and with a great prospect of success; while the demand for their admission into professions and occupations hitherto closed against them becomes every year more urgent. Though there are not in this country, as there are in the United States, periodical Conventions and an organized party to agitate for the Rights of Women, there is a numerous and active Society organized and managed by women, for the more limited object of obtaining the political franchise. Nor is it only in our own country and in America that women are beginning to protest, more or less collectively, against the disabilities under which they labour. France, and Italy, and Switzerland, and Russia now afford examples of the same thing. How many more women there are who silently cherish similar aspirations, no one can possibly know; but there are abundant tokens how many *would* cherish them, were they not so strenuously taught to repress them as contrary to the proprieties of their sex. . . .

All causes, social and natural, combine to make it unlikely that women should be collectively rebellious to the power of men. They are so far in a position different from all other subject classes, that their masters require something more from them than actual service. Men do not want solely the obedience of women, they want their sentiments. All men, except the most brutish, desire to have, in the woman most nearly connected with them, not a forced slave but a willing one; not a slave merely, but a favourite. They have therefore put everything in practice to enslave their minds. The masters of all other slaves rely, for maintaining obedience, on fear; either fear of themselves, or religious fears. The masters of women wanted more than simple obedience, and they turned the whole force of education to effect their purpose. All women are brought up from the very earliest years in the belief that their ideal of character is the very opposite to that of men; not self-will, and government by self-control, but submission, and yielding to the control of others. All the moralities tell them that it is the duty of women, and all the current sentimentalities that it is their nature, to live for others; to make complete abnegation of themselves, and to have no life but in their affections. And by their affections are meant the only ones they are allowed to have — those to the men with whom they are connected, or to the children who constitute an additional and indefeasible tie between them and a man. When we put together three things — first, the natural attraction between opposite sexes; secondly, the wife's entire dependence on the husband, every privilege or pleasure she has being either his gift, or depending entirely on his will; and lastly, that the principal object of human pursuit, consideration, and all objects of social ambition, can in general be sought or obtained by her only through him — it would be a miracle if the object of being attractive to men had not become the polar star of feminine education and formation of character. And, this great means of influence over the minds of women having been acquired, an instinct of selfishness made men avail themselves of it to the utmost as a means of holding women in subjection, by representing to them meekness, submissiveness, and resignation of all individual will into the hands of a man, as an essential part of sexual attractiveness. Can it be doubted that any of the other yokes which mankind have succeeded in breaking would have subsisted till now if the same means had existed, and had been as sedulously used to bow down their minds to it?

E. SYLVIA PANKHURST

Lady Constance Lytton, Suffragette

Agitation in Great Britain for women's suffrage reached a peak during the turbulent years of parliamentary reform, 1909–1911. Under the leadership of Emmeline Pankhurst and her daughter Christabel, women engaged in demonstrations, disrupted political meetings, and when dragged to jail, resorted to passive resistance and hunger strikes. Some hunger strikers were subjected to the cruelty of force-feeding. The following passage taken from *The Suffragette* by E. Sylvia Pankhurst (second daughter of Emmeline Pankhurst) illustrates the dedication of one of the suffragettes, Lady Constance Lytton, who was imprisoned in 1910 for organizing and leading a demonstration protesting the imprisonment of suffragettes.

Now Lady Constance Lytton, in spite of her fragile constitution and the [heart] disease from which she suffered, again determined to place herself beside the women in the fighting ranks who were enduring the greatest hardship. . . . She and Mrs. Baines [a militant suffragette] organised a procession to Walton Gaol [in Liverpool]. A halt was called opposite the prison, and, having told the story of what was happening inside Lady Constance called the people to follow her to its gates, and demand the release of the tortured women. Then she moved forward and, as she had foreseen, she was immediately placed under arrest. . . . Lady Constance had disguised herself by cutting her hair, wearing spectacles, and dressing herself in poor and plain garments, and now she gave Jane Warton, seamstress, as her name and occupation. Next morning she was sentenced to fourteen days' hard labour without the option of a fine, whilst Elsie Howey [who had smashed a window of the Prison Governor's house] was sent to prison for six weeks' hard labour. Then they were dragged ruthlessly away to the torture which they well knew was to come. On arriving at the prison, on Saturday, January 15th, they made the usual claim to be treated as political prisoners, and, on this being refused, signified their intention of refusing to conform to any of the prison rules. Thereupon they were forcibly stripped by the wardresses and dressed in the prison clothes. At five

o'clock, on Tuesday, the doctor entered Lady Constance Lytton's cell with four wardresses and the forcible feeding apparatus. Then, without testing her heart or feeling her pulse, though she had not been medically examined since entering the prison, he ordered that she should be placed in position. She did not resist, but lay down on the bed board voluntarily, well knowing that she would need all her strength for the ordeal that was to come. Her poor heart was palpitating wildly, but she set her teeth and tried to calm herself. The doctor then produced a wooden and a steel gag and told her that he would not use the latter, which would hurt, unless she resisted him; but, as she would not unlock her teeth, he threw the milder wooden instrument aside and pried her mouth open with the steel one. Then the stomach tube was forced down and the whole hateful feeding business was gone through. "The reality surpassed all that I had anticipated," she said. "It was a living nightmare of pain, horror and revolting degradation. The sense is of being strangled, suffocated by the thrust down of the large rubber tube, which arouses great irritation in the throat and nausea in the stomach. The anguish and effort of retching whilst the tube is forcibly pressed back into the stomach and the natural writhing of the body restrained, defy description. I forgot what I was in there for, I forgot women, I forgot everything, except my own sufferings, and I was completely overcome by them." The doctor, annoyed by her one effort to resist, affected to consider her distress assumed, and struck her contemptuously on the cheek as he rose to leave, but the wardresses showed pity for her weakness, and they helped her to wipe her clothes, over which she had been sick. They promised to bring her others in the morning, but she was obliged to pass the night as she was, for, owing both to the low temperature of the cell and her own lack of vitality, she was always so cold that she wore her nightdress and all her clothes both night and day; even then her limbs remained stiff with cold, and though, at last, as a special favour, she was allowed first one, and then another extra blanket and the cape which the prisoners wear at exercise, she remained cold, for she says, "It was like clothing a stone to warm it." When she was fed the second time the vomiting was more excessive and the doctor's clothes suffered. He was angry and left her cell hastily, saying, "You did that on purpose. If you do it again to-morrow I shall feed you twice."

. . . The third time she was fed she vomited continuously, but the doctor kept pouring in more food until she was seized with a violent fit of shivering. Then he became alarmed. He hastily told the wardresses to lay her on the floor and called in his assistant to test her heart, but, after a brief and superficial investigation, it was pronounced "quite sound" and the pulse "steady." Next time he appeared he pleaded with her, saying, "I do beg of you, I appeal to you, not as a prison doctor, but as a man, to give over. You are a delicate woman, you are not fit for this sort of thing." "Is anybody fit for it?" she answered. "I beg of you, I appeal to you, not as a prisoner, but as a woman, to refuse to continue this inhuman treatment."

From Wednesday, January 19th, and onwards, she began to find that not only did she receive greater consideration from the doctor, but that there was a marked change in her treatment generally. This led her to conclude that her identity had been discovered. . . . The authorities made up their minds that she was not Jane Warton, and on Sunday morning both the governor and doctor appeared and told her that she was to be released. . . .

Lady Constance Lytton now sent a careful statement to Mr. Gladstone asserting that the forcible feeding was performed with unnecessary cruelty and without proper care. He declared that all her charges were unfounded, and the visiting magistrates, having held a one-sided enquiry into the matter, announced that the regulations had been carried out with the greatest care and consideration.

HUBERTINE AUCLERT
La Citoyenne

The leading voice for women's rights in late-nineteenth-century France was the newspaper *La Citoyenne (The Female Citizen)*, started in 1881 by Hubertine Auclert (1848–1914). But in socially conservative France, progress was slow — women did not receive the vote until 1944. In the following passage, Auclert stated the case for female equality.

It is the humiliating law that, for purposes of giving verbal or written testimony, lumps women together with male idiots and men deprived by law of their civil rights. Women are not allowed to act as witness to the registration of a birth or a marriage, or the execution of an act of sale. What am I saying? A woman is not even allowed to attest to the identity of another woman for the notarization of a signature.

By the civil emancipation of woman, I

mean, in a word, the abrogation of every one of these laws of exception that release men from responsibilities and weigh down women with the heaviest burdens. . . .

Now, what do we mean by the political emancipation of woman? We mean women's receiving the right that confers the power to make laws: by itself, if one is elected deputy; by delegation, if one is a voter.

Thus, it is evident that political rights are for women the keystone that will give her all other rights.

When women are able to intervene in public affairs, their first concern will be to reform unjust legislation; their first act will be to use the right given them to change their situation.

But since woman does not have the power to weaken the laws that oppress her, whom can she count on to do it? On man? But it is man who has established the existing laws and these laws do not trouble him. On the contrary, they give him all the facilities to trouble us; thus, instead of suppressing these laws that enslave woman, man busies himself with creating laws that will further enlarge his horizons. In this country where there are seventeen million sovereigns — men — and more than seventeen million slaves — women — the reforms that men perceive as essential are the reforms that will grant them still more privileges.

This means that it is beyond any doubt that as long as woman does not possess this weapon — the vote — she will suffer the rule of masculine law. All her efforts to conquer her civil and economic liberties will be in vain.

What women need to free themselves from masculine tyranny — made law — is the possession of their share of sovereignty; they need the title of *citoyenne française;* they need the ballot.

The French citizeness: this means that woman invested with the highest social rights will, by freedom, have her dignity restored; by the sense of responsibility, her character enlarged.

The French citizeness will promptly rise out of her distressing economic situation; the State and the laws will no longer render her inferior; the schooling of woman being, like that of man, essentially useful, every career, every profession will be open to her; and whatever her work, woman will no longer see it deprecated under the ridiculous pretext that it was done by a woman.

The French citizeness will quintuple the effectiveness of her maternal influence; she will raise the child not for herself alone, or for itself, but for society. She will inculcate those private and public virtues that will contribute to the child's happiness and that of his fellow-creatures.

The woman invested with the highest social rights, the French citizeness, will have the power to endow generations with such a sweeping moral vision, that fraternity will replace egoism in human relationships, and harmony — the goal to which all aspire — will supplant the present conflict in society.

In as much as we believe that from the emancipation of woman will flow a source of good for all humanity, we can do no better than to consecrate all our efforts to this cause.

Review Questions

1. In John Stuart Mill's view, what was the ultimate origin of the subjection of women?

2. What examples of female subjection did Mill provide?

3. According to Mill, what character qualities did men seek to instill in women?

4. What do you find most noteworthy in the story of Lady Constance Lytton's dedication to the women's suffrage movement?

5. What evidence of class distinction in British society do you find in the story about Lady Lytton?

6. What were the "laws that enslave women" in France, according to Hubertine Auclert?

7. What did Hubertine Auclert mean by "the political emancipation of women"?

4 | Social Reform

Prince Otto von Bismarck (1815–1898), first chancellor of the German Empire, was the architect of a united Germany under Prussian auspices. A conservative Prussian aristocrat, he nevertheless adopted the liberal goal of national unity, giving the German Empire a broad political base. He was concerned with the need to tie the emerging industrial working class to his state by supporting "state socialism." To establish itself in the world, the New Germany could not afford domestic discord or class struggle.

The workers in the fast-expanding German industries, however, were attracted to the Social Democratic party inspired by Marx and Engels, which favored a democratic republic and even talked of a socialist revolution. After an attempt on the emperor's life in 1878 was blamed on the Social Democrats, Bismarck stepped forward with his Anti-Socialist Law — he called it the "exceptional law" — designed to suppress Social Democratic agitation. Aware that repression alone would not yield tranquility, he introduced positive measures during the 1880s in the form of state-organized social insurance for industrial workers. The program guaranteed workers a minimum income in case of sickness, accident, disability, and old age. By giving workers a stake in the social order, Bismarck effectively undercut revolutionary fervor.

Bismarck's pioneer program in state socialism set a model for other countries as well. As part of Liberal party reforms in 1910–1911, Britain adopted a state-sponsored social insurance scheme, the beginning of the British welfare state.

OTTO VON BISMARCK
Promotion of the Workers' Welfare

Bismarck's motives for state socialism — as well as aspects of his political philosophy, with its religious overtones — are evident in the following selection from a speech he gave to the Reichstag — the German national assembly — on March 10, 1884.

The positive efforts began really only in the year . . . 1881 . . . with the imperial message . . . in which His Majesty William I said: "Already in February of this year, we have expressed our conviction that the healing of social ills is not to be sought exclusively by means of repression of Social Democratic excesses, but equally in the positive promotion of the workers' welfare. . . ."

In consequence of this, first of all, the insurance law against accidents was submitted. . . .

And . . . it reads . . . "But those who have, through age or disability, become incapable of working have a confirmed claim on all for a higher degree of state care than could have been their share heretofore. . . ."

The plan of reform which we adhere

to according to the will of the Emperor and of the allied governments cannot be implemented in a short time; it needs a period of years for its accomplishment. We have bestirred ourselves to improve the laborers' position in three directions. One, at a time when opportunity for work is slight and wages have become low, we have taken the necessary steps to protect work in our native land against competition; in other words, we have introduced protective tariffs to protect domestic labor. As a result of these measures, a real improvement of wages and a diminution of unemployment has taken place. Since then, work has reappeared more and more, and you trouble yourself in vain in seeking other grounds for that. On the contrary, I believe this event must have a considerable effect in the quietening down of socialist efforts. The person who still remembers the period from 1877 and 1878 and the conditions at the time will not deny that even in foreign writings the hope of connecting their revolutionary plans to the workers' dissatisfaction has declined to some degree. Therefore, this protective tariff system has usefulness for the goal.

A second plan, which is in the government's mind, is the improvement of tax conditions, in that a fit division of them is sought, by which particularly oppressive [sales taxes] on account of small amounts are, if not eliminated, then, at least, decreased, which perhaps will lead to a further decrease. [Sales taxes] have earlier destroyed and broken down many small individuals in the working class and the few groschen [pennies] which they brought in taxes at the stipulated time also often were the reason why a family, which did not stand right on the lowest rung of affluence, was thrown back into want. . . .

The third branch of reforms, which we strive for, lies in direct provision for the workers. The question of labor time and wage increases is extraordinarily difficult to solve through state intervention, through legislation at all; for in any settlement that one makes, one runs the dan-

ger of interfering very considerably and unnecessarily in the personal freedom of getting value for one's services. . . . Then the worker suffers from that as well as the entrepreneur. That therefore is the governing borderline, and every legislative intervention must stop before that. . . . The workers' real sore point is the insecurity of his existence. He is not always sure he will always have work. He is not sure he will always be healthy, and he foresees some day he will be old and incapable of work. But also if he falls into poverty as a result of long illness, he is completely helpless with his own powers, and society hitherto does not recognize a real obligation to him beyond ordinary poor relief, even when he has worked ever so faithfully and diligently before. But ordinary poor relief leaves much to be desired, especially in the great cities where it is extraordinarily much worse than in the country. . . . We read in Berlin newspapers of suicide because of difficulty in making both ends meet, of people who died from direct hunger and have hanged themselves because they have nothing to eat, of people who announce in the paper they were tossed out homeless and have no income. . . .

. . . For the worker it is always a fact that falling into poverty and onto poor relief in a great city is synonymous with misery, and this insecurity makes him hostile and mistrustful of society. That is humanly not unnatural, and as long as the state does not meet him halfway, just as long will this trust in the state's honesty be taken from him by accusations against the government, which he will find where he wills; always running back again to the socialist quacks . . . and, without great reflection, letting himself be promised things, which will not be fulfilled. On this account, I believe that accident insurance, with which we show the way, especially as soon as it covers agriculture completely, the construction industry above all, and all trades, will still work amelioratingly on the anxieties and ill-feeling of the working class. The sickness is not entirely curable, but through suppression of its external symptoms by coercive legislation we only arrest it and drive it inward. I cannot have anything to do with that alone. . . .

. . . I have, of course, said: We derive our right to let the exceptional law continue from duty and from the fulfillment of the duty of Christian legislation. On the Progressive side, you call it "socialist legislation"; I prefer the term "Christian." At the time of the Apostles, socialism went very much further still. If perhaps you will read the Bible once, you will find out various things about it in the Acts of the Apostles. I don't go as far in our own times. But I get the courage for repressive measures only from my good intention of working to the end that, so far as a Christian-minded state society may do it, the real grievances, the real hardships of fate, about which the workers have to complain, will be alleviated and will be redressed. How far? That, indeed, is a matter of implementation, but the duty of doing what one recognizes to be a duty is not annulled by the difficulty of implementation, and . . . our action is completely independent of success.

Review Questions

1. What were the political motives behind Otto von Bismarck's social reforms?
2. What, according to Bismarck, were the causes of revolution?
3. What economic program did Bismarck propose for improving the conditions of the working class?
4. What means did Bismarck propose to ameliorate the insecurity of the working class?
5. Describe the Christian strains in Bismarck's arguments.
6. Did Bismarck believe that the state has a moral obligation to care for the welfare of the working class? Explain your answer.

5 | Revisionism

Even before the end of the nineteenth century, it had become clear that Marx's prediction of capitalism's impending collapse was unrealistic. With the growth of labor unions and more responsive governments, the conditions of the working class visibly improved. Possessing the right to vote, workers began to make their voices heard in politics; their revolutionary zeal was waning. Meanwhile, the middle class, far from sinking into the ranks of the impoverished proletariat as Marx had prophesied, was growing larger and more prosperous.

EDUARD BERNSTEIN
Evolutionary Socialism

Observing these trends, German Marxist Eduard Bernstein (1850–1932) sought to adapt Marxism to the new realities. He recommended that workers carry on their struggle within the existing order, that a gradual advance toward socialism was superior to a violent revolutionary upheaval. As the author of Marxist revisionism, Bernstein was bitterly denounced by militant Marxists in countries like tsarist Russia, where the absence of democratic institutions seemed to make revolution a necessity. In the preface to his book *Evolutionary Socialism,* which follows, Bernstein outlined the reasons for his objections to revolutionary Marxism.

I set myself against the notion that we have to expect shortly a collapse of the bourgeois economy, and that social democracy should be induced by the prospect of such an imminent, great, social catastrophe to adapt its tactics to that assumption. That I maintain most emphatically.

The adherents of this theory of a catastrophe, base it especially on the conclusions of the *Communist Manifesto.* This is a mistake in every respect.

The theory which the *Communist Manifesto* sets forth of the evolution of modern society was correct as far as it characterised the general tendencies of that evolution. But it was mistaken in several special deductions, above all in the estimate of the *time* the evolution would take. The last has been unreservedly acknowledged by Friedrich Engels, the joint author with Marx of the *Manifesto,* in his preface to the *Class War in France.* But it is evident that if social evolution takes a much greater period of time than was assumed, it must also take upon itself *forms* and lead to forms that were not foreseen and could not be foreseen then.

Social conditions have not developed to such an acute opposition of things and classes as is depicted in the *Manifesto.* It is not only useless, it is the greatest folly to attempt to conceal this from ourselves. The number of members of the possessing classes is to-day not smaller but larger. The enormous increase of social wealth is not accompanied by a decreasing number of large capitalists but by an increasing number of capitalists of all degrees. The middle classes change their character but they do not disappear from the social scale. . . .

In all advanced countries we see the privileges of the capitalist bourgeoisie yielding step by step to democratic organisations. Under the influence of this, and driven by the movement of the working classes which is daily becoming stronger, a social reaction has set in against the exploiting tendencies of capital, a counteraction which, although it still proceeds timidly and feebly, yet does exist, and is always drawing more departments of economic life under its influence. Factory legislation, the democratising of local government, and the extension of its area of work, the freeing of trade unions and systems of co-operative trading from legal restrictions, the consideration of standard conditions of labour in the work undertaken by public authorities — all these characterise this phase of the evolution.

But the more the political organisations of modern nations are democratised the more the needs and opportunities of great political catastrophes are diminished. He who holds firmly to the catastrophic theory of evolution must, with all his power, withstand and hinder the evolution described above, which, indeed, the logical defenders of that theory formerly did. But is the conquest of political power by the proletariat simply to be by a political catastrophe? Is it to be the appropriation and utilisation of the power of the State by the proletariat exclusively against the whole nonproletarian world? . . .

No one has questioned the necessity for the working classes to gain the control of government. The point at issue is between the theory of a social cataclysm and the question whether with the given social development in Germany and the present advanced state of its working classes in the towns and the country, a sudden catastrophe would be desirable in the interest of the social democracy. I have denied it and deny it again, because in my judgment a greater security for lasting success lies in a steady advance than in the possibilities offered by a catastrophic crash.

Review Questions

1. On what grounds did Eduard Bernstein disagree with Marx?
2. On what social and political trends did Bernstein base his "revisionism"?
3. What did Bernstein mean when he spoke of Marx's "theory of a social cataclysm"?
4. According to Bernstein, how did the progress of democracy affect the working-class struggle?

6 | Anarchism

Anarchism, a social and political philosophy that values individual freedom and repudiates the coercive authority of states, took several forms in the nineteenth century. Mikhail Alexsandrovich Bakunin (1814–1876), the son of a Russian noble, was instrumental in shaping a socialist anarchism. Leaving Russia in 1840, Bakunin studied in the West, where he absorbed radical socialist and anarchist ideas. In 1848–1849, he participated in liberal-democratic uprisings in the German states and in Bohemia, then part of the Austro-Hungarian Empire. After spending two years in German and Austrian prisons, Bakunin was extradited to Russia to continue his sentence; exiled to Siberia, he escaped in 1861. Immediately after gaining freedom, Bakunin devoted his energies to fomenting revolutions by Russian peasants and Polish nationalists; later he became active in the international socialist movement.

MIKHAIL BAKUNIN
Destruction of the State

Like Marx, Bakunin denounced capitalist exploitation of the working class and envisioned a stateless society. However, on two crucial issues, Bakunin was Marx's great antagonist. First, Marx believed that inevitable historical process, together with a working class conscious of its historical role, would bring about the revolution. To generate class consciousness among the workers and to increase their political clout, Marxists were organizing mass political parties, particularly in Germany. Bakunin, eschewing the mass political party, insisted that a handful of dedicated revolutionaries organized in secret societies could bring down the capitalist state. Second, Marx taught that the proletariat would overthrow the capitalist state and establish a temporary dictatorship, and in time, as the classless society became more pronounced, the state would wither away. Bakunin feared that once in control, socialist leaders would never relinquish power and would become the new rulers and exploiters of the masses. Hence, said Bakunin, the Marxist revolution would lead to the intensification of, and not the disappearance of, state power. For this reason, Bakunin called for the immediate destruction of the state once the capitalist order had been overthrown.

In the following excerpts from Bakunin's writings, the italic headings at the beginnings of paragraphs are the annotations of G. P. Maximoff, who compiled and edited Bakunin's works.

Exploitation and Government. Exploitation and Government are two inseparable expressions of that which is called politics, the first furnishing the means with which the process of governing is carried on, and also constituting the necessary base as well as the goal of all government, which in turn guarantees and legalizes the power to exploit. From the beginning of history both have constituted the real life of all States: theocratic, monarchic, aristocratic, and even democratic States. Prior to the Great Revolution toward the end of the eighteenth century, the intimate bond between exploitation and government was disguised by religious, loyalist, knightly fictions; but ever since the brutal hand of the bourgeoisie has torn off these rather transparent veils, ever since the revolutionary whirlwind scattered all the vain fancies behind which the Church, the State, the theocracy [government empowered by God], monarchy, and aristocracy were carrying on serenely and for such a long time their historic abominations; ever since the bourgeoisie, tired of being the anvil, in turn became the hammer, and inaugurated the modern State, this inevitable bond has revealed itself as a naked and incontestable truth. . . .

Perpetual War Is the Price of the State's Existence. The rights of peoples, as well as the treaties regulating the relations of States, lack any moral sanction. In every definite historic epoch they are the material expression of the equilibrium resulting from the mutual antagonism of States. So long as States exist, there will be no peace. There will be only more or less prolonged respites, armistices concluded by the perpetually belligerent States; but as soon as a State feels sufficiently strong to destroy this equilibrium to its advantage, it will never fail to do so. The history of humanity fully bears out this point.

Crimes Are the Moral Climate of the States. This explains to us why ever since history began, that is, ever since States came into existence, the political world has always been and still continues to be the stage for high knavery and unsurpassed brigandage — brigandage and knavery which are held in high honor, since they are ordained by patriotism, transcendent morality [morality derived from a higher world], and by the supreme interest of the State. This explains to us why all the history of ancient and modern States is nothing more than a series of revolting crimes; why present and past kings and ministers of all times and of all countries — statesmen, diplomats, bureaucrats, and warriors — if judged from the point of view of simple morality and human justice, deserve a thousand times the gallows or penal servitude.

For there is no terror, cruelty, sacrilege, perjury, imposture, infamous transaction, cynical theft, brazen robbery, or foul treason which has not been committed and all are still being committed daily by representatives of the State, with no other excuse than this elastic, at times so convenient and terrible phrase *reason of State.* A terrible phrase indeed! For it has corrupted and dishonored more people in official circles and in the governing classes of society than Christianity itself. As soon as it is uttered everything becomes silent and drops out of sight: honesty, honor, justice, right, pity itself vanishes and with it logic and sound sense; black becomes white and white becomes black, the horrible becomes humane, and the most dastardly felonies and most atrocious crimes become meritorious acts. . . .

Doctrinaire Socialists Are the Friends of the State. Now it is clear why the doctrinaire Socialists who have for their aim the overthrow of the existing authorities and re-gimes in order to build upon the ruins of the latter a dictatorship of their own, never were and never will be enemies of the State, but on the contrary that they were and ever will be its zealous champions. They are enemies of the powers-that-be only because they cannot take their places. They are enemies of the existing political institutions because such institutions pre-clude the possibility of carrying out their own dictatorship, but they are at the same time the most ardent friends of State power, without which the Revolution, by freeing the toiling masses, would deprive this would-be revolutionary minority of all hope of putting the people into a new harness and heap upon them the bless-ings of their governmental mea-sures. . . .

The Fiction of the People's State. . . . But the State connotes domination, and dom-ination connotes exploitation, which proves that the term *the People's State (Volks-Staat),* which unfortunately still remains the watchword of the German Social-Demo-cratic Party, is a ridiculous contradiction, a fiction, a falsehood — doubtless an un-conscious falsehood — and for the prole-tariat a very dangerous pitfall. The State, however popular it be made in form, will always be an institution of domination and exploitation, and it will therefore ever re-main a permanent source of slavery and misery. Consequently there is no other means of emancipating the people eco-nomically and politically, of providing them with well-being and freedom, but to abolish the State, all States, and once and for all do away with that which until now has been called *politics.*

The Implication of the Dictatorship of the Proletariat. One may ask then: if the pro-letariat is to be the ruling class, over whom will it rule? The answer is that there will remain another proletariat which will be subjected to this new domination, this new State. It may be, for example, the peas-ant "rabble," which, as we know, does not stand in great favor with the Marxists, and who, finding themselves on a lower level

of culture, probably will be ruled by the city and factory proletariat. . . .

If there is a State, there must necessar-ily be domination, and therefore slavery; a State without slavery, overt or con-cealed, is unthinkable — and that is why we are enemies of the State.

What does it mean: "the proletariat raised into a ruling class?" Will the pro-letariat as a whole be at the head of the government? There are about forty mil-lion Germans. Will all the forty million be members of the government? The whole people will govern and there will be no one to be governed. It means that there will be no government, no State, but if there is a State in existence there will be people who are governed, and there will be slaves.

This dilemma is solved very simply in the Marxist theory. By a people's gov-ernment they mean the governing of people by means of a small number of representatives elected by the people. Universal suffrage — the right of the whole people to elect its so-called repre-sentatives and rulers of the State — this is the last word of the Marxists as well as of the democratic school. And this is a false-hood behind which lurks the despotism of a governing minority, a falsehood which is all the more dangerous in that it ap-pears as the ostensible expression of a people's will.

Thus, from whatever angle we ap-proach the problem, we arrive at the same sorry result: the rule of great masses of people by a small privileged minority. But, the Marxists say, this minority will consist of workers. Yes, indeed, of *ex-workers,* who, once they become rulers or repre-sentatives of the people, cease to be work-ers and begin to look down upon the toil-ing people. From that time on they represent not the people but themselves and their own claims to govern the peo-ple. Those who doubt this know precious little about human nature.

Powerfully Centralized State the Goal of the Marxists. While the political and social theory of the anti-State Socialists or Anarchists leads them steadily toward a full break with all governments, and with all varieties of bourgeois policy, leaving no other way out but a social revolution, the opposite theory of the State Communists and scientific authority also inevitably draws and enmeshes its partisans, under the pretext of political tactics, into cease-less compromises with governments and political parties; that is, it pushes them toward downright reaction. . . .

The proletariat ought to wage a revo-lution in order to capture the State — a rather heroic undertaking. And in our opinion, once the proletariat captures the State, it should immediately proceed with its destruction as the everlasting prison for the toiling masses. Yet according to the theory of M. Marx, the people not only should not destroy the State but should strengthen and reinforce it, and transfer it in this form into the hands of its bene-factors, guardians, and teachers, the chiefs of the Communist Party — in a word, to M. Marx and his friends, who will begin to emancipate it in their own fashion.

They will concentrate all the powers of government in strong hands, because the very fact that the people are ignorant ne-cessitates strong, solicitous care by the government. They will create a single State bank, concentrating in its hands all the commercial, industrial, agricultural, and even scientific production; and they will divide the mass of people into two ar-

mies — industrial and agricultural armies under the direct command of the State engineers who will constitute the new privileged scientific-political class.

One can see then what a shining goal the German Communist school has set up before the people.

Preliminary Conditions of a Revolu-tion. But States do not crumble by them-selves; they are overthrown by a universal international social organization. And organizing popular forces to carry out that revolution — such is the only task of those who sincerely aim at emancipation.

Industrial Workers and Peasants in the Revolution. The initiative in the new movement will belong to the people . . . in Western Europe, to the city and factory workers — in Russia, Poland and most of the Slavic countries, to the peasants.

But in order that the peasants rise up, it is absolutely necessary that the initiative in this revolutionary movement be taken by the city workers, for it is the latter who combine in themselves the instincts, ideas, and conscious will of the Social Revolu-tion. Consequently, the whole danger threatening the existence of the States is focused in the city proletariat.

Revolution: An Act of Justice. The social transformation to which we whole-heart-edly aspire is the great act of justice, find-ing its basis in the rational organization of society with equal rights for all.

Review Questions

1. Why did Mikhail Bakunin hate the state?
2. Why did Bakunin reject Marx's idea of the dictatorship of the proletariat?
3. Which of Bakunin's predictions about the Marxist state have materialized in the twentieth century?

7 | Russian Modernization

To the east of Germany stretched the vastness of Imperial Russia, which extended from the Russian heartland deep into Central Asia and to Siberia and the shores of the Pacific. By any comparison with western Europe — and all of Europe west of Russia was called the West — Russia was backward. Although liberal democracy advanced in western Europe, the Russian tsars embodied repressive monarchism. By the end of the nineteenth century, Russia was a police state; this was the only form in which the tsarist regime could hold its government together in this strikingly poor country, inhabited mostly by peasants barely emancipated from serfdom. Western travelers found Russia lacking in sanitation and other "essentials" of civilization, a situation that worsened the further east they ventured. Even though Russian intellectuals familiar with western Europe cherished their homeland, they deplored their country's inferiority in government and material culture. In spite of its backwardness, though, Russia played an important role in European politics.

SERGEI WITTE
A Report for Tsar Nicholas II

In 1899, Sergei Witte (1849–1915), Russia's Minister of Finance, prepared a report for Tsar Nicholas II (1894–1917) on the necessity of industrialization. This report offers unusual insights into the tsarist empire's economic weakness and the problems of trying to overcome that weakness. Witte's emphasis on the need for economic mobilization with the help of a carefully planned system foreshadows the subsequent industrialization drive under the Communist regime.

The Witte system, as it came to be called, justified the high tariff on imports originally imposed in 1891. The tariff raised the prices of imported manufactured goods (as well as of luxuries), which upset the landed nobility — Russia's chief agricultural producers and exporters and the tsar's major support group. The nobility not only preferred Western manufactured goods and resented having to pay more for them but also feared that European nations would impose a retaliatory tariff on Russian agricultural exports. The spokesmen for Russian agriculture demanded free trade and opposed Witte who, in promoting industrial development with the help of foreign capital and know-how, also had to combat widespread nationalist hostility toward foreigners.

In his report, Witte left no doubt that rapid economic development would bring much hardship for the Russian people, and he therefore pressed the emperor to be bold in his support for these policies. His "firm and strict economic system" was absolutely necessary if the Russian Empire, virtually a colony of western Europe, were to become as strong economically as the United States, already in 1900 serving as a yardstick for Russia's progress. Excerpts from Witte's report follow.

Russia remains even at the present essentially an agricultural country. It pays for all its obligations to foreigners by exporting raw materials, chiefly of an agricultural nature, principally grain. It meets its demand for finished goods by imports from abroad. The economic relations of Russia with western Europe are fully comparable to the relations of colonial countries with their [ruling states]. The latter consider their colonies as advantageous markets in which they can freely sell the products of their labor and of their industry and from which they can draw with a powerful hand the raw materials necessary for them. This is the basis of the economic power of the governments of western Europe, and chiefly for that end do they guard their existing colonies or acquire new ones. Russia was, and to a considerable extent still is, such a hospitable colony for all industrially developed states, generously providing them with the cheap products of her soil and buying dearly the products of their labor. But there is a radical difference between Russia and a colony: Russia is an independent and strong power. She has the right and the strength not to want to be the eternal handmaiden of states which are more developed economically. She should know the price of her raw materials and of the natural riches hidden in the womb of her abundant territories, and she is conscious of the great, not yet fully displayed, capacity for work among her people. She is proud of her great might, by which she jealously guards not only the political but also the economic independence of her empire. She wants to be a metropolis herself. On the basis of the people's labor, liberated from the bonds of serfdom, there began to grow our own national economy, which bids fair to become a reliable counterweight to the domination of foreign industry.

The creation of our own national industry — that is the profound task, both economic and political, from which our protectionist system arises. . . . The task of our present commercial and industrial policy is thus still a very difficult one. It is necessary not only to create industries but to force them to work cheaply; it is necessary to develop in our growing industrial community an energetic and active life — in a word, to raise our industries qualitatively and quantitatively to such a high level that they cease to be a drain and become a source of prosperity in our national economy.

What do we need to accomplish that? We need capital, knowledge, and the spirit of enterprise. Only these three factors can speed up the creation of a fully independent national industry. But, unfortunately, not all these forces can be artificially implanted. They are mutually interconnected; their own proper development depends upon the very growth of industry. . . .

We have . . . neither capital, nor knowledge, nor the spirit of enterprise. The extension of popular education through general, technical, and commer-

cial schools can have, of course, a beneficial influence; and Your Majesty's government is working on that. But no matter how significant the promotion of enlightenment, that road is too slow; by itself it cannot realize our goal. The natural school of industry is first of all a lively industry. Institutions of learning serve only as one aid toward that end. The first investment of savings awakens in man the restlessness of enterprise, and with the first investment in industry the powerful stimulus of personal interest calls forth such curiosity and love of learning as to make an illiterate peasant into a railway builder, a bold and progressive organizer of industry, and a versatile financier.

Industry gives birth to capital; capital gives rise to enterprise and love of learning; and knowledge, enterprise, and capital combined create new industries. Such is the eternal cycle of economic life, and by the succession of such turns our national economy moves ahead in the process of its natural growth. In Russia this growth is yet too slow, because there is yet too little industry, capital, and spirit of enterprise. But we cannot be content with the continuation of such slow growth. . . .

We must give the country such industrial perfection as has been reached by the United States of America, which firmly bases its prosperity on two pillars — agriculture and industry. . . . I have now analysed the chief bases of the economic system which has been followed in Russia since the reign of Alexander III. . . .

To obtain cheaper goods, of which the population stands in such urgent need, by a substantial tariff reduction would be too expensive. It would forever deprive the country of the positive results of the protective system, for which a whole generation has made sacrifices; it would upset the industries which we have created with so much effort just when they were ready to repay the nation for its sacrifices.

It would be very dangerous to rely on the competition of foreign goods for the lowering of our prices. But we can attain the same results with the help of the competition of foreign capital, which, by coming into Russia, will help Russian enterprise to promote native industry and speed up the accumulation of native capital. Any obstructions to the influx of foreign capital will only delay the establishment of a mature and all-powerful industry. The country cannot afford to defer that goal for long. . . .

Your Imperial Highness may see from the foregoing that the economic policy which the Russian government has followed for the last eight years is a carefully planned system, in which all parts are inseparably interconnected.

Review Questions

1. What assessment did Sergei Witte make of the economic position of Russia in relation to the major states of western Europe and to the United States?

2. In what respects did Witte consider Russia an economic colony of western Europe? What difference did he see between Russia and the colonies of European states?

3. What, according to Witte, did Russia lack in comparison with the economically developed countries?

4. What measures did Witte propose in order to create a Russian "national industry"?

5. What evidence of Russia's political ambition do you see in this document?

8 | The Revolution of 1905

Revolution had long been brewing in the Russian Empire. The peasants had always been restless, ready for an uprising whenever conditions seemed favorable. The government regarded industrial workers, numerous in towns and cities, as troublemakers. The leaders of business and finance cautiously favored a constitution, and liberal intellectuals had been agitating for one for decades. Meanwhile, the revolutionary underground waited in the wings. Then war broke out with Japan in 1904 as a result of Russian expansion into Manchuria after the completion of the Trans-Siberian railway. When the Russian forces were defeated, the disastrous loss of prestige encouraged the revolutionists. In 1905, violence spread in the countryside, followed by uprisings in the industrial centers that culminated in a general strike in October. At its height, a workers' council (or *soviet*) was formed in St. Petersburg to run the city. Nicholas II, his army still in the Far East, feared losing his throne unless he quickly granted a constitution.

In late October, the tsar issued the October Manifesto allowing limited popular participation in the government. Order was gradually restored when the army returned, and the country entered an era of pseudoconstitutionalism, which lasted into World War I. A few observers realized, however, that if the army should suffer a worse defeat, the country could explode and overthrow the tsar's regime.

GEORGE GAPON AND IVAN VASIMOV
Russian Workers' Petition to the Tsar

The opening shots in the revolution of 1905 did not come from revolutionaries but from soldiers aiming at a peaceful procession of workers led by Father George Gapon (1870–1906), an Orthodox priest known for his loyalty to the throne. The workers intended to petition the tsar to relieve their plight; instead they were fired on by order of officials afraid of mob violence in front of the imperial palace. Several hundred people were killed or injured. The mishandling of this incident, called "Bloody Sunday," further revealed the government's incompetence; it became the signal for revolutionary action throughout the country. Father Gapon himself fled and was murdered the following year in Finland by socialist revolutionaries. The tone of the petition, parts of which follow, was certainly peaceful, although the workers called for a freely elected constituent assembly that would limit the tsar's powers. The petition's contents provide insight into Russian workers' conditions.

Sovereign!

We, the workers and the inhabitants of various social strata of the city of St. Petersburg, our wives, children, and helpless old parents, have come to you, Sovereign, to seek justice and protection. We are impoverished; our employers oppress us, overburden us with work, insult us, consider us inhuman, and treat us as slaves who must suffer a bitter fate in silence. Though we have suffered, they push us deeper and deeper into a gulf of misery, disfranchisement, and ignorance. Despotism and arbitrariness strangle us and we are gasping for breath. Sovereign, we have no strength left. We have reached the limit of endurance. We have reached that terrible moment when death is preferable to the continuance of unbearable sufferings.

And so we left our work and informed our employers that we shall not resume work until they meet our demands. We do not demand much; we only want what is indispensable to life and without which life is nothing but hard labor and eternal suffering. Our first request was that our employers discuss our needs jointly with us. But they refused to do this; they even denied us the right to speak about our needs, saying that the law does not give us such a right. Also unlawful were our requests to reduce the working day to eight

hours, to set wages jointly with us; to examine our disputes with lower echelons of factory administration; to increase the wages of unskilled workers and women to one ruble [about $1.00] per day; to abolish overtime work; to provide medical care without insult. . . .

Sovereign, there are thousands of us here; outwardly we resemble human beings, but in reality neither we nor the Russian people as a whole enjoy any human right, have any right to speak, to think, to assemble, to discuss our needs, or to take measures to improve our conditions. They have enslaved us and they did it under the protection of your officials, with their aid and with their cooperation. They imprison and [even] send into exile any one of us who has the courage to speak on behalf of the interests of the working class and of the people. They punish us for our good heartedness and sympathy as if for a crime. To pity a downtrodden, disfranchised, and oppressed man is to commit a major crime. All the workers and the peasants are at the mercy of bureaucratic administrators consisting of embezzlers of public funds and thieves who not only disregard the interests of the people but also scorn these interests. The bureaucratic administration has brought the country to complete ruin, has brought upon it a disgraceful war, and continues to lead it further and further into destruction. We, the workers and the people, have absolutely nothing to say in the matter of expenditure of huge taxes that are collected from us. In fact, we do not know where or for what the money collected from the impoverished people goes. The people are deprived of the opportunity to express their wishes and their demands and to participate in determining taxes and expenditures. The workers are deprived of the opportunity to organize themselves in unions to protect their interests.

Sovereign! Is all this compatible with God's laws, by the grace of which you reign? And is it possible to live under such laws? Wouldn't it be better for all of us if we, the toiling people of all Russia, died? Let the capitalist-exploiters of the working class, the bureaucratic embezzlers of public funds, and the pillagers of the Russian people live and enjoy themselves. Sovereign, these are the problems that we face and these are the reasons that we have gathered before the walls of your palace. Here we seek our last salvation. Do not refuse to come to the aid of your people; lead them out of the grave of disfranchisement, poverty, and ignorance; grant them an opportunity to determine their own destiny, and remove from them the unbearable yoke of bureaucrats. Tear down the wall that separates you from your people and let them rule the country with you. . . . Russia is too great, her needs too diverse and numerous to be administered by bureaucrats only. It is essential to have a popular representation; it is essential that the people help themselves and that they govern themselves. Only they

know their real needs. Do not spurn their help; accept it; decree immediately to summon at once representatives of the Russian land from all classes, from all strata, including workers' representatives. Let there be present a capitalist, a worker, a bureaucrat, a priest, a doctor, and a teacher — let everyone regardless of who they are elect their own representatives. Let everyone be equal and free to elect or be elected, and toward that end decree that the elections to the Constituent Assembly be carried out on the basis of universal, secret, and equal suffrage. . . .

Here, Sovereign, are our principal needs with which we came to you. Only if and when they are fulfilled will it be possible to free our country from Slavery and poverty; will it be possible for it to flourish; will it be possible for the workers to organize themselves to protect their interests against the insolent exploitation of the capitalists and the thievish government of bureaucrats who strangle the people. Decree and swear that you will realize these [requests] and you will make Russia happy, famous and will imprint forever your name in our hearts and in the hearts of our descendants. And if you will not decree it, if you will not respond to our plea, we shall die here, in this square, before your palace. We have nowhere else to go and it is useless to go. We have only two roads open to us: one leading to freedom and happiness, the other to the grave. Let our life be a sacrifice for suffering Russia. We do not regret this sacrifice. We offer it willingly.

George Gapon, Priest
Ivan Vasimov, Worker

Review Questions

1. What, according to the petition, were the conditions of life and work for Russian workers?

2. What was the workers' view of the government?

3. What was their attitude toward the tsar?

4. What were the workers' demands?

5. Do their demands indicate that these workers were revolutionaries? Explain your answer.

9 | Anti-Semitism

Anti-Semitism, a European phenomenon of long standing, rose to new prominence in the late nineteenth century. Formerly segregated by law into ghettoes, Jews, under the aegis of the Enlightenment and the French Revolution, had gained legal equality in most European lands. In the nineteenth century, Jews participated in the economic and cultural progress of the times and often achieved distinction in business, the professions, and the arts and sciences. However, driven by irrational fears and mythical conceptions that had survived from the Middle Ages, many people regarded Jews as a dangerous race of international conspirators and foreign intruders who threatened their nations.

Throughout the nineteenth century, anti-Semitic outrages occurred in many European lands. Russian anti-Semitism assumed a particularly violent form of the infamous pogroms — murderous mob attacks on Jews — occasionally fomented by government officials. Even in highly civilized France, anti-Semitism proved a powerful force. At the time of the Dreyfus affair, Catholic and nationalist zealots demanded that Jews be deprived of their civil rights. In Germany, anti-Semitism became associated with the ideological defense of a distinctive German culture, the volkish thought popular in the last part of the nineteenth century. After the foundation of the German Empire in 1871, the pace of economic and cultural change quickened, and with it the cultural disorientation that fanned anti-Semitism. Volkish thinkers, who valued traditional Germany — the landscape, the peasant, and the village — associated Jews with the changes brought about by rapid industrialization and modernization. Compounding the problem was the influx into Germany of Jewish immigrants from Russia, who were searching for a better life and brought with them their own distinctive culture and religion. Conservative politicians running for election to the Reichstag were able to use anti-Semitism to gain a mass following. Racial-national considerations were the decisive force behind modern anti-Semitism. Racists said that Jews were a wicked race, condemned by their genes, a view that they expressed in the pseudoscientific language of Social Darwinism (see page 181).

HERMANN AHLWARDT

The Semitic versus the Teutonic Race

In the following reading, Hermann Ahlwardt, an anti-Semitic member of the Reichstag, addresses the chamber on March 6, 1895, with a plea to close Germany's borders to Jewish immigrants. His speech reflects the anti-Semitic rhetoric popular among German conservatives before World War I. The material in parentheses is by Paul W. Massing, translator and editor.

It is certainly true that there are Jews in our country of whom nothing adverse can be said. Nevertheless, the Jews as a whole must be considered harmful, for the racial traits of this people are of a kind that in the long run do not agree with the racial traits of the Teutons.[1] Every Jew who at this very moment has not as yet transgressed is likely to do so at some future time under given circumstances because his racial characteristics drive him on in that direction. . . .

"My political friends do not hold the view that we fight the Jews because of their religion. . . . We would not dream of waging a political struggle against anyone because of his religion. . . . We hold the view that the Jews are a different race, a different people with entirely different character traits.

Experience in all fields of nature shows that innate racial characteristics which have been acquired by the race in the course of many thousands of years are the strongest and most enduring factors that exist, and that therefore we can rid ourselves of the characteristics of our race no more than can the Jews. One need not fight the Jew individually, and we are not doing that, by the way. But, when countless specimens prove the existence of certain racial characteristics and when these characteristics are such as to make impossible a common life, well, then I believe that we who are natives here, who have tilled the soil and defended it against all enemies — that we have a duty to take a stand against the Jews who are of a quite different nature.

We Teutons are rooted in the cultural soil of labor. . . . The Jews do not believe in the culture of labor, they do not want to create values themselves, but want to appropriate, without working, the values which others have created; that is the cardinal difference that guides us in all our considerations. . . .

Herr Deputy Rickert[2] here has just ex-

pounded how few Jews we have altogether and that their number is steadily declining. Well, gentlemen, why don't you go to the main business centers and see for yourselves whether the percentages indicated by Herr Rickert prevail there too. Why don't you walk along the Leipzigerstrasse (in Berlin) or the Zeil in Frankfurt and have a look at the shops? Wherever there are opportunities to make money, the Jews have established themselves, but not in order to work — no, they let others work for them and take what the others have produced by their labor.

Deputy Hasse . . . has committed the grave mistake of putting the Jews and other peoples on the same level, and that is the worst mistake that we could possibly make.

The Jews have an attitude toward us which differs totally from that of other peoples. It is one thing when a Pole, a Russian, a Frenchman, a Dane immigrates to our country, and quite another thing when a Jew settles here. . . . Once our (Polish, etc.) guests have lived here for ten, twenty years, they come to resemble us. For they have stood with us on the same cultural soil of labor. . . . After thirty, forty years they have become Germans and their grandchildren would be indistinguishable from us except for the strange-sounding names they still bear. The Jews have lived here for 700, 800 years, but have they become Germans? Have they placed themselves on the cultural soil of labor? They never even dreamed of such a thing; as soon as they arrived, they started to cheat and they have been doing that ever since they have been in Germany. . . .

The Jews should not be admitted, whether or not there is overpopulation, for they do not belong to a productive race, they are exploiters, parasites. . . .

[1] Teutons refers to the quintessential Germans. The name comes from a German tribe that once defeated a Roman army.
[2] Heinrich Rickert, a leader of the Progressives and an outspoken opponent of anti-Semitism, had pointed out that the Jews constituted only

1.29 percent of the population of Prussia. What enraged the German Right was that the Jews accounted for 9.58 percent of the university students in Prussia.

(Answering Rickert's arguments that . . . it would be a shame if fifty million Germans were afraid of a few Jews, Ahlwardt continued:). . .

Herr Rickert, who is just as tall as I am, is afraid of one single cholera bacillus — well, gentlemen, the Jews are just that, cholera bacilli!

Gentlemen, the crux of the matter is Jewry's capacity for contagion and exploitation. . . . How many thousands of Germans have perished as a result of this Jewish exploitation, how many may have hanged themselves, shot themselves, drowned themselves, how many may have ended by the wayside as tramps in America or drawn their last breath in the gutter, all of them people who had worked industriously on the soil their fathers had acquired, perhaps in hundreds of years of hard work. . . . Don't you feel any pity for those countless Germans? Are they to perish unsung? Ah, why were they foolish enough to let themselves be cheated? But the Germans are by no means so foolish, they are far more intelligent than the Jews. All inventions, all great ideas come from the Germans and not from the Jews. No, I shall tell you the national difference: The German is fundamentally trusting, his heart is full of loyalty and confidence. The Jew gains this confidence, only to betray it at the proper moment, ruining and pauperizing the German. This abuse of confidence on the part of the Jews is their main weapon. And these Jewish scoundrels are to be defended here! Is there no one to think of all those hundreds of thousands, nor of those millions of workers whose wages grow smaller and smaller because Jewish competition brings the prices down? One always hears: you must be humane toward the Jews. The humanitarianism of our century . . . is our curse. Why aren't you for once humane toward the oppressed? You'd better exterminate those beasts of prey and you'd better start by not letting any more of them into our country. . . .

(Taking issue with the liberals' argu-ment of Jewish achievements in the arts, Ahlwardt declared:)

Art in my opinion is the capacity for expressing one's innermost feelings in such a way as to arouse the same feelings in the other person. Now the Jewish world of emotions (*Gefühlswelt*) and the Teutonic world of emotions are two quite different things. German art can express only German feelings; Jewish art only Jewish feelings. Because Jewry has been thrusting itself forward everywhere, it has also thrust itself forward in the field of art and therefore the art that is now in the foreground is Jewish art. Nowadays the head of a family must be very careful when he decides to take his family to the theater lest his Teutonic feelings be outraged by the infamous Jewish art that has spread everywhere.

The Jew is no German. If you say, the Jew was born in Germany, he was nursed by a German wetnurse, he abides by German laws, he has to serve as a soldier — and what kind of a soldier at that! let's not talk about it — he fulfills all his obligations, he pays his taxes — then I say that all this is not the crucial factor with regard to his nationality; the crucial factor is the race from which he stems. Permit me to make a rather trite comparison which I have already used elsewhere in my speeches: a horse that is born in a cowshed is far from being a cow.

A Jew who was born in Germany does not thereby become a German; he is still a Jew. Therefore it is imperative that we realize that Jewish racial characteristics differ so greatly from ours that a common life of Jews and Germans under the same laws is quite impossible because the Germans will perish. . . .

. . . I beg you from the bottom of my heart not to take this matter* lightly but as a very serious thing. It is a question of life and death for our people. . . .

We wouldn't think of going as far as

---

*Prohibition of Jewish immigration.

have the Austrian anti-Semites in the Federal Council (*Reichsrat*) and to move that a bounty be paid for every Jew shot or to decree that he who kills a Jew shall inherit his property. We have no such intention. We shall not go as far as that. What we want is a clear and reasonable separation of the Jews from the Germans.

An immediate prerequisite is that we slam the door and see to it that no more of them get in.*

---

*At the end of the debate a vote was taken, with 218 representatives present. Of these, 51 voted for, 167 against the motion.

Review Questions

1. What, according to Hermann Ahlwardt, were the racial characteristics of Jews? What, in contrast, were the racial characteristics of Germans?

2. What, said Ahlwardt, would be the ultimate result if Jewish immigration into Germany were not stopped?

3. Judging by Ahlwardt's specific arguments and their emotional tone, to what kind of people and to what class in society do you think he was appealing?

4. Anti-Semitism is a regression to mythical modes of thinking. Discuss this statement.

10 | The Spirit of British Imperialism

In 1872, British statesman Benjamin Disraeli (1804–1881) delivered a speech at the Crystal Palace in London that expressed the ambitions driving the British to imperialist expansion. Disraeli posed a choice for his country: comfortable insignificance in world affairs or imperial power with prosperity and global prestige. Disraeli's espousal of the second alternative met with support from many Englishmen.

CECIL RHODES
Confession of Faith

One ardent supporter of British expansion was Cecil Rhodes (1853–1902). Raised in a parsonage north of London, Rhodes went to southern Africa at the age of seventeen for his health and to join his brother. Within two years he had established himself in the diamond industry. In the 1870s, he divided his time between Africa and studying at Oxford University. While at Oxford, Rhodes heard John Ruskin (1819–1900), social reformer and Slade Professor of Art, deliver an address echoing Disraeli's Crystal Palace speech. Ruskin expressed great pride in the British race and great enthusiasm for imperial ventures. He urged England "to found colonies as fast and as far as she is able, formed of the most energetic and worthiest of men." To the impressionable Rhodes, Ruskin was a prophet outlining England's future. Ruskin inspired Rhodes to write a "Confession of Faith," which represented an extravagant dream of a world empire ruled by "the most honorable race the world possesses."

The "Confession of Faith" guided Rhodes's life to the end. His company, De Beers Consolidated Mines, Ltd., controlled 90 percent of the world's diamond production and had a large stake in South Africa's gold fields. Never regarding wealth as an end in itself, Rhodes sought to extend British influence and institutions into the interior of Africa and to bring lands settled and dominated by Dutch-descended Boers under the British flag. Through his efforts, Rhodesia (now Zimbabwe) was added to the British Empire.

Excerpts follow from "Confession of Faith" of 1877. The "Confession" is included in the appendix of John E. Flint's biography of Cecil Rhodes. Flint reproduced the document "in its original form without any editing of spelling or punctuation."

It often strikes a man to inquire what is the chief good in life; to one the thought comes that it is a happy marriage, to another great wealth, and as each seizes on his idea, for that he more or less works for the rest of his existence. To myself thinking over the same question the wish came to render myself useful to my country. I then asked myself how could I and after reviewing the various methods I have felt that at the present day we are actually limiting our children and perhaps bringing into the world half the human beings we might owing to the lack of country for them to inhabit that if we had retained America there would at this moment be millions more of English living. I contend that we are the finest race in the world and that the more of the world we inhabit the better it is for the human race. Just fancy those parts that are at present inhabited by the most despicable specimens of human beings what an alteration there would be if they were brought under Anglo-Saxon influence, look again at the extra employment a new country added to our dominions gives. I contend that every acre added to our territory means in the future birth to some more of the English race who otherwise would not be brought into existence. Added to this the absorption of the greater portion of the world under our rule simply means the end of all wars. . . .

The idea gleaming and dancing before ones eyes like a will-of-the-wisp at last frames itself into a plan. Why should we not form a secret society with but one object the furtherance of the British Empire and the bringing of the whole uncivilised world under British rule for the recovery of the United States for the making the Anglo-Saxon race but one Empire. What a dream, but yet it is probable, it is possible. I once heard it argued by a fellow in my own college, I am sorry to own it by an Englishman, that it was a good thing for us that we have lost the United States. There are some subjects on which there can be no arguments, and to an Englishman this is one of them, but even from an American's point of view just picture what they have lost, look at their government, are not the frauds that yearly come before the public view a disgrace to any country and especially their's which is the finest in the world. Would they have occurred had they remained under English rule great as they have become how infinitely greater they would have been with the softening and elevating influences of English rule, think of those countless 000's [thousands] of Englishmen that during the last 100 years would have crossed the Atlantic and settled and populated the United States. Would they have not made without any prejudice a finer country of it than the low class Irish and German emigrants? All this we have lost and that country loses owing to whom? Owing to two or three ignorant pig-headed statesmen of the last century, at their door lies the blame. Do you ever feel mad? do you ever feel murderous. I think I do with those men. I bring facts to prove my assertion. Does an English father when his sons wish to emigrate ever think of suggesting emigration to a country under another flag, never — it would seem a disgrace to suggest such a thing I think that we all think that poverty is better under our own flag than wealth under a foreign one.

Put your mind into another train of thought. Fancy Australia discovered and colonised under the French flag. . . . We learn from having lost to cling to what we possess. We know the size of the world we know the total extent. Africa is still lying ready for us it is our duty to take it. It is our duty to seize every opportunity of acquiring more territory and we should keep this one idea steadily before our eyes that more territory simply means more of the Anglo-Saxon race more of the best the most human, most honourable race the world possesses.

To forward such a scheme what a splendid help a secret society would be a society not openly acknowledged but who would work in secret for such an object.

I contend that there are at the present moment numbers of the ablest men in the world who would devote their whole lives to it. . . . What has been the main cause of the success of the Romish Church? The fact that every enthusiast, call it if you like every madman finds employment in it. Let us form the same kind of society a Church for the extension of the British Empire. A society which should have its members in every part of the British Empire working with one object and one idea. . . .

(In every Colonial legislature the Society should attempt to have its members prepared at all times to vote or speak and advocate the closer union of England and the colonies, to crush all disloyalty and every movement for the severance of our Empire. The Society should inspire and even own portions of the press for the press rules the mind of the people. The Society should always be searching for members who might by their position in the world by their energies or character forward the object but the ballot and test for admittance should be severe). . . .[1]

For fear that death might cut me off before the time for attempting its development I leave all my worldly goods in trust to S. G. Shippard and the Secretary for the Colonies at the time of my death to try to form such a Society with such an object.

---

[1] It is not clear why Rhodes placed this paragraph in parentheses.

JOSEPH CHAMBERLAIN
The British Empire: Colonial Commerce and the White Man's Burden

British imperialists like Joseph Chamberlain (1836–1914) argued that the welfare of Britain depended upon the preservation and extension of the empire, for colonies fostered trade and served as a source of raw materials. In addition, Chamberlain asserted that the British Empire had a sacred duty to carry civilization, Christianity, and British law to the "backward" peoples of Africa and Asia. As a leading statesman, Chamberlain made many speeches both in Parliament and before local political groups, that endorsed imperialist ventures. Excerpts from these speeches later collected and published under the title *Foreign and Colonial Speeches,* follow.

[June 10, 1896]

. . . The Empire, to parody a celebrated expression, is commerce. It was created by commerce, it is founded on commerce, and it could not exist a day without commerce. (Cheers). . . . The fact is history teaches us that no nation has ever achieved real greatness without the aid of commerce, and the greatness of no nation has survived the decay of its trade. Well, then, gentlemen, we have reason to be proud of our commerce and to be resolved to guard it from attack. (Cheers.) . . .

[March 31, 1897]

. . . We have suffered much in this country from depression of trade. We know how many of our fellow-subjects are at this moment unemployed. Is there any man in his senses who believes that the crowded population of these islands could exist for a single day if we were to cut adrift from us the great dependencies which now look to us for protection and assistance, and which are the natural markets for our trade? (Cheers.) The area of the United Kingdom is only 120,000 miles; the area of the British Empire is over 9,000,000 square miles, of which nearly 500,000 are to be found in the portion of Africa with which we have been dealing. If tomorrow it were possible, as some people apparently desire, to reduce by a stroke of the pen the British Empire to the dimensions of the United Kingdom, half at least of our population would be starved (cheers). . . .

[January 22, 1894]

We must look this matter in the face, and must recognise that in order that we may have more employment to give we must create more demand. (Hear, hear.) Give me the demand for more goods and then I will undertake to give plenty of employment in making the goods; and the only thing, in my opinion, that the Government can do in order to meet this great difficulty that we are considering, is so to arrange its policy that every inducement shall be given to the demand; that new markets shall be created, and that old markets shall be effectually developed. (Cheers.) . . . I am convinced that it is a necessity as well as a duty for us to uphold the dominion and empire which we now possess. (Loud cheers.) . . . I would never lose the hold which we now have over our great Indian dependency — (hear, hear) — by far the greatest and most valuable of all the customers we have or ever shall have in this country. For the same reasons I approve of the continued occupation of Egypt; and for the same reasons I have urged upon this Government, and upon previous Governments, the necessity for using every legitimate opportunity to extend our influence and control in that great African continent which is now being opened up to civilisation and to commerce; and, lastly, it is for the same reasons that I hold that our navy should be strengthened — (loud cheers) — until its supremacy is so assured that we cannot be shaken in any of the possessions which we hold or may hold hereafter.

Believe me, if in any one of the places to which I have referred any change took place which deprived us of that control and influence of which I have been speaking, the first to suffer would be the working-men of this country. Then, indeed, we should see a distress which would not be temporary, but which would be chronic, and we should find that England was entirely unable to support the enormous population which is now maintained by the aid of her foreign trade. If the working-men of this country understand, as I believe they do — I am one of those who have had good reason through my life to rely upon their intelligence and shrewdness — if they understand their own interests, they will never lend any countenance to the doctrines of those politicians who never lose an opportunity of pouring contempt and abuse upon the brave Englishmen, who, even at this moment, in all parts of the world are carving out new dominions for Britain, and are opening up fresh markets for British commerce, and laying out fresh fields for British labour. (Applause.) . . .

March 31, 1897

. . . We feel now that our rule over these territories can only be justified if we can show that it adds to the happiness and prosperity of the people — (cheers) — and I maintain that our rule does, and has, brought security and peace and comparative prosperity to countries that never knew these blessings before. (Cheers.)

In carrying out this work of civilisation we are fulfilling what I believe to be our national mission, and we are finding scope for the exercise of those faculties and qualities which have made of us a great governing race. (Cheers.) I do not say that our success has been perfect in every case, I do not say that all our methods have been beyond reproach; but I do say that in almost every instance in which the rule of the Queen has been established and the great *Pax Britannica* has been enforced, there has come with it greater security to life and property, and a material improvement in the condition of the bulk of the population. (Cheers.) No doubt, in the first instance, when these conquests have been made, there has been bloodshed, there has been loss of life among the native populations, loss of still more precious lives among those who have been

sent out to bring these countries into some kind of disciplined order, but it must be remembered that that is the condition of the mission we have to fulfil. . . .

. . . You cannot have omelettes without breaking eggs; you cannot destroy the practices of barbarism, of slavery, of superstition, which for centuries have desolated the interior of Africa, without the use of force; but if you will fairly contrast the gain to humanity with the price which we are bound to pay for it, I think you may well rejoice in the result of such expeditions as those which have recently been conducted with such signal success — (cheers) — in Nyassaland, Ashanti, Benin, and Nupé [regions in Africa] — expeditions which may have, and indeed have, cost valuable lives, but as to which we may rest assured that for one life lost a hundred will be gained, and the cause of civilisation and the prosperity of the people will in the long run be eminently advanced. (Cheers.) But no doubt such a state of things, such a mission as I have described, involve heavy responsibility. . . . and it is a gigantic task that we have undertaken when we have determined to wield the sceptre of empire. Great is the task, great is the responsibility, but great is the honour — (cheers); and I am convinced that the conscience and the spirit of the country will rise to the height of its obligations, and that we shall have the strength to fulfil the mission which our history and our national character have imposed upon us. (Cheers.)

KARL PEARSON
Social Darwinism: Imperialism Justified by Nature

In the last part of the nineteenth century, the spirit of expansionism was buttressed by application of Darwin's theory of evolution to human society. Theorists called Social Darwinists argued that nations and races, like the species of animals, were locked in a struggle for existence in which only the fittest survived and deserved to survive. British and American imperialists employed the language of Social Darwinism to promote and justify Anglo-Saxon expansion and domination of other peoples.

Social Darwinist ideas spread to Germany, which was inspired by the examples of British and American expansion. In a lecture given in 1900 and titled "National Life from the Standpoint of Science," Karl Pearson (1857–1936), a British professor of mathematics, expressed the beliefs of Social Darwinists.

What I have said about bad stock seems to me to hold for the lower races of man. How many centuries, how many thousands of years, have the Kaffir [a tribe in southern Africa] or the negro held large districts in Africa undisturbed by the white man? Yet their intertribal struggles have not yet produced a civilization in the least comparable with the Aryan[1] [western European]. Educate and nurture them as you will, I do not believe that you will succeed in modifying the stock. History shows me one way, and one way only, in which a high state of civilization has been produced, namely, the struggle of race with race, and the survival of the physically and mentally fitter race. . . .

. . . Let us suppose we could prevent the white man, if we liked, from going to lands of which the agricultural and mineral resources are not worked to the full; then I should say a thousand times better for him that he should not go than that he should settle down and live alongside the inferior race. The only healthy alternative is that he should go and completely drive out the inferior race. That is practically what the white man has done in North America. . . . But I venture to say that no man calmly judging will wish either that the whites had never gone to America, or would desire that whites and Red Indians were to-day living alongside each other as negro and white in the Southern States, as Kaffir and European in South Africa, still less that they had mixed their

blood as Spaniard and Indian in South America. . . . I venture to assert, then, that the struggle for existence between white and red man, painful and even terrible as it was in its details, has given us a good far outbalancing its immediate evil. In place of the red man, contributing practically nothing to the work and thought of the world, we have a great nation, mistress of many arts, and able, with its youthful imagination and fresh, untrammelled impulses, to contribute much to the common stock of civilized man. . . .

But America is but one case in which we have to mark a masterful human progress following an inter-racial struggle. The Australian nation is another case of great civilization supplanting a lower race unable to work to the full the land and its resources. . . . The struggle means suffering, intense suffering, while it is in progress; but that struggle and that suffering have been the stages by which the white man has reached his present stage of development, and they account for the fact that he no longer lives in caves and feeds on roots and nuts. This dependence of progress on the survival of the fitter race, terribly black as it may seem to some of you, gives the struggle for existence its redeeming features; it is the fiery crucible out of which comes the finer metal. You may hope for a time when the sword shall be turned into the ploughshare, when American and German and English traders shall no longer compete in the markets of the world for their raw material and for their food supply, when the white man and the dark shall share the soil between them, and each till it as he lists. But, believe me, when that day comes mankind will no longer progress; there will be nothing to check the fertility of inferior stock; the relentless law of heredity will not be controlled and guided

---

[1] Most European languages derive from the Aryan language spoken by people who lived thousands of years ago in the region from the Caspian Sea to the Hindu Kush Mountains. Around 2000 B.C., some Aryan-speaking people migrated to Europe and India. Nineteenth-century racialist thinkers held that Europeans, descendants of the ancient Aryans, were racially superior to other peoples.

by natural selection. Man will stagnate. . . .

The . . . great function of science in national life . . . is to show us what national life means, and how the nation is a vast organism subject as much to the great forces of evolution as any other gregarious type of life. There is a struggle of race against race and of nation against nation. In the early days of that struggle it was a blind, unconscious struggle of barbaric tribes. At the present day, in the case of the civilized white man, it has become more and more the conscious, carefully directed attempt of the nation to fit itself to a continuously changing environment. The nation has to foresee how and where the struggle will be carried on; the maintenance of national position is becoming more and more a conscious preparation for changing conditions, an insight into the needs of coming environments. . . .

. . . If a nation is to maintain its position in this struggle, it must be fully provided with trained brains in every department of national activity, from the government to the factory, and have, if possible, a *reserve of brain and physique* to fall back upon in times of national crisis. . . .

You will see that my view — and I think it may be called the scientific view of a nation — is that of an organized whole, kept up to a high pitch of internal efficiency by insuring that its numbers are substantially recruited from the better stocks, and kept up to a high pitch of external efficiency by contest, chiefly by way of war with inferior races, and with equal races by the struggle for trade-routes and for the sources of raw material and of food supply. This is the natural history view of mankind, and I do not think you can in its main features subvert it. . . .

. . . Is it not a fact that the daily bread of our millions of workers depends on their having somebody to work for? that if we give up the contest for trade-routes and for free markets and for waste lands, we indirectly give up our food-supply? Is it not a fact that our strength depends on these and upon our colonies, and that our colonies have been won by the ejection of inferior races, and are maintained against equal races only by respect for the present power of our empire? . . .

. . . We find that the law of the survival of the fitter is true of mankind, but that the struggle is that of the gregarious animal. A community not knit together by strong social instincts, by sympathy between man and man, and class and class, cannot face the external contest, the competition with other nations, by peace or by war, for the raw material of production and for its food supply. This struggle of tribe with tribe, and nation with nation, may have its mournful side; but we see as a result of it the gradual progress of mankind to higher intellectual and physical efficiency. It is idle to condemn it; we can only see that it exists and recognise what we have gained by it — civilization and social sympathy. But while the statesman has to watch this external struggle, . . . he must be very cautious that the nation is not silently rotting at its core. He must insure that the fertility of the inferior stocks is checked, and that of the superior stocks encouraged; he must regard with suspicion anything that tempts the physically and mentally fitter men and women to remain childless. . . .

. . . The path of progress is strewn with the wrecks of nations; traces are everywhere to be seen of the hecatombs [slaughtered remains] of inferior races, and of victims who found not the narrow way to perfection. Yet these dead people are, in very truth, the stepping stones on which mankind has arisen to the higher intellectual and deeper emotional life of today.

Review Questions

1. What nationalistic views were expressed in Cecil Rhodes's "Confession of Faith"?
2. What role did the concept of race — the English or Anglo-Saxon race — play in the arguments of Rhodes? Compare his views with those advanced by Hermann Ahlwardt in the preceding selection.
3. How do Joseph Chamberlain's arguments in favor of British expansion compare with those of Rhodes?
4. What, according to Chamberlain, were the economic benefits of British expansion?
5. How did Chamberlain define the national mission of the "great governing race," the English?
6. What does the phrase, "you cannot make omelettes without breaking eggs," have to do with British imperialism?
7. What, according to Karl Pearson, was the "natural history view of mankind"?
8. How did Pearson define the difference between inferior and superior races?
9. What measures did Pearson advocate for keeping the race fit?
10. How did Pearson portray the effects of the survival of the fittest on international relations?

11 | German Imperialism

The unification of Germany in 1871 created a powerful state in the heart of Europe. Aware of their country's new political significance, ambitious Germans soon expanded their designs from Europe to the world at large. Impressed by British imperialism, they suggested that Germany establish its own colonial empire, and claimed that Germany, like Britain, had a civilizing mission. While Otto von Bismarck was in power, he discouraged such global ambitions, preoccupied as he was with Germany's security within Europe. Under popular pressure, however, he took part at the Congress of Berlin (1884) in the partition of Africa, from which Germany gained several African colonies.

Agitation for more colonies and for a global role for Germany advanced during the reign of Kaiser William II (1888–1918). Following the British example, Germany built up its navy and demanded its rightful "place in the sun." This competition with England contributed to the tensions that led to World War I.

FRIEDRICH FABRI

Does Germany Need Colonies?

The following reading comes from a popularly written book *Does Germany Need Colonies?* published in Germany in 1879 by Friedrich Fabri (1824–1891). Fabri, who had seen long service as a colonial administrator in Southwest Africa, supported colonization as a force for both national growth and the spread of German culture.

Should not the German nation, so seaworthy, so industrially and commercially minded, more than other peoples geared to agricultural colonization, and possessing a rich and available supply of labor. all these to a greater extent than other modern culture-peoples, should not this nation successfully hew a new path on the road of imperialism? We are convinced beyond doubt that the colonial question has become a matter of life-or-death for the development of Germany. Colonies will have a salutary effect on our economic situation as well as on our entire national progress.

Here is a solution for many of the problems that face us. In this new Reich of ours there is so much bitterness, so much unfruitful, sour, and poisoned political wrangling, that the opening of a new, promising road of national effort will act as a kind of liberating influence. Our national spirit will be renewed, a gratifying thing, a great asset. A people that has been led to a high level of power can maintain its historical position only as long as it understands and proves itself to be *the bearer of a culture-mission*. At the same time, this is the only way to stability and to the growth of national welfare, the necessary foundation for a lasting expansion of power.

At one time Germany contributed only intellectual and literary activity to the tasks of our century. That era is now over. As a people we have become politically minded and powerful. But if political power becomes the primal goal of a nation, it will lead to harshness, even to barbarism. We must be ready to serve for the ideal, moral, and economic culture-tasks of our time. The French national-economist, Leroy Beaulieu, closed his work on colonization with these words: "That nation is the greatest in the world which colonizes most; if she does not achieve that rank today, she will make it tomorrow."

No one can deny that in this direction England has by far surpassed all other countries. Much has been said, even in Germany, during the last few decades about the "disintegrating power of England." . . . It has been customary in our age of military power to evaluate the strength of a state in terms of its combat-ready troops. But anyone who looks at the globe and notes the steadily increasing colonial possessions of Great Britain, how she extracts strength from them, the skill with which she governs them, how the Anglo-Saxon strain occupies a dominant position in the overseas territories, he will begin to see the military argument as the reasoning of a philistine.

The fact is that England tenaciously holds on to its world-wide possessions with scarcely one-fourth the manpower of our continental military state. That is not only a great economic advantage but also a striking proof of the solid power and cultural fiber of England. Great Britain, of course, isolates herself far from the mass warfare of the continent, or only goes into action with dependable allies; hence, the insular state has suffered and will suffer no real damage. In any case, it would be wise for us Germans to learn about colonial skills from our Anglo-Saxon cousins and to begin a friendly competition with them. When the German Reich centuries ago stood at the pinnacle of the states of Europe, it was the Number One trade and sea power. If the New Germany wants to protect its newly won position of power for a long time, it must heed its *Kultur-mission* and, above all, delay no longer in the task of renewing the call for colonies.

Review Questions

1. Why did Friedrich Fabri view the colonial question as a matter of life or death for Germany?

2. What did Fabri see as the benefits of colonial expansion for Germany?

3. According to Fabri, what were Germany's assets for colonial expansion?
4. What qualities did Fabri say England possessed that the Germans still needed to learn?
5. What was seen as Germany's "culture-mission" in the world?

12 | Anti-imperialism

The early protests of non-European victims of colonialism were reinforced by anti-imperialist agitation within Europe itself. Although the statesmen in power, with the support of parliamentary majorities, backed colonial expansion, the spokesmen of the opposition, labor leaders and socialist intellectuals, spoke out on behalf of the colonized peoples.

JOHN ATKINSON HOBSON
An Early Critique of Imperialism

One of the early English critics of imperialism was the social reformer and economist John Atkinson Hobson (1858–1940). Hobson's primary interest was social reform, and he turned to economics to try to solve the problem of poverty. Like Rhodes, he was influenced by Ruskin's ideas, but his interpretation of them led him to a diametrically opposed view of colonialism. As an economist, he argued that the unequal distribution of income made capitalism unproductive and unstable. It could not maintain itself except through investing in less-developed countries on an increasing scale, thus fostering colonial expansion. Lenin, leader of the Russian Revolution, later adopted this thesis. Hobson's stress upon the economic causes of imperialism has been disputed by historians who see the desire for national power and glory as a far more important cause. Hobson attacked imperialism in the following passages from his book *Imperialism*.

. . . The decades of Imperialism have been prolific in wars; most of these wars have been directly motived by aggression of white races upon "lower races," and have issued in the forcible seizure of territory. Every one of the steps of expansion in Africa, Asia, and the Pacific has been accompanied by bloodshed; each imperialist Power keeps an increasing army available for foreign service; rectification of frontiers, punitive expeditions, and other euphemisms for war are in incessant progress. The *pax Britannica*, always an impudent falsehood, has become of recent years a grotesque monster of hypocrisy; along our Indian frontiers, in West Africa, in the Soudan, in Uganda, in Rhodesia fighting has been well-nigh incessant. Although the great imperialist Powers have kept their hands off one another, save where the rising empire of the United States has found its opportunity in the falling empire of Spain, the self-restraint has been costly and precarious. Peace as a national policy is antagonised not merely by war, but by militarism, an even graver injury. Apart from the enmity of France and Germany, the main cause of the vast armaments which are draining the resources of most European countries is their conflicting interests in territorial and commercial expansion.

Where thirty years ago there existed one sensitive spot in our relations with France, or Germany, or Russia, there are a dozen now; diplomatic strains are of almost monthly occurrence between Powers with African or Chinese interests, and the chiefly business nature of the national antagonisms renders them more dangerous, inasmuch as the policy of Governments passes more under the influence of distinctively financial juntos. . . .

Our economic analysis has disclosed the fact that it is only the interests of competing cliques of business men — investors, contractors, export manufacturers, and certain professional classes — that are antagonistic; that these cliques, usurping the authority and voice of the people, use the public resources to push their private businesses, and spend the blood and money of the people in this vast and disastrous military game, feigning national antagonisms which have no basis in reality. It is not to the interest of the British people, either as producers of wealth or as tax-payers, to risk a war with Russia and France in order to join Japan in preventing Russia from seizing [K]orea; but it may serve the interests of a group of commercial politicians to promote this dangerous policy. The South African war [the Boer War, 1899–1902], openly fomented by gold speculators for their private purposes, will rank in history as a leading case of this usurpation of nationalism. . . .

. . . So long as this competitive expansion for territory and foreign markets is permitted to misrepresent itself as "national policy" the antagonism of interests seems real, and the peoples must sweat and bleed and toil to keep up an ever more expensive machinery of war. . . .

. . . The industrial and financial forces of Imperialism, operating through the party, the press, the church, the school, mould public opinion and public policy by the false idealisation of those primitive lusts of struggle, domination, and acquisitiveness which have survived throughout the eras of peaceful industrial order and whose stimulation is needed once again for the work of imperial aggression, expansion, and the forceful exploitation of lower races. For these business politicians biology and sociology weave thin convenient theories of a race struggle for the subjugation of the inferior peoples, in order that we, the Anglo-Saxon, may take their lands and live upon their labours; while economics buttresses the argument by representing our work in conquering and ruling them as our share in the division of labour among nations, and history devises reasons why the lessons of past empire do not apply to ours, while social ethics paints the motive of "Imperialism" as the desire to bear the "burden" of educating and elevating races of "children." Thus are the "cultured" or semi-cultured classes indoctrinated with the intellectual and moral grandeur of Imperialism. For the masses there is a cruder appeal to hero-worship and sensational glory, adventure and the sporting spirit: current history falsified in coarse flaring colours, for the direct stimulation of the combative instincts. But while various methods are employed, some delicate and indirect, others coarse and flamboyant, the operation everywhere resolves itself into an incitation and direction of the brute lusts of human domination which are everywhere latent in civilised humanity, for the pursuance of a policy fraught with material gain to a minority of co-operative vested interests which usurp the title of the commonwealth. . . .

. . . The presence of a scattering of white officials, missionaries, traders, mining or plantation overseers, a dominant male caste with little knowledge of or sympathy for the institutions of the people, is ill-calculated to give to these lower races even such gains as Western civilisation might be capable of giving.

The condition of the white rulers of these lower races is distinctively parasitic; they live upon these natives, their chief work being that of organising native labour for their support. The normal state of such a country is one in which the most fertile lands and the mineral resources are owned by white aliens and worked by natives under their direction, primarily for their gain: they do not identify themselves with the interests of the nation or its people, but remain an alien body of sojourners, a "parasite" upon the carcass of its "host,² destined to extract wealth from the country and retire to consume it at home. All the hard manual or other severe routine work is done by natives. . . .

Nowhere under such conditions is the theory of white government as a trust for civilisation made valid; nowhere is there any provision to secure the predominance of the interests, either of the world at large or of the governed people, over those of the encroaching nation, or more commonly a section of that nation. The relations subsisting between the superior and the inferior nations, commonly established by pure force, and resting on that basis, are such as preclude the genuine sympathy essential to the operation of the best civilising influences, and usually resolve themselves into the maintenance of external good order so as to forward the profitable development of certain natural resources of the land, under "forced" native labour, primarily for the benefit of white traders and investors, and secondarily for the benefit of the world of white Western consumers.

This failure to justify by results the forcible rule over alien peoples is attributable to no special defect of the British or other modern European nations. It is inherent in the nature of such domination. . . .

Review Questions

1. Why, in J. A. Hobson's opinion, was the *pax Britannica* an "impudent falsehood"?

2. According to Hobson, what were the driving forces behind imperialism? And how did the special interests behind imperialism dominate public opinion?

3. How was imperialism endangering international relations among western European nations, according to Hobson?

4. One ideal of imperialism was to spread civilizing influences among native populations. How did Hobson interpret this sense of mission?

5. If, as Hobson asserted, "the brute lusts of human domination . . . are everywhere latent in civilised humanity," why did he especially blame "the competing cliques of business men" for the inhumanities and violence of imperialism?

CHAPTER 7

Changing Patterns of Thought and Culture

Romanticism dominated European art, literature, and music in the early nineteenth century. Stressing the feelings and the free expression of personality, the Romantic Movement was a reaction against the rationalism of the Enlightenment. In the middle decades of the century, realism and its close successor naturalism supplanted romanticism as the chief mode of cultural expression. Rejecting religious, metaphysical, and romantic interpretations of reality, realists aspired to an exact and accurate portrayal of the external world and daily life. Realist and naturalist writers like Émile Zola used the empirical approach: the careful collection, ordering, and interpretation of facts employed in science, which was advancing steadily in the nineteenth century. Among the most important scientific theories formulated was Charles Darwin's on evolution, which revolutionized conceptions of time and the origins of the human species.

The closing decades of the nineteenth century and the opening of the twentieth witnessed a crisis in Western thought. Rejecting the Enlightenment belief in the essential rationality of human beings, some thinkers — such as Fyodor Dostoyevsky, Friedrich Nietzsche, and Sigmund Freud — stressed the immense power of the nonrational in individual and social life. They held that subconscious drives, impulses, and instincts lay at the core of human nature, that people were moved more by religious-mythic images and symbols than by logical thought, that feelings determine human conduct more than reason does. This new image of the individual led to unsettling conclusions. If human beings are not fundamentally rational, then what are the prospects of resolving the immense problems of an industrial civilization? Although most thinkers shared the Enlightenment's vision of humanity's future progress, doubters were also heard.

The crisis of thought also found expression in art and literature. Artists like Pablo Picasso and writers like James Joyce and Franz Kafka exhibited a a growing fascination with the nonrational — with dreams, fantasies, sexual conflicts, and guilt, with tortured, fragmented, and dislocated inner lives. In the process, they rejected traditional esthetic standards established during the Renaissance and the Enlightenment and experimented with new forms of artistic and literary representation.

These developments in thought and culture produced insights into human nature and society and opened up new possibilities in art and literature. But such changes also contributed to the disorientation and insecurity that characterizes the twentieth century.

1 | Realism and Naturalism

The middle decades of the nineteenth century were characterized by the growing importance of science and industrialization in European life. A movement known as positivism sought to apply the scientific method to the study of society. Rejecting theological and metaphysical theories as unscientific, positivists sought to arrive at the general laws that underlie society by carefully assembling and classifying data.

This stress on a rigorous observation of reality also characterized realism and naturalism, the dominant movements in art and literature. In several ways, realism differed from romanticism, the dominant cultural movement in the first half of the century. Romantics were concerned with the inner life — with feelings, intuition, and imagination. They sought escape from the city into natural beauty, and they venerated the past, particularly the Middle Ages, which they viewed as noble, idyllic, and good in contrast to the spiritually impoverished present. Realists, on the other hand, shifted attention away from individual human feelings to the external world, which they investigated with the meticulous care of the scientist. Preoccupied with reality as it actually is, realist writers and artists depicted ordinary people, including the poor and humble, in ordinary circumstances. With a careful eye for detail and in a matter-of-fact way devoid of romantic exuberance and exaggeration, realists described peasants, factory workers, laundresses, beggars, criminals, and prostitutes.

Realism quickly evolved into naturalism. Naturalist writers held that human behavior was determined by the social environment, that certain social and economic conditions produced predictable traits in men and women, that cause and effect operated in society as well as in physical nature.

ÉMILE ZOLA
The Experimental Novel

In the following reading from *The Experimental Novel*, Émile Zola (1840–1902), the leading French naturalist novelist, asserted that literature too can be a science. In his novels, he blended the realist's passion for exact observation with the poet's imagination, subjective insights, and use of imagery, as the second reading (from *Germinal*) shows.

. . . Some day the physiologist[1] will explain to us the mechanism of the thoughts and the passions; we shall know how the individual machinery of each man works; how he thinks, how he loves, how he goes from reason to passion and folly; but these phenomena, resulting as they do from the mechanism of the organs, acting under the influence of an interior condition, are not produced in isolation or in the bare void. Man is not alone; he lives in society, in a social condition; and consequently, for us novelists, this social condition unceasingly modifies the phenomena. Indeed our great study is just there, in the reciprocal effect of society on the individual and the individual on society. For the physiologist, the exterior and interior conditions are purely chemical and physical, and this aids him in finding the laws which govern them easily. We are not yet able to prove that the social condition is also physical and

---

[1] Physiology is the study of the functions of living organisms.

chemical. It is that certainly, or rather it is the variable product of a group of living beings, who themselves are absolutely submissive to the physical and chemical laws which govern alike living beings and inanimate. From this we shall see that we can act upon the social conditions, in acting upon the phenomena of which we have made ourselves master in man. And this is what constitutes the experimental novel: to possess a knowledge of the mechanism of the phenomena inherent in man, to show the machinery of his intellectual and sensory manifestations, under the influences of heredity and environment, such as physiology shall give them to us, and then finally to exhibit man living in social conditions produced by himself, which he modifies daily, and in the heart of which he himself experiences a continual transformation. Thus, then, we lean on physiology; we take man from the hands of the physiologist solely, in order to continue the solution of the problem, and to solve scientifically the question of how men behave when they are in society. . . .

I have reached this point: the experimental novel is a consequence of the scientific evolution of the century; it continues and completes physiology, which itself leans for support on chemistry and medicine; it substitutes for the study of the abstract and the metaphysical[2] man the study of the natural man, governed by physical and chemical laws, and modified by the influences of his surroundings; it is in one word the literature of our scientific age. . . .

. . . The metaphysical man is dead; our whole territory is transformed by the advent of the physiological man. No doubt "Achilles' Anger," "Dido's Love,"[3] will last

forever on account of their beauty; but today we feel the necessity of analyzing anger and love, of discovering exactly how such passions work in the human being. This view of the matter is a new one; we have become experimentalists instead of philosophers. In short, everything is summed up in this great fact: the experimental method in letters, as in the sciences, is on the way to explain the natural phenomena, both individual and social, of which metaphysics, until now, has given only irrational and supernatural explanations.

In Germinal, *Zola's greatest novel, Étienne, a bright young man who has wandered the roads in search of work, becomes a coal miner. The following passage treats Étienne's adjustment to life in the mines. Later, he revolts against these oppressive conditions. The passage reveals Zola as both a naturalist writer and a social critic.*

Germinal

On the next day, and the days that followed, Étienne continued his work at the pit. He grew accustomed to it; his existence became regulated by this labour and to these new habits which had seemed so hard to him at first. Only one episode interrupted the monotony of the first fortnight: a slight fever which kept him in bed for forty-eight hours with aching limbs and throbbing head, dreaming in a state of semi-delirium that he was pushing his tram in a passage that was so narrow that his body would not pass through. It was simply the exhaustion of his apprenticeship, an excess of fatigue from which he quickly recovered.

And days followed days, until weeks and months had slipped by. Now, like his mates, he got up at three o'clock, drank

---

[2] Metaphysics is a branch of philosophy concerned with the first principle of things, with the ultimate reality beyond the physical appearance of things.
[3] "Achilles' anger" is a reference to Homer's *Iliad;* Achilles, the great Greek warrior, is infuriated when King Agamemnon deprives him of his prize, the captive girl Briseis. "Dido's

love" is a reference to Virgil's *Aeneid;* Dido, the Queen of Carthage, has a great love for Aeneas, the Trojan prince.

his coffee, and carried off the double slice of bread and butter which Madame Rasseneur had prepared for him the evening before. Regularly as he went every morning to the pit, he met old Bonnemort who was going home to sleep, and on leaving in the afternoon he crossed Bouteloup who was going to his task. He had his cap, his breeches and canvas jacket, and he shivered and warmed his back in the shed before the large fire. Then came the waiting with naked feet in the receiving-room, swept by furious currents of air. But the engine, with its great steel limbs starred with copper shining up above in the shade, no longer attracted his attention, nor the cables which flew by with the black and silent motion of a nocturnal bird, nor the cages rising and plunging unceasingly in the midst of the noise of signals, of shouted orders, of trams shaking the metal floor. His lamp burnt badly, that confounded lamp-man could not have cleaned it; and he only woke up when Mouquet bundled them all off, roguishly smacking the girls' flanks. The cage was unfastened, and fell like a stone to the bottom of a hole without causing him even to lift his head to see the daylight vanish. He never thought of a possible fall; he felt himself at home as he sank into the darkness beneath the falling rain. Below at the pit-eye, when Pierron had unloaded them with his air of hypocritical mildness, there was always the same tramping as of a flock, the yard-men each going away to his cutting with trailing steps. He now knew the mine galleries better than the streets of Montsou; he knew where he had to turn, where he had to stoop, and where he had to avoid a puddle. He had grown so accustomed to these two kilometres beneath the earth, that he could have traversed them without a lamp, with his hands in his pockets. And every time the same meetings took place: a captain lighting up the faces of the passing workmen, Father Mouque leading a horse, Bébert conducting the snorting Bataille, Jeanlin running behind the train to close the ventilation doors, and big Mouquette and lean Lydie pushing their trams.

After a time, also, Étienne suffered much less from the damp and closeness of the cutting. The chimney or ascending passage seemed to him more convenient for climbing up, as if he had melted and could pass through cracks where before he would not have risked a hand. He breathed the coal-dust without difficulty, saw clearly in the obscurity, and sweated tranquilly, having grown accustomed to the sensation of wet garments on his body from morning to night. Besides, he no longer spent his energy recklessly; he had gained skill so rapidly that he astonished the whole stall. In three weeks he was named among the best putters in the pit; no one pushed a tram more rapidly to the upbrow, nor loaded it afterwards so correctly. His small figure allowed him to slip about everywhere, and though his arms were as delicate and white as a woman's, they seemed to be made of iron beneath the smooth skin, so vigorously did they perform their task. He never complained, out of pride no doubt, even when he was panting with fatigue. The only thing they had against him was that he could not take a joke, and grew angry as soon as any one trod on his toes. In all other respects he was accepted and looked upon as a real miner, reduced beneath this pressure of habit, little by little, to a machine.

Review Questions

1. How did Émile Zola define the experimental novel?
2. What relationship did Zola draw between the experimental novel and the scientific age?

3. What does Zola's description of Étienne's apprenticeship reveal about conditions in the mines in late-nineteenth-century France?

4. How does this passage reveal Zola as both a naturalist writer and a social critic?

2 | Theory of Evolution

In a century of outstanding scientific discoveries, none was more significant than the theory of evolution formulated by the English naturalist Charles Darwin (1809–1882). From December 1831 to 1836, Darwin had served as naturalist at sea on the *H.M.S. Beagle,* which surveyed parts of South America and some Pacific islands. He collected and classified many specimens of animal and plant life and from his investigations eventually drew several conclusions that startled the scientific community and enraged many clergy.

Before Darwin's theory of evolution, most people adhered to the biblical account of creation found in Genesis, which said that God had created the universe, the various species of animal and plant life, and human beings, all in six days. The creation account also said that God had given each species of animal and plant a form that distinguished it from every other species. It was commonly held that the creation of the universe and of the first human beings had occurred some six thousand years ago.

Based on his study, Darwin maintained that all life on earth had descended from earlier living forms; that human beings had evolved from lower, nonhuman species; and that the process had taken millions of years. Adopting the Malthusian idea that population reproduces faster than the food supply increases, Darwin held that within nature there is a continual struggle for existence. He said that the advantage lies with those living things that are stronger, faster, better camouflaged from their enemies, or better fitted in some way for survival than are other members of their species; those more fit to survive pass along the advantageous trait to offspring. This principle of *natural selection* explains why some members of a species survive and reproduce and why those less fit perish.

CHARLES DARWIN
Natural Selection

According to Darwin, members of a species inherit variations that distinguish them from others in the species, and over many generations these variations become more pronounced. In time, a new variety of life evolves that can no longer breed with the species from which it descended. In this way, new species emerge and older ones die out. Human beings were also a product of natural selection, evolving from earlier, lower, nonhuman forms of life. In this first passage, from his autobiography, Darwin described his empirical method and his discovery of a general theory that coordinated and illuminated the data he found. Succeeding excerpts are from his *Origin of Species* and *Descent of Man.*

[Darwin's Description of His Method and Discovery]

From September 1854 I devoted my whole time to arranging my huge pile of notes, to observing, and to experimenting in relation to the transmutation of species. During the voyage of the *Beagle* I had been deeply impressed by discovering in the Pampean formation[1] great fossil animals covered with armour like that on the existing armadillos; secondly, by the manner in which closely allied animals replace one another in proceeding southwards over the Continent; and thirdly, by the South American character of most of the productions of the Galapagos archipelago,[2] and more especially by the manner in which they differ slightly on each island of the group; none of the islands appearing to be very ancient in a geological sense.

It was evident that such facts as these, as well as many others, could only be explained on the supposition that species gradually become modified; and the subject haunted me. But it was equally evident that neither the action of the surrounding conditions, nor the will of the organisms (especially in the case of plants) could account for the innumerable cases in which organisms of every kind are beautifully adapted to their habits of life — for instance, a woodpecker or a tree-frog to climb trees, or a seed for dispersal by hooks or plumes. I had always been much struck by such adaptations, and until these could be explained it seemed to me almost useless to endeavour to prove by indirect evidence that species have been modified.

After my return to England it appeared to me that by following the example of Lyell[3] in Geology, and by collecting all facts which bore in any way on the variation of animals and plants under domestication and nature, some light might perhaps be thrown on the whole subject. My first note-book was opened in July 1837. I worked on true Baconian principles,[4] and without any theory collected facts on a wholesale scale, more especially with respect to domesticated productions, by printed enquiries, by conversation with skilful breeders and gardeners, and by extensive reading. When I see the list of books of all kinds which I read and abstracted, including whole series of Journals and Transactions, I am surprised at my industry. I soon perceived that selection was the keystone of man's success in making useful races of animals and plants. But how selection could be applied to organisms living in a state of nature remained for some time a mystery to me.

In October 1838, that is, fifteen months after I had begun my systematic enquiry, I happened to read for amusement Malthus[5] on *Population,* and being well prepared to appreciate the struggle for existence which everywhere goes on from long-continued observation of the habits of animals and plants, it at once struck me that under these circumstances favourable variations would tend to be preserved and unfavourable ones to be destroyed. The result of this would be the formation of new species. Here, then, I had at last got a theory by which to work. . . .

---

[1] The Pampean formation refers to the vast plain that stretches across Argentina, from the Atlantic Ocean to the foothills of the Andes Mountains.

[2] The Galapagos Islands, a Pacific archipelago 650 miles west of Ecuador, are noted for their unusual wildlife, which Darwin observed.

[3] Sir Charles Lyell (1797–1875) was a Scottish geologist whose work showed that the planet had evolved slowly over many ages. Like Lyell, Darwin sought to interpret natural history by observing processes still going on.

[4] "Baconian principles" refers to Sir Francis Bacon (1561–1626), one of the first to insist that new knowledge should be acquired through experimentation and the accumulation of data.

[5] Thomas Malthus (1766–1834) was an English economist who maintained that population increases geometrically (2, 4, 8, 16, and so on) while the food supply increases arithmetically (1, 2, 3, 4, and so on). (See page 135.)

It has sometimes been said that the success of the *Origin [of Species]* proved "that the subject was in the air," or "that men's minds were prepared for it." I do not think that this is strictly true, for I occasionally sounded not a few naturalists, and never happened to come across a single one who seemed to doubt about the permanence of species. Even Lyell and Hooker,[6] though they would listen with interest to me, never seemed to agree. I tried once or twice to explain to able men what I meant by Natural selection, but signally failed. What I believe was strictly true is that innumerable well-observed facts were stored in the minds of naturalists ready to take their proper places as soon as any theory which would receive them was sufficiently explained. . . .

My *Descent of Man* was published in February 1871. As soon as I had become, in the year 1837 or 1838, convinced that species were mutable productions, I could not avoid the belief that man must come under the same law.

———————— ➤ •❖• ◀ ————————

In the following excerpt from The Origin of Species *(1859), Darwin explained the struggle for existence and the principle of natural selection.*

———————— ➤ •❖• ◀ ————————

The Origin of Species

. . . Owing to this struggle [for existence], variations, however slight . . . , if they be in any degree profitable to the individuals of a species, in their infinitely complex relations to other organic beings and to their physical conditions of life, will tend to the preservation of such individuals, and will generally be inherited by the offspring. The offspring, also, will thus have a better chance of surviving, for, of the many individuals of any species which are periodically born, but a small number

can survive. I have called this principle, by which each slight variation, if useful, is preserved, by the term Natural Selection, in order to mark its relation to man's power of selection. But the expression often used by Mr. Herbert Spencer[7] of the Survival of the Fittest is more accurate, and is sometimes equally convenient. . . .

A struggle for existence inevitably follows from the high rate at which all organic beings tend to increase. Every being, which during its natural lifetime produces several eggs or seeds, must suffer destruction during some period of its life, and during some season or occasional year, otherwise, on the principle of geometrical increase, its numbers would quickly become so inordinately great that no country could support the product. Hence, as more individuals are produced than can possibly survive, there must in every case be a struggle for existence, either one individual with another of the same species, or with the individuals of distinct species, or with the physical conditions of life. It is the doctrine of Malthus applied with manifold force to the whole animal and vegetable kingdoms; for in this case there can be no artificial increase of food, and no prudential restraint from marriage. Although some species may be now increasing, more or less rapidly, in numbers, all cannot do so, for the world would not hold them.

There is no exception to the rule that every organic being naturally increases at so high a rate, that, if not destroyed, the earth would soon be covered by the progeny of a single pair. Even slow-breeding man has doubled in twenty-five years, and at this rate, in less than a thousand years, there would literally not be standing-room for his progeny. . . . The elephant is reckoned the slowest breeder of all known animals, and I have taken some pains to estimate its probable minimum rate of

———————————————

[6] Sir Joseph Dalton Hooker (1817–1911) was an English botanist who supported Darwin's ideas.

[7] The British philosopher Herbert Spencer (1820–1903) coined the term *survival of the fittest.* (See page 151.)

natural increase; it will be safest to assume that it begins breeding when thirty years old, and goes on breeding till ninety years old, bringing forth six young in the interval, and surviving till one hundred years old; if this be so, after a period of from 740 to 750˙ years there would be nearly nineteen million elephants alive, descended from the first pair. . . .

. . . Can we doubt (remembering that many more individuals are born than can possibly survive) that individuals having any advantage, however slight, over others, would have the best chance of surviving and of procreating their kind? On the other hand, we may feel sure that any variation in the least degree injurious would be rigidly destroyed. This preservation of favourable individual differences and variations, and the destruction of those which are injurious, I have called Natural Selection, or the Survival of the Fittest. . . .

. . . Natural selection acts solely through the preservation of variations in some way advantageous, which consequently endure. Owing to the high geometrical rate of increase of all organic beings, each area is already fully stocked with inhabitants; and it follows from this, that as the favoured forms increase in number, so, generally, will the less favoured decrease and become rare. . . .

From these several considerations I think it inevitably follows, that as new species in the course of time are formed through natural selection, others will become rarer and rarer, and finally extinct. The forms which stand in closest competition with those undergoing modification and improvement will naturally suffer most. And we have seen in the chapter on the Struggle for Existence that it is the most closely-allied forms — varieties of the same species, and species of the same genus or of related genera — which, from having nearly the same structure, constitution, and habits, generally come into the severest competition with each other; consequently, each new variety or species, during the progress of its formation, will

generally press hardest on its nearest kindred, and tend to exterminate them. We see the same process of extermination amongst our domesticated productions, through the selection of improved forms by man.

--------→ •●• ←--------

In The Descent of Man *(1871), Darwin argued that human beings have evolved from lower forms of life.*

--------→ •●• ←--------

The Descent of Man

The main conclusion here arrived at, and now held by many naturalists who are well competent to form a sound judgment, is that man is descended from some less highly organised form. The grounds upon which this conclusion rests will never be shaken, for the close similarity between man and the lower animals in embryonic development, as well as in innumerable points of structure and constitution, both of high and of the most trifling importance, — the rudiments which he retains, and the abnormal reversions to which he is occasionally liable, — are facts which cannot be disputed. They have long been known, but until recently they told us nothing with respect to the origin of man. Now when viewed by the light of our knowledge of the whole organic world, their meaning is unmistakable. The great principle of evolution stands up clear and firm, when these groups of facts are considered in connection with others, such as the mutual affinities of the members of the same group, their geographical distribution in past and present times, and their geological succession. It is incredible that all these facts should speak falsely. He who is not content to look, like a savage, at the phenomena of nature as disconnected, cannot any longer believe that man is the work of a separate act of creation. He will be forced to admit that the close resemblance of the embryo of man to that, for instance, of a dog — the construction of his skull, limbs and whole frame on the same plan with that of other mammals, independently of the uses to which the parts may be put — the occasional reappearance of various structures, for instance of several muscles, which man does not normally possess, but which are common to the Quadrumana[1] — and a crowd of analogous facts — all point in the plainest manner to the conclusion that man is the co-descendant with other mammals of a common progenitor.

We have seen that man incessantly presents individual differences in all parts of his body and in his mental faculties. These differences or variations seem to be induced by the same general causes, and to obey the same laws as with the lower animals. In both cases similar laws of inheritance prevail. Man tends to increase at a greater rate than his means of subsistence; consequently he is occasionally subjected to a severe struggle for existence, and natural selection will have ef-

[1] An order of mammals, Quadrumana includes all primates (monkeys, apes, and baboons) except human beings; the primates' hind and forefeet can be used as hands as they have opposable first digits.

fected whatever lies within its scope. A succession of strongly-marked variations of a similar nature is by no means requisite; slight fluctuating differences in the individual suffice for the work of natural selection. . . .

Man may be excused for feeling some pride at having risen, though not through his own exertions, to the very summit of the organic scale; and the fact of his having thus risen, instead of having been aboriginally placed there, may give him hope for a still higher destiny in the distant future. But we are not here concerned with hopes or fears, only with the truth as far as our reason permits us to discover it; and I have given the evidence to the best of my ability. We must, however, acknowledge, as it seems to me, that man with all his noble qualities, with sympathy which feels for the most debased, with benevolence which extends not only to other men but to the humblest living creature, with his god-like intellect which has penetrated into the movements and constitution of the solar system — with all these exalted powers — Man still bears in his bodily frame the indelible stamp of his lowly origin.

Review Questions

1. How did Darwin make use of Malthus's theory of population growth?
2. To what did Darwin attribute the struggle for existence?
3. How did Darwin account for the extinction of old species and the emergence of new ones?
4. What did Darwin mean when he said that man "with his god-like intellect . . . still bears in his bodily frame the indelible stamp of his lowly origins"?

3 | Darwinism and Religion

Many clergymen regarded the theory of evolution as a threat to the infallibility of the Bible. Darwinism attacked the traditional belief that some six thousand years ago God had created all animal and plant species and had given each one a permanent form; evolution seemed to relegate Adam and Eve to the realm of myth. The conflict between fundamentalists — those who believed in a literal interpretation of the Bible — and advocates of the new biology was marked by bitter acrimony. In time, however, many Christians reconciled the theory of evolution and the biblical account of creation. They maintained that God directed the evolutionary process and that the timespan of six days for creation given in Genesis is not meant to be taken literally.

In the early seventeenth century, Galileo (see Chapter 1) had insisted that on questions concerning nature, scientists should not turn to the Bible as an authority, but should rely on the evidence of observation and experiments. The controversy over evolution reaffirmed this conviction for the scientific community, which more than ever saw the scientific method as the incontestable authority for interpreting nature. The theory of evolution also contributed to a growing secularism. The central doctrine of Christianity — that human beings were created by God and that salvation was the ultimate aim of life — rested more than ever on faith rather than on reason.

ANDREW D. WHITE

A History of the Warfare of Science with Theology

In the following passage, Andrew D. White (1832–1918), scholar, diplomat, and president of Cornell University in Ithaca, New York, described the controversy that raged over the publication of *The Origin of Species* and *The Descent of Man*. A founder of Cornell, White himself came under attack by clergy who feared that the new institution of higher learning would teach "atheism" and "infidelity."

Darwin's *Origin of Species* had come into the theological world like a plough into an ant-hill. Everywhere those thus rudely awakened from their old comfort and repose had swarmed forth angry and confused. Reviews, sermons, books light and heavy, came flying at the new thinker from all sides.

The keynote was struck at once in the *Quarterly Review* by Wilberforce, Bishop of Oxford. He declared that Darwin was guilty of "a tendency to limit God's glory in creation"; that "the principle of natural selection is absolutely incompatible with the word of God"; that it "contradicts the revealed relations of creation to its Creator"; that it is "inconsistent with the fulness of his glory"; that it is "a dishonouring view of Nature"; and that there is "a simpler explanation of the presence of these strange forms among the works of God": that explanation being — "the fall of Adam." Nor did the bishop's efforts end here; at the meeting of the British Association for the Advancement of Science he again disported himself in the tide of popular applause. Referring to the ideas of Darwin, who was absent on account of illness, he congratulated himself in a public speech that he was not descended from a monkey. The reply came from Huxley,[1] who said in substance: "If I had to choose, I would prefer to be a descendant of a humble monkey rather than of a man who employs his knowledge and eloquence in misrepresenting those who are wearing out their lives in the search for truth."

This shot reverberated through Eng-

---

[1] Thomas Henry Huxley (1825–1895) was an English biologist and a staunch defender of Darwin.

land, and indeed through other countries.

The utterances of this the most brilliant prelate of the Anglican Church received a sort of antiphonal response from the leaders of the English Catholics. . . . Cardinal Manning declared his abhorrence of the new view of Nature, and described it as "a brutal philosophy — to wit, there is no God, and the ape is our Adam."

These attacks from such eminent sources set the clerical fashion for several years. . . . Another distinguished clergyman, vice-president of a Protestant institute to combat "dangerous" science, declared Darwinism "an attempt to dethrone God." . . . Another spoke of Darwin's views as suggesting that "God is dead," and declared that Darwin's work "does open violence to everything which the Creator himself has told us in the Scriptures of the methods and results of his work." Still another theological authority asserted: "If the Darwinian theory is true, Genesis is a lie, the whole framework of the book of life falls to pieces, and the revelation of God to man, as we Christians know it, is a delusion and a snare." Another, who had shown excellent qualities as an observing naturalist, declared the Darwinian view "a huge imposture from the beginning."

Echoes came from America. One review . . . denounced Darwin's views as "infidelity"; another, representing the American branch of the Anglican Church. . . . plunged into an exceedingly dangerous line of argument in the following words: "If this hypothesis be true, then is the Bible an unbearable fiction; . . . then have Christians for nearly two thousand years been duped by a monstrous lie. . . . Darwin requires us to disbelieve the authoritative word of the Creator." . . .

Nor was the older branch of the Church to be left behind in this chorus. Bayma, in the *Catholic World*, declared, "Mr. Darwin is, we have reason to believe, the mouthpiece or chief trumpeter of that infidel clique whose well-known object is to do away with all idea of a God."

Worthy of especial note as showing the determination of the theological side at that period was the foundation of sacro-scientific organizations to combat the new ideas. First to be noted is the "Academia," planned by Cardinal Wiseman. In a circular letter the cardinal, usually so moderate and just, sounded an alarm and summed up by saying, "Now it is for the Church, which alone possesses divine certainty and divine discernment, to place itself at once in the front of a movement which threatens even the fragmentary remains of Christian belief in England." The necessary permission was obtained from Rome, the Academia was founded. . . . A similar effort was seen in Protestant quarters; the "Victoria Institute" was created, and perhaps the most noted utterance which ever came from it was the declaration of its vice-president, the Rev. Walter Mitchell, that "Darwinism endeavours to dethrone God."

In France the attack was even more violent. Fabre d'Envieu brought out the heavy artillery of theology, and in a long series of elaborate propositions demonstrated that any other doctrine than that of the fixity and persistence of species is absolutely contrary to Scripture. . . .

In Germany . . . Catholic theologians vied with Protestants in bitterness. Prof. Michelis declared Darwin's theory "a caricature of creation." Dr. Hagermann asserted that it "turned the Creator out of doors." Dr. Schund insisted that "every idea of the Holy Scriptures, from the first to the last page, stands in diametrical opposition to the Darwinian theory"; and, "if Darwin be right in his view of the development of man out of a brutal condition, then the Bible teaching in regard to man is utterly annihilated." Rougemont in Switzerland called for a crusade against the obnoxious doctrine. Luthardt, Professor of Theology at Leipsic, declared: "The idea of creation belongs to religion and not to natural science; the whole superstructure of personal religion is built upon the doctrine of creation"; and he showed the evolution theory to be in direct contradiction to Holy Writ. . . .

In 1871 was published Darwin's *Descent of Man*. Its doctrine had been anticipated by critics of his previous books, but it made, none the less, a great stir; again the opposing army trooped forth, though evidently with much less heart than before. A few were very violent. The *Dublin University Magazine*, . . . charged Mr. Darwin with . . . being "resolved to hunt God out of the world." . . .

From America there came new echoes. . . . The Rev. Dr. Hodge, of Princeton . . . denounced it as thoroughly "atheistic"; he insisted that Christians "have a right to protest against the arraying of probabilities against the clear evidence of the Scriptures"; . . . and declared that the Darwinian theory of natural selection is "utterly inconsistent with the Scriptures," and that "an absent God, who does nothing, is to us no God"; that "to ignore design as manifested in God's creation is to dethrone God"; that "a denial of design in Nature is virtually a denial of God." . . .

Fortunately, at about the time when Darwin's *Descent of Man* was published, there had come into Princeton University a Dr. James McCosh. Called to the presidency, he at once took his stand against teachings so dangerous to Christianity as those of Drs. Hodge, Duffield, and their associates. . . . He saw that the most dangerous thing which could be done to Christianity at Princeton was to reiterate in the university pulpit, week after week, solemn declarations that if evolution by natural selection, or indeed evolution at all, be true, the Scriptures are false. He tells us that he saw that this was the certain way to make the students unbelievers; he therefore not only checked this dangerous preaching but preached an opposite doctrine. With him began the inevitable compromise, and, in spite of mutterings against him as a Darwinian, he carried the day. Whatever may be thought of his general system of philosophy, no one can deny his great service in neutralizing the teachings of his predecessors and colleagues — so dangerous to all that is essential in Christianity.

Other divines of strong sense in other parts of the country began to take similar ground — namely, that men could be Christians and at the same time Darwinians. . . .

In view of the proofs accumulating in favour of the new evolutionary hypothesis, the change in the tone of controlling theologians was now rapid. From all sides came evidences of desire to compromise with the theory. . . .

Whatever additional factors may be added to natural selection — and Darwin himself fully admitted that there might be others — the theory of an evolution process in the formation of the universe and of animated nature is established, and the old theory of direct creation is gone forever. In place of it science has given us conceptions far more noble, and opened the way to an argument for design infinitely more beautiful than any ever developed by theology.

Review Questions

1. For what reasons did the clergy denounce Charles Darwin's theories?

2. Darwin and the clergy who attacked his theories perceived truth differently. Discuss this statement.

4 | The Futility of Reason and the Power of the Will

The outlook of the Enlightenment, which stressed science, political freedom, the rational reform of society, and the certainty of progress, was the dominant intellectual current in the late nineteenth century. However, in the closing decades of the century, several thinkers challenged and rejected the Enlightenment outlook. In particular, they maintained that people are not fundamentally rational, that below surface rationality lie impulses, instincts, and drives that constitute a deeper reality.

A powerful attack on the rational-scientific tradition of the Enlightenment came from Fyodor Dostoyevsky (1821–1881), a Russian novelist and essayist whose masterpieces include *Crime and Punishment* (1866), *The Idiot* (1868), and *The Brothers Karamazov* (1879–1880).

FYODOR DOSTOYEVSKY
Notes from the Underground

In *Notes from the Underground* (1864), Dostoyevsky attacked thinkers who enshrined reason and science and believed that scientific laws govern human behavior. He rejected the notion that once these laws were understood, people could create (as socialists in fact tried to do) utopian communities in which society would be rationally planned and organized to promote human betterment. The narrator in the novel, called the Underground Man, rebels against the efforts of rationalists, positivists, liberals, and socialists to define human nature according to universal principles and to reform society so as to promote greater happiness and security. For the Underground Man, there are no objective truths; there are only individuals with subjective desires and unpredictable, irrepressible wills.

Dostoyevsky maintained that human beings cannot be defined by reason alone — human nature is too dynamic, too diversified, too volcanic to be schematized and programmed by the theoretical mind. He urged a new definition of human beings, one that would affirm each person's individuality and subjectivity and encompass the total personality — feelings and will as well as reason.

In the first part of *Notes from the Underground*, the Underground Man addresses an imaginery audience. In a long monologue, he expresses a revulsion for the rationalist's assertion that with increased enlightenment, people would "become good and noble"; they would realize that it was to their advantage to pursue "prosperity, wealth, [political] freedom, peace." The Underground Man retorts that the individual's principal concern is not happiness or security but a free and unfettered will.

. . . Oh, tell me, who first declared, who first proclaimed, that man only does nasty things because he does not know his own real interests; and that if he were enlightened, if his eyes were opened to his real normal interests, man would at once cease to do nasty things, would at once become good and noble because, being enlightened and understanding his real advantage, he would see his own advantage in the good and nothing else, and we all know that not a single man can knowingly act to his own disadvantage. Consequently, so to say, he would begin doing good through necessity. Oh, the babe! Oh, the pure, innocent child! Why, in the first place, when in all these thousands of years has there ever been a time when man has acted only for his own advantage? What is to be done with the millions of facts that bear witness that men, *knowingly*, that is, fully understanding their real advantages, have left them in the background and have rushed headlong on another path, to risk, to chance, compelled to this course by nobody and by nothing, but, as it were, precisely because they did not want the beaten track, and stubbornly, wilfully, went off on another difficult, absurd way seeking it almost in the darkness. After all, it means that this stubbornness and willfulness were more pleasant to them than any advantage. Advantage! What is advantage? And will you take it upon yourself to define with perfect accuracy in exactly what the advantage of man consists of? And what if it so happens that a man's advantage *sometimes* not only may, but even must, consist exactly in his desiring under certain conditions what is harmful to himself and not what is advantageous. . . . After all, you, [imaginary] gentlemen, so far as I know, have taken your whole register of human advantages from the average of statistical figures and scientific-economic formulas. After all, your advantages are prosperity, wealth, freedom, peace — and so on, and so on. So that a man who, for instance, would openly and knowingly oppose that whole list would, to your thinking, and indeed to mine too, of course, be an obscurantist or an absolute madman, would he not? But, after all, here is something amazing: why does it happen that all these statisticians, sages and lovers of humanity, when they calculate human advantages invariably leave one out? . . .

. . . The fact is, gentlemen, it seems that something that is dearer to almost every man than his greatest advantages must really exist, or (not to be illogical) there is one most advantageous advantage (the very one omitted of which we

spoke just now) which is more important and more advantageous than all other advantages, for which, if necessary, a man is ready to act in opposition to all laws, that is, in opposition to reason, honor, peace, prosperity — in short, in opposition to all those wonderful and useful things if only he can attain that fundamental, most advantageous advantage which is dearer to him than all. . . .

. . . Why, one may choose what is contrary to one's own interests, and sometimes one *positively ought* (that is my idea). One's own free unfettered choice, one's own fancy, however wild it may be, one's own fancy worked up at times to frenzy — why that is that very "most advantageous advantage" which we have overlooked, which comes under no classification and through which all systems and theories are continually being sent to the devil. And how do these sages know that man must necessarily need a rationally advantageous choice? What man needs is simply *independent* choice, whatever that independence may cost and wherever it may lead. Well, choice, after all, the devil only knows. . . .

---•—•·•—•---

Life is more than reasoning, more than "simply extracting square roots," declares the Underground Man. The will, which is "a manifestation of all life," is more precious than reason. Simply to have their own way, human beings will do something stupid, self-destructive, irrational. Reason constitutes only a small part of the human personality.

---•—•·•—•---

. . . You see, gentlemen, reason, gentlemen, is an excellent thing, there is no disputing that, but reason is only reason and can only satisfy man's rational faculty, while will is a manifestation of all life, that is, of all human life including reason as well as all impulses. And although our life, in this manifestation of it, is often worthless, yet it is life nevertheless and not simply extracting square roots. After all, here I, for instance, quite naturally want to live, in order to satisfy all my faculties for life, and not simply my rational faculty, that is, not simply one-twentieth of all my faculties for life. What does reason know? Reason only knows what it has succeeded in learning (some things it will perhaps never learn; while this is nevertheless no comfort, why not say so frankly?) and human nature acts as a whole, with everything that is in it, consciously or unconsciously, and, even if it goes wrong, it lives. I suspect, gentlemen, that you are looking at me with compassion; you repeat to me that an enlightened and developed man, such, in short, as the future man will be, cannot knowingly desire anything disadvantageous to himself, that this can be proved mathematically. I thoroughly agree, it really can — by mathematics. But I repeat for the hundredth time, there is one case, one only, when man may purposely, consciously, desire what is injurious to himself, what is stupid, very stupid — simply in order *to have the right* to desire for himself even what is very stupid and not to be bound by an obligation to desire only what is rational. After all, this very stupid thing, after all, this caprice of ours, may really be more advantageous for us, gentlemen, than anything else on earth, especially in some cases. And in particular it may be more advantageous than any advantages even when it does us obvious harm, and contradicts the soundest conclusions of our reason about our advantage — because in any case it preserves for us what is most precious and most important — that is, our personality, our individuality. Some, you see, maintain that this really is the most precious thing for man; desire can, of course, if it desires, be in agreement with reason; particularly if it does not abuse this practice but does so in moderation, it is both useful and sometimes even praiseworthy. But very often, and even most often, desire completely and stubbornly opposes reason, and . . . and . . . and do you know that that, too, is useful and sometimes even praiseworthy?

To intellectuals who want to "cure men of their old habits and reform their will in accordance with science and common sense," the Underground Man asks: Is it possible or even desirable to reform men? Perhaps they prefer uncertainty and caprice, chaos and destruction, or just living in their own way. How else do they preserve their uniqueness?

. . . In short, one may say anything about the history of the world — anything that might enter the most disordered imagination. The only thing one cannot say is that it is rational. The very word sticks in one's throat. And, indeed, this is even the kind of thing that continually happens. After all, there are continually turning up in life moral and rational people, sages, and lovers of humanity, who make it their goal for life to live as morally and rationally as possible, to be, so to speak, a light to their neighbors, simply in order to show them that it is really possible to live morally and rationally in this world. And so what? We all know that those very people sooner or later toward the end of their lives have been false to themselves, playing some trick, often a most indecent one. Now I ask you: What can one expect from man since he is a creature endowed with such strange qualities? Shower upon him every earthly blessing, drown him in bliss so that nothing but bubbles would dance on the surface of his bliss, as on a sea; give him such economic prosperity that he would have nothing else to do but sleep, eat cakes and busy himself with ensuring the continuation of world history and even then man, out of sheer ingratitude, sheer libel, would play you some loathsome trick. He would even risk his cakes and would deliberately desire the most fatal rubbish, the most uneconomical absurdity, simply to introduce into all this positive rationality his fatal fantastic element. It is just his fantastic dreams, his vulgar folly, that he will desire to retain, simply in order to prove to himself (as though that were so necessary) that men still are men and not piano keys, which even if played by the laws of nature themselves threaten to be controlled so completely that soon one will be able to desire nothing but by the calendar. And, after all, that is not all: even if man really were nothing but a piano key, even if this were proved to him by natural science and mathematics, even then he would not become reasonable, but would purposely do something perverse out of sheer ingratitude, simply to have his own way. And if he does not find any means he will devise destruction and chaos, will devise sufferings of all sorts, and will thereby have his own way. He will launch a curse upon the world, and, as only man can curse (it is his privilege, the primary distinction between him and other animals) then, after all, perhaps only by his curse will he attain his object, that is, really convince himself that he is a man and not a piano key! If you say that all this, too, can be calculated and tabulated, chaos and darkness and curses, so that the mere possibility of calculating it all beforehand would stop it all, and reason would reassert itself — then man would purposely go mad in order to be rid of reason and have his own way! I believe in that, I vouch for it, because, after all, the whole work of man seems really to consist in nothing but proving to himself continually that he is a man and not an organ stop. It may be at the cost of his skin! But he has proved it; he may become a caveman, but he will have proved it. And after that can one help sinning, rejoicing that it has not yet come, and that desire still depends on the devil knows what! . . .

. . . Gentlemen, I am tormented by questions; answer them for me. Now you, for instance, want to cure men of their old habits and reform their will in accordance with science and common sense. But how do you know, not only that it is possible, but also that it is *desirable*, to reform man in that way? And what leads you to the conclusion that it is so *necessary* to reform man's desires? In short, how do you know that such a reformation will really be advantageous to man? And go to the heart of the matter, why are you *so sure* of your conviction that not to act against his real normal advantages guaranteed by the conclusions of reason and arithmetic is always advantageous for man and must be a law for all mankind? . . .

And why are you so firmly, so triumphantly convinced that only the normal and the positive — in short, only prosperity — is to the advantage of man? Is not reason mistaken about advantage? After all, perhaps man likes something besides prosperity? Perhaps he likes suffering just as much? Perhaps suffering is just as great an advantage to him as prosperity? Man is sometimes fearfully, passionately in love with suffering and that is a fact. There is no need to appeal to universal history to prove that; only ask yourself, if only you are a man and have lived at all. As far as my own personal opinion is concerned, to care only for prosperity seems to me somehow even ill-bred. Whether it's good or bad, it is sometimes very pleasant to smash things, too. After all, I do not really insist on suffering or on prosperity either. I insist on my caprice, and its being guaranteed to me when necessary. Suffering would be out of place in vaudevilles, for instance; I know that. In the crystal palace it is even unthinkable; suffering means doubt, means negation, and what would be the good of a crystal palace if there could be any doubt about it? And yet I am sure man will never renounce real suffering, that is, destruction and chaos.

Review Questions

1. Why did Fyodor Dostoyevsky believe that people will act in opposition to their own interest?

2. How did Dostoyevsky regard intellectuals who sought to "cure men of their old habits and reform their will in accordance with science and common sense"?

3. What did Dostoyevsky mean when he said that "the whole work of man seems really to consist in nothing but proving to himself continually that he is a man and not an organ stop"?

4. What role did reason play in Dostoyevsky's view of human nature and society?

5 | The Overman and the Will to Power

Few modern thinkers have aroused more controversy than the German philosopher Friedrich Nietzsche (1844–1900). Although scholars pay tribute to Nietzsche's originality and genius, they are often in sharp disagreement over the meaning and influence of his work. Nietzsche was a relentless critic of modern society. He attacked democracy, universal suffrage, equality, and socialism for suppressing a higher type of human existence. Nietzsche was also critical of the Western rational tradition. The theoretical outlook, the excessive intellectualizing of philosophers, he said, smothers the will, thereby stifling creativity and nobility; reason also falsifies life through the claim that it allows apprehension of universal truth. Nietzsche was not opposed to the critical use of the intellect, but like the romantics, he focused on the immense vitality of the emotions. He also held that life is a senseless flux devoid of any overarching purpose. There are no moral values revealed by God. Indeed, Nietzsche proclaimed that God is dead. Nor are values and certainties woven into the fabric of nature that can be apprehended by reason — the "natural rights of man," for example. All the values taught by Christian and bourgeois thinkers are without foundation, said Nietzsche. There is only naked man living in a godless and absurd world.

Nietzsche called for the emergence of the *overman,* a higher type of man who asserts his will, gives order to chaotic passions, makes great demands on himself, and lives life with a fierce joy. The overman aspires to self-perfection. Without fear or guilt, he creates his own values and defines his own life. In this way, he overcomes nihilism — the belief that there is nothing of ultimate value. It is such rare individuals, the highest specimens of humanity, that concern Nietzsche, not the herdlike masses.

The overman grasps the central reality of human existence — that people instinctively, uncompromisingly, ceaselessly strive for power. The will to power is the determining factor in domestic politics and international affairs. Life is a contest in which the enhancement of power is the ultimate purpose of our actions; it brings supreme enjoyment: "the love of power is the demon of men. Let them have everything — health, food, a place to live, entertainment — they are and remain unhappy and low-spirited: for the demon waits and waits and will be satisfied. Take everything from them and satisfy this and they are almost happy — as happy as men and demons can be."

FRIEDRICH NIETZSCHE

The Birth of Tragedy, the Will to Power, and the Antichrist

Three of Nietzsche's works are represented in the following readings: *The Birth of Tragedy, The Will to Power,* and *The Antichrist.* In *The Birth of Tragedy* (1872), his first major work, Nietzsche offered an unconventional interpretation of ancient Greek culture. Traditionally, scholars and philosophes had lauded the Greeks for their rationality — for conceiving scientific and philosophic thought and for aspiring to balance, harmony, and moderation both in the arts and in ethics. Nietzsche chose to emphasize the emotional roots of Greek culture — the Dionysian spirit that springs from the soil of myth and ritual, passion and frenzy, instinct and intuition, heroism and suffering. He maintained that this Dionysian spirit, rooted in the nonrational, was the source of Greek creativity in art and drama.

In the following excerpt from *The Birth of Tragedy,* Nietzsche attributed to Socrates the rise of scientific thought, which aspires to separate truth from myth, illusion, and error. He said that this scientific outlook, which began essentially with Socrates and achieved its height in the ancient world in Alexandria, has become the basis of modern culture. Modern westerners admire the theoretical man and not the man of instinct and action. But he said in modern times that doubts have arisen about science's claim to the attainment of certainty. Westerners are beginning to recognize the limitations of reason and to appreciate the creative potential inherent in the nonrational side of human nature.

The Birth of Tragedy

Once we have fully realized how, after Socrates, the mystagogue of science, one school of philosophers after another came upon the scene and departed; how generation after generation of inquirers, spurred by an insatiable thirst for knowledge, explored every aspect of the universe; and how by that ecumenical concern a common net of knowledge was spread over the whole globe, affording glimpses into the workings of an entire solar system — once we have realized all this, and the monumental pyramid of present-day knowledge, we cannot help viewing Socrates as the vortex and turning point of Western civilization. . . .

. . . Socrates represents the archetype of the theoretical optimist, who, strong in the belief that nature can be fathomed, considers knowledge to be the true panacea and error to be radical evil. To Socratic man the one noble and truly human occupation was that of laying bare the workings of nature, of separating true knowledge from illusion and error. So it happened that ever since Socrates the mechanism of concepts, judgments, and syllogisms has come to be regarded as the highest exercise of man's powers, nature's most admirable gift. Socrates and his successors, down to our own day, have considered all moral and sentimental accomplishments — noble deeds, compassion, self-sacrifice, heroism, even that spiritual calm, so difficult of attainment, which the Apollonian[1] Greek called *sophrosyne* — to be ultimately derived from the dialectic of knowledge, and therefore teachable. Whoever has tasted the delight of a Socratic perception, experienced how it moves to encompass the

---

[1] *Apollonian* derives from Apollo — the Greek god of sunlight, prophecy, music, and poetry — and refers to calm, measured, balanced form. Nietzsche opposes the term to *Dionysian.*

whole world of phenomena in ever widening circles, knows no sharper incentive
to life than his desire to complete the conquest, to weave the net absolutely
tight. . . .

Our whole modern world is caught in
the net of Alexandrian culture and recognizes as its ideal the man of theory,
equipped with the highest cognitive powers, working in the service of science, and
whose archetype and progenitor is Socrates. All our pedagogic devices are oriented toward this ideal. Any type of existence that deviates from this model has
a hard struggle and lives, at best, on suf-
ferance. It is a rather frightening thought
that for centuries the only form of educated man to be found was the scholar.
Even our literary arts have been forced to
develop out of learned imitations, and the
important role rhyme plays in our poetry
still betokens the derivation of our poetic
forms from artificial experiments with a
language not vernacular but properly
learned. To any true Greek, that product
of modern culture, *Faust*,[2] would have
seemed quite unintelligible, though we
ourselves understand it well enough. We
have only to place Faust, who storms un-
satisfied through all the provinces of
knowledge and is driven to make a bar-
gain with the powers of darkness, beside
Socrates in order to realize that modern
man has begun to be aware of the limits
of Socratic curiosity and to long, in the
wide, waste ocean of knowledge, for a
shore. Goethe once said to Eckermann,
referring to Napoleon: "Yes indeed, my
friend, there is also a productivity of actions." This *aperçu* [insight] suggests that
for us moderns the man of action is something amazing and incredible, so that the
wisdom of a Goethe was needed to find

such a strange mode of existence compre-
hensible, even excusable.

We should acknowledge, then, that
Socratic culture is rooted in an optimism
which believes itself omnipotent. . . .

The blight which threatens theoretical
culture has only begun to frighten modern man, and he is groping uneasily for
remedies out of the storehouse of his experience, without having any real conviction that these remedies will prevail against
disaster. In the meantime, there have
arisen certain men of genius who, with
admirable circumspection and consequence, have used the arsenal of science
to demonstrate the limitations of science
and of the cognitive faculty itself. They
have authoritatively rejected science's claim
to universal validity and to the attainment
of universal goals and exploded for the
first time the belief that man may plumb
the universe by means of the law of causa-
tion. The extraordinary courage and
wisdom of Kant and Schopenhauer[3] have
won the most difficult victory, that over
the optimistic foundations of logic, which
form the underpinnings of our culture.
Whereas the current optimism had treated
the universe as knowable, in the presumption of eternal truths, and space,
time, and causality as absolute and universally valid laws, Kant showed how these
supposed laws serve only to raise appearance . . . to the status of true reality,
thereby rendering impossible a genuine
understanding of that reality: in the words
of Schopenhauer, binding the dreamer
even faster in sleep. . . .

. . . Socratic culture has been shaken
and has begun to doubt its own infallibility. . . . The man of theory, having be-

[2] *Faust* is a play written by Johann Goethe (1749–1832), often considered Germany's greatest writer. In the play, Dr. Faustus, a man of learning, determines that reason cannot solve the mysteries of the universe. Seeking to experience life fully, Faust enters into a pact with the devil.

[3] Immanuel Kant (1724–1804), a German philosopher, held that scientific knowledge is based on appearances (phenomena) and that absolute knowledge of reality is unattainable. Arthur Schopenhauer (1788–1860), another German philosopher, declared that beneath the conscious intellect is the will, a striving, demanding force that is the real basis of human behavior.

gun to dread the consequences of his views, no longer dares commit himself freely to the icy flood of existence but runs nervously up and down the bank.

———————————◆•◆—————————————

First published in 1901, one year after Nietzsche's death, The Will to Power *consists of the author's notes written in the years 1883 to 1888. The following passages from this work show Nietzsche's contempt for democracy and socialism and proclaim the will to power.*

———————————◆•◆—————————————

The Will to Power

720 (1886–1887)

The most fearful and fundamental desire in man, his drive for power — this drive is called "freedom"— must be held in check the longest. This is why ethics . . . has hitherto aimed at holding the desire for power in check: it disparages the tyrannical individual and with its glorification of social welfare and patriotism emphasizes the power-instinct of the herd.

728 (March–June 1888)

. . . A society that definitely and *instinctively* gives up war and conquest is in decline: it is ripe for democracy and the rule of shopkeepers — In most cases, to be sure, assurances of peace are merely narcotics.

751 (March–June 1888)

"The will to power" is so hated in democratic ages that their entire psychology seems directed toward belittling and defaming it. . . .

752 (1884)

. . . Democracy represents the disbelief in great human beings and an elite society: "Everyone is equal to everyone else." "At bottom we are one and all self-seeking cattle and mob."

753 (1885)

I am opposed to 1. socialism, because it dreams quite naively of "the good, true, and beautiful" and of "equal rights" (—

anarchism also desires the same ideal, but in a more brutal fashion);

2. parliamentary government and the press, because these are the means by which the herd animal becomes master.

762 (1885)

European democracy represents a release of forces only to a very small degree. It is above all a release of laziness, of weariness, of *weakness*.

765 (Jan.–Fall 1888)

. . . Another Christian concept, no less crazy, has passed even more deeply into the tissue of modernity: the concept of the "equality of souls before God." This concept furnishes the prototype of all theories of equal rights: mankind was first taught to stammer the proposition of equality in a religious context, and only later was it made into morality: no wonder that man ended by taking it seriously, taking it practically! — that is to say, politically, democratically, socialistically, in the spirit of the pessimism of indignation.

854 (1884)

In the age of *suffrage universel*, i.e., when everyone may sit in judgment on everyone and everything, I feel impelled to reestablish *order of rank*.

855 (Spring–Fall 1887)

What determines rank, sets off rank, is only quanta of power, and nothing else.

857 (Jan.–Fall 1888)

I distinguish between a type of ascending life and another type of decay, disintegration, weakness. Is it credible that the question of the relative rank of these two types still needs to be posed?

858 (Nov. 1887–March 1888)

What determines your rank is the quantum of power you are: the rest is cowardice.

861 (1884)

A declaration of war on the masses by *higher men* is needed! Everywhere the mediocre are combining in order to make themselves master! Everything that makes soft and effeminate, that serves the ends of the "people" or the "feminine," works in favor of *suffrage universel*, i.e., the dominion of *inferior* men. But we should take reprisal and bring this whole affair (which in Europe commenced with Christianity) to light and to the bar of judgment.

862 (1884)

A doctrine is needed powerful enough to work as a breeding agent: strengthening the strong, paralyzing and destructive for the world-weary.

The annihilation of the decaying races. Decay of Europe. — The annihilation of slavish evaluations. — Dominion over the earth as a means of producing a higher type. — The annihilation of the tartuffery [hypocrisy] called "morality." . . . The annihilation of *suffrage universel;* i.e., the system through which the lowest natures prescribe themselves as laws for the higher. — The annihilation of mediocrity and its acceptance. (The onesided, individuals — peoples; to strive for fullness of nature through the pairing of opposites: race mixture to this end). — The new courage — no *a priori* [innate and universal] truths (such truths were sought by those accustomed to faith!), but a *free* subordination to a ruling idea that has its time: e.g., time as a property of space, etc.

870 (1884)

The root of all evil: that the slavish morality of meekness, chastity, selflessness, absolute obedience, has triumphed — ruling natures were thus condemned (1) to hypocrisy, (2) to torments of conscience — creative natures felt like rebels against God, uncertain and inhibited by eternal values. . . .

In summa: the best things have been slandered because the weak or the immoderate swine have cast a bad light on them — and the best men have remained hidden — and have often misunderstood themselves.

874 (1884)

The degeneration of the rulers and the ruling classes has been the cause of the greatest mischief in history! Without the Roman Caesars and Roman society, the insanity of Christianity would never have come to power.

When lesser men begin to doubt whether higher men exist, then the danger is great! And one ends by discovering that there is *virtue* also among the lowly and subjugated, the poor in spirit, and that *before God* men are equal — which has so far been the . . . [height] of nonsense on earth! For ultimately, the higher men measured themselves according to the standard of virtue of slaves — found they were "proud," etc., found all their higher qualities reprehensible.

997 (1884)

I teach: that there are higher and lower men, and that a single individual can under certain circumstances justify the existence of whole millennia — that is, a full, rich, great, whole human being in relation to countless incomplete fragmentary men.

998 (1884)

The highest men live beyond the rulers, freed from all bonds; and in the rulers they have their instruments.

999 (1884)

Order of rank: He who *determines* values and directs the will of millenia by giving direction to the highest natures is the *highest* man.

1001 (1884)

Not "mankind" but *overman* is the goal!

1067 (1885)

. . . *This world is the will to power — and nothing besides!* And you yourselves are also this will to power — and nothing besides!

———— •••• ————

Nietzsche regarded Christianity as a life-denying religion that appeals to the masses. Fear-

ful and resentful of their betters, he said, the masses espouse a faith that preaches equality and compassion. He maintained that Christianity has "waged a war to the death against (the) higher type of man." The following passages are from The Antichrist *written in 1888.*

The Antichrist

2. What is good? — All that heightens the feeling of power, the will to power, power itself in man.

What is bad? — All that proceeds from weakness.

What is happiness? — The feeling that power *increases* — that a resistance is overcome.

Not contentment, but more power; *not* peace at all, but war; *not* virtue, but proficiency (virtue in the Renaissance style, *virtù,* virtue free of moralic acid).

The weak and ill-constituted shall perish: first principle of *our* philanthropy. And one shall help them to do so.

What is more harmful than any vice? — Active sympathy for the ill-constituted and weak — Christianity. . . .

3. The problem I raise here is not what ought to succeed mankind in the sequence of species (— the human being is an *end* —): but what type of human being one ought to *breed,* ought to *will,* as more valuable, more worthy of life, more certain of the future.

This more valuable type has existed often enough already: but as a lucky accident, as an exception, never as *willed. He* has rather been the most feared, he has hitherto been virtually *the* thing to be feared — and out of fear the reverse type has been willed, bred, *achieved:* the domestic animal, the herd animal, the sick animal man — the Christian. . . .

5. One should not embellish or dress up Christianity: it has waged *a war to the death* against this *higher* type of man, it has excommunicated all the fundamental instincts of this type, it has distilled evil, the *Evil One,* out of these instincts — the strong human being as the type of reprehensi-

bility, as the "outcast." Christianity has taken the side of everything weak, base, ill-constituted, it has made an ideal out of *opposition* to the preservative instincts of strong life; it has depraved the reason even of the intellectually strongest natures by teaching men to feel the supreme values of intellectuality as sinful, as misleading, as *temptations.* The most deplorable example: the depraving of Pascal,[1] who believed his reason had been depraved by original sin while it had only been depraved by his Christianity!

6. . . . Christianity is a revolt of everything that crawls along the ground directed against that which is elevated. . . .

7. Christianity is called the religion of *pity.* — Pity stands in antithesis to the tonic emotions which enhance the energy of the feeling of life: it has a depressive effect. One loses force when one pities. . . .

15. In Christianity neither morality nor religion come into contact with reality at any point. Nothing but imaginary *causes* ("God," "soul," "ego," "spirit," "free will" — or "unfree will"): nothing but imaginary *effects* ("sin," "redemption," "grace," "punishment," "forgiveness of sins"). . . .

18. The Christian conception of God — God as God of the sick, God as spider, God as spirit — is one of the most corrupt conceptions of God arrived at on earth: perhaps it even represents the low-water mark in the descending development of the God type. God degenerated to the *contradiction of life,* instead of being its transfiguration and eternal *Yes!* In God a declaration of hostility towards life, nature, the will to life! God the formula for every calumny of "this world," for every lie about 'the next world'! In God nothingness deified, the will to nothingness sanctified! . . .

21. In Christianity the instincts of the subjugated and oppressed come into the

---

[1] Blaise Pascal (1623–1662) was a French mathematician, philosopher, and eloquent defender of the Christian faith.

foreground: it is the lowest classes which seek their salvation in it. . . .

43. The poison of the doctrine *"equal rights for all"* — this has been more thoroughly sowed by Christianity than by anything else; from the most secret recesses of base instincts, Christianity has waged a war to the death against every feeling of reverence and distance between man and man, against, that is, the *precondition* of every elevation, every increase in culture — it has forged out of the *ressentiment* of the masses its *chief weapon* against *us,* against everything noble, joyful, high-spirited on earth, against our happiness on earth. . . . "Immortality" granted to every Peter and Paul has been the greatest and most malicious outrage on *noble* mankind ever committed. — *And* let us not underestimate the fatality that has

crept out of Christianity even into politics! No one any longer possesses today the courage to claim special privileges or the right to rule, the courage to feel a sense of reverence towards himself and towards his equals — the courage for a *pathos of distance.* . . . Our politics is *morbid* from this lack of courage! — The aristocratic outlook has been undermined most deeply by the lie of equality of souls; and if the belief in the "prerogative of the majority" makes revolutions and *will continue to make them* — it is Christianity, let there be no doubt about it, *Christian* value judgement which translates every revolution into mere blood and crime! Christianity is a revolt of everything that crawls along the ground directed against that which is *elevated:* the Gospel of the "lowly" *makes* low. . . .

Review Questions

1. Why did Friedrich Nietzsche criticize Socrates?

2. According to Nietzsche, how was "Socratic culture" undermined in the nineteenth century?

3. What did Nietzsche consider to be a human being's most elemental desire?

4. Why did Nietzsche attack democracy and socialism? How do you respond to his attack?

5. What were Nietzsche's criticisms of Christianity? How do you respond to this attack?

6. How does Nietzsche's philosophy stand in relation to the Enlightenment?

6 | The Unconscious

After graduating from medical school in Vienna, Sigmund Freud (1856–1939), the founder of psychoanalysis, specialized in the treatment of nervous disorders. By encouraging his patients to speak to him about their troubles, Freud was able to probe deeper into their minds. These investigations led him to conclude that childhood fears and experiences, often sexual in nature, accounted for neuroses — hysteria, anxiety, depression, obsessions, and so on. So threatening and painful were these childhood emotions and experiences that his patients banished them from conscious memory to the realm of the unconscious. To understand and treat neurotic behavior, Freud said, it is necessary to look behind overt symptoms and bring to the surface emotionally charged experiences and fears — childhood traumas — that lie buried in the unconscious. Freud probed the unconscious by urging his patients to say whatever came to their minds. This procedure, called free association, rests on the premise that spontaneous and uninhibited talk reveals a person's underlying preoccupations, his or her inner world. A second avenue to the unconscious is the analysis of dreams; an individual's dreams, said Freud, reveal his or her secret wishes.

SIGMUND FREUD

The Unconscious, Psychoanalysis, and Civilization and Its Discontents

Readings from these three works of Freud are included: *A Note on the Unconscious in Psychoanalysis, Five Lectures on Psychoanalysis,* and *Civilization and Its Discontents.* Freud's scientific investigation of psychic development led him to conclude that powerful mental processes hidden from consciousness govern human behavior more than reason does. His exploration of the unconscious produced a new image of the human being that has had a profound impact on twentieth-century thought. In the following excerpt from *A Note on the Unconscious in Psychoanalysis* (1912), Freud defined the term *unconscious.*

A Note on the Unconscious in Psychoanalysis

I wish to expound in a few words and as plainly as possible what the term 'unconscious' has come to mean in psychoanalysis and in psychoanalysis alone. . . .

. . . The well-known experiment, . . . of the 'post-hypnotic suggestion' teaches us to insist upon the importance of the distinction between *conscious* and *unconscious* and seems to increase its value.

In this experiment, as performed by Bernheim,[1] a person is put into a hypnotic state and is subsequently aroused. While he was in the hypnotic state, under the influence of the physician, he was ordered to execute a certain action at a certain fixed moment after his awakening, say half an hour later. He awakes, and seems fully conscious and in his ordinary condition; he has no recollection of his hypnotic state, and yet at the prearranged moment there rushes into his mind the

impulse to do such and such a thing, and he does it consciously, though not knowing why. It seems impossible to give any other description of the phenomenon than to say that the order had been present in the mind of the person in a condition of latency, or had been present unconsciously, until the given moment came, and then had become conscious. But not the whole of it emerged into consciousness: only the conception of the act to be executed. All the other ideas associated with this conception — the order, the influence of the physician, the recollection of the hypnotic state, remained unconscious even then. . . .

The mind of the hysterical patient is full of active yet unconscious ideas; all her symptoms proceed from such ideas. It is in fact the most striking character of the hysterical mind to be ruled by them. If the hysterical woman vomits, she may do so from the idea of being pregnant. She has, however, no knowledge of this idea, although it can easily be detected in her mind, and made conscious to her, by one of the technical procedures of psychoanalysis. If she is executing the jerks and movements constituting her 'fit', she does

---

[1] Hippolyte Bernheim (1840–1919), a French physician, used hypnosis in the treatment of his patients and published a successful book on the subject.

not even consciously represent to herself the intended actions, and she may perceive those actions with the detached feelings of an onlooker. Nevertheless analysis will show that she was acting her part in the dramatic reproduction of some incident in her life, the memory of which was unconsciously active during the attack. The same preponderance of active unconscious ideas is revealed by analysis as the essential fact in the psychology of all other forms of neurosis. . . .

. . . The term *unconscious* . . . designates . . . ideas with a certain dynamic character, ideas keeping apart from consciousness in spite of their intensity and activity.

———————— ♦•♦ ————————

This passage from a lecture given in 1909 describes Freud's attempt to penetrate the world of the unconscious.

———————— ♦•♦ ————————

Five Lectures on Psychoanalysis

. . . At first, I must confess, this seemed a senseless and hopeless undertaking. I was set the task of learning from the patient something that I did not know and that he did not know himself. How could one hope to elicit it? But there came to my help a recollection of a most remarkable and instructive experiment which I had witnessed when I was with Bernheim at Nancy [in 1889]. Bernheim showed us that people whom he had put into a state of hypnotic somnambulism, and who had had all kinds of experiences while they were in that state, only *appeared* to have lost the memory of what they had experienced during somnambulism; it was possible to revive these memories in their normal state. It is true that, when he questioned them about their somnambulistic experiences, they began by maintaining that they knew nothing about them; but if he refused to give way, and insisted, and assured them that they *did* know about them, the forgotten experiences always reappeared.

So I did the same thing with my pa-

tients. When I reached a point with them at which they maintained that they knew nothing more, I assured them that they *did* know it all the same, and that they had only to say it; and I ventured to declare that the right memory would occur to them at the moment at which I laid my hand on their forehead. In that way I succeeded, without using hypnosis, in obtaining from the patients whatever was required for establishing the connection between the pathogenic scenes they had forgotten and the symptoms left over from those scenes. But it was a laborious procedure, and in the long run an exhausting one; and it was unsuited to serve as a permanent technique.

I did not abandon it, however, before the observations I made during my use of it afforded me decisive evidence. I found confirmation of the fact that the forgotten memories were not lost. They were in the patient's possession and were ready to emerge in association to what was still known by him; but there was some force that prevented them from becoming conscious and compelled them to remain unconscious. The existence of this force could be assumed with certainty, since one became aware of an effort corresponding to it if, in opposition to it, one tried to introduce the unconscious memories into the patient's consciousness. The force which was maintaining the pathological condition became apparent in the form of *resistance* on the part of the patient.

It was on this idea of resistance, then, that I based my view of the course of psychical events in hysteria. In order to effect a recovery, it had proved necessary to remove these resistances. Starting out from the mechanism of cure, it now became possible to construct quite definite ideas of the origin of the illness. The same forces which, in the form of resistance, were now offering opposition to the forgotten material's being made conscious, must formerly have brought about the forgetting and must have pushed the pathogenic experiences in question out of consciousness. I gave the name of "*repres-*

sion" to this hypothetical process, and I considered that it was proved by the undeniable existence of resistance.

The further question could then be raised as to what these forces were and what the determinants were of the repression in which we now recognized the pathogenic mechanism of hysteria. A comparative study of the pathogenic situations which we had come to know through the cathartic procedure made it possible to answer this question. All these experiences had involved the emergence of a wishful impulse which was in sharp contrast to the subject's other wishes and which proved incompatible with the ethical and aesthetic standards of his personality. There had been a short conflict, and the end of this internal struggle was that the idea which had appeared before consciousness as the vehicle of this irreconcilable wish fell a victim to repression, was pushed out of consciousness with all its attached memories, and was forgotten. Thus the incompatibility of the wish in question with the patient's ego was the motive for the repression; the subject's ethical and other standards were the repressing forces. An acceptance of the incompatible wishful impulse or a prolongation of the conflict would have produced a high degree of unpleasure; this unpleasure was avoided by means of repression, which was thus revealed as one of the devices serving to protect the mental personality.

To take the place of a number of instances, I will relate a single one of my cases, in which the determinants and advantages of repression are sufficiently evident. For my present purpose I shall have once again to abridge the case history and omit some important underlying material. The patient was a girl, who had lost her beloved father after she had taken a share in nursing him — a situation analogous to that of Breuer's[2] patient. Soon

afterwards her elder sister married, and her new brother-in-law aroused in her a peculiar feeling of sympathy which was easily masked under a disguise of family affection. Not long afterwards her sister fell ill and died, in the absence of the patient and her mother. They were summoned in all haste without being given any definite information of the tragic event. When the girl reached the bedside of her dead sister, there came to her for a brief moment an idea that might be expressed in these words: 'Now he is free and can marry me.' We may assume with certainty that this idea, which betrayed to her consciousness the intense love for her brother-in-law of which she had not herself been conscious, was surrendered to repression a moment later, owing to the revolt of her feelings. The girl fell ill with severe hysterical symptoms; and while she was under my treatment it turned out that she had completely forgotten the scene by her sister's bedside and the odious egoistic impulse that had emerged in her. She remembered it during the treatment and reproduced the pathogenic moment with signs of the most violent emotion, and, as a result of the treatment, she became healthy once more.

———— • • • ————

In the tradition of the Enlightenment philosophes, Freud valued reason and science, but he did not share the philosophes' confidence in human goodness and humanity's capacity for future progress. In Civilization and Its Discontents *(1930), Freud posited the frightening theory that human beings are driven by an inherent aggressiveness that threatens civilized life — that civilization is fighting a losing battle with our aggressive instincts. Although Freud's pessimism was no doubt influenced by the tragedy of World War I, many ideas expressed in* Civilization and Its Discontents *derived from views that he had formulated decades earlier.*

———— • • • ————

Civilization and Its Discontents

The element of truth behind all this, which people are so ready to disavow, is that men

---

[2] Joseph Breuer (1842–1925) was an Austrian physician and Freud's early collaborator.

are not gentle creatures who want to be loved, and who at most can defend themselves if they are attacked; they are, on the contrary, creatures among whose instinctual endowments is to be reckoned a powerful share of aggressiveness. As a result, their neighbour is for them not only a potential helper or sexual object, but also someone who tempts them to satisfy their aggressiveness on him, to exploit his capacity for work without compensation, to use him sexually without his consent, to seize his possessions, to humiliate him, to cause him pain, to torture and to kill him. *Homo homini lupus.* [Man is wolf to man.] Who, in the face of all his experience of life and of history, will have the courage to dispute this assertion? As a rule this cruel aggressiveness waits for some provocation or puts itself at the service of some other purpose, whose goal might also have been reached by milder measures. In circumstances that are favourable to it, when the mental counter-forces which ordinarily inhibit it are out of action, it also manifests itself spontaneously and reveals man as a savage beast to whom consideration towards his own kind is something alien. Anyone who calls to mind the atrocities committed during the racial migrations or the invasions of the Huns, or by the people known as Mongols under Jenghiz Khan and Tamerlane, or at the capture of Jerusalem by the pious Crusaders, or even, indeed, the horrors of the recent World War — anyone who calls these things to mind will have to bow humbly before the truth of this view.

The existence of this inclination to aggression, which we can detect in ourselves and justly assume to be present in others, is the factor which disturbs our relations with our neighbour and which forces civilization into such a high expenditure [of energy]. In consequence of this primary mutual hostility of human beings, civilized society is perpetually threatened with disintegration. The interest of work in common would not hold it together; instinctual passions are stronger than reasonable interests. Civilization has to use

its utmost efforts in order to set limits to man's aggressive instincts and to hold the manifestations of them in check by psychical reaction-formations. Hence, therefore, the use of methods intended to incite people into identifications and aim-inhibited relationships of love, hence the restriction upon sexual life, and hence too the ideal's commandment to love one's neighbour as oneself — a commandment which is really justified by the fact that nothing else runs so strongly counter to the original nature of man. In spite of every effort, these endeavours of civilization have not so far achieved very much. It hopes to prevent the crudest excesses of brutal violence by itself assuming the right to use violence against criminals, but the law is not able to lay hold of the more cautious and refined manifestations of human aggressiveness. The time comes when each one of us has to give up as illusions the expectations which, in his youth, he pinned upon his fellowmen, and when he may learn how much difficulty and pain has been added to his life by their ill-will. At the same time, it would be unfair to reproach civilization with trying to eliminate strife and competition from human activity. These things are undoubtedly indispensable. But opposition is not necessarily enmity; it is merely misused and made an *occasion* for enmity.

The communists believe that they have found the path to deliverance from our evils. According to them, man is wholly good and is well-disposed to his neighbour; but the institution of private property has corrupted his nature. The ownership of private wealth gives the individual power, and with it the temptation to ill-treat his neighbour; while the man who is excluded from possession is bound to rebel in hostility against his oppressor. If private property were abolished, all wealth held in common, and everyone allowed to share in the enjoyment of it, ill-will and hostility would disappear among men. Since everyone's needs would be satisfied, no one would have any reason to regard another as his enemy; all would willingly undertake the work that was necessary. I have no concern with any economic criticisms of the communist system. . . . But I am able to recognize that the psychological premisses on which the system is based are an untenable illusion. In abolishing private property we deprive the human love of aggression of one of its instruments, certainly a strong one, though certainly not the strongest; but we have in no way altered the differences in power and influence which are misused by aggressiveness, nor have we altered anything in its nature. Aggressiveness was not created by property. It reigned almost without limit in primitive times, when property was still very scanty, and it already shows itself in the nursery almost before property has given up its primal, anal form; it forms the basis of every relation of affection and love among people (with the single exception, perhaps, of the mother's relation to her male child). If we do away with personal rights over material wealth, there still remains prerogative in the field of sexual relationships, which is bound to become the source of the strongest dislike and the most violent hostility among men who in other respects are on an equal footing. If we were to remove this factor, too, by allowing complete freedom of sexual life and thus abolishing the family, the germ-cell of civilization, we cannot, it is true, easily foresee what new paths the development of civilization could take; but one thing we can expect, and that is that this indestructible feature of human nature will follow it there.

It is clearly not easy for men to give up the satisfaction of this inclination to aggression. They do not feel comfortable without it. . . .

If civilization imposes such great sacrifices not only on man's sexuality but on his aggressivity, we can understand better why it is hard for him to be happy in that civilization. . . .

In all that follows I adopt the standpoint, therefore, that the inclination to aggression is an original, self-subsisting instinctual disposition in man, and I return to my view that it constitutes the greatest impediment to civilization.

Review Questions

1. What was Sigmund Freud's definition of the *unconscious*? What examples of the power of the unconscious did he provide?

2. What did Freud mean by *repression*? What examples of repression did he provide?

3. Compare and contrast the approaches of Freud and Nietzsche to the nonrational.

4. What did Freud consider the "greatest impediment to civilization"? Why?

5. How did Freud react to the Marxist view that private property is the source of evil?

PART III

Western Civilization in Crisis

CHAPTER · 8

World War I

To many Europeans, the opening years of the twentieth century seemed full of promise. Advances in science and technology, the rising standard of living, the expansion of education, and the absence of wars between the Great Powers since the Franco-Prussian War (1870–1871) all contributed to a general feeling of optimism. Yet these accomplishments hid disruptive forces that were propelling Europe toward a cataclysm. On June 28, 1914, Archduke Francis Ferdinand, heir to the throne of Austria-Hungary, was assassinated by Gavrilo Princip, a young Serbian nationalist (and Austrian subject), at Sarajevo in the Austrian province of Bosnia, inhabited largely by South Slavs. The assassination triggered those explosive forces that lay below the surface of European life, and six weeks later, Europe was engulfed in a general war that altered the course of Western civilization.

Belligerent, irrational, and extreme nationalism was a principal cause of World War I. Placing their country above everything, nationalists in various countries fomented hatred of other nationalities and called for the expansion of their nation's borders — attitudes that fostered belligerence in foreign relations. Wedded to nationalism was a militaristic view that regarded war as heroic and as the highest expression of individual and national life.

Yet Europe might have avoided world war had the nations not been divided into hostile alliance systems. By 1907, the Triple Alliance of Germany, Austria-Hungary, and Italy confronted the loosely organized Triple Entente of France, Russia, and Great Britain. What German Chancellor Otto von Bismarck said in 1879 was just as true in 1914: "The great powers of our time are like travellers, unknown to one another, whom chance has brought together in a carriage. They watch each other, and when one of them puts his hand into his pocket, his neighbor gets ready his own revolver in order to be able to fire the first shot."

A danger inherent in an alliance is that a country, knowing that it has the support of allies, may pursue an aggressive foreign policy and may be less likely to compromise during a crisis; also, a war between two states may well draw in the other allied powers. These dangers materialized in 1914.

In the diplomatic furor of July and early August 1914, following the assassination of Francis Ferdinand, several patterns emerged. Austria-Hungary, a multinational empire dominated by Germans and Hungarians, feared the nationalist aspirations of its Slavic minorities. The nationalist yearnings of neighboring Serbia aggravated Austria-Hungary's problems, for the Serbs, a South Slav people, wanted to create a Greater Serbia by uniting with South Slavs of Austria-Hungary. If Slavic nationalism gained in intensity, the Austro-Hungarian (or Hapsburg) Empire would be broken into states based on nationality. Austria-Hungary decided to use the assassination as justification for crushing Serbia.

The system of alliances escalated the tensions between Austria-Hungary and Serbia into a general European war. Germany saw itself threatened by the Triple Entente (a conviction based more on paranoia than on objective fact) and regarded Austria-Hungary as its only reliable ally. Holding that at all costs its ally must be kept strong, German officials supported Austria-Hungary's decision to crush Serbia. Fearing that Germany and Austria-Hungary aimed to extend their power into southeastern Europe, Russia would not permit the destruction of Serbia. With the support of France, Russia began to mobilize, and when it moved to full mobilization, Germany declared war. Since German battle plans, drawn up years before, called for a war with both France and Russia, France was drawn into the conflict; Germany's invasion of neutral Belgium brought Great Britain into the war.

Most European statesmen and military men believed the war would be over in a few months. Virtually no one anticipated that it would last more than four years and that the casualties would number in the millions.

World War I was a turning point in Western history. In Russia, it led to the downfall of the tsarist autocracy and the rise of the Soviet state. The war created unsettling conditions that led to the emergence of fascist movements in Italy and Germany, and it shattered, perhaps forever, the Enlightenment belief in the inevitable and perpetual progress of Western civilization.

1 | Militarism

Historians regard a surging militarism as an underlying cause of World War I. One sign of militarism was the rapid increase in expenditures for armaments in the years prior to 1914. Between 1910 and 1914, both Austria-Hungary and Germany, for example, doubled their military budgets. The arms race intensified suspicion among the Great Powers. A second danger was the increased power of the military in policy making, particularly in Austria-Hungary and Germany, and in the crisis following the assassination, generals tended to press for a military solution.

HEINRICH VON TREITSCHKE
The Greatness of War

Coupled with the military's influence on state decisions was a romantic glorification of the nation and war, an attitude shared by both the elite and the masses. Although militarism generally pervaded Europe, it was particularly strong in Germany. In the following reading from *Politics,* German historian Heinrich von Treitschke (1834–1896) glorified warfare.

. . . One must say with the greatest determination: War is for an afflicted people the only remedy. When the State exclaims: My very existence is at stake! then social self-seeking must disappear and all party hatred be silent. The individual must forget his own *ego* and feel himself a member of the whole, he must recognize how negligible is his life compared with the good of the whole. Therein lies the greatness of war that the little man completely vanishes before the great thought of the State. The sacrifice of nationalities for one another is nowhere invested with such beauty as in war. At such a time the corn is separated from the chaff. All who lived through 1870 will understand the saying of Niebuhr[1] with regard to the year 1813, that he then experienced the "bliss of sharing with all his fellow citizens, with the scholar and the ignorant, the one common feeling—no

man who enjoyed this experience will to his dying day forget how loving, friendly and strong he felt."

It is indeed political idealism which fosters war, whereas materialism rejects it. What a perversion of morality to want to banish heroism from human life. The heroes of a people are the personalities who fill the youthful souls with delight and enthusiasm, and amongst authors we as boys and youths admire most those whose words sound like a flourish of trumpets. He who cannot take pleasure therein, is too cowardly to take up arms himself for his fatherland. All appeal to Christianity in this matter is perverted. The Bible states expressly that the man in authority shall wield the sword; it states likewise that: "Greater love hath no man than this that he giveth his life for his friend." Those who preach the nonsense about everlasting peace do not understand the life of the Aryan race,[2] the Aryans are before all

---

[1] Barthold G. Niebuhr (1776–1831) was a Prussian historian. The passage refers to the German War of Liberation against Napoleon, which German patriots regarded as a glorious episode in their national history.

[2] Most European languages derive from the Aryan language spoken by people who lived thousands of years ago in the region from the Caspian Sea to the Hindu Kush Mountains.

brave. They have always been men
enough to protect by the sword what they
had won by the intellect. . . .

To the historian who lives in the realms
of the Will, it is quite clear that the fur-

Around 2000 B.C., some Aryan-speaking people migrated to Europe and India. Racists
claimed that the Germans were descended from
the ancient Aryans and racially superior to other
peoples.

therance of an everlasting peace is fundamentally reactionary. He sees that to
banish war from history would be to banish all progress and becoming. It is only
the periods of exhaustion, weariness and
mental stagnation that have dallied with
the dream of everlasting peace. . . . The
living God will see to it that war returns
again and again as a terrible medicine for
humanity.

Review Questions

1. Why did Heinrich von Treitschke regard war as a far more desirable condition
   than peace?
2. According to Treitschke, what is the individual's highest responsibility?
3. According to Treitschke, what function does the hero serve in national life?

2 | Pan-Serbism: Nationalism and Terrorism

The conspiracy to assassinate Archduke Francis Ferdinand was organized by a secret
Serbian society called Union or Death, more popularly known as the Black Hand.
Founded in 1911, the Black Hand aspired to create a Greater Serbia by uniting with
their kinsmen, the South Slavs dwelling in Austria-Hungary. Thus, Austrian officials
regarded the aspirations of Pan-Serbs as a significant threat to the Hapsburg Empire.

The Black Hand

In 1914, the Black Hand had some 2,500 members, most of them army officers. The
society indoctrinated members with a fanatic nationalism and trained them in terrorist methods. The initiation ceremony, designed to strengthen a new member's commitment to the cause and to foster obedience to the society's leaders, had the appearance of a sacred rite. The candidate entered a dark room in which a table stood
covered with a black cloth; resting on the table were a dagger, a revolver, and a
crucifix. When the candidate declared his readiness to take the oath of allegiance, a
masked member of the society's elite entered the room and stood in silence. After
the initiate pronounced the oath, the masked man shook his hand and departed
without uttering a word. Excerpts of the Black Hand's by-laws, including the oath
of allegiance, follow.

By-Laws of the Organization Union or Death

Article 1. This organization is created for the purpose of realizing the national ideal: the union of all Serbs. Membership is open to every Serb, without distinction of sex, religion, or place of birth, and to all those who are sincerely devoted to this cause.

Article 2. This organization prefers terrorist action to intellectual propaganda, and for this reason it must remain absolutely secret.

Article 3. The organization bears the name *Ujedinjenje ili Smirt* (Union or Death).

Article 4. To fulfill its purpose, the organization will do the following:

(1) Exercise influence on government circles, on the various social classes, and on the entire social life of the kingdom of Serbia, which is considered the Piedmont[1] of the Serbian nation;

(2) Organize revolutionary action in all territories inhabited by Serbs;

(3) Beyond the frontiers of Serbia, fight with all means the enemies of the Serbian national idea;

(4) Maintain amicable relations with all states, peoples, organizations, and individuals who support Serbia and the Serbian element;

(5) Assist those nations and organizations that are fighting for their own national liberation and unification. . . .

Article 24. Every member has a duty to recruit new members, but the member shall guarantee with his life those whom he introduces into the organization.

Article 25. Members of the organization are forbidden to know each other personally. Only members of the central committee are known to each other.

Article 26. In the organization itself, the members are designated by numbers. Only the central committee in Belgrade knows their names.

Article 27. Members of the organization must obey absolutely the commands given to them by their superiors.

Article 28. Each member has a duty to communicate to the central committee at Belgrade all information that may be of interest to the organization.

Article 29. The interests of the organization stand above all other interests.

Article 30. On entering the organization, each member must know that he loses his own personality, that he can expect neither personal glory nor personal profit, material or moral. Consequently, any member who endeavors to exploit the organization for personal, social, or party motives, will be punished. If by his acts he harms the organization itself, his punishment will be death.

Article 31. Those who enter the organization may never leave it, and no one has the authority to accept a member's resignation.

Article 32. Each member must aid the organization with weekly contributions. If need be, the organization may procure funds through coercion. . . .

Article 33. When the central committee of Belgrade pronounces a death sentence the only thing that matters is that the execution is carried out unfailingly. The method of execution is of little importance.

Article 34. The organization's seal is composed as follows. On the center of the seal a powerful arm holds in its hand an unfurled flag. On the flag, as a coat of arms, are a skull and crossed bones; by the side of the flag are a knife, a bomb and poison. Around, in a circle, are inscribed the following words reading from left to right: "Unification or Death," and at the base "The Supreme Central Directorate."

Article 35. On joining the organization, the recruit takes the following oath:

"I (name), in becoming a member of the organization, "Unification or Death,"

---

[1]The Piedmont was the Italian state that served as the nucleus for the unification of Italy.

do swear by the sun that shines on me, by the earth that nourishes me, by God, by the blood of my ancestors, on my honor and my life that from this moment until my death, I shall be faithful to the regulations of the organization and that I will be prepared to make any sacrifice for it. I swear before God, on my honor and on my life, that I shall carry with me to the grave the organization's secrets. May God condemn me and my comrades judge me if I violate or do not respect, consciously or not, my oath.

Article 36. These regulations come into force immediately.

Article 37. These regulations must not be changed.

                                        Belgrade, 9 May 1911.

BARON VON GIESL

Austrian Response to the Assassination

Austrian officials who wanted to use the assassination as a pretext to crush Serbia feared that Pan-Serbism would lead to revolts among Slavs living in the Hapsburg Empire. This attitude was expressed in a memorandum written on July 21, 1914, three weeks after the assassination, by Baron von Giesl, the Austrian ambassador to Serbia, to foreign minister Count Leopold von Berchtold.

Belgrade, July 21, 1914.

After the lamentable crime of June 28th, I have now been back at my post for some time, and I am able to give some judgment as to the tone which prevails here.

After the annexation crisis[1] the relations between the Monarchy and Servia [Serbia] were poisoned on the Servian side by national chauvinism, animosity and an effective propaganda of Great-Servian aspirations carried on in that part of our territory where there is a Servian population; since the last two Balkan Wars [in 1912 and 1913], the success of Servia has increased this chauvinism to a paroxysm, the expression of which in some cases bears the mark of insanity.

I may be excused from bringing proof and evidence of this; they can be had easily everywhere among all parties, in political circles as well as among the lower classes. I put it forward as a well-known axiom that the policy of Servia is built up on the separation of the territories inhabited by Southern Slavs, and as a corollary to this on the abolition of the [Hapsburg] Monarchy as a Great Power; this is its only object.

No one who has taken the trouble to move and take part in political circles here for a week can be blind to this truth. . . .

The crime at Serajevo [the assassination of Ferdinand] has aroused among the Servians an expectation that in the immediate future the Hapsburg States will fall to pieces; it was this on which they had set their hopes even before; there has been dangled before their eyes the cession of those territories in the Monarchy which are inhabited by the Southern Slavs, a revolution in Bosnia and Herzegovina and the unreliability of the Slav regiments — this is regarded as ascertained fact and had brought system and apparent justification into their nationalist madness.

Austria-Hungary, hated as she is, now appears to the Servians as powerless, and as scarcely worthy of waging war with; contempt is mingled with hatred; she is

---

[1] Since 1878, Austria-Hungary had administered the provinces of Bosnia and Herzegovina, which were officially a part of the Ottoman Empire. The population of these lands consisted mainly of South Slavs, ethnic cousins of the Serbs. When Austria-Hungary annexed Bosnia and Herzegovina in 1908, Serbia was enraged.

ripe for destruction, and she is to fall without trouble into the lap of the Great-Servian Empire, which is to be realised in the immediate future.

Newspapers, not among the most extreme, discuss the powerlessness and decrepitude of the neighbouring Monarchy in daily articles, and insult its officials without reserve and without fear of reprimand. They do not even stop short of the exalted person of our ruler. Even the official organ refers to the internal condition of Austria-Hungary as the true cause of this wicked crime. There is no longer any fear of being called to account. For decades the people of Servia has been educated by the press, and the policy at any given time is dependent on the party press; the Great-Servian propaganda and its monstrous offspring the crime of June 28th, are a fruit of this education. . . .

. . . The electoral campaign has united all parties on a platform of hostility against Austria-Hungary. None of the parties which aspire to office will incur the suspicion of being held capable of weak compliance towards the Monarchy. The campaign, therefore, is conducted under the catchword of hostility towards Austria-Hungary.

For both internal and external reasons the Monarchy is held to be powerless and incapable of any energetic action, and it is believed that the serious words which were spoken by leading men among us are only "bluff." . . .

I have allowed myself to trespass too long on the patience of Your Excellency, not because I thought that in what I have said I could tell you anything new, but because I considered this picture led up to the conclusion which forces itself upon me that a reckoning with Servia, a war for the position of the Monarchy as a Great Power, even for its existence as such, cannot be permanently avoided.

If we delay in clearing up our relations with Servia, we shall share the responsibility for the difficulties and the unfavourable situation in any future war which must, however, sooner or later be carried through.

For any observer on the spot, and for the representative of Austro-Hungarian interests in Servia, the question takes the form that we cannot any longer put up with any further injury to our prestige. . . .

Half measures, the presentation of demands, followed by long discussions and ending only in an unsound compromise, would be the hardest blow which could be directed against Austria-Hungary's reputation in Servia and her position in Europe.

Review Questions

1. How did Union or Death seek to accomplish its goal of uniting all Serbs?

2. What type of people do you think were attracted to the objectives and methods of the Black Hand?

3. According to Baron von Giesl, how did Serbia view the Hapsburg monarchy? What policy toward Serbia did he advocate?

3 | British Fear of German Power

The completion of German unification under Prussian leadership in 1870–1871 upset the European balance of power. A militarily powerful, rapidly industrializing, and increasingly nationalist Germany aroused fear among other European states, particularly after Chancellor Otto von Bismarck (1815–1898) was forced out of office in 1890. The new German leadership became increasingly more aggressive and more susceptible to nationalist demands. German nationalists argued that the unification of Germany was more than the culmination of a deeply felt German goal; it was the starting point for German world power.

EYRE CROWE
Germany's Yearning for Expansion and Power

Fearful of Germany's growing industrial might, acquisition of colonies, and military preparations, particularly in naval armament, Britain ended its "splendid isolation" and entered into what was in effect a loose alliance with France in 1904 and with Russia in 1907. In 1907, Sir Eyre Crowe, an official in the British Foreign Office, assessed Germany's *Weltpolitik* — its desire to play a greater role on the world stage. Some historians regard that desire as a primary cause of World War I. Excerpts from Crowe's memorandum follow.

The general character of England's foreign policy is determined by the immutable conditions of her geographical situation on the ocean flank of Europe as an island State with vast oversea colonies and dependencies, whose existence and survival as an independent community are inseparably bound up with the possession of preponderant sea power. . . .

. . . It would, therefore, be but natural that the power of a State supreme at sea should inspire universal jealousy and fear, and be ever exposed to the danger of being overthrown by a general combination of the world. Against such a combination no single nation could in the long run stand, least of all a small island kingdom not possessed of the military strength of a people trained to arms, and dependent for its food supply on oversea commerce. The danger can in practice only be averted — and history shows that it has been so averted — on condition that the national policy of the insular and naval State is so directed as to harmonize with the general desires and ideals common to all mankind, and more particularly that it is closely identified with the primary and vital interests of a majority, or as many as

possible, of the other nations. Now, the first interest of all countries is the preservation of national independence. It follows that England, more than any other non-insular Power, has a direct and positive interest in the maintenance of the independence of nations, and therefore must be the natural enemy of any country threatening the independence of others, and the natural protector of the weaker communities. . . .

History shows that the danger threatening the independence of this or that nation has generally arisen, at least in part, out of the momentary predominance of a neighbouring State at once militarily powerful, economically efficient, and ambitious to extend its frontiers or spread its influence, the danger being directly proportionate to the degree of its power and efficiency, and to the spontaneity or "inevitableness" of its ambitions. The only check on the abuse of political predominance derived from such a position has always consisted in the opposition of an equally formidable rival, or of a combination of several countries forming leagues of defence. The equilibrium established by such a grouping of forces is technically known as the balance of power, and it has become almost an historical truism to identify England's secular policy with the maintenance of this balance by throwing her weight now in this scale and now in that, but ever on the side opposed to the political dictatorship of the strongest single State or group at a given time.

If this view of British policy is correct, the opposition into which England must inevitably be driven to any country aspiring to such a dictatorship assumes almost the form of a law of nature. . . .

By applying this general law to a particular case, the attempt might be made to ascertain whether, at a given time, some powerful and ambitious State is or is not in a position of natural and necessary enmity towards England; and the present position of Germany might, perhaps, be so tested. Any such investigation must take the shape of an inquiry as to whether Germany is, in fact, aiming at a political hegemony with the object of promoting purely German schemes of expansion, and establishing a German primacy in the world of international politics at the cost and to the detriment of other nations.

For purposes of foreign policy the modern German Empire may be regarded as the heir, or descendant of Prussia. . . .

. . . With "blood and iron" Prussia had forged her position in the councils of the Great Powers of Europe. In due course it came to pass that, with the impetus given to every branch of national activity by the newly-won unity, and more especially by the growing development of oversea trade flowing in ever-increasing volume . . . , the young empire found opened to its energy a whole world outside Europe, of which it had previously hardly had the opportunity to become more than dimly conscious. Sailing across the ocean in German ships, German merchants began for the first time to divine the true position of countries such as England, the United States, France, and even the Netherlands, whose political influence extends to distant seas and continents.

The colonies and foreign possessions of England more especially were seen to give to that country a recognized and enviable status in a world where the name of Germany, if mentioned at all, excited no particular interest. The effect of this discovery upon the German mind was curious and instructive. Here was a vast province of human activity to which the mere title and rank of a European Great Power were not in themselves a sufficient passport. Here in a field of portentous magnitude, dwarfing altogether the proportions of European countries, others, who had been perhaps rather looked down upon as comparatively smaller folk, were at home and commanded, whilst Germany was at best received but as an honoured guest. Here was distinct inequality, with a heavy bias in favour of the maritime and colonizing Powers.

Such a state of things was not welcome to German patriotic pride. Germany had won her place as one of the leading, if not, in fact, the foremost Power on the European continent. But over and beyond the European Great Powers there seemed to stand the "World Powers." It was at once clear that Germany must become a "World Power." The evolution of this idea and its translation into practical politics followed with singular consistency the line of thought that had inspired the Prussian Kings in their efforts to make Prussia great. "If Prussia," said Frederick the Great, "is to count for something in the councils of Europe, she must be made a Great Power." And the echo: "If Germany wants to have a voice in the affairs of the larger oceanic world she must be made a 'World Power.'" "I want more territory," said Prussia. "Germany must have Colonies," says the new world-policy. And Colonies were accordingly established, in such spots as were found to be still unappropriated, or out of which others could be pushed by the vigorous assertion of a German demand for "a place in the sun." . . .

Meanwhile the dream of a Colonial Empire had taken deep hold on the

German imagination. Emperor, statesmen, journalists, geographers, economists, commercial and shipping houses, and the whole mass of educated and uneducated public opinion continue with one voice to declare: We *must* have real Colonies, where German emigrants can settle and spread the national ideals of the Fatherland, and we *must* have a fleet and coaling stations to keep together the Colonies which we are bound to acquire. To the question, "Why *must?*" the ready answer is: "A healthy and powerful State like Germany, with its 60,000,000 inhabitants, must expand, it cannot stand still, it must have territories to which its overflowing population can emigrate without giving up its nationality." When it is objected that the world is now actually parcelled out among independent States, and that territory for colonization cannot be had except by taking it from the rightful possessor, the reply again is: "We cannot enter into such considerations. Necessity has no law. The world belongs to the strong. A vigorous nation cannot allow its growth to be hampered by blind adherence to the *status quo.* We have no designs on other people's possessions, but where States are too feeble to put their territory to the best possible use, it is the manifest destiny of those who can and will do so to take their places." . . .

The significance of these individual utterances may easily be exaggerated. Taken together, their cumulative effect is to confirm the impression that Germany distinctly aims at playing on the world's political stage a much larger and much more dominant part than she finds allotted to herself under the present distribution of material power. . . .

. . . No modern German would plead guilty to a mere lust of conquest for the sake of conquest. But the vague and undefined schemes of Teutonic expansion . . . are but the expression of the deeply rooted feeling that Germany has by the strength and purity of her national purpose, the fervour of her patriotism, the depth of her religious feeling, the high standard of competency, and the perspicuous honesty of her administration, the successful pursuit of every branch of public and scientific activity, and the elevated character of her philosophy, art, and ethics, established for herself the right to assert the primacy of German national ideals. And as it is an axiom of her political faith that right, in order that it may prevail, must be backed by force, the transition is easy to the belief that the "good German sword," which plays so large a part in patriotic speech, is there to solve any difficulties that may be in the way of establishing the reign of those ideals in a Germanized world. . . .

So long . . . as Germany competes for an intellectual and moral leadership of the world in reliance on her own national advantages and energies England can but admire, applaud, and join in the race. If, on the other hand, Germany believes that greater relative preponderance of material power, wider extent of territory, inviolable frontiers, and supremacy at sea are the necessary and preliminary possessions without which any aspirations to such leadership must end in failure, then England must expect that Germany will surely seek to diminish the power of any rivals, to enhance her own by extending her dominion, to hinder the co-operation of other States, and ultimately to break up and supplant the British Empire.

Now, it is quite possible that Germany does not, nor ever will, consciously cherish any schemes of so subversive a nature. Her statesmen have openly repudiated them with indignation. Their denial may be perfectly honest, and their indignation justified. If so, they will be most unlikely to come into any kind of armed conflict with England, because, as she knows of no causes of present dispute between the two countries, so she would have difficulty in imagining where, on the hypothesis stated, any such should arise in the future. England seeks no quarrels, and will never give Germany cause for legitimate offence.

But this is not a matter in which England can safely run any risks. . . .

. . . A German maritime supremacy

must be acknowledged to be incompatible with the existence of the British Empire, and even if that Empire disappeared, the union of the greatest military with the greatest naval Power in one State would compel the world to combine for the riddance of such an incubus [nightmare].

Review Questions

1. How did Sir Eyre Crowe interpret the principle of the balance of power as it applied to Britain? How was Britain's foreign policy related to its geographic position?

2. According to Crowe, what did Germany's foreign policy owe to its Prussian background?

3. How did Crowe regard German demands for colonies?

4 | War as Celebration

An outpouring of patriotism greeted the proclamation of war. Huge crowds thronged the avenues and squares of capital cities to express their devotion to their nations and their willingness to bear arms. Many Europeans regarded war as a sacred moment that held the promise of adventure and an escape from a humdrum and purposeless daily existence. Going to war seemed to satisfy a yearning to surrender oneself to a noble cause: the greatness of the nation. The image of the nation united in a spirit of fraternity and self-sacrifice was immensely appealing.

STEFAN ZWEIG
War Fever in Vienna

Some intellectuals viewed the war as a way of regenerating Europe; nobility and glory would triumph over life's petty concerns. In the following reading, Stefan Zweig (1881–1942), a prominent Austrian literary figure, recalled the scene in Vienna, the capital of the Austro-Hungarian Empire, at the outbreak of World War I. This passage comes from Zweig's autobiography written in 1941.

The next morning I was in Austria. In every station placards had been put up announcing general mobilization. The trains were filled with fresh recruits, banners were flying, music sounded, and in Vienna I found the entire city in a tumult. The first shock at the news of war — the war that no one, people or government, had wanted — the war which had slipped, much against their will, out of the clumsy hands of the diplomats who had been bluffing and toying with it, had suddenly been transformed into enthusiasm. There were parades in the street, flags, ribbons, and music burst forth everywhere, young recruits were marching triumphantly, their faces lighting up at the cheering — they, the John Does and Richard Roes who usually go unnoticed and uncelebrated.

And to be truthful, I must acknowledge that there was a majestic, rapturous, and even seductive something in this first outbreak of the people from which one could escape only with difficulty. And in spite of all my hatred and aversion for war, I should not like to have missed the memory of those first days. As never before, thousands and hundreds of thousands felt what they should have felt in peace time, that they belonged together. A city of two million, a country of nearly fifty million, in that hour felt that they were participating in world history, in a moment which would never recur, and that each one was called upon to cast his infinitesimal self into the glowing mass, there to be purified of all selfishness. All differences of class, rank, and language were flooded over at that moment by the rushing feeling of fraternity. Strangers spoke to one another in the streets, people who had avoided each other for years shook hands, everywhere one saw excited faces. Each individual experienced an exaltation of his ego, he was no longer the isolated person of former times, he had been incorporated into the mass, he was part of the people, and his person, his hitherto unnoticed person, had been given meaning. The petty mail clerk, who ordinarily sorted letters early and late, who sorted constantly, who sorted from Monday until Saturday without interruption; the clerk, the cobbler, had suddenly achieved a romantic possibility in life: he could become a hero, and everyone who wore a uniform was already being cheered by the women, and greeted beforehand with this romantic appellation by those who had to remain behind. They acknowledged the unknown power which had lifted them out of their everyday existence. Even mothers with their grief, and women with their fears, were ashamed to manifest their quite natural emotions in the face of this first transformation. But it is quite possible that a deeper, more secret power was at work in this frenzy. So deeply, so quickly did the tide break over humanity that, foaming over the surface, it churned up the depths, the subconscious primitive instincts of the human animal — that which

Freud so meaningfully calls "the revulsion from culture," the desire to break out of the conventional bourgeois world of codes and statutes, and to permit the primitive instincts of the blood to rage at will. It is also possible that these powers of darkness had their share in the wild frenzy into which everything was thrown — self-sacrifice and alcohol, the spirit of adventure and the spirit of pure faith, the old magic of flags and patriotic slogans, that mysterious frenzy of the millions which can hardly be described in words, but which, for the moment, gave a wild and almost rapturous impetus to the greatest crime of our time. . . .

. . . What did the great mass know of war in 1914, after nearly half a century of peace? They did not know war, they had hardly given it a thought. It had become legendary, and distance had made it seem romantic and heroic. They still saw it in the perspective of their school readers and of paintings in museums; brilliant cavalry attacks in glittering uniforms, the fatal shot always straight through the heart, the entire campaign a resounding march of victory — "We'll be home at Christmas," the recruits shouted laughingly to their mothers in August of 1914. Who in the villages and the cities of Austria remembered "real" war? A few ancients at best, who in 1866 had fought against Prussia, which was now their ally. But what a quick, bloodless, far-off war that had been, a campaign that had ended in three weeks with few victims and before it had well started! A rapid excursion into the romantic, a wild, manly adventure — that is how the war of 1914 was painted in the imagination of the simple man, and the young people were honestly afraid that they might miss this most wonderful and exciting experience of their lives; that is why they hurried and thronged to the colors, and that is why they shouted and sang in the trains that carried them to the slaughter; wildly and feverishly the red wave of blood coursed through the veins of the entire nation.

Review Questions

1. Why, according to Stefan Zweig, did the prospects of war appeal so seductively to the emotions?

2. Do you think that human beings are aggressive by nature? Explain your answer.

3. How long did people think World War I would last? What does this tell you about their understanding of the nature of modern warfare?

5 | Trench Warfare

In 1914 the young men of European nations marched off to war believing that they were embarking on a glorious and chivalrous adventure. They were eager to serve their countries, to demonstrate personal valor, and to experience life at its most intense moments. But in the trenches, where unseen enemies fired machine guns and artillery that killed indiscriminately and relentlessly, this romantic illusion about combat disintegrated.

ERICH MARIA REMARQUE
All Quiet on the Western Front

The following reading is taken from Erich Maria Remarque's novel *All Quiet on the Western Front* (1929), the most famous literary work to emerge from World War I. A veteran of the trenches himself, Remarque graphically described the slaughter that robbed Europe of its young men. His narrator is a young German soldier.

We wake up in the middle of the night. The earth booms. Heavy fire is falling on us. We crouch into corners. We distinguish shells of every calibre.

Each man lays hold of his things and looks again every minute to reassure himself that they are still there. The dug-out heaves, the night roars and flashes. We look at each other in the momentary flashes of light, and with pale faces and pressed lips shake our heads.

Every man is aware of the heavy shells tearing down the parapet, rooting up the embankment and demolishing the upper layers of concrete. When a shell lands in the trench we note how the hollow, furious blast is like a blow from the paw of a raging beast of prey. Already by morn-

ing a few of the recruits are green and vomiting. They are too inexperienced. . . .

The bombardment does not diminish. It is falling in the rear too. As far as one can see spout fountains of mud and iron. A wide belt is being raked.

The attack does not come, but the bombardment continues. We are gradually benumbed. Hardly a man speaks. We cannot make ourselves understood.

Our trench is almost gone. At many places it is only eighteen inches high, it is broken by holes, and craters, and mountains of earth. A shell lands square in front of our post. At once it is dark. We are buried and must dig ourselves out. . . .

Towards morning, while it is still dark,

there is some excitement. Through the entrance rushes in a swarm of fleeing rats that try to storm the walls. Torches light up the confusion. Everyone yells and curses and slaughters. The madness and despair of many hours unloads itself in this outburst. Faces are distorted, arms strike out, the beasts scream; we just stop in time to avoid attacking one another. . . .

Suddenly it howls and flashes terrifically, the dug-out cracks in all its joints under a direct hit, fortunately only a light one that the concrete blocks are able to withstand. It rings metallically, the walls reel, rifles, helmets, earth, mud, and dust fly everywhere. Sulphur fumes pour in.

If we were in one of those light dug-outs that they have been building lately instead of this deeper one, none of us would be alive.

But the effect is bad enough even so. The recruit starts to rave again and two others follow suit. One jumps up and rushes out, we have trouble with the other two. I start after the one who escapes and wonder whether to shoot him in the leg — then it shrieks again, I fling myself down and when I stand up the wall of the trench is plastered with smoking splinters, lumps of flesh, and bits of uniform. I scramble back.

The first recruit seems actually to have gone insane. He butts his head against the wall like a goat. We must try to-night to take him to the rear. Meanwhile we bind him, but in such a way that in case of attack he can be released at once. . . .

Suddenly the nearer explosions cease. The shelling continues but it has lifted and falls behind us, our trench is free. We seize the hand-grenades pitch them out in front of the dug-out and jump after them. The bombardment has stopped and a heavy barrage now falls behind us. The attack has come.

No one would believe that in this howling waste there could still be men; but steel helmets now appear on all sides out of the trench, and fifty yards from us a machine-gun is already in position and barking.

The wire entanglements are torn to pieces. Yet they offer some obstacle. We see the storm-troops coming. Our artillery opens fire. Machine-guns rattle, rifles crack. The charge works its way across. Haie and Kropp begin with the hand-grenades. They throw as fast as they can, others pass them, the handles with the strings already pulled. Haie throws seventy-five yards, Kropp sixty, it has been measured, the distance is important. The enemy as they run cannot do much before they are within forty yards.

We recognize the smooth distorted faces, the helmets: they are French. They have already suffered heavily when they reach the remnants of the barbed wire entanglements. A whole line has gone down before our machine-guns; then we have a lot of stoppages and they come nearer.

I see one of them, his face upturned, fall into a wire cradle. His body collapses, his hands remain suspended as though he were praying. Then his body drops clean away and only his hands with the stumps of his arms, shot off, now hang in the wire.

The moment we are about to retreat three faces rise up from the ground in front of us. Under one of the helmets a dark pointed beard and two eyes that are fastened on me. I raise my hand, but I cannot throw into those strange eyes; for one mad moment the whole slaughter whirls like a circus round me, and these two eyes alone are motionless; then the head rises up, a hand, a movement, and my hand-grenade flies through the air and into him.

We make for the rear, pull wire cradles into the trench and leave bombs behind us with the strings pulled, which ensures us a fiery retreat. The machine-guns are already firing from the next position.

We have become wild beasts. We do not fight, we defend ourselves against annihilation. It is not against men that we fling our bombs, what do we know of men in this moment when Death is hunting us down — now, for the first time in three days we can see his face, now for the first time in three days we can oppose him; we feel a mad anger. No longer do we lie helpless, waiting on the scaffold, we can destroy and kill, to save ourselves, to save ourselves and to be revenged.

We crouch behind every corner, behind every barrier of barbed wire, and hurl heaps of explosives at the feet of the advancing enemy before we run. The blast of the hand-grenades impinges powerfully on our arms and legs; crouching like cats we run on, overwhelmed by this wave that bears us along, that fills us with ferocity, turns us into thugs, into murderers, into God only knows what devils; this wave that multiplies our strength with fear and madness and greed of life, seeking and fighting for nothing but our deliverance. If your own father came over with them you would not hesitate to fling a bomb at him.

The forward trenches have been abandoned. Are they still trenches? They are blown to pieces, annihilated — there are only broken bits of trenches, holes linked by cracks, nests of craters, that is all. But the enemy's casualties increase. They did not count on so much resistance.

*

It is nearly noon. The sun blazes hotly, the sweat stings in our eyes, we wipe it off on our sleeves and often blood with it. At last we reach a trench that is in a somewhat better condition. It is manned and ready for the counter-attack, it receives us. Our guns open in full blast and cut off the enemy attack.

The lines behind us stop. They can advance no farther. The attack is crushed by our artillery. We watch. The fire lifts a hundred yards and we break forward. Beside me a lance-corporal has his head torn off. He runs a few steps more while the blood spouts from his neck like a fountain.

It does not come quite to hand-to-hand fighting; they are driven back. We arrive once again at our shattered trench and pass on beyond it. . . .

We have lost all feeling for one another. We can hardly control ourselves when our glance lights on the form of some other man. We are insensible, dead men, who through some trick, some dreadful magic, are still able to run and to kill.

A young Frenchman lags behind, he is overtaken, he puts up his hands, in one he still holds his revolver — does he mean to shoot or to give himself! — a blow from a spade cleaves through his face. A second sees it and tries to run farther; a bayonet jabs into his back. He leaps in the air, his arms thrown wide, his mouth wide open, yelling; he staggers, in his back the bayonet quivers. A third throws away his rifle, cowers down with his hands before his eyes. He is left behind with a few other prisoners to carry off the wounded.

Suddenly in the pursuit we reach the enemy line.

We are so close on the heels of our retreating enemies that we reach it almost at the same time as they. In this way we suffer few casualties. A machine-gun barks, but is silenced with a bomb. Nevertheless, the couple of seconds has sufficed to give us five stomach wounds. With the butt of his rifle Kat smashes to pulp the face of one of the unwounded machine-gunners. We bayonet the others before they have time to get out their bombs. Then thirstily we drink the water they have for cooling the gun.

Everywhere wire-cutters are snapping, planks are thrown across the entanglements, we jump through the narrow entrances into the trenches. Haie strikes his spade into the neck of a gigantic Frenchman and throws the first hand-grenade; we duck behind a breastwork for a few seconds, then the straight bit of trench ahead of us is empty. The next throw whizzes obliquely over the corner and clears a passage; as we run past we toss handfuls down into the dug-outs, the earth shudders, it crashes, smokes and groans, we stumble over slippery lumps of flesh, over yielding bodies; I fall into an open belly on which lies a clean, new officer's cap.

The fight ceases. We lose touch with the enemy. We cannot stay here long but must retire under cover of our artillery to our own position. No sooner do we know this than we dive into the nearest dug-outs, and with the utmost haste seize on whatever provisions we can see, especially the tins of corned beef and butter, before we clear out.

We get back pretty well. There is no further attack by the enemy. We lie for an hour panting and resting before anyone speaks. We are so completely played out that in spite of our great hunger we do not think of the provisions. Then gradually we become something like men again.

Review Questions

1. How did the soldiers in the trenches react to artillery bombardment?
2. What ordeal did the attacking soldiers encounter as they neared the enemy trenches?
3. What were the feelings of the soldiers as they engaged the attackers?

6 | The War and British Women

At the outbreak of war, British suffragists set aside their political activism and responded to their country's wartime needs. To release men for military service, many women took jobs in offices, factories, and service industries. They drove ambulances, mail trucks, and buses; worked in munitions factories, read gas meters, and collected railway tickets. They worked as laboratory assistants, plumbers' helpers, and bank clerks. By performing effectively in jobs formerly reserved for men, women demonstrated that they had an essential role to play in Britain's economic life. By the end of the war, little opposition remained to granting women political rights, and in 1918 women over the age of thirty gained the vote. In 1928, Parliament lowered the voting age to twenty-one, the same as for men.

The War Cabinet Committee's Report on British Women in Industry

A British War Cabinet Committee investigated the wartime employment of women. The following excerpts are from the report the committee submitted to Parliament immediately after the war.

Increased Employment of Women during the War. — In the second half of 1915 unemployed women were rapidly absorbed in munition factories, and in January, 1916, in industry proper the number of women had already increased by over a quarter of a million, of whom about one-half were employed in the Metal and Chemical trades. From this time onwards the figure of female employment rose steadily until in July, 1918, the total number of occupied women had, according to Board of Trade figures, increased by 22½ per cent or from just under 6 million to nearly 7⅓ million as shown in . . . table [1]: —

. . . After industry the most important increases were in commerce — mostly clerks and shop assistants; in the National and Local Government — mainly the Civil Service, which took on some 168,000 women clerks, &c.; and in transport. The additions in the different branches of industry, their effect in altering the proportion of women to men in those branches and the extent to which females directly replaced males are shown in . . . table [2]: —

Employment of Women during the War. Munition Metal Trades. — First and foremost the requirements of munitions brought women into the Metal trades, but down to the end of December, 1914, the special munition problem had not emerged and the female employees in these trades only increased by some 3,000. During the next six months the shortage of munitions was recognised, but the attempt was made to meet it by ordinary methods, by a speeding up of contracts and by a gradual development of the agencies of supply. During this period, some 26,000 women came in. Their increased employment, though not unimportant, was, however, confined to a few well-defined but unskilled processes. Then followed in the second half of 1915 the initial [efforts] of the Ministry of Munitions when the engineering resources of the nation were mobilised and every possible step taken to expand them. Another 45,000 female workers were added to the Metal trades during this period . . . From the beginning of 1916 the forces set in motion gathered strength and produced results with uninterrupted acceleration. Between July, 1914, and July, 1918, the number of women rose from 170,000 to 594,000, or by 424,000, of whom about 90 per cent. were employed on work customarily done by men. To this last figure must be added a large proportion of the 223,000 women employed,

mostly on metal work, in National establishments where practically none had worked before, making a total addition to female metal workers of over 600,000. The most important single trade was shell-making. The women were soon some 60 per cent. of the workers, and made the shell throughout from the roughing and turning of the bodies to the final gauging of the completed shell. In general engineering shops and ship-yards, foundries, gun and aircraft factories, women were introduced on most varieties of men's work — light labouring, turning, shaping, slotting, drawing, filing, grinding, punching, shearing, machine riveting, gear-cutting, crane-driving, assembling, dressing castings, soldering, welding — and were sometimes promoted as "fitters" and "turners" in the tool-room and as "capstan lathe setters" and "toolsetters." In some munition factories the men's work was almost entirely carried out by women, but the processes were not generally the same as were the men's processes. In factories employing already semi-skilled workers, the job was sometimes identical, but in factories employing normally skilled tradesmen, either the machine was transformed by the adjustment of "jigs" or foolproof appliances, or the women performed only a part of the man's job and were confined to one of a comparatively narrow range of operations. "The usual position is that the women may do the whole operation on the machine except the setting-up of the work and setting-up the tool. In certain shops women who have been on their machines for a long time gradually get to setting-up their work and tools, but in general one may say that in skilled work the woman does not do the whole job."* . . .

In some factories, notably in shell factories, the output increased enormously, but this was attributed chiefly to improved methods of production. "A

---

* Mr. Baillie, Director of the Technical Section of the Labour Supply Department.

TABLE 1

Numbers of Women Working.	In July, 1914.	In July, 1918.	In July, 1918, over (+) or under (−) numbers in July, 1914.
On their own account or as Employers	430,000	470,000	+ 40,000
In Industry	2,178,600	2,970,600	+ 792,000
In Domestic Service	1,658,000	1,258,000	− 400,000
In Commerce, etc.	505,500	934,500	+ 429,000
In National and Local Government, including			
Education	262,200	460,200	+ 198,000
In Agriculture	190,000	228,000	+ 38,000
In employment of Hotels, Public Houses, Theatres, etc.	181,000	220,000	+ 39,000
In Transport	18,200	117,200	+ 99,000
In other, including Professional employment and as home workers	542,500	652,500	+ 110,000
Altogether in occupations	5,966,000	7,311,000	+1,345,000
Not [employed] but over 10 [years]	12,946,000	12,496,000	− 550,000
Under 10 [years of age]	4,809,000	4,731,000	− 78,000
Total Females [in Britain]	23,721,000	24,538,000	+ 817,000

TABLE 2

Trades.	Estimated number of Females employed in July, 1914.	Estimated number of Females employed in July, 1918.	Difference between numbers of Females employed in July, 1914, and July, 1918.	Percentage of Females to total number of Workpeople employed. July, 1914.	Percentage of Females to total number of Workpeople employed. July, 1918.	Estimated number of Females directly replacing Males in Jan., 1918.
Metal	170,000	594,000	+424,000	9	25	195,000
Chemical	40,000	104,000	+ 64,000	20	39	35,000
Textile	863,000	827,000	− 36,000	58	67	64,000
Clothing	612,000	568,000	− 44,000	68	76	43,000
Food, Drink, and Tobacco	196,000	235,000	+ 39,000	35	49	60,000
Paper and Printing	147,500	141,500	− 6,000	36	48	21,000
Wood	44,000	79,000	+ 35,000	15	32	23,000
China and Earthenware	32,000					
Leather	23,100	197,100	+ 93,000	4	10	62,000
Other	49,000					
Government Establishments.	2,000	225,000	+223,000	3	47	197,000
Total	2,178,600	2,970,600	+792,000	26	37	704,000

woman is doing it better, not because she has got very much greater speed, but she has got very much better methods laid out to enable her to do it. She has the quantity; she has the continuity of production."* Exact comparisons were therefore hard to make. The Engineering and National Employers' Federation submitted, however, the following general statement as to the comparative quality and quantity of men's and women's output and other factors affecting productive value in the trades represented by them: —

OUTPUT.
Quality.

    Sheet Metal. — Better than men's work.

    Engineering. — Women's work fair, equal to boys. Men far superior.

    Repetition Light Work. — Women and girls equal to men and boys.

    Aircraft Woodwork. — Equal in most branches.

    Cartridges. — Equal.

    Shells. — Men, then boys, women last.

Quantity.

    Sheet Metal. — Women 90 per cent. of men's output.

    Engineering. — Women fair. If work varies, women not so good as men. Approximate, two-thirds of men.

    Repetition Work. — Nearly same.

    Aircraft Woodwork. — Equal.

    Cartridges. — Generally equal, and in some cases as much as 20 per cent. more than men.

    Shells. — Boys, then men, and women last.

Cost to Employer.

    Women are considerably more costly than men by reason of the cost of tuition, setting up, &c., and larger percentage of scrap.

    One large firm employing thousands of women reports that the cost of them represents a standing weekly additional cost of 30 per cent., which figure does not include initial outlay on machinery, &c.

Timekeeping.

    Men are the best timekeepers, then boys, and women last. One firm employing 18,000 people state that men lose 3·4 per cent., as compared with 7·1 per cent. of time lost by women.

Length of Service.

    Men first, then boys, and women last. Women are constantly changing their place of employment.

    A large firm employing about 5,000 women state that of this number 60 per cent. is a "floating" quantity, *i.e.,* constantly changing; the remaining 40 per cent. could be considered as permanent employees.

Aptitude for Training.

    Boys first and then young girls, but, speaking generally, there is nothing to choose. Some firms report that women are only "fair." Repetition work they are quick to learn, but where it is of a jobbing nature, and requires special training, women have not been found equal to the work. In this connection, however, it is not surprising, because it has always taken at least four years to train a man as a mechanic. . . .

    Hotels, Public Houses, &c. — Under this head the number of women increased by 21 per cent., or 39,000. In catering establishments women have been brought into all branches of the industry and into departments they had never previously entered. The first-class hotels have drawn a considerable number of waiters from second-class hotels and restaurants, but even establishments of the best class now employ women in occupations in which men were almost exclusively employed before the war, viz., as lift and cloak room attendants, in clerical work, including audit, stocktaking and bill office duties, in cellar work, window cleaning, electro-plate washing and, in some cases, in cooking. Women have also replaced men waiters in some establishments employing all men

---

*Mr. Bean, Managing Director of the Dudley National Projectile Factory.

before the war, or employing men for the late dinner service. In most occupations the women are not quite equal to the men, but mainly for lack of experience. Waitresses, for example, cannot undertake even in normal times the same number of tables as men waiters, and, although their time-keeping is as good as the men's, the normal employer has to keep an additional 10 per cent. of women on active service, *i.e.*, supposing a firm has 100 waitresses in employment, it must have 110 on its list. Women have not replaced men to a very great extent as cooks and are not looked upon in the same way as a chef. The most important opening for women after the war is the boarding-house service, where large numbers of Germans and Austrians were employed before.

Teaching and other Professions. — The main fact with regard to the teaching profession in the war is that towards making good the loss of 22,000 men teachers, some 13,000 women were drawn into the service. The temporary displacement will probably accelerate the change in the proportion of the two sexes engaged which had been going on for some years before the war. The impossibility of allowing it to exceed certain limits in the interests of boys' education was emphasized by Sir Robert Blair, who gave evidence in the matter on behalf of the London County Council.

As an indirect result of the war and of the grant of the parliamentary suffrage to women some new professions are being opened to them. In January, 1918, the Society of Incorporated Accountants and Auditors obtained permission from the Chancery Court to alter their articles of association so as to permit of the admission of women as members. In March, 1918, a Bill to admit of women qualifying as Barristers and Solicitors passed the House of Lords.

Employment of Women in Men's Occupations. — From the foregoing examination of the evidence and returns submitted to the Committee, it appears that the principal changes made by the war in the direction of introducing women into men's occupations have been: —

(1) To bring or bring back women into manual labour and outdoor occupations, viz., agriculture, transport, chemical manufacture.

(2) To admit women into skilled trades of an apprenticeship or "craft" character, *e.g.*, "all round" engineering and wood-working, and scientific instrument making.

(3) To hasten the normal movement of women into "repetition" and routine processes of trades or other occupations, such as specialised engineering, wood-working, or clerical work.

These changes resulted from shortage of male labour, and were rendered possible by the patriotic enthusiasm of women and, in the case of the organised trades, by the relaxation of Trade Union restrictions.

Review Questions

1. How did the needs of the war lead to women's employment in British industry?

2. What professions admitted women for the first time?

3. The commission reported that Sir Robert Blair believed that the education of boys would be adversely affected if they were subjected to too many women teachers. Why do you think he held this view?

7 | The Paris Peace Conference

The most terrible war the world had experienced ended in November 1918; in January 1919, representatives of the victorious powers assembled in Paris to draw up a peace settlement. The principal figures at the Paris Peace Conference were Woodrow Wilson (1856–1924), president of the United States; David Lloyd George (1863–1945), prime minister of Great Britain; Georges Clemenceau (1841–1929), premier of France; and Vittorio Orlando (1860–1952), premier of Italy. Disillusioned intellectuals and the war-weary masses turned to Wilson as the prince of peace who would fashion a new and better world.

WOODROW WILSON
The Idealistic View

Wilson sought a peace of justice and reconciliation, one based on democratic and Christian ideals, as the following excerpts from his speeches illustrate.

(May 26, 1917)

We are fighting for the liberty, the self-government, and the undictated development of all peoples, and every feature of the settlement that concludes this war must be conceived and executed for that purpose. Wrongs must first be righted and then adequate safeguards must be created to prevent their being committed again. . . .

. . . No people must be forced under sovereignty under which it does not wish to live. No territory must change hands except for the purpose of securing those who inhabit it a fair chance of life and liberty. No indemnities must be insisted on except those that constitute payment for manifest wrongs done. No readjustments of power must be made except such as will tend to secure the future peace of the world and the future welfare and happiness of its peoples.

And then the free peoples of the world must draw together in some common covenant, some genuine and practical coöperation that will in effect combine their force to secure peace and justice in the dealings of nations with one another.

The following are excerpts from Wilson's Fourteen Points of January 18, 1918.

IV. Adequate guarantees given and taken that national armaments will be reduced to the lowest point consistent with domestic safety.

V. A free, open-minded, and absolutely impartial adjustment of all colonial claims, based upon a strict observance of the principle that in determining all such questions of sovereignty the interests of the populations concerned must have equal weight with the equitable claims of the government whose title is to be determined. . . .

VIII. All French territory should be freed and the invaded portions restored, and the wrong done to France by Prussia in 1871 in the matter of Alsace-Lorraine, which has unsettled the peace of the world for nearly fifty years, should be righted, in order that peace may once more be made secure in the interest of all.

IX. A readjustment of the frontiers of Italy should be effected along clearly recognizable lines of nationality.

X. The peoples of Austria-Hungary, whose place among the nations we wish to see safeguarded and assured, should be accorded the freest opportunity of autonomous development. . . .

XII. The Turkish portions of the present Ottoman Empire should be assured a secure sovereignty, but the other nationalities which are now under Turkish rule should be assured an undoubted security of life and an absolutely unmolested opportunity of autonomous development, and the Dardanelles should be permanently opened as a free passage to the ships and commerce of all nations under international guarantees.

XIII. An independent Polish state should be erected which should include the territories inhabited by indisputably Polish populations, which should be assured a free and secure access to the sea, and whose political and economic independence and territorial integrity should be guaranteed by international covenant.

XIV. A general association of nations must be formed under specific covenants for the purpose of affording mutual guarantees of political independence and territorial integrity to great and small states alike.

(February 11, 1918)

. . . The principles to be applied [in the peace settlement] are these:

First, that each part of the final settlement must be based upon the essential justice of that particular case and upon such adjustments as are most likely to bring a peace that will be permanent;

Second, that peoples and provinces are not to be bartered about from sovereignty to sovereignty as if they were mere chattels and pawns in a game, even the great game, now forever discredited, of the balance of power; but that

Third, every territorial settlement involved in this war must be made in the interest and for the benefit of the populations concerned, and not as a part of any mere adjustment or compromise of claims amongst rival states; and

Fourth, that all well-defined national aspiration shall be accorded the utmost satisfaction that can be accorded them without introducing new or perpetuating old elements of discord and antagonism that would be likely in time to break the peace of Europe and consequently of the world.

(April 6, 1918)

. . . We are ready, whenever the final reckoning is made, to be just to the German people, deal fairly with the German power, as with all others. There can be no difference between peoples in the final judgment, if it is indeed to be a righteous judgment. To propose anything but justice, even-handed and dispassionate justice, to Germany at any time, whatever the outcome of the war, would be to renounce and dishonor our own cause. For we ask nothing that we are not willing to accord.

(December 16, 1918)

. . . The war through which we have just passed has illustrated in a way which never can be forgotten the extaordinary wrongs which can be perpetrated by arbitrary and irresponsible power.

It is not possible to secure the happiness and prosperity of the world, to establish an enduring peace, unless the repetition of such wrongs is rendered impossible. This has indeed been a people's war. It has been waged against absolutism and militarism, and these enemies of liberty must from this time forth be shut out from the possibility of working their cruel will upon mankind.

(January 3, 1919)

. . . Our task at Paris is to organize the friendship of the world, to see to it that all the moral forces that make for right and justice and liberty are united and are given a vital organization to which the peoples of the world will readily and gladly respond. In other words, our task is no less colossal than this, to set up a new international psychology, to have a new atmosphere.

(January 25, 1919)

. . . We are . . . here to see that every people in the world shall choose its own masters and govern its own destinies, not as we wish, but as it wishes. We are here to see, in short, that the very foundations of this war are swept away. Those foundations were the private choice of small coteries of civil rulers and military staffs. Those foundations were the aggression of great powers upon the small. Those foundations were the holding together of empires of unwilling subjects by the duress of arms. Those foundations were the power of small bodies of men to work their will upon mankind and use them as pawns in a game. And nothing less than the emancipation of the world from these things will accomplish peace.

GEORGES CLEMENCEAU
French Demands for Security and Revenge

Wilson's promised new world clashed with French demands for security and revenge. Almost all the fighting on the war's western front had taken place in France; its industries and farmlands lay in ruins, and many of its young men had perished. France had been invaded by Germany in 1870 as well as in 1914, so the French believed that only by crippling Germany could they gain security. Premier Clemenceau, who was called "the Tiger," dismissed Wilson's vision of a new world as mere noble sentiment divorced from reality, and he fought tenaciously to gain security for France. Clemenceau's profound hatred and mistrust of Germany is revealed in his book *Grandeur and Misery of Victory* (1930), written a decade after the Paris Peace Conference.

War and peace, with their strong contrasts, alternate against a common background. For the catastrophe of 1914 the Germans are responsible. Only a professional liar would deny this. . . .

What after all is this war, prepared, undertaken, and waged by the German people, who flung aside every scruple of conscience to let it loose, hoping for a peace of enslavement under the yoke of a militarism destructive of all human dignity? It is simply the continuance, the recrudescence, of those never-ending acts of violence by which the first savage tribes carried out their depredations with all the resources of barbarism. The means improve with the ages. The ends remain the same. . . .

Germany, in this matter, was unfortunate enough to allow herself (in spite of her skill at dissimulation) to be betrayed into an excess of candour by her characteristic tendency to go to extremes.

Deutschland über alles. Germany above everything! That, and nothing less, is what she asks, and when once her demand is satisfied she will let you enjoy a peace under the yoke. Not only does she make no secret of her aim, but the intolerable arrogance of the German aristocracy, the servile good nature of the intellectual and the scholar, the gross vanity of the most competent leaders in industry, and the widespread influence of a violent popular poetry conspire to shatter throughout the world all the time-honoured traditions of individual, as well as international, dignity. . . .

On November 11, 1918, the fighting ceased.

It is not I who will dispute the German soldier's qualities of endurance. But he had been promised a *fresh and frolicsome war,* and for four years he had been pinned down between the anvil and the hammer. It was a famous German, Planck, who set before us the new theory of the *quanta*, according to which cosmic energy is discontinuous, exerted in a series of determinate shocks. Byzantium attained to dominion over Athens and Rome. Her quantum was soon exhausted. The quantum of a hypothetical German civilization would not take us very far, because she is today still too close to barbarism, while the quantum of a Hellenic civilization, even though conquered, is nowhere near exhaustion. Our defeat would have resulted in a relapse of human civilization into violence and bloodshed. The question is to know what contribution to moral progress our victory can and must furnish, if it be maintained. . . .

Outrages against human civilization are in the long run defeated by their own excess, and thus I discern in the peculiar mentality of the German soldier, with his *"Deutschland über alles,"* the cause of the premature exhaustion that brought him to beg for an armistice before the French soldier, who was fighting for his independence. . . .

And what is this "Germanic civilization," this monstrous explosion of the will to power, which threatens openly to do away entirely with the diversities established by many evolutions, to set in their place the implacable mastery of a race whose lordly part would be to substitute itself, by force of arms, for all national developments? We need only read [General Friedrich von] Bernhardi's famous pamphlet *Our Future*, in which it is alleged that Germany sums up within herself, as the historian Treitschke asserts, the greatest manifestation of human supremacy, and finds herself condemned, by her very greatness, either to absorb all nations in herself or to return to nothingness.

From the German point of view the monstrous problem thus set must inevitably be solved by the apotheosis of the German peoples. In the meantime, far from "German culture" seeming disposed to reform itself, we hear it proclaiming louder than ever a universal right to supreme domination, which confers on it the

right of life and death over the nations, to be asserted and enforced by all possible means. Ought we not all to feel menaced in our very vitals by this mad doctrine of universal Germanic supremacy over England, France, America, and every other country? . . .

What document more suitable to reveal the direction of "German culture" than the famous manifesto of the ninety-three super-intellectuals of Germany,[1] issued to justify the bloodiest and the least excusable of military aggressions against the great centres of civilization? At the moment when violated Belgium lay beneath the heel of the malefactor (October 1914) all the *élite* of "German culture" arose to take sides against the respect for treaties and to lay down the doctrine of a victory that seemed to them assured by means of perjury.

In itself the actual manifestation is not without apparent justification. Politicians, in all countries, are not necessarily intellectuals. It is therefore not astonishing that those who profess "culture" are overcome by the desire to enlighten them. For a long time still our rulers and governors will no doubt continue to be haphazard empirics. And so we need not be surprised if men, very different in doctrine, willingly set about spreading their light among those who are spending themselves in the blind convulsions of their times. However, since it is well known that learned men themselves may sometimes make mistakes, perhaps it would be a good thing if they consented to pause a moment before expressing themselves.

The case of the greatest war in history, let loose for no overt reason, offered a great chance to thinkers, qualified in the different realms of human knowledge, to appeal against the outrage done to public faith merely to open the way to the rav-

---

[1] Shortly after the outbreak of war, ninety-three leading German scholars and scientists addressed a letter to the world, defending Germany's actions.

aging of French territory, from the razing of great historical buildings to the ground to the burning down of libraries. It would need a whole book to tell of the infamous treatment inflicted upon noncombatants, to reckon up those who were shot down, or put to death, or deported, or condemned to forced labour. . . .

Well, this was the hour chosen by German intellectuals to make themselves heard. Let all the nations give ear! . . .

. . . Their learning made of them merely Germans better than all others qualified to formulate, on their own account, the extravagances of Germanic arrogance. The only difference is that they speak louder than the common people, those docile automatons. The fact is that they really believe themselves to be the representatives of a privileged *"culture"* that sets them above the errors of the human race, and confers on them the prerogative of a superior power, the very abuse of which can but be hailed by the nations with gratitude and joy.

The whole document is nothing but denials without the support of a single proof. *"It is not true* that Germany wanted the War."* William II had for years been *"mocked at by his adversaries of today on account of his unshakable love of peace."* They neglect to tell us whence they got this lie. They forget that from 1871 till 1914 we received from Germany a series of war threats in the course of which Queen Victoria and also the Czar had to intervene with the *Kaiser* direct for the maintenance of peace.

I have already recalled how our German intellectuals account for the violation of the Belgian frontier:

> *It is not true that we criminally violated Belgian neutrality. It can be proved that France and England had made up their minds to violate it. It can be proved that Belgium was willing. It would have been suicide not to forestall them.* . . .

. . . And when a great chemist such as Ostwald tells us, with his colleagues, that our struggle *"against the so-called German militarism"* is really directed *"against German culture,"* we must remember that *this same savant published a history of chemistry* IN WHICH THE NAME OF [eighteenth-century French chemist Antoine] LAVOISIER WAS NOT MENTIONED.

The "intellectuals" take their place in public opinion as the most ardent propagandists of the thesis which makes Germany the very model of the *"chosen people."* The same Professor Ostwald had already written, *"Germany has reached a higher stage of civilization than the other peoples, and the result of the War will be an organization of Europe under German leadership."* Professor Haeckel had demanded *the conquest of London, the division of Belgium between Germany and Holland, the annexation of North-east France, of Poland, the Baltic Provinces, the Congo, and a great part of the English colonies.* Professor Lasson went further still:

> *We are morally and intellectually superior to all men. We are peerless.* So too are our organizations and our institutions. *Germany is the most perfect creation known in history,* and the Imperial Chancellor, Herr von Bethmann-Hollweg, is *the most eminent of living men.*

Ordinary laymen who talked in this strain would be taken off to some safe asylum. Coming from duly hallmarked professors, such statements explain all German warfare by alleging that Germany's destiny is universal domination, and that for this very reason she is bound either to disappear altogether or to exercise violence on all nations with a view to their own betterment. . . .

May I further recall, since we have to emphasize the point, that on September 17, 1914, Erzberger, the well-known German statesman, an eminent member of the Catholic Party, wrote to the Minister of War, General von Falkenhayn, *"We must not worry about committing an offence against the rights of nations nor about violating the laws of humanity. Such feelings today are of secondary importance"*? A month later, on October 21, 1914, he wrote in *Der Tag,* *"If a way was found of entirely wiping out the whole of London it would be more humane to employ it* than to allow the blood of A SINGLE GERMAN SOLDIER to be shed on the battlefield!" . . .

. . . General von Bernhardi himself, the best pupil, as I have already said, of the historian Treitschke, whose ideas are law in Germany, has just preached the doctrine of "World power or Downfall" at us. So there is nothing left for other nations, as a way of salvation, but to be conquered by Germany. . . .

I have sometimes penetrated into the sacred cave of the Germanic cult, which is, as every one knows, the *Bierhaus.* A great aisle of massive humanity where there accumulate, amid the fumes of tobacco and beer, the popular rumblings of a nationalism upheld by the sonorous brasses blaring to the heavens the supreme voice of Germany, *"Deutschland über alles!"* Men, women, and children, all petrified in reverence before the divine stoneware pot, brows furrowed with irrepressible power, eyes lost in a dream of infinity, mouths twisted by the intensity of will-power, drink in long draughts the celestial hope of vague expectations. These only remain to be realized presently when the chief marked out by Destiny shall have given the word. There you have the ultimate framework of an old but childish race.

Review Questions

1. What principles did Woodrow Wilson want to serve as the basis of the peace settlement?

2. What were Wilson's objectives for the peoples of Austria-Hungary? The Poles? Alsace and Lorraine?

3. According to Wilson, what were the principal reasons for the outbreak of war in 1914?

4. What accusations did Georges Clemenceau make against the German national character? What contrasts did he draw between the Germans and the French?

5. How did Clemenceau respond to the manifesto of the German intellectuals?

6. Why, more than a decade after the war, did Clemenceau believe that Germany should still be feared?

8 | German Denunciation of the Versailles Treaty

A debate raged over the Versailles Treaty, the peace settlement imposed on Germany by the Paris Peace Conference. The treaty's defenders argued that if Germany had won the war, it would have forced far more ruthless terms on France and other losing countries. These defenders pointed to the Treaty of Brest-Litovsk, which Germany compelled the new and weak revolutionary Russian government to sign in 1918, as an example of German peacemaking. Through this treaty, Germany seized 34 percent of Russia's population, 32 percent of its farmland, 54 percent of its industrial enterprise, and 89 percent of its coal mines.

The Germans denounced the Versailles Treaty, which they regarded both as a violation of Wilson's principles as enunciated in the Fourteen Points and other statements and as an Anglo-French plot to keep Germany economically and militarily weak. Leaders of the new German Weimar Republic, formed after a revolution had forced the emperor to abdicate, protested that in punishing and humiliating the new republic for the sins of the monarchy and the military, the peacemakers weakened the foundations of democracy in Germany, kept alive old hatreds, and planted the seeds of future conflicts. Enraged nationalists swore to erase this blot on German honor.

GERMAN DELEGATION TO THE PARIS PEACE CONFERENCE
A Peace of Might

In the excerpts that follow, the German delegation to the Paris Peace Conference voiced its criticism of the Versailles Treaty.

The peace to be concluded with Germany was to be a peace of right, not a peace of might.

In his address to the Mexican journalists on the 9th of June, 1918, President Wilson promised to maintain the principle that the interests of the weakest and of the strongest should be equally sacred. . . . And in his speech before Congress on the 11th of February 1918, the President described the aim of peace as follows: "What we are striving for is a new international order based upon broad and universal principles of right and justice — no mere peace of shreds and patches." . . .

To begin with the territorial questions:

In the West, a purely German territory on the Saar with a population of at least 650,000 inhabitants is to be separated from the German Empire for at least fifteen years merely for the reason that claims are asserted to the coal abounding there.

The other cessions in the West, German-Austria and German-Bohemia will be mentioned in connection with the right of self-determination.

In Schleswig, the line of demarcation for voting has been traced through purely German districts and goes farther than Denmark herself wishes.

In the East, Upper Silesia is to be separated from Germany and given to Poland, although it has had no political connexion with Poland for the last 750 years. Contrary to this, the provinces of Posen and almost the whole of West Prussia are to be separated from the German Empire in consideration of the former extent of the old Polish state, although millions of Germans are living there. Again, the district of Memel is separated from Germany quite regardless of its historical past, in the obvious attempt to separate Germany from Russia for economic reasons. For the purpose of securing to Poland free access to the sea, East Prussia is to be completely cut off from the rest of the Empire and thereby condemned to economic and national decay. The purely German city of Danzig is to become a Free State under the suzerainty of Poland. Such terms are not founded on any principle of justice. Quite arbitrarily, here the idea of an imprescribable historical right, there the idea of ethnographical possession, there the standpoint of economic interest shall prevail, in every case the decision being unfavourable to Germany.

The settlement of the colonial question is equally contradictory to a peace of justice. For the essence of activity in colonial work does not consist in capitalistic exploitation of a less developed human race, but in raising backward peoples to a higher civilization. This gives the Powers which are advanced in culture a natural claim to take part in colonial work. Germany, whose colonial accomplishments cannot be denied, has also this natural claim, which is not recognized by a treaty of peace that deprives Germany of all of her colonies.

Not only the settlement of the territorial questions but each and every provision of the treaty of peace is governed by the ill-renowned phrase: "Might above Right!" — Here are a few illustrations: . . .

Although President Wilson . . . has acknowledged that "no single fact caused the war, but that in the last analysis the whole European system is in a deeper sense responsible for the war, with its combination of alliances and understandings, a complicated texture of intrigues and espionage that unfailingly caught the whole family of nations in its meshes," . . . Germany is to acknowledge that Germany and her allies are responsible for all damages which the enemy Governments or their subjects have incurred by her and her allies' aggression. . . . Apart from the consideration that there is no incontestable legal foundation for the obligation for reparation imposed upon Germany, the amount of such compensation is to be determined by a commission nominated solely by Germany's enemies, Germany taking no part in the findings of the commission. The commission is plainly to have power to administer Germany like the estate of a bankrupt. . . .

. . . Germany must promise to pay an indemnity, the amount of which at present is not even stated. . . .

These few instances show that that is not the just peace we were promised, not the peace "the very principle of which", according to a word of President Wilson, "is equality and the common participation in a common benefit. The equality of nations upon which peace must be founded if it is to last must be an equality of rights." . . .

In this war, a new fundamental law has arisen which the statesmen of all belligerent peoples have again and again ac-

knowledged to be their aim: the right of self-determination. To make it possible for all nations to put this privilege into practice was intended to be one achievement of the war. . . . On February 11, 1918, President Wilson said in Congress: "Peoples and provinces are not to be bartered about from sovereignty to sovereignty as if they were mere chattels and pawns in a game." . . .

Neither the treatment described above of the inhabitants of the Saar region . . . of consulting the population in the districts of Eupen, Malmédy, and Prussian Moresnet — which, moreover, shall not take place before they have been put under Belgian sovereignty — comply in the least with such a solemn recognition of the right of self-determination.

The same is also true with regard to Alsace-Lorraine. If Germany has pledged herself "to right the wrong of 1871," this does not mean any renunciation of the right of self-determination of the inhabitants of Alsace-Lorraine. A cession of the country without consulting the population would be a new wrong, if for no other reason, because it would be inconsistent with a recognized principle of peace.

On the other hand, it is incompatible with the idea of national self-determination for two and one-half million Germans to be torn away from their native land against their own will. By the proposed demarcation of the boundary, unmistakably German territories are disposed of in favor of their Polish neighbours. Thus, from the Central Silesian districts of Guhrau and Militsch certain portions are to be wrenched away, in which, besides 44,900 Germans, reside at the utmost 3,700 Poles. The same may be said with reference to the towns of Schneidemühl and Bromberg of which the latter has, at the utmost, eighteen per cent. Polish inhabitants, whereas in the rural district of Bromberg the Poles do not form even forty per cent. of the population. . . . This disrespect of the right of self-determination is shown most grossly in the fact that Danzig is to be separated from the German Empire and made a free state. Neither historical rights nor the present ethnographical conditions of ownership of the Polish people can have any weight as compared with the German past and the German character of that city. Free access to the sea, satisfying the economic wants of Poland, can be secured by guarantees founded on international law, by the creating of free ports. Likewise the cession of the commercial town of Memel, which is to be exacted from Germany, is in no way consistent with the right of self-determination. The same may be said with reference to the fact that millions of Germans in German-Austria are to be denied the union with Germany which they desire and that, further, millions of Germans dwelling along our frontiers are to be forced to remain part of the newly created Czecho-Slovakian State.

PHILIPP SCHEIDEMANN
The Debate Within Germany

The following reading is taken from the memoirs of Philipp Scheidemann (1865–1939), Prime Minister of the Weimar Republic during the time of the debate over signing the Versailles Treaty.

On the afternoon of 12th May a meeting of the National Assembly took place in the new Aula [assembly hall] of the University. As Prime Minister, I spoke on behalf of the Government on the Versailles Treaty. A few extracts from the speech may be given here:

On strange premises in emergency quarters, the representatives of the nation have met together, like a last remnant of loyal men, at a time when the Fatherland is in the gravest danger. All are present except the Alsace-Lorrainers, from whom the right of being here represented has been taken away, as well as the right of exercising their privilege of self-determination as free men.

When I see lined up here the representatives of German stock and nationality, men chosen from the Rhineland, the Saar Basin, West and East Prussia, Posen, Silesia and Memel, side by side with Parliamentarians from [regions] that are not threatened and men from [regions] that are, who, if the will of our enemies becomes law, will now for the last time meet Germans as Germans, I am conscious of being one with you in spirit at this sad and solemn hour when we have only one command to obey: We must hold together. We must stick together. We are one flesh and one blood, and he who tries to separate us cuts with a murderous knife into the live flesh of the German people. To preserve the life of our people is our highest duty.

We are chasing no nationalistic phantoms; no question of prestige and no thirst of power have any part or lot in our deliberations. For country and people we must save life — a bare, poor life now, when everyone feels the throttling hand on his throat. Let me speak without mincing my words; what lies at the root of our deliberations is this thick book (pointing to the Peace Terms), in which hundreds of paragraphs begin with "Germany renounces — renounces — renounces" — this *malleus maleficarum* [hammer of evil-doing countries] by which the confession of our own unworthiness, the consent to our own merciless dismemberment, the agreement to our enslavement and bondage, are to be wrung and extorted from a great people — this book shall not be our law manual for the future!

Then followed comparisons of the dictated Peace with Wilson's fourteen points, and a description of the devastating effect of the Treaty for Germany in home and foreign policy.

Then I continued:

> I ask you: who can, as an honest man, I will not say as a German, but only as an honest, straightforward man, accept such terms? What hand would not wither that binds itself and us in these fetters? (Great applause.) And now I've said enough, more than enough. We have made counter proposals; we shall make others. We see, with your approval, that our sacred duty lies in negotiation. This Treaty, in the opinion of the Government, cannot be accepted. (Tumultuous cheering, lasting for minutes in the Hall and galleries. The meeting rises.)

PRESIDENT: I ask you to allow the speaker to continue his speech.

SCHEIDEMANN, THE PRIME MINISTER: This Treaty is so impossible that I cannot yet realize the world containing such a book without millions and trillions of throats in all lands and of all parties yelling out: "Away with this organized murder."

My speech ended with these words:

> We have done with fighting; we want peace. We behold in horror from the example of our enemies what convulsions a policy of force and brutal militarism have caused. With a shudder we turn our heads away from these long years of murder.
>
> Yes, we do. Woe to them who have conjured up the War. But threefold woe to them who postpone a real peace for a single day.

Vociferous cheers and clapping of hands followed. . . .

The Peace delegates returned from Versailles to Weimar on 17th June. .... Count Brockdorff-Rantzau [head of the Foreign Office] reported to the Government on behalf of the delegates on 18th June. He asked for the rejection of the Treaty as being intolerable and impracticable. "There is no one in Germany who considers the Peace proposed to us can be carried out. In our eyes honesty is the best policy. This precept does not admit of our accepting impossible obligations." In the last sentence it says: "If our enemies intend using force against us, we can be sure that the peaceable course of the world will soon set up for us an impartial tribunal, before which we shall plead for our rights."

The pros and cons were debated from late at night till three o'clock in the morning. It was out of the question that one side would persuade the other. . . . Why continue this quibbling that could lead to nothing? I cried off this cruel game by . . . tendering my resignation. . . .

. . . The new Cabinet, now consisting of members of the Centre [Catholic Center party] and the S.P.D. [Social Democratic party] made frantic efforts to get concessions here and there and also tried to amend certain reservations. Clémenceau brutally put a stop to this by saying: "You have only twenty-four hours to decide. The time allowed for discussion is past. Either — yes or no."

. . . The People's Representatives were flocking to the National Assembly. There they decided by 237 votes to 138 to sign the peace proposals. Five members abstained from voting. . . .

. . . Generals von Hindenburg and Groener frankly admitted, when asked by the Government, that no serious resistance could be offered. If such were not the case why had they asked for an armistice and peace? Hindenburg supplemented his opinion with the words that he, as a soldier, would prefer utter ruin to a disgraceful peace. This was the soldier's point of view, who was ready to give his own life, not the politician's point of view, who was responsible for the life of the entire people and had to try to keep them together. . . .

On the top of all these unheard-of difficulties came many others. The people were without clothing, underlinen, boots and shoes and — bread. The people must go on starving. "Sign! Then there'll be bread" — that was the hope of millions.

Many hundreds of thousands racked with worry had their kith and kin in foreign prison camps. We were required to return our prisoners of war at once, but when would our fathers, brothers and sons who had been captured be released from bondage? No one knew, but all knew that they were badly treated, especially in France, and were badly fed.

Review Questions

1. According to the German delegation, how did the Treaty of Versailles violate the principle of self-determination championed by Woodrow Wilson?

2. In addition to the loss of territory, what other features of the Treaty of Versailles angered the Germans?

3. Why, despite their hatred of the treaty, did the German government ratify it?

9 | The War and European Consciousness

World War I caused many intellectuals to have grave doubts about the Enlightenment tradition and the future of Western civilization. More than ever the belief in human goodness, reason, and the progress of humanity seemed an illusion. Despite its many accomplishments, intellectuals contended that Western civilization was flawed and might die.

PAUL VALÉRY
Disillusionment

Shortly after World War I, Paul Valéry (1871–1945), a prominent French writer, expressed the mood of disillusionment that gripped many intellectuals. The following reading was written in 1919; the second reading is from a 1922 speech. Both were published in *Variety*, a collection of some of Valéry's works.

We modern civilizations have learned to recognize that we are mortal like the others.

We had heard tell of whole worlds vanished, of empires foundered with all their men and all their engines, sunk to the inexplorable depths of the centuries with their gods and laws, their academies and their pure and applied sciences, their grammars, dictionaries, classics, romantics, symbolists, their critics and the critics of their critics. We knew that all the apparent earth is made of ashes, and that ashes have a meaning. We perceived, through the misty bulk of history, the phantoms of huge vessels once laden with riches and learning. We could not count them. But these wrecks, after all, were no concern of ours.

Elam, Nineveh, Babylon were vague and splendid names; the total ruin of these worlds, for us, meant as little as did their existence. But *France, England, Russia . . .* these names, too, are splendid. . . . And now we see that the abyss of history is deep enough to bury all the world. We feel that a civilization is fragile as a life. The circumstances which will send the works of [John] Keats [English poet] and the works of [Charles] Baudelaire [French poet] to join those of Menander[1] are not at all inconceivable; they are found in the daily papers.

———————◆•◆—————

The following passage is from an address that Valéry delivered at the University of Zurich on November 15, 1922.

———————◆•◆—————

The storm has died away, and still we are restless, uneasy, as if the storm were about to break. Almost all the affairs of men remain in a terrible uncertainty. We think of what has disappeared, we are almost destroyed by what has been destroyed; we do not know what will be born, and we

———————————

[1] Menander was an ancient Greek poet whose works were lost until fragments were found in Egypt at the end of the nineteenth century.

fear the future, not without reason. We hope vaguely, we dread precisely; our fears are infinitely more precise than our hopes; we confess that the charm of life is behind us, abundance is behind us, but doubt and disorder are in us and with us. There is no thinking man, however shrewd or learned he may be, who can hope to dominate this anxiety, to escape from this impression of darkness, to measure the probable duration of this period when the vital relations of humanity are disturbed profoundly.

We are a very unfortunate generation, whose lot has been to see the moment of our passage through life coincide with the arrival of great and terrifying events, the echo of which will resound through all our lives.

One can say that all the fundamentals of our world have been affected by the war, or more exactly, by the circumstances of the war; something deeper has been worn away than the renewable parts of the machine. You know how greatly the general economic situation has been disturbed, and the polity of states, and the very life of the individual; you are familiar with the universal discomfort, hesitation, apprehension. *But among all these injured things is the Mind.* The Mind has indeed been cruelly wounded; its complaint is heard in the hearts of intellectual man; it passes a mournful judgment on itself. It doubts itself profoundly.

———————————————————

ERICH MARIA REMARQUE
The Lost Generation

In Erich Maria Remarque's *All Quiet on the Western Front*, a wounded German soldier reflects on the war and his future. He sees himself as part of a lost generation.

Gradually a few of us are allowed to get up. And I am given crutches to hobble around on. But I do not make much use of them; I cannot bear Albert's gaze as I move about the room. His eyes always follow me with such a strange look. So I

sometimes escape to the corridor; — there I can move about more freely.

On the next floor below are the abdominal and spine cases, head wounds and double amputations. On the right side of the wing are the jaw wounds, gas cases, nose, ear, and neck wounds. On the left the blind and the lung wounds, pelvis wounds, wounds in the joints, wounds in the kidneys, wounds in the testicles, wounds in the intestines. Here a man realizes for the first time in how many places a man can get hit.

Two fellows die of tetanus. Their skin turns pale, their limbs stiffen, at last only their eyes live — stubbornly. Many of the wounded have their shattered limbs hanging free in the air from a gallows; underneath the wound a basin is placed into which drips the pus. Every two or three hours the vessel is emptied. Other men lie in stretching bandages with heavy weights hanging from the end of the bed. I see intestine wounds that are constantly full of excreta. The surgeon's clerk shows me X-ray photographs of completely smashed hip-bones, knees, and shoulders.

A man cannot realize that above such shattered bodies there are still human faces in which life goes its daily round. And this is only one hospital, one single station; there are hundreds of thousands in Germany, hundreds of thousands in France, hundreds of thousands in Russia. How senseless is everything that can ever be written, done, or thought, when such things are possible. It must be all lies and of no account when the culture of a thousand years could not prevent this stream of blood being poured out, these torture-chambers in their hundreds of thousands. A hospital alone shows what war is.

I am young, I am twenty years old; yet I know nothing of life but despair, death, fear, and fatuous superficiality cast over an abyss of sorrow. I see how peoples are set against one another, and in silence, unknowingly, foolishly, obediently, innocently slay one another. I see that the keenest brains of the world invent weapons and words to make it yet more refined and enduring. And all men of my age, here and over there, throughout the whole world see these things; all my generation is experiencing these things with me. What would our fathers do if we suddenly stood up and came before them and proffered our account? What do they expect of us if a time ever comes when the war is over? Through the years our business has been killing; — it was our first calling in life. Our knowledge of life is limited to death. What will happen afterwards? And what shall come out of us?

TRISTAN TZARA

Contempt for Western Values: Dada

One example of the intellectual disorientation fostered by the war was the Dadaist Movement, which arose in 1916 in Zurich, Switzerland. The artists and writers who founded Dada intended to express their contempt for the war and the civilization that produced it. The movement spread from neutral Switzerland to Germany and Paris, attracting disillusioned intellectuals. Rejecting God, reason, and traditional standards of culture, Dadaists viewed life as absurd and nonsensical (Dada itself is a nonsense term). Tristan Tzara (1896–1945), a Rumanian-French poet and essayist, one of the founders of Dada and its chief spokesman, expressed this revulsion for the Western tradition in a series of manifestos. Below are excerpts from a lecture Tzara gave in 1922.

I know that you have come here today to hear explanations. Well, don't expect to hear any explanations about Dada. You explain to me why you exist. You haven't the faintest idea. You will say: I exist to make my children happy. But in your hearts you know that isn't so. You will say: I exist to guard my country against barbarian invasions. That's a fine reason. You will say: I exist because God wills. That's a fairy tale for children. You will never be able to tell me why you exist but you will always be ready to maintain a serious attitude about life. You will never understand that life is a pun, for you will never be alone enough to reject hatred, judgments, all these things that require such an effort, in favor of a calm and level state of mind that makes everything equal and without importance. . . .

These observations of everyday conditions have led us to a realization which constitutes our minimum basis of agreement, aside from the sympathy which binds us and which is inexplicable. It would not have been possible for us to found our agreement on principles. For everything is relative. What are the Beautiful, the Good, Art, Freedom? Words that have a different meaning for every individual. Words with the pretension of creating agreement among all, and that is why they are written with capital letters. Words which have not the moral value and objective force that people have grown accustomed to finding in them. Their meaning changes from one individual, one epoch, one country to the next. Men are different. It is diversity that makes life interesting. There is no common basis in men's minds. The unconscious is inexhaustible and uncontrollable. Its force surpasses us. It is as mysterious as the last particle of a brain cell. Even if we knew it, we could not reconstruct it.

What good did the theories of the philosophers do us? Did they help us to take a single step forward or backward? What is forward, what is backward? Did they alter our forms of contentment? We are. We argue, we dispute, we get excited. The rest is sauce. Sometimes pleasant, sometimes mixed with a limitless boredom, a swamp dotted with tufts of dying shrubs.

We have had enough of the intelligent movements that have stretched beyond measure our credulity in the benefits of science. What we want now is spontane-

ity. Not because it is better or more beautiful than anything else. But because everything that issues freely from ourselves, without the intervention of speculative ideas, represents us. We must intensify this quantity of life that readily spends itself in every quarter. Art is not the most precious manifestation of life. Art has not the celestial and universal value that people like to attribute to it. Life is far more interesting. Dada knows the correct measure that should be given to art: with subtle, perfidious methods, Dada introduces it into daily life. And vice versa. In art, Dada reduces everything to an initial simplicity, growing always more relative. It mingles its caprices with the chaotic wind of creation and the barbaric dances of savage tribes. It wants logic reduced to a personal minimum. . . . The absurd has no terrors for me, for from a more exalted point of view everything in life seems absurd to me. . . . The Beautiful and the True in art do not exist; what interests me is the intensity of a personality transposed directly, clearly into the work; the man and his vitality; the angle from which he regards the elements and in what manner he knows how to gather sensation, emotion, into a lacework of words and sentiments. . . .

We are often told that we are incoherent, but into this word people try to put an insult that it is rather hard for me to fathom. Everything is incoherent. The gentleman who decides to take a bath but goes to the movies instead. The one who wants to be quiet but says things that haven't even entered his head. Another who has a precise idea on some subject but succeeds only in expressing the opposite in words which for him are a poor translation. There is no logic. Only relative necessities discovered *a posteriori* [after the fact], valid not in any exact sense but only as explanations.

The acts of life have no beginning or end. Everything happens in a completely idiotic way. That is why everything is alike. Simplicity is called Dada.

Any attempt to conciliate an inexplicable momentary state with logic strikes me as a boring kind of game. The convention of the spoken language is ample and adequate for us, but for our solitude, for our intimate games and our literature we no longer need it.

The beginnings of Dada were not the beginnings of an art, but of a disgust. Disgust with the magnificence of philosophers who for 3000 years have been explaining everything to us (what for?), disgust with the pretensions of these artists-God's-representatives-on-earth, disgust with passion and with real pathological wickedness where it was not worth the bother; disgust with a false form of domination and restriction *en masse,* that accentuates rather than appeases man's instinct of domination, disgust with all the catalogued categories, with the false prophets who are nothing but a front for the interests of money, pride disease, disgust with the lieutenants of a mercantile art made to order according to a few infantile laws, disgust with the divorce of good and evil, the beautiful and the ugly (for why is it more estimable to be red rather than green, to the left rather than the right, to be large or small?). Disgust finally with the Jesuitical dialectic which can explain everything and fill people's

minds with oblique and obtuse ideas without any physiological basis or ethnic roots, all this by means of blinding artifice and ignoble charlatan's promises.

As Dada marches it continuously destroys, not in extension but in itself. From all these disgusts, may I add, it draws no conclusion, no pride, no benefit. It has even stopped combating anything, in the realization that it's no use, that all this doesn't matter. What interests a Dadaist is his own mode of life. But here we approach the great secret.

Dada is a state of mind. That is why it transforms itself according to races and events. Dada applies itself to everything, and yet it is nothing, it is the point where the yes and the no and all the opposites meet, not solemnly in the castles of human philosophies, but very simply at street corners, like dogs and grasshoppers.

Like everything in life, Dada is useless.

Dada is without pretension, as life should be.

Perhaps you will understand me better when I tell you that Dada is a virgin microbe that penetrates with the insistence of air into all the spaces that reason has not been able to fill with words or conventions.

ERNST VON SALOMON
Brutalization of the Individual

The war also produced a fascination for violence that persisted after peace had been declared. Many returned veterans, their whole being enveloped by the war, continued to yearn for the excitement of battle and the fellowship of the trenches. Brutalized by the war, these men became ideal recruits for fascist parties that relished violence and sought the destruction of the liberal state.

Immediately after the war ended, thousands of soldiers and adventurers joined the Free Corps — volunteer brigades that defended Germany's eastern borders against encroachments by the new states of Poland, Latvia, and Estonia, and fought communist revolutionaries. Many of these freebooters later became members of Hitler's movement. Ernst von Salomon, a leading spokesman of the Free Corps movement, was a sixteen-year-old student in Berlin when the defeated German army marched home. In the passage that follows, he described the soldiers who "will always carry the trenches in their blood."

The soldiers walked quickly, pressed closely to each other. Suddenly the first four came into sight, looking lifeless. They had stony, rigid faces. . . .

Then came the others. Their eyes lay deep in dark, gray, sharp-edged hollows under the shadow of their helmets. They looked neither right nor left, but straight ahead, as if under the power of a terrifying target in front of them; as if they peered from a mud hole or a trench over torn-up earth. In front of them lay emptiness. They spoke not a word. . . .

O God, how these men looked, as they came nearer — those utterly exhausted, immobile faces under their steel helmets, those bony limbs, those ragged dusty uniforms! And around them an infinite void. It was as if they had drawn a magic circle around themselves, in which dangerous forces, invisible to outsiders, worked their secret spell. Did they still carry in their minds the madness of a thousand battles compressed into whirling visions, as they carried in their uniforms the dirt and the dust of shell-torn fields? The sight was unbearable. They marched like envoys of death, of dread, of the most deadly and solitary coldness. And here was their homeland, warmth, and happiness. Why were they so silent? Why did they not smile?

. . . When I saw these deadly determined faces, these faces as hard as if hacked out of wood, these eyes that glanced past the onlookers, unresponsive, hostile — yes, hostile indeed — then I knew — it suddenly came over me in a fright — that everything had been utterly different from what we had thought, all of us who stood here watching. . . . What did we know about these men? About the war in the trenches? About our soldiers? Oh God, it was terrible: What we had been told was all untrue. We had been told lies. These were not our beloved heroes, the protectors of our homes — these were men who did not belong to us, gathered here to meet them. They did not want to belong to us; they came from other worlds with other laws and other friendships. And all of a sudden everything that I had hoped and wished for, that had inspired me, turned shallow and empty. . . . What an abysmal error it had been to believe for four years that these men belonged to us. Now that misunderstanding vanished. . . .

Then I suddenly understood. These were not workers, peasants, students; no, these were not mechanics, white-collar employees, businessmen, officials — these were soldiers. . . . These were men who had responded to the secret call of blood, of spirit, volunteers one way or the other, men who had experienced exacting comradeship and the things behind things — who had found a home in war, a fatherland, a community, and a nation. . . .

The homeland belonged to them; the nation belonged to them. What we had blabbered like marketwomen, they had actually lived. . . . The trenches were their home, their fatherland, their nation. And they had never used these words; they never believed in them; they believed in themselves. The war held them in its grip and dominated them; the war will never discharge them; they never will return home; they will always carry the trenches in their blood, the closeness of death, the dread, the intoxication, the iron. And suddenly they were to become peaceful citizens, set again in solid every-day routines? Never! That would mean a counterfeit that was bound to fail. The war is over; the warriors are still marching, . . . dissatisfied when they are demobilized, explosive when they stay together. The war had not given them answers; it had achieved no decision. The soldiers continue to march. . . .

Appeals were posted on the street corners for volunteer units to defend Germany's eastern borders. The day after the troops marched into our town, I volunteered. I was accepted and outfitted. Now I too was a soldier.

Review Questions

1. What did Paul Valéry mean in saying that the mind of Europe doubts itself profoundly?

2. Why do you think many veterans felt that they were part of a lost generation?

3. What value did Tristan Tzara give to art? What relationship did he draw between art and life?

4. Why was Tzara critical of philosophy and science? What did he value?

5. "The acts of life have no beginning or end?" What did Tzara mean by this statement?

6. What reasons can you think of why many Germans were attracted to paramilitary organizations immediately after the war?

Developments in Painting
from Impressionism to
the Abstract

THE BATHERS (1883–1884) by Georges Seurat (1859–1891), 79½ × 118½ in. Impressionist in its subject, colors, and sunlit effect, the painting is composed of carefully composed flicks of color. *(The National Gallery, London)*

THE JOY OF LIFE (1905–1906) by Henri Matisse (1869–1954), 68½×93¼ in. Fauvism, the first movement of twentieth-century painting, can be summed up in this picture: Classical poses rendered with radical simplicity, and the essence of nature captured in line and color. *(Photograph © 1987 by The Barnes Foundation)*

STREET DRESDEN (1908, dated on painting 1907) by Ernst Ludwig Kirchner (1880–1938), oil on canvas, 59¼ in. × 6 ft. 6⅞ in. A German expressionist influenced by Matisse and by Edvard Munch, Kirchner used strong, simple lines and bright color. *(Collection, The Museum of Modern Art, New York. Purchase)*

LES DEMOISELLES D'AVIGNON (1907) by Pablo Picasso (1881–1974), oil on canvas, 8 ft. × 7 ft. 8 in. Stimulated by the fauves and the post impressionists, Picasso created a new abstract style, cubism. *(Collection, The Museum of Modern Art, New York. Acquired through the Lillie P. Bliss Bequest)*

I AND THE VILLAGE (1911) by Marc Chagall (1887–1985), oil on canvas, 6 ft. 3⅝ in. × 59⅝ in. Chagall drew upon his childhood experience when painting this cubist fantasy of Russian Jewish village life. *(Collection, The Museum of Modern Art, New York. Mrs. Simon Guggenheim Fund)*

PAINTING (1933) by Joan Miró (1893–1983), oil on canvas 51⅜ × 64⅛ in. Beginning as a cubist, Miro developed an imaginative surrealism characterized by its fluid and vigorous shapes, as shown in this work. *(Wadsworth Atheneum, Hartford)*

CHAPTER · 9

The Russian Revolution and the Soviet Union

On the eve of World War I the Russian Empire faced a profound crisis. Ever-closer contact with the West, industrialization, and socioeconomic mobility resulting from a new railroad network were undermining the traditional foundations of state and society. Peasant uprisings were frequent; the new factories had spawned a rebellious working class. The tsar had never trusted the country's intellectuals — too many of them had turned into revolutionaries. Defeat in the war with Japan had led to the Revolution of 1905, nearly toppling the tsarist regime. Less than a decade later, as worldwide war approached, conservatives recognized and dreaded the prospect of military collapse followed by revolutionary anarchy. Liberals, less realistically, hoped for a constitutional regime that would let backward Russia catch up to the West. Radicals of utopian vision, like V. I. Lenin, expected the Russian workers to become the vanguard of a revolutionary advance that would bring freedom and justice to oppressed peoples all over the world.

Toward the end of World War I, the conservatives' fears came true. Nicholas II was overthrown in the March revolution of 1917; in the ensuing civic disorganization, the Russian state faced dissolution. The Germans were ready to partition the country. The liberal coalition that had formed a provisional government after the abdication of Nicholas II broke apart in early November. At that point, Lenin's Bolsheviks seized power, supported by the workers and soldiers in the country's capital of Petrograd (formerly St. Petersburg and after 1924 called Leningrad). In the civil war that followed, the Bolsheviks proved to be the only force capable of holding together a country faced with defeat, revolution, civil war, foreign intervention, and economic ruin. The government became a socialist dictatorship with Lenin at its head. Soviet Russia was guided by Marxist ideology adapted by Lenin to Russian conditions, and it was run by the professional revolutionaries of the Communist party in the name of elected councils (called Soviets) of workers and peasants. To counter the prevailing anarchy, Lenin preached discipline, the discipline of responsible social cooperation, which in Western countries had become, to a large extent, part of civic routine. Lenin believed that among the raw and violence-prone peoples of Russia discipline had to be enforced by compulsion and even terror. By the end of the civil war, however, even the workers and soldiers of Petrograd protested against the Communist dictatorship, and the garrison at the nearby Kronstadt naval base rose in revolt in 1921.

The years after the Kronstadt uprising were relatively calm. Russia re-gained its prewar standards of productivity, but it did not overcome the weaknesses that had led to catastrophe in World War I. To guard Soviet Russia against a similar fate was the burning ambition of Joseph Stalin, who in 1929, after a prolonged struggle, took over the leadership role vacated when Lenin died in 1924. The product of violence and revolutionary agi-tation since youth, Stalin started a second revolution far more brutal than Lenin's.

Rapid industrialization under successive Five-Year Plans led to appalling confusion, waste, and hardship, yet also to an impressive increase in produc-tivity. The forcible collectivization of agriculture, designed to crush the spirit of ever-rebellious peasants and to bring agricultural production under the planned economy, proved a savage process. By the end of the 1930s, how-ever, there was more food for everybody. All along, Stalin's revolution was accompanied by well-orchestrated methods of disciplining the country's het-erogeneous, stubborn, and willful peoples into docile citizens ready for the sacrifices of overly rapid industrialization and driven by patriotic dedication. The second revolution created a sense of citizenship among the peoples of Russia that was unique in the country's history.

Stalin burned to achieve the age-old Russian dream of overcoming the country's backwardness and matching the advanced Western countries in world power and prestige. His program was a desperate effort to create deliberately by compulsion and in the shortest time possible a modern Rus-sian state that would hold its own in a ruthlessly competitive, modern world. With harsh and cruel methods, so repulsive to Western values, Stalin trans-formed the Soviet Union into an industrial and world power.

1 | Intimations of Revolution

In the years before 1914, many Russians felt that they were sitting on top of an active volcano. After the Russian defeat in the Japanese war, the Revolution of 1905 forced Tsar Nicholas II (1894–1917) to grant the October Manifesto, a limited constitution with an elected Parliament, the State Duma. The tsar's armies subsequently returned from the Far East, restoring order and shoring up tsarist rule. Yet what would happen if the Russian army were destroyed, as was likely in the case of a much-predicted war with Germany?

PETER DURNOVO
Memorandum to Nicholas II

Peter Durnovo (1844–1914), a conservative official who was a former minister of the interior, foresaw the collapse of the tsarist regime in a war with Germany. He doubted — correctly as events proved — that in the case of a war-induced revolution, the constitutional opposition parties (the conservative Octobrists and the liberal Cadets) could establish a viable parliamentary regime. Instead, he anticipated revolutionary chaos. The following passages conclude a memorandum that he wrote to Nicholas II in February 1914, three years before the revolution broke out.

. . . An especially favorable soil for social upheavals is found in Russia, where the masses undoubtedly profess, unconsciously, the principles of Socialism. In spite of the spirit of antagonism to the Government in Russian society, as unconscious as the Socialism of the broad masses of the people, a political revolution is not possible in Russia, and any revolutionary movement inevitably must degenerate into a Socialist movement. The opponents of the Government have no popular support. The people see no difference between a Government official and an intellectual. The Russian masses, whether workmen or peasants, are not looking for political rights, which they neither want nor comprehend.

The peasant dreams of obtaining a gratuitous share of somebody else's land; the workman, of getting hold of the entire capital and profits of the manufacturer. Beyond this, they have no aspirations. If these slogans are scattered far and wide among the populace, and the Government permits agitation along these lines, Russia will be flung into anarchy, such as she suffered in the ever-memorable period of troubles in 1905–6. War with Germany would create exceptionally favorable conditions for such agitation. As already stated, this war is pregnant with enormous difficulties for us, and cannot turn out to be a mere triumphal march to Berlin. Both military disasters — partial ones, let us hope — and all kinds of shortcomings in our supply are inevitable. In the excessive nervousness and spirit of opposition of our society, these events will be given an exaggerated importance, and all the blame will be laid on the Government.

It will be well if the Government does not yield, but declares directly that in time of war no criticism of the governmental authority is to be tolerated, and resolutely suppresses all opposition. In the absence of any really strong hold on the people by the opposition, this would settle the affair. . . .

But a worse thing may happen: the Government authority may make concessions, may try to come to an agreement with the opposition, and thereby weaken

itself just when the Socialist elements are
ready for action. Even though it may
sound like a paradox, the fact is that
agreement with the opposition in Russia
positively weakens the Government. The
trouble is that our opposition refuses to
reckon with the fact that it represents no
real force. The Russian opposition is intellectual throughout, and this is its weakness, because between the intelligentsia and
the people there is a profound gulf of
mutual misunderstanding and distrust.
We need an artificial election law, indeed,
we require the direct influence of the
governmental authority, to assure the
election to the State Duma of even the most
zealous champions of popular rights. Let
the Government refuse to support the
elections, leaving them to their natural
course, and the legislative institutions
would not see within their walls a single
intellectual, outside of a few demogogic
agitators. However insistent the members of our legislative institutions may be
that the people confide in them, the peasant would rather believe the landless
Government official than the Octobrist
landlord in the Duma, while the working-
man treats the wage-earning factory in-
spector with more confidence than the
legislating manufacturer, even though the
latter professes every principle of the Ca-
det Party.

It is more than strange, under these
circumstances, that the governmental authority should be asked to reckon seriously with the opposition, that it should
for this purpose renounce the role of impartial regulator of social relationships,
and come out before the broad masses of
the people as the obedient organ of the
class aspirations of the intellectual and
propertied minority of the population.
The opposition demands that the Government should be responsible to it, rep-

resentative of a class, and should obey the
parliament which it artificially created. . . . In other words, the opposition demands that the Government should
adopt the psychology of a savage, and
worship the idol which he himself
made. . . .

. . . If the war ends in victory, the
putting down of the Socialist movement
will not offer any insurmountable obstacles. There will be agrarian troubles, as a
result of agitation for compensating the
soldiers with additional land allotments;
there will be labor troubles during the
transition from the probably increased
wages of war time to normal schedules;
and this, it is to be hoped, will be all, so
long as the wave of the German social
revolution has not reached us. But in the
event of defeat, the possibility of which in
a struggle with a foe like Germany cannot
be overlooked, social revolution in its most
extreme form is inevitable.

As has already been said, the trouble
will start with the blaming of the Government for all disasters. In the legislative
institutions a bitter campaign against the
Government will begin, followed by revolutionary agitations throughout the
country, with Socialist slogans, capable of
arousing and rallying the masses, beginning with the division of the land and succeeded by a division of all valuables and
property. The defeated army, having lost
its most dependable men, and carried away
by the tide of primitive peasant desire for
land, will find itself too demoralized to
serve as a bulwark of law and order. The
legislative institutions and the intellectual
opposition parties, lacking real authority
in the eyes of the people, will be powerless to stem the popular tide, aroused by
themselves, and Russia will be flung into
hopeless anarchy, the issue of which cannot be foreseen.

Review Questions

1. What was Peter Durnovo's view of the liberal opposition in tsarist Russia and
   its popular support?

2. What was Durnovo's assessment of the Russian masses and their political views?

3. What did Durnovo think of the Russian intellectuals?

4. What policies did he recommend for the government in case of war and unrest?

5. What, in Durnovo's opinion, would be the worst consequences of war with Germany?

2 | Theory and Practice of Bolshevism

As Durnovo had foreseen and events in 1917 proved, Russian liberals were not capable of ruling the country in times of supreme crisis. The question then became what political system and ideology could overcome "the hopeless anarchy" Durnovo anticipated. Could the rebellious peasants and workers — the working class — mount a successful revolution and build a Russian government more effective than that of the tsars? That question had long agitated Russian revolutionary leaders, and the answer would determine not only the fate of the revolution but also the survival of Russia as an independent state.

V. I. LENIN
What Is to Be Done?

Lenin (Vladimir Ilyich Ulyanov, 1870–1924) believed that on their own, the working class could never achieve a successful revolution; workers without leadership could not rise above petty trade unionism. Throughout his career, Lenin contrasted ignorant working-class "spontaneity" with revolutionary "consciousness," meaning deliberate action guided by the proper comprehension of the conditions under which revolutionaries must work. Under his leadership, the guiding ideology of the Soviet Union became Marxism-Leninism, that is, Marxist theory as applied by Lenin to the special conditions of Russia.

A seminal document of Marxism-Leninism was Lenin's pamphlet *What Is to Be Done?* published in 1902, fifteen years before the tsar's overthrow. In this tract Lenin addressed the big questions facing Russian Marxists (who sometimes called themselves Social Democrats after the German Social Democratic party that served as their model). How could they effectively channel the mounting discontent in Russian society and especially in the new industrial working class? How could they prevail against the secret police in the tsarist police state (referred to by Lenin as autocracy)? How could they find Russia's way among the complexities of the modern world and master them? The answers Lenin offered to these difficult questions — found in the following passages — helped shape the Soviet regime.

Without revolutionary theory there can be no revolutionary movement. This idea cannot be insisted upon too strongly at a time when the fashionable preaching of opportunism goes hand in hand with an infatuation for the narrowest forms of practical activity. Yet, for Russian Social-Democrats the importance of theory is enhanced by three other circumstances, which are often forgotten: first, by the fact that our Party is only in process of formation, its features are only just becoming defined, and it has as yet far from settled accounts with the other trends of revolutionary thought that threaten to divert the movement from the correct path. . . .

Secondly, the Social-Democratic movement is in its very essence an international movement. This means, not only that we must combat national chauvinism, but that an incipient movement in a young country can be successful only if it makes use of the experiences of other countries. In order to make use of these experiences it is not enough merely to be acquainted with them, or simply to copy out the latest resolutions. What is required is the ability to treat these experiences critically and to test them independently. He who realises how enormously the modern working-class movement has grown and branched out will understand what a reserve of theoretical forces and political (as well as revolutionary) experience is required to carry out this task.

Thirdly, the national tasks of Russian Social-Democracy are such as have never confronted any other socialist party in the world. We shall have occasion further on to deal with the political and organisational duties which the task of emancipating the whole people from the yoke of autocracy imposes upon us. At this point, we wish to state only that the *role of vanguard fighter can be fulfilled only by a party that is guided by the most advanced theory*. . . .

We have said that there *could not have been* Social-Democratic consciousness among the workers. It would have to be brought to them from without. The history of all countries shows that the working class, exclusively by its own effort, is able to develop only trade-union consciousness, i.e. the conviction that it is necessary to combine in unions, fight the employers, and strive to compel the government to pass necessary labour legislation, etc. The theory of socialism, however, grew out of the philosophic, historical, and economic theories elaborated by educated representatives of the propertied classes, by intellectuals. By their social status, the founders of modern scientific socialism, Marx and Engels, themselves belonged to the bourgeois intelligentsia. In the very same way, in Russia, the theoretical doctrine of Social-Democracy arose altogether independently of the spontaneous growth of the working-class movement; it arose as a natural and inevitable outcome of the development of thought among the revolutionary socialist intelligentsia. . . .

--- ◆ ◆ ◆ ---

Given the ignorance of the working class, said Lenin, revolutionary leadership had to come from a close-knit vanguard of dedicated and disciplined professional revolutionaries as well trained as the tsarist police and always in close touch with the masses. The revolutionary leaders had to raise working-class awareness to a comprehensive understanding of the coming crisis in Russia and the capitalist world generally.

--- ◆ ◆ ◆ ---

. . . I assert: (1) that no revolutionary movement can endure without a stable organisation of leaders maintaining continuity; (2) that the broader the popular mass drawn spontaneously into the struggle, which forms the basis of the movement and participates in it, the more urgent the need for such an organisation, and the more solid this organisation must be (for it is much easier for all sorts of demagogues to side-track the more backward sections of the masses); (3) that such an organisation must consist chiefly of people professionally engaged in revolutionary activity; (4) that in an autocratic state, the more we *confine* the membership of such an organisation to people who are professionally engaged in revolutionary activity and who have been professionally trained in the art of combating the political police, the more difficult will it be to unearth the organisation; and (5) the *greater* will be the number of people from the working class and from the other social classes who will be able to join the movement and perform active work in it. . . .

. . . Social-Democracy leads the struggle of the working class, not only for better terms for the sale of labour-power, but for the abolition of the social system that compels the propertyless to sell themselves to the rich. Social-Democracy represents the working class, not in its relation to a given group of employers alone, but in its relation to all classes of modern society and to the state as an organised political force. Hence, it follows that not only must Social-Democrats not confine themselves exclusively to the economic struggle, but that they must not allow the organisation of economic exposures to become the predominant part of their activities. We must take up actively the political education of the working class and the development of its political consciousness. . . .

--------------- ►•♦•◄ ---------------

Lenin did not think there was a danger that the secret, tightly centralized revolutionary organization would establish a dictatorship over the proletariat. He trusted that close comradeship and a sense of responsibility would lead to a superior revolutionary "democratism." He looked to the Russian revolutionaries as the vanguard of the international revolutionary movement.

--------------- ►•♦•◄ ---------------

. . . We can never give a mass organisation that degree of secrecy without which there can be no question of persistent and continuous struggle against the government. To concentrate all secret functions in the hands of as small a number of professional revolutionaries as possible does not mean that the latter will "do the thinking for all" and that the rank and file will not take an active part in the *movement.* On the contrary, the membership will promote increasing numbers of the professional revolutionaries from its ranks; for it will know that it is not enough for a few students and for a few working men waging the economic struggle to gather in order to form a "committee," but that it takes years to train oneself to be a professional revolutionary. . . . Centralisation of the most secret functions in an organisation of revolutionaries will not diminish, but rather increase the extent and enhance the quality of the activity of a large number of other organisations, that are intended for a broad public and are therefore as loose and as non-secret as possible, such as workers' trade unions; workers' self-education circles and circles for reading illegal literature; and socialist, as well as democratic, circles among *all* other sections of the population; etc., etc. We must have such circles, trade unions, and organisations everywhere in *as large a number as possible* and with the widest variety of functions. . . .

. . . The only serious organisational principle for the active workers of our movement should be the strictest secrecy, the strictest selection of members, and the training of professional revolutionaries. Given these qualities, something even more than "democratism" would be guaranteed to us, namely, complete, comradely, mutual confidence among revolutionaries. . . . They have a lively sense of their *responsibility,* knowing as they do from experience that an organisation of real revolutionaries will stop at nothing to rid itself of an unworthy member. . . .

. . . Our worst sin with regard to organisation consists in the fact that *by our primitiveness we have lowered the prestige of revolutionaries in Russia.* A person who is flabby and shaky on questions of theory, who has a narrow outlook, who pleads the spontaneity of the masses as an excuse for his own sluggishness, who resembles a trade-union secretary more than a spokesman of the people, who is unable to conceive of a broad and bold plan that would command the respect even of opponents, and who is inexperienced and clumsy in his own professional art — the art of combating the political police — such a man is not a revolutionary, but a wretched amateur! . . .

The Russian proletariat will have to . . . fight a monster compared with which an anti-socialist law in a constitutional country seems but a dwarf. History has not confronted us with an immediate task which is the *most revolutionary* of all the *immediate* tasks confronting the proletariat of any country. The fulfilment of this task, the destruction of the most powerful bulwark, not only of European, but (it may now be said) of Asiatic reaction, would make the Russian proletariat the vanguard of the international revolutionary proletariat. And we have the right to count upon acquiring this honourable title, already earned by our predecessors, the revolutionaries of the seventies, if we succeed in inspiring our movement, which is a thousand times broader and deeper, with the same devoted determination and vigour.

Review Questions

1. Why, in V. I. Lenin's thinking, did revolutionary theory play a crucial role in the overthrow of the tsarist regime?

2. How did Lenin think revolutionary theory that originated outside the working class could be in the interest of the working class?

3. According to Lenin, why did the revolutionary movement in Russia call for an elite of professional revolutionaries?

4. What did Lenin say were the qualities of the revolutionary elite?

5. How democratic was the organization of the revolutionary elite as described by Lenin?

6. Do you see an element of Russian nationalism in the special role Lenin assigned to the Russian workers?

3 | The Bolshevik Revolution

In March 1917, in the middle of World War I, Russians were demoralized. The army, poorly trained, inadequately equipped, and incompetently led, had suffered staggering losses; everywhere soldiers were deserting. Food shortages and low wages drove workers to desperation; the loss of fathers and sons at the front embittered peasants. Discontent was keenest in Petrograd, where on March 9, 200,000 striking workers shouting "Down with autocracy!" packed the streets. After some bloodshed, government troops refused to fire on the workers. Faced with a broad and debilitating crisis — violence and anarchy in the capital, breakdown of transport, uncertain food and fuel supplies, and general disorder — Tsar Nicholas II was forced to turn over authority to a provisional government, thereby ending three centuries of tsarist rule under the Romanov dynasty.

V. I. LENIN
The Call to Power

The Provisional Government, after July 1917 guided by Alexander Kerensky (1881–1970), sought to transform Russia into a Western-style liberal state, but the government failed to comprehend the urgency with which the Russian peasants wanted the landlords' land, and soldiers and the masses wanted peace. Resentment spiraled. Kerensky's increasing unpopularity and the magnitude of popular unrest seemed to Lenin, then in hiding, to offer the long-expected opportunity for the Bolsheviks to seize power. On November 6 (October 24 by the old-style calendar then in use in Russia) he urged immediate action, as the following document reveals.

. . . The situation is critical in the extreme. In fact it is now absolutely clear that to delay the uprising would be fatal.

With all my might I urge comrades to realise that everything now hangs by a thread; that we are confronted by problems which are not to be solved by conferences or congresses (even congresses of Soviets), but exclusively by peoples, by the masses, by the struggle of the armed people.

The bourgeois onslaught of the Kornilovites [followers of General Kornilov, who tried to establish a military dictatorship] show that we must not wait. We must at all costs, this very evening, this very night, arrest the government, having first disarmed the officer cadets (defeating them, if they resist), and so on.

We must not wait! We may lose everything!

Who must take power?

That is not important at present. Let the Revolutionary Military Committee [Bolshevik organization working within the army and navy] do it, or "some other institution" which will declare that it will relinquish power only to the true representatives of the interests of the people, the interests of the army (the immediate proposal of peace), the interests of the peasants (the land to be taken immediately and private property abolished), the interests of the starving.

All districts, all regiments, all forces must be mobilised at once and must immediately send their delegations to the Revolutionary Military Committee and to the Central Committee of the Bolsheviks [governing organization of the Bolshevik party] with the insistent demand that under no circumstances should power be left in the hands of Kerensky and Co. . . . not under any circumstances; the matter must be decided without fail this very evening, or this very night.

History will not forgive revolutionaries for procrastinating when they could be victorious today (and they certainly will be victorious today), while they risk losing much tomorrow, in fact, they risk losing everything.

If we seize power today, we seize it not in opposition to the Soviets but on their behalf.

The seizure of power is the business of the uprising; its political purpose will become clear after the seizure. . . .

. . . It would be an infinite crime on the part of the revolutionaries were they to let the chance slip, knowing that the *salvation of the revolution,* the offer of peace, the salvation of Petrograd, salvation from famine, the transfer of the land to the peasants depend upon them.

The government is tottering. It must be *given the death-blow* at all costs.

To delay action is fatal.

N. N. SUKHANOV
Changing the Guard

On the morning of November 7, 1917, the Bolsheviks struck. Their political headquarters was located at the Smolny Institute, formerly a school for aristocratic young ladies and now the seat of the Petrograd Soviet of Workers and Soldiers' Deputies formed in March 1917 when Nicholas II had been overthrown. The military leaders of the Bolsheviks were members of the Military-Revolutionary Committee, which controlled the garrison of Petrograd; this committee, under the command of Ensign V. A. Antonov-Ovseyenko, was in charge of seizing the capital. The following description of the overthrow of the Provisional Government is from *Russian Revolution, 1917*, written by N. N. Sukhanov, a prominent Menshevik (a Social Democratic moderate), who closely observed the events.

The decisive operations of the Military Revolutionary Committee started around 2 in the morning.

. . . Antonov says it was his plan that was accepted. It consisted in occupying first of all those parts of the city adjoining the Finland Station [railroad station]: the Vyborg Side [working-class suburb], the outskirts of the Petersburg Side [located on the city side of the Neva River], etc. Together with the units arrived from Finland [Russian sailors stationed in Finland] it would then be possible to launch an offensive against the centre of the capital. But of course — that was only in an extremity, in case of serious resistance, which was considered possible.

But no resistance was shown. Beginning at 2 in the morning the stations, bridges, lighting installations, telegraphs, and telegraphic agency were gradually occupied by small forces brought from the barracks. . . . In general the military operations in the politically important centres of the city rather resembled a changing of the guard. The weaker defence force . . . retired; and a strengthened defence force, of Guards [Red Guards of workers], took its place.

From evening on there were rumours of shootings and of armed cars racing round the city attacking Government pickets. But these were manifestly fancies. In any case the decisive operations that had begun were quite bloodless; not one casualty was recorded. The city was absolutely calm. Both the centre and the suburbs were sunk in a deep sleep, not suspecting what was going on in the quiet of the cold autumn night.

. . . When all the important points of the city were occupied without any resistance and the ranks, so-called, were placed not very far from the Winter Palace [seat of the Provisional Government; formerly the tsars' winter residence] and the Staff [Army headquarters], the Military Revolutionary Committee struck the bell. By 10 o'clock in the morning it had already written and had sent to be printed this proclamation: "To the citizens of Russia: The Provisional Government is overthrown. The state power has passed into the hands of the organ of the Petersburg Soviet of Workers' and Soldiers' Deputies, the Military Revolutionary Committee, which stands at the head of the Petersburg garrison and proletariat. The cause the people have been fighting for — the immediate proposal of a democratic peace, the elimination of private property in land, workers' control of production, and the formation of a Soviet Government — is assured. Long live the revolution of the workers, soldiers, and peasants! . . ."

Roughly the same thing was broadcast by wireless to the whole country and the front. There it was also added that the "new Government will convoke a Constituent Assembly" [an elective body to write a constitution for postrevolutionary Russia], and that "the workers were victorious without any bloodshed."

Review Questions

1. What promises did V. I. Lenin hold out to his supporters should the revolution succeed?

2. How would you characterize Lenin's mood on the eve of the Bolshevik seizure of power?

3. According to N. N. Sukhanov, how violent was the Bolshevik seizure of power in Russia's capital? How much opposition did it encounter?

4. How would you relate the revolution's promise to workers, soldiers, and peasants to Durnovo's prediction (see Selection 1) of utter anarchy should the tsarist government be overthrown?

4 | Russians and Westerners: A Comparison

Lenin and his Bolsheviks wanted to fashion a socialist society in which the proletariat would voluntarily submit to a superior work discipline. As Lenin was keenly aware — and as his successors have endlessly repeated — a socialist society requires redoubled discipline and efficiency, qualities not easily found among the Russian masses. The peoples of Russia were not like those of Western Europe or the United States. They had passed through an entirely different historical experience. Nature had always been hostile; cruel foreign invaders had roamed through their midst; tsars and landlords had imposed a harsh servitude; life had always been nasty, brutish, and short. The liberal-rational tradition of the West had hardly penetrated into Russian lands. Russia also lacked a strong, progressive, and influential middle class that had spurred reforms in Western lands. To many Westerners, Russia had always appeared as medieval, barbaric, and backward. Most Russians, of course, and the communists especially, were reluctant to admit these facts, but there is no dearth of evidence in the works of modern Russian writers, including those of Maxim Gorki (1868–1936).

MAXIM GORKI
On the Russian Peasantry

Aleksei Maksimovich Peshkov (Gorki was a pen name, meaning "the bitter one") was familiar with the dark side of Russian life from his own upbringing. He grew up amid physical and emotional violence imposed by a brutish grandfather, an impoverished tradesman in the city of Nizhni Novgorod (now renamed Gorki), and under the loving care of his long-suffering grandmother. On his own from an early age, he tramped through Russia, observing at close quarters how people lived and interacted. Self-taught, Gorki subsequently put his experiences into short stories, novels, and plays, becoming a well-known literary figure with a decided revolutionary bent long before the revolution. Gorki was a realist, honestly describing "our bestial Russian life," yet also convinced that "the Russian remains spiritually so young and sound that he can and does transcend" all brutality. In his essay "On the Russian Peasantry," written in 1922, he provided some insight into the temper of the people as revealed in the years of World War I, revolution, and civil war between the Bolsheviks (Reds) and their opponents (Whites) from 1918 to 1920.

From early childhood, as soon as he can get up on his hindlegs, Western man sees everywhere around him the monumental results of his ancestors' labour. From the canals of Holland to the tunnels of the Italian riviera and the vineyards of Vesuvius, from the great works of England to the mighty Silesian factories, the whole of Europe is closely covered by the grandiose incarnations of the organised will of the people, a will which set itself a proud aim: to subordinate the elemental forces of nature to the rational interests of man. The land is in the hands of man and man is its real ruler. The child of the West absorbs this impression, and it makes him aware of the worth of man, gives him a respect for his labour and a feeling for his personal significance, as the heir of the marvels of his ancestor's labour and creativity. . . .

Such thoughts, such feelings and values cannot arise in the heart of the Russian peasant. The boundless, flat country, in which straw-thatched, wooden hamlets closely huddle together, has a poisonous quality which devastates a man, and empties him of desire. When a peasant goes beyond the limits of his hamlet and looks at the emptiness around him, after a time he feels that this emptiness has filled his heart. Nowhere around are these stable traces of labour and creative work to be seen. The seats of the landlords? But they are few and occupied by enemies. The towns? But they are distant and are little more significant culturally than the hamlet. Around is a limitless plain, in its centre an insignificant little man, cast up on this boring earth for hard labour. Man is overcome by indifference, which kills his ability to think, to remember what he has seen, to generate his own ideas from his experience. A historian of Russian culture described the peasantry as: "a multitude of superstitions and no ideas."

This sad judgment is confirmed by the whole of Russian folklore. . . .

. . . Now, after the terrible madness of the European war and the bloody events of the revolution . . . I would note that Russian cruelty does not seem to evolve, its forms do not apparently change. . . .

. . . The peasants in Siberia dug pits and lowered Red Army prisoners into them upside down, leaving their legs to the knees above ground; then they gradually filled in the pit with soil, watching by the convulsions of the legs which of the victims was more resistant, livelier, and which would be the last to die.

The Trans-Baikal [to the east of Lake Baikal in Siberia] Cossacks trained their young men in the use of the sabre on prisoners.

In Tambov Guberniya [Tambov Province] Communists were nailed with railway spikes by their left hand and left foot to trees a metre above the soil, and they watched the torments of these deliberately oddly-crucified people.

They would open a prisoner's belly, take out the small intestine and nailing it to a tree or telegraph pole they drove the man around the tree with blows, watching the intestine unwind through the wound. Stripping a captured officer naked, they tore strips of skin from his shoulders in the form of shoulder straps, and knocked in nails in place of pips; they would pull off the skin along the lines of the sword belt and trouser stripes — this operation was called "to dress in uniform." It, no doubt, demanded much time and considerable skill.

Many similar horrors were perpetrated, but revulsion prevents me from adding to the number of descriptions of these bloody amusements. Who was crueller, Whites or Reds? Probably they were equal; after all, both of them were Russians. In any event, history gives a very clear answer to the question of degrees of cruelty: he who is the most active is the most cruel. . . .

. . . A soldier of the European War, now commander of a considerable detachment of the Red Army [said]:

An internal war, that's nothing! But internecine strife against others, that sticks in the gullet. I'll tell you straight, comrade, it's easier to kill a Russian. Our people are many, our economy is poor; well, if a hamlet is burnt, what's the loss. It would have burnt down itself in due course. And anyway, it's our own internal affair, a sort of manoeuvres, for learning, you might say. But when I happened to be in Prussia early in the other war — my God, I was so sorry for the people there, their villages, the towns and the whole set-up! What a splendid economy we destroyed for no known cause. It made you sick! . . . When I was wounded I was almost glad, it was so hard to look at the ugliness of life. Then I was in the Caucasus against Yudenich [a general in the anti-Bolshevik army], there there were Turks and other darkies. Very poor people, good chaps, smiling, you know, but nobody knows why. You beat him, and he smiles. I was sorry for them, too, I mean, each of them has his job, they're attached to life in their own way. . . .

This was said by a man, humane in his own fashion, on good terms with his soldiers and evidently respected and even loved by them, who loves his military profession. . . .

In discussing cruelty, one can hardly ignore the nature of the Jewish pogroms in Russia. The fact that these were permitted by the evil idiots who held power exonerates no-one and justifies nothing. In allowing the beating and pillaging of Jews, the idiots did not enjoin the terrorist hundreds taking part in the pogroms to cut off the breasts of Jewish women, beat their children, drive nails into Jewish skulls — all these bloody abominations must be seen as "manifestations of the personal initiative of the masses." . . .

To conclude this joyless sketch, I quote a story of a member of a scientific expedition which worked in the Urals [Ural Mountains] in 1921. A peasant turned to

the expedition with the following question: "You are educated people, tell me then, what's to happen to me; a Bashkir [one of the ethnic minority groups in the Soviet Union] killed my cow, so *of course,* I killed the Bashkir and then I took the cow away from his family, so tell me: shall I be punished for the cow?"

When they asked him whether he did not expect to be punished for the murder of the man, the muzhik [ignorant peasant] answered calmly: "That's nothing, people are cheap nowadays."

The phrase "of course" is here characteristic; it shows that murder has become a simple, usual matter. This is a result of the Civil War and of banditry.

Here is an example of how, sometimes, ideas new to the rural mind are perceived.

A rural teacher, the son of a peasant, wrote to me.

Since the celebrated scientist, Darwin, has established scientifically the necessity for a merciless struggle for existence and has no objection to the destruction of weak and useless people, and since in olden times old people were taken off to die of hunger in ravines or set in trees and shaken down to their death, so, protesting against such harshness, I propose that useless people should be destroyed by more compassionate means. For example, poison them with something tasty, and so on. Such measures would alleviate the universal struggle for existence, i.e. its methods. We should deal similarly with weak-minded idiots, with madmen and congenital criminals, and perhaps also with the incurably sick, the hunch-backed, the blind and suchlike. Such legislation, of course, will not please our whining intelligentsia, but the time has come to stop paying attention to their conservative and counterrevolutionary ideology. Keeping useless people costs the nation too much and this item of expenditure should be reduced to nil.

Many such and similar projects, letters and reports are now being written in Russia; they are very depressing, but also, despite their monstrosity, they make us feel that thought has been awakened in the countryside and, though clumsily, it is working in a direction completely new to it; the village is attempting to think of the state as a whole.

Review Questions

1. What, according to Maxim Gorki, were the differences between "Western man" and the Russian peasant?
2. What were some characteristic qualities of Russian peasants in these years of turmoil?
3. The final paragraph in this reading is cautiously optimistic. What reason did Gorki give for coming to this conclusion?

5 | Modernize or Perish

Joseph Stalin (1879–1953) was the communist leader who made the Soviet Union into a superpower. He was born Iosif Vissarionovich Dzhugashvili in Trans-Caucasus Georgia. A shiftless rebel from childhood, he was one of Lenin's favored professional revolutionaries, trained in the tough schools of underground agitation, tsarist prisons, and Siberian exile. Unscrupulous, energetic, and endowed with a keen nose for the realities of power within the party and the country as a whole, Stalin surpassed his political rivals in strength of will and organizational astuteness. After he was appointed secretary-general of the Communist party (then considered a minor post) in 1922, he concentrated on building, amid the disorganization caused by war, revolution, and civil war, an effective party organization adapted to the temper of the Russian people. With this structure's help, he established himself as Lenin's successor. Stalin, more powerful and more ruthless than Lenin, was determined to force his country to overcome the economic and political weakness that had led to defeat and ruin in 1917. After Lenin's death, Stalin preached the "Leninist style of work," which combined "Russian revolutionary sweep" with "American efficiency."

JOSEPH STALIN
The Hard Line

Firmly entrenched in power by 1929, Stalin started a second revolution (called the Stalin revolution), mobilizing at top speed the potential of the country, however limited the human and material resources available, whatever the obstacles, and whatever the human price. The alternative, he was sure, was foreign domination that would totally destroy his country's independence. In this spirit, he addressed a gathering of industrial managers in 1931, talking to them not in Marxist-Leninist jargon, but in terms of hard-line Russian nationalism.

It is sometimes asked whether it is not possible to slow down the tempo a bit, to put a check on the movement. No, comrades, it is not possible! The tempo must not be reduced! On the contrary, we must increase it as much as is within our powers and possibilities. This is dictated to us by our obligations to the workers and peasants of the U.S.S.R. This is dictated to us by our obligations to the working class of the whole world.

To slacken the tempo would mean falling behind. And those who fall behind get beaten. But we do not want to be beaten. No, we refuse to be beaten! One feature of the history of old Russia was the continual beatings she suffered for falling behind, for her backwardness. She was beaten by the Mongol Khans. She was beaten by the Turkish beys. She was beaten by the Swedish feudal lords. She was beaten by the Polish and Lithuanian gentry. She was beaten by the British and French capitalists. She was beaten by the Japanese barons. All beat her — for her backwardness: for military backwardness, for cultural backwardness, for political backwardness, for industrial backwardness, for agricultural backwardness. She was beaten because to do so was profitable and could be done with impunity. Do you remember the words of the pre-revolutionary poet [Nikolai Nekrassov]: "You are poor and abundant, mighty and impotent, Mother Russia." These words of the old poet were well learned by those gentlemen. They beat her, saying: "You are abundant," so one can enrich oneself at your expense. They beat her, saying: "You are poor and impotent," so you can be beaten and plundered with impunity. Such is the law of the exploiters — to beat the backward and the weak. It is the jungle law of capitalism. You are backward, you are weak — therefore you are wrong; hence, you can be beaten and enslaved. You are mighty — therefore you are right; hence, we must be wary of you.

That is why we must no longer lag behind.

In the past we had no fatherland, nor could we have one. But now that we have overthrown capitalism and power is in the hands of the working class, we have a fatherland, and we will defend its independence. Do you want our socialist fatherland to be beaten and to lose its independence? If you do not want this you must put an end to its backwardness in the shortest possible time and develop genuine Bolshevik tempo in building up its socialist system of economy. There is no other way. That is why Lenin said during the October Revolution: "Either perish, or overtake and outstrip the advanced capitalist countries."

We are fifty or a hundred years behind the advanced countries. We must make good this distance in ten years. Either we do it, or they crush us.

This is what our obligation to the workers and peasants of the U.S.S.R. dictate to us.

Review Questions

1. Why did Joseph Stalin argue that the tempo of industrialization could not be slowed down?

2. Which sentences in Stalin's statement seem to you the most quotable or the most important?

6 | Forced Collectivization

The forced collectivization of agriculture from 1929 to 1933 was an integral part of the Stalin revolution. His argument in favor of it was simple: an economy divided against itself cannot stand — planned industrial mobilization was incompatible with small-scale private agriculture in the traditional manner. Collectivization meant combining many small peasant holdings into a single large unit run in theory by the peasants (now called collective farmers), but in practice by the collective farm chairman guided by the government's Five-Year Plan.

JOSEPH STALIN
Liquidation of the Kulaks

Collectivization, not surprisingly, met with fierce resistance, especially from the more efficient peasants called kulaks, who were averse to surrendering their private plots and their freedom in running their households. Their resistance therefore had to be broken, and the Communist party fomented a rural class struggle, seeking help in this effort from the poorer peasants. Sometimes even the poorest peasants sided with the local kulaks. Under these conditions, Stalin did not shrink from unleashing violence in the countryside aimed at the "liquidation of the kulaks as a class." For Stalin the collectivization drive meant an all-out war on what was for him the citadel of backwardness: the peasant tradition and rebelliousness so prominent under the tsars. The following reading — Stalin's address to the Conference of Marxist Students of the Agrarian Question, December 1929 — conveys his intentions.

The characteristic feature of our work during the past year is: (a) that we, the party and the Soviet government, have developed an offensive on the whole front against the capitalist elements in the countryside; and (b) that this offensive, as you know, has brought about and is bringing about very palpable, *positive* results.

What does this mean? It means that we have passed from the policy of *restricting* the exploiting proclivities of the kulaks to the policy of *eliminating* the kulaks as a class. This means that we have made, and are still making, one of the most decisive turns in our whole policy.

. . . Could we have undertaken such an offensive against the kulaks five years or three years ago? Could we then have counted on success in such an offensive? No, we could not. That would have been the most dangerous adventurism! That

would have been playing a very dangerous game at offensive. We would certainly have come to grief and, once we had come to grief, we would have strengthened the position of the kulaks. Why? Because we did not yet have strongholds in the rural districts in the shape of a wide network of state farms and collective farms upon which to rely in a determined offensive against the kulaks. Because at that time we were not yet able to *substitute* for the capitalist production of the kulaks socialist production in the shape of the collective farms and state farms. . . .

But today? What is the position? Today, we have an adequate material base which enables us to strike at the kulaks, to break their resistance, to eliminate them as a class, and to *substitute* for their output the output of the collective farms and state farms. . . .

Now, as you see, we have the material

base which enables us to *substitute* for kulak output the output of the collective farms and state farms. That is why our offensive against the kulaks is now meeting with undeniable success. That is how the offensive against the kulaks must be carried on, if we mean a real offensive and not futile declamations against the kulaks.

That is why we have recently passed from the policy of *restricting* the exploiting proclivities of the kulaks to the policy of *eliminating the kulaks as a class.*

Well, what about the policy of expropriating the kulaks? Can we permit the expropriation of kulaks in the regions of solid collectivization? This question is asked in various quarters. A ridiculous question! We could not permit the expropriation of the kulaks as long as we were pursuing the policy of restricting the exploiting proclivities of the kulaks, as long as we were unable to launch a determined offensive against the kulaks, as long as we were unable to substitute for kulak output the output of the collective farms and state farms [run under state management]. At that time the policy of not permitting the expropriation of the kulaks was

necessary and correct. But now? Now the situation is different. Now we are able to carry on a determined offensive against the kulaks, to break their resistance, to eliminate them as a class and substitute for their output the output of the collective farms and state farms. Now, the kulaks are being expropriated by the masses of poor and middle peasants themselves, by the masses who are putting solid collectivization into practice. Now the expropriation of the kulaks in the regions of solid collectivization is no longer just an administrative measure. Now, the expropriation of the kulaks is an integral part of the formation and development of the collective farms. That is why it is ridiculous and fatuous to expatiate today on the expropriation of the kulaks. You do not lament the loss of the hair of one who has been beheaded.

There is another question which seems no less ridiculous: whether the kulak should be permitted to join the collective farms. Of course not, for he is a sworn enemy of the collective farm movement. Clear, one would think.

ANONYMOUS

A Kulak Story

The liquidation of the kulaks began in late 1929, extending through the length and breadth of the country during the winter. The killing rose to a brutal climax in the following spring and continued for another two years, by which time the bulk of the private farms had been eliminated. By some estimates, almost five million people were liquidated. Some were driven from their huts, deprived of all possessions, and left destitute in the dead of winter; the men were sent to forced labor and their families left abandoned. Others killed themselves or were killed outright, sometimes in pitched battles involving a whole village — men, women, and children.

The upheaval destroyed agricultural production in these years; farm animals died or were killed in huge numbers; fields lay barren. In 1932 and 1933, famine stalked the south and southeast, killing additional millions. The vast tragedy caused by collectivization did not deter Stalin from pursuing his goals: the establishment of state farms run like factories and the subordination of the rebellious and wilful peasantry to state authority.

The following reading, taken from an unpublished short novel, sheds some light on events in the countryside during the war against the kulaks. Roy Medvedev, a dissident Russian historian living in Moscow, quoted the following extract in his book

On Stalin and Stalinism. He identified the author only as ". . . A. M. who himself took part in the collectivization drive." The unknown author describes the eviction of a peasant named Terentyev, accused of being a kulak agent.

. . . The door opened and the brigade burst into the house. The OGPU [Secret Police] officer in charge of the operation was in front, holding a revolver.

"Hands up!"

Morgunov [the officer in charge] was barely able to distinguish the frail figure of the class enemy. He was barefoot, wearing white drawers and a dark under-shirt; a dishevelled beard stuck out on a face that was long unshaven. His eyes, wide with terror, darted from place to place. The lined face flinched, the coarse brown hands were trembling. Hanging from a worn-out cord on his bare chest was a little cross, grown dark with age.

"Lord Jesus, save us, have mercy on us!"

Gusts of freezing air came through the open door into the well-heated little hut. Members of the dekulakization brigade were already standing at each window, their faces stern. Expecting something dreadful to happen, they all were ready to rush into battle for their cause, for soviet power, for socialism. But the kulak-agent Terentyev never thought of resisting. He kept blinking and crossing himself, shifting from one foot to the other, as though he were standing on something hot, and suddenly he began to sob, his whole body shaken by convulsive gasps. He was bending over in a peculiar position, shuddering, and small, glisten-ing tears, one after another, rolled down the coarsened, weather-beaten face. His wife, no longer young, jumped down from the high sleeping bench and began to wail at the top of her voice; the children started to cry; and a calf, apparently rather sick

and lying beside the stove, added to the clamour. Morgunov looked around, quite horrified. He saw that the hut contained only the one room and the large Russian stove. In the front corner beneath the icons were two simple wooden benches and a crude table put together from planks. There was no sign of a dresser, or a bed, or a chair. On the shelves there were some simple wooden bowls, worn by years of use, and some old wooden spoons. Some oven forks and buckets of water stood by the stove, and on the left against the wall, a large old-fashioned trunk.

The class enemy!

The representatives of authority had already informed Terentyev that he was under arrest. He was to be dekulakized and deported straight away. All his pos-sessions would be confiscated. His family would follow shortly, but their destina-tion was not known. He could take with him only the clothes on his back and a change of underwear.

Terentyev trembled and wept. "How can you call us kulaks? What for? What have I done?" He got no reply. Roughly breaking the locks, they opened the trunk and the food cupboard and pulled out some sort of footgear, sackcloth, and foodstuffs.

"What for? What have I done?"

"Nothing. You're a kulak, a kulak-agent. You're against the collective farm. You don't want to join and you're upset-ting everything. And that's all there is to it!" And they started making a list of all his goods and possessions.

Review Questions

1. How, in Joseph Stalin's view, did socialist farming differ from capitalist farming?
2. Why were the kulaks selected as special targets in the drive for collectivization?

3. Can you detect in the first selection a distinctly Stalinist style of argument?

4. Describe the physical appearance of the peasant Terentyev and his hut. What significance did the cross on his chest have?

5. What was the attitude of Morgunov, the officer in charge of the dekulakization brigade?

6. Describe any relationships you see between the scenes described by A. M. and the incidents reported in the reading from Gorki in selection 4.

7 | Soviet Indoctrination

Pressed by the necessity to transform their country into a modern state, the communist leaders used every opportunity to force the population to adopt the attitudes and motivation necessary to effect such a transformation. Education, from nursery school to university, provided special opportunities to mold attitudes. The Soviet regime made impressive gains in promoting education among its diverse people; it also used education to foster dedication to hard work, discipline in social cooperation, and pride in the nation. For a backward country that, as Lenin had said, must "either perish or overtake and outstrip the advanced capitalist countries," such changes were essential.

During the Stalin era, artists and writers were compelled to promote the ideals of the Stalin revolution. In the style of "socialist realism," their heroes were factory workers and farmers who labored tirelessly and enthusiastically to build a new society. Even romance served a political purpose. Novelists wrote love stories following limited, prosaic themes. For example, a young girl might lose her heart to a co-worker who is a leader in the communist youth organization and who outproduces his comrades at his job; since the newly married couple is needed at the factory, they choose to forgo a honeymoon.

B. P. ESIPOV

I Want to Be Like Stalin

The following passage is a sample of Stalinist educational theory designed to inculcate among Soviet children the habits of "the new man." This reading is taken from a Russian text of pedagogy by B. P. Esipov. These habits include self-discipline, social responsibility, and patriotic loyalty in individual and collective conduct.

The basic mark of the new man — a member of communist society — is his new attitude toward labor, *a communist attitude toward labor*. Under the conditions of a socialist society labor is an expression of a need of a healthy organism. With us labor is not a grievous burden; nor is it performed under compulsion. On the contrary, it brings joy. In our country, as Comrade Stalin has said, labor "is a matter of *honor*, a matter of *glory*, a matter of *valor* and *heroism*." The communist attitude toward labor is associated with man's desire to serve society more fully, to work consciously and with highest productivity for the general welfare. . . .

The communist attitude toward labor is most intimately related to the *communist attitude toward public ownership* and to the solicitous attitude toward socialist property produced by social labor. "It is the duty of every citizen of the USSR," says the Stalin Constitution, "to safeguard and strengthen public, socialist property as the sacred and inviolable foundation of the Soviet system, as the source of the wealth and power of the Motherland, as the source of a prosperous and cultured life for all working people. . . .

Discipline is one of the basic conditions for the development of the communist attitude toward labor. For pupils labor is first of all studying. The cultivation of discipline in children has as its purpose the ensuring of successful schoolwork, the fostering of a conscious striving for perfect knowledge, and the preparation for organized and disciplined labor in higher schools, in production, and in the service of the Red Army.

A communist attitude toward labor signifies concern for the general good and for the interest of the Soviet state. To be of greatest possible usefulness to the Soviet Motherland through deeds is patriotism. People who work devotedly for society, who strive to contribute as much as possible to the state, and who are ready when necessary to give their lives for the Motherland — such people are patriots.

The cultivation of the spirit of Soviet patriotism in the younger generation is the most important task of moral education in our country. . . .

Duty to the Motherland is duty to the people; the feeling of love for one's fatherland is the feeling of devotion to the people. Our best men and women are banded together in our Communist Party which directs the entire life of the country. Soviet patriotism is expressed in devotion to the Communist Party and supreme readiness to serve the cause of Lenin and Stalin.

To educate the young in the spirit of Soviet patriotism means also to plant in their consciousness the understanding that the interests of our people and the interests of the toiling masses of the entire world are indivisible.

We set ourselves the task of educating every school child to grasp clearly the fact that the Soviet Union is a multi-national state, where the friendship of peoples is strengthened, where culture national in form and socialistic in content develops, where national antagonisms do not exist, and where creative constructive work is carried on in building a communist society. This will enable him to understand the leading role of our country in peaceful social life. . . .

. . . We must cultivate in our children the realization that the Union of Soviet Socialist Republics is a land where a socialist society is being constructed for the first time in history. We must develop in them a feeling of pride in the most revolutionary class, the working class, and in its vanguard, the Communist Party. This party, the party of Lenin and Stalin, was able to organize the toiling masses for the construction of a new communist society. Through the victories of the Stalin five-year plans, our land was transformed into a mighty industrial country, the most advanced and most cultured. We must make every school child aware of the grandeur of our struggle and our victories; we must show him the cost of these great successes in labor and blood; we must tell him how the great people of our epoch — Lenin, Stalin, and their companions in arms — organized the workers in the struggle for a new and happy life.

Our youth must be trained in militant readiness for the defense of their socialist fatherland. . . .

In his utterances Comrade Stalin emphasizes again and again the necessity of an attentive and careful attitude toward people. And in his own actions he offers a model of such an attitude by recognizing and honoring the best workers in the different branches of technology, military affairs, economy, science, and art.

Such is the morality of socialist humanism. We must cultivate in our children such an attitude toward people and such a consciousness of interdependence and of unity of interests of individual and society.

YEVGENY YEVTUSHENKO
Literature as Propaganda

After Stalin's death in 1953, Soviet intellectuals breathed more freely, and they protested against the rigid Stalinist controls. In the following extract from his *Precocious Autobiography,* Russian poet Yevgeny Yevtushenko (b. 1933) looks back from the stability provided by Soviet Russia's victory in World War II to the raw days of intellectual repression under Stalin.

Blankly smiling workers and collective farmers looked out from the covers of books. Almost every novel and short story had a happy ending. Painters more and more often took as their subject state banquets, weddings, solemn public meetings, and parades.

The apotheosis of this trend was a movie which in its grand finale showed thousands of collective farmers having a gargantuan feast against the background of a new power station.

Recently I had a talk with its producer, a gifted and intelligent man.

"How could you produce such a film?" I asked. "It is true that I also once wrote verses in that vein, but I was still wet behind the ears, whereas you were adult and mature."

The producer smiled a sad smile. "You know, the strangest thing to me is that I was absolutely sincere. I thought all this was a necessary part of building communism. And then I believed Stalin."

So when we talk about "the cult of personality," we should not be too hasty in accusing all those who, one way or another, were involved in it, debasing themselves with their flattery. There were of course sycophants [servile flatterers] who used the situation for their own ends. But that many people connected with the arts sang Stalin's praises was often not vice but tragedy.

How was it possible for even gifted and intelligent people to be deceived?

To begin with, Stalin was a strong and vivid personality. When he wanted to, Stalin knew how to charm people. He charmed Gorky and Barbusse. In 1937, the cruelest year of the purges, he managed to charm that tough and experienced observer, Lion Feuchtwanger. [Barbusse and Feuchtwanger were Western European writers.]

In the second place, in the minds of the Soviet people, Stalin's name was indissolubly linked with Lenin's. Stalin knew how popular Lenin was and saw to it that history was rewritten in such a way as to make his own relations with Lenin seem much more friendly than they had been in fact. The rewriting was so thorough that perhaps Stalin himself believed his own version in the end.

There can be no doubt of Stalin's love for Lenin. His speech on Lenin's death, beginning with the words, "In leaving us, Comrade Lenin has bequeathed . . ." reads like a poem in prose. He wanted to stand as Lenin's heir not only in other people's eyes, but in his own eyes too. He deceived himself as well as the others. Even [Boris] Pasternak put the two names side by side:

> Laughter in the village,
> Voice behind the plow,
> Lenin and Stalin,
> And these verses now . . .

In reality, however, Stalin distorted Lenin's ideas, because to Lenin — and this

was the whole meaning of his work —
communism was to serve man, whereas
under Stalin it appeared that man served
communism.

Stalin's theory that people were the little cogwheels of communism was put into
practice and with horrifying results. . . .
Russian poets, who had produced some
fine works during the war, turned dull
again. If a good poem did appear now
and then, it was likely to be about the war
— this was simpler to write about.

Poets visited factories and construction
sites but wrote more about machines than
about the men who made them work. If
machines could read, they might have
found such poems interesting. Human
beings did not.

The size of a printing was not determined by demand but by the poet's official standing. As a result bookstores were
cluttered up with books of poetry which
no one wanted. . . . A simple, touching
poem by the young poet Vanshenkin,
about a boy's first love, caused almost a
sensation against this background of
industrial-agricultural verse. Vinoku-
rov's first poems, handsomely disheveled
among the general sleekness, were avidly
seized upon — they had human warmth.
But the general situation was unchanged.
Poetry remained unpopular. The older
poets were silent, and when they did break

their silence, it was even worse. The generation of poets that had been spawned
by the war and that had raised so many
hopes had petered out. Life in peacetime
turned out to be more complicated than
life at the front. Two of the greatest Russian poets, Zabolotsky and Smelyakov,
were in concentration camps. The young
poet Mandel (Korzhavin) had been deported. I don't know if Mandel's name
will be remembered in the history of Russian poets but it will certainly be remembered in the history of Russian social
thought.

He was the only poet who openly wrote
and recited verses against Stalin while
Stalin was alive. That he recited them
seems to be what saved his life, for the
authorities evidently thought him insane.
In one poem he wrote of Stalin:

There in Moscow, in whirling
    darkness,
Wrapped in his military coat,
Not understanding Pasternak,
A hard and cruel man stared at the
    snow.

. . . Now that ten years have gone by,
I realize that Stalin's greatest crime was
not the arrests and the shootings he ordered. His greatest crime was the corruption of the human spirit.

VLADIMIR POLYAKOV

An Attack on Censorship: The Story of Fireman Prokhorchuk

The following reading by Soviet writer Vladimir Polyakov was published in Moscow
the year Stalin died. This "story of a story" is a humorous attack on censorship.

(The action takes place in the editorial offices of a Soviet magazine. A woman
writer — a beginner — shyly enters the
editors' office.)
    SHE Pardon me. . . . please excuse me.
. . . You're the editor of the magazine,
aren't you?

HE That's right.
    SHE My name is Krapivina. I've writ-
ten a little short story for your magazine.
    HE All right, leave it here.
    SHE I was wondering whether I
couldn't get your opinion of it right away.
If you'll permit me, I'll read it to you. It

won't take more than three or four minutes. May I?

HE All right, read it.

SHE It is entitled "A Noble Deed." (She begins to read.)

It was the dead of night — three o'clock. Everybody in the town was asleep. Not a single electric light was burning. It was dark and quiet. But suddenly a gory tongue of flame shot out of the fourth-floor window of a large gray house. "Help!" someone shouted. "We're on fire!" This was the voice of a careless tenant who, when he went to bed, had forgotten to switch off the electric hot plate, the cause of the fire. Both the fire and the tenant were darting around the room. The siren of a fire engine wailed. Firemen jumped down from the engine and dashed into the house. The room where the tenant was darting around was a sea of flames. Fireman Prokhorchuk, a middle-age Ukrainian with large black mustachios, stopped in front of the door. The fireman stood and thought. Suddenly he rushed into the room, pulled the smoldering tenant out, and aimed his extinguisher at the flames. The fire was put out, thanks to the daring of Prokhorchuk. Fire Chief Gorbushin approached him. "Good boy, Prokhorchuk," he said, "you've acted according to the regulations!" Whereupon the fire chief smiled and added: "You haven't noticed it, but your right mustachio is aflame." Prokhorchuk smiled and aimed a jet at his mustachio. It was dawning.

HE The story isn't bad. The title's suitable too: "A Noble Deed." But there are some passages in it that must be revised. You see, it's a shame when a story is good and you come across things that are different from what you'd wish. Let's see, how does it start, your story?

SHE It was the dead of night — three o'clock. Everybody in the town was asleep. . . .

HE No good at all. It implies that the police are asleep, and those on watch are asleep, and. . . . No, won't do at all. It indicates a lack of vigilance. That passage must be changed. Better write it like this: It was dead of night — three o'clock. No one in the town was asleep.

SHE But that's impossible, it's night-time and people do sleep.

HE Yes, I suppose you're right. Then let's have it this way: Everybody in the town was asleep but was at his post.

SHE Asleep at their posts?

HE No, that's complete nonsense. Better write: Some people slept while others kept a sharp lookout. What comes next?

SHE Not a single electric light was burning.

HE What's this? Sounds as if, in our country, we make bulbs that don't work?

SHE But it's night. They were turned off.

HE It could reflect on our bulbs. Delete it! If they aren't lit, what need is there to mention them?

SHE (reading on) But suddenly a gory tongue of flame shot out of the fourth-floor window of a large gray house. "Help!" someone shouted, "we're on fire!"

HE What's that, panic?

SHE Yes.

HE And it is your opinion that panic ought to be publicized in the columns of our periodicals?

SHE No, of course not. But this is fiction, . . . a creative work. I'm describing a fire.

HE And you portray a man who spreads panic instead of a civic-minded citizen? If I were you, I'd replace that cry of "help" by some more rallying cry.

SHE For instance?

HE For instance, say . . . ". . . We shall put it out!" someone shouted. "Nothing to worry about, there's no fire."

SHE What do you mean, "there's no fire," when there *is* a fire?

HE No, "there's no fire" in the sense of "we shall put it out, nothing to worry about."

SHE It's impossible.

HE It's possible. And then, you could do away with the cry.

SHE (reads on) This was the voice of

the careless tenant who, when he went to bed, had forgotten to switch off the electric hot plate.

HE The what tenant?

SHE Careless.

HE Do you think that carelessness should be popularized in the columns of our periodicals? I shouldn't think so. And then why did you write that he forgot to switch off the electric hot plate? Is that an appropriate example to set for the education of the readers?

SHE I didn't intend to use it educationally, but without the hot plate there'd have been no fire.

HE And would we be much worse off?

SHE No, better, of course.

HE Well then, that's how you should have written it. Away with the hot plate and then you won't have to mention the fire. Go on, read, how does it go after that? Come straight to the portrayal of the fireman.

SHE Fireman Prokhorchuk, a middle-aged Ukrainian . . .

HE That's nicely caught.

SHE . . . with large black mustachios, stopped in front of the door. The fireman stood there and thought.

HE Bad. A fireman mustn't think. He must put the fire out without thinking.

SHE But it is a fine point in the story.

HE In a story it may be a fine point but not in a fireman. Then also, since we have no fire, there's no need to drag the fireman into the house.

SHE But then, what about his dialogue with the fire chief?

HE Let them talk in the fire house. How does the dialogue go?

SHE (reads) Fire Chief Gorbushin approached him. "Good boy, Prokhorchuk," he said, "you've acted according to regulations!" Whereupon the fire chief smiled and added: "You haven't noticed it, but your right mustachio is aflame." Prokhorchuk smiled and aimed a jet at his mustachio. It was dawning.

HE Why must you have that?

SHE What?

HE The burning mustachio.

SHE I put it in for the humor of the thing. The man was so absorbed in his work that he didn't notice that his mustache was ablaze.

HE Believe me, you should delete it. Since there's no fire, the house isn't burning and there's no need to burn any mustachios.

SHE And what about the element of laughter?

HE There'll be laughter all right. When do people laugh? When things are good for them. And isn't it good that there's no fire? It's very good. And so everybody will laugh. Read what you have now.

SHE (reading) "A Noble Deed." It was the dead of night — three o'clock. Some people slept while others kept a sharp lookout. From the fourth-floor window of a large gray house somebody shouted: "We are not on fire!" "Good boy, Prokhorchuk!" said Fire Chief Gorbushin to Fireman Prokhorchuk, a middle-aged Ukrainian with large black mustachios, "you're following the regulations." Prokhorchuk smiled and aimed a jet of water at his mustachio. It was dawning.

HE There we have a good piece of writing! Now it can be published!

Review Questions

1. According to Soviet pedagogy, what is the communist attitude toward labor?

2. What, according to these guidelines, is the role of the Communist party?

3. From the B. P. Esipov reading, how were communists supposed to feel about Lenin and Stalin?

4. How do these guidelines promote pride in the Soviet Union?

5. What were Yevgeny Yevtushenko's reasons for denouncing Stalin?

6. Describe the contrasting attitudes in Yevtushenko's reading: first, before Stalin's death and then afterward.

7. What do you think Yevtushenko meant by "the corruption of the human spirit" under Stalin?

8. What values did the censor strive to uphold in Vladimir Polyakov's story?

9. What does the story suggest about the impact of censorship on creativity?

8 | Stalin's Terror

The victims of Stalin's terror number in the tens of millions. Stalin had no qualms about sacrificing multitudes of people to build up the Soviet Union's strength and to make it a powerful factor in world politics. In addition, he felt entitled to settle his own private scores as well as national ones against secessionist Ukrainians.

NIKITA KHRUSHCHEV
Khrushchev's Secret Speech

Nikita Khrushchev (1894–1971), first secretary of the Communist party (1953–1964) and premier of the Soviet Union (1958–1964) delivered a famous speech to an unofficial, closed session of the 20th Party Congress on February 25, 1956. Although the speech was considered confidential, it was soon leaked to outsiders. While safeguarding the moral authority of Lenin, Khrushchev attacked Stalin, revealing some of the crimes committed by him and his closest associates in the 1930s. The following passages from the speech draw on evidence collected by a special commission of inquiry.

We have to consider seriously and analyze correctly this matter [the crimes of the Stalin era] in order that we may preclude any possibility of a repetition in any form whatever of what took place during the life of Stalin, who absolutely did not tolerate collegiality in leadership and in work, and who practiced brutal violence, not only toward everything which opposed him, but also toward that which seemed to his capricious and despotic character, contrary to his concepts.

Stalin acted not through persuasion, explanation, and patient co-operation with people, but by imposing his concepts and demanding absolute submission to his opinion. Whoever opposed this concept or tried to prove his viewpoint, and the correctness of his position, was doomed to removal from the leading collective and to subsequent moral and physical annihilation. This was especially true during the period following the XVIIth Party Congress [1934], when many prominent Party leaders and rank-and-file Party workers, honest and dedicated to the cause of Communism, fell victim to Stalin's despotism. . . .

Stalin originated the concept "enemy of the people." This term automatically rendered it unnecessary that the ideological errors of a man or men engaged in a controversy be proven; this term made possible the usage of the most cruel repression, violating all norms of revolutionary legality, against anyone who in any way disagreed with Stalin, against those who were only suspected of hostile intent, against those who had bad reputations. This concept, "enemy of the people," actually eliminated the possibility of any kind of ideological fight or the making of one's views known on this or that issue, even those of a practical character. In the main, and in actuality, the only proof of guilt used, against all norms of current legal science, was the "confession" of the accused himself; and, as subsequent probing proved, "confessions" were acquired through physical pressures against the accused.

This led to glaring violations of revolutionary legality, and to the fact that many entirely innocent persons, who in the past had defended the Party line, became victims. . . .

The Commission [of Inquiry] has become acquainted with a large quantity of materials in the NKVD [secret police, forerunner to the KGB] archives and with other documents and has established many facts pertaining to the fabrication of cases against Communists, to false accusations, to glaring abuses of socialist legality — which resulted in the death of innocent people. It became apparent that many Party, Soviet and economic activists who were branded in 1937–1938 as "enemies" were actually never enemies, spies, wreckers, etc., but were always honest Communists; they were only so stigmatized, and often, no longer able to bear barbaric tortures, they charged themselves (at the order of the investigative judges — falsifiers) with all kinds of grave and unlikely crimes. . . .

Lenin used severe methods only in the most necessary cases, when the exploiting classes were still in existence and were vigorously opposing the revolution, when the struggle for survival was decidedly assuming the sharpest forms, even including a civil war.

Stalin, on the other hand, used extreme methods and mass repressions at a time when the revolution was already victorious, when the Soviet state was strengthened, when the exploiting classes were already liquidated and Socialist relations were rooted solidly in all phases of national economy, when our Party was politically consolidated and had strengthened itself both numerically and ideologically. It is clear that here Stalin showed in a whole series of cases his intolerance, his brutality and his abuse of power. Instead of proving his political correctness and mobilizing the masses, he often chose the path of repression and physical annihilation, not only against actual enemies, but also against individuals who had not committed any crimes against the Party and the Soviet government. . . .

An example of vile provocation, of odious falsification and of criminal violation of revolutionary legality is the case of the former candidate for the Central Committee Political Bureau, one of the most eminent workers of the Party and of the Soviet government, Comrade Eikhe, who was a Party member since 1905. *(Commotion in the hall.)*

Comrade Eikhe was arrested on April 29, 1938 on the basis of slanderous materials, without the sanction of the Prosecutor of the USSR, which was finally received 15 months after the arrest.

Investigation of Eikhe's case was made in a manner which most brutally violated Soviet legality and was accompanied by willfulness and falsification.

Eikhe was forced under torture to sign ahead of time a protocol of his confession prepared by the investigative judges, in which he and several other eminent Party workers were accused of anti-Soviet activity.

On October 1, 1939, Eikhe sent his declaration to Stalin in which he categorically denied his guilt and asked for an examination of his case. In the declaration he wrote: "There is no more bitter misery than to sit in the jail of a government for which I have always fought."

A second declaration of Eikhe has been preserved which he sent to Stalin on October 27, 1939; in it he cited facts very convincingly and countered the slanderous accusations made against him, arguing that this provocatory accusation was on the one hand the work of real Trotskyites whose arrests he had sanctioned as First Secretary of the West Siberian Krai Party Committee and who conspired in order to take revenge on him, and, on the other hand, the result of the base falsification of materials by the investigative judges. . . .

It would appear that such an important declaration was worth an examination by the Central Committee. This, however, was not done and the declaration was transmitted to Beria [head of the NKVD] while the terrible maltreatment of the Political Bureau candidate, Comrade Eikhe, continued.

On February 2, 1940 Eikhe was brought before the court. Here he did not confess any guilt and said as follows:

> In all the so-called confessions of mine there is not one letter written by me with the exception of my signatures under the protocols which were forced from me. I have made my confession under pressure from the investigative judge who from the time of my arrest tormented me. After that I began to write all this nonsense. . . . The most important thing for me is to tell the court, the Party and Stalin that I am not guilty. I have never been guilty of any conspiracy. I will die believing in the truth of Party policy as I have believed in it during my whole life.

On February 4 Eikhe was shot. (*Indignation in the hall.*)

Review Questions

1. Why was Nikita Khrushchev careful to distinguish Stalin from Lenin?

2. What charges against Stalin did Khrushchev highlight in his speech?

3. What image of Stalin did Khrushchev draw?

4. How did Stalin use the concept of the "enemy of the people"?

5. What attitude did Comrade Eikhe express in court about the party policy just before he was shot? What did this reveal about his character and about the strength of communist ideology?

CHAPTER 10

Fascism and World War II

Following World War I, fascist movements arose in Italy, Germany, and many other European countries. Although these movements differed — each a product of separate national histories and the outlook of each movement's leader — they shared a hatred of liberalism, democracy, and communism; a commitment to aggressive nationalism; and a glorification of the party leader. Fascist leaders cleverly utilized myths, rituals, and pageantry to mobilize and manipulate the masses.

Several conditions fostered the rise of fascism. One factor was the fear of communism among the middle and upper classes. Inspired by the success of the Bolsheviks in Russia, communists in other lands were calling for the establishment of Soviet-style republics. Increasingly afraid of a communist takeover, industrialists, landowners, government officials, army leaders, professionals, and shopkeepers were attracted to fascist movements that promised to protect their nations from this threat. A second factor contributing to the growth of fascism was the disillusionment of World War I veterans and the mood of violence bred by the war. The thousands of veterans facing unemployment and poverty made ideal recruits for fascist parties that glorified combat and organized private armies. A third contributing factor was the inability of democratic parliamentary governments to cope with the problems that burdened postwar Europe. Having lost confidence in the procedures and values of democracy, many people joined fascist movements that promised strong leadership, an end to party conflicts, and a unified national will.

Fascism's appeal to nationalist feelings also drew people into the movement. In a sense, fascism expressed the aggressive racial nationalism that had emerged in the late nineteenth century. Fascists saw themselves as dedicated idealists engaged in a heroic struggle to rescue their nations from domestic and foreign enemies; they aspired to regain lands lost by their countries in World War I or to acquire lands denied them by the Paris Peace Conference.

Fascists glorified instinct, will, and blood as the true forces of life; they openly attacked the ideals of reason, liberty, and equality — the legacies of the Enlightenment and the French Revolution. At the center of German fascism (National Socialism or Nazism) was a bizarre racial mythology that preached the superiority of the German race and the inferiority of others, particularly Jews and Slavs.

Benito Mussolini founder of the Italian Fascist party came to power in 1922. Although he established a one-party state, he was less successful than Adolf Hitler, the leader of the German National Socialists, in controlling the state and the minds of the people. After gaining power as chancellor of the German government in 1933, Hitler moved to establish a totalitarian state that controlled all phases of political, social, and cultural life. Utilizing modern methods of administration and communication, the Nazi state manipulated the lives and thoughts of its citizens to a much greater extent than had absolute and tyrannical governments of the past. Rejecting central liberal principles, it outlawed competing political parties, made terror a government policy, and drew no distinction between the individual's private life and the interests of the state. The Nazi regime aspired to shape a "new man," one who possessed a sense of mission and was willing to devote body and soul to the party, its ideology, and its leader, *Der Fuehrer,* who was endowed with attributes of infallibility.

Hitler's goal, which he pursued obsessively, was to forge a vast German empire in central and eastern Europe and to subjugate "inferior" races. Hitler explicitly laid out his philosophy of *Lebensraum* (living space) and racial nationalism, but Britain and France did not properly assess his intentions. Believing that the German dictator could be reasoned with and fearful of engulfing their nations in another disastrous world war, British and French statesmen gave in to Hitler's demands during the 1930s. This policy of appeasement only made Germany stronger and did not avert World War II.

Perhaps as many as fifty million people, both soldiers and civilians, died in World War II; of those, about twenty million were Russians, the Soviet Union suffering the most severe losses. Millions of people were murdered by the Nazis, including six million Jews, whom the Nazis aimed to exterminate. Nazi atrocities demonstrated anew the immense power of the irrational and the precariousness of Western civilization. The U.S. dropping of atomic bombs on the Japanese cities of Hiroshima and Nagasaki compounded doubts about humanity's future.

1 | Italian Fascism

Benito Mussolini (1883–1945) started his political life as a socialist and in 1912 was appointed editor of *Avanti*, the leading socialist newspaper. During World War I, Mussolini was expelled from the Socialist party for advocating Italy's entry into the conflict. Immediately after the war, he organized the Fascist party. Exploiting labor unrest, fear of communism, and thwarted nationalist hopes, Mussolini gained followers among veterans and the middle class. Powerful industrialists and landowners, viewing the Fascists as a bulwark against communism, helped to finance the young movement. An opportunist, Mussolini organized a march on Rome in 1922 to bring down the government. King Victor Emmanuel, fearful of civil war, appointed the Fascist leader prime minister. Had Italian liberals and the king taken a firm stand, the government could have crushed the 20,000 lightly armed marchers.

BENITO MUSSOLINI

Fascist Doctrines

Ten years after he seized power, Mussolini, assisted by philosopher Giovanni Gentile (1875–1944), contributed an article to the *Italian Encyclopedia* in which he discussed fascist political and social doctrines. In this piece, Mussolini lauded violence as a positive experience; attacked Marxism for denying idealism by subjecting human beings to economic laws and for dividing the nation into warring classes; and denounced liberal democracy for promoting individual selfishness at the expense of the national community and for its inability to solve the nation's problems. The fascist state, he said, required unity and power, not individual freedom. The following excerpts are from Mussolini's article.

. . . Above all, Fascism, the more it considers and observes the future and the development of humanity quite apart from political considerations of the moment, believes neither in the possibility nor the utility of perpetual peace. It thus repudiates the doctrine of Pacifism — born of a renunciation of the struggle and an act of cowardice in the face of sacrifice. War alone brings up to its highest tension all human energy and puts the stamp of nobility upon the peoples who have the courage to meet it. All other trials are substitutes, which never really put men into the position where they have to make the great decision — the alternative of life or death. Thus a doctrine which is founded upon this harmful postulate of peace is hostile to Fascism. And thus hostile to the spirit of Fascism, though accepted for what use they can be in dealing with particular political situations, are all the international leagues and societies which, as history will show, can be scattered to the winds when once strong national feeling is aroused by any motive — sentimental, ideal, or practical. This antipacifist spirit is carried by Fascism even into the life of the individual; the proud motto of the *Squadrista,* "Me ne frego" [It doesn't matter], written on the bandage of the wound, is an act of philosophy not only stoic, the summary of a doctrine not only political — it is the education to combat, the acceptation of the risks which combat implies, and a new way of life for Italy. Thus the Fascist accepts life and loves it, knowing nothing of and despising suicide: he rather conceives of life as duty and struggle and conquest, life which should be high and full, lived for oneself, but above all for others — those who are at hand and those who are far distant, contemporaries, and those who will come after. . . .

. . . Fascism [is] the complete opposite of . . . Marxian Socialism, the materialist conception of history; according to which the history of human civilization can be explained simply through the conflict of interests among the various social groups and by the change and development in the means and instruments of production. That the changes in the economic field — new discoveries of raw materials, new methods of working them, and the inventions of science — have their importance no one can deny; but that these factors are sufficient to explain the history of humanity excluding all others is an absurd delusion. Fascism, now and always, believes in holiness and in heroism; that is to say, in actions influenced by no economic motive, direct or indirect. And if the economic conception of history be denied, according to which theory men are no more than puppets, carried to and fro by the waves of chance, while the real directing forces are quite out of their control, it follows that the existence of an unchangeable and unchanging class-war is also denied — the natural progeny of the economic conception of history. And above all Fascism denies that class-war can be the preponderant force in the transformation of society. . . .

After Socialism, Fascism combats the whole complex system of democratic ideology, and repudiates it, whether in its theoretical premises or in its practical application. Fascism denies that the majority, by the simple fact that it is a majority, can direct human society; it denies that numbers alone can govern by means of a periodical consultation, and it affirms the immutable, beneficial, and fruitful inequality of mankind, which can never be permanently leveled through the mere operation of a mechanical process such as universal suffrage. . . .

. . . Fascism denies, in democracy, the absur[d] conventional untruth of political equality dressed out in the garb of collective irresponsibility, and the myth of "happiness" and indefinite progress. . . .

. . . Given that the nineteenth century was the century of Socialism, of Liberalism, and of Democracy, it does not necessarily follow that the twentieth century must also be a century of Socialism, Liberalism, and Democracy: political doctrines pass, but humanity remains; and it may rather be expected that this will be a century of authority, . . . a century of Fascism. For if the nineteenth century was a century of individualism (Liberalism always signifying individualism) it may be expected that this will be the century of collectivism, and hence the century of the State. . . .

The foundation of Fascism is the conception of the State, its character, its duty, and its aim. Fascism conceives of the State as an absolute, in comparison with which all individuals or groups are relative, only to be conceived of in their relation to the State. The conception of the Liberal State is not that of a directing force, guiding the play and development, both material and spiritual, of a collective body, but merely a force limited to the function of recording results: on the other hand, the Fascist State is itself conscious and has itself a will and a personality — thus it may be called the "ethic" State. . . .

. . . The Fascist State organizes the nation, but leaves a sufficient margin of liberty to the individual; the latter is deprived of all useless and possibly harmful freedom, but retains what is essential; the deciding power in this question cannot be the individual, but the State alone. . . .

. . . For Fascism, the growth of empire, that is to say the expansion of the nation, is an essential manifestation of vitality, and its opposite a sign of decadence. Peoples which are rising, or rising again after a period of decadence, are always imperialist; any renunciation is a sign of decay and of death. Fascism is the doctrine best adapted to represent the tendencies and the aspirations of a people, like the people of Italy, who are rising again after many centuries of abasement and foreign servitude. But empire demands discipline, the coordination of all forces and a deeply felt sense of duty and sacrifice: this fact explains many aspects of the practical working of the régime, the character of many forces in the State, and the necessarily severe measures which must be taken against those who would oppose this spontaneous and inevitable movement of Italy in the twentieth century, and would oppose it by recalling the outworn ideology of the nineteenth century — re-pudiated wheresoever there has been the courage to undertake great experiments of social and political transformation; for never before has the nation stood more in need of authority, of direction, and of order. If every age has its own characteristic doctrine, there are a thousand signs which point to Fascism as the characteristic doctrine of our time. For if a doctrine must be a living thing, this is proved by the fact that Fascism has created a living faith; and that this faith is very powerful in the minds of men is demonstrated by those who have suffered and died for it.

Review Questions

1. Why did Benito Mussolini consider pacifism to be the enemy of fascism?
2. Why did Mussolini attack Marxism?
3. How did Mussolini view majority rule and equality?
4. What relationship did Mussolini see between the individual and the state?

2 | The World-View of Nazism

In November 1918 a revolution forced the German emperor, Kaiser William II, to flee and a republic was proclaimed in Germany. Immediately afterward, the new government (soon to be called the Weimar Republic) signed an armistice agreement ending the war. The Weimar Republic, headed by democratic socialists, faced attacks from both the left and the right. In early 1919, German communists, seeking to establish a proletarian state, took up arms against the republic. Although the communists were easily subdued, the middle and upper classes were deeply scarred by the uprising. Fear of communism led many of these people to support the right-wing parties that sought to bring down the republic.

The rightist attack on the republic was multifaceted. Traditional conservatives — aristocrats, army leaders, and industrialists — were contemptuous of democracy and sought a strong government that would protect the nation from communism and check the power of the working class. Nationalists, in a peculiar twist of logic, blamed the defeat in the war and the humiliation of the Versailles Treaty on the republic.

Many extreme racist-nationalist and paramilitary organizations sprang up in postwar Germany. Adolf Hitler, a veteran of World War I, joined one of these organizations, which became known as the National Socialist German Worker's party (commonly called the Nazi party). Hitler (1889–1945) had uncanny insight into the state of mind of postwar Germans and at mass meetings employed his power as an orator to play on their dissatisfactions with the Weimar Republic.

ADOLF HITLER

Mein Kampf

In November 1923, Hitler attempted to overthrow the state government in Bavaria as the first step in bringing down the Weimar Republic. But the Nazis quickly scattered when the Bavarian police opened fire. Hitler was arrested and sentenced to five years' imprisonment — he served only nine months. While in prison, Hitler wrote *Mein Kampf* (*My Struggle*) in which he presented his views. The book came to be regarded as an authoritative expression of the Nazi world-view and served as a kind of sacred writing for the Nazi movement.

Hitler's thought — a patchwork of nineteenth-century anti-Semitic, Volkish, Social Darwinist, and anti-Marxist ideas — contrasted sharply with the core values of both the Judeo-Christian and the Enlightenment traditions. Central to Hitler's world-view was a racial mythology: a heroic Germanic race that was descended from the ancient Aryans who once swept across Europe, and was battling for survival against racial inferiors. In the following passages excerpted from *Mein Kampf*, Hitler presents his views of race, of propaganda, and of the National Socialist territorial goals.

[The Primacy of Race]

No more than Nature desires the mating of weaker with stronger individuals, even less does she desire the blending of a higher with a lower race, since, if she did, her whole work of higher breeding, over perhaps hundreds of thousands of years, might be ruined with one blow.

Historical experience offers countless proofs of this. It shows with terrifying clarity that in every mingling of Aryan blood with that of lower peoples the result was the end of the cultured people. North America, whose population consists in by far the largest part of Germanic elements who mixed but little with the lower colored peoples, shows a different humanity and culture from Central and South America, where the predominantly Latin immigrants often mixed with the aborigines on a large scale. By this one example, we can clearly and distinctly recognize the effect of racial mixture. The Germanic inhabitant of the American continent, who has remained racially pure and unmixed, rose to be master of the continent; he will remain the master as long as he does not fall a victim to defilement of the blood.

The result of all racial crossing is therefore in brief always the following:

(a) Lowering of the level of the higher race;

(b) Physical and intellectual regression and hence the beginning of a slowly but surely progressing sickness.

To bring about such a development is, then, nothing else but to sin against the will of the eternal creator. . . .

Everything we admire on this earth today — science and art, technology and inventions — is only the creative product of a few peoples and originally perhaps of *one* race. On them depends the existence of this whole culture. If they perish, the beauty of this earth will sink into the grave with them. . . .

All great cultures of the past perished only because the originally creative race died out from blood poisoning.

The ultimate cause of such a decline was their forgetting that all culture depends on men and not conversely; hence that to preserve a certain culture the man who creates it must be preserved. This preservation is bound up with the rigid law of necessity and the right to victory of the best and stronger in this world. . . .

If we were to divide mankind into three groups, the founders of culture, the bearers of culture, the destroyers of culture, only the Aryan could be considered as the representative of the first group. From him originate the foundations and walls of all human creation. . . .

Blood mixture and the resultant drop in the racial level is the sole cause of the dying out of old cultures; for men do not perish as a result of lost wars, but by the loss of that force of resistance which is contained only in pure blood.

All who are not of good race in this world are chaff. . . .

A state which in this age of racial poisoning dedicates itself to the care of its best racial elements must some day become lord of the earth.

Modern anti-Semitism was a powerful legacy of the Middle Ages and the unsettling changes brought about by rapid industrialization; it was linked to racist doctrines that asserted the Jews were inherently wicked and bore dangerous racial qualities. Hitler grasped the political potential of anti-Semitism: by concentrating all evil in one enemy, he could provide non-Jews with an emotionally satisfying explanation for all their misfortunes and thus manipulate and unify the German people.

[Anti-Semitism]

The mightiest counterpart to the Aryan is represented by the Jews. . . .

. . . The Jewish people, despite all apparent intellectual qualities, is without any true culture, and especially without any culture of its own. For what sham culture the Jew today possesses is the property of other peoples, and for the most part it is ruined in his hands.

In judging the Jewish people's attitude on the question of human culture, the most essential characteristic we must always bear in mind is that there has never been a Jewish art and accordingly there is none today either; that above all the two queens of all the arts, architecture and music, owe nothing original to the Jews. What they do accomplish in the field of art is either patchwork or intellectual theft. Thus, the Jew lacks those qualities which distinguish the races that are creative and hence culturally blessed. . . .

On this first and greatest lie, that the Jews are not a race but a religion, more and more lies are based in necessary consequence. Among them is the lie with regard to the language of the Jew. For him it is not a means for expressing his thoughts, but a means for concealing them. When he speaks French, he thinks Jewish, and while he turns out German verses, in his life he only expresses the nature of his nationality. As long as the Jew has not become the master of the other peoples, he must speak their languages whether he likes it or not, but as soon as they became his slaves, they would all have to learn a universal language. . . .

With satanic joy in his face, the black-haired Jewish youth lurks in wait for the unsuspecting girl whom he defiles with his blood, thus stealing her from her people. With every means he tries to destroy the racial foundations of the people he has set out to subjugate. . . .

For a racially pure people which is conscious of its blood can never be enslaved by the Jew. In this world he will forever be master over bastards and bastards alone.

And so he tries systematically to lower the racial level by a continuous poisoning of individuals.

And in politics he begins to replace the idea of democracy by the dictatorship of the proletariat.

In the organized mass of Marxism he has found the weapon which lets him dispense with democracy and in its stead allows him to subjugate and govern the peoples with a dictatorial and brutal fist.

He works systematically for revolutionization in a twofold sense: economic and political.

Around peoples who offer too violent a resistance to attack from within he weaves a net of enemies, thanks to his international influence, incites them to war, and finally, if necessary, plants the flag of revolution on the very battlefields.

In economics he undermines the states

until the social enterprises which have become unprofitable are taken from the state and subjected to his financial control.

In the political field he refuses the state the means for its self-preservation, destroys the foundations of all national self-maintenance and defense, destroys faith in the leadership, scoffs at its history and past, and drags everything that is truly great into the gutter.

Culturally he contaminates art, literature, the theater, makes a mockery of natural feeling, overthrows all concepts of beauty and sublimity, of the noble and the good, and instead drags men down into the sphere of his own base nature.

Religion is ridiculed, ethics and morality represented as outmoded, until the last props of a nation in its struggle for existence in this world have fallen. . . .

And so the Jew today is the great agitator for the complete destruction of Germany. Wherever in the world we read of attacks against Germany, Jews are their fabricators, just as in peacetime and during the War the press of the Jewish stock exchange and Marxists systematically stirred up hatred against Germany until state after state abandoned neutrality and, renouncing the true interests of the peoples, entered the service of the World War coalition.

The Jewish train of thought in all this is clear. The Bolshevization of Germany — that is, . . . to make possible the sweating of the German working class under the yoke of Jewish world finance [which] is conceived only as a preliminary to the further extension of this Jewish tendency of world conquest. As often in history, Germany is the great pivot in the mighty struggle. If our people and our state become the victim of these bloodthirsty and avaricious Jewish tyrants of nations, the whole earth will sink into the snares of this octopus; if Germany frees herself from this embrace, this greatest of dangers to nations may be regarded as broken for the whole world. . . .

———————— ◆•◆ ————————

Hitler was a master propagandist and advanced his ideas on propaganda techniques in

Mein Kampf. He mocked the learned and book-oriented German liberals and socialists whom he felt were entirely unsuited for modern mass politics. The successful leader, he said, must win over the masses through the use of simple ideas and images, constantly repeated, to control the mind by evoking primitive feelings. Hitler contended that mass meetings were the most effective means of winning over followers. What counted most at these demonstrations, he said, was will power, strength, and unflagging determination radiating from the speaker to every single individual in the crowd.

———————— ◆•◆ ————————

[Propaganda and Mass Rallies]

The function of propaganda does not lie in the scientific training of the individual, but in calling the masses' attention to certain facts, processes, necessities, etc., whose significance is thus for the first time placed within their field of vision.

The whole art consists in doing this so skillfully that everyone will be convinced that the fact is real, the process necessary, the necessity correct, etc. . . . Its effect for the most part must be aimed at the emotions and only to a very limited degree at the so-called intellect.

All propaganda must be popular and its intellectual level must be adjusted to the most limited intelligence among those it is addressed to. Consequently, the greater the mass it is intended to reach, the lower its purely intellectual level will have to be. . . .

The art of propaganda lies in understanding the emotional ideas of the great masses and finding, through a psychologically correct form, the way to the attention and thence to the heart of the broad masses. . . .

The receptivity of the great masses is very limited, their intelligence is small, but their power of forgetting is enormous. In consequence of these facts, all effective propaganda must be limited to a very few points and must harp on these in slogans until the last member of the public understands what you want him to understand by your slogan. As soon as you sacrifice this slogan and try to be many-sided, the effect will piddle away, for the crowd can neither digest nor retain the material offered. In this way the result is weakened and in the end entirely cancelled out.

Thus we see that propaganda must follow a simple line and correspondingly the basic tactics must be psychologically sound. . . .

The function of propaganda is, for example, not to weigh and ponder the rights of different people, but exclusively to emphasize the one right which it has set out to argue for. Its task is not to make an objective study of the truth, in so far as it favors the enemy, and then set it before the masses with academic fairness; its task is to serve our own right, always and unflinchingly. . . .

But the most brilliant propagandist technique will yield no success unless one fundamental principle is borne in mind constantly and with unflagging attention. It must confine itself to a few points and repeat them over and over. Here, as so often in this world, persistence is the first and most important requirement for success. . . .

The purpose of propaganda is not to provide interesting distraction for blasé young gentlemen, but to convince, and what I mean is to convince the masses. But the masses are slow-moving, and they always require a certain time before they are ready even to notice a thing, and only after the simplest ideas are repeated thousands of times will the masses finally remember them.

When there is a change, it must not alter the content of what the propaganda is driving at, but in the end must always say the same thing. For instance, a slogan must be presented from different angles, but the end of all remarks must always and immutably be the slogan itself. Only in this way can the propaganda have a unified and complete effect. . . .

All advertising, whether in the field of business or politics, achieves success through the continuity and sustained uniformity of its application. . . .

The mass meeting is . . . necessary for the reason that in it the individual, who at first,

while becoming a supporter of a young movement, feels lonely and easily succumbs to the fear of being alone, for the first time gets the picture of a larger community, which in most people has a strengthening, encouraging effect. The same man, within a company or a battalion, surrounded by all his comrades, would set out on an attack with a lighter heart than if left entirely on his own. In the crowd he always feels somewhat sheltered, even if a thousand reasons actually argue against it.

But the community of the great demonstration not only strengthens the individual, it also unites and helps to create an *esprit de corps*. The man who is exposed to grave tribulations, as the first advocate of a new doctrine in his factory or workshop, absolutely needs that strengthening which lies in the conviction of being a member and fighter in a great comprehensive body. And he obtains an impression of this body for the first time in the mass demonstration. When from his little workshop or big factory, in which he feels very small, he steps for the first time into a mass meeting and has thousands and thousands of people of the same opinions around him, when, as a seeker, he is swept away by three or four thousand others into the mighty effect of suggestive intoxication and enthusiasm, when the visible success and agreement of thousands confirm to him the rightness of the new doctrine and for the first time arouse doubt in the truth of his previous conviction — then he himself has succumbed to the magic influence of what we designate as "mass suggestion." The will, the longing, and also the power of thousands are accumulated in every individual. The man who enters such a meeting doubting and wavering leaves it inwardly reinforced: he has become a link in the community. . . .

———— ◆ •◆• ◆ ————

Hitler was an extreme nationalist who wanted a reawakened, racially united Germany to expand eastward at the expense of the Slavs, whom he viewed as racially inferior.

———— ◆ •◆• ◆ ————

[Lebensraum]

Only an adequately large space on this earth assures a nation of freedom of existence. . . .

If the National Socialist movement really wants to be consecrated by history with a great mission for our nation, it must be permeated by knowledge and filled with pain at our true situation in this world; boldly and conscious of its goal, it must take up the struggle against the aimlessness and incompetence which have hitherto guided our German nation in the line of foreign affairs. Then, without consideration of "traditions" and prejudices, it must find the courage to gather our people and their strength for an advance along the road that will lead this people from its present restricted living space to new land and soil, and hence also free it from the danger of vanishing from the earth or of serving others as a slave nation.

The National Socialist movement must strive to eliminate the disproportion between our population and our area — viewing this latter as a source of food as well as a basis for power politics — between our historical past and the hopelessness of our present impotence. . . .

. . . The demand for restoration of the frontiers of 1914 is a political absurdity of such proportions and consequences as to make it seem a crime. Quite aside from the fact that the Reich's frontiers in 1914 were anything but logical. For in reality they were neither complete in the sense of embracing the people of German nationality, nor sensible with regard to geo-military expediency. . . .

As opposed to this, we National Socialists must hold unflinchingly to our aim in foreign policy, namely, *to secure for the German people the land and soil to which they are entitled on this earth.* And this action is the only one which, before God and our German posterity, would make any sacrifice of blood seem justified. . . .

. . . Just as our ancestors did not receive the soil on which we live today as a gift from Heaven, but had to fight for it at the risk of their lives, in the future no folkish grace will win soil for us and hence life for our people, but only the might of a victorious sword.

Much as all of us today recognize the necessity of a reckoning with France, it would remain ineffectual in the long run if it represented the whole of our aim in foreign policy. It can and will achieve meaning only if it offers the rear cover for an enlargement of our people's living space in Europe. . . .

If we speak of soil in Europe today, we can primarily have in mind only *Russia* and her vassal border states. . . .

A state which in this age of racial poisoning dedicates itself to the care of its best racial elements must some day become lord of the earth.

May the adherents of our movement never forget this.

Review Questions

1. How did Adolf Hitler account for cultural greatness? Cultural decline?

2. What comparisons did Hitler draw between Aryans and Jews?

3. What kind of evidence did Hitler offer for his anti-Semitic arguments?

4. Theodor Mommsen, a nineteenth-century German historian, said that anti-Semites do not listen to "logic and ethical arguments. . . . They listen only to their own envy and hatred, to the meanest instincts." Discuss this statement.

5. What insights did Hitler have about mass psychology and propaganda?

6. What foreign policy goals did Hitler have for Germany? How did he expect them to be achieved?

3 | The Great Depression and Hitler's Rise to Power

Had it not been for the Great Depression that began in late 1929, the National Socialists might have remained a relatively small and insignificant party, a minor irritant outside the mainstream of German politics. In 1928 the Nazis had 810,000 votes; in 1930, during the Depression, their share of votes soared to 6,400,000. To many Germans, the Depression was final evidence that the Weimar Republic had failed. The traumatic experience of unemployment and the sense of hopelessness led millions to embrace Hitler.

HEINRICH HAUSER
With Germany's Unemployed

The following article excerpted from *Die Tat,* a National Socialist periodical, describes the loss of dignity suffered by the unemployed wandering Germany's roads and taking shelter in municipal lodging houses. Conditions in 1932 as described in the article radicalized millions of Germans, particularly young people.

An almost unbroken chain of homeless men extends the whole length of the great Hamburg–Berlin highway.

There are so many of them moving in both directions, impelled by the wind or making their way against it, that they could shout a message from Hamburg to Berlin by word of mouth.

It is the same scene for the entire two hundred miles, and the same scene repeats itself between Hamburg and Bremen, between Bremen and Kassel, between Kassel and Würzburg, between Würzburg and Munich. All the highways in Germany over which I traveled this year presented the same aspect. . . .

. . . Most of the hikers paid no attention to me. They walked separately or in small groups, with their eyes on the ground. And they had the queer, stumbling gait of barefooted people, for their shoes were slung over their shoulders. Some of them were guild members, — carpenters with embroidered wallets, knee breeches, and broad felt hats; milkmen with striped red shirts, and bricklayers with tall black hats, — but they were in a mi-

nority. Far more numerous were those whom one could assign to no special profession or craft — unskilled young people, for the most part, who had been unable to find a place for themselves in any city or town in Germany, and who had never had a job and never expected to have one. There was something else that had never been seen before — whole families that had piled all their goods into baby carriages and wheelbarrows that they were pushing along as they plodded forward in dumb despair. It was a whole nation on the march.

I saw them — and this was the strongest impression that the year 1932 left with me — I saw them, gathered into groups of fifty or a hundred men, attacking fields of potatoes. I saw them digging up the potatoes and throwing them into sacks while the farmer who owned the field watched them in despair and the local policeman looked on gloomily from the distance. I saw them staggering toward the lights of the city as night fell, with their sacks on their backs. What did it remind me of? Of the War, of the worst periods of starvation in 1917 and 1918, but even then people paid for the potatoes. . . .

I saw that the individual can know what is happening only by personal experience. I know what it is to be a tramp. I know what cold and hunger are. I know what it is to spend the night outdoors or behind the thin walls of a shack through which the wind whistles. I have slept in holes such as hunters hide in, in hayricks, under bridges, against the warm walls of boiler houses, under cattle shelters in pastures, on a heap of fir-tree boughs in the forest. But there are two things that I have only recently experienced — begging and spending the night in a municipal lodging house.

I entered the huge Berlin municipal lodging house in a northern quarter of the city. . . .

. . . There was an entrance arched by a brick vaulting, and a watchman sat in a little wooden sentry box. His white coat made him look like a doctor. We stood waiting in the corridor. Heavy steam rose from the men's clothes. Some of them sat down on the floor, pulled off their shoes, and unwound the rags that were bound around their feet. More people were constantly pouring in the door, and we stood closely packed together. Then another door opened. The crowd pushed forward, and people began forcing their way almost eagerly through this door, for it was warm in there. Without knowing it I had already caught the rhythm of the municipal lodging house. It means waiting, waiting, standing around, and then suddenly jumping up.

We now stand in a long hall, down the length of which runs a bar dividing the hall into a narrow and a wide space. All the light is on the narrow side. There under yellow lamps that hang from the ceiling on long wires sit men in white smocks. We arrange ourselves in long lines, each leading up to one of these men, and the mill begins to grind. . . .

. . . As the line passes in single file the official does not look up at each new person to appear. He only looks at the paper

that is handed to him. These papers are for the most part invalid cards or unemployment certificates. The very fact that the official does not look up robs the homeless applicant of self-respect, although he may look too beaten down to feel any. . . .

. . . Now it is my turn and the questions and answers flow as smoothly as if I were an old hand. But finally I am asked, "Have you ever been here before?"

"No."

"No?" The question reverberates through the whole room. The clerk refuses to believe me and looks through his card catalogue. But no, my name is not there. The clerk thinks this strange, for he cannot have made a mistake, and the terrible thing that one notices in all these clerks is that they expect you to lie. They do not believe what you say. They do not regard you as a human being but as an infection, something foul that one keeps at a distance. He goes on. "How did you come here from Hamburg?"

"By truck."

"Where have you spent the last three nights?"

I lie coolly.

"Have you begged?"

I feel a warm blush spreading over my face. It is welling up from the bourgeois world that I have come from. "No."

A coarse peal of laughter rises from the line, and a loud, piercing voice grips me as if someone had seized me by the throat: "Never mind. The day will come, comrade, when there's nothing else to do." And the line breaks into laughter again, the bitterest laughter I have ever heard, the laughter of damnation and despair. . . .

Again the crowd pushes back in the kind of rhythm that is so typical of a lodging house, and we are all herded into the undressing room. It is like all the other rooms except that it is divided by benches and shelves like a fourth-class railway carriage. I cling to the man who spoke to me. He is a Saxon with a friendly manner and he has noticed that I am a stranger here. A certain sensitiveness, an almost perverse, spiritual alertness makes me like him very much.

Out of a big iron chest each of us takes a coat hanger that would serve admirably to hit somebody over the head with. As we undress the room becomes filled with the heavy breath of poverty. We are so close together that we brush against each other every time we move. Anyone who has been a soldier, anyone who has been to a public bath is perfectly accustomed to the look of naked bodies. But I have never seen anything quite so repulsive as all these hundreds of withered human frames. For in the homeless army the majority are men who have already been defeated in the struggle of life, the crippled, old, and sick. There is no repulsive disease of which traces are not to be seen here. There is no form of mutilation or degeneracy that is not represented, and the naked bodies of the old men are in a disgusting state of decline. . . .

It is superfluous to describe what follows. Towels are handed out by the same methods described above. Then nightgowns — long, sacklike affairs made of plain unbleached cotton but freshly washed. Then slippers. All at once a new sound goes up from the moving mass that has been walking silently on bare feet. The shuffling and rattling of the hard soles of the slippers ring through the corridor.

Distribution of spoons, distribution of enameled-ware bowls with the words "Property of the City of Berlin" written on their sides. Then the meal itself. A big kettle is carried in. Men with yellow smocks have brought it and men with yellow smocks ladle out the food. These men, too, are homeless and they have been expressly picked by the establishment and given free food and lodging and a little pocket money in exchange for their work about the house.

Where have I seen this kind of food distribution before? In a prison that I once helped to guard in the winter of 1919 during the German civil war. There was

the same hunger then, the same trembling, anxious expectation of rations. Now the men are standing in a long row, dressed in their plain nightshirts that reach to the ground, and the noise of their shuffling feet is like the noise of big wild animals walking up and down the stone floor of their cages before feeding time. The men lean far over the kettle so that the warm steam from the food envelops them and they hold out their bowls as if begging and whisper to the attendant, "Give me a real helping. Give me a little more." A piece of bread is handed out with every bowl.

My next recollection is sitting at table in another room on a crowded bench that is like a seat in a fourth-class railway carriage. Hundreds of hungry mouths make an enormous noise eating their food. The men sit bent over their food like animals who feel that someone is going to take it away from them. They hold their bowl with their left arm part way around it, so that nobody can take it away, and they also protect it with their other elbow and with their head and mouth, while they move the spoon as fast as they can between their mouth and the bowl. . . .

We shuffle into the sleeping room, where each bed has a number painted in big letters on the wall over it. You must find the number that you have around your neck, and there is your bed, your home for one night. It stands in a row with fifty others and across the room there are fifty more in a row. . . .

I curl up in a ball for a few minutes and then see that the Saxon is lying the same way, curled up in the next bed. We look at each other with eyes that understand everything. . . .

. . . Only a few people, very few, move around at all. The others lie awake and still, staring at their blankets, wrapped up in themselves but not sleeping. Only an almost soldierly sense of comradeship, an inner self-control engendered by the presence of so many people, prevents the despair that is written on all these faces from expressing itself. The few who are moving about do so with the tormenting consciousness of men who merely want to kill time. They do not believe in what they are doing.

Going to sleep means passing into the unconscious, eliminating the intelligence. And one can read deeply into a man's life by watching the way he goes to sleep. For we have not always slept in municipal lodgings. There are men among us who still move as if they were in a bourgeois bedchamber. . . .

. . . The air is poisoned with the breath of men who have stuffed too much food into empty stomachs. There is also a sickening smell of lysol. It seems completely terrible to me, and I am not merely pitying myself. It is painful just to look at the scene. Life is no longer human here. Today, when I am experiencing this for the first time, I think that I should prefer to do away with myself, to take gas, to jump into the river, or leap from some high place, if I were ever reduced to such straits that I had to live here in the lodging house. But I have had too much experience not to mistrust even myself. If I ever were reduced so low, would I really come to such a decision? I do not know. Animals die, plants wither, but men always go on living.

LILO LINKE
Mass Suggestion

The Nazis exploited the misery of the German people during the Depression. In mass rallies, Hitler provided simple explanations for Germany's misfortunes, attacked the Versailles Treaty, and denounced the Jews and the Weimar Republic. In the following passage from *Restless Days: A German Girl's Autobiography*, Lilo Linke described her experience at such a rally during the Depression.

At this moment the whole audience rose from their seats, most of them with wild cheers — from the back, behind an S.A. [Nazi stormtrooper] man who carried a large swastika flag, and a drumming and blowing and [deafening] band, a procession of S.A. men and Hitler Youth [Nazi youth movement] marched towards the platform. I enjoyed the right to remain seated as a member of the press. When they were half-way through the hall, the curtain draped behind the platform opened and Hitler, wearing a dark suit, stepped forward to the decorated desk. The audience howled with enthusiastic madness, lifting their right arms in the Fascist salute.

Hitler stood unmoved. At last, when the crowd was already hoarse with shouting, he made a commanding gesture to silence them, and slowly obeying, they grew calmer, as a dog, called to order by its master after wild play, lies down, exhaustedly snarling.

For an hour and a half Hitler spoke, every few minutes interrupted by fanatic acclamations which grew into a frenzy after such phrases as:

"Today the world treats us like outcasts. But they will respect us again when we show them our good old German sword, flashing high above our heads!"

Or: "Pacifism is the contemptible religion of the weak; a real man is not afraid of defending his rights by force."

Or: "Those foreign blood-suckers, those degenerate asphalt-democrats, those cunning Jews, those whining pacifists, those corrupted November criminals[1] — we'll

---

[1] "November criminals" is a derogatory reference to the revolutionaries who overthrew the kaiser in November 1918 and established a republic.

knock them all down with our fists without pardoning a single one of them."

He thrust his chin forward. His voice,
hammering the phrases with an obsessed
energy, became husky and shrill and began to squeak more and more frequently.
His whole face was covered with sweat; a
greasy tress kept on falling on his forehead, however often he pushed it back.

Speaking with a stern face, he crossed
his arms over his breast — the imposing
attitude of one who stood under his own
supreme control. But a moment later a
force bursting out of him flung them into
the air, where they implored, threatened,
accused, condemned, assisted by his hands
and fists. Later, exhausted, he crossed
them on his back and began to march a
few steps to and fro along the front of the
platform, a lion behind the bars of his cage,
waiting for the moment when the door will
be opened to jump on the terror-stricken
enemy.

The audience was breathlessly under
his spell. This man expressed their
thoughts, their feelings, their hopes; a new
prophet had arisen — many saw in him
already another Christ, who predicted the
end of their sufferings and had the power
to lead them into the promised land if they
were only prepared to follow him.

Every word he said was true. They had
won the war — yes. Been deprived of the
reward for their heroism by a number of
traitors — yes. Had suffered incessantly
ever since — yes. Been enslaved, suppressed, exploited — yes, yes, yes. But the
day had arrived when they would free and
revenge themselves — *yes*.

A single question as to reason or proof
or possibility would have shattered the
whole argument, but nobody asked it —
the majority because they had begun to
think with their blood, which condemns
all logic, and the others because they sat
amazed, despairing, and hopeless in a
small boat tossed about by the foaming
waves of emotional uproar which surrounded it.

Under the sound of brass bands we
pushed out of the hall. Intimidated, I took
hold of Rolf's arm:

"Oh, Rolf, this is terrible — so inhuman — so full of hatred against all we value
— they don't understand what we want —
you'll see, they'll demolish all we built up
with our love and pains. The milkman,
revenging his inferiority with a shining
sword in his [swollen] hand and forcing
his suppressors under his will — what a
prospect for us, what a prospect for Germany!"

"Yet, my dear, something of what he
said —"

"Good heavens, Rolf, what is the matter with you? Are you going Nazi, too?"

"You are absurd. But if you are just,
you must admit that in many ways he is
right."

"My dear Rolf, to 'admit that in many
ways . . .' is always the beginning of the
end. Of course, the Nazis are not mere
villains, and they are striving for an ideal
for which they are willing to suffer. On
the other hand, much is rotten in the Republic and in the Republican parties. But
that doesn't mean that Hitler is right and
we are wrong, and you should know that
well enough."

"Yes, but we are democrats, and we
have to give them a chance —"

"To cut our throats. What a fool you
are! You can't treat like a gentleman
somebody who wants to murder you. The
protection of the democratic rules can only
be granted to those who follow them
themselves. The others must be stamped
out before they lift their heads too high."

"That is Bolshevism!"

"If you are right, I'll gladly be a Bol-
shevist, because I refuse to be made a
Nazi."

Review Questions

1. How did the Depression dehumanize people?
2. Judging from the description of the Nazi rally, what were the consequences of the Depression for German politics?
3. Account for Hitler's success at rallies.

4 | Nazism and Youth

Young people, in particular, were attracted to Nazism, in which they saw a cause worthy of their devotion. Victims of Nazi propaganda and led astray by their youthful idealism, they equated a total commitment to the Nazi movement with a selfless devotion to the nation.

ALICE HAMILTON
The Youth Who Are Hitler's Strength

Dr. Alice Hamilton (1869–1970) wrote the following article in 1933 after her second post–World War I trip to Germany. An international authority on industrial diseases who was known for her social consciousness, she was the first woman on the faculty of the Medical School of Harvard University. Her familiarity with Germany had begun in the late nineteenth century when she pursued postgraduate studies there. Her article, which appeared in the *New York Times Magazine* eight months after Hitler gained power, shows how the Nazis exploited patriotism, idealism, and a deep-seated desire of youth for fellowship.

Hitler's movement is called a youth movement and during the first months of the Nazi rule, while I was in Germany, this certainly seemed to be true. The streets of every city swarmed with brown shirts [trademark Nazi uniform], echoed to the sound of marching men and Hitler songs; there were parades, monster mass meetings, celebrations of all kinds, day in and day out. The swastika flag flapped from every building. In Frankfort-on-Main where I had spent, years ago, delightful student days, I went to the beautiful Römer Platz, only to find it unrecognizable, its lovely buildings hidden under fifty-three Nazi banners. Rathenau Square had been changed to Horst Wessel Square, for Wessel, the young organizer of storm detachments in the slums of Berlin, who died at the hands of Communists, is the new hero of Germany. . . .

To understand Hitler's enormous success with the young we must understand what life has meant to the post-war generation in Germany, not only the children of the poor but of the middle class as well. They were children during the years of the war when the food blockade kept them half starved, when fathers were away at the front and mothers distracted with the effort to keep their families fed. They came to manhood in a country which seemed to have no use for them. Even compulsory military training was no more and there was nothing to take its place. . . .

. . . A settlement worker told me that she knew families in which the children had come to manhood without ever realizing the connection between work and food. They had never had work, and food had come scantily and grudgingly from some governmental agency.

To these idle, hopeless youths two stirring calls to action came — one from the Communists, the other from Hitler; and to both of them German youth responded. Both appealed to hatred, both held out an ideal of a changed Germany, but Hitler's propaganda was cleverer than the Communists', because his program is narrower, more concrete. The Communist is internationally minded, his brothers are all over the world, his ideal State embraces all lands. Hitler repudiates internationalism; he is against all who are not German; his ideal State is a self-contained Germany, an object of fear to all her neighbors. The Communist is taught to hate a class, the capitalistic, the Hitlerite to hate each individual Jew. Many young Communists were brought under the banner of Hitler by appeals to national pride and race antagonism, but also by the ideal of a united Germany without class hatred.

Hitler made each insignificant, poverty-stricken, jobless youth of the slums feel himself one of the great of the earth, since the youth was a German, a Nordic, far superior to the successful Jew who was to be driven out of office and counting house to make place for the youth and his like. Hitler told the young men that the fate of Germany was in their hands, that if they joined his army they would battle with the Communists for the streets, they would see Jewish blood flow in streams, they would capture the government, deliver Germany from the Versailles treaty and then sweep triumphantly over the borders to reconquer Germany's lost land. He put them into uniforms, he taught them to march and sing together, he aroused that sense of comradeship and esprit de corps so precious to the young, and gave them what is even more pre-

cious — an object for hero worship. Life suddenly took on meaning and importance, with the call to danger, sacrifice, even death.

Among the hundreds of thousands who make up the audiences at Hitler's or Goebbels's meetings, and who seem to an outsider to be carried away by a kind of mass hysteria, there are many who are actuated by real idealism, who long to give themselves unreservedly to the great vision of a resurgent Germany. Being young they are of course contemptuous of the slow and moderate methods of the republic; they are for action, quick, arrogant, ruthless.

But their program calls for a changed Germany, one purged of all selfishness and materialism. They repudiate liberalism, for that means to them capitalism, it means the profit-making system, it means class distinctions, inequalities. The Germany the young are planning will have no division between the classes and will substitute the common good for individual profit. They really believe that Hitler will bring about a genuine socialism without class warfare and this part of their program is highly idealistic and fine, but, as is to be expected, it is mixed with the intolerance of youth, it calls for the forcible repression of opposition within the country and a battling front to be presented to the outside world. This is the outpouring of a student writing in the official organ of the Nazi students' league:

A people organically united and filled with the spirit of sacrifice for the common good, strong and eager for battle. A people fused into an unconquerable fighting unit against a hostile world. This is what we must achieve in these incomparably important days. The millions who stand aside from our movement must be made to believe in it. He is a traitor who now holds back. Our revolution marches on, over saboteurs and counter-revolutionaries, whoever they be.

The students . . . dream of a reform in the courts of justice which is to be brought about by requiring each candidate for the bar to serve for eight weeks in a labor camp, working shoulder to shoulder with men from all walks of life. In every way the barriers between workers and students must be abolished. "We must strive against intellectualism and liberalism which are Jewish. We wish to be red-blooded men. Students, show the peasant and worker that you are not intellectuals." . . .

And here is one of the songs which the boys and girls sing as they march through the streets.

Seest thou the morning red in the East, a promise of sun and of freedom? We hold together for life or for death, no matter what may threaten. Many a year were we slaves to traitor Jews, but now has arisen a son of the people — he gives to Germany new hope and faith. Brothers, to arms! Young and old flock to the hooked cross banner, peasants and workers with sword and with hammer. For Hitler, for freedom, for work and for bread. Germany, awaken! Death to the Jew! Brothers, to arms! . . .

In spite of the strict censorship of the press, we heard many a bloody tale of the Storm Troopers, but we heard even more about their high-handed methods in business houses and in the universities. While we were in Berlin the struggle was going on between the Nazi students and the rector of the university. It was on the issue of academic freedom. The students had nailed up twelve theses in the entrance hall of the main building and refused to take them down at the command of the rector. These were the theses that called for the expulsion of all "non-German teachers," that demanded that Jews should write only

in Hebrew and that repudiated "Jewish intellectualism." . . .

It was only too clear that whatever group had put up the theses ruled the university, and there were proofs aplenty that this was true. The rector threatened to resign if the proclamation was not removed. He did resign and his successor declared himself to be unreservedly behind the Nazi student movement. The new "Cultus-minister" soon afterward dissolved all student organizations and announced that there would be in the future one only, the Nazi students' league. He went on to praise the part played by the students in the revolution and to warn the faculties that they must no longer lag behind when youth led the way.

No wonder the students took things into their own hands, howled down the few Jewish professors who had received exceptional treatment because of war service, raided libraries, denounced suspected liberals right and left! The students of Kiel University demanded the discharge of twenty-eight professors. In Hamburg, when the university formally opened after the Spring holidays, a student arose and addressed the rector and faculty, telling them that any young Nazi was worth more to the Fatherland than the whole lot of them. His speech was received in silence.

Some two months later, also in Hamburg, a professor in the Medical School who was in the war and had declared himself an admirer of Hitler, was turned out of his position because a student reported that he had said something derogatory of the Nazis. The Berlin students undertook a "cleansing" of Magnus Hirschfeld's Institute of the Science of Sex. A procession of students in white shirts (for purity) drove to the institute in trucks bearing signs such as "German students march against the un-German spirit," and at a blare of trumpets they entered the library of the institute, seized books and pamphlets, threw them into the trucks and drove off. I suppose the books were consigned to the purifying flames.

All this seemed simply stupid and ugly and primitive to an American, an incomprehensible swing-back to a day when physical force was the only thing respected and men of thought shut themselves in monasteries and were not always safe there. But this is an aspect which the students with whom I talked could not see. They were passionately behind the new movement, the revolt against intellectualism, against scientific objectivity, against all that the German universities had stood for. The burning of the books was their work and they were proud of it.

This revolt of youth against modern education is a part of Hitler's program, for Hitler has long preached the necessity for a new pedagogy, one that is directed first toward physical prowess, then character training, while purely intellectual subjects are to be left for specialists. Herr Frick, Minister of the Interior, said while I was there: "The mistake of the past was for the school to train the child as an individual. This led, especially after the war, to the destruction of nation and State. We will supplant it by a training which will sink into the blood and flesh and cannot be uprooted for generations, a training which will fuse the German into his nation and bind him by the closest ties to his history and the destiny of his people."

The most important subject in the new curriculum is history, with the emphasis laid on German heroes, German inventors, German rulers, poets, artists. The German child must be taught that his nation is superior to every other in every field. Next to this comes politics and then everything that has to do with agriculture. Such subjects as mathematics and the physical sciences take a secondary place. Physical training and mental training find their culminating point in the last year, which is the year of compulsory service in labor camps. The training in these camps is military, for "defense warfare." For girls, education ends in a year of domestic service, with training for wifehood and motherhood.

Of course all the young men and girls accept Hitler's fantastic theories about "pure Germanism" and the superiority of the Aryan type, and that girl is most envied who can display two long braids of yellow hair. It is true that yellow hair and blue eyes are not as common in many parts of Germany as the Nazis could wish, but peroxide helps, and there is said to be a great demand for it now. It is a little ironical that the prophet of the Nordic religion should himself be black-haired and round-headed, a good example of the Alpine type he so despises. . . .

In his autobiography and in his voluminous speeches Hitler reveals himself as a man with the ambitions, the ideals, the crudities and the virtues of the adolescent. His physical courage and daring are those of the perfect soldier; he cares nothing for ease and comfort; he adores display, applause; he worships force and despises persuasion and mutual concession; he is intolerant of dissent, convinced of his own absolute rightness, and ready to commit any cruelty to carry out his own will.

It is this violent, fanatical, youthful despot, backed by some millions of like-minded youths, who now rules Germany. Truly it is a new thing in the world — a great modern country submitting itself to the will of its young men.

Review Questions

1. How did Alice Hamilton interpret repression and coercion in the universities?

2. What educational theory did the Nazis espouse?

3. The idealism of youth has often been praised. What dangers did Hamilton see in this idealism?

5 | Nazification of Culture

The Nazis aspired to more than political power; they also wanted to have the German people view the world in accordance with National Socialist ideology. Toward this end the Nazis strictly regulated cultural life. Believing that the struggle of racial forces occupied the center of world history, Nazi ideologists tried to strengthen the racial consciousness of the German people. Numerous courses in "race science" introduced in schools and universities emphasized the superiority of the Nordic soul and the worthlessness of Jews, and their threat to the nation.

JAKOB GRAF
Heredity and Racial Biology for Students

The following assignments from a textbook entitled *Hereditary and Racial Biology for Students* (1935) show how young people were indoctrinated with racist teachings.

How We Can Learn to Recognize a Person's Race

Assignments

1. Summarize the spiritual characteristics of the individual races.

2. Collect from stories, essays, and poems examples of ethnological illustrations. Underline those terms which describe the type and mode of the expression of the soul.

3. What are the expressions, gestures, and movements which allow us to make conclusions as to the attitude of the racial soul?

4. Determine also the physical features which go hand in hand with the specific racial soul characteristics of the individual figures.

5. Try to discover the intrinsic nature of the racial soul through the characters in stories and poetical works in terms of their inner attitude. Apply this mode of observation to persons in your own environment.

6. Collect propaganda posters and caricatures for your race book and arrange them according to a racial scheme. What image of beauty is emphasized by the artist (a) in posters publicizing sports

and travel? (b) in publicity for cosmetics? How are hunters, mountain climbers, and shepherds drawn?

7. Collect from illustrated magazines, newspapers, etc., pictures of great scholars, statesmen, artists, and others who distinguish themselves by their special accomplishments (for example, in economic life, politics, sports). Determine the preponderant race and admixture, according to physical characteristics. Repeat this exercise with the pictures of great men of all nations and times.

8. When viewing monuments, busts, etc., be sure to pay attention to the race of the person portrayed with respect to figure, bearing, and physical characteristics. Try to harmonize these determinations with the features of the racial soul.

9. Observe people whose special racial features have drawn your attention, also with respect to their bearing when moving or when speaking. Observe their expressions and gestures.

10. Observe the Jew: his way of walking, his bearing, gestures, and movements when talking.

11. What strikes you about the way a Jew talks and sings?

12. What are the occupations engaged in by the Jews of your acquaintance?
13. What are the occupations in which Jews are not to be found? Explain this phenomenon on the basis of the character of the Jew's soul.

LOUIS P. LOCHNER
Book Burning

The antiintellectualism of the Nazis was demonstrated on May 10, 1933, when the principal German student body organized students for a book-burning festival. In university towns, students consigned to the flames books that were considered a threat to the Germanic spirit. Louis P. Lochner (1887–1975), head of the Associated Press Bureau in Berlin, gave an eyewitness account of the scene in the German capital in *The Goebbels Diaries 1942–1943*.

The whole civilized world was shocked when on the evening of May 10, 1933, the books of authors displeasing to the Nazis, including even those of our own Helen Keller, were solemnly burned on the immense Franz Joseph Platz between the University of Berlin and the State Opera on Unter den Linden. I was a witness to the scene.

All afternoon Nazi raiding parties had gone into public and private libraries, throwing onto the streets such books as Dr. [Joseph] Goebbels [Nazi Propaganda Minister] in his supreme wisdom had decided were unfit for Nazi Germany. From the streets Nazi columns of beer-hall fighters had picked up these discarded volumes and taken them to the square above referred to.

Here the heap grew higher and higher, and every few minutes another howling mob arrived, adding more books to the impressive pyre. Then, as night fell, students from the university, mobilized by the little doctor, performed veritable Indian dances and incantations as the flames began to soar skyward.

When the orgy was at its height, a cavalcade of cars drove into sight. It was the Propaganda Minister himself, accompanied by his bodyguard and a number of fellow torch bearers of the new Nazi *Kultur*.

"Fellow students, German men and women!" he said as he stepped before a microphone for all Germany to hear him. "The age of extreme Jewish intellectualism has now ended, and the success of the German revolution has again given the right of way to the German spirit. . . .

"You are doing the right thing in committing the evil spirit of the past to the flames at this late hour of the night. It is a strong, great, and symbolic act — an act that is to bear witness before all the world to the fact that the spiritual foundation of the November Republic has disappeared. From these ashes there will rise the phoenix of a new spirit. . . .

"The past is lying in flames. The future will rise from the flames within our own hearts. . . . Brightened by these flames our vow shall be: The Reich and the Nation and our Fuehrer Adolf Hitler: *Heil! Heil! Heil!*"

The few foreign correspondents who had taken the trouble to view this "symbolic act" were stunned. What had happened to the "Land of Thinkers and Poets?" they wondered.

Review Questions

1. How does racism impede rational thought? Draw examples from the race science assignments.
2. What were the purposes of book burning?
3. What did Joseph Goebbels mean by "the age of extreme Jewish intellectualism has now ended"?
4. What type of "new spirit" did the Nazis seek to mold?

6 | The Anguish of the Intellectuals

A somber mood gripped European intellectuals in the postwar period. The memory of World War I, the rise of totalitarianism, and the Great Depression caused intellectuals to have grave doubts about the nature and destiny of Western civilization. To many European liberals it seemed that the sun was setting on the Enlightenment tradition, that the ideals of reason and freedom, already gravely weakened by World War I, could not endure the threats posed by economic collapse and totalitarian ideologies.

JOHAN HUIZINGA
In the Shadow of Tomorrow

Dutch historian Johan Huizinga (1872–1945) wrote that European civilization was at the breaking point in his *In the Shadow of Tomorrow* (1936).

We are living in a demented world. And we know it. It would not come as a surprise to anyone if tomorrow the madness gave way to a frenzy which would leave our poor Europe in a state of distracted stupor, with engines still turning and flags streaming in the breeze, but with the spirit gone.

Everywhere there are doubts as to the solidity of our social structure, vague fears of the imminent future, a feeling that our civilization is on the way to ruin. They are not merely the shapeless anxieties which beset us in the small hours of the night when the flame of life burns low. They are considered expectations founded on observation and judgment of an overwhelming multitude of facts. How to

avoid the recognition that almost all things which once seemed sacred and immutable have now become unsettled, truth and humanity, justice and reason? We see forms of government no longer capable of functioning, production systems on the verge of collapse, social forces gone wild with power. The roaring engine of this tremendous time seems to be heading for a breakdown. . . .

If, then, this civilization is to be saved, if it is not to be submerged by centuries of barbarism but to secure the treasures of its inheritance on new and more stable foundations, there is indeed need for those now living fully to realise how far the decay has already progressed.

It is but a little while since the apprehension of impending doom and of a progressive deterioration of civilization has become general. For the majority of men it is the economic crisis with its direct material effects (most of us being more sensitive in body than in spirit), which has first prepared the soil for thoughts and sentiments of this nature. Obviously those whose occupation it is to deal systematically and critically with problems of human society and civilization, philosophers and sociologists, have long ago realised that all was not well with our vaunted modern civilization. They have recognised from the outset that the economic dislocation is only one aspect of a transformation-process of much wider import.

The first ten years of this century have known little if anything in the way of fears and apprehensions regarding the future of our civilization. Friction and threats, shocks and dangers, there were then as ever. But except for the revolution menace which Marxism had hung over the world, they did not appear as evils threatening mankind with ruin. . . .

To-day, however, the sense of living in the midst of a violent crisis of civilization, threatening complete collapse, has spread far and wide. Oswald Spengler's *Untergang des Abendlandes*[1] has been the alarm signal for untold numbers the world over. This is not to say that all those who have read Spengler's famous work have become converts to his views. But it has jolted them out of their unreasoning faith in the providential nature of Progress and familiarised them with the idea of a decline of existing civilization and culture in our own time. Unperturbed optimism is at present only possible for those who through lack of insight fail to realise what is ailing civilization, having themselves been affected by the disease, and for those who in their social or political creed of

salvation think to have the key to the hidden treasure-room of earthly weal from which to scatter on humanity the blessings of the civilization to come. . . .

How naïve the glad and confident hope of a century ago, that the advance of science and the general extension of education assured the progressive perfection of society, seems to us to-day! Who can still seriously believe that the translation of scientific triumphs into still more marvellous technical achievements is enough to save civilization, or that the eradication of illiteracy means the end of barbarism! Modern society, with its intensive development and mechanisation, indeed looks very different from the dream vision of Progress! . . .

Delusion and misconception flourish everywhere. More than ever men seem to be slaves to a word, a motto, to kill one another with, to silence one another in the most literal sense. The world is filled with hate and misunderstanding. There is no way of measuring how great the percentage of the deluded is and whether it is greater than formerly, but delusion and folly have more power to harm and speak with greater authority. For the shallow, semi-educated person the beneficial restraints of respect for tradition, form and cult are gradually falling away. Worst of all is that widely prevalent indifference to truth which reaches its peak in the open advocacy of the political lie.

Barbarisation sets in when, in an old culture which once, in the course of many centuries, had raised itself to purity and clarity of thought and understanding, the vapours of the magic and fantastic rise up again from the seething brew of passions to cloud the understanding: when the *muthos* [myth] supplants the *logos* [reason].

Again and again the new creed of the heroic will to power, with its exaltation of life over understanding, is seen to embody the very tendencies which to the believer in the Spirit spell the drift towards barbarism. For the "life-philosophy" does exactly this: it extols *muthos* over *logos*. To the prophets of the life-philosophy bar-

---

[1] Oswald Spengler was the author of *Untergang des Abendlandes (The Decline of the West;* volume 1, 1918; volume 2, 1922), which maintained that Western civilization was dying.

barism has no deprecatory implications. The term itself loses its meaning. The new rulers desire nothing else. . . .

. . . Against all that seems to presage decline and ruin, contemporary humanity, except for a few fatalists, for once unanimously [asserts] the energetic declaration . . . we *will* not perish. This world of ours is, with all its misery, too fine to allow it to sink into a night of human deg-

radation and blindness of the spirit. We no longer count with an early end of all time. This heirloom of centuries called Western civilization has been entrusted to us to pass it on to coming generations, preserved, safeguarded, if possible enriched and improved, if it must be, impoverished, but at any rate as pure as it is in our power to keep it.

JOSÉ ORTEGA Y GASSET
The Revolt of the Masses

Another thinker who feared for the ideals of reason and freedom was Spanish philosopher José Ortega y Gasset (1883–1955). In *Revolt of the Masses* (1930), Ortega held that European civilization was degenerating into barbarism because of the growing power of the intellectually undisciplined and culturally unrefined masses. Ortega did not equate the masses with the working class and the elite with the nobility. For him, what distinguished the "mass-man" was an attitude that renounced rational dialogue in favor of violence and compulsion, and demanded uniformity of thought. These threats to Western civilization, he said, were exemplified in both communism and fascism. Excerpts from *The Revolt of the Masses* follow.

There is one fact which, whether for good or ill, is of utmost importance in the public life of Europe at the present moment. This fact is the accession of the masses to complete social power. As the masses, by definition, neither should nor can direct their own personal existence, and still less rule society in general, this fact means that actually Europe is suffering from the greatest crisis that can afflict peoples, nations, and civilisation. . . .

Strictly speaking, the mass, as a psychological fact, can be defined without waiting for individuals to appear in mass formation. In the presence of one individual we can decide whether he is "mass" or not. The mass is all that which sets no value on itself — good or ill — based on specific grounds, but which feels itself "just like everybody," and nevertheless is not concerned about it; is, in fact, quite happy to feel itself as one with everybody else. . . .

. . . I believe that the political innovations of recent times signify nothing less

than the political domination of the masses. The old democracy was tempered by a generous dose of liberalism and of enthusiasm for law. By serving these principles the individual bound himself to maintain a severe discipline over himself. Under the shelter of liberal principles and the rule of law, minorities could live and act. Democracy and law — life in common under the law — were synonymous. To-day we are witnessing the triumphs of a hyperdemocracy in which the mass acts directly, outside the law, imposing its aspirations and its desires by means of material pressure. . . . The mass believes that it has the right to impose and to give force of law to notions born in the café. I doubt whether there have been other periods of history in which the multitude has come to govern more directly than in our own. . . .

. . . *The characteristic of the hour is that the commonplace mind, knowing itself to be commonplace, has the assurance to proclaim the rights of the commonplace and to impose them wherever it will.* As they say in the United States: "to be different is to be indecent." The mass crushes beneath it everything that is different, everything that is excellent, individual, qualified and select. Anybody who is not like everybody, who does not think like everybody, runs the risk of being eliminated. And it is clear, of course, that this "everybody" is not "everybody." "Everybody" was normally the complex unity of the mass and the divergent, specialised minorities. Nowadays, "everybody" is the mass alone. Here we have the formidable fact of our times, described without any concealment of the brutality of its features. . . .

. . . It is illusory to imagine that the mass-man of to-day . . . will be able to control, by himself, the process of civilisation. I say process, and not progress. The simple process of preserving our present civilisation is supremely complex, and demands incalculably subtle powers. Ill-fitted to direct it is this average man who has learned to use much of the machinery of civilisation, but who is characterised by root-ignorance of the very principles of that civilisation. . . .

The command over public life exercised to-day by the intellectually vulgar is perhaps the factor of the present situation which is most novel, least assimilable to anything in the past. At least in European history up to the present, the vulgar had never believed itself to have "ideas" on things. It had beliefs, traditions, experiences, proverbs, mental habits, but it never imagined itself in possession of theoretical opinions on what things are or ought to be. . . . To-day, on the other hand, the average man has the most mathematical "ideas" on all that happens or ought to happen in the universe. Hence he has lost the use of his hearing. Why should he listen if he has within him all that is necessary? There is no reason now for listening, but rather for judging, pronouncing, deciding. There is no question concerning public life, in which he does not intervene, blind and deaf as he is, imposing his "opinions."

But, is this not an advantage? Is it not a sign of immense progress that the masses should have "ideas," that is to say, should be cultured? By no means. The "ideas" of the average man are not genuine ideas, nor is their possession culture. . . . Whoever wishes to have ideas must first prepare himself to desire truth and to accept the rules of the game imposed by it. It is no use speaking of ideas when there is no acceptance of a higher authority to regulate them, a series of standards to which it is possible to appeal in a discussion. These standards are the principles on which culture rests. I am not concerned with the form they take. What I affirm is that there is no culture where there are no standards to which our fellow-men can have recourse. There is no culture where there are no principles of legality to which to appeal. There is no culture where there is no acceptance of certain final intellectual positions to which a dispute may be referred. There is no culture where economic relations are not subject to a regulating principle to protect interests involved. There is no culture where aesthetic controversy does not recognise the necessity of justifying the work of art.

When all these things are lacking there is no culture; there is in the strictest sense of the word, barbarism. And let us not deceive ourselves, this is what is beginning to appear in Europe under the progressive rebellion of the masses. The traveller who arrives in a barbarous country knows that in that territory there are no ruling principles to which it is possible to appeal. Properly speaking, there are no barbarian standards. Barbarism is the absence of standards to which appeal can be made. . . .

. . . Under . . . Fascism there appears for the first time in Europe a type of man who does not want to give reasons or to be right, but simply shows himself resolved to impose his opinions. This is the new thing: the right not to be reasonable, the "reason of unreason." Here I see the most palpable manifestation of the new mentality of the masses, due to their having decided to rule society without the capacity for doing so. In their political conduct the structure of the new mentality is revealed in the rawest, most convincing manner. . . . The average man finds himself with "ideas" in his head, but he lacks the faculty of ideation. He has no conception even of the rare atmosphere in which ideas live. He wishes to have opinions, but is unwilling to accept the conditions and presuppositions that underlie all opinion. Hence his ideas are in effect nothing more than appetites in words. . . .

To have an idea means believing one is in possession of the reasons for having it, and consequently means believing that there is such a thing as reason, a world of intelligible truths. To have ideas, to form opinions, is identical with appealing to such an authority, submitting oneself to it, accepting its code and its decisions, and

therefore believing that the highest form of intercommunion is the dialogue in which the reasons for our ideas are discussed. But the mass-man would feel himself lost if he accepted discussion, and instinctively repudiates the obligation of accepting that supreme authority lying outside himself. Hence the "new thing" in Europe is "to have done with discussions," and detestation is expressed for all forms of intercommunion which imply acceptance of objective standards, ranging from conversation to Parliament, and taking in science. This means that there is a renunciation of the common life based on culture, which is subject to standards, and a return to the common life of barbarism. All the normal processes are suppressed in order to arrive directly at the imposition of what is desired. The hermetism [closing off] of the soul which, as we have seen before, urges the mass to intervene in the whole of public life. . . .

THOMAS MANN
An Appeal to Reason

Dismayed by the spread of fascism in Italy, Germany, and other lands, several thinkers attempted to reassert the ideals of reason and freedom. In 1931, two years before Hitler took power, the internationally prominent German author Thomas Mann (1875–1955) wrote an article entitled "An Appeal to Reason," in which he discussed the crisis in the European soul that gave rise to fascism. He saw National Socialism and the extreme nationalism it espoused as a rejection of the Western rational tradition and as a regression to primitive and barbaric modes of behavior. Some excerpts from Mann's article follow.

. . . The economic decline of the middle classes was accompanied — or even preceded — by a feeling which amounted to an intellectual prophecy and critique of the age: the sense that here was a crisis which heralded the end of the bourgeois epoch that came in with the French revolution and the notions appertaining to it. There was proclaimed a new mental attitude for all mankind, which should have nothing to do with bourgeois principles such as freedom, justice, culture, optimism, faith in progress. As art, it gave vent to expressionistic soul-shrieks; as

philosophy it repudiated . . . reason, and the . . . ideological conceptions of bygone decades; it expressed itself as an irrationalistic throwback, placing the conception *life* at the centre of thought, and raised on its standard the powers of the unconscious, the dynamic, the darkly creative, which alone were life-giving. Mind, quite simply the intellectual, it put under a taboo as destructive of life, while it set up for homage as the true inwardness of life . . . the darkness of the soul, the holy procreative underworld. Much of this nature-religion, by its very essence inclining to the orgiastic and to . . . [frenzied] excess, has gone into the nationalism of our day, making of it something quite different from the nationalism of the nineteenth century, with its bourgeois, strongly cosmopolitan and humanitarian cast. It is distinguished in its character as a nature-cult, precisely by its absolute unrestraint, its orgiastic, radically anti-humane, frenziedly dynamic character. . . .

. . . And there is even more: there are other intellectual elements come to strengthen this national-social political movement — a certain ideology, a Nordic creed, a Germanistic romanticism, from philological, academic, professorial spheres. It addresses the Germany of 1930 in a highflown wishy-washy jargon full of mystical good feeling, with hyphenated prefixes like race- and folk- and fellowship-, and lends to the movement a . . . fanatical cult-barbarism, . . . dangerous and estranging, with . . . power to clog and stultify the brain. . . .

Fed, then, by such intellectual and pseudo-intellectual currents as these, the movement which we sum up under the name of national-socialism and which has displayed such a power of enlisting recruits to its banner, mingles with the mighty wave — a wave of anomalous barbarism, of primitive popular vulgarity — that sweeps over the world to-day, assailing the nerves of mankind with wild, bewildering, stimulating, intoxicating sensations. . . . Humanity seems to have run

like boys let out of school away from the humanitarian, idealistic nineteenth century, from whose morality — if we can speak at all of morality in this connection — our time represents a wide and wild reaction. Everything is possible, everything permitted as a weapon against human decency; if we have got rid of the idea of freedom as a relic of the bourgeois state of mind, as though an idea so bound up with all European feeling, upon which Europe has been founded, for which she has made such sacrifices, could ever be utterly lost — it comes back again, this castoff conception, in a guise suited to the time: as demoralization, as a mockery of all human authority, as a free rein to instincts, as the emancipation of brutality, the dictatorship of force. . . . In all this violence demonstrates itself, and demonstrates nothing but violence, and even that is unnecessary, for all other considerations are fallen away, man does not any longer believe in them, and so the road is free to vulgarity without restraint.

This fantastic state of mind, of a humanity that has outrun its ideas, is matched by a political scene in the grotesque style, with Salvation Army methods, hallelujahs and bell-ringing and dervishlike repetition of monotonous catchwords, until everybody foams at the mouth. Fanaticism turns into a means of salvation, enthusiasm into epileptic ecstasy, politics becomes an opiate for the masses, . . . and reason veils her face.

ARTHUR KOESTLER
The Appeal of Communism

The 1930s have been called the Pink Decade, because many intellectuals, anguished by the Depression and fascism, found a new hope in communism and the Soviet Union. One such intellectual was Arthur Koestler (1905–1983), who joined the Communist party of Germany on December 31, 1931. However, disillusioned by Stalin's purges, he left the party in 1938. In the following passage, written in 1949, Koestler recalled the attraction communism had held for him.

A faith is not acquired by reasoning. One does not fall in love with a woman, or enter the womb of a church, as a result of

logical persuasion. Reason may defend an act of faith — but only after the act has been committed, and the man committed to the act. Persuasion may play a part in a man's conversion; but only the part of bringing to its full and conscious climax a process which has been maturing in regions where no persuasion can penetrate. A faith is not acquired; it grows like a tree. Its crown points to the sky; its roots grow downward into the past and are nourished by the dark sap of the ancestral humus. . . .

I became converted because I was ripe for it and lived in a disintegrating society thirsting for faith. But the day when I was given my Party card was merely the climax of a development which had started long before I had read about the drowned pigs or heard the names of Marx and Lenin. Its roots reach back into childhood; and though each of us, comrades of the Pink Decade, had individual roots with different twists in them, we are products of, by and large, the same generation and cultural climate. It is this unity underlying diversity which makes me hope that my story is worth telling.

I was born in 1905 in Budapest; we lived there till 1919, when we moved to Vienna. Until the First World War we were comfortably off, a typical Continental middle-middle-class family: my father was the Hungarian representative of some old-established British and German textile manufacturers. In September, 1914, this form of existence, like so many others, came to an abrupt end; my father never found his feet again. He embarked on a number of ventures which became the more fantastic the more he lost self-confidence in a changed world. He opened a factory for radioactive soap; he backed several crank-inventions (everlasting electric bulbs, self-heating bed bricks and the like); and finally lost the remains of his capital in the Austrian inflation of the early 'twenties. I left home at twenty-one, and from that day became the only financial support of my parents.

At the age of nine, when our middle-class idyl collapsed, I had suddenly become conscious of the economic Facts of Life. As an only child, I continued to be pampered by my parents; but, well aware of the family crisis, and torn by pity for my father, who was of a generous and somewhat childlike disposition, I suffered a pang of guilt whenever they bought me books or toys. This continued later on, when every suit I bought for myself meant so much less to send home. Simultaneously, I developed a strong dislike of the obviously rich; not because they could afford to buy things (envy plays a much smaller part in social conflict than is generally assumed) but because they were able to do so without a guilty conscience. Thus I projected a personal predicament onto the structure of society at large.

It was certainly a tortuous way of acquiring a social conscience. But precisely because of the intimate nature of the conflict, the faith which grew out of it became an equally intimate part of my self. It did not, for some years, crystallize into a political creed; at first it took the form of a mawkishly sentimental attitude. Every contact with people poorer than myself was unbearable — the boy at school who had no gloves and red chilblains [inflamed swellings produced by exposure to cold] on his fingers, the former traveling salesman of my father's reduced to [begging] occasional meals — all of them were additions to the load of guilt on my back. The analyst would have no difficulty in showing that the roots of this guilt-complex go deeper than the crisis in our household budget; but if he were to dig even deeper, piercing through the individual layers of the case, he would strike the archetypal pattern which has produced millions of particular variations on the same theme — "Woe, for they chant to the sound of harps and anoint themselves, but are not grieved for the affliction of the people."

Thus sensitized by a personal conflict, I was ripe for the shock of learning that wheat was burned, fruit artificially spoiled and pigs were drowned in the depression years to keep prices up and enable fat capitalists to chant to the sound of harps, while Europe trembled under the torn boots of hunger-marchers and my father hid his frayed cuffs under the table. The frayed cuffs and drowned pigs blended into one emotional explosion, as the fuse of the archetype was touched off. We sang the "Internationale" [the communists' anthem], but the words might as well have been the older ones: "Woe to the shepherds who feed themselves, but feed not their flocks."

In other respects, too, the story is more typical than it seems. A considerable proportion of the middle classes in central Europe was, like ourselves, ruined by the inflation of the 'twenties. It was the beginning of Europe's decline. This disintegration of the middle strata of society started the fatal process of polarization which continues to this day. The pauperized bourgeois became rebels of the Right or Left; Schickelgrüber [Hitler] and Djugashwili [Stalin] shared about equally the benefits of the social migration. Those who refused to admit that they had become déclassé, who clung to the empty shell of gentility, joined the Nazis and found comfort in blaming their fate on Versailles and the Jews. Many did not even have that consolation; they lived on pointlessly, like a great black swarm of tired winterflies crawling over the dim windows of Europe, members of a class displaced by history.

The other half turned Left, thus confirming the prophecy of the "Communist Manifesto":

> Entire sections of the ruling classes are . . . precipitated into the proletariat, or are at least threatened in their conditions of existence. They . . . supply the proletariat with fresh elements of enlightenment and progress. . . .

I was ripe to be converted, as a result of my personal case-history; thousands of other members of the intelligentsia and the middle classes of my generation were ripe for it, by virtue of other personal case-histories; but, however much these differed from case to case, they had a common denominator: the rapid disintegration of moral values, of the pre-1914 pattern of life in postwar Europe, and the simultaneous lure of the new revelation which had come from the East.

I joined the Party (which to this day remains "the" Party for all of us who once belonged to it) in 1931. . . .

I lived at that time in Berlin. For the last five years, I had been working for the Ullstein chain of newspapers — first as a foreign correspondent in Palestine and the Middle East, then in Paris. Finally, in 1930, I joined the editorial staff in the Berlin "House." . . .

. . . With one-third of its wage-earners unemployed, Germany lived in a state of latent civil war, and if one wasn't prepared to be swept along as a passive victim by the approaching hurricane it became imperative to take sides. . . . The Communists, with the mighty Soviet Union behind them, seemed the only force capable of resisting the onrush of the primitive horde with its swastika totem. I began for the first time to read Marx, Engels and Lenin in earnest. By the time I had finished with *Feuerbach* and *State and Revolution*, something had clicked in my brain which shook me like a mental explosion. To say that one had "seen the light" is a poor description of the mental rapture which only the convert knows (regardless of what faith he has been converted to). The new light seems to pour from all directions across the skull; the whole universe falls into pattern like the stray pieces of a jigsaw puzzle assembled by magic at one stroke. There is now an answer to every question, doubts and conflicts are a matter of the tortured past — a past already remote, when one had lived in dismal ignorance in the tasteless, colorless world of those who *don't know*. Nothing henceforth can disturb the convert's inner peace and serenity — except the occasional fear of losing faith again, losing thereby what alone makes life worth living, and falling back into the outer darkness, where there is wailing and gnashing of teeth.

Review Questions

1. What contrasts did Johan Huizinga draw between Europe at the turn of the century and the Europe of his day?

2. How did José Ortega y Gasset define the "mass-man"?

3. According to Ortega, what were the attitudes of the mass-man toward liberal democracy, reason, and culture?

4. How did Ortega view fascism?

5. According to Thomas Mann, what new mental attitude emerged that heralded the end of the bourgeois age?

6. How did Mann view extreme nationalism and National Socialism?

7. What did Mann mean by "politics becomes an opiate of the masses"?

8. What factors led to Arthur Koestler's becoming a communist?

7 | The Munich Agreement

Hitler sought power to build a great German empire in Europe, a goal that he revealed in *Mein Kampf*. In 1935, Hitler declared that Germany was no longer bound by the Versailles Treaty and would restore military conscription. In 1936, Germany remilitarized the Rhineland and in 1938 incorporated Austria into the Third Reich. Although these actions violated the Versailles Treaty, Britain and France offered no resistance.

In 1938, Hitler also threatened war if Czechoslovakia did not cede to Germany the Sudetenland with its large German population — of the 3.5 million people living in the Czech Sudetenland, some 2.8 million were Germans. In September 1938, Hitler met with other European leaders at Munich. Prime Minister Neville Chamberlain (1869–1940) of Great Britain and Prime Minister Édouard Daladier (1884–1970) of France agreed to Hitler's demands, despite France's mutual assistance pact with Czechoslovakia and the Czechs' expressed determination to resist the dismemberment of their country. Both Chamberlain and Daladier were praised by their compatriots for ensuring, as Chamberlain said, "peace in our time."

NEVILLE CHAMBERLAIN
In Defense of Appeasement

Britain and France pursued a policy of appeasement — giving in to Germany in the hope that a satisfied Hitler would not drag Europe into another war. Appeasement expressed the widespread British desire to heal the wounds of World War I and to correct what many British officials regarded as the injustices of the Versailles Treaty. Some officials, lauding Hitler's anticommunism, regarded a powerful Germany as a bulwark against the Soviet Union. Britain's lack of military preparedness was another compelling reason for not resisting Hitler. On September 27, 1938, when negotiations between Hitler and Chamberlain reached a tense moment, the British prime minister addressed his nation. Excerpts of this speech and of another before the House of Commons, which appeared in his *In Search of Peace* (1939), follow.

First of all I must say something to those who have written to my wife or myself in these last weeks to tell us of their gratitude for my efforts and to assure us of their prayers for my success. Most of these letters have come from women — mothers or sisters of our own countrymen. But there are countless others besides — from France, from Belgium, from Italy, even from Germany, and it has been heartbreaking to read of the growing anxiety they reveal and their intense relief when they thought, too soon, that the danger of war was past.

If I felt my responsibility heavy before, to read such letters has made it seem almost overwhelming. How horrible, fantastic, incredible it is that we should be digging trenches and trying on gas masks here because of a quarrel in a far-away country between people of whom we know nothing. It seems still more impossible that a quarrel which has already been settled in principle should be the subject of war.

I can well understand the reasons why the Czech Government have felt unable to accept the terms which have been put before them in the German memorandum. Yet I believe after my talks with Herr Hitler that, if only time were allowed, it ought to be possible for the arrangements for transferring the territory that the Czech Government has agreed to give to Germany to be settled by agreement under conditions which would assure fair treatment to the population concerned. . . .

However much we may sympathise with a small nation confronted by a big and powerful neighbour, we cannot in all circumstances undertake to involve the whole British Empire in war simply on her account. If we have to fight it must be on larger issues than that. I am myself a man of peace to the depths of my soul. Armed conflict between nations is a nightmare to me; but if I were convinced that any nation had made up its mind to dominate the world by fear of its force, I should feel that it must be resisted. Under such a domination life for people who believe in liberty would not be worth living; but war is a fearful thing, and we must be very clear, before we embark on it, that it is really the great issues that are at stake, and that the call to risk everything in their defence, when all the consequences are weighed, is irresistible.

For the present I ask you to await as calmly as you can the events of the next few days. As long as war has not begun, there is always hope that it may be prevented, and you know that I am going to work for peace to the last moment. Good night.

--- ◆ •◆• ◆ ---

On October 6, 1938, in a speech to Britain's House of Commons, Chamberlain defended the Munich agreement signed on September 30.

--- ◆ •◆• ◆ ---

. . . When war starts . . . in the very first hour, before any professional soldier, sailor or airman has been touched, it will strike the workman, the clerk, the man-in-the-street or in the 'bus, and his wife and children in their homes. As I listened, I could not help being moved, as I am sure everybody was who heard the hon. Member for Bridgeton (Mr. Maxton) when he began to paint the picture which he himself had seen and realised what it would mean in war — people burrowing underground, trying to escape from poison gas, knowing that at any hour of the day or night death or mutilation was ready to come upon them. Remembering that the dread of what might happen to them or to those dear to them might remain with fathers and mothers for year after year — when you think of these things you cannot ask people to accept a prospect of that kind; you cannot force them into a position that they have got to accept it; unless you feel yourself, and can make them feel, that the cause for which they are going to fight is a vital cause — a cause that transcends all the human values, a cause to which you can point, if some day you win the victory, and say, "That cause is safe."

Since I first went to Berchtesgaden [to

confer with Hitler in Germany] more than 20,000 letters and telegrams have come to No. 10, Downing Street [British prime minister's residence]. Of course, I have only been able to look at a tiny fraction of them, but I have seen enough to know that the people who wrote did not feel that they had such a cause for which to fight, if they were asked to go to war in order that the Sudeten Germans might not join the Reich. That is how they are feeling. That is my answer to those who say that we should have told Germany weeks ago that, if her army crossed the border of Czechoslovakia, we should be at war with her. We had no treaty obligations and no legal obligations to Czechoslovakia and if we had said that, we feel that we should have received no support from the people of this country. . . .

. . . When we were convinced, as we became convinced, that nothing any longer would keep the Sudetenland within the Czechoslovakian State, we urged the Czech Government as strongly as we could to agree to the cession of territory, and to agree promptly. The Czech Government, through the wisdom and courage of President Benes, accepted the advice of the French Government and ourselves. It was a hard decision for anyone who loved his country to take, but to accuse us of having by that advice betrayed the Czechoslovakian State is simply preposterous. What we did was to save her from annihilation and give her a chance of new life as a new State, which involves the loss of territory and fortifications, but may perhaps enable her to enjoy in the future and develop a national existence under a neutrality and security comparable to that which we see in Switzerland to-day. Therefore, I think the Government deserve the approval of this House for their conduct of affairs in this recent crisis which has saved Czechoslovakia from destruction and Europe from Armageddon.

Does the experience of the Great War and of the years that followed it give us reasonable hope that, if some new war started, that would end war any more than the last one did? . . .

One good thing, at any rate, has come out of this emergency through which we have passed. It has thrown a vivid light upon our preparations for defence, on their strength and on their weakness. I should not think we were doing our duty if we had not already ordered that a prompt and thorough inquiry should be made to cover the whole of our preparations, military and civil, in order to see, in the light of what has happened during these hectic days, what further steps may be necessary to make good our deficiencies in the shortest possible time.

WINSTON CHURCHILL
A Disaster of the First Magnitude

On October 5, 1938, elder statesman Winston Churchill (1874–1965) delivered a speech in the House of Commons attacking the Munich agreement and British policy toward Germany.

. . . I will begin by saying what everybody would like to ignore or forget but which must nevertheless be stated, namely, that we have sustained a total and unmitigated defeat, and that France has suffered even more than we have. . . .

. . . The utmost my right hon. Friend the Prime Minister. . . . has been able to gain for Czechoslovakia and in the matters which were in dispute has been that the German dictator, instead of snatching his victuals from the table, has been content to have them served to him course by course. . . .

. . . And I will say this, that I believe the Czechs, left to themselves and told they

were going to get no help from the Western Powers, would have been able to make
better terms than they have got — they
could hardly have worse — after all this
tremendous perturbation. . . .

. . . I have always held the view that
the maintenance of peace depends upon
the accumulation of deterrents against the
aggressor, coupled with a sincere effort to
redress grievances. Herr Hitler's victory,
like so many of the famous struggles that
have governed the fate of the world, was
won upon the narrowest of margins. After
the seizure of Austria in March we faced
this problem in our Debates. I ventured
to appeal to the Government to go a little
further than the Prime Minister went, and
to give a pledge that in conjunction with
France and other Powers they would
guarantee the security of Czechoslovakia
while the Sudeten-Deutsch question was
being examined either by a League of
Nations Commission or some other impartial body, and I still believe that if that
course had been followed events would not
have fallen into this disastrous state. I
agree very much with my right hon. Friend
the Member for Sparkbrook (Mr. Amery)
when he said on that occasion — I cannot
remember his actual words — "Do one
thing or the other; either say you will dis-
interest yourself in the matter altogether
or take the step of giving a guarantee
which will have the greatest chance of securing protection for that country."

France and Great Britain together, especially if they had maintained a close
contact with Russia, which certainly was
not done, would have been able in those
days in the summer, when they had the
prestige, to influence many of the smaller
States of Europe, and I believe they could
have determined the attitude of Poland.
Such a combination, prepared at a time
when the German dictator was not deeply
and irrevocably committed to his new adventure, would, I believe, have given
strength to all those forces in Germany
which resisted this departure, this new
design. They were varying forces, those
of a military character which declared that

Germany was not ready to undertake a
world war, and all that mass of moderate
opinion and popular opinion which
dreaded war, and some elements of which
still have some influence upon the German Government. Such action would have
given strength to all that intense desire for
peace which the helpless German masses
share with their British and French fellow
men, and which, as we have been re-
minded, found a passionate and rarely
permitted vent in the joyous manifestations with which the Prime Minister was
acclaimed in Munich.

All these forces, added to the other deterrents which combinations of Powers,
great and small, ready to stand firm upon
the front of law and for the ordered remedy of grievances, would have formed,
might well have been effective. . . . I do
not think it is fair to charge those who
wished to see this course followed, and
followed consistently and resolutely, with
having wished for an immediate war. Between submission and immediate war there
was this third alternative, which gave a
hope not only of peace but of justice. It
is quite true that such a policy in order to
succeed demanded that Britain should
declare straight out and a long time beforehand that she would, with others, join
to defend Czechoslovakia against an un-
provoked aggression. His Majesty's Government refused to give that guarantee
when it would have saved the situation,
yet in the end they gave it when it was too
late, and now, for the future, they renew
it when they have not the slightest power
to make it good.

All is over. Silent, mournful, abandoned, broken, Czechoslovakia recedes
into the darkness. She has suffered in
every respect by her association with the
Western democracies and with the League
of Nations, of which she has always been
an obedient servant. She has suffered in
particular from her association with
France, under whose guidance and policy
she has been actuated for so long. . . .

We in this country, as in other Liberal
and democratic countries, have a perfect

right to exalt the principle of self-determination, but it comes ill out of the mouths of those in totalitarian States who deny even the smallest element of toleration to every section and creed within their bounds. But, however you put it, this particular block of land, this mass of human beings to be handed over, has never expressed the desire to go into the Nazi rule. I do not believe that even now — if their opinion could be asked, they would exercise such an option.

What is the remaining position of Czechoslovakia? Not only are they politically mutilated, but, economically and financially, they are in complete confusion. Their banking, their railway arrangements, are severed and broken, their industries are curtailed, and the movement of their population is most cruel. The Sudeten miners, who are all Czechs and whose families have lived in that area for centuries, must now flee into an area where there are hardly any mines left for them to work. It is a tragedy which has occurred. . . .

I venture to think that in future the Czechoslovak State cannot be maintained as an independent entity. You will find that in a period of time which may be measured by years, but may be measured only by months, Czechoslovakia will be engulfed in the Nazi régime. Perhaps they may join it in despair or in revenge. At any rate, that story is over and told. But we cannot consider the abandonment and ruin of Czechoslovakia in the light only of what happened only last month. It is the most grievous consequence which we have yet experienced of what we have done and of what we have left undone in the last five years — five years of futile good intention, five years of eager search for the line of least resistance, five years of uninterrupted retreat of British power, five years of neglect of our air defences. Those are the features which I stand here to declare and which marked an improvident stewardship for which Great Britain and France have dearly to pay. We have been reduced in those five years from a posi-

tion of security so overwhelming and so unchallengeable that we never cared to think about it. We have been reduced from a position where the very word "war" was considered one which would be used only by persons qualifying for a lunatic asylum. We have been reduced from a position of safety and power — power to do good, power to be generous to a beaten foe, power to make terms with Germany, power to give her proper redress for her grievances, power to stop her arming if we chose, power to take any step in strength or mercy or justice which we thought right — reduced in five years from a position safe and unchallenged to where we stand now.

When I think of the fair hopes of a long peace which still lay before Europe at the beginning of 1933 when Herr Hitler first obtained power, and of all the opportunities of arresting the growth of the Nazi power which have been thrown away, when I think of the immense combinations and resources which have been neglected or squandered, I cannot believe that a parallel exists in the whole course of history. So far as this country is concerned the responsibility must rest with those who have the undisputed control of our political affairs. They neither prevented Germany from rearming, nor did they rearm ourselves in time. . . . They neglected to make alliances and combinations which might have repaired previous errors, and thus they left us in the hour of trial without adequate national defence or effective international security. . . .

We are in the presence of a disaster of the first magnitude which has befallen Great Britain and France. Do not let us blind ourselves to that. It must now be accepted that all the countries of Central and Eastern Europe will make the best terms they can with the triumphant Nazi Power. The system of alliances in Central Europe upon which France has relied for her safety has been swept away, and I can see no means by which it can be reconstituted. The road down the Danube Valley to the Black Sea, the resources of corn and oil, the road which leads as far as Turkey, has been opened. In fact, if not in form, it seems to me that all those countries of Middle Europe, all those Danubian countries, will, one after another, be drawn into this vast system of power politics — not only power military politics but power economic politics — radiating from Berlin, and I believe this can be achieved quite smoothly and swiftly and will not necessarily entail the firing of a single shot. . . .

. . . The German army at the present time is more numerous than that of France, though not nearly so matured or perfected. Next year it will grow much larger, and its maturity will be more complete. Relieved from all anxiety in the East, and having secured resources which will greatly diminish, if not entirely remove, the deterrent of a naval blockade, the rulers of Nazi Germany will have a free choice open to them in what direction they will turn their eyes. If the Nazi dictator should choose to look westward, as he may, bitterly will France and England regret the loss of that fine army of ancient Bohemia [Czechoslovakia] which was estimated last week to require not fewer than 30 German divisions for its destruction. . . .

. . . Many people, no doubt, honestly believe that they are only giving away the interests of Czechoslovakia, whereas I fear we shall find that we have deeply compromised, and perhaps fatally endangered, the safety and even the independence of Great Britain and France. . . . The Prime Minister desires to see cordial relations between this country and Germany. There is no difficulty at all in having cordial relations with the German people. Our hearts go out to them. But they have no power. You must have diplomatic and correct relations, but there can

never be friendship between the British democracy and the Nazi Power, that Power which spurns Christian ethics, which cheers its onward course by a barbarous paganism, which vaunts the spirit of aggression and conquest, which derives strength and perverted pleasure from persecution, and uses, as we have seen, with pitiless brutality the threat of murderous force. That Power cannot ever be the trusted friend of the British democracy. . . .

I do not grudge our loyal, brave people, who were ready to do their duty no matter what the cost, who never flinched under the strain of last week — I do not grudge them the natural, spontaneous outburst of joy and relief when they learned that the hard ordeal would no longer be required of them at the moment; but they should know the truth. They should know that there has been gross neglect and deficiency in our defences; they should know that we have sustained a defeat without a war, the consequences of which will travel far with us along our road; they should know that we have passed an awful milestone in our history, when the whole equilibrium of Europe has been deranged, and that the terrible words have for the time being been pronounced against the Western democracies:

Thou art weighed in the balance and found wanting.

And do not suppose that this is the end. This is only the beginning of the reckoning. This is only the first sip, the first foretaste of a bitter cup which will be proffered to us year by year unless by a supreme recovery of moral health and martial vigour, we arise again and take our stand for freedom as in the olden time.

Review Questions

1. In Neville Chamberlain's view, how did the British people regard a war with Germany over the Sudetenland?

2. How did Chamberlain respond to the accusation that Britain and France had betrayed Czechoslovakia?

3. What did Chamberlain consider to be the "one good thing" to come out of the Sudetenland crisis?

4. Why did Winston Churchill believe that "there can never be friendship between the British democracy and the Nazi Power"?

5. Why did Churchill believe that the Munich agreement was "a disaster of the first magnitude" for Britain and France?

6. According to Chamberlain, how did Czechoslovakia benefit from the Munich agreement? What was Churchill's assessment of the impact of the Munich agreement on Czechoslovakia? What prediction did he make regarding post-Munich Czechoslovakia?

7. What policy toward Nazi Germany did Churchill advocate?

8 | Britain's Finest Hour

On September 1, 1939, German troops crossed into Poland, precipitating World War II. Poland fell in four weeks to the Nazi blitzkrieg, that is, lightning war marked by fast-moving mechanized columns. In the months that followed, land battles consisted only of a few skirmishes on the Franco-German border. Then in April 1940, Germany attacked Denmark and Norway. The swift conquest of these countries discredited the leadership of Britain's Neville Chamberlain, who was replaced as prime minister by Winston Churchill on May 10, the very day that Hitler struck against Holland, Belgium, Luxembourg, and France.

WINSTON CHURCHILL
Blood, Toil, Tears, and Sweat

Churchill, at the age of sixty-six, proved to be an undaunted leader, sharing the perils faced by all and able by example and by speeches to rally British morale. When he first addressed Parliament as prime minister on May 13, 1940, he left no doubt about the grim realities that lay ahead. Excerpts from his speeches in 1940 follow.

May 13, 1940

I would say to the House, as I said to those who have joined this Government: "I have nothing to offer but blood, toil, tears, and sweat." We have before us an ordeal of the most grievous kind. We have before us many, many long months of struggle and suffering. You ask: "What is our policy?" I will say: "It is to wage war by sea, land, and air with all our might, and with all the strength that God can give us; to wage war against a monstrous tyranny, never surpassed in the dark lamentable catalogue of human crime." That is our policy.

You ask: "What is our aim?" I can answer in one word: "Victory!" Victory at all costs, victory in spite of all terror, victory however long and hard the road may be; for without victory there is no survival.

→ •◦• ←

When Churchill spoke next, on May 19, the Dutch had surrendered to the Germans, and

the French and British armies were in retreat.
Still, Churchill promised that "conquer we shall."

———— •••• ————

May 19, 1940

This is one of the most awe-striking periods in the long history of France and Britain. It is also beyond doubt the most sublime. Side by side, unaided except by their kith and kin in the great Dominions and by the wide Empires which rest beneath their shield — side by side, the British and French peoples have advanced to rescue not only Europe but mankind from the foulest and most soul-destroying tyranny which has ever darkened and stained the pages of history. Behind them — behind us — behind the armies and fleets of Britain and France — gather a group of shattered states and bludgeoned races: the Czechs, the Poles, the Norwegians, the Danes, the Dutch, the Belgians — upon all of whom the long night of barbarism will descend unbroken even by a star of hope, unless we conquer, as conquer we must; as conquer we shall.

———— •••• ————

By early June the Belgians had surrendered to the Germans and the last units of the British Expeditionary Force in France had been evacuated from Dunkirk; the French armies were in full flight. Again Churchill spoke out in defiance of events across the Channel.

———— •••• ————

June 4, 1940

We shall not flag or fail. We shall go on to the end. We shall fight in France, we shall fight on the seas and oceans, we shall fight with growing confidence and growing strength in the air. We shall defend our island, whatever the cost may be. We shall fight on the beaches, we shall fight on the landing-grounds, we shall fight in the fields and in the streets, we shall fight in the hills. We shall never surrender; and even if, which I do not for a moment believe, this island or a large part of it were subjugated and starving, then our Em-

pire beyond the seas, armed and guarded by the British Fleet, would carry on the struggle, until, in God's good time, the New World, with all its power and might, steps forth to the rescue and liberation of the Old.

———— •••• ————

By June 18 the battle of France was lost; on June 22 France surrendered. Now Britain itself was under siege. Churchill again found the right words to sustain his people:

———— •••• ————

June 18, 1940

What General [Maxime] Weygand [commander of the French army] called the Battle of France is over. . . . The Battle of Britain is about to begin. Upon this battle depends the survival of Christian civilization. Upon it depends our own British life and the long continuity of our institutions and our Empire. The whole fury and might of the enemy must very soon be turned upon us. Hitler knows that he will have to break us in this island or lose the war.

If we can stand up to him, all Europe may be free and the life of the world may move forward into broad sunlit uplands. But if we fail, then the whole world, including the United States, including all that we have known and cared for, will sink into the abyss of a new Dark Age made more sinister and perhaps more prolonged by the lights of a perverted science.

Let us therefore brace ourselves to our duty and so bear ourselves that if the British Empire and Commonwealth last for a thousand years, men will still say, "This was their finest hour."

———— •••• ————

The bombing of Britain began, in advance of the Germans' planned invasion, in July, reaching a climax in September with great raids on London and other cities. The Battle of Britain was fought in the air by British pilots defending their country. Early in the battle Churchill acknowledged the courage of British airmen and their contribution to Britain's survival.

———— •••• ————

August 20, 1940

The gratitude of every home in our island, in our Empire, and indeed throughout the world, except in the abodes of the guilty, goes out to the British airmen who, undaunted by odds, unwearied in their constant challenge and mortal danger, are turning the tide of world war by their prowess and by their devotion. Never in the field of human conflict was so much owed by so many to so few. All hearts go out to the fighter pilots whose brilliant actions we see with our own eyes day after day.

Review Questions

1. According to Winston Churchill, what did a Nazi victory mean for Europe?
2. On whose help did Churchill ultimately count for the liberation of Europe?
3. Both Hitler and Churchill were gifted orators. Compare their styles.

9 | Stalingrad: A Turning Point

In July 1942, the Germans resumed their advance into the U.S.S.R. begun the previous summer, seeking to conquer Stalingrad, a vital transportation center located on the Volga River. Germans and Russians battled with dogged ferocity over every part of the city; 99 percent of Stalingrad was reduced to rubble. A Russian counteroffensive in November trapped the German Sixth Army. Realizing that the Sixth Army, exhausted and short of weapons, ammunition, food, and medical supplies, faced annihilation, German generals pleaded in vain with Hitler to permit withdrawal before the Russians closed the ring. On February 2, 1943, the remnants of the Sixth Army surrendered. More than a million people — Russian civilians and soldiers, Germans and their Italian, Hungarian, and Rumanian allies — perished in the epic struggle for Stalingrad. The Russian victory was a major turning point in the war.

Diary of a German Soldier

The following entries in the diary of a German soldier who perished at Stalingrad reveal the decline in German confidence as the battle progressed. While the German army was penetrating deeply into Russia, he believed that victory was not far away and dreamed of returning home with medals. Then the terrible struggles in Stalingrad made him curse the war.

Today, after we'd had a bath, the company commander told us that if our future operations are as successful, we'll soon reach the Volga, take Stalingrad and then the war will inevitably soon be over. Perhaps we'll be home by Christmas.

July 29. . . . The company commander says the Russian troops are completely broken, and cannot hold out any longer. To reach the Volga and take Stalingrad is not so difficult for us. The Führer knows where the Russians' weak point is. Victory is not far away. . . .

August 2. . . . What great spaces the Soviets occupy, what rich fields there are to be had here after the war's over! Only let's get it over with quickly. I believe that the Führer will carry the thing through to a successful end.

August 10. . . . The Führer's orders were read out to us. He expects victory of us. We are all convinced that they can't stop us.

August 12. We are advancing towards Stalingrad along the railway line. Yesterday Russian "katyushi" and then tanks halted our regiment. "The Russians are throwing in their last forces," Captain Werner explained to me. Large-scale help is coming up for us, and the Russians will be beaten.

This morning outstanding soldiers were presented with decorations. . . . Will I really go back to Elsa without a decoration? I believe that for Stalingrad the Führer will decorate even me. . . .

August 23. Splendid news — north of Stalingrad our troops have reached the Volga and captured part of the city. The Russians have two alternatives, either to flee across the Volga or give themselves up. Our company's interpreter has interrogated a captured Russian officer. He was wounded, but asserted that the Russians would fight for Stalingrad to the last round. Something incomprehensible is, in fact, going on. In the north our troops capture a part of Stalingrad and reach the Volga, but in the south the doomed divisions are continuing to resist bitterly. Fanaticism. . . .

August 27. A continuous cannonade on all sides. We are slowly advancing. Less than twenty miles to go to Stalingrad. In the daytime we can see the smoke of fires, at night-time the bright glow. They say that the city is on fire; on the Führer's orders our Luftwaffe has sent it up in flames. That's what the Russians need, to stop them from resisting . . .

September 4. We are being sent northward along the front towards Stalingrad. We marched all night and by dawn had reached Voroponovo Station. We can already see the smoking town. It's a happy thought that the end of the war is getting nearer. That's what everyone is saying.

If only the days and nights would pass more quickly . . .

September 5. Our regiment has been ordered to attack Sadovaya station — that's nearly in Stalingrad. Are the Russians really thinking of holding out in the city itself? We had no peace all night from the Russian artillery and aeroplanes. Lots of wounded are being brought by. God protect me . . .

September 8. Two days of non-stop fighting. The Russians are defending themselves with insane stubbornness. Our regiment has lost many men from the "katyushi," which belch out terrible fire. I have been sent to work at battalion H.Q. It must be mother's prayers that have taken me away from the company's trenches . . .

September 11. Our battalion is fighting in the suburbs of Stalingrad. We can already see the Volga; firing is going on all the time. Wherever you look is fire and flames. . . . Russian cannon and machine-guns are firing out of the burning city. Fanatics . . .

September 13. An unlucky number. This morning "katyushi" attacks caused the company heavy losses: twenty-seven dead and fifty wounded. The Russians are fighting desperately like wild beasts, don't give themselves up, but come up close and then throw grenades. Lieutenant Kraus was killed yesterday, and there is no company commander.

September 16. Our battalion, plus tanks, is attacking the [grain storage] elevator, from which smoke is pouring — the grain in it is burning, the Russians seem to have set light to it themselves. Barbarism. The battalion is suffering heavy losses. There are not more than sixty men left in each company. The elevator is occupied not by men but by devils that no flames or bullets can destroy.

September 18. Fighting is going on inside the elevator. The Russians inside are condemned men; the battalion commander says: "The commissars have ordered those men to die in the elevator."

If all the buildings of Stalingrad are

defended like this then none of our soldiers will get back to Germany. I had a letter from Elsa today. She's expecting me home when victory's won.

September 20. The battle for the elevator is still going on. The Russians are firing on all sides. We stay in our cellar; you can't go out into the street. Sergeant-Major Nuschke was killed today running across a street. Poor fellow, he's got three children.

September 22. Russian resistance in the elevator has been broken. Our troops are advancing towards the Volga. . . .

. . . Our old soldiers have never experienced such bitter fighting before.

September 26. Our regiment is involved in constant heavy fighting. After the elevator was taken the Russians continued to defend themselves just as stubbornly. You don't see them at all, they have established themselves in houses and cellars and are firing on all sides, including from our rear — barbarians, they use gangster methods.

In the blocks captured two days ago Russian soldiers appeared from somewhere or other and fighting has flared up with fresh vigour. Our men are being killed not only in the firing line, but in the rear, in buildings we have already occupied.

The Russians have stopped surrendering at all. If we take any prisoners it's because they are hopelessly wounded, and can't move by themselves. Stalingrad is hell. Those who are merely wounded are lucky; they will doubtless be at home and celebrate victory with their families. . . .

September 28. Our regiment, and the whole division, are today celebrating victory. Together with our tank crews we have taken the southern part of the city and reached the Volga. We paid dearly for our victory. In three weeks we have occupied about five and a half square miles. The commander has congratulated us on our victory. . . .

October 3. After marching through the night we have established ourselves in a shrub-covered gully. We are apparently going to attack the factories, the chimneys of which we can see clearly. Behind them is the Volga. We have entered a new area. It was night but we saw many crosses with our helmets on top. Have we really lost so many men? Damn this Stalingrad!

October 4. Our regiment is attacking the Barrikady settlement. A lot of Russian tommy-gunners have appeared. Where are they bringing them from?

October 5. Our battalion has gone into the attack four times, and got stopped each time. Russian snipers hit anyone who shows himself carelessly from behind shelter.

October 10. The Russians are so close to us that our planes cannot bomb them. We are preparing for a decisive attack. The Führer has ordered the whole of Stalingrad to be taken as rapidly as possible.

October 14. It has been fantastic since morning: our aeroplanes and artillery have been hammering the Russian positions for hours on end; everything in sight is being blotted from the face of the earth. . . .

October 22. Our regiment has failed to break into the factory. We have lost many men; every time you move you have to jump over bodies. You can scarcely breathe in the daytime: there is nowhere and no one to remove the bodies, so they are left there to rot. Who would have thought three months ago that instead of the joy of victory we would have to endure such sacrifice and torture, the end of which is nowhere in sight? . . .

The soldiers are calling Stalingrad the mass grave of the Wehrmacht [German army]. There are very few men left in the companies. We have been told we are soon going to be withdrawn to be brought back up to strength.

October 27. Our troops have captured the whole of the Barrikady factory, but we cannot break through to the Volga. The Russians are not men, but some kind of cast-iron creatures; they never get tired and are not afraid of fire. We are absolutely exhausted; our regiment now has barely the strength of a company. The Russian artillery at the other side of the

Volga won't let you lift your head. . . .

October 28. Every soldier sees himself as a condemned man. The only hope is to be wounded and taken back to the rear. . . .

November 3. In the last few days our battalion has several times tried to attack the Russian positions, . . . to no avail. On this sector also the Russians won't let you lift your head. There have been a number of cases of self-inflicted wounds and malingering among the men. Every day I write two or three reports about them.

November 10. A letter from Elsa today. Everyone expects us home for Christmas. In Germany everyone believes we already hold Stalingrad. How wrong they are. If they could only see what Stalingrad has done to our army.

November 18. Our attack with tanks yesterday had no success. After our attack the field was littered with dead.

November 21. The Russians have gone over to the offensive along the whole front. Fierce fighting is going on. So, there it is — the Volga, victory and soon home to our families! We shall obviously be seeing them next in the other world.

November 29. We are encircled. It was announced this morning that the Führer has said: "The army can trust me to do everything necessary to ensure supplies and rapidly break the encirclement."

December 3. We are on hunger rations and waiting for the rescue that the Führer promised.

I send letters home, but there is no reply.

December 7. Rations have been cut to such an extent that the soldiers are suffering terribly from hunger; they are is-

suing one loaf of stale bread for five men.

December 11. Three questions are obsessing every soldier and officer: When will the Russians stop firing and let us sleep in peace, if only for one night? How and with what are we going to fill our empty stomachs, which, apart from $3\frac{1}{2}$–7 ozs of bread, receive virtually nothing at all? And when will Hitler take any decisive steps to free our armies from encirclement?

December 14. Everybody is racked with hunger. Frozen potatoes are the best meal, but to get them out of the ice-covered ground under fire from Russian bullets is not so easy.

December 18. The officers today told the soldiers to be prepared for action. General Manstein is approaching Stalingrad from the south with strong forces. This news brought hope to the soldiers' hearts. God, let it be!

December 21. We are waiting for the order, but for some reason or other it has been a long time coming. Can it be that it is not true about Manstein? This is worse than any torture.

December 23. Still no orders. It was all a bluff with Manstein. Or has he been defeated at the approaches to Stalingrad?

December 25. The Russian radio has announced the defeat of Manstein. Ahead of us is either death or captivity.

December 26. The horses have already been eaten. I would eat a cat; they say its meat is also tasty. The soldiers look like corpses or lunatics, looking for something to put in their mouths. They no longer take cover from Russian shells; they haven't the strength to walk, run away and hide. A curse on this war! . . .

Review Questions

1. What were the expectations of the German soldier in July and August? How did he view Hitler and the war?

2. How did he view the Russians?

3. How did the hard fighting at Stalingrad alter his conception of the war and his attitude toward the Russians?

10 | The Holocaust

Over conquered Europe the Nazis imposed a "New Order" marked by exploitation, torture, and mass murder. The Germans took some 5.5 million Russian prisoners of war, of whom more than 3.5 million perished; many of these prisoners were deliberately starved to death. The Germans imprisoned and executed many Polish intellectuals and priests and slaughtered vast numbers of Gypsies. Using the modern state's organizational capacities and the instruments of modern technology, the Nazis murdered six million Jews, including one and a half million children — two-thirds of the Jewish population of Europe. Gripped by the mythical, perverted world-view of Nazism, the SS, Hitler's elite guard, carried out these murders with dedication and idealism; they believed that they were exterminating subhumans who threatened the German nation.

HERMANN GRAEBE
Slaughter of Jews in the Ukraine

While the regular German army penetrated deeply into Russia, special SS units, the *Einsatzgruppen,* rounded up Jews for mass executions, killing about a million and a half people. Hermann Graebe, a German construction engineer, saw such a mass slaughter in Dubno in the Ukraine. He gave a sworn affidavit before the Nuremberg tribunal, a court at which the Allies tried Nazi war criminals after the end of World War II.

Graebe had joined the Nazi party in 1931 but later renounced his membership, and during the war he rescued Jews from the SS. Graebe was the only German citizen to volunteer to testify at the Nuremberg trials, an act that earned him the enmity of his compatriots. Socially ostracized, Graebe emigrated to the United States, where he died in 1986 at the age of eighty-five.

On October 5, 1942, when I visited the building office at Dubno, my foreman told me that in the vicinity of the site, Jews from Dubno had been shot in three large pits, each about 30 metres long and 3 metres deep. About 1,500 persons had been killed daily. All the 5,000 Jews who had still been living in Dubno before the pogrom were to be liquidated. As the shooting had taken place in his presence, he was still much upset.

Thereupon, I drove to the site accompanied by my foreman and saw near it great mounds of earth, about 30 metres long and 2 metres high. Several trucks stood in front of the mounds. Armed Ukrainian militia drove the people off the trucks under the supervision of an S.S. man. The militiamen acted as guards on the trucks and drove them to and from the pit. All these people had the regulation yellow patches on the front and back of their clothes, and thus could be recognized as Jews.

My foreman and I went directly to the pits. Nobody bothered us. Now I heard rifle shots in quick succession from behind one of the earth mounds. The people who had got off the trucks — men, women and children of all ages — had to undress upon the orders of an S.S. man, who carried a riding or dog whip. They had to put down their clothes in fixed places, sorted according to shoes, top clothing and underclothing. I saw a heap of shoes of about 800 to 1,000 pairs, great piles of underlinen and clothing.

Without screaming or weeping, these

people undressed, stood around in family groups, kissed each other, said farewells, and waited for a sign from another S.S. man, who stood near the pit, also with a whip in his hand. During the fifteen minutes that I stood near I heard no complaint or plea for mercy. I watched a family of about eight persons, a man and a woman both about fifty with their children of about one, eight and ten, and two grown-up daughters of about twenty to twenty-nine. An old woman with snow-white hair was holding the one-year-old child in her arms and singing to it and tickling it. The child was cooing with delight. The couple were looking on with tears in their eyes. The father was holding the hand of a boy about ten years old and speaking to him softly; the boy was fighting his tears. The father pointed to the sky, stroked his head, and seemed to explain something to him.

At that moment the S.S. man at the pit shouted something to his comrade. The latter counted off about twenty persons and instructed them to go behind the earth mound. Among them was the family which I have mentioned. I well remember a girl, slim and with black hair, who, as she passed close to me, pointed to herself and said "23." I walked around the mound and found myself confronted by a tremendous grave. People were closely wedged together and lying on top of each other so that only their heads were visible. Nearly all had blood running over their shoulders from their heads. Some of the people shot were still moving. Some were lifting their arms and turning their heads to show that they were still alive. The pit was already two-thirds full. I estimated that it already contained about 1,000 people.

I looked for the man who did the shooting. He was an S.S. man, who sat at the edge of the narrow end of the pit, his feet dangling into the pit. He had a tommy-gun on his knees and was smoking a cigarette. The people, completely naked, went down some steps which were cut in the clay wall of the pit and clambered over the heads of the people lying there, to the place to which the S.S. man directed them. They lay down in front of the dead or injured people; some caressed those who were still alive and spoke to them in a low voice.

Then I heard a series of shots. I looked into the pit and saw that the bodies were twitching or the heads lying motionless on top of the bodies which lay before them. Blood was running from their necks. I was surprised that I was not ordered away, but I saw that there were two or three postmen in uniform nearby. The next batch was approaching already. They went down into the pit, lined themselves up against the previous victims and were shot.

When I walked back round the mound, I noticed another truckload of people which had just arrived. This time it included sick and infirm persons. An old, very thin woman with terribly thin legs was undressed by others who were already naked, while two people held her up. The woman appeared to be paralyzed. The naked people carried the woman around the mound. I left with my foreman and drove in my car back to Dubno.

On the morning of the next day, when I again visited the site, I saw about thirty naked people lying near the pit — about 30 to 50 metres away from it. Some of them were still alive; they looked straight in front of them with a fixed stare and seemed to notice neither the chilliness of the morning nor the workers of my firm who stood around. A girl of about twenty spoke to me and asked me to give her clothes and help her escape. At that moment we heard a fast car approach and I noticed that it was an S.S. detail. I moved away to my site. Ten minutes later we heard shots from the vicinity of the pit. The Jews alive had been ordered to throw the corpses into the pit, then they had themselves to lie down in it to be shot in the neck.

RUDOLF HOESS
Commandant of Auschwitz

To speed up the "final solution of the Jewish problem," the SS established death camps in Poland. Jews from all over Europe were crammed into cattle cars and shipped to these camps to be gassed or worked to death. At Auschwitz, the most notorious of the concentration camps, the SS used five gas chambers to kill 9,000 or more people a day. Special squads of prisoners, called *Sonderkommando*, were forced to pick over the corpses for gold teeth, jewelry, and anything else of value for the German war effort. Some two million Jews perished at Auschwitz. In the following passage from *Commandant of Auschwitz*, Rudolf Hoess (1900–1947) who commanded the camp and was executed by Poland after the war, recalled the murder process when he was in a Polish prison.

In the spring of 1942 the first transports of Jews, all earmarked for extermination, arrived from Upper Silesia.

They were taken from the detraining platform to the "cottage" — to bunker I — across the meadows where later building site II was located. The transport was conducted by Aumeier and Palitzsch and some of the block leaders. They talked with the Jews about general topics, inquiring concerning their qualifications and trades, with a view to misleading them. On arrival at the "cottage," they were told to undress. At first they went calmly into the rooms where they were supposed to be disinfected. But some of them showed signs of alarm, and spoke of death by suffocation and of annihilation. A sort of panic set in at once. Immediately all the Jews still outside were pushed into the chambers, and the doors were screwed shut. With subsequent transports the difficult individuals were picked out early and most carefully supervised. At the first signs of unrest, those responsible were unobtrusively led behind the building and killed with a small-caliber gun, that was inaudible to the others. The presence and calm behavior of the Special Detachment [of *Sonderkommando*] served to reassure those who were worried or who suspected what was about to happen. A further calming effect was obtained by members of the Special Detachment accompanying them into the rooms and remaining with them until the last moment, while an SS man also stood in the doorway until the end.

It was most important that the whole business of arriving and undressing should take place in an atmosphere of the greatest possible calm. People reluctant to take off their clothes had to be helped by those of their companions who had already undressed, or by men of the Special Detachment.

The refractory ones were calmed down and encouraged to undress. The prisoners of the Special Detachment also saw to it that the process of undressing was carried out quickly, so that the victims would have little time to wonder what was happening. . . .

Many of the women hid their babies among the piles of clothing. The men of the Special Detachment were particularly on the lookout for this, and would speak words of encouragement to the woman until they had persuaded her to take the child with her. The women believed that the disinfectant might be bad for their smaller children, hence their efforts to conceal them.

The smaller children usually cried because of the strangeness of being undressed in this fashion, but when their mothers or members of the Special Detachment comforted them, they became calm and entered the gas chambers, playing or joking with one another and carrying their toys.

I noticed that women who either

guessed or knew what awaited them nevertheless found the courage to joke with the children to encourage them, despite the mortal terror visible in their own eyes.

One woman approached me as she walked past and, pointing to her four children who were manfully helping the smallest ones over the rough ground, whispered:

"How can you bring yourself to kill such beautiful, darling children? Have you no heart at all?"

One old man, as he passed by me, hissed:

"Germany will pay a heavy penance for this mass murder of the Jews."

His eyes glowed with hatred as he said this. Nevertheless he walked calmly into the gas chamber, without worrying about the others.

One young woman caught my attention particularly as she ran busily hither and thither, helping the smallest children and the old women to undress. During the selection she had had two small children with her, and her agitated behavior and appearance had brought her to my notice at once. She did not look in the least like a Jewess. Now her children were no longer with her. She waited until the end, helping the women who were not undressed and who had several children with them, encouraging them and calming the children. She went with the very last ones into the gas chamber. Standing in the doorway, she said:

"I knew all the time that we were being brought to Auschwitz to be gassed. When the selection took place I avoided being put with the able-bodied ones, as I wished to look after the children. I wanted to go through it all, fully conscious of what was happening. I hope that it will be quick. Goodbye!"

From time to time women would suddenly give the most terrible shrieks while undressing, or tear their hair, or scream like maniacs. These were immediately led away behind the building and shot in the back of the neck with a small-caliber weapon.

It sometimes happened that, as the men of the Special Detachment left the gas chamber, the women would suddenly realize what was happening, and would call down every imaginable curse upon our heads.

I remember, too, a woman who tried to throw her children out of the gas chamber, just as the door was closing. Weeping, she called out:

"At least let my precious children live."

There were many such shattering scenes, which affected all who witnessed them.

During the spring of 1942 hundreds of vigorous men and women walked all unsuspecting to their death in the gas chambers, under the blossom-laden fruit trees of the "cottage" orchard. This picture of death in the midst of life remains with me to this day.

The process of selection, which took place on the unloading platforms, was in itself rich in incident.

The breaking up of families, and the separation of the men from the women and children, caused much agitation and spread anxiety throughout the whole transport. This was increased by the further separation from the others of those capable of work. Families wished at all costs to remain together. Those who had been selected ran back to rejoin their relations. Mothers with children tried to join their husbands, or old people attempted to find those of their children who had been selected for work, and who had been led away.

Often the confusion was so great that the selections had to be begun all over again. The limited area of standing room did not permit better sorting arrangements. All attempts to pacify these agitated mobs were useless. It was often necessary to use force to restore order.

As I have already frequently said, the Jews have strongly developed family feelings. They stick together like limpets. . . .

Then the bodies had to be taken from the gas chambers, and after the gold teeth had been extracted, and the hair cut off, they had to be dragged to the pits or to the crematoria. Then the fires in the pits had to be stoked, the surplus fat drained off, and the mountain of burning corpses constantly turned over so that the draught might fan the flames. . . .

It happened repeatedly that Jews of the Special Detachment would come upon the bodies of close relatives among the corpses, and even among the living as they en-tered the gas chambers. They were obviously affected by this, but it never led to any incident.[1]

---

[1]On October 7, 1944, the *Sonderkommando* attacked the SS. Some SS guards were killed and one crematorium was burned. Most of the prisoners who escaped were caught and killed.

Y. PFEFFER
Concentration Camp Life and Death

Jews not immediately selected for extermination faced a living death in the concentration camp, which also included non-Jewish inmates, many of them opponents of the Nazi regime. The SS, who ran the camps, took sadistic pleasure in humiliating and brutalizing their helpless Jewish victims. In 1946, Y. Pfeffer, a Jewish survivor of Majdanek concentration camp in Poland, described the world created by the SS and Nazi ideology.

You get up at 3 a.m. You have to dress quickly, and make the "bed" so that it looks like a matchbox. For the slightest irregularity in bed-making the punishment was 25 lashes, after which it was impossible to lie or sit for a whole month.

Everyone had to leave the barracks immediately. Outside it is still dark — or else the moon is shining. People are trembling because of lack of sleep and the cold. In order to warm up a bit, groups of ten to twenty people stand together, back to back so as to rub against each other.

There was what was called a washroom, where everyone in the camp was supposed to wash — there were only a few faucets — and we were 4,500 people in that section (no. 3). Of course there was neither soap nor towel or even a handkerchief, so that washing was theoretical rather than practical. . . . In one day, a person there came a lowly person indeed.

At 5 a.m. we used to get half a litre of black, bitter coffee. That was all we got for what was called "breakfast." At 6 a.m. — a headcount (*Appell* in German). We all had to stand at attention, in fives, according to the barracks, of which there were 22 in each section. We stood there until the SS men had satisfied their game-playing instincts by "humorous" orders to take off and put on caps. Then they received their report, and counted us. After the headcount — work.

We went in groups — some to build railway tracks or a road, some to the quarries to carry stones or coal, some to take out manure, or for potato-digging, latrine-cleaning, barracks — or sewer — repairs. All this took place inside the camp enclosure. During work the SS men beat up the prisoners mercilessly, inhumanly and for no reason.

They were like wild beasts and, having found their victim, ordered him to present his backside, and beat him with a stick or a whip, usually until the stick broke.

The victim screamed only after the first blows, afterwards he fell unconscious and the SS man then kicked at the ribs, the face, at the most sensitive parts of a man's body, and then, finally convinced that the the victim was at the end of his strength, he ordered another Jew to pour one pail of water after the other over the beaten person until he woke and got up.

A favorite sport of the SS men was to make a "boxing sack" out of a Jew. This was done in the following way: Two Jews were stood up, one being forced to hold the other by the collar, and an SS man trained giving him a knock-out. Of course, after the first blow, the poor victim was likely to fall, and this was prevented by the other Jew holding him up. After the fat, Hitlerite murderer had "trained" in this way for 15 minutes, and only after the poor victim was completely shattered, covered in blood, his teeth knocked out, his nose broken, his eyes hit, they released him and ordered a doctor to treat his wounds. That was their way of taking care and being generous.

Another customary SS habit was to kick a Jew with a heavy boot. The Jew was forced to stand to attention, and all the while the SS man kicked him until he broke some bones. People who stood near enough to such a victim, often heard the breaking of the bones. The pain was so terrible that people, having undergone that treatment, died in agony.

Apart from the SS men there were other expert hangmen. These were the so-called Capos. The name was an abbreviation for "barracks police." The Capos were German criminals who were also camp inmates. However, although they belonged to "us," they were privileged. They had a special, better barracks of their own, they had better food, better, almost normal clothes, they wore special red or green riding pants, high leather boots, and fulfilled the functions of camp guards. They were worse even than the SS men. One of them, older than the others and the worst murderer of them all, when he descended on a victim, would not revive him later with water but would choke him to death. Once, this murderer caught a boy of 13 (in the presence of his father) and hit his head so that the poor child died instantly. This "camp elder" later boasted in front of his peers, with a smile on his beast's face and with pride, that he managed to kill a Jew with one blow.

In each section stood a gallows. For being late for the head count, or similar crimes, the "camp elder" hanged the offenders.

Work was actually unproductive, and its purpose was exhaustion and torture.

At 12 noon there was a break for a meal. Standing in line, we received half a litre of soup each. Usually it was cabbage soup, or some other watery liquid, without fats, tasteless. That was lunch. It was eaten — in all weather — under the open sky, never in the barracks. No spoons were allowed, though wooden spoons lay on each bunk — probably for show, for Red Cross committees. One had to drink the soup out of the bowl and lick it like a dog.

From 1 p.m. till 6 p.m. there was work again. I must emphasize that if we were lucky we got a 12 o'clock meal. There were "days of punishment" — when lunch was given together with the evening meal, and it was cold and sour, so that our stomach was empty for a whole day.

Afternoon work was the same: blows, and blows again. Until 6 p.m.

At 6 there was the evening headcount. Again we were forced to stand at attention. Counting, receiving the report. Usually we were left standing at attention for an hour or two, while some prisoners were called up for "punishment parade" — they were those who in the Germans' eyes had transgressed in some way during the day, or had not been punctilious in their performance. They were stripped naked publicly, laid out on specially constructed benches, and whipped with 25 or 50 lashes.

The brutal beating and the heart-rending cries — all this the prisoners had to watch and hear.

Review Questions

1. How did the SS view their victims?

2. In your opinion what is the meaning of the Holocaust for Western civilization? For Jews? For Christians? For Germans?"

11 | Allied Preparations for the D-Day Invasion

On June 6, 1944, the allied forces launched their invasion of Nazi-occupied France. The invasion, called Operation Overlord, had been planned with meticulous care. Under the supreme command of General Dwight D. Eisenhower (1890–1969), the Allies organized the biggest amphibious operation of the war. It involved 5,000 ships of all kinds, 11,000 aircraft, and 2 million soldiers, 1.5 million of them Americans, all equipped with the latest military gear. Two artificial harbors and several oil pipelines stood ready to supply the troops once the invasion was underway.

The success of D-Day depended on what happened during the first few hours. If the Allies had failed to secure beachheads, the operation would have ended in disaster. Allied control of the air was an important factor in the success of D-Day. A second factor was the fact that the Germans were caught by surprise. Although expecting an invasion, they did not believe that it would take place in the Normandy area of France, and they dismissed June 6 as a possible date because weather conditions were unfavorable.

DWIGHT D. EISENHOWER
Operation Overlord

In the following passage from his book *Crusade in Europe*, General Eisenhower described the intricate planning for Operation Overlord.

. . . The venture the United States and Great Britain were now about to undertake could not be classed as an ordinary tactical movement in which consequences would be no greater than those ordinarily experienced through success or failure in a battle. The two countries were definitely placing all their hopes, expectations, and assets in one great effort to establish a theater of operations in western Europe. Failure would carry with it consequences that would be almost fatal. Such a catastrophe might mean the complete redeployment to other theaters of all United States forces accumulated in the United Kingdom, while the setback to Allied morale and determination would be so profound that it was beyond calculation. Finally, such a failure would certainly react violently upon the Russian situation and it was not unreasonable to assume that, if that country should consider her Allies completely futile and helpless in doing anything of a major character in Europe, she might consider a separate peace. . . .

The timing of the operation was a difficult matter to decide. At Teheran the

President [Franklin D. Roosevelt] and the Prime Minister [Winston Churchill] had promised Generalissimo Stalin that the attack would start in May but we were given to understand that any date selected in that period of the year would fulfill the commitments made by our two political leaders.

In order to obtain the maximum length of good campaigning weather, the earlier the attack could be launched the better. Another factor in favor of an early attack was the continuing and frantic efforts of the German to strengthen his coastal defenses. Because of weather conditions in the [English] Channel, May was the earliest date that a landing attempt could be successfully undertaken and the first favorable combination of tides and sunrise occurred early in the month. Thus early May was the original and tentatively selected target date.

Alarming Intelligence reports concerning the progress of the Germans in developing new long-range weapons of great destructive capacity also indicated the advisability of attacking early. . . .

Two considerations, one of them decisive in character, combined to postpone the target date from May to June. The first and important one was our insistence that the attack be on a larger scale than that originally planned by the staff assembled in London under Lieutenant General Frederick Morgan. He was an extraordinarily fine officer and had, long before my arrival, won the high admiration and respect of General Marshall. I soon came to place an equal value upon his qualifications: He had in the months preceding my arrival accomplished a mass of detailed planning, accumulation of data, and gathering of supply that made D-day possible. My ideas were supported by General Morgan personally but he had been compelled to develop his plan on the basis of a fixed number of ships, landing craft, and other resources. Consequently he had no recourse except to work out an attack along a three-division front, whereas I insisted upon five and informed the

Combined Chiefs of Staff that we had to have the additional landing craft and other gear essential to the larger operation, even if this meant delaying the assault by a month. To this the Combined Chiefs of Staff agreed.

Another factor that made the later date a desirable one was the degree of dependence we were placing upon the preparatory effort of the air force. An early attack would provide the air force with only a minimum opportunity for pinpoint bombing of critical transportation centers in France, whereas the improved weather anticipated for the month of May would give them much more time and better opportunity to impede the movement of German reserves and demolish German defenses along the coast line. The virtual destruction of critical points on the main roads and railroads leading into the selected battle area was a critical feature of the battle plan. Nevertheless, acceptance of the later date was disappointing. We wanted all the summer weather we could get for the European campaign.

Along with the general plan of operations we thoroughly considered means of deceiving the enemy as to the point and timing of attack. Our purpose was to convince him that we intended to strike directly across the Channel at its narrowest point, against the stronghold of Calais. In many ways great advantages would have accrued to us could we have successfully attacked in this region. Not only were the beaches the best along the coast, they were closest to the British ports and to the German border. The enemy, fully appreciating these facts, kept strong forces in the area and fortified that particular section of coast line more strongly than any other. The defenses were so strong that none of us believed that a successful assault from the sea could be made except at such terrific cost that the whole expedition might find itself helpless to accomplish anything of a positive character, after it got ashore. But we counted upon the enemy believing that we would be tempted into this operation, and the wide variety of measures we took for convincing him were given extraordinary credence by his Intelligence division. . . .

One of the most difficult problems, which invariably accompanies planning for a tactical offensive, involves measures for maintenance, supplies, evacuation, and replacement.

Prior to the late war it had always been assumed that any major amphibious attack had to gain permanent port facilities within a matter of several days or be abandoned. The development of effective landing gear by the Allies, including LSTs, LCTs, ducks, and other craft, did much to lessen immediate dependence upon established port facilities. It is not too much to say that Allied development of great quantities of revolutionary types of equipment was one of the greatest factors in the defeat of the plans of the German General Staff.

Nevertheless, possession of equipment and gear that permit the landing of material on open beaches does not by any means eliminate the need for ports. This was particularly true in Overlord. The history of centuries clearly shows that the English Channel is subject to destructive storms at all times of the year, with winter by far the worst period. The only certain method to assure supply and maintenance was by capture of large port facilities.

Since the nature of the defenses to be encountered ruled out the possibility of gaining adequate ports promptly, it was necessary also to provide a means for sheltering beach supply from the effect of storms. We knew that even after we captured Cherbourg its port capacity and the lines of communication leading out of it could not meet all our needs. To solve this apparently unsolvable problem we undertook a project so unique as to be classed by many scoffers as completely fantastic. It was a plan to construct artificial harbors on the coast of Normandy.

The first time I heard this idea tentatively advanced was by [British] Admiral [Louis] Mountbatten, in the spring of 1942. At a conference attended by a number of service chiefs he remarked, "If ports are not available, we may have to construct them in pieces and tow them in." Hoots and jeers greeted his suggestion but two years later it was to become reality.

Two general types of protected anchorages were designed. The first, called a "gooseberry," was to consist merely of a line of sunken ships placed stem to stem in such numbers as to provide a sheltered coast line in their lee on which small ships and landing craft could continue to unload in any except the most vicious weather. The other type, named "mulberry," was practically a complete harbor. Two of these were designed and constructed in Great Britain, to be towed piecemeal to the coast of Normandy. The principal construction unit in the mulberry was an enormous concrete ship, called a "phoenix," boxlike in shape and so heavily constructed that when numbers of them were sunk end to end along a strip of coast they would probably provide solid protection against almost any wave action. Elaborate auxiliary equipment to facilitate unloading and all types of gear required in the operation of a modern port were planned for and provided. The British and American sectors were each to have one of the mulberry ports. Five gooseberries were to be installed. . . .

At a secluded spot in eastern England the British Army constructed every type of tactical obstacle that the German might use in defending against our attack. The British built pillboxes, massive stone walls, and great areas of barbed-wire entanglements. They planted mine fields, erected steel obstacles for underwater and land use, and dug anti-tank ditches. Each of these was a replica of similar defenses we knew the Germans had already installed. Then the British set about the task of designing equipment that would facilitate destruction of these obstacles. They used the area for actual test of the equipment so developed and for trying out new battle techniques.

An interesting example of this experimentation was a new method for using the Bangalore torpedo. This torpedo is nothing but a long tube filled with explosive. It is thrust out into a mine field and upon detonation explodes all the mines planted along its length. Thus is created a narrow path through the mine field, along which troops can advance and continue the attack while others in the rear come forward to clear up the remaining portions of the field. These torpedoes had long been used in warfare but the British developed a novel way of employing them. They did this by covering a Sherman tank with a series of pipes, each of which contained a Bangalore torpedo. The pipes pointed straight to the front and were, in effect, guns with light charges of black powder at the rear. As the tank advanced it automatically fired these makeshift guns in succession so that, as each of the torpedoes flew out in the air and exploded some thirty feet in front of the tank, it cleared a continuous path through the mine field. Each tank carried a sufficient number of torpedoes to clear a path approximately fifty yards long. The idea was that, instead of depending upon defenseless foot soldiers to do this hazardous work, it would be done by a tank crew, from the comparative safety afforded by its protecting armor. I never saw this particular piece of equipment used in action but it is an example of the methods by which we tried to ease the problem of the foot soldier. Transportable bridges to span anti-tank ditches, flame-throwing tanks, and flails, plows, and heavy rollers for destroying mines were other items constantly under development and test.

As always, the matter of the Army's morale attracted the constant attention of all senior commanders. Sometimes this attention had to be directed toward particular and specific points. For example, a columnist estimated that any attempt to

land on the defended coast of northwest Europe would result in eighty to ninety per cent losses in the assaulting units. This irresponsible statement was sufficiently circulated to cause doubt and uneasiness in the command. [U.S. General Omar] Bradley and others immediately took occasion, during numerous visits to troops, to brand this statement for just what it was — a fearful, false, and completely misguided statement by someone who knew nothing of warfare or of the facts. Bradley predicted that the attacking losses would be no greater than in any other stiff battle of comparable size. We went so far as to give publicity to his estimate in the papers and used every other means available to us to prevent the doleful prediction from shaking the confidence of the troops.

The air plan, in both its preparatory and supporting phases, was worked out in minute detail, and as the spring wore on the results obtained in the preparatory phrase were reviewed weekly. Reconnaissance by submarine and airplane was unending, while information was gathered from numbers of sources. The naval plan involved general protection, mine sweeping, escorting, supporting fire, and, along with all else, erection of artificial ports, repair of captured ports, and maintenance of cross-Channel supply. The coastal defenses were studied and specific plans made for the reduction of every strong point, every pillbox. Pictures were studied and one of the disturbing things these continued to show was the growing profusion of beach obstacles, most of them under water at high tide. Embarkation plans for troops, equipment, and supplies were voluminous, and exact in detail. Routes to ports, timings of departures and arrivals, locations, protection and camouflage of temporary camps, and a thousand related matters were all carefully predetermined and, so far as feasible, tested in advance.

Senior commanders used every possible moment in visiting and inspecting troops. Records left by a staff officer show that in four months, from February 1 to June 1, I visited twenty-six divisions, twenty-four airfields, five ships of war, and numerous depots, shops, hospitals, and other important installations. [Military commanders] Bradley, Montgomery, Spaatz, and Tedder maintained similar schedules. Such visits, sandwiched between a seemingly endless series of conference and staff meetings, were necessary and highly valuable.

Soldiers like to see the men who are directing operations; they properly resent any indication of neglect or indifference to them on the part of their commanders and invariably interpret a visit, even a brief one, as evidence of the commander's concern for them. Diffidence or modesty must never blind the commander to his duty of showing himself to his men, of speaking to them, of mingling with them to the extent of physical limitations. It pays big dividends in terms of morale, and morale, given rough equality in other things, is supreme on the battlefield.

After the abandonment of the May target date, the next combination of moon, tide, and time of sunrise that we considered practicable for the attack occurred on June 5, 6, and 7. We wanted to cross the Channel with our convoys at night so that darkness would conceal the strength and direction of our several attacks. We wanted a moon for our airborne assaults. We need approximately forty minutes of daylight preceding the ground assault to complete our bombing and preparatory bombardment. We had to attack on a relatively low tide because of beach obstacles which had to be removed while uncovered. These principal factors dictated the general period; but the selection of the actual day would depend upon weather forecasts.

If none of the three days should prove satisfactory from the standpoint of weather, consequences would ensue that were almost terrifying to contemplate. Secrecy would be lost. Assault troops would be unloaded and crowded back into assembly areas enclosed in barbed wire, where their original places would already have been taken by those to follow in subsequent waves. Complicated movement tables would be scrapped. Morale would drop. A wait of at least fourteen days, possibly twenty-eight, would be necessary — a sort of suspended animation involving more than 2,000,000 men! The good-weather period available for major campaigning would become still shorter and the enemy's defenses would become still stronger! The whole of the United Kingdom would become quickly aware that something had gone wrong and national discouragement there and in America could lead to unforeseen results. Finally, always lurking in the background was the knowledge that the enemy was developing new, and presumably effective, secret weapons on the French coast. What the effect of these would be on our crowded harbors, especially at Plymouth and Portsmouth, we could not even guess.

It was a tense period, made even worse by the fact that the one thing that could give us this disastrous setback was entirely outside our control. Some soldier once said, "The weather is always neutral." Nothing could be more untrue. Bad weather is obviously the enemy of the side that seeks to launch projects requiring good weather, or of the side possessing great assets, such as strong air forces, which depend upon good weather for effective operations. If really bad weather should endure permanently, the Nazi would need nothing else to defend the Normandy coast! . . .

The staffs that were developing, coordinating, and recording all these details were, of course, working in constant cooperation with numerous agencies and personalities in London and Washington. During the preparatory period an endless stream of staff officers from Washington visited our headquarters to provide information on the availability of needed items, confirm dates of shipment, discuss plans for personnel replacements, for security, for photographic coverage, and a thousand related items.

One of General Somervell's principal assistants, Major General LeRoy Lutes, remained with us in Britain several weeks, investigating arrangements for insuring the uninterrupted flow of supplies all the way from the factories in the United States to the front line. . . .

. . . The big question mark always before us was the weather that would prevail during the only period of early June that we could use, the fifth, sixth, and seventh.

All southern England was one vast military camp, crowded with soldiers awaiting final word to go, and piled high with supplies and equipment awaiting transport to the far shore of the Channel. The whole area was cut off from the rest of England. The government had established a deadline, across which no unauthorized person was allowed to go in either direction. Every separate encampment, barrack, vehicle park, and every unit was carefully charted on our master maps. The scheduled movement of each unit had been so worked out that it would reach the embarkation point at the exact time the vessels would be ready to receive it. The southernmost camps where assault troops were assembled were all surrounded by barbed-wire entanglements to prevent any soldier leaving the camp after he had once been briefed as to his part in the attack. The mighty host was tense as a coiled spring, and indeed that is exactly what it was — a great human spring, coiled for the moment when its energy should be released and it would vault the English Channel in the greatest amphibious assault ever attempted.

We met with the Meteorologic Committee twice daily, once at nine-thirty in the evening and once at four in the morning. The committee, comprising both British and American personnel, was headed by a dour but canny Scot, Group Captain J. M. Stagg. At these meetings every bit of evidence was carefully presented, carefully analyzed by the experts, and carefully studied by the assembled commanders. With the approach of the critical period the tension continued to mount as prospects for decent weather became worse and worse.

The final conference for determining the feasibility of attacking on the tentatively selected day, June 5, was scheduled for 4:00 a.m. on June 4. However, some of the attacking contingents had already been ordered to sea, because if the entire force was to land on June 5, then some of the important elements stationed in northern parts of the United Kingdom could not wait for final decision on the morning of June 4.

When the commanders assembled on the morning of June 4 the report we received was discouraging. Low clouds, high winds, and formidable wave action were predicted to make landing a most hazardous affair. The meteorologists said that air support would be impossible, naval gunfire would be inefficient, and even the handling of small boats would be rendered difficult. Admiral Ramsay thought that the mechanics of landing could be handled, but agreed with the estimate of the difficulty in adjusting gunfire. His position was mainly neutral. General Montgomery, properly concerned with the great disadvantages of delay, believed that we should go. Tedder disagreed.

Weighing all factors, I decided that the attack would have to be postponed. This decision necessitated the immediate dispatch of orders to the vessels and troops already at sea and created some doubt as to whether they could be ready twenty-four hours later in case the next day should prove favorable for the assault. Actually the maneuver of the ships in the Irish Sea proved most difficult by reason of the storm. That they succeeded in gaining ports, refueling, and readying themselves to resume the movement a day later represented the utmost in seamanship and in brilliant command and staff work.

The conference on the evening of June 4 presented little, if any, added brightness to the picture of the morning, and tension mounted even higher because the inescapable consequences of postponement were almost too bitter to contemplate.

At three-thirty the next morning our little camp was shaking and shuddering under a wind of almost hurricane proportions and the accompanying rain seemed to be traveling in horizontal streaks. The mile-long trip through muddy roads to the naval headquarters was anything but a cheerful one, since it seemed impossible that in such conditions there was any reason for even discussing the situation.

When the conference started the first report given us by Group Captain Stagg and the Meteorologic Staff was that the bad conditions predicted the day before for the coast of France were actually prevailing there and that if we had persisted in the attempt to land on June 5 a major disaster would almost surely have resulted. This they probably told us to inspire more confidence in their next astonishing declaration, which was that by the following morning a period of relatively good weather, heretofore completely unexpected, would ensue, lasting probably thirty-six hours. The long-term prediction was not good but they did give us assurance that this short period of calm weather would intervene between the exhaustion of the storm we were then experiencing and the beginning of the next spell of really bad weather.

The prospect was not bright because of the possibility that we might land the first several waves successfully and then find later build-up impracticable, and so have to leave the isolated original attacking forces easy prey to German counteraction. However, the consequences of the delay justified great risk and I quickly announced the decision to go ahead with the attack on June 6. The time was then 4:15 a.m., June 5. No one present disagreed and there was a definite brightening of faces as, without a further word, each went off to his respective post of duty to flash out to his command the messages that would set the whole host in motion.

Review Questions

1. What did Dwight Eisenhower consider to be the consequences if Operation Overlord failed?

2. Why did Eisenhower believe that the invasion should begin in May or June rather than later in the year?

3. Give illustrations of the meticulous planning that went into operation Overlord.

4. How did senior commanders try to maintain high morale among the troops as they prepared for the invasion?

5. After the abandonment of the May target date, why did Eisenhower consider it absolutely vital that the invasion start on June 5, 6, or 7?

12 | The Decision to Drop the Bomb

The dropping of the two atomic bombs on Hiroshima and Nagasaki ended the war with Japan at a stroke. The two bombs also introduced a new era: for the first time in human history, humanity possesses weapons with the potential to destroy civilization and life. Hiroshima and Nagasaki became the symbols of a new age that requires, as Albert Einstein observed in 1946, new modes of thinking if the world is to escape unparalleled catastrophe.

Predictably, the world-shaking change wrought by nuclear weapons produced prolonged controversy over whether the bombs should have been dropped on Japan. Some people contend that the United States acted to prevent the even greater loss of life that would have resulted from an U.S. invasion of Japan. Others argue that Japan was set to surrender in any case and that the real intent in dropping the bomb was to frighten Stalin into compliance with U.S. policy in Europe and the Far East.

HENRY L. STIMSON
The Atomic Bomb and the Surrender of Japan

Henry L. Stimson (1867–1950), who served as secretary of war under Presidents Franklin Roosevelt and Harry Truman, supervised the atomic development program. In 1947 in an article incorporated that year into a book, *On Active Service in Peace and War*, Stimson discussed the decision to drop the bomb. The major part of the article as reproduced in the book follows.

The principal political, social, and military objective of the United States in the summer of 1945 was the prompt and complete surrender of Japan. Only the complete destruction of her military power could open the way to lasting peace.

Japan, in July, 1945, had been seriously weakened by our increasingly violent attacks. It was known to us that she had gone so far as to make tentative proposals to the Soviet Government, hoping to use the Russians as mediators in a negotiated peace. These vague proposals contemplated the retention by Japan of important conquered areas and were therefore not considered seriously. There was as yet no indication of any weakening in the Japanese determination to fight rather than accept unconditional surrender. If she should persist in her fight to the end, she had still a great military force.

In the middle of July, 1945, the intelligence section of the War Department General Staff estimated Japanese military strength as follows: in the home islands, slightly under 2,000,000; in Korea, Manchuria, China proper, and Formosa, slightly over 2,000,000; in French Indo-China, Thailand, and Burma, over 200,000; in the East Indies area, including the Philippines, over 500,000; in the by-passed Pacific islands, over 100,000. The total strength of the Japanese Army was estimated at about 5,000,000 men. These estimates later proved to be in very close agreement with official Japanese figures.

The Japanese Army was in much better condition than the Japanese Navy and Air Force. The Navy had practically ceased to exist except as a harrying force against an invasion fleet. The Air Force had been reduced mainly to reliance upon Kamikaze, or suicide, attacks. These latter, however, had already inflicted serious damage on our seagoing forces, and their possible effectiveness in a last ditch fight was a matter of real concern to our naval leaders.

As we understood it in July, there was a very strong possibility that the Japanese Government might determine upon resistance to the end, in all the areas of the Far East under its control. In such an event the Allies would be faced with the enormous task of destroying an armed force of five million men and five thousand suicide aircraft, belonging to a race which had already amply demonstrated its ability to fight literally to the death.

The strategic plans of our armed forces for the defeat of Japan, as they stood in July, had been prepared without reliance upon the atomic bomb, which had not yet been tested in New Mexico. We were planning an intensified sea and air blockade, and greatly intensified strategic air bombing, through the summer and early fall, to be followed on November 1 by an invasion of the southern island of Kyushu. This would be followed in turn by an invasion of the main island of Honshu in the spring of 1946. The total U.S. military and naval force involved in this grand design was of the order of 5,000,000 men; if all those indirectly concerned are included, it was larger still. . . .

We estimated that if we should be forced to carry this plan to its conclusion, the major fighting would not end until the latter part of 1946, at the earliest. I was informed that such operations might be expected to cost over a million casualties, to American forces alone. Additional large losses might be expected among our allies and, of course, if our campaign were successful and if we could judge by previous experience, enemy casualties would be much larger than our own.

It was already clear in July that even before the invasion we should be able to inflict enormously severe damage on the Japanese homeland by the combined application of "conventional" sea and air power. The critical question was whether this kind of action would induce surrender. It therefore became necessary to consider very carefully the probable state of mind of the enemy, and to assess with accuracy the line of conduct which might end his will to resist.

With these considerations in mind, I wrote a memorandum for the President, on July 2, which I believe fairly represents the thinking of the American Government as it finally took shape in action. . . .

In the last item of his memorandum, Stimson suggested giving Japan a warning that it faced inevitable and complete destruction if it did not agree to a surrender and military occupation.

It is important to emphasize the double character of the suggested warning. It was designed to promise destruction if Japan resisted, and hope, if she surrendered.

It will be noted that the atomic bomb is not mentioned in this memorandum. On grounds of secrecy the bomb was never mentioned except when absolutely necessary, and furthermore, it had not yet been tested. It was of course well forward in our minds, as the memorandum was written and discussed, that the bomb would be the best possible sanction if our warning were rejected. . . .

There was much discussion in Washington about the timing of the warning to Japan. The controlling factor in the end was the date already set for the Potsdam [Germany] meeting of the Big Three [Truman, Stalin, and Churchill, the leaders of the Allies]. It was President Truman's decision that such a warning should be solemnly issued by the U.S. and the U.K. from this meeting [following the surrender of Germany], with the concurrence of the head of the Chinese Government, so that it would be plain that *all* of Japan's principal enemies were in entire unity. This was done, in the Potsdam ultimatum of July 26, which very closely followed the . . . memorandum of July 2, with the exception that it made no mention of the Japanese Emperor.

On July 28 the Premier of Japan, Suzuki, rejected the Potsdam ultimatum by announcing that it was "unworthy of public notice." In the face of this rejection we could only proceed to demonstrate that the ultimatum had meant exactly what it said when it stated that if the Japanese continued the war, "the full application of our military power, backed by our resolve, will mean the inevitable and complete destruction of the Japanese armed

forces and just as inevitably the utter dev-
astation of the Japanese homeland."

For such a purpose the atomic bomb
was an eminently suitable weapon. The
New Mexico test occurred while we were
at Potsdam, on July 16. It was immediately clear that the power of the bomb
measured up to our highest estimates. We
had developed a weapon of such a revolutionary character that its use against the
enemy might well be expected to produce
exactly the kind of shock on the Japanese
ruling oligarchy which we desired,
strengthening the position of those who
wished peace, and weakening that of the
military party. . . .

Hiroshima was bombed on August 6,
and Nagasaki on August 9. These two
cities were active working parts of the
Japanese war effort. One was an army
center; the other was naval and industrial. Hiroshima was the headquarters of
the Japanese Army defending southern
Japan and was a major military storage and
assembly point. Nagasaki was a major
seaport and it contained several large industrial plants of great wartime importance. We believed that our attacks had
struck cities which must certainly be important to the Japanese military leaders,
both Army and Navy, and we waited for
a result. We waited one day.

Many accounts have been written about
the Japanese surrender. After a prolonged Japanese Cabinet session in which
the deadlock was broken by the Emperor
himself, the offer to surrender was made
on August 10. . . .

The two atomic bombs which we had
dropped were the only ones we had ready,
and our rate of production at the time was
very small. Had the war continued until
the projected invasion on November 1,
additional fire raids of B-29's would have
been more destructive of life and property than the very limited number of
atomic raids which we could have executed in the same period. But the atomic
bomb was more than a weapon of terrible
destruction; it was a psychological weapon.
In March, 1945, our Air Forces had

launched the first great incendiary raid on
the Tokyo area. In this raid more damage was done and more casualties were
inflicted than was the case at Hiroshima.
Hundreds of bombers took part and
hundreds of tons of incendiaries were
dropped. Similar successive raids burned
out a great part of the urban area of Japan, but the Japanese fought on. On August 6 one B-29 dropped a single atomic
bomb on Hiroshima. Three days later a
second bomb was dropped on Nagasaki
and the war was over. So far as the Japanese could know, our ability to execute
atomic attacks, if necessary by many planes
at a time, was unlimited. As Dr. Karl
Compton[1] has said, "it was not one atomic
bomb, or two, which brought surrender;
it was the experience of what an atomic
bomb will actually do to a community, *plus
the dread of many more*, that was effective."*

The bomb thus served exactly the purpose we intended. The peace party was
able to take the path of surrender, and
the whole weight of the Emperor's prestige was exerted in favor of peace. When
the Emperor ordered surrender, and the
small but dangerous group of fanatics who
opposed him were brought under control, the Japanese became so subdued that
the great undertaking of occupation and
disarmament was completed with unprecedented ease. . . .

---

*In a "personal summary" Stimson reviewed the
"compelling and clear" reasons for the course
taken by the United States.*

Two great nations were approaching
contact in a fight to a finish which would

---

[1] K. T. Compton, "The Atomic Bomb and the
Surrender of Japan," *Atlantic Monthly*, January,
1947.
*Karl T. Compton (1887–1954) was an edu-
cator (president of the Massachusetts Institute
of Technology) and physicist closely associated
with the development of the atomic bomb and
radar.

begin on November 1, 1945. Our enemy, Japan, commanded forces of somewhat over 5,000,000 armed men. Men of these armies had already inflicted upon us, in our break-through of the outer perimeter of their defenses, over 300,000 battle casualties. Enemy armies still unbeaten had the strength to cost us a million more. *As long as the Japanese Government refused to surrender,* we should be forced to take and hold the ground, and smash the Japanese ground armies, by close-in fighting of the same desperate and costly kind that we had faced in the Pacific islands for nearly four years.

In the light of the formidable problem which thus confronted us, I felt that every possible step should be taken to compel a surrender of the homelands, and a withdrawal of all Japanese troops from the Asiatic mainland and from other positions, before we had commenced an invasion. . . .

In order to end the war in the shortest possible time and to avoid the enormous losses of human life which otherwise confronted us, I felt that we must use the Emperor as our instrument to command and compel his people to cease fighting and subject themselves to our authority through him, and that to accomplish this we must give him and his controlling advisers a compelling reason to accede to our demands. This reason furthermore must be of such a nature that his people could understand his decision. The bomb seemed to me to furnish a unique instrument for that purpose.

My chief purpose was to end the war in victory with the least possible cost in the lives of the men in the armies which I had helped to raise. In the light of the alternatives which, on a fair estimate, were open to us I believe that no man, in our position and subject to our responsibilities, holding in his hands a weapon of such possibilities for accomplishing this purpose and saving those lives, could have failed to use it and afterwards looked his countrymen in the face. . . .

. . . The decision to use the atomic bomb was a decision that brought death to over a hundred thousand Japanese. No explanation can change that fact and I do not wish to gloss it over. But this deliberate, premeditated destruction was our least abhorrent choice. The destruction of Hiroshima and Nagasaki put an end to the Japanese war. It stopped the fire raids, and the strangling blockade; it ended the ghastly specter of a clash of great land armies.

Review Questions

1. What casualties were estimated if the United States invaded Japan? Why were such high casualties anticipated?

2. What comparison did Henry Stimson draw between the incendiary raid on Tokyo and the bombing of Hiroshima? What conclusion did he draw from the incendiary raids?

3. What alternatives to dropping the bombs did Stimson describe?

PART IV

The Contemporary World

CHAPTER 11

The West in an Age of Globalism

Four major themes pervade the years since World War II: the Cold War, decolonization and independent statehood in the Third World, human rights, and humanity's prospects for survival amid the unprecedented changes in global conditions during the past half-century. The final selections in this volume reflect significant issues within these broad themes.

The Cold War between the United States and the Soviet Union dominates world politics and is the principal reason for global anxiety. The consequences of nuclear war threaten human life everywhere; the high costs of the arms race deepen the poverty of developing countries; the tension between the superpowers poisons international relations generally. The causes of the Cold War have deep roots. On one side the countries of Western liberal democracy, above all the United States, advance their power and influence around the world. On the other side a large but historically backward country has labored — first under the tsars, and since 1917, under the Soviet dictatorship — to rise from humiliating defeats early in this century to global prestige and power.

At the end of World War II the two mutually incompatible political systems came into direct confrontation. At issue were not only the new U.S. pre-eminence in the world and Soviet penetration into central Europe and into Manchuria in the Far East, but also the competition between two systems of government and two approaches to fulfilling human aspirations for escape from backwardness and poverty. In this competition, each side dreads the expansionism of the other, convinced of the worthlessness and immorality of the other's political system. All along, both sides have built up their military power to the utmost. Arguments first advanced by Churchill and Khrushchev still inspire current policies.

Superpower rivalry has also entangled former colonial peoples; both the United States and the Soviet Union have tried to win the newcomers in world politics to their sides. The human attitudes motivating the relations between the former colonial masters and their subjects, to whom they taught the ideals of freedom and self-determination, cover a wide spectrum. The colonial peoples' attitudes range from plain envy to outright rejection.

These conflicting attitudes still swirl around the world, reflected in world politics as well as in the efforts of the developing countries to escape from poverty and instability. Decolonization, which began with high hopes, has produced turmoil in many lands; with political independence came civil strife, economic distress, and further economic dependence on the West. Western imperialism had bred high expectations in African and Asian lands. However, when former colonies with different and conflicting cultural traditions attempted to copy the trappings of Western civilization, the result was often cultural disorientation and political discord.

In the relations between the superpowers, as well as in global politics generally, the issue of human rights has played an important role. Having reasonably secured human rights in their own society, the Western democracies have promoted them as part of their responsibility in world affairs; Americans especially have pressed the issue. Unfortunately, in other parts of the world the preconditions that led to the evolution of human rights in Western society are patently lacking. The majority of people around the world are compelled to conform to alien Western institutions of statehood and industrialization. The historically conditioned attitudes needed for orderly constitutional government and respect for individual liberty are often lacking in non-Western nations; consequently, these lands have often experienced revolutions and rule by force and terror.

In addition to international tensions and violations of human rights, humanity also faces serious social, economic, and environmental problems, including a population explosion that has tripled in less than one hundred years the number of people to be fed and employed. The immensity of human progress has raised expectations to a high level, while the earth's resources and the capacity of humankind to fulfill such expectations are burdened by a mushrooming population, cultural disorientation, political discord, and national antagonisms.

1 | The Cold War

After World War II, the first Western statesman to express publicly his alarm over Soviet expansionism was Winston Churchill, the doughty and articulate wartime leader of Great Britain. Churchill surveyed the postwar world scene and noted that the United States stood "at the pinnacle of world power." But he also warned that "a shadow has fallen" on Europe and Asia, a shadow cast by Soviet hostility to the liberties that are a traditional part of Western democracy and had become embodied in the Charter of the United Nations as well. He still spoke of "our Russian friends," but the failure of appeasement and his war experiences prompted him to urge military strength and political unity for Western Europe and the United States in order to stop the communist advance.

WINSTON CHURCHILL
The Iron Curtain

In a famous speech at Fulton, Missouri, in early March 1946, when he was no longer in office, Churchill articulated his views on the duty of Western democracies in the face of Soviet expansion. Significant passages from that speech, in which the term *iron curtain* was first used, follow.

The United States stands at this time at the pinnacle of world power. It is a solemn moment for the American democracy. With primacy in power is also joined an awe-inspiring accountability to the future. As you look around you, you must feel not only the sense of duty done but also feel anxiety lest you fall below the level of achievement. Opportunity is here now, clear and shining, for both our countries. To reject it or ignore it or fritter it away will bring upon us all the long reproaches of the aftertime. . . .

. . . We cannot be blind to the fact that the liberties enjoyed by individual citizens throughout the British Empire are not valid in a considerable number of countries, some of which are very powerful. In these states, control is enforced upon the common people by various kinds of all-embracing police governments, to a degree which is overwhelming and contrary to every principle of democracy. The power of the state is exercised without restraint, either by dictators or by compact oligarchies operating through a privileged party and a political police. . . .

A shadow has fallen upon the scenes so lately lighted by the Allied victory. Nobody knows what Soviet Russia and its Communist international organization intends to do in the immediate future, or what are the limits, if any, to their expansive and proselytizing tendencies. I have a strong admiration and regard for the valiant Russian people and for my wartime comrade, Marshal Stalin. There is sympathy and good will in Britain — and I doubt not here also — toward the peoples of all the Russias and a resolve to persevere through many differences and rebuffs in establishing lasting friendships. We understand the Russians need to be secure on her western frontiers from all renewal of German aggression. We welcome her to her rightful place among the leading nations of the world. Above all we welcome constant, frequent and growing contacts between the Russian people and our own people on both sides of the

Atlantic. It is my duty, however, to place before you certain facts about the present position in Europe — I am sure I do not wish to, but it is my duty, I feel, to present them to you.

From Stettin in the Baltic to Triest in the Adriatic, an iron curtain has descended across the Continent. Behind that line lie all the capitals of the ancient states of central and eastern Europe. Warsaw, Berlin, Prague, Vienna, Budapest, Belgrade, Bucharest and Sofia, all these famous cities and the populations around them lie in the Soviet sphere and all are subject in one form or another, not only to Soviet influence but to a very high and increasing measure of control from Moscow. Athens alone, with its immortal glories, is free to decide its future at an election under British, American and French observation. The Russian-dominated Polish government has been encouraged to make enormous and wrongful inroads upon Germany, and mass expulsions of millions of Germans on a scale grievous and undreamed of are now taking place. The Communist parties, which were very small in all these eastern states of Europe, have been raised to pre-eminence and power far beyond their numbers and are seeking everywhere to obtain totalitarian control. Police governments are prevailing in nearly every case, and so far, except in Czechoslovakia, there is no true democracy. Turkey and Persia are both profoundly alarmed and disturbed at the claims which are made upon them and at the pressure being exerted by the Moscow government. An attempt is being made by the Russians in Berlin to build up a quasi-Communist party in their zone of occupied Germany by showing special favors to groups of Left-Wing German leaders. . . . Whatever conclusions may be drawn from these facts — and facts they are — this is certainly not the liberated Europe we fought to build up. Nor is it one which contains the essentials of permanent peace. . . . What we have to consider here today while time remains, is the permanent prevention of war and the establishment of conditions of freedom and democracy as rapidly as possible in all countries. Our difficulties and dangers will not be removed by closing our eyes to them. They will not be removed by mere waiting to see what happens; nor will they be relieved by a policy of appeasement. What is needed is a settlement and the longer this is delayed the more difficult it will be and the greater our dangers will become. From what I have seen of our Russian friends and allies during the war, I am convinced that there is nothing they admire so much as strength, and there is nothing for which they have less respect than for military weakness. . . . If the western democracies stand together in strict adherence to the principles of the United Nations Charter, their influence for furthering these principles will be immense and no one is likely to molest them. If, however, they become divided or falter in their duty, and if these all-important years are allowed to slip away, then indeed catastrophe may overwhelm us all.

NIKITA S. KHRUSHCHEV
Report to the Twentieth Party Congress

After Stalin's death, the Korean War, and the escalation of the nuclear arms race into the deployment of hydrogen bombs, the Soviets perceived themselves to be in a worldwide struggle with the Western capitalists. In the Russian view, the socialist system was advancing, while the capitalist system was in decline; the Cold War represented a desperate effort to preserve capitalism. Communists especially attacked the American desire to deal with the socialist countries from a position of superior strength.

Soviet international policy gave special attention to the aspirations of "the peoples of the East," the Asians and Africans emerging from colonial rule. Soviets described American aid to developing countries as a new form of imperialism, whereas Soviet aid was pictured as humanitarian assistance in the struggle against colonialism.

Nikita Khrushchev (1894–1971) summed up the Soviet perspective on world affairs for the benefit of a new generation of Soviet citizens. As first secretary of the Communist party, he delivered a report to the Congress in February 1956, on the eve of his famous denunciation of the crimes of the Stalin era (see page 289). He sounded an optimistic but militant note. Alarmed by the progress of the arms race, Khrushchev gave vigorous support to an old Soviet plea for the peaceful coexistence of the two competing sociopolitical systems — a coexistence in which victory would inevitably go to communism.

Soon after the Second World War ended, the influence of reactionary and militarist groups began to be increasingly evident in the policy of the United States of America, Britain and France. Their desire to enforce their will on other countries by economic and political pressure, threats and military provocation prevailed. This became known as the "positions of strength" policy. It reflects the aspiration of the most aggressive sections of present-day imperialism to win world supremacy, to suppress the working class and the democratic and national-liberation movements; it reflects their plans for military adventures against the socialist camp.

The international atmosphere was poisoned by war hysteria. The arms race began to assume more and more monstrous dimensions. Many big U.S. military bases designed for use against the U.S.S.R. and the People's Democracies [East European countries under Soviet control] were built in countries thousands of miles from the borders of the United States. "Cold war" was begun against the socialist camp. International distrust was artificially kindled, and nations set against one another. A bloody war was launched in Korea; the war in Indo-China dragged on for years.

The inspirers of the "cold war" began to establish military blocs, and many countries found themselves, against the will of their peoples, involved in restricted aggressive alignments — the North Atlantic bloc, Western European Union, SEATO (military bloc for South-East Asia) and the Baghdad pact.

The organizers of military blocs allege that they have united for defence, for protection against the "communist threat." But that is sheer hypocrisy. We know from history that when planning a redivision of the world, the imperialist powers have always lined up military blocs. Today the "anti-communism" slogan is again being used as a smokescreen to cover up the claims of one power for world domination. The new thing here is that the United States wants, by means of all kinds of blocs and pacts, to secure a dominant position in the capitalist world for itself, and to reduce all its partners in the blocs to the status of obedient executors of its will.

The inspirers of the "positions of strength" policy assert that this policy makes another war impossible, because it ensures a "balance of power" in the world arena. . . .

The winning of political freedom by the peoples of the former colonies and semi-colonies is the first and most important prerequisite of their full independence, that is, of the achievement of economic independence. The liberated Asian countries are pursuing a policy of building up their own industry, training their own technicians, raising the living standards of the people, and regenerating and developing their age-old national culture. History-making prospects for a better future are opening up before the countries which have embarked upon the path of independent development. . . .

To preserve, and in some places also to re-establish their former domination, the colonial powers are resorting to the suppression of the colonial peoples by the force of arms, a method which has been condemned by history. They also have recourse to new forms of colonial enslavement under the guise of so-called "aid" to underdeveloped countries, which brings colossal profits to the colonialists. Let us take the United States as an example. The United States renders such "aid" above all in the form of deliveries of American weapons to the underdeveloped countries. This enables the American monopolies to load up their industry with arms orders. Then the products of the arms industry, worth billions of dollars and paid for through the budget by the American taxpayers, are sent to the underdeveloped countries. States receiving such "aid" in the form of weapons, inevitably fall into dependence; they increase their armies, which leads to higher taxes and a decline in living standards. . . .

Naturally, "aid" to underdeveloped countries is granted on definite political terms, terms providing for their integration into aggressive military blocs, the conclusion of joint military pacts, and support for American foreign policy aimed at world domination, or "world leadership," as the American imperialists themselves call it. . . .

[In contrast,] the exceptionally warm and friendly welcome accorded the representatives of the great Soviet people has strikingly demonstrated the deep-rooted confidence and love the broad masses in the Eastern countries have for the Soviet Union. Analyzing the sources of this confidence, the Egyptian *Al Akhbar* justly wrote: "Russia does not try to buy the conscience of the peoples, their rights and liberty. Russia has extended a hand to the peoples and said that they themselves should decide their destiny, that she recognizes their rights and aspirations and does not demand their adherence to military pacts or blocs." Millions of men and women ardently acclaim our country for its uncompromising struggle against colonialism, for its policy of equality and friendship among all nations and for its consistent peaceful foreign policy. *(Stormy, prolonged applause.)*

. . . The Leninist principle of peaceful co-existence of states with different social systems has always been and remains the general line of our country's foreign policy. . . . To this day the enemies of peace allege that the Soviet Union is out to overthrow capitalism in other countries by "exporting" revolution. It goes without saying that among us Communists there are no supporters of capitalism. But this does not mean that we have interfered or plan to interfere in the internal affairs of countries where capitalism still exists. . . . It is ridiculous to think that revolutions are made to order. We often hear representatives of bourgeois countries reasoning thus: "The Soviet leaders claim that they are for peaceful co-existence between the two systems. At the same time they declare that they are fighting for communism, and say that communism is bound to win in all countries. Now if the Soviet Union is fighting for communism, how can there be any peaceful co-existence with it?" This view is the result of bourgeois propaganda. The ideologists of the bourgeoisie distort the facts and deliberately confuse questions of ideological struggle with questions of relations between states in order to make the Communists of the Soviet Union look like advocates of aggression.

When we say that the socialist system will win in the competition between the two systems — the capitalist and the socialist — this by no means signifies that its victory will be achieved through armed interference by the socialist countries in the internal affairs of the capitalist countries. Our certainty of the victory of communism is based on the fact that the socialist mode of production possesses decisive advantages over the capitalist mode of production. Precisely because of this, the ideas of Marxism-Leninism are more and more capturing the minds of the broad masses of the working people in the capitalist countries, just as they have captured the minds of millions of men and women in our country and the People's Democracies. *(Prolonged applause.)* We believe that all working men in the world, once they have become convinced of the advantages communism brings, will sooner or later take the road of struggle for the construction of socialist society.

Review Questions

1. Where did Winston Churchill observe evidence of Russian expansionism? Find on a map of Europe and Asia the areas he mentioned.

2. What were Churchill's recommendations for countering Soviet expansionism?

3. What, according to Nikita Khrushchev, were the "imperialist powers" (the United States, England, and France) trying to accomplish in their pursuit of a "position of strength"?

4. How did Khrushchev describe the aims of American policy in regard to the Soviet Union?

5. What were Khrushchev's hopes for the future? What were his reasons for viewing socialism as superior to capitalism?

2 | Imperialism: Its Decline and Legacy

Mohandas K. Gandhi (1869–1948) channeled Indian spirituality into an anti-British political force. Born into a prominent, tradition-oriented Hindu family, he broke Hindu taboo by studying law in London. After his return home, he confessed that next to India he "would rather live in London than in any other place in the world." From 1894 to 1914, however, he lived in South Africa, using his legal training to defend the local Indian community against white discrimination. There he put together from Indian and Western sources the philosophy and practice of nonviolent resistance, strengthening the self-confidence and the civil status of his clients.

On a trip to India in 1909, Gandhi spelled out his political program, called Indian Home Rule. Curtly, he announced, "If India copies England, it is my firm conviction that she will be ruined," not because of any special flaw in the English (indeed he rather liked them), but because of the nature of modern civilization in general. It was materialistic, hedonistic, and mechanical, and therefore, said Gandhi, diseased and in decline. After World War I, Gandhi became the leader of the Indian nationalist movement against British rule. Under Gandhi's guidance the movement advocated and carried out nonviolent noncooperation to achieve Indian independence, which was granted in 1947.

MOHANDAS K. GANDHI
Indian Home Rule: Passive Resistance

The following extracts are taken from Gandhi's *Indian Home Rule,* where he states his social and political views in the form of a dialogue between the author, called Editor, and a skeptical friend, called Reader. Central to Gandhi's (Editor's) creed is the acceptance of passive resistance or nonviolence as a superior political weapon. Passive resistance is based on "soul-force," the quintessential ascetic quality of Indian spirituality and the hope for the future.

READER According to what you say, it is plain that instances of this kind of passive resistance are not to be found in history. It is necessary to understand this passive resistance more fully. It will be better, therefore, if you enlarge upon it.

EDITOR Passive resistance is a method of securing rights by personal suffering; it is the reverse of resistance by arms. When I refuse to do a thing that is repugnant to my conscience, I use soul-force. For instance, the Government of the day has passed a law which is applicable to me. I do not like it. If, by using violence, I force the government to repeal the law I am employing what may be termed body-force. If I do not obey the law and accept the penalty for its breach, I use soul-force. It involves sacrifice of self.

Everybody admits that sacrifice of self is infinitely superior to sacrifice of others. Moreover, if this kind of force is used in a cause that is unjust, only the person using it suffers. He does not make others suffer for his mistakes. Men have before now done many things which were subsequently found to have been wrong. No man can claim to be absolutely in the right or that a particular thing is wrong because he thinks so, but it is wrong for him so long as that is his deliberate judgment. It is therefore, [proper] that he should not do that which he knows to be wrong, and suffer the consequence whatever it may be. This is the key to the use of soul-force.

READER You would then disregard laws — this is rank disloyalty. We have always been considered a law-abiding nation. You seem to be going even beyond the extremists. They say that we must obey the laws that have been passed but that if the laws be bad, we must drive out the law-givers even by force.

EDITOR Whether I go beyond them or whether I do not is a matter of no consequence to either of us. We simply want to find out what is right and to act accordingly. The real meaning of the statement that we are a law-abiding nation is that we are passive resisters. When we do not like certain laws, we do not break the heads of law-givers but we suffer and do not submit to the laws. That we should obey laws whether good or bad is a new-fangled notion. There was no such thing in former days. The people disregarded those laws they did not like and suffered the penalties for their breach. It is contrary to our manhood if we obey laws repugnant to our conscience. Such teaching is opposed to religion and means slavery. If the Government were to ask us to go about without any clothing, should we do so? If I were a passive resister I would say to them that I would have nothing to do with their law. But we have so forgotten ourselves and become so compliant, that we do not mind any degrading law.

A man who has realised his manhood, who fears only God, will fear no one else. Man-made laws are not necessarily binding on him. Even the Government do not expect any such thing from us. They do not say: "You must do such and such a thing," but they say: "If you do not do it, we will punish you." We are sunk so low, that we fancy that it is our duty and our religion to do what the law lays down. If man will only realise that it is unmanly to obey laws that are unjust, no man's tyranny will enslave him. This is the key to self-rule or home-rule.

It is a superstition and an ungodly thing to believe that an act of a majority binds a minority. Many examples can be given in which acts of majorities will be found to have been wrong and those of minorities to have been right. All reforms owe their origin to the initiation of minorities in opposition to majorities. If among a band of robbers, a knowledge of robbing is obligatory, is a pious man to accept the obligation? So long as the superstition that men should obey unjust laws exists, so long will their slavery exist. And a passive resister alone can remove such a superstition.

To use brute-force, to use gun-powder is contrary to passive resistance, for it means that we want our opponent to do by force that which we desire but he does not. And, if such a use of force is justifiable, surely he is entitled to do likewise by us. And so we should never come to an agreement. We may simply fancy, like the blind horse moving in a circle round a mill, that we are making progress. Those who believe that they are not bound to obey laws which are repugnant to their conscience have only the remedy of passive resistance open to them. Any other must lead to disaster.

READER From what you say, I deduce that passive resistance is a splendid weapon of the weak, but that when they are strong they may take up arms.

EDITOR This is gross ignorance. Passive resistance, that is, soul-force, is matchless. It is superior to the force of arms. How, then, can it be considered only a weapon of the weak? Physical-force men are strangers to the courage that is requisite in a passive resister. . . . A passive resister will say he will not obey a law that is against his conscience, even though he may be blown to pieces at the mouth of a cannon.

What do you think? Wherein is courage required — in blowing others to pieces from behind a cannon or with a smiling face to approach a cannon and to be blown to pieces? . . .

This, however, I will admit: that even a man weak in body is capable of offering this resistance. One man can offer it just as well as millions. Both men and women can indulge in it. It does not require the training of an army; it needs no Jiu-jitsu. Control over the mind is alone necessary and, when that is attained, man is free like the king of the forest and his very glance withers the enemy.

Passive resistance is an all sided sword; it can be used anyhow; it blesses him who uses it and him against whom it is used. Without drawing a drop of blood it produces far-reaching results. . . .

READER From what you say, then, it would appear that it is not a small thing to become a passive resister and, if that is so, I would like you to explain how a man may become a passive resister.

EDITOR To become a passive resister is easy enough but it is also equally difficult. I have known a lad of fourteen years become a passive resister; I have known also sick people doing likewise; and I have also known physically strong and otherwise happy people being unable to take up passive resistance. After a great deal of experience it seems to me that those who want to become passive resisters for the service of the country have to observe perfect chastity, adopt poverty, follow truth, and cultivate fearlessness.

FRANTZ FANON

The Wretched of the Earth: The Evils of Colonialism

One of the keenest modern critics of colonialism was Frantz Fanon (1925–1961). A black from the French West Indies, Fanon was familiar with racial discrimination, and he was influenced by Marxism. He was trained in France as a psychiatrist and decorated for valor in World War II. In the 1950s he sided with the Algerian rebels in their fight for independence from France, and became an embattled advocate of African decolonization. In his book *The Wretched of the Earth,* published in 1961 when colonial rule in Africa had virtually ended, he analyzed the relations between the colonial masters and their subject peoples with the keen eye of a psychoanalyst. Highlighting the tensions built up under colonialism and reflecting the fury of the Algerian war, he painted the relations between the colonizers and the colonized. He did not even spare the Christian churches from criticism, although they had often trained those who eventually led the anticolonial struggles.

Fanon also anticipated the ambitions of the emerging African leaders. As he observed, "The colonised man is an envious man," who wanted what the masters possessed — wealth and power in an independent state. Rejection of colonial domination did not rule out imitation of the colonial masters' way of life — an attitude that sometimes brought a new dependence, branded as neocolonialism. Yet the memory of colonial exploitation that Fanon so vividly described persists, kept alive by the poverty and powerlessness of the new African states. In the following passage from *The Wretched of the Earth,* Fanon starkly compares the two realms of the colonial world: ruler and ruled.

The colonial world is a world cut in two. The dividing line, the frontiers are shown by barracks and police stations. In the colonies it is the policeman and the soldier who are the official, instituted gobetweens, and spokesmen of the settler and his rule of oppression. In capitalist societies the educational system, whether lay or clerical, the structure of moral reflexes handed down from father to son, the exemplary honesty of workers who are given a medal after fifty years of good and loyal service, and the affection which springs from harmonious relations and good behaviour — all these esthetic expressions of respect for the established order serve to create around the exploited person an atmosphere of submission and of inhibition which lightens the task of policing considerably. In the capitalist countries a multitude of moral teachers, counsellors and "bewilderers" separate the exploited from those in power. In the colonial countries, on the contrary, the policeman and the soldier, by their immediate presence and their frequent and direct action maintain contact with the native and advise him by means of rifle-butts and napalm not to budge. It is obvious here that the agents of government speak the language of pure force. The intermediary does not lighten the oppression, nor seek to hide the domination; he shows them up and puts them into practice with the clear conscience of an upholder of the peace; yet he is the bringer of violence into the home and into the mind of the native.

The zone where the natives live is not complementary to the zone inhabited by the settlers. The two zones are opposed, but not in the service of a higher unity. . . .

. . . No conciliation is possible, for of the two terms, one is superfluous. The settlers' town is a strongly-built town, all made of stone and steel. It is a brightly-lit town; the streets are covered with asphalt, and the garbage-cans swallow all the leavings, unseen, unknown and hardly thought about. The settler's feet are never visible, except perhaps in the sea; but there you're never close enough to see them. His feet are protected by strong shoes although the streets of his town are clean and even, with no holes or stones. The settler's town is a well-fed town, an easygoing town; its belly is always full of good things. The settler's town is a town of white people, of foreigners.

The town belonging to the colonised

people, or at least the native town, the ne-gro village, the medina,[1] the reservation, is a place of ill fame, peopled by men of evil repute. They are born there, it mat-ters little where or how; they die there, it matters not where, nor how. It is a world without spaciousness; men live there on top of each other, and their huts are built one on top of the other. The native town is a hungry town, starved of bread, of meat, of shoes, of coal, of light. The native town is a crouching village, a town on its knees, a town wallowing in the mire. It is a town of niggers and dirty arabs. . . . The look that the native turns on the settler's town is a look of lust, a look of envy; it expresses his dreams of posses-sion — all manner of possession: to sit at the settler's table, to sleep in the settler's bed, with his wife if possible. The colo-nised man is an envious man. And this the settler knows very well; when their glances meet he ascertains bitterly, always on the defensive "They want to take our place". It is true, for there is no native who does not dream at least once a day of setting himself up in the settler's place.

This world divided into compart-ments, this world cut in two is inhabited by two different species. The originality of the colonial context is that economic reality, inequality and the immense dif-ference of ways of life never come to mask the human realities. When you examine at close quarters the colonial context, it is evident that what parcels out the world is to begin with the fact of belonging to or not belonging to a given race, a given spe-cies. In the colonies the economic sub-structure is also a superstructure. The cause is the consequence; you are rich because you are white, you are white be-cause you are rich. . . .

---

[1] The term *medina* here connotes a quarter of a North African city inhabited by indigenous people; the Saudi Arabian city of Medina is the sacred center of the Islamic faith.

. . . As if to show the totalitarian char-acter of colonial exploitation the settler paints the native as a sort of quintessence of evil. . . . Native society is not simply described as a society lacking in values. It is not enough for the colonist to affirm that those values have disappeared from, or still better never existed in, the colonial world. The native is declared insensible to ethics; he represents not only the ab-sence of values, but also the negation of values. He is, let us dare to admit, the enemy of values, and in this sense he is the absolute evil. . . .

. . . I speak of the Christian religion, and no one need be astonished. The Church in the colonies is the white peo-ple's Church, the foreigner's Church. She does not call the native to God's ways but to the ways of the white man, of the mas-ter, of the oppressor. And as we know, in this matter many are called but few chosen.

At times this Manicheism [conflict be-tween light and dark] goes to its logical conclusion and dehumanises the native, or to speak plainly it turns him into an ani-mal. In fact, the terms the settler uses when he mentions the native are zoologi-cal terms. He speaks of the yellow man's reptilian motions, of the stink of the na-tive quarter, of breeding swarms, of foul-ness, of spawn, of gesticulations. When the settler seeks to describe the native fully in exact terms he constantly refers to the bestiary. The European rarely hits on a picturesque style; but the native, who knows what is in the mind of the settler, guesses at once what he is thinking of. Those hordes of vital statistics, those hys-terical masses, those faces bereft of all hu-manity, those distended bodies which are like nothing on earth, that mob without beginning or end, those children who seem to belong to nobody, that laziness stretched out in the sun, that vegetative rhythm of life — all this forms part of the colonial vocabulary.

JACQUES ELLUL

The Betrayal of the West: A Reaffirmation of Western Values

In recent years a number of Western intellectuals have attacked the values and deeds of the West. At the same time, they exalt the other civilizations of the world. That many Westerners have lost confidence in their own tradition constitutes a profound spiritual crisis. Jacques Ellul (b. 1912), a French sociologist with a pronounced moralist bent, is known for his study of the impact of technology and bureaucracy on the modern world. In the following passages from *The Betrayal of the West*, he assessed the historical uniqueness and greatness of Western civilization.

. . . I am not criticizing or rejecting other civilizations and societies; I have deep admiration for the institutions of the Bantu and other peoples (the Chinese among them) and for the inventions and poetry and architecture of the Arabs. I do not claim at all that the West is superior. In fact, I think it absurd to lay claim to superiority of any kind in these matters. What criterion would you apply? What scale of values would you use? I would add that the greatest fault of the West since the seventeenth century has been precisely its belief in its own unqualified superiority in all areas.

The thing, then, that I am protesting against is the silly attitude of western intellectuals in hating their own world and then illogically exalting all other civilizations. Ask yourself this question: If the Chinese have done away with binding the feet of women, and if the Moroccans, Turks, and Algerians have begun to liberate their women, whence did the impulse to these moves come from? From the West, and nowhere else! Who invented the "rights of man"? The same holds for the elimination of exploitation. Where did the move to socialism originate? In Europe, and in Europe alone. The Chinese, like the Algerians, are inspired by western thinking as they move toward socialism. Marx was not Chinese, nor was Robespierre an Arab. How easily the intellectuals forget this! The whole of the modern world, for better or for worse, is following a western model; no one im-

posed it on others, they have adopted it themselves, and enthusiastically.

I shall not wax lyrical about the greatness and benefactions of the West. Above all, I shall not offer a defense of the material goods Europe brought to the colonies. We've heard that kind of defense too often: "We built roads, hospitals, schools, and dams; we dug the oil wells. . . ." And the reason I shall say nothing of this invasion by the technological society is that I think it to be the West's greatest crime, as I have said at length elsewhere. The worst thing of all is that we exported our rationalist approach to things, our "science," our conception of the state, our bureaucracy, our nationalist ideology. It is this, far more surely than anything else, that has destroyed the other cultures of the world and shunted the history of the entire world onto a single track.

But is that all we can say of the West? No, the essential, central, undeniable fact is that the West was the first civilization in history to focus attention on the individual and on freedom. Nothing can rob us of the praise due us for that. We have been guilty of denials and betrayals (of these we shall be saying something more), we have committed crimes, but we have also caused the whole of mankind to take a gigantic step forward and to leave its childhood behind.

This is a point we must be quite clear on. If the world is everywhere rising up and accusing the West, if movements of liberation are everywhere under way, what accounts for this? Its sole source is the proclamation of freedom that the West has broadcast to the world. The West, and the West alone, is responsible for the movement that has led to the desire for freedom and to the accusations now turned back upon the West.

Today men point the finger of outrage at slavery and torture. Where did that kind of indignation originate? What civilization or culture cried out that slavery was unacceptable and torture scandalous? Not Islam, or Buddhism, or Confucius, or Zen, or the religions and moral codes of Africa and India! The West alone has defended the inalienable rights of the human person, the dignity of the individual, the man who is alone with everyone against him. But the West did not practice what it preached? The extent of the West's fidelity is indeed debatable: the whole European world has certainly not lived up to its own ideal all the time, but to say that it has never lived up to it would be completely false.

In any case, that is not the point. The point is that the West originated values and goals that spread throughout the world (partly through conquest) and inspired man to demand his freedom, to take his stand in the face of society and affirm his value as an individual. I shall not be presumptuous enough to try to "define" the freedom of the individual. . . .

. . . The West gave expression to what man — every man — was seeking. The West turned the whole human project into a conscious, deliberate business. It set the goal and called it freedom, or, at later date, individual freedom. It gave direction to all the forces that were working in obscure ways, and brought to light the value that gave history its meaning. Thereby, man became man.

The West attempted to apply in a conscious, methodical way the implications of freedom. The Jews were the first to make freedom the key to history and to the whole created order. From the very beginning their God was the God who lib-

erates; his great deeds flowed from a will to give freedom to his people and thereby to all mankind. This God himself, moreover, was understood to be sovereignly free (freedom here was often confused with arbitrariness or with omnipotence). This was something radically new, a discovery with explosive possibilities. The God who was utterly free had nothing in common with the gods of eastern and western religions; he was different precisely because of his autonomy.

The next step in the same movement saw the Greeks affirming both intellectual and political liberty. They consciously formulated the rules for a genuinely free kind of thinking, the conditions for human freedom, and the forms a free society could take. Other peoples were already living in cities, but none of them had fought so zealously for the freedom of the city in relation to other cities, and for the freedom of the citizen within the city.

The Romans took the third step by inventing civil and institutional liberty and making political freedom the key to their entire politics. Even the conquests of the Romans were truly an unhypocritical expression of their intention of freeing peoples who were subject to dictatorships and tyrannies the Romans judged degrading. It is in the light of that basic thrust that we must continue to read Roman history. Economic motives undoubtedly also played a role, but a secondary one; to make economic causes the sole norm for interpreting history is in the proper sense superficial and inadequate. You can not write history on the basis of your suspicions! If you do, you only project your own fantasies.

I am well aware, of course, that in each concrete case there was darkness as well as light, that liberty led to wars and conquests, that it rested on a base of slavery. I am not concerned here, however, with the excellence or defects of the concrete forms freedom took; I am simply trying to say (as others have before me) that at the beginning of western history we find the awareness, the explanation, the proclamation of freedom as the meaning and goal of history.

No one has ever set his sights as intensely on freedom as did the Jews and Greeks and Romans, the peoples who represented the entire West and furthered its progress. In so doing, they gave expression to what the whole of mankind was confusedly seeking. In the process we can see a progressive approach to the ever more concrete: from the Jews to the Greeks, and from the Greeks to the Romans there is no growth in consciousness, but there is the ongoing search for more concrete answers to the question of how freedom can be brought from the realm of ideas and incarnated in institutions, behavior, thinking, and so on.

Today the whole world has become the heir of the West, and we Westerners now have a twofold heritage: we are heirs to the evil the West has done to the rest of the world, but at the same time we are heirs to our forefathers' consciousness of freedom and to the goals of freedom they set for themselves. Other peoples, too, are heirs to the evil that has been inflicted on them, but now they have also inherited the consciousness of and desire for freedom. Everything they do today and everything they seek is an expression of what the western world has taught them. . . .

. . . Everything used to be so organized that wealth and poverty were stable states, determined (for example) by the traditional, accepted hierarchy, and that this arrangement was regarded as due to destiny or an unchangeable divine will. The West did two things: it destroyed the hierarchic structures and it did away with the idea of destiny. It thus showed the poor that their state was not something inevitable. This is something Marx is often credited with having done, but only because people are ignorant. It was Christianity that did away with the idea of destiny and fate. . . .

Once Christianity had destroyed the idea of destiny or fate, the poor realized that they were poor, and they realized that their condition was not inevitable. Then the social organisms that had made it possible to gloss over this fact were challenged and undermined from within.

Against all this background we can see why the whole idea of revolution is a western idea. Before the development of western thought, and apart from it, no revolution ever took place. Without the individual and freedom and the contradictory extremes to which freedom leads, a society cannot engender a revolution. Nowhere in the world — and I speak as one with a knowledge of history — has there ever been a revolution, not even in China, until the western message penetrated that part of the world. Present-day revolutions, whether in China or among the American Indians, are the direct, immediate, unmistakable fruit of the western genius. The entire world has been pupil to the West that it now rejects. . . .

. . . I wish only to remind the reader that the West has given the world a certain number of values, movements, and orientations that no one else has provided. No one else has done quite what the West has done. I wish also to remind the reader that the whole world is living, and living almost exclusively, by these values, ideas, and stimuli. There is nothing original about the "new" thing that is coming into existence in China or Latin America or Africa: it is all the fruit and direct consequence of what the West has given the world.

In the fifties it was fashionable to say that "the third world is now entering upon the stage of history." The point was not, of course, to deny that Africa or Japan had a history. What the cliché was saying, and rightly saying, was that these peoples were now participating in the creative freedom of history and the dialectic of the historical process. Another way of putting it is that the West had now set the whole world in motion. It had released a tidal wave that would perhaps eventually drown it. There had been great changes in the past and vast migrations of peoples; there had been planless quests for power and the building of gigantic empires that collapsed overnight. The West represented something entirely new because it set the world in movement in every area and at every level; it represented, that is, a coherent approach to reality. Everything — ideas, armies, the state, philosophy, rational methods, and social organization — conspired in the global change the West had initiated.

It is not for me to judge whether all this was a good thing or bad. I simply observe that the entire initiative came from the West, that everything began there. I simply observe that the peoples of the world had abided in relative ignorance and [religious] repose until the encounter with the West set them on their journey.

Please, then, don't deafen us with talk about the greatness of Chinese or Japanese civilization. These civilizations existed indeed, but in a larval or embryonic state; they were approximations, essays. They always related to only one sector of the human or social totality and tended to be static and immobile. Because the West was motivated by the ideal of freedom and had discovered the individual, it alone launched society in its entirety on its present course.

Again, don't misunderstand me. I am not saying that European science was superior to Chinese science, nor European armies to Japanese armies; I am not saying that the Christian religion was superior to Buddhism or Confucianism; I am not saying that the French or English political system was superior to that of the Han dynasty. I am saying only that the West discovered what no one else had discovered; freedom and the individual, and that this discovery later set everything else in motion. Even the most solidly established religions could not help changing under the influence. . . .

It was not economic power or sudden technological advances that made the West what it is. These played a role, no doubt, but a negligible one in comparison with the great change — the discovery of freedom and the individual — that represents the goal and desire implicit in the history

of all civilizations. That is why, in speaking of the West, I unhesitatingly single out freedom from the whole range of values. After all, we find justice, equality, and peace everywhere. Every civilization that has attained a certain level has claimed to be a civilization of justice or peace. But which of them has ever spoken of the individual? Which of them has been reflectively conscious of freedom as a value?

The decisive role of the West's discovery of freedom and the individual is beyond question, but the discovery has brought with it . . . tragic consequences. First, the very works of the West now pass judgment on it. For, having proclaimed freedom and the individual, the West played false in dealing with other peoples. It subjected, conquered, and exploited them, even while it went on talking about freedom. It made the other peoples conscious of their enslavement by intensifying that enslavement and calling it freedom. It destroyed the social structures of tribes and clans, turned men into isolated atoms, and shaped them into a worldwide proletariat, and all the time kept on talking of the great dignity of the individual: his autonomy, his power to decide for himself, his capacity for choice, his complex and many-sided reality. . . .

. . . Reason makes it possible for the individual to master impulse, to choose the ways in which he will exercise his freedom, to calculate the chances for success and the manner in which a particular action will impinge upon the group, to understand human relations, and to communicate. Communication is the highest expression of freedom, but it has little meaning unless there is a content which, in the last analysis, is supplied by reason. . . . Here precisely we have the magnificent discovery made by the West: that the individual's whole life can be, and even is, the subtle, infinitely delicate interplay of reason and freedom.

This interplay achieved its highest form in both the Renaissance and classical literature since the Enlightenment. No other culture made this discovery. We of the

West have the most rounded and self-conscious type of man. For, the development of reason necessarily implied reason's critique of its own being and action as well as a critique of both liberty and reason, through a return of reason upon itself and a continuous reflection which gave rise to new possibilities for the use of freedom as controlled by new developments of reason. . . .

Let me return to my main argument. It was the West that established the splendid interplay of freedom, reason, self-control, and coherent behavior. It thus produced a type of human being that is unique in history: true western man. (I repeat: the type belongs neither to nature nor to the animal world; it is a deliberate construct achieved through effort.) I am bound to say that I regard this type as superior to anything I have seen or known elsewhere. A value judgment, a personal and subjective preference? Of course. But I am not ready on that account to turn my back on the construction and on the victory and affirmation it represents. Why? Because the issue is freedom itself, and because I see no other satisfactory model that can replace what the West has produced.

Review Questions

1. What justifications did Mohandas Gandhi offer for passive resistance and "soul-force"?

2. How did Gandhi believe that home rule (or independence) can be achieved?

3. What was Gandhi's reply to the objection that passive resistance is suited only to the weaker party in any conflict?

4. Why did Frantz Fanon think that no conciliation is possible between the colonial masters and their subjects?

5. How did Fanon define the "totalitarian character" of colonial exploitation?

6. In saying that colonized people are envious, does Fanon reject what colonial exploitation stands for?

7. What contribution, according to Jacques Ellul, did the West make to human life everywhere?

8. According to Ellul, what was the West's "greatest crime"?

9. Ellul asserts on one hand that he does "not claim at all that the West is superior," and on the other he characterizes Chinese or Japanese civilization as existing only "in a larval or embryonic state." Compare these statements in the context of the entire passage. Are they contradictory?

3 | Human Rights

The West has attempted to apply its liberal-democratic principles in condemning oppression, persecution, and terror, including international terrorism. Through the United Nations and other international bodies, the Western democracies, with the United States foremost, have attempted to uphold standards of human rights for the entire world. However, in most cases, efforts to police human rights violations have met with only limited success. In recent decades, women—particularly in the United States and Europe—have continued and intensified their struggle for equal rights.

The Universal Declaration of Human Rights

In September 1948, the General Assembly of the United Nations, implementing the UN Charter of 1945, issued the Universal Declaration of Human Rights. The declaration, drafted under U.S. leadership, not only summed up the quintessence of Western democratic tradition but also universalized it as "a common standard of achievement for all peoples and all nations." The declaration's key phrases are familiar from famous documents of the English, American, and French revolutions. "All human beings are born free and equal in dignity and rights. . . . Everyone has the right to life, liberty and the security of person. . . . Everyone . . . has the right to be presumed innocent until proved guilty. . . ." In short, the standards of Western politics (not always followed, even in the West) were proclaimed as models for all others, whatever their resources or convictions. In the United Nations debate on the declaration, Islamic countries protested the disregard of religious custom; Soviet spokesmen deplored the lack of attention to civic duty (only one sentence in the entire document — in Article 29 — refers to the subject of civic responsibility). The declaration was adopted by a large majority; Saudi Arabia, the Union of South Africa, and the Soviet-bloc countries abstained.

The declaration of rights drafted by the United Nations follows in its entirety. The discrepancy between the high ideals of this document and the prevailing practices worldwide is obvious.

PREAMBLE. Whereas recognition of the inherent dignity and of the equal and inalienable rights of all members of the human family is the foundation of freedom, justice and peace in the world,

Whereas disregard and contempt for human rights have resulted in barbarous acts which have outraged the conscience of mankind, and the advent of a world in which human beings shall enjoy freedom of speech and belief and freedom from fear and want has been proclaimed as the highest aspiration of the common people,

Whereas it is essential, if man is not compelled to have recourse, as a last resort, to rebellion against tyranny and oppression, that human rights should be protected by the rule of law,

Whereas it is essential to promote the development of friendly relations between nations,

Whereas the people of the United Nations have in the Charter reaffirmed their faith in fundamental human rights, in the dignity and worth of the human person and in the equal rights of men and women and have determined to promote social progress and better standards of life in larger freedom,

Whereas Member States have pledged themselves to achieve, in cooperation with the United Nations, the promotion of universal respect for and observance of human rights and fundamental freedoms,

Whereas a common understanding of these rights and freedoms is of the greatest importance for the full realization of this pledge,

Now, therefore,

The General Assembly

Proclaims this Universal Declaration of Human Rights, as a common standard of achievement for all peoples and all nations, to the end that every individual and every organ of society, keeping this Declaration constantly in mind, shall strive by teaching and education to promote respect for these rights and freedoms and by progressive measures, national and international, to secure their universal and effective recognition and observance, both among the peoples of Member States themselves and among the peoples of territories under their jurisdiction.

ARTICLE 1. All human beings are born free and equal in dignity and rights. They are endowed with reason and conscience and should act towards one another in a spirit of brotherhood.

ARTICLE 2. Everyone is entitled to all the rights and freedoms set forth in this Declaration, without distinction of any kind, such as race, colour, sex, language, religion, political or other opinion, national or social origin, property, birth or other status.

Furthermore, no distinction shall be made on the basis of the political, jurisdictional or international status of the country or territory to which a person belongs, whether it be independent, trust, non-self-governing or under any other limitation of sovereignty.

ARTICLE 3. Everyone has the right to life, liberty and the security of person.

ARTICLE 4. No one shall be held in slavery or servitude; slavery and the slave trade shall be prohibited in all their forms.

ARTICLE 5. No one shall be subjected to torture or to cruel, inhuman or degrading treatment or punishment.

ARTICLE 6. Everyone has the right to recognition everywhere as a person before the law.

ARTICLE 7. All are equal before the law and are entitled without any discrimination to equal protection of the law. All are entitled to equal protection against any discrimination in violation of this Declaration and against any incitement to such discrimination.

ARTICLE 8. Everyone has the right to an effective remedy by the competent national tribunals for acts violating the fundamental rights granted him by the constitution or by law.

ARTICLE 9. No one shall be subjected to arbitary arrest, detention or exile.

ARTICLE 10. Everyone is entitled in full equality to a fair and public hearing by an independent and impartial tribunal, in the determination of his rights and obligations and of any criminal charge against him.

ARTICLE 11. 1. Everyone charged with a penal offense has the right to be presumed innocent until proved guilty according to law in a public trial at which he has had all the guarantees necessary for his defence.

2. No one shall be held guilty of any penal offence on account of any act or omission which did not constitute a penal offence, under national or international law, at the time when it was committed. Nor shall a heavier penalty be imposed than the one that was applicable at the time the penal offence was committed.

ARTICLE 12. No one shall be subjected to arbitrary interference with his privacy, family, home or correspondence, nor to attacks upon his honour and reputation. Everyone has the right to the protection of the law against such interference or attacks.

ARTICLE 13. 1. Everyone has the right to freedom of movement and residence within the borders of each State.

2. Everyone has the right to leave any country including his own, and to return to his country.

ARTICLE 14. 1. Everyone has the right to seek and to enjoy in other countries asylum from persecution.

2. This right may not be invoked in the case of prosecutions genuinely rising from non-political crimes or from acts contrary to the purposes and principles of the United Nations.

ARTICLE 15. 1. Everyone has the right to a nationality.

2. No one shall be arbitrarily deprived of his nationality nor denied the right to change his nationality.

ARTICLE 16. 1. Men and women of full age, without any limitation due to race, nationality or religion, have the right to marry and to found a family. They are entitled to equal rights as to marriage, during marriage and at its dissolution.

2. Marriage shall be entered into only with the free and full consent of the intending spouses.

3. The family is the natural and fundamental group unit of society and is entitled to protection by society and the State.

ARTICLE 17. 1. Everyone has the right to own property alone as well as in association with others.

2. No one shall be arbitrarily deprived of his property.

ARTICLE 18. Everyone has the right to freedom of thought, conscience and religion; this right includes freedom to change his religion or belief, and freedom, either alone or in community with others and in public or private, to manifest his religion or belief in teaching, practice, worship and observance.

ARTICLE 19. Everyone has the right to freedom of opinion and expression; this right includes freedom to hold opinions without interference and to seek, receive and impart information and ideas through any media and regardless of frontiers.

ARTICLE 20. 1. Everyone has the right to freedom of peaceful assembly and association.

2. No one may be compelled to belong to an association.

ARTICLE 21. 1. Everyone has the right to take part in the government of his country, directly or through freely chosen representatives.

2. Everyone has the right to equal access to public service in his country.

3. The will of the people shall be the basis of the authority of government; this will shall be expressed in periodic and genuine elections which shall be by universal and equal suffrage and shall be held by secret vote or by equivalent free voting procedures.

ARTICLE 22. Everyone, as a member of society, has the right to social security and is entitled to realization, through national effort and international cooperation and in accordance with the organization and resources of each State, of the economic, social and cultural rights indispensable for his dignity and the free development of his personality.

ARTICLE 23. 1. Everyone has the right to work, to free choice of employment, to just and favourable conditions of work and to protection against unemployment.

2. Everyone, without any discrimination, has the right to equal pay for equal work.

3. Everyone who works has the right to just and favourable remuneration ensuring for himself and his family an existence worthy of human dignity, and supplemented, if necessary, by other means of social protection.

4. Everyone has the right to form and to join trade unions for the protection of his interests.

ARTICLE 24. Everyone has the right to rest and leisure, including reasonable limitation of working hours and periodic holidays with pay.

ARTICLE 25. 1. Everyone has the right to a standard of living adequate for the health and well-being of himself and of his family, including food, clothing, housing and medical care and necessary social services, and the right to security in the event of unemployment, sickness, disability, widowhood, old age or other lack of livelihood in circumstances beyond his control.

2. Motherhood and childhood are entitled to special care and assistance. All children, whether born in or out of wedlock, shall enjoy the same social protection.

ARTICLE 26. 1. Everyone has the right to education. Education shall be free, at least in the elementary and fundamental stages. Elementary education shall be compulsory. Technical and professional education shall be made generally available and higher education shall be equally accessible to all on the basis of merit.

2. Education shall be directed to the full development of the human personality and to the strengthening of respect for human rights and fundamental freedoms. It shall promote understanding, tolerance and friendship among all nations, racial or religious groups, and shall further the activities of the United Nations for the maintenance of peace.

3. Parents have a prior right to choose the kind of education that shall be given to their children.

ARTICLE 27. 1. Everyone has the right freely to participate in the cultural life of the community, to enjoy the arts and to share in scientific advancement and its benefits.

2. Everyone has the right to the protection of the moral and material interests resulting from any scientific, literary or artistic production of which he is the author.

ARTICLE 28. Everyone is entitled to a social and international order in which the rights and freedoms set forth in this Declaration can be fully realized.

ARTICLE 29. 1. Everyone has duties to the community in which alone the free and full development of his personality is possible.

2. In the exercise of his rights and freedoms, everyone shall be subject only to such limitations as are determined by law solely for the purpose of securing due recognition and respect for the rights and freedoms of others and of meeting the just requirements of morality, public order and the general welfare in a democratic society.

3. These rights and freedoms may in no case be exercised contrary to the purposes and principles of the United Nations.

ARTICLE 30. Nothing in this Declaration may be interpreted as implying for any State, group or person any right to engage in any activity or to perform any act aimed at the destruction of any of the rights and freedoms set forth herein.

AMNESTY INTERNATIONAL
Political Murder

Amnesty International was founded in England in 1961 by Peter Benenson, a lawyer long interested in upholding human rights. The organization now has chapters in forty-one countries around the world. Preferring a low-key approach to its work, Amnesty International tracks down evidence about the fate of political prisoners and tries to help them by sending supportive letters to unjustly imprisoned individuals and by writing to their governments and asking for their release. Amnesty International also issues occasional reports on the most flagrant violations of elemental human rights.

The following reading from *Political Killings by Governments* (1983) deals with large-scale, politically motivated killings "in most, if not all regions of the world." The worst excesses are reported from Third World countries trying to cope with the demands of modern times: building an effective state, creating unity among their faction-ridden peoples, and preserving public order. In many of these lands, dictators use violence and terror to produce obedience to their rule.

Hundreds of thousands of people in the past 10 years have been killed by the political authorities in their countries. The killings continue. Day after day Amnesty International receives reports of deliberate political killings by the army and the police, by other regular security forces, by special units created to function outside normal supervision, by "death squads" sanctioned by the authorities, by government assassins.

The killings take place outside any legal or judicial process; the victims are denied any protection from the law. Many are abducted, illegally detained, or tortured before they are killed.

Sometimes the killings are ordered at the highest level of government: in other cases the government deliberately fails to investigate killings or take measures to prevent further deaths.

Governments often try to cover up the fact that they have committed political killings. They deny that the killings have taken place, they attribute them to opposition forces, or they try to pass them off as the result of armed encounters with government forces or of attempts by the victim to escape from custody.

The pattern of killings is often accompanied by the suspension of constitutional rights, intimidation of witnesses and relatives of victims, suppression of evidence and a weakening of the independence of the judiciary.

These killings flout the absolute principle that governments must protect their citizens against arbitrary deprivation of life, which cannot be abandoned under any circumstances, however grave. These political killings are crimes for which governments and their agents are responsible under national and international law. Their accountability is not diminished by opposition groups committing similar abhorrent acts. Nor does the difficulty of proving who is ultimately answerable for a killing lessen the government's responsibility to investigate unlawful killings and take steps to prevent them. It is the duty of governments not to commit or condone political killings, but to take all legislative, executive and judicial measures to ensure that those responsible are brought to justice.

Political killings by governments have certain common features. These are summed up in the definition that Amnesty International uses: "unlawful and deliberate killings of persons by reason of their real or imputed political beliefs or activities, religion, other conscientiously held beliefs, ethnic origin, sex, colour or language, carried out by order of a government or with its complicity." The alternative term "extrajudicial executions" is also used to refer to these killings. They are committed outside the judicial process and in violation of national laws and international standards forbidding the arbitrary deprivation of life. They are unlawful and deliberate: this distinguishes them from accidental killings and from deaths resulting from the use of reasonable force in law enforcement. It also separates them from the category of killings in war not forbidden under the international laws that regulate the conduct of armed conflicts. The fact that they are "extrajudicial" distinguishes them from the judicial death penalty — the execution of a death sentence imposed by a court after a prisoner has been convicted of a crime carrying the death penalty. These extrajudicial executions are political: the victims are selected because of their political beliefs or activities, religion, colour, sex, language or ethnic origin.

* * *

Political killings by governments take place in different parts of the world and in countries of widely differing ideologies. They range from individual assassinations to the wholesale slaughter of mass opposition movements or entire ethnic groups. The scale of the crime is sometimes not known to the international community before it has reached proportions that will damage a whole society for generations to come. . . .

The Killings

Political killings by governments have been committed in most, if not all, the regions of the world. The cases in this report show that they are not confined to any one political system or ideology. Further examples are given here of political killings since 1980 believed to have been carried out by official forces or others linked to the government. The circumstances of the killings and the nature of government involvement vary from country to country. Some governments have been shown to be responsible by their wilful failure to investigate adequately or to prevent further killings.

The victims — individuals and entire families — have come from all walks of life and from many political persuasions and religious faiths. Politicians, government officials, judges, lawyers, military officers, trade unionists, journalists, teachers, students and schoolchildren, religious workers and peasants: all have lost their lives. In some cases well-known political figures have been publicly assassinated; in others whole villages have been wiped out, and the news has not reached the outside world for weeks or months. Often the victims belonged to the political opposition — often they were simply members of a particular ethnic group or lived in an area targeted for security operations.

In El Salvador, thousands of people have been killed by the security forces since the military coup of October 1979. The victims have included not only people suspected of opposition to the authorities, but thousands of unarmed peasant farmers living in areas targeted for military operations in the government's counter-guerrilla campaign. People monitoring government abuses such as journalists, church activists, community workers, political militants and trade unionists have been intimidated, arrested and killed. Patients have even been abducted from hospital beds by security forces and killed.

On 3 January 1982 Archbishop Arturo Rivera y Damas of San Salvador stated that he estimated that 11,723 non-combatants had been killed in El Salvador during 1981. In July 1981 the Centre of Information and Documentation of the University of Central America in San Salvador estimated that some 6,000 civilians had been killed in the first six months of the year. In the same month another Roman Catholic source put the death toll in the previous 18 months at 22,000. . . .

In Libya the Third Congress of the Libyan Revolutionary Committees issued a declaration in February 1980 calling for the "physical liquidation" of enemies of the 1969 revolution living abroad. Since then at least 14 Libyan citizens have been killed or wounded in assassination attempts outside Libya.

In Uganda, the widespread unlawful killings of the eight-year military government of President Idi Amin ended only with the overthrow of the regime in 1979. In the aftermath of the armed conflict, a high level of criminal violence continued, with many unexplained but possibly politically motivated murders. Opponents and supporters of the government and members of the security forces were killed under the successive governments of Yusuf Lule, Godfrey Binaisa, and the Military Commission. Former President Milton Obote returned to power after elections in 1980. Instability continued, and early 1981 saw a series of guerrilla attacks. Many civilians — particularly alleged political opponents — were arrested by the army and there were reports of torture and killings in military custody. Unarmed civilians are also reported to have been killed by security forces operating against guerrillas in the countryside.

In Iran, in addition to the large number of officially announced executions which have taken place since the revolution of February 1979 (more than 4,500 at the end of November 1982), Amnesty International has received many reports of executions which have not been announced and may not have been preceded by a trial. In other cases it is clear from the circumstances of the killings that no legal proceedings took place. Because of the difficulty of obtaining reliable and detailed information from all parts of Iran, it is often not possible to know whether a death is the result of a judicial decision or could be described as an extrajudicial execution. Sometimes prisoners who have previously been sentenced to a term of imprisonment have been executed, but it is not known whether this is the result of an arbitrary decision, or whether new legal proceedings have taken place. . . .

Members of the Baha'i religion have been killed in circumstances suggesting official involvement. Amnesty International knows of no case in which anyone has been prosecuted in Iran in connection with such a killing. On 12 January 1981 Professor Manuchihr Hakim was shot dead by unknown assailants in his office. He was a physician and professor at the University of Tehran and had been a member of the supreme governing body of the Baha'is of Iran for many years. Three days before his assassination Professor Hakim had been visited by two Revolutionary Guards and interrogated at length about his activities as a Baha'i. Before this interrogation Professor Hakim had received threats to his life. . . .

A report received in October 1982 referred to the killing by Revolutionary Guards of 51 people in the village of Dehgaz in the Caspian region between June and September 1981. The reason for these killings was reported to be the villagers' alleged sympathy with the opposition People's Mujahadeen Organization of Iran (PMOI).

In Colombia members of the political opposition have been killed by the security forces, and peasant farmers summarily executed by the army in rural areas where counter-insurgency operations are carried out.

Extensive isolated regions of the country have been "militarized" to combat guerrilla groups operating there, and other special security measures imposed to control the local population. Freedom of movement in these areas is strictly controlled, and supplies of food, clothing and medical goods limited to deprive guerrilla forces of material support. Controls have been enforced through the threat of arbitrary detention, interrogation and torture at local army posts or temporary bivouacs, and death. People have been detained on suspicion of aiding guerrillas and then killed by army units. Others have been killed after routinely reporting to a local army post to have their safe-conduct passes stamped as required.

On 20 June 1982, the state of siege that had been in force in Colombia for most of the past 34 years was lifted. However, reports of killings of peasants by army counter-guerrilla units in rural areas, particularly Central Colombia, have continued since 20 June 1982. . . .

In Namibia, where South African military forces are in conflict with nationalist guerrillas of the South West Africa People's Organisation (SWAPO), church leaders and others have reported that civilians have been killed by South African soldiers because they were thought to support or sympathize with SWAPO. . . .

In Chile, during the first few months after the 1973 military coup thousands of people were reported to have been summarily executed; between 1973 and 1979 hundreds — mainly political activists, trade unionists and peasants — "disappeared" after being arrested by the security forces of the army, navy, air force and *carabineros* (uniformed police), all coordinated by the *Dirección de Inteligencia Nacional* (DINA), National Intelligence Directorate. The "disappearances" and killings which took place between 1973 and 1979 remain officially unexplained. In August 1977 the DINA was dissolved and replaced by the *Central Nacional de Informaciones* (CNI) — Chilean secret police.

Since 1977, a number of alleged members of banned political parties and organizations, such as the *Movimiento de Izquierda Revolucionaria* (MIR), Movement of the Revolutionary Left, have died in the custody of the CNI, in circumstances which indicate that they may have died after torture, or may have been deliberately killed by other methods. A number of other killings have been described officially as the result of "confrontations" with members of the security forces, such as the CNI. Some victims were reportedly abducted by members of the security forces before being killed. . . .

In the Republic of Korea (South Korea) at least 40 people were killed when army paratroopers dispersed a peaceful student demonstration in Kwangju on 18 May 1980. Amnesty International has received reports and eye-witness accounts alleging that paratroopers clubbed people on the head indiscriminately and bayonetted them; that many of the dead were shot in the face, and that others were stabbed to death. Reportedly, at least 1,200 civilians died in disturbances in the following nine days; the South Korean authorities said that 144 civilians, 22 soldiers and four police officers died. Amnesty International has also received allegations that eight people arrested in connection with disturbances in Kwangju were beaten to death on 16 July 1980 by Special Forces troops and their bodies buried in the prison grounds.

In Syria since 1980 there have been several reported incidents of killings by the security forces. On 27 July 1980 hundreds of prisoners — most of them believed to have been members of the outlawed Muslim Brotherhood — were reported to have been killed in Palmyra (Tadmur) desert prison by the *Saray al-Difa'*, Special Defence Units, a special military force under the command of President Assad's brother, Rifa'at Assad. On the night of 23 April 1981 Syrian security forces reportedly sealed off parts of the town of Hama, carried out house-to-house searches, dragged people from their homes, lined them up in the streets and shot them. Amnesty International received the names of over 100 of those reported killed.

On 2 February 1982 violent clashes between security forces and Muslim Brotherhood fighters, following the discovery of a hidden cache of arms, developed into a near-insurrection in the town of Hama. The town was encircled by Syrian troops and security forces and subsequently bombarded from the air and the ground. A news blackout was imposed by the authorities. In early March, after the fighting had ended, reports of massacres and atrocities began to reach the outside world. Most reports indicated that at the start of the fighting government officials and their families in Hama were systematically sought out and killed by the rebels. Later, however, massacres were reported to have been committed by government forces partly through aerial bombardment but also by troops on the ground as they regained control of the town. Unofficial estimates put the killings by security forces at over 10,000, but Amnesty International was not able to make its own assessment of the number killed.

Syrian security forces have also allegedly been responsible for the assassination abroad since 1980 of several prominent opponents of the Assad government.

Mass Liquidation

Several governments in the past two decades have decided on the wholesale liquidation of political opposition. The death toll in these purges has run into the tens and hundreds of thousands, sometimes in a matter of months. . . .

In Kampuchea [formerly Cambodia] under *Khmer Rouge* rule (1975–1979) at least 300,000 people were killed in a series of purges directed at "counter-revolutionaries" and other "undesirable elements." Nearly all high-ranking officers of the former Lon Nol government, senior officials, police officers, customs officials and members of the military police appear to have been executed during the days immediately after the *Khmers Rouges* came to power. Subsequent purges were directed at lower officials of the former Lon Nol government; at intellectuals, teachers and students, often described by the *Khmers Rouges* as "the worthless ones"; at members of ethnic minorities, especially the Cham, a Muslim people; at currents within the ruling movement who were out of line with the leadership; and at alleged "counter-revolutionaries."

In Uganda at least 100,000 and possibly as many as half a million people were killed by the security forces during the eight years of President Idi Amin's rule (1971–1979). The victims included members of particular ethnic groups, religious leaders, judges, lawyers, students, intellectuals and foreign nationals.

In Ethiopia thousands of people were unlawfully and deliberately killed by the security forces after the Provisional Military Government assumed power in 1974 — particularly during the government's "Red Terror" campaign of 1977 and 1978. In February 1977 the government publicly ordered the security forces, including armed civilian officials, to "apply red-terror and revolutionary justice" to the members and supporters of the opposition Ethiopian People's Revolutionary Party, which it accused of being "counter-revolutionary" and spreading "white terror." At the peak of the "red terror," from November 1977 until about February 1978, an estimated 5,000 political opponents of the government were killed in Addis Ababa alone.

In Burundi [in south-central Africa] at least 80,000 people are believed to have been killed in just two months — May and June 1972. There had been a power struggle between the dominant Tutsi ethnic group and the numerically larger Hutu for some years, and a Hutu-inspired rebellion began on 29 April 1972 in the capital, Bujumbura, and in several provinces. Two provincial capitals were overrun in the course of the uprising and some 2,000 people killed, including a brother-in-law of the president and a provincial governor.

On 30 April a government counterattack began. Martial law was declared and a curfew imposed. The army, assisted by the *Jeunesse révolutionnaire Rwagasore*, Revolutionary Rwagasore Youth, the paramilitary youth movement of the ruling party, began killing anyone believed to be connected with the uprising, as well as any other Hutu leaders or potential Hutu leaders. In the capital and in the provinces Hutu were loaded into jeeps and lorries, clubbed to death and buried in mass graves. There were also a number of killings arising from personal disputes, and a number of Tutsi were killed as well.

According to a British reporter, David Martin, who visited Burundi during this period:

. . . at Bujumbura bulldozer tracks could clearly be seen from the air near the main airport where victims had been buried in mass graves and open trenches were waiting for more bodies. To be educated — albeit only to primary level — or to have a job, was a death sentence for a Hutu. Diplomats were hiding their cooks and gardeners at their official residences. The banks in the capital said they had lost over 100 Hutu employees from clerks upwards; all of whom were believed to be dead. At the cable office, where before the uprising and repression twenty-five Hutu had worked, only two were left. One large Belgian company said that every single Hutu employee had disappeared and almost all of them were thought to be dead. One of the few surviving Hutu employees I spoke to in Bujumbura said that he had tried to escape but had been stopped at a road block, beaten up and told to go back. He had not been involved in the uprising so could not understand why they should do anything to him. He knew many of his friends who had also not been involved but had been killed. Subsequently I learned he too had disappeared.

SIMONE DE BEAUVOIR
The Second Sex

Simone de Beauvoir (1908–1986), the French philosopher and feminist, published *The Second Sex* in 1949. It described the role of women in a traditional society, in which the majority of women were married, depended on men for their role in society, and were tied to their home and their children; only a minority of women (including the author) led independent lives. De Beauvoir traced the role of women through history and through their contemporary life cycle as evidence for her thesis:

because the forces of social tradition are controlled by men, women have been relegated to a secondary place in the world.

In the excerpts that follow, de Beauvoir argued that despite considerable change in their social status, women are still prevented from becoming autonomous individuals and taking their places as men's equals. Marriage is still expected to be women's common destiny, with their identity defined in relation to their husbands. In discussing the status of newly independent women, de Beauvoir implied that because of their failure to escape the pyschological trap of secondary status, they lack confidence and creativity in their work.

. . . Woman has always been man's dependant, if not his slave; the two sexes have never shared the world in equality. And even today woman is heavily handicapped, though her situation is beginning to change. Almost nowhere is her legal status the same as man's, and frequently it is much to her disadvantage. Even when her rights are legally recognized in the abstract, long-standing custom prevents their full expression in the mores. In the economic sphere men and women can almost be said to make up two castes; other things being equal, the former hold the better jobs, get higher wages, and have more opportunity for success than their new competitors. In industry and politics men have a great many more positions and they monopolize the most important posts. In addition to all this, they enjoy a traditional prestige that the education of children tends in every way to support, for the present enshrines the past — and in the past all history has been made by men. At the present time, when women are beginning to take part in the affairs of the world, it is still a world that belongs to men — they have no doubt of it at all and women have scarcely any. To decline to be the Other, to refuse to be a party to the deal — this would be for women to renounce all the advantages conferred upon them by their alliance with the superior caste. Man-the-sovereign will provide woman-the-liege with material protection and will undertake the moral justification of her existence; thus she can evade at once both economic risk and the metaphysical risk of a liberty in which ends and aims must be contrived without assistance. Indeed, along with the ethical urge

of each individual to affirm his subjective existence, there is also the temptation to forgo liberty and become a thing. This is an inauspicious road, for he who takes it — passive, lost, ruined — becomes henceforth the creature of another's will, frustrated in his transcendence and deprived of every value. But it is an easy road; on it one avoids the strain involved in undertaking an authentic existence. When man makes of woman the *Other*, he may, then, expect to manifest deep-seated tendencies towards complicity. Thus, woman may fail to lay claim to the status of subject because she lacks definite resources, because she feels the necessary bond that ties her to man regardless of reciprocity, and because she is often very well pleased with her role as the *Other*. . . .

Marriage is the destiny traditionally offered to women by society. It is still true that most women are married, or have been, or plan to be, or suffer from not being. The celibate woman is to be explained and defined with reference to marriage, whether she is frustrated, rebellious, or even indifferent in regard to that institution. We must therefore continue this study by analysing marriage.

Economic evolution in woman's situation is in process of upsetting the institution of marriage: it is becoming a union freely entered upon by the consent of two independent persons; the obligations of the two contracting parties are personal and reciprocal; adultery is for both a breach of contract; divorce is obtainable by the one or the other on the same conditions. Woman is no longer limited to the reproductive function, which has lost in large part its character as natural servitude and has come to be regarded as a function to be voluntarily assumed; and it is compatible with productive labour, since, in many cases, the time off required by a pregnancy is taken by the mother at the expense of the State or the employer. In the Soviet Union marriage was for some years a contract between individuals based upon the complete liberty of the husband and wife; but it would seem that it is now a duty that the State imposes upon them both. Which of these tendencies will prevail in the world of tomorrow will depend upon the general structure of society, but in any case male guardianship of woman is disappearing. Nevertheless, the epoch in which we are living is still, from the feminist point of view, a period of transition. Only a part of the female population is engaged in production, and even those who are belong to a society in which ancient forms and antique values survive. Modern marriage can be understood only in the light of a past that tends to perpetuate itself.

Marriage has always been a very different thing for man and for woman. The two sexes are necessary to each other, but this necessity has never brought about a condition of reciprocity between them; women, as we have seen, have never constituted a caste making exchanges and contracts with the male caste upon a footing of equality. A man is socially an independent and complete individual; he is regarded first of all as a producer whose existence is justified by the work he does for the group: we have seen why it is that the reproductive and domestic role to which woman is confined has not guaranteed her an equal dignity. Certainly the male needs her; in some primitive groups it may happen that the bachelor, unable to manage his existence by himself, becomes a kind of outcast; in agricultural societies a woman co-worker is essential to the peasant; and for most men it is of advantage to unload certain drudgery upon a mate; the individual wants a regular sexual life and posterity, and the State requires him to contribute to its perpetua-

tion. But man does not make his appeal directly to woman herself; it is the men's group that allows each of its members to find self-fulfilment as husband and father; woman, as slave or vassal, is integrated within families dominated by fathers and brothers, and she has always been given in marriage by certain males to other males. In primitive societies the paternal clan, the gens, disposed of woman almost like a thing: she was included in deals agreed upon by two groups. The situation is not much modified when marriage assumes a contractual form in the course of its evolution; when dowered or having her share in inheritance, woman would seem to have civil standing as a person, but dowry and inheritance still enslave her to her family. During a long period the contracts were made between father-in-law and son-in-law, not between wife and husband; only widows then enjoyed economic independence. The young girl's freedom of choice has always been much restricted; and celibacy — apart from the rare cases in which it bears a sacred character — reduced her to the rank of parasite and pariah; marriage is her only means of support and the sole justification of her existence. It is enjoined upon her for two reasons.

The first reason is that she must provide the society with children; only rarely — as in Sparta and to some extent under the Nazi régime — does the State take woman under direct guardianship and ask only that she be a mother. But even the primitive societies that are not aware of the paternal generative role demand that woman have a husband, for the second reason why marriage is enjoined is that woman's function is also to satisfy a male's sexual needs and to take care of his household. These duties placed upon woman by society are regarded as a *service* rendered to her spouse: in return he is supposed to give her presents, or a marriage settlement, and to support her. Through him as intermediary, society discharges its debt to the woman it turns over to him. The rights obtained by the wife in fulfilling her duties are represented in obligations that the male must assume. He cannot break the conjugal bond at his pleasure; he can repudiate or divorce his wife only when the public authorities so decide, and even then the husband sometimes owes her compensation in money; the practice even becomes an abuse in Egypt under Bocchoris [Egyptian King] or, as the demand for alimony, in the United States today. Polygamy has always been more or less openly tolerated: man may bed with slaves, concubines, mistresses, prostitutes, but he is required to respect certain privileges of his legitimate wife. If she is maltreated or wronged, she has the right — more or less definitely guaranteed — of going back to her family and herself obtaining a separation or divorce.

Thus for both parties marriage is at the same time a burden and a benefit; but there is no symmetry in the situations of the two sexes; for girls marriage is the only means of integration in the community, and if they remain unwanted, they are, socially viewed, so much wastage. . . .

It must be said that the independent woman is justifiably disturbed by the idea that people do not have confidence in her. As a general rule, the superior caste is hostile to newcomers from the inferior caste: white people will not consult a Negro physician, nor males a woman doctor; but individuals of the inferior caste, imbued with a sense of their specific inferiority and often full of resentment towards one of their kind who has risen above their usual lot, will also prefer to turn to the masters. Most women, in particular, steeped in adoration for man, eagerly seek him out in the person of the doctor, the lawyer, the office manager, and so on. Neither men nor women like to be under a woman's orders. Her superiors, even if they esteem her highly, will always be somewhat condescending; to be a woman, if not a defect, is at least a peculiarity. Woman must constantly win the confidence that is not at first accorded her: at the start she is suspect, she has to prove herself. If she has worth she will pass the tests, so they say. But worth is not a given essence; it is the outcome of a successful development. To feel the weight of an unfavourable prejudice against one is only on very rare occasions a help in overcoming it. The initial inferiority complex ordinarily leads to a defence reaction in the form of an exaggerated affectation of authority.

Most women doctors, for example, have too much or too little of the air of authority. If they act naturally, they fail to take control, for their life as a whole disposes them rather to seduce than to command; the patient who likes to be dominated will be disappointed by plain advice simply given. Aware of this fact, the woman doctor assumes a grave accent, a peremptory tone; but then she lacks the bluff good nature that is the charm of the medical man who is sure of himself.

Man is accustomed to asserting himself; his clients believe in his competence; he can act naturally: he infallibly makes an impression. Woman does not inspire the same feeling of security; she affects a lofty air, she drops it, she makes too much of it. In business, in administrative work, she is precise, fussy, quick to show aggressiveness. As in her studies, she lacks ease, dash, audacity. In the effort to achieve she gets tense. Her activity is a succession of challenges and self-affirmations. This is the great defect that lack of assurance engenders: the subject cannot forget himself. He does not aim gallantly towards some goal: he seeks rather to make good in prescribed ways. In boldly setting out towards ends, one risks disappointments; but one also obtains unhoped-for results; caution condemns to mediocrity.

We rarely encounter in the independent woman a taste for adventure and for experience for its own sake, or a disinterested curiosity; she seeks "to have a career" as other women build a nest of happiness; she remains dominated, surrounded, by the male universe, she lacks the audacity to break through its ceiling, she does not passionately lose herself in her projects. She still regards her life as an immanent enterprise: her aim is not at an objective but, through the objective, at her subjective success. This is a very conspicuous attitude, for example, among American women; they like having a job and proving to themselves that they are capable of handling it properly; but they are not passionately concerned with the *content* of their tasks. Woman similarly has a tendency to attach too much importance to minor setbacks and modest successes; she is turn by turn discouraged or puffed up with vanity. When a success has been anticipated, one takes it calmly; but it becomes an intoxicating triumph when one has been doubtful of obtaining it. This is the excuse when women become addled with importance and plume themselves ostentatiously over their least accomplishments. They are for ever looking back to see how far they have come, and that interrupts their progress. By this procedure they can have honourable careers, but not accomplish great things. It must be added that many men are also unable to build any but mediocre careers. It is only in comparison with the best of them that woman — save for very rare exceptions — seems to us to be trailing behind. The reasons I have given are sufficient explanation, and in no way mortgage the future. What woman essentially lacks today for doing great things is forgetfulness of herself; but to forget oneself it is first of all necessary to be firmly assured that now and for the future one has found oneself. Newly come into the world of men, poorly seconded by them, woman is still too busily occupied to search for herself.

Review Questions

1. What demands do the rights listed under articles 22 to 26 of the United Nations' declaration make on a country's society and government?

2. On what grounds does Amnesty International condemn political killings by governments?

3. What is Amnesty International's definition for political killings by governments?

4. What, in Simone de Beauvoir's view, is the position of women in regard to men and in regard to marriage?

5. Why, from de Beauvoir's feminist perspective, is the epoch in which we are living a period of transition?

6. What are the obstacles, according to de Beauvoir, that face "the independent woman" with "a taste for adventure and experience for its own sake"?

4 | Global Problems

The *global village*, meaning the world, is a term in common use today. This phrase succinctly states a truth that has become self-evident in the past decades: the interdependence of all nations in the vital areas of food, energy, economics, and the environment. Given this interdependence, the problems that affect one part of the world impact on the rest of it. For example, the burgeoning population, especially in Third World countries, puts pressure on increasing the food supply, but such increase has limits, with finite land, water, and other resources. Larger populations also mean dwindling forests and subsequent soil erosion as people clear trees for fuel and farmland. More people need more energy, using up nonrenewable energy sources as well as renewable sources; more people seek more jobs for their livelihood. Another problem that adds to the economic distress of many Third World countries is the immense debt that they have accumulated. A more volatile and immediate problem is the arms race of the superpowers and other countries. Not only does it drain their nations' gross national product, but the stockpiling of nuclear weaponry carries the threat of the annihilation of humanity. All these threats and pressures on the global village and its inhabitants present the greatest challenge humankind has ever faced.

AMADOU-MAHTAR M'BOW

Where the Future Begins

Amadou-Mahtar M'Bow served as Director General of the United Nations Educational, Scientific, and Cultural Organization (UNESCO) from 1974 to 1986. Born in the French colony of Senegal in 1921 and educated in Paris, he returned to his native land as an educator; after independence, he served as a government minister. In 1970, he joined UNESCO, becoming its head four years later.

In 1984, M'Bow wrote *Where the Future Begins,* a perceptive survey of the global situation which pointed to significant features of the contemporary age, including the interdependence that makes the network of world problems significant to all humanity.

One World

From whatever angle the major questions which mankind has to answer are approached, it is clear that the future of modern societies will take place in a context already expanding to a worldwide scale. Indications can be found in the upsurge of international trade, which has increased sixfold in just a quarter of a century, and the flood-tide of international migration, which has now reached the point where 20 million workers are living outside their country of origin, not counting the millions of tourists and businessmen moving to and fro over the globe, the many students living abroad temporarily and the 10 million refugees who have been driven from their countries by fear or compulsion. As for the exchange of messages and data and other non-material exchanges, the growth rate is considerably greater than that of world trade in raw materials and finished products.

As a result, societies which had been able to live in almost total ignorance of each other up to a few decades ago are now in increasingly regular contact. Reciprocal influences are ever more numerous and interdependence is becoming a multidimensional reality. While interdependence is certainly a source of mutual enrichment, receptivity, initiative and creativity, it also leads to frustrations when accompanied by a deterioration in the lot of some peoples, a reduction in the scope for manoeuvre, increased unpredictability and greater vulnerability. The decisions taken by states in some fields take account of a growing number of given factors beyond their control and these decisions may, conversely, cause repercussions of varying degrees beyond their borders.

Ecological damage caused by the activities of some is inflicted on others: from major oil spills to the increase in the level of carbon dioxide in the atmosphere and the threat of nuclear contamination, the risks of pollution are spreading to ever-larger areas and lasting for incomparably longer periods. Whether for sources of energy or raw materials such as oil, cereals and minerals or a large number of primary or manufactured products, users have come to depend increasingly on a distant producer who is himself engaged in a constant effort to open up new outlets abroad. Moreover, the intensification of financial flows further accentuates dependence. Many countries, caught up in this system, are obliged to give precedence to export production to keep their balance of payments in equilibrium, to service foreign debt or to purchase capital equipment. A large number of them have to give lower priority to production of items vital to the subsistence of their own populations, thus increasing their dependence on others for food and the means of development. . . .

It is perhaps in the cultural field that these contradictory demands of new world relationships are most readily discernible. The context of communication among human beings is becoming world wide, while the quantity of knowledge and information and, with the development of computer technology, the means of collecting and storing them and transferring them from one point of the globe to another are constantly increasing. Telecommunication techniques are becoming more and more sophisticated and they combine with the traditional means of propagation — books, periodicals, printed matter — to offer opportunities for communication which can be at the one time universal and instantaneous. Satellites extend the range of the media, wipe out national frontiers, increase the flow of messages and facilitate access to computerized data banks that enrich each other and are interconnected in multiple networks. At some levels, these exchanges and contacts are accompanied by a growing tendency towards standardization of tastes and behaviour and homogenization of certain patterns of life, thought and ac-

tion, of production and consumption propagated by uniform dissemination of the same television series, the same musical beats, the same clothes and the same escapist dreams. On the other hand, as a kind of reaction to this trend, a renewed, explosive upsurge of distinctive characteristics is taking place. Everywhere, ethnic or national, rural or urban communities and cultural or religious entities are asserting their originality and striving to assume and vigorously defend those features which define their identity. These contradictory phenomena are spreading in a series of shock waves from one region of the globe to another.

Asymmetries and Inequalities

The growing interdependence which is characteristic of the way things are moving in the second half of the twentieth century has been accompanied by a heightening of the contrasts between countries. Overall, the world has enjoyed a rapid rate of economic growth, probably unprecedented in history, in the decades since the end of the Second World War. For the world as a whole, value added in industry rose from $234 billion in 1948 to about $1,200 billion in 1980 (at 1970 prices). . . . But despite the progress achieved, especially in setting up processing industries and developing basic industries, the share of the Third World in overall industrial production has grown only slightly, from 6.2 per cent in 1952 to roughly 9 per cent at the end of the 1970s. . . .

It may be noted, for instance, that in 1979 four industrialized countries alone accounted for just over half of the world gross product, and in 1980, whereas the average per capita product in the industrialized market-economy countries amounted to $10,660, in the so-called low-income countries it came to only $250 — that is to say forty-two times less.

These economic statistics provide blunt evidence of the scale of the disparities between nations and groups of nations. But inequalities also persist within most societies and are in some cases even becoming more pronounced. The prosperity of many industrialized countries may conceal an uneven distribution of income, and some sections of the population in those countries lead a difficult, sometimes even precarious, existence. In the Third World, vast populations frequently enjoy none of the benefits of progress, and towns and cities — in many cases and at least as regards certain social categories — are like islands of modernity cut off from the hinterland.

The picture of destitution, concentrated for the most part in countries of the Third World, is a familiar one. An age-old word — poverty — has today become a central concept of economies. It betokens serious deficiencies in food, housing, health and education and an extremely low income level. Depending on the criteria adopted, it may be reckoned that there are some 800 million people in the world living in a state of absolute poverty (World Bank) or about 1,100 million poor (International Labour Office). Other equally disquieting figures have to be taken into account to form a more detailed picture of various categories of unfulfilled needs: 430 million people severely undernourished, 1,000 million badly housed, 1,300 million without access to drinking-water, and, according to statistics established by Unesco, 814 million adult illiterates and 123 million children of school age not attending school. . . .

Obviously, it is the poorest who are worst hit by undernourishment or malnutrition, in certain urban areas or in rural areas where particular land-tenure systems and various economic factors lead to the formation of vast landless and jobless population groups who are unable either to produce or to purchase enough food to live on; and it is they who also have the least access to health and welfare services and education. Malnutrition has particularly serious effects on young children, whose physical and mental development it may seriously impair. In many countries, indeed, the effectiveness of education is severely reduced as a result of the fact that large numbers of pre-school and school-age children are underfed or improperly nourished.

Poverty has direct effects on the lives of many population groups. Whereas the mean expectation of life at birth is roughly seventy-two years in the industrialized countries, it is only fifty-five years in the countries of the Third World and only fifty in some of them. The mortality rate of children in the 1 to 5 age-group is only one per thousand in most industrialized countries, but averages twenty in many developing countries and exceeds thirty in some regions. Of every thousand children born in the least developed countries, 200 will die before the age of 1 and a 100 more before the age of 5; only 500 will survive to the age of 40.

People suffering from food deficiencies are indeed particularly susceptible to disease. Various diseases in some of the developing countries are so chronic and debilitating that they sharply reduce the capacity for work of part of the population at precisely those times of the year when agricultural work requires the greatest efforts.

Whereas two people in every hundred are illiterate in the industrialized countries, the number reaches forty-one in the developing countries and in some cases sixty. Illiteracy thrives on the inadequacy of primary education and is a direct consequence of the economic difficulties under which the developing countries are labouring, which diminish the resources available for education. The 123 million or so children who are of primary-school age but have no opportunity to attend school will subsequently join the ranks of the adult illiterate population, of whom 60 per cent, in 1980, were women. . . . Many of these people are born, grow up and die amid poverty, hunger and ignorance. Illiteracy, which is also a denial of the right to education, is thus an indicator and together with all its consequences constitutes one of the major challenges to the international community.

On top of illiteracy come unemployment and underemployment. The International Labour Organisation (ILO) estimates that over 600 million jobs would have to be created by 1987 in the Third World as a whole in order to absorb unemployment, provide jobs for those reaching working age, and enable everyone to enjoy decent living conditions. Apart from a privileged or relatively sheltered sector consisting of the national civil service and a few enterprises in what is termed the modern sector, the vast majority of the labour force — in some countries virtually the whole of it — have only casual and irregular jobs which are poorly paid and inadequately protected, or else are engaged in agricultural work characterized by such low productivity that it barely provides the wherewithal to live. . . .

Peace and the Arms Race

At this stage it appears essential to raise a question: is it possible to cope with the fundamental problems confronting mankind, particularly the problem of development conceived of in worldwide terms, as long as human societies are pitted against one another and humanity is threatened with nuclear war, that is to say with annihilation?

The nature of war has changed today. The quantity and destructive capacity of modern nuclear weapons and of chemical and biological weapons are such that a conflict between the great powers, in which such weapons would inevitably be used, would result in the destruction of the human race. The feature that makes the present era radically different from previous ones is this capacity of the human race to destroy itself. It is a state of affairs unique in the history of mankind, and one that must be constantly borne in mind at a time when it is sometimes asserted that

with tactical nuclear weapons, a nuclear conflict could remain localized and its consequences be surmounted. In practice there is no guarantee that, once set off, a nuclear conflagration could ever be contained. The aftereffects of atomic explosions would be so extensive that there would be a strong likelihood of the threshold being quickly reached where the scale of destruction would prove lethal for the whole of mankind. . . .

The arms race, originating in many cases from the will to predominate or from a sense of insecurity which, far from mitigating, it makes worse, accelerates under its own momentum. It has undeniably become a phenomenon which, by virtue of its scale and implications, dominates the international scene. Total military expenditure in 1980 may be estimated at over $500,000 million — a sheer waste of these colossal resources, it may be said, since they do not enhance the security of those who foot the bill, the balance of power tending to be set at a constantly higher level.

It has been observed that total military expenditure represents about twenty times total official development assistance. The whole course of things would be altered if a substantial portion of the resources now taken up by military expenditure could be devoted to development.

The developing countries themselves have to set aside large resources, in proportion to their means, for military expenditure. . . .

As far as the developed countries are concerned, it goes without saying that a reduction of arms expenditure, by easing the burden on national budgets, would make it possible to eliminate all the areas of poverty within those countries and to step up development assistance considerably.

It should also be pointed out that the arms race at present ties up valuable human resources and, especially, very large numbers of top scientists. The number of scientists and engineers, among the world's best, currently engaged in military research and development is estimated at between 400,000 and 500,000. Roughly a quarter of world research-and-development expenditure is for military purposes. Some sources think the proportion to be as high as 40 per cent. This amounts to a diversion of scientific activity from the improvement of the human condition. If this huge research-and-development potential were used for purposes of human welfare, considerable progress could be made towards solving some of man's major problems, such as those in the fields of health, education or agricultural production. Quite obviously, such a redeployment has an ethical aspect and is one of the major issues in the current debate on the ultimate purposes of science and technology. . . .

Human Rights

. . . Massive violations of human rights continue; foremost among them, mention must yet again be made of the apartheid regime that still prevails in South Africa, despite repeated condemnations by the international community. That regime continues to institutionalize racism and to deny, by its very existence, the most fundamental principle on which human rights are based: the oneness of the human race and the equal dignity of all human beings. . . .

As was said earlier, there are some 10 million refugees in the world today; their situation is particularly grave because of the precariousness of their living conditions, the fact of their having been uprooted and the difficulty of finding sound solutions, in the prevailing political and economic circumstances.

No less disquieting is the trend with regard to individual freedoms, which are jeopardized in various ways, either by blind terrorism that strikes even at the totally innocent in the name of particular aspirations or principles, or by the established authorities. Authorities in many countries have curbed political liberties and freedom of association and put down op-

position movements. In some cases, the law itself is used to redouble the attacks upon human rights, for instance by retroactive, repressive legislation, the widening of the interpretation of national security, or the institutionalization of emergency measures. There is a disquieting tendency to "criminalize" opposition by bringing mere political disagreement within the scope of the penal code. Furthermore, normal legal safeguards are often set aside, with the resultant development of various forms of detention without trial.

No less serious, and perhaps even more serious, is the tendency to adopt, parallel to official and legal repression, procedures beyond the pale of legality and state power, involving undercover operations of kidnapping or murder whose perpetrators enjoy a sort of impunity.

Moreover, although prohibited by legislation in most states, torture and, more generally, humiliating and degrading treatment are still practised. In some places they are inflicted, seemingly on a systematic basis, when suspects are arrested and during their interrogation and detention. . . .

The Environment and Natural Resources

Attention is now also focused, as the result of a new awareness that has become especially marked over recent decades, on the pressure that man's activities, based on technological advance, exert on the environment, either through the unchecked consumption of resources and space, or through the production of waste material that the natural environment can no longer absorb without suffering far-reaching effects. The major risks emerging in the relationship between man and nature are the exhaustion or scarcity of certain non-renewable resources essential for human activities, and irreversible damage that might jeopardize the balance of the biosphere. . . .

But in the particular case of energy resources, given their crucial importance and the fact that consumption is set to go on rising in the coming decades, the prospect of oil and gas resources dwindling over a period that is difficult to measure but can be estimated in terms of decades rather than centuries means that thought must be given in the medium term to the problem of the transition to other sources of energy, the transition from the present economy, heavily reliant on the combustion of hydrocarbons, to one based on more diversified sources, above all renewable ones. In the long term, that is to say beyond the early decades of the twenty-first century, a massive input of renewable and virtually inexhaustible energies in the shape of nuclear fusion and solar energy can perhaps be envisaged. . . .

As for the state of resources of the earth and the human environment, despite some signs of improvement in such matters as atmospheric pollution in certain major urban centres, there are considerable grounds for concern. Large areas are threatened by desertification, erosion and soil salination; the area of the land where yields are drastically reduced by desertification in any given year is estimated at a minimum of 6 million hectares.

This situation contributes to the aggravation of the food problems affecting the greater part of mankind, while population pressure is giving rise to greater needs. Agricultural output must grow on a worldwide scale to meet the foodstuff needs of over 4,000 million human beings, whose number will exceed 6,000 million by the end of the century. This growth can be achieved only through the cultivation of unused lands, more irrigation and, above all, increased yields. But resources must be rationally managed if what is being done is not to be compromised or even cancelled out by soil deterioration.

Furthermore, deforestation is proceeding apace, particularly in the tropical forests which are dwindling by some 10 million hectares a year as a combined result of clearances to make more land available for cultivation and felling to provide firewood and timber for export. Serious consequences may ensue from the disappearance of plant and animal species, which impoverishes the genetic heritage of the planet, and also from an often irreversible deterioration of the soil.

A further vitally important matter is that of water resources. Although these are still abundant, a very large number of people are still deprived of drinking-water: in 1980, only 29 per cent of the world's rural population had access to water of satisfactory quality, and sewerage was provided for only 13 per cent; in the urban centres, the percentages were 75 and 56 respectively. The scarcity of water resources that is making itself felt in many regions, often combined with the irrational use of those still available, hinders economic development and social progress. Despite what has been done in pollution control, rivers and lakes are still threatened with pollution by industrial and even agricultural activities. . . .

But our thinking about the environment, the setting of man's life, cannot overlook the problems raised by population trends. Between 1950 and 1975, the world population increased from 2,500 million to 4,000 million, a growth unprecedented in the history of mankind. It is now estimated at 4,600 million and by the year 2000 will probably have reached between 5,800 and 6,600 million. The growth rate will, it is true, vary from one region of the world to another. The increase in the population will be much greater in what are at present the developing countries, whose share in the world population will rise considerably, while that of the industrialized countries will decrease. It can in fact be expected that, in the year 2000, the developing countries will reach a total of between 4,500 and 5,200 million inhabitants according to the different projections (as against 2,800 million in 1975) and the industrialized countries a total of between 1,300 and 1,400 million (as against 1,100 million in 1975). . . .

. . . Situations of underdevelopment,

in themselves, also have unfortunate implications for the environment. Poverty leads to over-use or irrational use of the productive capacities of ecosystems, of soil, water and wood. It also leads to uncontrolled extension of urbanization, which has today become a major problem in many countries.

Urbanization in the industrialized countries has involved considerable economic and social costs in terms of congested infrastructures, transport difficulties, air pollution and noise; it has produced slum areas, on the outskirts, or in some cases in the very centre, of cities, where people, often belonging to ethnic or linguistic minorities, experience serious problems in fitting into social and cultural life. Current urbanization in the Third World is marked chiefly by its rapidity and scale; it is accelerated, in a situation of high population growth, by the movement towards the towns of rural populations impelled by necessity — food shortages, famine and sometimes the collapse of traditional production systems — and by the often illusory hope of a better life. Huge settlements thus come into being where millions of people live in dire poverty. The evils from which these areas suffer are known to all, including as they do insanitary housing, wretched shanty towns, heaps of rubbish, shortage of drinking-water and lack of recreation facilities. The people themselves are very largely unemployed, and such phenomena as prostitution and delinquency take root among them all too easily.

For the first time in history, the Third World has now outstripped the industrialized countries in terms of the number of cities with over a million inhabitants. According to United Nations estimates, this number will double before the end of the century.

ARNOLD TOYNBEE
For the First Time in 30,000 Years

Appropriately, this volume ends with the observations of Arnold Toynbee (1889–1975). Toynbee authored the monumental work *The Study of History,* which traces the rise and fall of civilizations; as Director of the Royal Institute of International Affairs in London, he was for years a perceptive analyst of events around the world. In the following passages from an essay written in 1972, Toynbee sets his assessment of the contemporary age and its problems into the historical context of the past thirty millennia, combining in his person the roles of historian, observer of his own times, and prophet of human destiny.

As a prophet, Toynbee hardly offers a reassuring message: humankind's future is once again in doubt. Like M'Bow, he points to the threat of nuclear weapons, the despoliation of the human habitat, and the effects of the population explosion. Assessing the causes of political hostility in the world, he stresses the dangers of nationalism, pleading for a voluntary union of all humankind on a global scale as the main hope for survival.

Till now, mankind has either taken it as a matter of course that it is going to survive, or, alternatively, assumed that its destiny will be decided by forces beyond human control: the gods or God or Nature. We have now woken up to the truth that, today, we are in greater danger of extinction than we have been at any time since the date — perhaps 30,000 years ago — at which our ancestors gained the upper hand over all other forms of life on this planet except microbes and viruses. In the present age we have discovered and conquered the microbes, and we have hopes of getting the better of the viruses. But our recent victories over non-human menaces to human life are far outweighed by new threats to us from ourselves. These threats have no precedents; for man, armed with the power of science applied to technology, is a vastly more formidable enemy for man than any non-human enemy that man has yet encountered.

The present human threats to mankind's survival are notorious. The three principal current man-made menaces are nuclear weapons, the pollution of mankind's habitat on this planet, together with the using up of the planet's irreplaceable natural resources, and the population explosion produced by a reduction in the death-rate without a simultaneous corresponding reduction in the birth-rate.

Taken together, these man-made menaces threaten mankind with extinction, because they threaten to make the surface of our planet uninhabitable, and this limited area is the only habitat we have or are likely ever to have. At least this seems to be the lesson of the progressive increase in the range of astronomical observation and of the recent feat of breaking out into the nearest reaches of outer space. . . .

. . . It is surely clear that the first business on mankind's agenda ought now to be securing its own survival by making sure that its habitat on Earth, which is mankind's sole patrimony, should continue to be habitable by human beings. It is also surely clear that, since the whole habitable and traversable and exploitable and pollutable part of the Earth's crust and air-envelope has been knit together, for technological purposes, into a global unity, the necessary effort to conserve it for human use must be a united and concerted effort by the whole human race. The menaces of nuclear armaments, pollution, prodigality, and overcrowding threaten us on a global scale. They cannot be dealt with

effectively by a cooperative human effort of less than global comprehensiveness.

The technological unification of our habitat is now an accomplished fact. Its economic unification is hardly less complete, and even its social and cultural unification has been accomplished at some levels. This is the result of the global radiation during the last five centuries of West European technology, trade, investment, government, population, institutions, ideas, and ideals. For the non-Western majority of mankind, these West-European exports were originally alien imports, intrusions, and impositions, but gradually they have begun to become common possessions of all mankind. From being something specifically Western, they are turning into something generically modern, to which the living non-Western civilizations are making increasingly important contributions. On the cultural and professional planes, there are now people who are already citizens of the world — for instance, the members of the medical profession, and of university faculties and student bodies. The global bond of feeling that unites people in these walks of life is stronger than their juridical segregation from each other as citizens, in the political sense, of the planet's present 140 local sovereign states.

The present situation and, still more, the current tendency on the political plane presents a disturbing contrast to the situation and tendency on other planes of human activity. On these other planes, the history of human affairs during the last five hundred years has resulted in at least a beginning of the process of unification which is the outcome that we should expect. On the political plane, on the other hand, there has so far been little discernible progress toward unification.

Indeed, there has been a quite marked accentuation of political disunity, both in fact and in feeling. This increasing disharmony between politics and other human activities has now reached a degree at which it is manifestly threatening mankind with catastrophe. Why are we exposing ourselves to this fearful risk? Why, in our political life, are we so allergic to the unifying tendency which has prevailed in other fields? It is important to try to identify and understand the causes of this political misfit. To lay bare the causes is the most promising first step toward finding a cure.

The most obvious cause is the persistent disunity of the Western civilization, since it is the Western peoples who, within the last five hundred years, have initiated the global unification of mankind on a number of non-political planes. Since the collapse of the Roman Empire in its western provinces in the fifth century, the new Western civilization that has sprung up out of the Roman Empire's ruins has been disunited politically, though united culturally, technologically and to some extent also economically.

This initial combination of political disunity with unity on other planes is not peculiar to the West. Other civilizations — for instance, the Sumerian, the "classical" Greek, the Chinese — have started life with the same cultural and political configuration. The peculiarity of the Western civilization's political disunity has been its persistence. Its predecessor, the "classical" Greek civilization, was eventually unified politically in the Roman Empire, and similarly the Sumerian civilization in the Akkadian Empire and the Chinese civilization in the Chinese Empire — a political union that survives today, in the form of the People's Republic, nearly 2,200 years after its original establishment in 221 B.C. Moreover, when the Roman Empire disintegrated in its western provinces, it survived in its Levantine heartland; and when, in the seventh century, it broke down here too, it was quickly re-established, first as the Byzantine Greek Empire and then as the Ottoman Turkish Empire. The Ottoman Empire maintained itself till within living memory; it was not till after the First World War that it was extinguished by the youngest of its national successor-states, the present Turkish Republic.

These examples indicate that normally a cultural unity becomes a political unity as well — in course of time. But, if this is the normal rule, the political history of the Western civilization has been a conspicuous exception to it so far. In the West, the Roman Empire was replaced first by a number of local successor-states carved out by invading barbarian war-bands; and here, in contrast to the Levant, the attempt to re-establish the Roman Empire was a failure. The so-called "Holy Roman Empire" of Charlemagne and his successors never embraced the whole of the contemporary domain of the Western civilization, and its authority became more and more ineffective. The "Holy Roman Empire" was defeated by the medieval Papacy, but the Papacy's apparently promising attempt to unify the West under ecclesiastical auspices failed in its turn. In the Western Middle Ages, the most effective forms of political organization were the local city-states in Italy, Flanders, and Germany. In the modern age of Western history, the nation-state has supplanted the city-state as the standard form of Western polity. The global unification of mankind on the non-political planes within the last five hundred years has been accomplished through a competition between half-a-dozen rival West European nation-states — each of them expanding its trade, planting its settlers, and annexing territory all around the globe in chronic warfare with each of the others.

This political division of the modern Westerners into a number of mutually hostile nation-states has now been imitated by the non-Western majority of mankind. During the two centuries and a half that ended in the two world wars, the West was manifestly dominant in the world. Consequently, Western institutions acquired prestige. Non-Western peoples who revolted against Western domination adopted the Western political ideology of nationalism because they believed this had been the source of the West's strength. The dissolution of the West European national states' colonial empires during and since the Second World War has resulted in a doubling of the number of the world's local sovereign independent states. Each formerly subject territory that has recovered its political independence has set itself up as a national state in imitation of the Western national state whose rule it has shaken off.

The tendency to increase the number and to reduce the average size of local sovereign states has been stimulated, both in the West and elsewhere, by the nineteenth-century Western political doctrine of self-determination. . . .

Nationalism is the most potent of the causes of the political disunity of the present-day world. Another cause is a revulsion from the impersonalness of modern life. Today, human beings feel that they are being dehumanized; they are being reduced to ciphers, to serial numbers, or to clusters of holes punched in cards made for "processing" through a computer. People recognize that this dehumanization is a consequence of the increase in the number of persons and things, e.g., in the size of the populations of states. They know by experience that personal relations between human beings are more satisfactory than impersonal relations. They infer that life would become more human in a state in which it was possible for all the citizens to be acquainted with each other personally, and they argue from this premise that the breakup of states into smaller and smaller pieces is to be welcomed.

The premise is correct, but the conclusion drawn from it is fallacious because the objective is unattainable. A sovereign independent state small enough to become a family affair would not be viable. No state — not even a non-sovereign component of a federation — has ever been as small as that. In the smallest of the historical city-states, the political rela-

tions between the citizens have always been impersonal. They are inevitably impersonal in a population of, say, as many as 10,000 men, women, and children all told; when once this figure is reached, it makes no difference if it is increased to one million or to ten million or to five hundred million. Present-day Scottish and Welsh nationalists dream that they would find life more cosy in a separate Scottish or Welsh sovereign national state. In truth, they would find themselves no less depersonalized in a state of this smaller scale than they find themselves today as citizens of the United Kingdom. . . .

In most previous cases, political unity has been imposed eventually by military conquest. The cost, psychological as well as physical, of this barbarous method of unification has proved, again and again, to be prohibitively high. Unification by conquest has sometimes postponed the dissolution of a civilization, but it has seldom averted it and, insofar as the dissolution of a forcibly unified civilization has been postponed, the civilization has been preserved in most cases only in a state of petrification. However, in the age of atomic weapons by which mankind has now been overtaken, the traditional violent method of unification is no longer practicable anyway. A world war fought with atomic weapons could not unify mankind; it would only annihilate it. In the atomic age, the only possible method of unification is some form of voluntary association.

It has been noted already that since 1945 — the year in which the Second World War culminated and ended in the invention and use of atomic weaponry — some of the sovereign national states of Western Europe have taken the radically new departure of entering into a voluntary association in the E.E.C. This is a good augury, considering how deeply ingrained is nationalism in the tradition of Western European peoples and how often one or other of them has tried to subjugate the rest by force. If the Western European peoples can unite with each other voluntarily, as they are now demonstrating they can, a voluntary union of all mankind, on a global scale, is not a utopian objective.

The objective is not utopian, but will it be achieved? That is to say, will it be achieved in time to avert the catastrophe which is the alternative to it? This question will be answered by the three present superpowers [United States, Soviet Union, and China]; their answer is still unknown — probably even to themselves. Will the superpowers' governments and peoples recognize in time that the winning of successes in their competition with each other is not the paramount interest of any one of them? Will they recognize that their paramount interest is the preservation of the human race; that this interest is common to them all and also to the rest of mankind; and that the pursuit of this objective is not only their interest but their duty, both to themselves and to their fellow men? If and when the views and intentions of the superpowers become clear, we shall be better able than we are today to forecast the future of mankind. Today we know only that mankind's future is once again in doubt for the first time, perhaps, within the last 30,000 years.

Review Questions

1. What are the key conditions that according to Amadou-Mahtar M'Bow will shape the future?

2. What effects do telecommunications have on human relations in one world?

3. How does M'Bow describe the nature of modern war?

4. What, according to M'Bow, is the impact of the rapidly growing human population on the earth's environment?

5. What, according to Arnold Toynbee, is "the present human threat to mankind's survival"?

6. What obstacles to political unity in the world did Toynbee observe?

7. What did Toynbee identify as the causes of modern nationalism?

8. What hopes for the future did Toynbee hold out?

List of Sources

Chapter 1

Selection 1: P. 6 — Extract from *On the Revolutions* by Copernicus translated by Edward Rosen and edited by Jerry Dobrzycki. Reprinted by permission of Macmillan, London and Basingstoke. P. 9 — Extracts from E. Garin, "Alle origini della polemica anticopernica," in *Studia Copernica VI — Colloquia Copernicana II*, in E. Rosen, *Copernicus and the Scientific Revolution*. Reprinted by permission of Robert E. Krieger Publishing Co. *Selections 2 & 3:* Pp. 11 & 14 — Excerpts from *Discoveries and Opinions of Galileo* translated by Stillman Drake. Copyright © 1957 by Stillman Drake. Reprinted by permission of Doubleday & Company, Inc. *Selection 3:* P. 16 — Excerpts from Galileo Galilei, *Dialogue Concerning the Two Chief World Systems*, Trans. Stillman Drake, © 1967 The Regents of the University of California. Used by permission of the University of California Press. *Selection 4:* P. 17 — Reprinted from *Novum Organum*, in *The Works of Francis Bacon*, Vol. VIII, collected, ed., and trans. James Spedding, Robert Leslie Ellis, and Douglas Dennon Heath (Boston: Taggard and Thompson, 1863), pp. 67–69, 71–72, 135–136, 142. *Selection 5:* P. 19 — Extracts reprinted with permission of Macmillan Publishing Company from René Descartes, *Discourse on Method*, translated by Laurence J. Lafleur. Copyright 1956 by Macmillan Publishing Company, renewed 1984 by Adele S. Lafleur and Robert H. Lafleur. *Selection 6:* P. 23 — Reprinted from Sir Isaac Newton, *The Mathematical Principles of Philosophy, Book III, Vol. II*, trans. Andrew Motte (London: H. D. Symonds, 1803), pp. 160–162. *Selection 7:* P. 24 — Reprinted from William Harvey, "The Motion of the Heart and Blood in Animals," in *The Works of William Harvey*, trans. Robert Willis (London: Sydenham Society, 1847), pp. 19–20, 48–49.

Chapter 2

Selection 1: P. 30 — Extracts from *The Philosophy of Kant*, by Immanuel Kant, translated, edited with an Introduction by Carl J. Friedrich. Copyright © 1949 by Random House Inc. Reprinted by permission of the publisher. *Selection 2:* P. 32 — Reprinted from John Locke, *Two Treatises of Civil Government* (London: 1688, 7th reprinting by J. Whiston et al., 1772, pp. 315–316, 292, 354–355, 358–359, 361–362. *Selection 3:* Pp. 35–39 — Excerpts from *Candide and Other Writings*, by Voltaire, edited by Haskell M. Block. Copyright © 1956 by Random House, Inc. Reprinted by permission of the publisher. P. 36, col. 1, lines between bullets — Reprinted from an excerpt in E. L. Higgins, ed., *The French Revolution as Told by Contemporaries* (Boston: Houghton Mifflin, 1938), pp. 35–36. Copyright © 1938 by Houghton Mifflin Company. *Selection 4:* P.

39 — Reprinted from Thomas Paine, *Age of Reason being an investigation of True and Fabulous Theology* (New York: Peter Eckler, 1892), pp. 5–11. P. 41 — Reprinted from Paul Heinrich Dietrich Baron d'Holbach, *Good Sense or Natural Ideas opposed to Ideas that are Supernatural* (New York: G. Vale, 1856), pp. vii–xi. *Selection 5:* P. 43 — Extracts from Denis Diderot, *The Encyclopedia: Selections*, Stephen J. Gendzier. Ed. and Trans., reprinted by permission of Stephen J. Gendzier. *Selection 6:* P. 46 — Extracts reprinted with permission of Macmillan Publishing Company from Denis Diderot, *Rameau's Nephew and Other Works*, translated by Jacques Barzun and Ralph H. Bowen. Copyright © 1956 by Jacques Barzun and Ralph H. Bowen; copyright renewed 1984. *Selection 7:* P. 50 — Extracts from Jean Jacques Rousseau, *Emile*, Barbara Foxley, Trans. Everyman's Library Series, reprinted by permission of J. M. Dent & Sons Ltd. Publishers. *Selection 8:* P. 52 — Extracts reprinted with permission of Macmillan Publishing Company from Caesara Beccaria, *On Crimes and Punishments*, translated by Henry Paolucci. Copyright © 1963 by Macmillan Publishing Company. *Selection 9:* P. 54 — Excerpts from Antoine-Nicolas de Condorcet, *Sketch for a Historical Picture of the Progress of the Human Mind*, translated by June Barraclough, reprinted by permission of Weidenfeld & Nicholson Ltd.

Chapter 3

Selection 1: P. 61 — Reprinted from Arthur Young, *Travels During the Years 1787, 1788, and 1789* (London: Printed for W. Richardson, 1792), pp. 533–540. P. 63 — Selections reprinted with permission of Macmillan Publishing Company from *A Documentary Survey of the French Revolution* by John Hall Stewart. Copyright 1951 by Macmillan Publishing Company, renewed 1979 by John Hall Stewart. P. 65 — Extracts from Emmanuel Joseph Sieyès, *What Is the Third Estate?*, trans., M. Blondel, 1964, reprinted by permission of Praeger and Phaedon Press Ltd. *Selection 2:* P. 67 — Reprinted from Alexis de Tocqueville, *On the State of Society in France Before the Revolution of 1789*, trans. Henry Reeve (London: John Murray, 1856), pp. 253–257, 259–260, 266–269. *Selection 3:* P. 69 — Reprinted from Thomas Paine, *Rights of Man* (New York: Peter Eckler, 1892), pp. 94–96. *Selection 4:* P. 71 — Reprinted from Edmund Burke, *Reflections on the Revolution in France* (London: Printed for J. Dodsley, 1791), pp. 51–55, 90–91, 116–117, 127, 129. P. 73 — Reprinted from Thomas Paine, *Rights of Man* (New York: Peter Eckler, 1892), pp. 9, 127, 162–164, 167. *Selection 5:* P. 75 — Selections reprinted with permission of Macmillan Publishing Company from *A Documentary Survey of the French Revolution* by John Hall Stewart. Copyright 1951 by Macmillan Publishing Company, renewed

1979 by John Hall Stewart. P. 76 — Reprinted from George Rudé, ed., *Robespierre* (Englewood Cliffs: Prentice-Hall, 1967), pp. 58–59. P. 77 — Reprinted from E. L. Higgins, ed., *The French Revolution As Told By Contemporaries* (Boston: Houghton Mifflin, 1938), p. 301. *Selection 6:* P. 78 — Selections reprinted with permission of Macmillan Publishing Company from *A Documentary Survey of the French Revolution* by John Hall Stewart. Copyright 1951 by Macmillan Publishing Company, renewed 1979 by John Hall Stewart. *Selection 7:* P. 79 — Reprinted from Frank Malloy Anderson, ed., *The Constitutions and other Select Documents Illustrative of the History of France 1789–1907* (Minneapolis: H. W. Wilson, 1908), pp. 312–313.

Chapter 4

Selection 1: P. 84 — Reprinted from Wordsworth and Coleridge, *The Lyrical Ballads 1798–1805*, introduction and notes by George Sampson (London: Methuen, 1940), pp. 20–26. P. 85 — Reprinted from *The Complete Poetical Works of William Wordsworth* (Philadelphia: Porter and Coates, 1851), p. 194. P. 86 — Reprinted from William Blake, *Milton A Poem in Two Books* (London: Printed by William Blake, 1804), pp. 42, 44. *Selection 2:* P. 88 — Reprinted from Klemens von Metternich, *Memoirs*, trans. Mrs. Alexander Napier (London: Richard Bentley & Son, 1881), Vol. III, pp. 458–459, 461–463, 465–475. *Selection 3:* P. 91 — Excerpts from W. M. Simon, Ed., *French Liberalism*, reprinted by permission of John Wiley & Sons. P. 93 — Reprinted from John Stuart Mill, *On Liberty* (Boston: Ticknor and Fields, 1863), pp. 22–23, 27–29, 35–36. *Selection 4:* P. 95 — Extracts from *The Dynamics of Nationalism: Readings in Its Meaning and Development*, Louis L. Snyder, Ed., © 1964 by D. Van Nostrand Company, Inc. Reprinted by permission of Wadsworth. P. 96 — Excerpts from Mack Walker, Ed., *Metternich's Europe*, reprinted by permission of Mack Walker. P. 97 — Reprinted from Great Britain, *Annual Register*, 1819, pp. 159–160. *Selection 5:* P. 99 — Reprinted from John Comstock, *History of the Greek Revolution* (New York: William W. Reed, 1828), pp. 499–500. P. 100 — Extracts from Anatole G. Mazur, *The First Russian Revolution, 1825*, reprinted by permission of The University of California Press. *Selection 6:* P. 102 — Reprinted from *Joseph Mazzini: His Life, Writings, and Political Principles* (New York: Hurd and Houghton, 1872), pp. 62, 69, 71–74. *Selection 7:* P. 104 — Reprinted from *The Recollections of Alexis de Tocqueville*, trans. A. T. De Mattos (New York: Macmillan, 1896), pp. 14, 187–189, 197–200. P. 107 — Reprinted from *The Reminiscences of*

Carl Schurz, Vol. I (New York: The McClure Co., 1907), pp. 112–117.

Chapter 5

Selection 1: P. 113 — Reprinted from Edward Baines, *The History of the Cotton Manufacture in Great Britain* (London: Fisher, Fisher and Jackson, 1835), pp. 85–89, 184–185. *Selection 2:* P. 116 — Reprinted from Edward Baines, *The History of the Cotton Manufacture in Great Britain* (London: Fisher, Fisher and Jackson, 1835), pp. 148, 183, 195–196. *Selection 3:* P. 118 — Excerpts from A. Schroter and Walter Becker, *Die deutsche Maschinenbau industrie in der industriellen Revolution*, in S. Pollard and C. Holmes, Documents of European Economic History, reprinted by permission of Colin Holmes. *Selection 4:* P. 120 — Reprinted from Report from the Committee on the Bill to Regulate the Labour of Children in the Mills and Factories of the United Kingdom, *British Sessional Papers 1831–1832*, House of Commons, Vol. XV, pp. 5–6, 95–96, 99–100. P. 124 — Extracts from Frederick Engels, *The Condition of the Working Class in England*, W. O. Henderson and W. H. Chaloner, Eds. and Trans., reprinted by permission of Basil Blackwell Ltd. *Selection 5:* P. 126 — Reprinted from Andrew Ure, *The Philosophy of Manufactures* (London: Charles Knight, 1835), pp. 309–311, 347, 353–354. *Selection 6:* P. 128 — Reprinted from R. G. Gammage, *History of the Chartist Movement 1837–1854* (London: Truslove & Hanson, 1894), pp. 87–90. P. 130 — Excerpt from W. O. Henderson, *The Industrial Revolution in Europe*, reprinted by permission of Random House, Inc./Alfred A. Knopf. *Selection 7:* P. 131 — Reprinted from Adam Smith, *An Inquiry into the Nature and Causes of the Wealth of Nations*; reprint of the edition of 1812; ed. J. R. McCulloch (London: Ward Lock [n.d.]), pp. 19, 22, 20, 23–25, 352, 354–355, 385, 356. *Selection 8:* P. 135 — Reprinted from Thomas Robert Malthus, *First Essay on Population, 1798*, reprinted for the Royal Economic Society (London: Macmillan & Co. Ltd., 1926), pp. 7, 11–14, 16–17. P. 136 — Reprinted from Thomas Robert Malthus, *An Essay on the Principle of Population, or, a View of Its Past and Present Effects on Human Happiness*, 7th ed. (London: Reeves and Turner, 1872), pp. 6–8. *Selection 9:* P. 138 — Excerpts from Karl Marx and Frederick Engels, *Manifesto of the Communist Party*, Authorized English Translation edited and annotated by Frederick Engels, reprinted by permission of the Charles B. Kerr Publishing Company, Chicago.

Chapter 6

Selection 1: P. 148 — Extracts from *The Crystal Palace Exhibition: Illustrated Catalogue, London, 1851*, introduction by John Gloag, reprinted by courtesy of Dover Publications, Inc. *Selection 2:* P. 151 — Reprinted from Herbert Spencer, *The Man versus the State* (London: William & Norgate, 1884), pp. 28, 33, 34, 38–39, 41, 107. P. 152 — Reprinted from Thomas Hill Green, *Liberal Legislation and Freedom of Contract, A Lecture* (Oxford: Slattery & Rose and London: Simpkin, Marshall & Co., 1881), pp. 9–15. *Selection 3:* P. 156 — Reprinted from John Stuart Mill, *The Subjection of Women* (London: Longmans, 1909), pp. 29, 32–33, 41–43. P. 158 — Reprinted from E. Sylvia Pankhurst, *The Suffragette: the History of the Women's Militant Suffrage Movement, 1905–1910* (London: Gay & Hancock, 1911), pp. 483–487. P. 159 — Extract from Hubertine Auclert, *La Citoyenne,* from *Victorian Women: A Documentary History of Women's Lives in Nineteenth Century England, France and the United States,* trans. by Karen M. Offen, edited by Erna Olafson Hellerstein, Leslie Parker Hume, and Karen M. Offen. Reprinted with the permission of the publishers, Stanford University Press. © 1981 by the Board of Trustees of the Leland Stanford Junior University and Harvester Press Ltd. *Selection 4:* P. 161 — Excerpts reprinted from Frederick B. M. Hollyday, Ed., *Bismarck.* Prentice-Hall, Inc., Englewood Cliffs, N.J. 1970. Used by permission of the publisher. *Selection 5:* P. 163 — Reprinted from Eduard Bernstein, *Evolutionary Socialism: a Criticism and Affirmation,* trans. Edith C. Harvey (New York: B. W. Huebsch, 1911), pp. x–xii, xiv. *Selection 6:* P. 165 — Excerpts reprinted with permission of The Free Press, a Division of Macmillan, Inc., from *The Political Philosophy of Bakunin* edited by G. P. Maximoff. Copyright 1953 by The Free Press: copyright renewed 1981. *Selection 7:* P. 169 — Extracts from pp. 66, 68–69, & 73 in *The Journal of Modern History,* XXVI (March 1954) by Sergei Witte. Reprinted by permission of the University of Chicago. All rights reserved. *Selection 8:* P. 172 — Excerpts from *Imperial Russia: A Sourcebook, 1700–1917,* 2/e by Basil Dmytryshyn. Copyright © 1974 by the Dryden Press. Used by permission of CBS College Publishing. *Selection 9:* P. 174 — Excerpts from p. 147 in *Rehearsal for Destruction: A Study of Political Anti-Semitism in Imperial Germany* by Paul W. Massing. Copyright 1949 by the American Jewish Committee. Reprinted by permission of Harper & Row, Publishers, Inc. *Selection 10:* P. 177 — Reprinted from Cecil Rhodes, "Confession of Faith," in John E. Flint, *Cecil Rhodes* (Boston: Little, Brown, 1974), pp. 248–252. P. 179 — Reprinted from Joseph Chamberlain, *Foreign and Colonial Speeches* (London: G. Routledge and Sons, 1897), pp. 102, 202, 131–133, 244–246. P. 181 — Reprinted from Karl Pearson, *National Life from the Standpoint of Science* (London: Adam and Charles Black, 1905), pp. 21, 23–27, 36–37, 44, 46–47, 60–61, 64. *Selection 11:* P. 184 — Extracts from Louis L. Snyder, Ed. and Trans., *The Imperialism Reader,* reprinted by permission of Louis L. Snyder. *Selection 12:* P. 186 — Reprinted from J. A. Hobson, *Imperialism* (London: James Nisbet & Co. Ltd., 1902), pp. 132–134, 139, 234–235, 295–297.

Chapter 7

Selection 1: P. 191 — Reprinted from Émile Zola, *The Experimental Novel and other Essays,* trans. Belle M. Sherman (New York: The Lassell Publishing Co., 1893), pp. 20–21, 23, 54. P. 191 — Extract from Émile Zola, *Germinal,* Trans. Havelock Ellis, Everyman's Library edition, reprinted by permission of J. M. Dent & Sons Ltd. *Selection 2:* P. 194 — Reprinted from Charles Darwin, *His Life Told in an Autobiographical Chapter and in a Selected Series of his Published Letters,* edited by his son Francis Darwin (New York: D. Appleton, 1893), pp. 41–43, 45, 49. P. 196 — Reprinted from Charles Darwin, *The Origin of Species* (New York: D. Appleton, 1872), Vol. I, pp. 77, 79, 98, 133–134. P. 197 — Reprinted from Charles Darwin, *The Descent of Man* (New York: D. Appleton, 1876), pp. 606–607, 619. *Selection 3:* P. 199 — Reprinted from Andrew D. White, *A History of the Warfare of Science with Theology in Christendom* (New York: Appleton, 1896), Vol. 1, pp. 70–74, 78–81, 86. *Selection 4:* P. 202 — Excerpts from *Notes from the Underground and the Grand Inquisitor,* Fyodor Dostoevsky, translated by Ralph E. Matlaw. Copyright © 1960 by E. P. Dutton. Reprinted by permission of the publisher, E. P. Dutton, a division of New American Library. *Selection 5:* P. 207 — Extracts from *The Birth of Tragedy and the Genealogy of Morals* by Friedrich Nietzsche, translated by Francis Golffing. Translation copyright © 1956 by Doubleday & Company, Inc. Reprinted by permission of the publisher. P. 209 — Excerpts from *The Will to Power,* by Friedrich Nietzsche, edited with commentary by Walter Kaufmann, translated by R. J. Hollingdale and Walter Kaufmann. Copyright © 1967 by Walter Kaufmann. Reprinted by permission of Random House, Inc. P. 211 — Excerpts from Friedrich Nietzsche, *Twilight of the Idols/The Anti-Christ,* translated by R. J. Hollingdale (Penguin Classics, 1968), copyright © R. J. Hollingdale, 1968. *Selection 6:* P. 213 — Extract from "A Note on the Unconscious in Psychoanalysis" from *The Standard Edition of the Complete Psychological Works of Sigmund Freud,* Volume XII, translated and edited by James Strachey. Reprinted by permission of Sigmund Freud Copyrights Ltd., The Institute of Psycho-Analysis, The Hogarth Press. From *Collected Papers of Sigmund Freud,* authorized translation under the supervision of Joan Riviere. Published by Basic Books, Inc. by arrangement with Hogarth Press and The Institute of Psycho-Analysis. Reprinted by permission. P. 214 — Extracts from "Five Lectures on Psychoanalysis" from *The Standard Edition of the Complete Psychological Works of Sigmund Freud,* Volume XI, translated and edited by James Strachey. Reprinted by permission of Sigmund Freud Copyrights, Ltd., The Institute of Psycho-Analysis, The Hogarth Press and W. W. Norton & Company, Inc. Copyright © 1977. All rights reserved. P. 215 — Extracts from "Civilization and Its Discontents" from *The Standard Edition of the Complete Psychological Works of Sigmund Freud,* translated and edited by James Strachey. Reprinted by permission of Sigmund Freud Copyrights, Ltd., The Institute of Psycho-Analysis, The Hogarth Press and W. W. Norton & Company, Inc. Copyright © 1961 by James Strachey.

Chapter 8
Selection 1: P. 223 — Reprinted from Heinrich von Treitschke, *Die Politik,* excerpted in *Germany's War Mania* (New York: Dodd Mead, 1915), pp. 221–223. *Selection 2:* P. 224 — Translated by Marvin Perry from M. Boghitchevitch, *Le Procès de Salonique, Juin 1917,* André Delpeuch, ed., (Paris, 1927), pp. 41–42, 46–48. P. 226 — Reprinted from Great Britain, Foreign Office, *Collected Diplomatic Documents Relating to the Outbreak of the European War* (London: His Majesty's Stationery Office, 1915), *The Austro-Hungarian Red Book,* Document No. 6, pp. 450–452. *Selection 3:* P. 228 — Reprinted from G. P. Gooch and H. Temperley, eds., *British Documents on the Origins of the War 1898–1914* (New York: Johnson Reprint Corp., 1928), vol. III, pp. 402–406, 416. *Selection 4:* P. 231 — Selection from *The World of Yesterday* by Stefan Zweig. English translation copyright 1943, renewed © 1970 by The Viking Press, Inc. Reprinted by permission of Viking Penguin Inc. and William Verlag AG. *Selection 5:* P. 233 — *All Quiet on the Western Front* by Erich Maria Remarque. "Im Westen Nichts Neues," copyright 1928 by Ullstein A.G.; copyright renewed © 1956 by Erich Maria Remarque; *All Quiet on the Western Front* copyright 1929, 1930 by Little, Brown and Company; copyright renewed © 1957, 1958 by Erich Maria Remarque. All rights reserved. *Selection 6:* P. 236 — Reprinted from *Report of the War Cabinet Committee on Women in Industry* (London: His Majesty's Stationery Office, 1919), pp. 80–83, 99, 102–103. *Selection 7:* P. 241 — Reprinted from Ray Stannard Baker, ed., *The Public Papers of Woodrow Wilson: War and Peace* (New York: Harper, 1927), part III, vol. I, pp. 50–51, 159–161, 182–183, 199, 326, 363–364, 398–399. P. 243 — Extracts from Georges Clemenceau, *The Grandeur and Misery of Victory,* reprinted by permission of Georges P. Clemenceau. *Selection 8:* P. 247 — Excerpts reprinted from *A History of The Peace Conference of Paris* edited by H. W. V. Temperley, vol. II (1920) by permission of Oxford University Press for the Royal Institute of International Affairs. P. 249 — Extracts from Philipp Scheidemann, *The Making of New Germany: The Memoirs of Philipp Scheidemann,* Trans. James Edward Michell, reprinted by permission of Hodder and Stoughton Ltd. and Carl Reissener. *Selection 9:* P. 251 — Reprinted from *Variety* by Paul Valéry (New York: Harcourt, Brace, 1927). P. 252 — *All Quiet on the Western Front* by Erich Maria Remarque. "Im Westen Nichts Neues," copyright 1928 by Ullstein A.G.; copyright renewed © 1956 by Erich Maria Remarque; *All Quiet on the Western Front* copyright 1929, 1930 by Little, Brown and Company; copyright renewed © 1957, 1958 by Erich Maria Remarque. All rights reserved. P. 253 — Excerpts from Tristan Tzara, "Lecture on Dada," (1922), Trans. Ralph Mannheim, in Robert Motherwell, Ed., *The Dada Painters and Poets,* reprinted by permission of Wittenborn Art Books Inc. P. 255 — Translated by T. H. Von Laue from Ernst von Salomon, *Die Geächteten* (Berlin: Ernst Rowohlt Verlag, 1931), pp. 28–30, 34–35.

Chapter 9
Selection 1: P. 267 — Reprinted from Peter Durnovo, "Memorandum to Nicholas II," *Documents of Russian History, 1914–1917,* ed. Frank A. Golder (New York: The Century Co., 1927), pp. 19–20. *Selection 2:* P. 269 — Reprinted from V. I. Lenin, "What Is To Be Done," *Collected Works of V. I. Lenin,* Vol. 5 (Moscow: Progress Publishers, 1964), pp. 369–370, 373, 375, 400, 464–466, 480. *Selection 3:* P. 273 — Reprinted from V. I. Lenin, *Collected Works of V. I. Lenin,* Vol. 26 (Moscow: Progress Publishers, 1964), pp. 234–235. P. 273 — Excerpts from N. N. Sukhanov, *The Russian Revolution, 1917,* Trans. Joel Carmichael, reprinted by permission of the Oxford University Press. *Selection 4:* P. 275 — Extracts from Maxim Gorki, R. E. F. Smith, Ed., *The Russian Peasant 1920 and 1984.* © 1977 Frank Cass & Co. Reprinted by permission of Frank Cass & Co. Ltd. *Selection 5:* P. 278 — Extracts from Joseph Stalin, *Leninism: Selected Writings,* reprinted by permission of International Publishers Company. *Selection 6:* P. 280 — Extracts from Joseph Stalin, *Leninism: Selected Writings,* reprinted by permission of International Publishers Company. P. 281 — Selec-

tion from Roy A. Medvedev, *On Stalin and Stalinism,* reprinted by permission of Oxford University Press. *Selection 7:* P. 283 — Excerpts from *I Want to Be Like Stalin,* by B. P. Esipov, trans. by George S. Counts and Nucia P. Lodge (Thomas Y. Crowell) copyright 1947 by Harper & Row Publishers, Inc. Reprinted by permission of Harper & Row, Publishers, Inc. P. 285 — Excerpts from *A Precocious Autobiography* by Yevgeny Yevtushenko, translated by Andrew R. MacAndrew. English translation copyright © 1963 by E. P. Dutton. Reprinted by permission of the publisher, E. P. Dutton, a division of New American Library and Collins Publishers (London). P. 286 — Reprinted from Vladimir Polyakov, "The Story of a Story of Fireman Prokhorchuk," *Partisan Review* (28), 1961, pp. 515–518. *Selection 8:* P. 289 — Excerpts from Columbia University, Russian Institute, Ed., *The Anti-Stalin Campaign and International Communism, 1956* copyright © 1956 Columbia University Press. By permission.

Chapter 10
Selection 1: P. 295 — Extracts from Benito Mussolini, *The Political and Social Doctrine of Fascism,* reprinted by permission of the Carnegie Endowment for International Conciliation. *Selection 2:* P. 298 — Excerpts from *Mein Kampf* by Adolf Hitler, translated by Ralph Mannheim. Copyright 1943 and copyright © renewed 1971 by Houghton Mifflin Company. Reprinted by permission of Houghton Mifflin Company and Century Hutchinson Publishing Group (Hurst & Blackett edition). *Selection 3:* P. 303 — Reprinted from Heinrich Hauser, "With Germany's Unemployed," *Living Age,* vol. 344, no. 4398 (March, 1933), pp. 27–31, 34–38; translated from *Die Tat.* P. 306 — Excerpts from *Restless Days: A German Girl's Autobiography,* by Lilo Linke. Copyright 1935 by Alfred A. Knopf, Inc., and renewed 1963 by Lilo Linke. Reprinted by permission of the publisher. *Selection 4:* P. 308 — Excerpt from *The New York Times Magazine,* Oct. 8, 1933, copyright © 1933 by The New York Times Company. Reprinted by permission. *Selection 5:* P. 312 — Extracts from *Nazi Culture* reprinted by permission of George L. Mosse. P. 313 — Reprinted from Louis B. Lochner, ed., *The Goebbels Diaries, 1942–1943* (Garden City, New York: Doubleday, 1948), pp. 17–18. *Selection 6:* P. 314 — Excerpts from Johan Huizinga, *In the Shadow of Tomorrow* (London: Heinemann, 1936). Reprinted by permission of William Heinemann Limited and Robert Harben Literary Agency. P. 316 — Extracts reprinted from *The Revolt of the Masses* by José Ortega y Gasset by permission of W. W. Norton & Company, Inc., and Allen & Unwin. Copyright 1932 by W. W. Norton & Com-

pany, Inc. Copyright renewed 1960 by Teresa Carey. P. 318 — Material reprinted from *Order of the Day: Political Essays and Speeches of Two Decades* by Thomas Mann translated by H. T. Loew-Porter. Copyright 1942 and renewed 1970 by Alfred A. Knopf, Inc. Reprinted by permission of the publisher and S. Fischer Verlag GmbH. P. 319 — Excerpts on pages 15–25 from *The God that Failed* edited by Richard Crossman. Copyright 1949 by Richard Crossman. Reprinted by permission of Harper & Row, Publishers, Inc., and Hamish Hamilton, Ltd. *Selection 7:* P. 322 — Reprinted from Neville Chamberlain, *In Search of Peace* (New York: Putnam, 1939), pp. 173–175, 213–215, 217. P. 324 — Reprinted from *Parliamentary Debates, House of Commons* (London: His Majesty's Stationery Office, 1938), vol. 339, 12th, vol. of session 1937–1938, pp. 361–363, 363–364, 365–366, 367–369, 373. *Selection 8:* P. 328 — Extracts from Charles Eade, Ed., *The War Speeches of the Rt. Hon. Winston S. Churchill,* reprinted by kind permission of Curtis Brown, Ltd., on behalf of the Estate of Sir Winston Churchill. Copyright the Estate of Sir Winston Churchill. *Selection 9:* P. 330 — Extracts from Vasili Chuikov, *The Battle for Stalingrad,* reprinted by permission of Grafton Books, a Division of the Collins Publishing Group. *Selection 10:* P. 334 — Reprinted from *Nazi Conspiracy and Aggression* (Washington, D.C.: United States Government Printing Office, 1946), Vol. V, pp. 696–699, Document PS 2992. P. 336 — Extracts from Rudolph Hoess, *Commandant of Auschwitz,* reprinted by permission of George Weidenfeld & Nicholson Ltd. P. 338 — Extracts from the book, *History of the Holocaust* by Yehuda Bauer. Copyright © 1982. Reprinted with permission of the publisher, Franklin Watts. *Selection 11:* P. 340 — Excerpts from *Crusade in Europe* by Dwight D. Eisenhower. Copyright 1948 by Doubleday & Company, Inc. Reprinted by permission of the Publisher. *Selection 12:* P. 347 — Excerpts from pages 617–619, 624–626, 631–632 from *On Active Service in Peace and War* by Henry L. Stimson and McGeorge Bundy. Copyright 1947, 1948 by Henry L. Stimson. Reprinted by permission of Harper & Row, Publishers, Inc.

Chapter 11
Selection 1: P. 355 — Extracts reprinted by permission of *Vital Speeches of the Day.* P. 356 — Extracts reprinted from *Current Soviet Policies II. The Documentary Record of the Twentieth Party Congress and its Aftermath* published by *The Current Digest of the Soviet Press,* Columbus, Ohio. Used by permission. *Selection 2:* P. 360 — Reprinted from Mohandas K. Gandhi, *Hind Suaraj or Indian Home Rule* (Vithalnagar, India: published by Jivanji Dahyabhai Desai, at

Vithal Mudranalaya Congress Camp, 1938), pp. 131–138, 142. P. 361 — Extracts reprinted by permission of Grove Press, Inc., from Frantz Fanon, *The Wretched of the Earth*. P. 364 — Excerpts from *The Betrayal of the West* by Jacques Ellul, translated by Matthew J. O'Connell. Copyright © 1978 by the Continuum Publishing Company. Reprinted by permission. *Selection 3:* P. 369 — Reprinted from "Text of the Universal Declaration of Human Rights," *Yearbook of the United Nations, 1948–1949* (New York: Columbia University Press in cooperation with the United Nations, 1950), pp. 535–537. P. 372 — Excerpts from *Political Killings by Governments, An Amnesty Interna-*

tional Report, 1983, reprinted by permission of Amnesty International. P. 377 — Excerpts from *The Second Sex,* by Simone de Beauvoir, translated and edited by H. M. Parshley. Copyright 1952 by Alfred A. Knopf, Inc. Reprinted by permission of Alfred A. Knopf and Jonathan Cape Ltd. *Selection 4:* P. 382 — Extracts from *Where the Future Begins* © Unesco 1982. Reproduced by permission of Unesco. P. 388 — Material excerpted with permission of the Carnegie Council on Ethics and International Affairs from Arnold Toynbee, "For the First Time in 30,000 Years," *Worldview,* 15, March 1972, pp. 5–9.